The Student's Companion to Social Policy

Fifth Edition

Edited by
Pete Alcock, Tina Haux,
Margaret May and Sharon Wright

This edition first published 2016
© 2016 John Wiley & Sons Ltd

Edition history: Blackwell Publishers Ltd (1e, 1998); Blackwell Publishing Ltd (2e, 2003 and 3e, 2008); John Wiley & Sons Ltd (4e, 2012)

Wiley-Blackwell is an imprint of John Wiley & Sons, formed by the merger of Wiley's global Scientific, Technical and Medical business with Blackwell Publishing.

Registered Office
John Wiley & Sons Ltd, The Atrium, Southern Gate, Chichester, West Sussex, PO19 8SQ, UK

Editorial Offices

350 Main Street, Malden, MA 02148-5020, USA
9600 Garsington Road, Oxford, OX4 2DQ, UK
The Atrium, Southern Gate, Chichester, West Sussex, PO19 8SQ, UK

For details of our global editorial offices, for customer services and for information about how to apply for permission to reuse the copyright material in this book please see our website at www.wiley.com/wiley-blackwell.

The right of Pete Alcock, Tina Haux, Margaret May and Sharon Wright to be identified as the authors of the editorial material in this work has been asserted in accordance with the UK Copyright, Designs and Patents Act 1988.

Library of Congress Cataloging-in-Publication Data

Names: Alcock, Peter, 1951- editor. | Haux, Tina, editor. | May, Margaret,
   1947- editor. | Wright, Sharon (Sharon Elizabeth), editor.
Title: The student's companion to social policy / edited by Pete Alcock, Tina
   Haux, Margaret May, and Sharon Wright.
Description: Fifth edition. | Chichester, UK ; Hoboken, NJ : John Wiley &
   Sons, 2016. | Includes index.
Identifiers: LCCN 2016014402| ISBN 9781118965979 (pbk.) | ISBN 9781118965948
   (epub)
Subjects: LCSH: Great Britain–Social policy. | Public welfare–Great
   Britain. | Social policy–Study and teaching.
Classification: LCC HN390 .S78 2016 | DDC 306.0941–dc23 LC record available at
   https://lccn.loc.gov/2016014402

A catalogue record for this book is available from the British Library.

Cover image: Getty/Rogotanie

Set in 9.5/11.5 pt MinionPro-Regular by Thomson Digital, Noida, India

Printed in the UK

Contents

Part VIII   Welfare Domains   335

Part IX   Experiencing Welfare   401

Part X   International and Comparative Context   453

Notes on Contributors

Stuart Adam is a Senior Research Economist at the Institute for Fiscal Studies. His research and writing focus on analysing the design of the tax and benefit system, including income tax and National Insurance, capital gains tax, property taxation, tax credits, work incentives and redistribution, support for families with children and local government finance.

Pete Alcock is Professor of Social Policy and Administration at the University of Birmingham. He has been teaching and researching in social policy for over thirty years, and has written widely on social policy, the voluntary sector, social security, poverty and social exclusion, and anti-poverty policy.

Rob Baggott is Professor of Public Policy and Director of the Health Policy Research Unit at De Montfort University. His main research interests, on which he has published widely, include public health and preventive medicine, patient and public involvement, the role of business and voluntary organisations in the policy process and global health policy and health systems.

Saul Becker is Pro-Vice-Chancellor and Head of College of Social Sciences at the University of Birmingham and Professor of Social Policy and Social Work. He has been recognised as the world leader in research on children who are informal family carers ('young carers').

Derek Birrell is Professor of Social Policy and Administration at Ulster University. His main research and teaching interests include the government of Northern Ireland, social policy and devolution, the governance of welfare, health and social care policy, and cross-border relations.

Catherine Bochel is Reader in Policy Studies at the University of Lincoln. Her main research interests include the policy process, participation and petitions systems, on which she has published widely. She teaches on a range of policy-related courses.

Hugh Bochel is Professor of Public Policy at the University of Lincoln. His wide-ranging teaching and research interests across social policy come together around concerns with the policy process and the politics of social policy.

Edward Brunsdon is an Honorary Research Fellow in Social Policy at the University of Birmingham and has taught a range of Social Policy, Research Methods and Human Resource Management courses. His main areas of research include workplace welfare, pensions policy, executive reward and the mixed economy of welfare.

Claire Callender is Professor of Higher Education Policy both at Birkbeck and University College London, Institute of Education and Deputy Director of the ESRC/HEFCE Centre for Global Higher Education at UCL. Her research focuses on issues about student funding and finances in higher education and related topics which has informed the deliberations of government-commissioned inquiries into student funding.

Eleanor Carter is a PhD student at the University of Sheffield who has worked in policy roles in the voluntary sector. Her research centres on post-2010 welfare-to-work reforms in the UK, and also includes the broader application of outcome-based commissioning and the use of social investment in public services.

Paul Chaney is Professor of Politics and Policy at Cardiff University and Co-Director of Wales Institute of Social, Economic Research and Data. His research and teaching interests include territorial politics, public policy, civil society, and equality and human rights.

Jochen Clasen is Professor of Comparative Social Policy at the University of Edinburgh where his teaching centres on European social policy and the political economy of the welfare state. He has researched and written widely in the areas of social security, labour-market policy and the cross-national analysis of welfare states.

Daniel Clegg is Senior Lecturer in Social Policy at the University of Edinburgh. His research and teaching focus on the comparison of social policies across European countries, particularly in the areas of unemployment and working-age poverty.

Bob Coles is an Honorary Fellow at the University of York. He has a long-standing interest in youth policy and helped to establish it as a sub-area within social policy, developing links between policy, research and practice. His research has focused on vulnerable young people.

Guy Daly is Professor and Executive Dean, Faculty of Health and Life Sciences at Coventry University. His research interests are in social care, housing policy, local government and the governance of public services generally, on which he has published widely.

Howard Davis is Professor of Social and Local Policy at Coventry University. His interests include communities and community well-being, and the challenges and opportunities of an ageing society and later life. More widely, he has long been involved in advising on and evaluating the modernisation and improvement of public services in the UK and internationally.

Hartley Dean is Professor of Social Policy at the London School of Economics. Before his academic career he was a welfare rights worker in one of London's most deprived multicultural neighbourhoods. His principal research interests stem from concerns with poverty and social justice.

Peter Dwyer is Professor of Social Policy at the University of York. His teaching and research focus on issues related to social citizenship, inclusion/exclusion, welfare and migration and welfare conditionality.

Nick Ellison is Professor of Social Policy at the University of York. His research and teaching interests are wide ranging and include UK welfare politics in historical and contemporary perspective, citizenship in theory and practice, and global and international social policy.

Jane Falkingham is Professor of Demography and International Social Policy at the University of Southampton, where she is Dean of the Faculty of Social and Human Sciences and Director of the ESRC Centre for Population Change. Her research interests lie at the intersection of demographic change and social policy and span both developed and developing country contexts, with a particular focus on ageing and the changing life course.

Kevin Farnsworth is Senior Lecturer in Comparative, International and Global Social Policy at the University of York. His work focuses on broad questions relating to the political economy of welfare states, including the influence of business on social policy, welfare states and economic crisis and corporate welfare.

Tony Fitzpatrick is a Reader at the University of Nottingham. His main interests lie in the fields of social, ethical and political theories of social policy; the implications of climate change and environmental issues for the welfare state.

Deirdre Flanigan is a trainee solicitor specialising in social welfare law and human rights. She has a background in human rights promotion and protection, working for the Scottish Human Rights Commission and a human rights NGO in Nepal, and has written widely on various aspects of human rights accountability.

Jon Glasby is Professor of Health and Social Care at the University of Birmingham. A qualified social worker and former board member of the Social Care Institute for Excellence, he leads a national programme of research, consultancy and teaching to support more effective inter-agency working between social care and the NHS.

Howard Glennerster is Professor Emeritus of Social Policy at the London School of Economics. His research and teaching have focused on the finance and economics of social policy and its post-war history. He has published widely on these areas and also been an adviser to HM Treasury and the Secretary of State for Health.

Ann Marie Gray is a Senior Lecturer in Social Policy at Ulster University and Policy Director of Access Research Knowledge, a joint Ulster University/Queen's University research organisation. Her teaching and research interests are in the area of adult social care, devolution and social policy, and gender and social policy.

Ian Greener is Professor of Social Policy and Executive Director of the Wolfson Research Institute for Health and Wellbeing at Durham University. His research and teaching cross a range of areas, but focus particularly on health policy and healthcare, public management and governance and organisational change.

Scott L. Greer is Associate Professor of Health Management and Policy at the University of Michigan School of Public Health and a Senior Expert Adviser on Health Governance at the European Observatory on Health Systems and Policies. His research focuses primarily on these areas.

Jackie Gulland is Lecturer in Social Work at the University of Edinburgh. Her research and teaching interests include socio-legal studies, citizens' disputes with the state, social security policy, ageing and disability. Before entering academia, she worked in the voluntary and local authority sectors as a welfare rights adviser and trainer.

Kate Hamblin is a Senior Research Fellow at the Oxford Institute of Population Ageing. Her research has included projects exploring how people combine work and care in European countries; older entrepreneurs in the technology sector; the role of museums and galleries in supporting an ageing population; and technology support for older adults living independently with frailty, dementia or dual-sensory impairment.

Linda Hantrais is Emeritus Professor in European Social Policy at Loughborough University. She has served on a number of European committees as expert adviser. Her main research interests are in international comparative research theory, methodology and practice, with particular reference to socio-economic change, social and family policy in Europe, and international perspectives on evidence-based policy.

Bernard Harris is Professor of Social Policy at the University of Strathclyde. In addition to the history of social policy, he has conducted research into different aspects of the history of health, height, morbidity and mortality.

Tina Haux is Lecturer in Social Policy at the University of Kent. Her main research and teaching interests are on families, parenting and welfare to work. Her recent work focuses on the role of fathers in family life before and after separation, as well as the biographies and influence of the second generation of social policy scholars.

John Hills is Richard Titmuss Professor of Social Policy at the London School of Economics, where he is also Director of the Centre for Analysis of Social Exclusion and Co-Director of the International Inequalities Institute. His research interests include inequalities of income and wealth, the distributional effects of public policy and the evolution of the welfare state.

Chris Holden is Reader in International Social Policy at the University of York where he teaches on a range of social policy courses. He has published widely on the relationships between the global economy, transnational corporations, and health and social policy.

Alison Hosie has been the Research Officer at the Scottish Human Rights Commission since its creation in 2008. Prior to this she taught and researched in social policy for over fifteen years, with a particular interest in young people's right to healthcare; pregnant and parenting teenagers' right to education and methodological approaches to researching sensitive questions.

John Hudson is Professor of Social Policy and Co-Director of the Centre for Research in Comparative and Global Social Policy at the University of York. His research and teaching interests include the politics of social policy, the policymaking process and the comparative political economy of welfare.

Shona Hunter is Lecturer in Sociology and Social Policy Governance at the University of Leeds. Her research and teaching interests span a range of critical social policy. She is particularly interested in the relationship between subjectivities, emotion, power and politics in welfare

Zoë Irving is Senior Lecturer in Comparative, International and Global Social Policy at the University of York. Her work includes publications on the social politics of economic crisis and austerity, the relationship between population size and social policy development, and the social policy of Iceland and other small island states.

Misa Izuhara is Reader and Head of the Centre for Urban and Public Policy Research at the University of Bristol. Her research centres, both nationally and internationally, in the areas of housing and social change, ageing and intergenerational relations, and comparative policy analysis.

Rana Jawad is Senior Lecturer in Social Policy at the University of Bath where she teaches on social policy and the sociology of religion. Her main research interests, on which she has published widely, are the welfare systems of the MENA region and the role of religion in social policy.

Jeremy Kendall is Senior Lecturer in Social Policy at the University of Kent. His research interests cover theories and models of civil society; voluntary organisations, charities and social enterprises, especially those operating in fields of welfare, nationally and internationally; and the social policy process and the third sector.

Patricia Kennett is Reader in Comparative and International Policy Studies, and Director of Research at the School for Policy Studies, University of Bristol. Her research interests intersect the fields of social policy, urban and transnational studies, with a particular focus on Asia and Europe.

Majella Kilkey is Reader in Social Policy at the University of Sheffield. She researches at the intersections between migration and family and labour market studies with a focus on policies and lived experiences, particularly in Europe. She has undertaken research on intra-EU mobility in the context of enlargement and economic crisis, and also researches the outward migration of British citizens leaving to work abroad.

Stephen McKay is Professor of Social Research at the University of Lincoln. He conducts research on poverty, inequality, family change and the effects of social security policy. He has recently looked at the state of financial inclusion in the UK and conducted research on the system of child maintenance.

Nick Manning is Professor of Sociology at King's College London, following twenty years as Professor of Social Policy and Sociology at the University of Nottingham where he founded the Nottingham Institute of Mental Health and an International Centre for Mental Health in Shanghai. He has written widely on sociological aspects of social policy, health, mental health, Russia and China.

Margaret May is an Honorary Research Fellow in Social Policy at the University of Birmingham and has taught across the span of both Social Policy and Human Resource Management. Her research interests include employment policy and human resource management, occupational welfare, social security and comparative social policy.

David Mullins is Professor of Social Policy at the University of Birmingham where he leads the Housing and Communities Research Group, which undertakes research on community-led housing, social housing and the role of the private rented sector in housing low income groups. He has published widely on UK housing policy.

Catherine Needham is Reader in Public Policy and Public Management at the University of Birmingham. Her research focuses on public services in the UK, explaining why reforms take place and their impacts on front-line staff, citizens and broader notions of publicness. She teaches public policy, with a particular focus on evidence-based policy.

Tim Newburn is Professor of Criminology and Social Policy at the London School of Economics. His major areas of research centre on policing and security, comparative criminology and the history of criminal justice.

Robert M. Page is Reader in Democratic Socialism and Social Policy at the University of Birmingham. He has written on a wide range of social policy topics. His current work focuses on Conservative and Labour approaches to the welfare state since 1940.

Louisa Parks is Lecturer in Politics at the University of Lincoln. Her research and teaching has focused on social movements and their impacts on European Union legislation, anti-austerity protest, European politics and, more recently, local community organisations and environmental governance throughout the world.

Richard Parry is Honorary Fellow in the Centre on Constitutional Change at the University of Edinburgh. His main research interests are in politics and resource allocation in British social policy, especially the role of the Treasury and of the devolved administrations.

Ruth Patrick is a Postgraduate Researcher at the University of Leeds, where she worked with a group of out-of-work benefit claimants to make a short animated film highlighting key findings from her study of their experiences. Her research interests include participatory methods, welfare reform, social citizenship, poverty and disability.

Linda Pickard is an Associate Professorial Research Fellow at the London School of Economics. Her research interests are primarily concerned with unpaid care and long-term care policy on which she has conducted studies for the Royal Commission on Long Term Care and the Audit Commission.

Lucinda Platt is Professor of Social Policy and Sociology at the London School of Economics. She teaches social stratification, social advantage and disadvantage, ethnicity and immigration. She researches and publishes on ethnicity, immigration, child poverty and well-being, child and adult disability, and income and employment inequalities.

Lynne Poole is Lecturer in Social Policy at the University of the West of Scotland. She has researched and written on a range issues, including Scottish social policy and devolution, housing and health policy, the non-profit sector and Roma migration. Her current research interests include asylum-seeker policy and destitution.

Martin Powell is Professor of Health and Social Policy at the University of Birmingham. His main research interests and publications are in the areas of historical and geographical aspects of social and health policy, with specialism in the 'Third Way'.

Mark Priestley is Professor of Disability Policy at the University of Leeds and Scientific Director of the Academic Network of European Disability experts. He teaches courses in disability and public policy, and has published extensively in the disability policy field. His current research focuses mainly on disability policies in the EU and its member states.

Carol Propper is Professor of Economics at Imperial College London. Her research interests include the use of market and financial incentives to enhance quality, productivity and innovation in healthcare and the determinants of health.

Jessica Pykett is Senior Lecturer in Human Geography at the University of Birmingham. Her research to date has focused on the geographies of citizenship, education, behavioural forms of governance and the influence of applied and popular neuroscience on policy and practice. She teaches on the spatial politics of welfare, work and wealth.

Tess Ridge is Professor of Social Policy at the University of Bath. Her research interests include childhood poverty and social exclusion, and she has developed child-centred research methods which explore the lives and experiences of perspectives of low-income children themselves. She lectures on child and family policy and the sociology of childhood and the family.

Barra Roantree is a Research Economist at the Institute for Fiscal Studies. He researches income taxation, redistribution and the labour market, including the effects of social security contributions on earnings, redistribution across the life cycle, and how women's work choices have responded to incentives over time.

Karen Rowlingson is Professor of Social Policy, Deputy Director of the Centre for Household Assets and Savings Management, and Director of Research and Knowledge Transfer for the College of Social Sciences at the University of Birmingham. Her research interests lie in the financial security of individuals and families, including asset-based welfare, wealth and inequality, social security and financial capability.

Phillip M. Singer is a doctoral student at the University of Michigan School of Public Health. He studies the politics of healthcare and health reform. In particular, his research interests focus on state health policy, the politics of Medicaid waivers, and the implementation of the Affordable Care Act.

Rebecca Surender is Associate Professor in Social Policy at the University of Oxford and a Visiting Professor at Rhodes University in South Africa. Her research and teaching focus on health policy and policy and development, in particular South African social policy.

Peter Taylor-Gooby has been Professor of Social Policy at the University of Kent since 1989. His main research interests lie in social policy theory, attitudes to the welfare state and comparative social policy.

Athina Vlachantoni is Associate Professor in Gerontology at the University of Southampton. Her research interests span the broader areas of ageing and social policy, and she is currently involved in research projects on the topics of pension protection, informal care, social care, and living arrangements across the life course and in later life.

Aniela Wenham is Lecturer in Social Policy at the University of York. Her teaching and research interests include youth transitions, youth policy and qualitative longitudinal methods with 'hard to reach' groups.

Anne West is Professor of Education Policy and Director of the Education Research Group at the London School of Economics. Her research and many publications focus on educational policy, in particular market-oriented reforms in schools and their impacts on equity, financing education and accountability.

Noel Whiteside is Professor of Comparative Public Policy at the University of Warwick and Visiting Professor in Social Sciences at the University of Oxford. Her research focuses on systems of governance and public accountability in historical and comparative perspective. She has specific interests in labour markets and constructions of social dependency.

Adam Whitworth is Lecturer in Human Geography at the University of Sheffield. His research focuses on the analysis of activation reforms in the UK, their design, governance and concomitant outcomes for different claimants and geographical areas. More broadly, his interests lie in harnessing quantitative spatial methodologies to address applied policy concerns.

Jay Wiggan is Lecturer in Social Policy at the University of Edinburgh, where he teaches on the politics of public policy and social policy in an international context. His research interests and publications focus on the governance of public employment services and social security administration, lone parents, disabled people and 'welfare reform' and the politics of active labour market policy.

Sharon Wright is Senior Lecturer in Public Policy at the University of Glasgow, where she teaches social and public policy, specialising in the policy process, work, welfare and the politics of reform. Her research interests are in the lived experiences of poverty, social security, welfare reform and the implementation of employment services.

Nicola Yeates is Professor of Social Policy at the Open University. She teaches and has researched and published extensively on issues of social policy internationally and globally and has worked for the International Social Security Association, the World Bank, UNICEF, UNRISD and UNESCO.

Introduction

This *Student's Companion to Social Policy* is a resource book that will be of practical use to students of social policy throughout their undergraduate or postgraduate study of the subject. It aims to acquaint students with the study of social policy by covering all the main themes and issues likely to be included in any curriculum in the UK and, indeed, in many other countries. Readers are introduced to current theoretical and ideological debates, historical developments, service areas, key policy issues and the broader international context in which social policy operates. Each chapter includes a short guide to further sources, which points to some of the literature that pursues the issues addressed in the chapter in more depth and also alerts readers to major web-based sources. The *Companion* will be of value to students studying social policy on its own, as part of other undergraduate or postgraduate programmes (for instance, sociology, politics, applied social science or management studies) or as part of a professional course in a related field (for instance, social care work, nursing and health studies, public and voluntary sector management or criminology).

This fifth edition of the *Companion* has been much expanded and updated from the previous editions. New sections on Devolution and Social Policy in the UK and Welfare Governance have been included, and new chapters have been added to take account of recent policy developments and debates, and changing political and economic configurations. Existing authors have updated their contributions; and in some cases previous authors have been replaced with others leading in research and teaching in those areas.

As in the last edition, we have asked contributors to provide readers with a short bullet-point summary of key points at the beginning of each chapter and to conclude with some brief speculation on emerging issues. To provide further support for readers, as in the last edition, this fifth edition includes end of chapter review questions and is accompanied by a new dedicated website (www.wiley.com/go/alcocksocialpolicy). This provides a range of supplementary resources designed to facilitate further reading and reflection and to enable students to make the most of the text and their study of social policy. These include:

- Internet links to websites referred to in each chapter.
- Guides with internet links to key UK governmental, international and other useful resources.
- Help sheets
- Guidance on managing the main forms of assignments in social policy, including examples from the end of chapter questions.
- Careers advice.
- A glossary.

The Student's Companion to Social Policy, Fifth Edition. Edited by Pete Alcock, Tina Haux, Margaret May and Sharon Wright.
© 2016 John Wiley & Sons, Ltd. Published 2016 by John Wiley & Sons, Ltd.

The glossary is based on and links to *The Blackwell Dictionary of Social Policy*. This is a sister volume to the *Companion*, offering short definitions of all key terms and concepts and longer discussion of major items, and, as with previous editions, we hope that readers will be able to use the two together.

There has been an expansion of the editorial tram for this fifth edition. Tina Haux has joined Pete Alcock, Margaret May and Sharon Wright. We are pleased that Tina has been able to join us, and her role has meant that the editorial process has remained much the same for this latest edition, with a spreading of the load to cover the growing scale of the book.

All the contributors to this book, both old and new, are researchers and teachers in the forefront of social policy studies in the UK. They were selected on the basis that their expertise in their particular areas would provide readers with an authoritative introduction to a range of thinking and scholarship. Because the book has been prepared as a handbook and guide, rather than as a single text that focuses on one or two main themes, not all readers will necessarily want to read it from cover to cover. Indeed, most readers are likely to use it as a source of reference for consultation; hence, the chapters have been written so that they can be read in any order, separately or in groups.

- Part I introduces students to the concepts and approaches that underpin the study of social policy. These include a brief history of the scope and development of the subject and the ways in which it is studied and researched, together with discussion of the key concepts that students are likely to encounter in their studies.
- Part II provides readers with a guide to the theoretical and ideological context of social policy. Readers are introduced to the central themes and perspectives that provide the intellectual foundations of debates about the focus and aims of the subject.
- Part III surveys key themes and issues in the historical development of social policy in the UK, including consideration of nineteenth-century welfare arrangements, the growth of state welfare in the first half of the twentieth century, and the policies of Conservative and Labour administrations over recent decades.

- Part IV examines the impact of the devolution of political powers to the separate administrations in Scotland, Wales and Northern Ireland.
- Part V explores the social, political and economic context in which policies are developed and implemented, and some of the crucial challenges that they face.
- Part VI focuses on the organisation and production of social policy. The different providers of welfare are examined by looking at the five main sectors of welfare – state, commercial, occupational, voluntary and informal – setting these in the context of a brief examination of the ways in which welfare is financed and how taxation policy operates.
- Part VII considers different dimensions of the governance of welfare, including the role of local government and the European Union.
- Part VIII comprises chapters that examine the key domains of welfare service provision, with each providing up-to-date summaries of policy developments, planning and current debates.
- Part IX focuses on the provision of services to particular social groups and analyses the extent to which these groups are advantaged or disadvantaged by different aspects of policy provision.
- Part X explores the international context of social policy. There are introductory chapters on comparative analysis and policy learning and transfer, followed by a number of chapters summarising the differing policy experiences of different groups of nations across the world.

As editors we are very grateful for the work put into this volume by the contributors. The *Companion* first set out to produce a collection of chapters written by some of the most distinguished teachers and lecturers in social policy in the UK, and in this fifth edition we have followed this with an expanded range of contributions. We asked all our contributors to write in as accessible a way as possible, while introducing complex issues in a short space. Authors in social policy are no different from other authors, however; some write sharply and clearly, others are more difficult to follow and pack difficult ideas together. This collection reflects the range of styles of writing and the array of ideological and political positions that students of social policy are likely to encounter. All the chapters, of course, also provide only a short summary of a wide range of issues and information in their area. The aim therefore is to encourage readers to investigate further and read more widely.

While we, as editors, made the difficult, and occasionally contentious, decisions about what should be included, what should be left out and who should be asked to write, we were successful in persuading many of our authors to contribute to the *Companion* because of its long-standing links with the Social Policy Association (SPA) – the professional association for academics in Social Policy (see Appendix). We should also like to thank Justin Vaughan and Ben Thatcher at Wiley-Blackwell for their support in the production of this new edition, and the anonymous reviewers of the proposals for revision who all gave us such helpful advice. We hope that what we have produced is worthy of all this support and will continue to be of value to the social policy community as a whole. Any shortcomings in the collection as a whole are, however, our responsibility.

Pete Alcock
Tina Haux
Margaret May
Sharon Wright

PART I
Concepts and Approaches

1

What is Social Policy?

Pete Alcock

Overview

- Social policy is the use of policy measures to promote the welfare of citizens and social well-being.
- It is also the term for the academic study of these measures, having changed its name from 'social administration' to reflect a broadening concern with the theory as well as the practice of welfare arrangements.
- The welfare reforms in the UK in the period following the Second World War were critical in establishing the context for subsequent policy development.
- Social policy analysts adopt a range of theoretical perspectives, leading to varying conclusions about the viability and desirability of different measures and interventions
- Much social policy has been developed by national governments, but the role of international and global agencies has become more important, as have moves to shift policy to local and community levels.

The Subject of Social Policy

Social policy has a dual meaning. It is used to refer to the actions taken by politicians and policy-makers to introduce or amend provisions aimed at promoting individual welfare and social well-being. Social policy is what societies do to promote welfare. However, it is also used to refer to the academic study of these policy actions and their outcomes. Students study social policy as an academic subject, perhaps in a single honours degree, or perhaps alongside other social science

The Student's Companion to Social Policy, Fifth Edition. Edited by Pete Alcock, Tina Haux, Margaret May and Sharon Wright.
© 2016 John Wiley & Sons, Ltd. Published 2016 by John Wiley & Sons, Ltd.

subjects such as sociology or politics, or as part of professional training for social work or nursing and a wide range of careers in public, commercial and voluntary organisations. In essence, social policy is both social action and the study of it.

The later chapters in this book explore in more detail some of the key concepts and perspectives that have underpinned the study of social policy, the major issues that inform policy development and the main areas of policy practice. Much social policy analysis concerns the actions of national governments; and most of the chapters focus on the national context of the UK. However, as is discussed in Part IV, since the turn of the century much policymaking in the UK has been devolved to the separate administrations in Scotland, Wales and Northern Ireland; and the national programmes pursued by the parliaments and assemblies there are increasingly different to the policies developed for England by the UK parliament at Westminster.

Social policy is not just a UK phenomenon, however. Most countries across the world have developed measures to promote the welfare of their citizens. Some, particularly in the developed West, follow similar patterns of public support to that found in the UK, although the organisational forms and political priorities differ significantly. In the global South and in East Asia, however, social policy often takes a very different form. The study of social policy includes the comparative analysis of these differences (and similarities) and the varying histories of policy development in countries across the world; and the chapters in Part X of this book take up some examples of this comparative and international research

This does not just involve exploring and comparing the different models of policy developed in different countries – sometimes referred to as welfare regimes. Comparative scholars also use statistical data gathered across different countries to analyse international trends in welfare arrangements. Such data are gathered by international bodies such as the Office for Economic Cooperation and Development (OECD), and in Europe by the Commission of the European Union (EU); and have been used to explore to what extent social policies may be 'converging' on a common model, or to what extent economic pressures may be leading to reduced commitments to policy action – sometimes referred to as welfare 'retrenchment'.

An introduction to some of these aspects of international and comparative analysis is provided in Chapter 63. And Chapter 64 explores another dimension of international policy development, the extent to which comparative analysis of different welfare regimes can be used to inform policy development in others, through 'policy transfer'. International bodies like the OCED and EU do not just gather comparative data about social policy action, however. In the case of the EU, the Commission has the power to introduce policy measures that apply across all member states, as highlighted in Chapters 46 and 65. There are other international bodies seeking to influence policy developments on a global scale, such as the World Bank and the International Monetary Fund (IMF); and, as discussed in Chapter 71, these agencies have become more powerful and influential in shaping social policy on an international scale.

The study of social policy therefore includes not just the actions of national governments and their impacts on the citizens living in their jurisdictions, but also the comparative analysis of different welfare regimes across the world, their influences on each other, and the role of international agencies seeking to shape policy development on a global scale. Although many of the chapters in this book focus on the UK, and in many cases England only, students of social policy will need to address the wider international dimensions introduced in the later chapters. The study of social policy in the UK, however, also needs to take account of both the history of policy development in this country and changes in its analysis, for to some extent current issues and current practices are a product of that historical journey.

The Development of Social Policy

Social policy action has a long history in the UK; for instance, the first Poor Laws were introduced in 1601 at the time of Elizabeth I (see Chapter 16). However, much recent policy development, in particular, public policy, has its roots in the political and policy debates of the early twentieth century and the reforms that followed from these.

At the centre of the arguments for public action at this time was the *Fabian Society*, established in 1884 to campaign for state intervention to tackle the social problems and economic inequalities which its members argued had failed to be addressed by the capitalist markets of nineteenth-century Britain. Leading members of the Society were Sidney and Beatrice Webb. Sidney was a civil servant who later became a Labour MP, and Beatrice served on the Poor Law Commission discussed below. The Fabians used research evidence, such as the pioneering work by Booth and Rowntree, whose research revealed that the extent and depth of poverty in the UK at the end of the nineteenth century were both serious and widespread. This challenged conservative political assumption that markets could meet the welfare needs of all; and the Fabians used it to promote policy intervention through the state to protect people where the market had failed them.

As Sidney Webb's role as a Labour MP revealed, however, the Fabians' academic arguments were closely linked to the establishment and growth of the Labour Party as the political vehicle through which policy innovation and reform through the state could be achieved. In fact, it was some time before the Labour Party gained political power, and it was the Liberal governments of the early twentieth century who introduced some of the first major state measures for social policy.

These early reforms to social policy were informed by the recommendations of a Royal Commission established in 1905 to review the *Poor Laws*, the mainstay of nineteenth-century welfare policy. The commissioners themselves could not agree on the right way forward and so they produced two separate reports:

- a *Minority* Report, which was largely the work of Beatrice Webb; and
- a *Majority* Report, which was largely the work of Helen Bosanquet, who, with her husband Bernard, was a leading figure in the Charity Organisation Society (COS), a body which coordinated voluntary action to relieve poverty.

Both reports stressed the need for reforms to improve welfare provision; but, whilst the Minority Fabian report saw the public provision of state services as the means of achieving this, the Majority COS report envisaged a continuing central role for voluntary and philanthropic activity. This debate about the balance between state and non-state provision of welfare continued to influence the development of social policy throughout the twentieth century, as the chapters in Part III reveal; and, as is discussed in subsequent chapters, the issue of securing the appropriate mix between public and other provision remains a key element in social policy planning.

In practice, however, it was the Fabian arguments of the Minority Report that largely won the day in the development of social policy in the early twentieth century. The Liberal government of Asquith and Lloyd George in the early twentieth century introduced a range of measures to provide public resources through the state to tackle the social and economic problems identified by the Fabian researchers (as is discussed in Chapter 17). What is more, academic study and research evidence were expanded to support this, in particular, by the establishment by the Webbs of the London School of Economics (LSE) and the incorporation within it of the COS's School of Sociology to form a new Department of Social Sciences and Administration. This was the first major academic base for the study of social policy. Its first new lecturer was Clement Attlee, who became prime minister in the reforming Labour government after the Second World War; and it remains a major centre for teaching and research on social policy today.

The Welfare State and the Welfare Consensus

The welfare reforms of the early twentieth century were followed in the middle of the century by what was probably the most important period of policy reform in the UK. As mentioned, a Labour government under the leadership of Attlee was elected after the war with a manifesto commitment to introduce a range of comprehensive measures to provide for the welfare of citizens – to create what later came to be called a 'welfare state'.

This commitment had been prefigured to some extent in Beveridge's famous report on the need for comprehensive social security reform, published in 1942 and included in Labour's manifesto promises. Beveridge had written about the *Five Giant Social Evils* that had undermined British society before the war: ignorance, disease, idleness, squalor and want. He argued that it was in the interests of all citizens to remove these evils from British society, and it was the duty of the state, as the representative body of all citizens, to act to do this.

In the years following, between 1945 and 1951, comprehensive state provision to combat each of Beveridge's evils was introduced:

- free education up to the age of 15 (later 16), to combat ignorance;
- a national health service (NHS) free at the point of use, to combat disease;
- state commitment to securing full employment, to combat idleness;
- public housing for all citizens to rent, to combat squalor;
- national insurance benefits for all in need, to combat want.

All these required the development of major state services for citizens, and they resulted in a major extension of state responsibility – and state expenditure. The reforms were not only supported by the Labour government, however; indeed, the state education plans were introduced by a Conservative member of the wartime coalition government (R. A. Butler) in 1944. And the Conservative governments that followed in the 1950s supported the spirit of the reforms and maintained their basic structure. This cross-party consensus on state welfare was so strong that it even acquired an acronym – *Butskellism* – comprising the names of the Labour Chancellor (Gaitskell) and his Conservative successor (Butler).

For Fabian social policy, therefore, the postwar welfare state could be seen as the culmination of academic and political influence on government, after which analysis and debate focused more on the problems of how to administer and improve existing state welfare programmes than on the question of whether these were appropriate mechanisms for the social promotion of wellbeing. However, this narrow Fabian focus within post-war social policy provision and analysis did not last for long. It was soon under challenge from other perspectives which queried both the success and the desirability of state welfare.

Theoretical Pluralism

From the 1970s onwards the focus of the study and analysis of social policy began to move beyond the narrow confines of the Fabian welfare state and to consider both non-state forms of provision and a wider range of political and policy issues. This was symbolised most dramatically by a change (at the annual conference of the academic association in 1987) in the name of the subject from social administration to social policy, primarily because it was felt that *administration* was associated too closely with a focus on analysing the operation of existing welfare services, whereas *policy* encompassed a more general concern with the political and ideological bases of welfare provision. This change was representative of more general trends within academic and political debate to embrace a wider range of conflicting perspectives challenging the orthodoxy of Fabianism, and moved the study of social policy towards a more open theoretical pluralism in which questions of *whether* or *why* to pursue state welfare became as important as questions of *how* or *when*.

The New Left

The predominant focus of Fabianism on the success and desirability of state welfare was challenged in the 1960s and 1970s by critics on the left. Drawing on Marxist analysis of capitalist society, they argued that welfare services had not replaced the exploitative relationships of the labour market; and that, although they had provided some benefits for the poor and the working class, these services had also helped to support future capitalist development by providing a secure base for the market economy to operate. Unlike the Fabian socialists of the early twentieth century, these New Left critics did not necessarily see the further expansion of the existing state welfare base of social policy as resolving this dilemma. Indeed, for them state welfare was in a constant state of contradiction, or conflict, between the pressure to meet the welfare needs of citizens and the pressure to support the growth of capitalist markets.

The New Right

In the 1970s and 1980s rather different criticisms of state welfare began to appear from the right of the political spectrum. Right-wing proponents of free market capitalism, most notably Hayek, had been critical of the creation of the welfare state in the 1940s, but at the time these had been marginal voices in academic and political debate. In the 1970s, as the advent of economic recession revealed some of the limitations of state welfare, these voices became both more vocal and more widely supported – especially after the move to the right of the Conservative Party following the election of Margaret Thatcher as leader in 1975. The essence of the New Right critique is that the development of extensive state welfare services is incompatible with the maintenance of a successful market economy, and that this problem will get worse as welfare expands to meet more and more social needs. For its proponents the desirability of state welfare itself is called into question.

New social movements

The failings and limitations of state welfare were also questioned in the late twentieth century from perspectives outside the traditional left/right political spectrum. Most significant here was the challenge by feminism to the unequal treatment of men and women in the development and delivery of welfare services. As feminists point out, the provision of welfare is 'gendered'. Others have also challenged traditional analysis of state welfare to address a wider range of social divisions and social issues in analysing social policy. Anti-racists have pointed out that welfare services can be discriminatory and exclusive; disability campaigners have suggested that the needs of certain social groups can be systematically ignored; and environmentalists have argued that existing service provision is predicated upon forms of economic development which cannot be sustained.

The new pragmatism

The new radical voices that began to influence social policy towards the end of the twentieth century have widely varying, and sometimes mutually conflicting, implications. They challenged state welfare and the orthodoxy of Fabianism, but they were also critical of the New Left and the New Right. At the beginning of this century, these differing perspectives have resulted in a theoretical pluralism which has not only transformed academic study but also shifted the focus of policymaking itself. The Labour governments at

the beginning of the new century openly eschewed the policy programmes of the Fabian left and the New Right, and appealed instead to a 'third way' for social policy, combining private and public provision in a 'mixed economy' of welfare rather than a welfare state. They also argued that, rather than policy being determined by theoretical or ideological preferences, it should be based on empirical evidence of the impact of policy measures – captured in the phrase 'what counts is what works'.

Public austerity

Following the economic recession of 2007–8 and the change of government in the 2010 general election, however, the incremental expansion in social policy that had accompanied third-way pragmatism came under challenge. Under Labour public expenditure on welfare had begun to rise (see Chapter 20), and initially this was retained at the time of recession. However, as explained in Chapter 21, the Coalition government of 2010 was committed to reducing the growing public deficit left by Labour through extensive reductions in public spending – referred to by commentators as the introduction of a new public austerity. This was defended by the Coalition as the promotion of a *Big Society* approach to social policy development, to replace the 'big state' commitments to public spending; and it has continued under the Conservative government elected in 2015. In practice, however, the cuts in public spending, particularly on social security benefits and tax credits, have not been accompanied by any major expansion of community and citizen-led welfare support; and by 2015 the Big Society rhetoric had largely been abandoned by government.

Emerging Issues: the Future of Social Policy

Contemporary social policymaking and analysis has developed from its Fabian roots and its support for the welfare state reforms of the early post-war years to encompass a wide range of diverse – and conflicting – theoretical debates about both the value and the success of public welfare provision and a wider conceptualisation of the role of local and global action as well as national politics in policymaking. Social policy is now characterised by theoretical and geographical pluralism. It is also characterised by 'welfare pluralism': the recognition that state provision is only one feature of a broader mixture of differing forms and levels of welfare service. This is sometimes referred to as the shift from the *welfare state* to the *welfare mix*.

Quite how this mix will continue to evolve in the future is always hard to predict, although some broad trends are likely to continue to be influential both in policymaking and implementation and its analysis. In particular, as the rest of the later chapters in this book suggest, there are likely to be further moves:

- away from centralised public services of the welfare state towards partnerships between public and other welfare providers, and a focus on the role of the state as a contractor, a subsidiser or a regulator of the actions of others;
- away from the 'provider culture' focus on who delivers welfare services, towards a greater emphasis on the role of citizens and users in defining and delivering welfare, including the transfer of power to service users through mechanisms such as personal budgets and co-production and greater reliance on self-provision;
- towards a 'hollowing out' of the welfare state to include a greater emphasis on the role of global forces and global actors in shaping social policy, and to address the impact of devolution on policymaking and the pressures for greater localism in the development and delivery of welfare services, even down to neighbourhood level.

Guide to Further Sources

There are no textbooks dealing with the history and development of the study of social policy, but M. Bulmer, J. Lewis and D. Piachaud (eds) (1989), *The Goals of Social Policy*, London: Unwin Hyman, is an interesting, if dated, review and history of the work of the leading department at the LSE. And an overview of the crucial role of collective investment in welfare as the core of social policy can be found in P. Alcock (2016),

Why We Need Welfare: Collective Action for the Common Good, Bristol: Policy Press.

A number of authors have sought to provide introductory guides to the subject. The most well established is M. Hill and Z. Irving (2009), *Understanding Social Policy*, 8th edn, Chichester: Wiley-Blackwell, which provides a service-based review of welfare policy. P. Alcock, with M. May (2014), *Social Policy in Britain*, 4th edn, Basingstoke: Palgrave, takes a broader approach covering key questions of structure, context and issues, and also includes extensive coverage of the impact of devolution in the UK on social policy. J. Baldock, L. Mitton, N. Manning and S. Vickerstaff (eds) (2011), *Social Policy*, 4th edn, Oxford: Oxford University Press, is a collection covering both contextual issues and service areas.

F. Castles, S. Leibfried, J. Lewis, H. Obinger and C. Pierson (eds) (2010), *The Oxford Handbook of the Welfare State*, Oxford: Oxford University Press, is an extensive collection on the international and comparative analysis of social policy. P. Alcock and M. Powell (eds) (2011), *Welfare Theory and Development*, 4 vols, London: Sage, is an international collection of previously published key texts. The Policy Press publishes a major series of textbooks on social policy in their *Understanding Welfare* series, edited by Saul Becker. Finally, the Social Policy Association and the Policy Press produce an annual collection of topical essays, *Social Policy Review*.

A useful website providing introductory material on social policy is maintained by Paul Spicker at: www.spicker.uk.

Review and Assignment Questions

1 What is *Fabianism* and how did it influence the development of social policy in the twentieth century?

2 What was *Butskellism* and how did it shape post-war policy development in the UK?

3 To what extent did the New Left and New Right agree that the 'welfare state' had failed?

4 What is *welfare pluralism* and how accurately does it describe current social policy planning?

5 Do we still have a 'welfare state' in the UK?

Visit the book companion site at www.wiley.com/go/alcocksocialpolicy to make use of the resources designed to accompany the textbook. There you will find chapter-specific guides to further resources, including governmental, international, thinktank, pressure groups and relevant journal sources. You will also find a glossary based on *The Blackwell Dictionary of Social Policy*, help sheets, guidance on managing assignments in social policy and career advice.

2

Researching Social Policy

Pete Alcock and Saul Becker

Overview

- Social policy is a research-informed and research-orientated academic subject.
- Research requires rigorous theoretical inquiry and informed empirical data.
- Students of social policy need to have a good understanding of the wide range of approaches and methods in social policy research.
- Social policy draws from the full range of social science research approaches, including quantitative, qualitative and mixed methods.
- The use of research in evidence-based policymaking has become more common in policy planning and delivery, and includes evaluation of policies and practices.

Why We Need Research

Social policy needs research. As an academic subject it requires the linking of rigorous theoretical analysis with informed empirical enquiry; and as a field of social action and practice (see Chapter 1) it needs evidence to inform decision-making. This does not make social policy unique, but it does mean that research for social policy is central to study and practice; and the Social Policy Association's (SPA) *Guidelines on Research Ethics* argue that

social policy research has four features which differentiate it to some extent from other social science disciplines:

- it tends to address both academic and policy/practice questions;
- it engages with users of welfare services;
- it works with a range of disciplines and research methodologies;
- it has a responsibility to disseminate results to a range of audiences, both academic and policy/practice.

The Student's Companion to Social Policy, Fifth Edition. Edited by Pete Alcock, Tina Haux, Margaret May and Sharon Wright.
© 2016 John Wiley & Sons, Ltd. Published 2016 by John Wiley & Sons, Ltd.

Students of social policy are therefore expected to have a good knowledge of research methods and approaches. They will need to:

- be aware, and make use of, the more significant sources of data about social welfare and the main research methods used to collect and analyse data;
- seek out, use, evaluate and analyse qualitative, quantitative and mixed methods data derived from social surveys and other research publications;
- understand the strengths, weaknesses and uses of social research and research methods;
- develop a critical ability to assess, summarise, synthesise and comment on different forms of research evidence;
- undertake investigations of social questions, issues and problems, requiring skills in problem identification; collection, storage, management, manipulation and analysis of data; the construction of coherent and reasoned arguments and the presentation of clear conclusions and recommendations.

While there are various ways in which policy-making and delivery might be informed, including the experiences of service users and the expertise of service providers, evidence from research is arguably more reliable, and more persuasive. Research evidence, unlike other forms of knowledge, can be systematically tested, refuted or verified using long-established procedures.

This raises the question of what 'counts' as research. There is no formal definition of this; but academics in particular agree that it must be conducted in a systematic, disciplined and rigorous way, making use of the most appropriate research designs and methods to collect and analyse data and to answer specific research questions. We explore these issues in a little more detail below; but there are a large number of textbooks and guides to social science research that readers can use for more extensive analysis of different methods and procedures; in particular, the edited text by Becker et al. (2012), which focuses specifically on understanding research for social policy.

A distinction is sometimes made between research for policy and research of policy, although much social policy research is simultaneously of both types. Research *for policy* is concerned to analyse, understand and inform the various stages of the policy process – from before the formulation of policy through to its implementation – and, as we discuss below, the role of evidence in policymaking has become more important in recent times. Research *of policy* is concerned with how social problems and issues are defined, agendas are set, policy is formulated and decisions are made, and how policy is delivered in the real world, and later evaluated and changed (see Chapter 42).

Approaches, Methods and Designs

Social policy draws from the full range of approaches, research designs and methods that are used in the social sciences. In terms of *approaches*, these can include, for example, feminist research, service user-led research, action research, evaluation research and post-structuralist approaches . These each have their own assumptions about the nature of the social world and the researcher's and research participants' place within it, and about knowledge creation and the research process itself. These assumptions help to inform the way in which the research is carried out, the selection of methods, the data analysis techniques and the way in which research is written up and reported.

A *research method* is a technique for gathering data, such as a questionnaire, interview or observation. A *research design* is a structure or framework within which data are collected, for example, an experimental or longitudinal design. Research methods can serve different designs. Thus, a method of data collection such as a questionnaire can be employed in connection with many, if not all, research designs. Decisions about appropriate research methods are in a sense subsidiary to decisions about an appropriate design, since it is the design that provides the framework for answering research questions; and the choice of research design will be critically informed by what is already known about an issue and what still needs to be found out.

An early stage of the research process therefore involves a review of the available literature. This needs to be as comprehensive as possible – there may be answers here already to the questions that are of current concern. It is important to have an explicit and transparent way of distinguishing between different publications and for deciding which to include in the literature review, not least because of the sheer volume of information that is now publicly available and the need to recognise that not everything can, or should, be read or included. 'Systematic reviews' are one way of conducting literature searches and reviews. These are comprehensive literature reviews with studies chosen in a systematic way and summarised according to explicit criteria. These forms of review are valued highly in medicine and health-care research and are increasingly being used, in developing forms, within social policy.

Depending on the specific research question(s) to be addressed, in some cases just one research method may be used within an overall design or approach. This could be a quantitative method or

a qualitative method, but in others research could include a mix of different methods (see Boxes 2.1, 2.2 and 2.3).

Each research design and method, or combination of methods, has its own strengths and limitations, therefore; and those conducting or studying social policy research need to be aware of the appropriateness or otherwise of the approaches, designs and methods used in any published enquiry. Students need to develop a critical ability to 'read' research-based publications, not just for their findings and conclusions, but also to make judgements about whether or not the research design and methods are appropriate for the research question or questions that are being examined.

There is another dimension of the research process of which researchers, and students, need

---

Box 2.1   Quantitative Methods

Quantitative research generally adopts an objectivist position with respect to the nature of social reality, linked to a natural science model of seeking to establish relationships between pieces of data (variables) from which causal inferences can be drawn. These usually involve the use of statistical tests on large sets of anonymous quantitative data, which can become quite complex and require training in mathematical and statistical methods to carry out – and even to interpret. Quantitative data can be gathered by researchers through the administration and analysis of a large-scale social survey – referred to as *primary* data. Or analysis could focus on an existing set of data that has already been established – referred to as *secondary* data. The latter is increasingly common because the costs of new surveys are expensive and there are a range of good datasets already available, including the decennial census, regular national and international surveys, and administrative data such as benefit claimant records.

Box 2.2   Qualitative Methods

Qualitative research tends to be associated with a constructionist position, which pays greater attention to the role that individuals play in constructing their social networks and their influence over them. There is a strong focus on the meanings that actors attribute to their social interactions, with an emphasis on description, context and process. Thus, qualitative researchers aim to understand the behaviour, values, beliefs and so on of the people that they are researching from the perspective of the participants themselves. Thus, qualitative researchers will use in depth interviews with participants, or perhaps bring them together in 'focus groups' to discuss their experiences; and more detailed exploration could take the form of ethnographic accounts of people's lifestyles and experiences. Qualitative research adopts an inductive approach to the relationship between theory and research whereby concepts and theory are generated out of the data, rather than as in the quantitative approach, whereby concepts and theoretical ideas often guide the collection of data.

Box 2.3 Mixed Methods

Quantitative and qualitative research methods are not mutually exclusive, of course. Indeed, each explore different dimensions of social issues and provide different insights into these. The causal inferences derived from statistical analysis can be explored in more depth through interviews that seek to discover why respondents acted in a particular way. Therefore, an integration of different methods can build on the advantages of both and improve the comprehensiveness of the data and analysis. This multi-strategy research is commonly referred to as a 'mixed methods' study, and has become more common over time, especially in larger research projects seeking to examine different aspects of social problems and inform policymaking across a range of different interventions. It is important though to give a coherent rationale for why different methods are being integrated in the way that they are rather than the alternative of using a single method or other approach.

to be aware, and that is the ethical issues that might be at stake in carrying out research. Ethical considerations underpin all social policy research. For example, it is unacceptable to conduct research that would harm research participants or place researchers themselves in danger. Data must be collected and stored in a way that is safe and secure, and that protects the anonymity of participants. Participants should give their informed consent to taking part in research rather than being coerced, bribed or misled. The SPA has developed a set of ethical guidelines that sit alongside those of other learned bodies (for example, the British Sociological Association) and relevant research groups (the Social Research Association), but ethics can be controversial and the SPA guidelines have generated dissension amongst some social policy researchers. Students need to be aware of the ethical implications of their own studies and be able to recognise good or poor ethics in published reports.

Evidence-based Policy and Evaluation

Evidence-based policy and practice are not new – there has been a long-term move in advanced industrialised countries towards using research and evaluation to guide the decisions and behaviour of policymakers and professionals. In the UK, since the early 1960s, government ministries have had their own research, statistics and evaluation departments which review research and commission their own studies, although in the current austere economic climate there is far less of this. In 2001, a UK Centre for Evidence Based Policy and Practice was established, funded initially by the Economic and Social Research Council (ESRC), who also fund a range of social science research of interest to policymakers and practitioners across the UK.

The belief that policy and professional practice *should* be informed by research evidence has accelerated in recent years, linked to concerns to ensure value for money and the effectiveness of policy action. This is generally associated with the impact of 'new public management' on policy practice (see Chapter 43), and has been captured in the slogan, 'what counts is what works'. Evidence-based policy, therefore, argues that effective and efficient public policy – and good returns to investment for taxpayers – requires that we understand what works before we spend.

This interest in evidence-based policy and practice has been influenced heavily by a parallel set of concerns in the fields of medicine and healthcare, which have developed systems for determining 'what counts as evidence' and what counts as the *most important* and trustworthy form of evidence. This approach can favour certain quantitative methods and methodologies – for example, quasi-experimental methods and randomised control trials, or meta-analyses and systematic reviews; and, in particular, is informed by the traditions of drug trials in medical research.

However, in social policy generally there is less reverence for experimental designs or for statistical meta-analyses, and there is little agreement that these methods and approaches are by themselves indicators of high quality. Indeed, it is more likely that research design and research methods will be selected on the basis of their relevance or appropriateness to the issues to be examined, rather than any intrinsic methodological quality, with a wide range of different methods all being used as evidence to inform policy and practice. The important message from this is that there is no universally superior research design or research method – they are only as good as their suitability to the research question(s) being asked.

In most cases of policy formulation, development and policy change, it is, however, difficult to be precise about the nature and degree of influence that research plays, if any, in informing policy and practice. Research can make a contribution to both policy and professional practice, even if it is not linear or direct. For example, *instrumental utilisation* of research can be said to have taken place when there is evidence of policymakers and service providers *acting* on the findings of specific research studies. *Conceptual utilisation* occurs when research *influences* how policymakers and practitioners *interpret* and *think* about a social issue or problem – where, for example, it provides alternative ways of understanding and informs their action strategies.

Many social policy researchers do want their research to make an impact on policy and practice, and to be seen as relevant evidence on which to base policy. To do this, however, research findings need to be communicated in some way to policymakers and practitioners. Research that does not come to the attention of policymakers or professionals cannot make an impact on their decision-making in any explicit or transparent way. How research is disseminated and communicated to target audiences, and what target audiences make or do with it – not just how research is 'done' and its 'trustworthiness' – are therefore critical to whether the evidence that it produces can have an impact on policy and practice.

Research evidence does not just aim to inform the creation of policy, however. Research can also be used to *evaluate* existing policies. Indeed, arguably, it is the evaluation of policies and practices that ought to be at the heart of researching social policy; and in practice much policy research is carried out to evaluate existing policies, often commissioned by the policymakers themselves to inform future planning.

It is governments in particular who are likely to commission evaluation research; and in their 'Green Book' the UK Treasury has even developed a sequential model of policymaking using the acronym, ROAMEF – Rationale, Objectives, Appraisal, Monitoring, Evaluation and Feedback (see too Chapter 42). Different types of evaluation take place at different stages of the policy process, and these are not consistently used. Nevertheless, we can differentiate between prospective, formative and summative evaluation in terms of the place of evaluation within the policy cycle, and in the type of research that is conducted:

- Prospective evaluation (including programme appraisal, option analysis, modelling and simulation, or feasibility evaluation) seeks to determine what worked in similar settings in the past or elsewhere, and takes place before the policy is implemented – what policy might work? This might involve a simulation exercise or reviewing the literature through techniques such as systematic review. The result of the appraisal may be not to proceed with the policy.

- Formative evaluation (including process, bottom-up or developmental) takes place when a policy is being implemented. It examines issues of process so as to determine whether guidelines have been followed: how is the policy working? The main aim is to provide feedback which may serve to improve the implementation process. Formative evaluation often involves qualitative methods such as interviews.

- Summative evaluation (including impact, retrospective or outcome) takes place after the policy and is typically quantitative. This examines the effects or impact of the policy: has the policy worked; what were its results? This is sometimes linked to policy goals. Successful policies achieve their initial goals, although this is problematic for three reasons. First, goals are often unclear. Second, the policy may have achieved its positive goals, but also with negative side effects. Third, it is difficult to attribute causality, with success being caused by other factors beyond the policy. Nevertheless, 'successful' policies are maintained or expanded, while failed policies are terminated.

It is often difficult to draw a hard and fast line between the different types of evaluation as policies are often ongoing rather than terminated, and so many evaluations have some elements of formative and summative assessment.

Emerging Issues

Research has always been at the centre of social policy practice and study. Evidence-based policymaking and policy evaluation have become more high profile in recent times, in particular because governments have been more willing to recognise the value of research in informing policy and more willing to commission policy researchers to carry this out. However, current pressures on public expenditure budgets for social policy are putting this under threat. New directions and new resources for policy research are always being developed, however; and in a number of areas the future prospects for the growth of research activity in social policy remain strong:

- Comparative research: social policy is now an international subject, and increasingly students are developing comparative analysis of policy activity in different countries (see Chapter 63). There are now a range of international datasets which can be used to inform such international research, in particular the information on the economic performance of countries collected by the Office for Economic Cooperation and Development (OECD) and the surveys carried out in Europe by the EU Commission.
- Administrative data: governments, including the UK and devolved governments, are becoming more aware of the information that is routinely collected about citizens that could be used as resources for research analysis, particularly secondary quantitative analysis. This includes benefit and tax data, as well as housing and crime records, and also that held by nongovernment bodies. There is now a national initiative to expand the availability and use of such 'big data', promoted by the ESRC.
- Longitudinal analysis: much quantitative and qualitative research is based on a 'snapshot' of social relations at a particular point in time. However, in order to understand social

change and to inform future changes, we need to engage in a longitudinal analysis of changes in people's social circumstances. This has become possible for quantitative analysis through the use of the panel data from a survey of a sample of respondents, collected on an annual basis by the ESRC's *Understanding Society*. There have also been some attempts to collect qualitative data about lifetime experiences, using small samples of selected respondents. These are time-consuming and expensive to undertake, but they provide an opportunity for greater understanding in the future of how social policies work to change people's lives.

Guide to Further Sources

There are literally hundreds of textbooks on research methods in the social sciences, but very few that have been specifically developed for social policy students. The main text is S. Becker, A. Bryman and H. Ferguson (eds) (2012), *Understanding Research for Social Policy and Social Work: Themes, Methods and Approaches*, Bristol: Policy Press, which provides an overview of all the main research methods and approaches, with research examples and illustrations from a wide range of social policy areas. This was thoroughly revised and updated in 2012, with new narratives and examples drawn from social policy and social work research. A superb 'generic' research methods text is A. Bryman (2014), *Social Research Methods*, 4th edn, Oxford: Oxford University Press; and a very accessible and useful guide is B. Matthews and L. Ross (2010), *Research Methods: A Practical Guide for the Social Sciences*, London: Longman.

For those interested in issues around how to determine 'quality' in social policy research, then S. Becker, A. Bryman and J. Sempik (2006), *Defining Quality in Social Policy Research*, Social Policy Association, provides the first study of how social policy researchers conceptualise 'quality' and offers a framework for discussion. It can be downloaded free from the SPA website at: www.social-policy.com. The SPA website has other useful research including the SPA's *Guidelines on Research Ethics*.

Review and Assignment Questions

1 What is it that makes research evidence more reliable than other forms of knowledge in informing policy planning?
2 Why are mixed methods studies becoming increasingly attractive to social policy researchers?
3 What are the differences between prospective, formative and summative policy evaluations?
4 Why is it important to consider the ethical issues underpinning policy research?
5 How would you design a research project to evaluate policies to provide care to vulnerable adults in their homes?

Visit the book companion site at www.wiley.com/go/alcocksocialpolicy to make use of the resources designed to accompany the textbook. There you will find chapter-specific guides to further resources, including governmental, international, thinktank, pressure groups and relevant journals sources. You will also find a glossary based on *The Blackwell Dictionary of Social Policy*, help sheets, guidance on managing assignments in social policy and career advice.

3

Social Needs, Social Problems, Social Welfare and Well-being

Nick Manning

Overview

■ An examination of the growth and structure of social welfare provision.
■ An identification of some basic definitions of need.
■ A review of debates about need, and the way it is used in practice.
■ A discussion of ideas about social problems.
■ A brief introduction to social problems, needs and well-being.

What is Social Welfare?

Social welfare refers to the various social arrangements that exist to meet the needs of individuals and groups in society, and to tackle social problems. Our use of the term social policy in modern times implies that social welfare means government welfare. This is not at all the case. Welfare for most people is still provided through other social mechanisms than the state. In addition to the state, there are three other types: family and friends; the market; and non-governmental organisations such as voluntary and charitable organisations (VCOs), and mutual associations. Social policy as an area of study is concerned with the way in which all these institutions affect the welfare of individuals and groups, and is taken up in more detail in some of the chapters in Part IX.

Social policy is a branch of social science. From this point of view, the basic conditions for the existence and survival of individual people are necessarily social. No individual, however resourceful, could survive for long in isolation. Human beings, in contrast to many other animals, are not capable of mediating directly with nature without mechanisms of cooperation and a

The Student's Companion to Social Policy, Fifth Edition. Edited by Pete Alcock, Tina Haux, Margaret May and Sharon Wright.
© 2016 John Wiley & Sons, Ltd. Published 2016 by John Wiley & Sons, Ltd.

Box 3.1 Types of Social Welfare Institution

- family
- market
- voluntary and community organisations (VCO)
- the welfare state

division of labour between individuals. This is illustrated well by the long period of dependence that children need for them to become adults. The family, then, may be taken as the archetypal social welfare institution, both in fact and as an ideal. Markets, governments and VCOs are by comparison modern developments.

The modern family provides less welfare than it did two hundred years ago. Hospitals, schools, shops, workplaces, transport and leisure facilities have developed to fulfil a variety of functions, which means that social welfare provision has become a more complex and mixed system than it used to be. Much of this change occurred in the nineteenth century, when hospitals, schools, shops and factories came to prominence. Two rival mechanisms underlay these changes: the market and VCOs. The market developed in two senses relevant to social welfare. The first sense is the market in labour as individual workers shifted increasingly from agriculture towards industrial wage labour. The vicissitudes of this means of livelihood threw up new insecurities whenever the availability of, or ability to, work stopped. The second sense is the market in goods and services, such as food, clothes and medical care, that accompanied these changes, and through which families increasingly met their various needs rather than through self-provisioning. Inability to pay could have disastrous consequences for a range of needs of family members.

Alongside the market, and very often in response to its failures to provide either adequately waged work or adequately priced goods and services, VCOs developed. However, this was not always for humanitarian reasons. On the one hand, for example, mutual associations such as friendly societies were indeed designed for the mutual benefit of members when social needs

arose. By contrast, however, the settlement house movement for the 'improvement' of working-class lives was also motivated by fear that upper-middle-class organisers had about the consequences for all social classes of poverty life styles, such as the spread of disease. In addition, there were also concerns about the costs of market failure, not to individual victims, but to those who might have to pick up the pieces. For example, in the latter part of the nineteenth century the provision of education was motivated by the employment needs of industrialists, while the provision of agreed compensation for industrial accidents was designed to avoid more expensive court proceedings.

For a while the market and VCOs enjoyed considerable independence from the attentions of government, but there was a growing concern by the end of the nineteenth century of the need to regulate their activities. In the twentieth century, regulation led on to the provision of financial support and eventually to state provision of welfare services. Motives for this were again mixed. Genuine humanitarian concern for the meeting of social needs coexisted with the fear of social problems threatening the wider social order, and the realisation that the costs of social reproduction (both the biological production of children for the future workforce and the daily replenishment of the capacity for work) might be better organised by the state. The climax of this process was the establishment of the British welfare state by the Labour government of the 1940s.

All these institutions of social welfare, family, market, state and VCOs continue to coexist, but with regular changes in their functions and scope, most recently under the impact of the Coalition government and its commitment to a reduction in state provision, alongside the encouragement of the 'Big Society', whereby families and VCOs will provide more welfare. This extends the previous New Labour government's growing emphasis on privatisation and market mechanisms to the point where social welfare was increasingly thought of as a consumption good. Nevertheless, the level of state expenditure on social welfare has remained at about 25 per cent of gross national product (GNP), albeit covering a steadily changing mix in favour of social security and health services, and away from education and housing.

What are Social Needs?

While I have suggested that there were mixed motives for organising social welfare institutions, the meeting of social needs remains their central concern. We must therefore review the definition of this crucial concept. A useful starting point is to distinguish needs from two related notions: wants and preferences. There are two important senses in which wants and needs differ. First, wants are more inclusive: we may want things that we do not need; indeed, marketing experts make great efforts to persuade us to do so. Second, we may need things that we do not want, either through ignorance or through our dislike of them. Medical intervention can often be of this type. Both these distinctions from want suggest that needs are more basic or essential to us than wants.

Preferences, a concept frequently used in economic analyses, differ from needs and wants in the sense that they are revealed only when we make choices, usually in the act of buying goods or services as consumers. The argument here is that it is difficult to really know what people need or want unless they act in some way to try to secure for themselves the things in question. This action component, however, has its limits, for of course wants cannot be revealed in the market if we do not have the money to pay for things, and needs cannot be revealed by individuals where they are not aware of them or there are no services to meet them. Needs, then, may well have to be discovered by those other than the individual concerned.

We should also make a distinction between needs and social needs. Needs (and problems and welfare) are 'social' in the sense that they are concerned not only with, for example, individual causes and experiences of illness and poverty, but also with the amount and distribution of illness and poverty in different social groups; the reasons for this that arise out of the shared conditions of life for those social groups; and the social structures and processes through which they might be ameliorated. For example, it is only necessary to vaccinate a proportion of the population to stop the spread of infectious disease. In this case, the population can be seen to have a need, but any specific individual may not necessarily feel, or be defined by others as, in need. Waiting in line for an injection, we may have all felt this way as children!

These considerations enable us to make some simple classification of types of need. First are those needs which we are aware of ourselves, felt needs. These are obvious when we feel ill or have an accident. The second type of needs is those defined for us by others, usually experts or professionals, such as doctors or teachers, but also importantly by family and friends. The third type of need is partly an extension of the second, to focus on needs as revealed, perhaps in surveys, in comparison with other people in the same social group. Here an individual can be said to be in comparative need because others have something that they do not.

An important aspect of needs, shared by all three types, has given rise to many debates in social policy. This is the question of how needs can be measured, particularly when we move away from the obvious examples such as major medical emergencies. The classic case is that of poverty. How much income do we need? One approach, drawing on the second type of need as defined by experts, is to think about the basic essentials, such as food, clothing and shelter, and to work out the amount of money needed to buy the cheapest minimal provision of these, and to define anyone with less money as poor or in need.

However, any close study of the way in which poor people live reveals that the notion of 'basic essentials' or 'cheapest minimal provision' varies with the way of life of the particular family and community in which an individual lives. Is television or internet access an essential? Is meat eating essential? What cultural prescriptions about dress codes are essential?

An alternative approach is to use the first type of need, and merely to ask poor people what they feel they need. However, where this has been done,

it seems that poor people often adjust to their
circumstances and feel less in need than they
'ought' to, especially if they are older people, while
others can feel poor where they 'ought' not to.
Finally, we could merely define as poor those
people with less than others as in the third type
of need, comparative need, for example, by ranking incomes and identifying, say, the bottom 10
per cent as poor.

This problem of measurement has resulted in
an oscillation in social policy debates between
those who favour an objective interpretation of
what is 'basic' or 'essential', for example, in terms
of the ability of an individual to remain alive, and
to retain the capacity to act as a 'person' in society;
and those who argue that needs are really more
subjectively defined by individuals themselves,
experts, and government agencies and others
who provide services designed to meet needs.

What is a Social Problem?

Social welfare institutions are also concerned with
social problems, which are related to, but not the
same as, social needs. For example, as C. Wright
Mills famously observed, one person suffering
from unemployment may be in acute need, but
it is only when unemployment becomes a more
widely shared experience in a community that
there may be said to be a social problem. Social
problems, then, are to be distinguished from
individual need.

A further distinction should be made between
the mere existence of a shared set of social mis-
fortunes in a community, whether or not they have
been defined as needs, and three further elements
of a social problem: the extent to which they are
perceived; the judgements made about them and
the values they threaten; and the actions recommended to deal with them. Needs . can exist
whether or not they are known about by anyone.
Social problems cannot. They exist within the
public domain rather than private experience.
The perceptions, judgements and recommended
actions are, in the broadest sense of the term, part
of the political process of a society or community.

Perceptions of social problems can occur
through the eyes of experts or the general public.
In the case of experts, social problems are typically
defined in relatively objective terms, for example,

Box 3.3 Elements and Types of
Social Problems

- Elements of social problems
  - social conditions
  - perceptions
  - judgements
  - solutions
- Types of social problems
  - open/contested
  - closed/uncontested

the incidence of divorce, where the rate of change
is a crucial issue. However, since many social
issues are less amenable to objective measurement,
for example, the effects of family neglect on children, experts can differ widely in their claims
about the objective state of a social problem. In
these cases, the general public, community groups,
pressure groups and so on may have widely varying views, such that a social problem is more
subjectively defined. Social problems, in the
extreme version of this view, become merely
'what people think they are'. Since most of our
experience of, and knowledge about, social issues
is indirect, the mass media are an important
influence not only on our knowledge of social
issues, but also on the way in which they are
framed, judged and dealt with.

These perceptions are heavily influenced by
judgements about the kind of values felt to be
under threat. This brings us to the heart of defining a social problem, since it is the sense that
something is wrong that motivates any attempt to
put things right. There are two aspects of this that
we have to consider. First is the issue of whose
values are threatened. Some issues command
widespread consensus, for example, that threats
to life are unacceptable. The judgement that the
spread of disease such as HIV-AIDS is a social
problem from this point of view is relatively
uncontested. Other issues, however, may be the
site of sharp value conflict, for example, the
relevance of people's sexuality to family life in
various ways.

However, a second important aspect of value
judgements in definitions of social problems can
sharply modify the effects of these value concerns.

This is the issue of who is to blame for the problem. In the case of HIV-AIDS, what might have been an ordinary medical issue was transformed in this regard by very sharp dissensus over the judgements of blame made about gay men, and therefore about the nature, status and solution to the problem. Where problems are the site of value conflict, or blame is attributed, we can speak of contested or open social problems, the solutions to which are far from clear. Where consensus and lack of blame are typical, we can think of social problems as closed or uncontested.

The solutions proffered to social problems have an intimate connection to perceptions and judgements made about them. Indeed, it has been argued that often the solution may in fact tend to determine these other aspects. An example of this process has been the development since the 1970s of the social problem of hyperactivity (ADHD) amongst children, at a time when a drug treatment to calm them down became available.

The UK Coalition government's approach to solving social problems illustrates the subjective nature of the perception and definition of social problems. It has defined state welfare itself as the problem. The deficit is too large, it is argued, and resources have been wasted on 'bureaucracy' (for example, in the NHS), while popular concerns have been ignored (for example, in school provision). The solution is to roll back state provision and regulation, and to encourage a 'Big Society' whereby more VCO and market provision will deliver greater efficiency and at the same time address popular concerns.

Conclusion

Social welfare institutions have evolved in their current form alongside the development of industrial society. As industrial societies change, so do their welfare institutions. This is most clearly observed in the countries of Russia and Eastern Europe, where a variety of neo-liberal social policy innovations have been developed, and already modified in response to economic and political forces. Western societies have not been immune to such influences, with the ubiquitous assumption of globalisation used to justify significant debates and changes in the trajectory of social policies for the twenty-first century. While they are chiefly

oriented to meeting social needs and tackling social problems, this has not been the only motive. The German chancellor, Bismarck, and Winston Churchill classically argued in favour of social welfare institutions as a buttress against the attractions of socialist ideas.

Social needs and social problems are subject to contested definitions. In both cases a major debate concerns the relative weight to be given to objective or subjective definitions. Can needs and problems be scientifically measured in some absolute sense, or are they inescapably subject to the relative social circumstances of both those in need and the particular interests of the definers? The genomic revolution, which seems to offer so many tantalising health benefits and yet to raise an even larger number of ethical uncertainties, illustrates well the interaction between industrial and scientific developments and public concerns. Public debate has never been more wide ranging, buttressed through public opinion surveys, focus groups and the development of professional committees and academic departments of ethics.

These points lead us back to the nature of social policy as a subject. The word 'policy' implies that it is a part of the political processes and institutions of modern society, and that social needs, social problems and social welfare are similarly political. While some observers have come to anticipate the decline of the nation-state in the wake of an increasingly globalised world (discussed further in Chapter 54), social policy issues have in reality grown in importance in regional affairs, whether at a sub-national level or more widely in multi-country regional welfare 'blocks', most noticeably in the development of a European social model, alongside the distinctive American or Asian patterns of welfare development.

Emerging Issues: from Needs to Well-being

With the steady expansion of consumer and individualist definitions of the 'good life' that have emerged with the economic growth of recent years, a new definition of needs in terms of our individual well-being has also developed. For example, healthcare is now focused on developing and sustaining good health as well as treating disease. The 2010 UK Coalition government's public health White Paper aimed to 'nudge' us to stop smoking, eat wisely and take exercise. This emphasis has also spread into concern for our personal relationships and mental health, such that stress generated by domestic or employment factors has become central to both public health and trade union actions. Economists have noted that the level of personal satisfaction reported in public surveys has risen very little over the last twenty-five years despite record levels of income and wealth, and there is a growing call for more balanced measures of well-being than the GNP. However, the arguments that we have reviewed in relation to defining needs and problems apply equally here. Well-being is a contested concept, open to subjective, objective, political and comparative definitions, and subject to the pressures of both professional and mass media fashions.

Guide to Further Sources

On social welfare institutions, see D. Fraser (2009), *The Evolution of the British Welfare State*, 4th edn, Basingstoke: Palgrave Macmillan, is the fourth edition of a comprehensive and balanced account of the growth of the British welfare state. J. R. Hay (1983), *The Origins of the Liberal Welfare Reforms 1906–1914*, Basingstoke: Macmillan, is a short book that gives a very clear account of the variety of different reasons for the rapid development of state welfare in the early twentieth century.

On social needs there are three classic statements on need: J. Bradshaw (1972), 'The concept of social need', *New Society*, 30 March 1972. This article was a milestone statement about different types of social need. D. Piachaud, 'Peter Townsend and the Holy Grail', *New Society*, 10 September 1981. This article presents a strong argument for the impossibility of finding an objective definition of need. L. Doyal and I. Gough (1985), 'A theory of human needs', *Critical Social Policy*, 10: 6–38. This work represents a cogent argument for returning to an objective basis for the definition of needs. A complete and accessible treatment of need is provided by H. Dean (2010), *Understanding Human Need*, Bristol: Policy Press.

On social problems, an early discussion in the UK is presented in N. Manning (ed.) (1985), *Social Problems and Welfare Ideology*, Aldershot: Gower. This book offers a detailed review of the theory of social problems, together with a range of case studies. In a more North American tradition is the seventh edition of a key textbook which presents a detailed analysis of seven different models of social problems: E. Rubington and M. Weinberg (2010). *The Study of Social Problems: Seven Perspectives*, Oxford: Oxford University Press. On well-being, there is useful presentation of data on the UK, and the relationship between needs and well-being in The Young Foundation (2009), *Sinking and Swimming, Understanding Britain's Unmet Needs*, London: Young Foundation.

Websites that include many examples of discussions about the way in which social policies should be organised, what legitimate social needs are, and how to tackle social problems can be found amongst thinktanks such as: www .centreforsocialjustice.org.uk; www.thebigsociety .co.uk; www.fabian-society.org.uk; www.demos .co.uk; www.youngfoundation.org; www.fawcett society.org.uk.

Review and Assignment Questions

1   What are the main sources of a person's welfare in modern society?
2   How does industrial development shape welfare states?
3   How can we establish what someone's needs are?
4   What is the difference between needs, wants and preferences?
5   Who defines social problems and how?

Visit the book companion site at www.wiley.com/ go/alcocksocialpolicy to make use of the resources designed to accompany the textbook. There you will find chapter-specific guides to further resources, including governmental, international, thinktank, pressure groups and relevant journal sources. You will also find a glossary based on *The Blackwell Dictionary of Social Policy*, help sheets, guidance on managing assignments in social policy and career advice.

4

Equality, Rights and Social Justice

Peter Taylor-Gooby

■■■

Overview

- Equality, rights and social justice are all political slogans, endlessly contested, endlessly renewed.
- Equality of opportunity has displaced equality of outcome as the central concern, despite compelling evidence of rapidly increasing inequality of income and life chances.
- Rights have been based on needs, capabilities and deserts. There are questions over how far people should take responsibility for meeting their own needs and whether government should encourage or compel them to do so.
- For justice, the big division is between those who base just allocations on individual contribution and circumstances and those who take social factors into account.
- In a more fluid, flexible, diverse, multi-faith, uncertain and globalised world the claims based on these concepts multiply, while the capacity of governments to respond to them diminishes.

■■■

Meanings and Definitions

'Equality', 'rights' and 'social justice' have been prominent among the rallying cries of those calling for radical reforms, whether to promote recognition of the equal value of women as human beings (De Beauvoir, in George and Page, 1995, ch. 14), to support social investment to meet the needs of future generations (Goodin, 1998: 237) or to argue that rich nations have a moral responsibility to the poor (Sen, 2009: Pt IV).

The Student's Companion to Social Policy, Fifth Edition. Edited by Pete Alcock, Tina Haux, Margaret May and Sharon Wright.
© 2016 John Wiley & Sons, Ltd. Published 2016 by John Wiley & Sons, Ltd.

Equality

In mathematics, equality refers to the relationship between two distinguishable elements of equal value. Note that claims about equality for elements that are the same in every respect are uninteresting. If they are completely identical you cannot distinguish them anyway. Similarly, no serious reformers who use a language of equality have argued for social uniformity, although detractors sometimes wish to treat them as if they do. The egalitarian claim of welfare reformers has been that different groups should be treated as of equal value as far as social policy goes. In practice, this has led to demands for equality in entitlement to benefits and services, in treatment by welfare authorities and in participation in decision-making.

Issues arise in two main areas. First, how do we set the limits to the range of egalitarianism? Views on the scope of equality will depend on theories about what influences people's behaviour. The view, associated with neo-classical economics, that people are inclined to maximise their individual utility, implies that egalitarianism may undermine work incentives and kill the goose that lays the golden egg. If being at the bottom of an increasingly unequal society gets you welfare benefits, why bother to be anything else? The view that individuals are more influenced by culture, social relationships and behavioural norms suggests that the impact of equalising policies will depend much more on the social framework within which they operate (Gintis et al., 2005; Rothstein, 2005: ch. 2; Taylor-Gooby, 2009: chs 5 and 6).

The second point concerns the practical rather than the moral scope of inequality. Many policy-makers have distinguished between 'equality of outcome' and 'equality of opportunity'. Policies directed at the former must aim to put people in positions of equal value, while those seeking the latter are more modest. The objective is simply to give individuals an equal starting point in an unequal society. Egalitarianism in this sense is entirely compatible with wide divergences in life chances.

As globalised capitalism increasingly dominates the societies in which welfare states exist and equality of outcome recedes as a practical goal for national governments, debates about equality have shifted to equal opportunities. The notion is immediately relevant to education and training,

and to policies in relation to the acknowledged social divisions of sex, disability, sexuality and ethnicity. It is surprising that the disturbing evidence of declining social mobility (Hills et al., 2010: ch. 11) does not attract more attention in policy debate.

Various groups have struggled to ensure that particular divisions are recognised as meriting equal opportunity intervention. These include sexuality, age, disability, region, linguistic facility, faith, ethnicity and (sometimes) social class.

Rights

The concept of rights refers to the legitimacy of an individual's claims. In the context of social policy, the question is whether claims to social benefits and services should be backed by state force, so that social rights become an element in citizenship. In practice, ideas about need, about capability and about desert are most important in legitimating such claims (Box 4.1).

Arguments about 'desert' are typically linked to normative systems. In our society two are paramount: the family ethic, linked to arguments about the gender division of labour, the spheres of childhood and adulthood, and appropriate forms of sexuality; and the work ethic, with its attendant assumptions about individual responsibility to provide for oneself, which stigmatise dependency among those deemed capable of paid work. These ethics are subject to modification, and the growing diversity of UK society adds extra impetus to this process. Ideas about the desert of particular groups are of considerable importance in relation to social rights and the way in which they are put into practice (see Horton and Gregory, 2009; and Box 4.2).

The assertion of a right provides powerful support to the political claims of exploited groups. However, mechanisms for enforcing rights are, in practice, often weak and favour those with the best access to the courts. They have failed to mitigate inequalities within rich nations, let alone between global North and South, and they may even entrench existing divisions.

The needs-based approach is particularly vulnerable to the problem of choosing between diverse competing needs. Capability approaches are criticised because they assume that people are

Box 4.1   Three Bases for Rights Claims

- The *need-based* approach starts out from a list of human needs and argues that government is under an obligation to meet such needs, as far as this is possible. Problems arise in providing a watertight justification for a specific list of needs. The approach has offered some of the most profound arguments for the legitimation of welfare as an inescapable duty of government (see Plant, 1991: ch. 5).

- The *capability-based* approach, developed in the path-breaking work of Nobel Laureate economist Amartya Sen (2009), understands well-being in terms of the capabilities a person has, 'the substantive freedoms he or she enjoys to lead the kind of life he or she has reason to value'. Poverty can be understood as the deprivation of capabilities. The onus lies on government to remedy this, if possible. People's capabilities can be established by comparing what more or less privileged groups are able to do or enjoy in a society.

The approach underlies the construction of the widely used UN *Human Development Index*, which, broadly speaking, seeks to compare the achievement of a range of capabilities in different countries. It has been expanded to support demands from systematically disadvantaged groups such as women and disabled people (Nussbaum 2000), and there have been attempts to apply the approach to practical policy issues.

- *Desert-based* claims are founded on the view that some quality or activity by a particular group imposes an obligation on society to provide them with certain services. For example, it may be claimed that motherhood, or contribution through work (however defined) or in war, is deserving of support, and that the duty to provide it should come home to the state. Such claims are typically linked to functional or reciprocal arguments or are part and parcel of a normative system.

Box 4.2   Entitlement through Desert

- Entitlement to social insurance benefits based on work records is more secure and, in practice, less subject to official harassment than entitlement to means-tested benefit based on need.

- Support services designed to help those caring for frail elderly people are sometimes effectively rationed by reference to

the status and the access to employment of the carer; receipt of the services is influenced by gender and age.

- Allocation of social housing of particular quality may involve the grading of tenants as suitable for higher or lower status estates.

autonomous, independent, reflective actors, not members of a complex society with vulnerabilities, interdependencies and social needs. They fail to take seriously the differing needs of various social groups for support and for access to a public realm to articulate and debate risks. Desert-based approaches entrench assumptions about the social worth of particular activities and possible damage from others. For these reasons recent debate has

stressed the importance of political action alongside rights and opportunities to press home the needs of the most vulnerable against the privileged (Lister, 2003: ch. 6; Dean 2010: ch. 9).

Social justice

Social justice is concerned with who ought to get what. Resource allocation in most welfare states is dominated by market systems which assume that goods are property to be owned, valued, bought and sold, and by normative systems of distribution closely linked to kin relationship. Arguments about rights and about equality have provided a basis for claims about justice which often cross-cut market and kin allocation. The most important positions of recent years have been those of Nozick and Rawls, and these illustrate individualistic and social approaches to social justice (see Box 4.3).

Both approaches have been extensively discussed and criticised. Nozick's position rests on

individualistic ideas about work. Production in modern society involves the interlinked activity of many people. The correct allocation of credit for work is highly controversial and is carried out in practice mainly through market institutions. Nozick's approach legitimates the market order and reinforces the work ethic.

The Rawlsian approach is attractive in that it rests on negotiation free from the biases that social position – class, gender, tenure, age, employment opportunities, state of health and so on – generates in the real politics of social policy. However, there are severe problems in deciding a priori the distribution of benefits and services people abstracted from their social circumstances would accept. There is nothing irrational in favouring a grossly unequal world and hoping to come out as a winner; or, if one felt more charitable, in supporting the highest average standard of living, providing the worst off are not too hard hit. It is difficult to devise approaches to social justice that both take seriously the autonomy of individual citizens and lay down the definitive policies a society must follow if it is to be labelled just – to put the seal of social justice on particular welfare arrangements.

Equality, Rights and Justice as Ideology

Equality

The conceptions of equality in policy debate increasingly centre on opportunity rather than outcome. New Labour policies in the early 2000s followed the Commission on Social Justice, which deprecated egalitarians as backward-looking 'levellers' and stressed 'the need to spread opportunities and life chances as widely as possible'. They also placed an increasing emphasis on individual responsibility to grasp opportunities and to contribute through paid work. The philosophy of the 2010–15 Coalition stressed individual responsibility even more strongly. This provided further justification for harsh cuts in benefit levels and in social spending and a restructuring of local government services, the NHS and much of education designed to encourage a shift to the private sector.

In general, the right in politics prioritises rights, derived from market and family, over claims based on considerations of equality. The left has regarded equality as important, but as only one policy objective among several. The

---

Box 4.3 Individualist and Social Approaches to Social Justice

■ Nozick argues that the core of just claims is labour: people have a right to what they have 'mixed their labour with', that is, improved by their work. As a matter of strict justice, it is a violation of individuals' autonomy to appropriate or redistribute the goods that people have gained through their work, although individuals may as a matter of charity choose to surrender property to those they view as needy and deserving (Plant, 1991: 210–13).

■ Rawls's approach rests on the notion of a 'veil of ignorance'. The central idea is that just arrangements are those that people would endorse if they did not know what position in society they themselves would come to occupy, if they had no vested interests themselves (Plant, 1991: 99–107). Rawls argues that it is in principle possible to 'second guess' the kind of choices about the allocation of goods (and bads) that individuals would arrive at under these circumstances. Uncertain whether they would end up at the bottom of an unequal and exploitative society, people would prefer a social order in which the only permitted inequalities were those that improved the position of the worst off; for example, by raising living standards throughout the community.

commitment is increasingly to equality of opportunity (with an obligation to group opportunities) rather than to equality of outcome, and to the linking of welfare to social contribution rather than to need.

Rights

Individual rights are closely linked to notions of social justice. Equality has been one of the principal foundations of rights claims in social policy debate, so that citizenship in itself is seen to justify rights to welfare. The other major foundation has been desert. In policy debate, ideas about desert, linked to work and family ethics, have become increasingly important, so that entitlement rules are drawn more stringently, the mechanisms for ensuring that able-bodied people pursue employment have been strengthened and obligations to maintain children after a relationship ends have been codified. Much reform is also concerned to reduce state spending, in line with a general emphasis on property rights. This requires collective spending decisions to be justified against a stricter criterion than is applied to individual spending.

The emphasis on desert is a central pillar of right-wing approaches to welfare. However, recent arguments on the left about reciprocity have also been concerned to emphasise individual contribution as part of a move towards more active policies. These are characterised by concern to expand opportunity and also to give weight to individual responsibility for outcomes, rather than simply provide maintenance through the passive receipt of benefits.

Social justice

Developments in relation to social justice follow largely from the above. The key shift is towards a more active notion of how social entitlements should be structured, in keeping with the move away from an egalitarian approach and towards one influenced by meritocracy or by ideas about property and family-linked desert.

The general trajectory of discussion of individual rights has been a shift from the notion of rights justified by equal citizenship to rights justified by desert. Benefit rights for unemployed people, for example, are ever more tightly linked to appropriate behaviour as 'job-seekers', through New Deal,

the Work Programme and Universal Credit. Work conditions are now being extended to single parents and some groups of sick and disabled people.

Emerging Issues

Debates about equality, rights and social justice have become both broader and narrower. On the one hand, increasing social diversity, more fluid patterns of family life and of employment, and struggles for the recognition of the rights by a broader range of groups have extended the range of claims for social policy interventions on the grounds of social justice. On the other hand, the ideological pressure justifying allocation on market and family-ethic principles and promoting individual rather than state responsibility is stronger than it has been for half a century. One view requires government to expand social policy, the other to spread welfare interventionism more thinly.

More recently there are indications of a move towards democratisation. Citizenship needs and social rights (Lister 2003; Taylor-Gooby, 2009: ch. 11; Dean, 2010: ch. 9) are increasingly seen as issues of public debate. The demand is for a broader and more vigorous public realm open equally to all and in which the principles underlying policy must be justified to the satisfaction of policy-users and not just policymakers.

Social policy is overshadowed by concerns about the impact of population ageing, technological un- or sub-employment, growing international competition, tax revolt, the weakening of kinship care networks, international migration, environmental concerns, general distrust of big government and the future sustainability of welfare states. The climate of policymaking is one of austerity and of scepticism about how far government can resolve social problems. Under these circumstances it is hardly surprising that conceptual debates turn away from an interventionist concern with the promotion of equality of outcome towards the nourishing of more equal opportunities. Moral arguments point out that equal opportunity policies may damage the interests of the most vulnerable unless we develop effective systems to protect rights. Equally, we can determine whether the final outcomes are morally acceptable only by comparison with standards of social justice.

Equality, rights and social justice remain central to social policy, especially in a more globalised, diverse and uncertain social world. They underlie many current political struggles about what states should do for their citizens. This is increasingly recognised by social policy writers, who repeatedly call for more inclusive democratic engagement so that disadvantaged groups can play a stronger role in determining outcomes. Recent years have seen severe cuts in state provision bearing harshly on the most vulnerable groups. This can only reinvigorate the appeal of social justice as a rallying point for the defence of the welfare state.

Guide to Further Sources

The best (and most clearly written) guide to the main relevant currents in contemporary political philosophy remains R. Plant (1991), *Modern Political Thought*, Oxford: Blackwell, especially chs 3–7.

R. Goodin (1998), *Reasons for Welfare*, Princeton: Princeton University Press, covers similar ground in more detail (see chs 2, 3 and 4). This book also reviews the moral aspects of exploitation and dependency and develops a principled case against New Right arguments. A. Sen (2009), *The Idea of Justice*, Cambridge, MA: Harvard University Press, summarises the capability approach in Part III. Part IV discusses the implications for democracy. This book is written from a global rather than a national perspective; see them.poly-log.org/3/fsa-en.htm for a typically readable and incisive article relating his work to other writers on social justice. M. Nussbaum (2000), *Women and Human Development: The Capabilities Approach*, Cambridge: Cambridge University Press, points to the relevance of the approach to gender inequality, from which it is a short step to embrace other dimensions of difference.

J. Hills et al. (2010), *An Anatomy of Economic Inequality in the UK*, Government Equalities Office and LSE, London, explores some of the recent evidence on social mobility. R. Lister (2003), *Citizenship: Feminist Perspectives*, Basingstoke: Palgrave, provides a detailed analysis of citizenship rights. H. Dean (2015), *Social Rights and Human Welfare*, London: Routledge, is an excellent discussion of rights- and needs-based

approaches. J. Foley (2004), *Sustainability and Social Justice*, London: IPPR, extends the focus to include issues of sustainability: environmentally, cross-nationally and inter-generationally.

P. Taylor-Gooby (2009), *Reframing Social Citizenship*, Oxford: Oxford University Press, analyses welfare, citizenship and social justice in a globalised world, paying particular attention to trust. J. Le Grand (2003), *Motivation, Agency and Public Policy*, Oxford: Oxford University Press, discusses theories of human agency (why people do what they do) and argues that social policy should be deliberately designed to respect diversity in values and motives.

B. Rothstein (2005), *Social Traps and the Problem of Trust*, Cambridge: Cambridge University Press, argues that trust and social cohesion are central to ensure that a moral social policy can be sustained. H. Gintis, S. Bowles, R. Boyd and E. Fehr (2005), *Moral Sentiments and Material Interests*, Cambridge, MA: MIT Press, is hard going, but rewarding: a principled critique of the view that we can understand how people behave in society simply by assuming that they follow self-interest. T. Horton and J. Gregory (2009), *The Solidarity Society*, London: Fabian Society, examine the idea of desert in relation to social rights.

V. George and R. Page (eds) (1995), *Modern Thinkers on Welfare*, London: Prentice Hall/Harvester Wheatsheaf, provide succinct accounts of the views of major policy commentators and critics. T. Fitzpatrick (2005), *New Theories of Welfare*, Basingstoke: Palgrave, provides an up-to-date review of theoretical concepts in social policy that includes genetics, information and surveillance. His (2010), *Voyage to Utopia*, Cambridge: Polity Press, is an entertaining guide to the whole field.

For the UN Human Development Report, influenced by Sen's work on capability, see: hdr.undp.org. Probably the best overall web resource on political ideas is Richard Kember's page at the University of Keele: www.psr.keele.ac.uk. Further material on the capability approach can be found at the Human Development and Capability Association at: hd-ca.org. The United Nations Human Development Reports are at: hdr.undp.org/en. The Centre for the Study of Social Justice, Oxford, has useful working papers and web-links, see: social-justice.politics.ox.ac.uk.

Review and Assignment Questions

1 What is the point of considering ethical issues such as equality, justice and desert in relation to practical social policy issues?

2 Dean argues that 'human needs must be satisfied in the context of our interdependency with others'. What does he mean? Is he right?

3 Retirement pensioners, single parents, single unemployed people without dependants and disabled people all receive different levels of state benefits. Is this fair? Why?

4 In an increasingly diverse world it is impossible to devise principles of social justice that can be applied across all groups: do you agree? Suggest some possible principles and point out their strengths and weaknesses.

5 What justification is there for the welfare state to direct benefits and services to its own citizens when people in other countries are in much greater need?

Visit the book companion site at www.wiley.com/go/alcocksocialpolicy to make use of the resources designed to accompany the textbook. There you will find chapter-specific guides to further resources, including governmental, international, thinktank, pressure groups and relevant journal sources. You will also find a glossary based on *The Blackwell Dictionary of Social Policy*, help sheets, guidance on managing assignments in social policy and career advice.

5

Human Rights and Equality

Deirdre Flanigan and Alison Hosie

Overview

- Debating human rights and equality involves reflecting on a number of conceptual ideas relating to human dignity, equality and non-discrimination, participation, empowerment and accountability.
- Human rights in the UK comes from the international system of human rights, specifically from the United Nations and the regional European Convention on Human Rights.
- Policies to promote equality in the UK progressed in a piecemeal way, leading to significant variance in the legal protections available to different social groups. These strands have now been brought together in a single piece of legislation.
- Approaches to achieving equality vary and are influenced extensively by the values of those with responsibility for implementing policy and practice to promote equality.
- The current political and economic environment calls into question the future direction of legislation and policy activity to promote human rights and equality.

Historical Context

Human rights

Human rights emerged, from a Western standpoint, from the horrors of the Holocaust and the misery of the Great Depression, although the evolution of concepts of rights, equality and the rule of law can also be traced back further to instruments like the Magna Carta and the French and American revolutions. The foundation document, the Universal Declaration of Human Rights (UDHR), adopted by the United Nations General

The Student's Companion to Social Policy, Fifth Edition. Edited by Pete Alcock, Tina Haux, Margaret May and Sharon Wright.
© 2016 John Wiley & Sons, Ltd. Published 2016 by John Wiley & Sons, Ltd.

Box 5.1 Core United Nations (UN) Human Rights Treaties

The core UN human rights treaties ratified by the UK are:

- International Covenant on Economic, Social and Cultural Rights.
- International Covenant on Civil and Political Rights.
- International Convention on the Elimination of all forms of Racial Discrimination.
- International Convention on the Elimination of all forms of Discrimination against Women and its Optional Protocol.
- Convention Against Torture and other forms of cruel, inhuman and degrading treatment or punishment and its Optional Protocol.
- Convention on the Rights of the Child.
- Convention on the Rights of Persons with Disabilities and its Optional Protocol.

Box 5.2 Human Rights Act 1998

- Article 2 Right to life.
- Article 3 Prohibition of torture and inhuman or degrading treatment or punishment.
- Article 4 Prohibition of slavery and forced labour.
- Article 5 Right to liberty and security.
- Article 6 Right to a fair trial.
- Article 7 No punishment without law.
- Article 8 Right to respect for private and family life.
- Article 9 Freedom of thought, conscience and religion.
- Article 10 Freedom of expression.
- Article 11 Freedom of assembly and association.
- Article 12 Right to marry.
- Article 14 Prohibition of discrimination.
- Article 16 Restrictions on political activity of aliens.
- Article 17 Prohibition of abuse of rights.
- Article 18 Limitation on use of restrictions on rights.

First Protocol.

- Article 1 Protection of property.
- Article 2 Right to education.
- Article 3 Right to free elections.

Assembly in 1948 declared that all human beings were born free and equal in dignity and rights. The UDHR spells out the full range of human rights in thirty articles and represents the standard for human rights across the world. These formed the basis for a wide range of international treaties known as UN Conventions, and the UK has voluntarily agreed to be bound by the majority of them in international law (see Box 5.1).

Almost at the same time, human rights developments were taking place in Europe. In 1950, the Council of Europe, not to be confused with the European Union, enacted the European Convention on Human Rights. The Convention is interpreted and enforced by the European Court of Human Rights. Similar regional instruments are found in the Americas and Africa.

Human rights were 'brought home' to the UK in 1998 with the coming into force of the Human Rights Act (see Box 5.2). Previous to this, people seeking to make human rights arguments in courts across the UK would have to exhaust their case using domestic law and then take the case to the European Court of Human Rights. The Human Rights Act brought two innovations, namely, people can now use human rights arguments directly in courts across the UK, and public bodies, or those exercising public functions, are bound to act in compliance with the European Convention on Human Rights.

Meanwhile, UN Conventions remain part of the UK's international obligations and exist as legal rights in international law. Consequently, courts throughout the UK are able to refer to UN Conventions in interpreting domestic law.

Moreover, the UK, as a member state at the UN Human Rights Council, is reviewed periodically for its compliance with human rights generally and by the UN Committees under specific UN Conventions.

There is, for those interested in human rights more generally, a wide range of information available through domestic case reports, the jurisprudence of the European Court of Human Rights and through the UK's engagement with the UN Human Rights Council and the UN Committees under the UN Conventions.

Equalities

Equality in the UK has developed from a system of different legal protections for separate groups to a consolidated legislative framework protecting seven characteristics: age, disability, gender, sexual orientation, marriage and civil partnership, pregnancy and maternity, and religion and belief. The promotion of equality law and policy can be traced back to the establishment of the European Community in 1957. An explicit commitment was made within that treaty to promote 'equality of opportunity', specifically the principle that women and men should receive equal pay for equal work. In the UK, legislation to promote equalities has developed in a piecemeal fashion since the late 1960s, which saw the first legislative measures to tackle racial discrimination. Throughout the 1970s in the UK there was a series of legislative developments focusing on equalities issues, including the Equal Pay Act 1970, the Sex Discrimination Act 1975 and the Race Relations Act 1976.

Legislation to tackle disability discrimination did not come until much later, with the introduction of the Disability Discrimination Act 1995. It has only been relatively recently that legislation has been introduced to promote equality on the grounds of sexual orientation (2003), religion or belief (2003), gender identity (2004) and age (2006). This piecemeal approach to the development of equalities legislation meant there was inconsistency in legal protections available to specific equality groups. The introduction of the Equality Act 2010 has addressed this by providing a single legal framework with streamlined law to tackle discrimination and promote equality. It should, however, be noted that the Equality Act 2010 does not apply to Northern Ireland, where responsibility for equality law and enforcement have been devolved.

Development of equality and human rights monitoring and enforcement bodies

In 2007, three legacy commissions – the Equal Opportunities Commission, the Commission for Racial Equality and the Disability Rights Commission – were brought together to create a single organisation, the Equality and Human Rights Commission (EHRC), with powers to promote and enforce equality and non-discrimination laws throughout Great Britain. The EHRC was also given the remit for monitoring all human rights obligations in England and Wales and those in Scotland which remained reserved to Westminster.

A number of other monitoring and regulatory bodies were created as a result of the processes of devolution in 1998. First, in compliance with the Belfast (Good Friday) Agreement of 10 April 1998, the Northern Ireland Human Rights Commission came into existence in March 1999, followed in October that year by the creation of the Northern Ireland Equality Commission which took over the functions of the four legacy commissions. In 2006, an Act of the Scottish Parliament created the Scottish Human Rights Commission.

The three national human rights institutions all have been awarded 'A' status at the UN (giving them speaking rights at the UN Human Rights Council) and they act as a bridge between the UN Human Rights System and the UK.

Conceptualising Human Rights and Equalities

Human rights

The conceptual basis of human rights is the recognition of the inherent dignity of all human lives; further, that the equal and inalienable rights of all members of the human family are the foundation of freedom, justice and peace in the world.

Human rights have been conceived as requiring both positive and negative duties on the state. Negative rights generally refer to the state refraining from doing things that interfere with human dignity, for example, the prohibition of torture. Positive rights require actions to fulfil rights such as providing due legal process to uphold fair trial rights. In reality, however, the fulfilment of most human rights protections requires positive duties on the state. For example, fulfilling the prohibition of torture requires the state to take a range of positive actions, including training officials involved in detention of prisoners that torture is a criminal act.

Human rights are not all absolute rights, although freedom from torture and slavery is an example of a right that can never be interfered with in any circumstance. Many human rights are qualified and can be derogated from in order to protect the rights of others, for reasons of national security, public safety or the economic well-being of the country, for the prevention of disorder or crime, or for the protection of health or morals. Other rights are limited in that they are restricted in particular circumstances, for example, the right to liberty can be restricted in order to effect a lawful arrest.

Equalities

Equality has been a central topic of debate in social policy analysis for many years, framing the development of the welfare state and playing out as a central point of debate by political leaders from both ends of the political spectrum (Coffey, 2004). However, equality means different things to different people, and is as contested as other central topics in social policy, including rights, freedom and social justice (see Chapter 4). White (2007) highlights five forms of equality (Box 5.3).

As well as different forms of equality, there are also different reasons for promoting equality. For example, economic equality may be valued to reduce poverty, while political equality may be valued in order to achieve status equality (an element of social equality) via each person having an equal right to vote. The reasons for promoting equality, and the type of equality promoted, will be influenced by a range of economic, political, social and ideological values.

Debates on equality within social policy have tended to highlight a distinction between equality of opportunity and equality of outcome. A minimal approach emphasises merit, with equality in access to opportunities in education, employment, etc. A broader approach recognises people's different histories and ensures equal chances on this

> **Box 5.3** Forms of Equality
>
> - Legal equality: having equal protection and treatment by the law.
> - Political equality: having equal opportunities to play a part in political life, including voting and standing for political office.
> - Social equality: having status equality with other social groups and an absence of domination of one group over another.
> - Economic equality: having opportunities to access economic resources; with recognition of the role played by the state in intervening to achieve this.
> - Moral equality: recognising, through the organisation of society, people's morally significant interests in relations to freedoms, resources, etc., that different people have equal claims in relation to their respective interests.

basis. A third approach involves taking affirmative action (for example, quotas) to address disadvantages. Positive action involves significant intervention to achieve equality of participation in public life and employment. Positive action involves favouring candidates from under-represented groups where they meet the core requirements for the role. Moving from minimalist to maximalist interventions corresponds with a move from concerns with promoting equality of opportunity towards measures that more directly influence equality of outcomes.

Three different approaches to promoting equality have been identified (see Box 5.4). These approaches were initially developed in analysis on gender equality, but are recognised as offering a valuable framework for promoting equality for a number of social groups (Squires, 2005).

Human Rights and Equalities: Making Links

Equalities and human rights approaches are mutually reinforcing. Fulfilling human rights

Box 5.4   Approaches to Equality

- Sameness: focuses on treating everyone in the same way. This would mean that we neither see particular group characteristics (for example, ethnicity, disability, gender, sexual orientation) as being relevant to someone's abilities, nor recognise these characteristics as meaning that a person is entitled to adaptations to current policies or practices.
- Difference: focuses on recognising and accommodating differences. This would mean recognising that different people have different needs and adapting policies and practices to take account of these differences.
- Transformative: focuses on fundamental change within policy and practice. A much more significant change to relations between groups is emphasised, with concern to design equalities issues into policies and practices rather than adapt or offer adjustments to meet the needs of specific groups.

involves the promotion of equality and non-discrimination, empowerment, participation, accountability and legality. Promoting equality involves progressing freedom, social justice and rights. The extent of policy intervention to achieve these aims, and the intended outcome of intervention (a minimalist or a maximalist approach, for example), will differ depending on the values of those promoting these goals. The capabilities approach brings together human rights and equality within a social justice framework.

The approach to equality promoted in the Equalities Review (2007) builds on the human rights principles developed by Amartya Sen through the *capabilities approach*, recognising the equal worth of every individual:

An equal society protects and promotes equal, real freedom and substantive opportunity to live in the ways people value and would choose, so that everyone can flourish. An equal society rec-ognises people's different needs, situations and goals and removes the barriers that limit what people can do and can be. (Equalities Review, 2007: 6)

The capabilities approach provides an overarching structure for understanding and measuring equality using human rights. It focuses on what matters most to people, recognises diverse needs, draws attention to the structural and institutional barriers framing life chances and recognises that people have diverse goals. Capabilities are the important things people can do or be in life, which make their lives fulfilling. Capabilities in this context do not refer to the internal skills or capacities of a person. Rather, the lack of a capability indicates a failure by society to provide real freedom for people (Burchardt and Vizard, 2007).

Martha Nussbaum's (1999) theorising on social justice and human rights builds on Sen's capabilities approach. By virtue of being human we are entitled to be treated with equal dignity and worth no matter what our social or economic position. The primary source through which we can articulate our worth is through our abilities in making choices that allow us to plan our lives in accordance with our own intended aims and outcomes. Critics have highlighted the limitations of its individualistic focus, arguing that it is incomplete in its current form and it is potentially unworkable in practice. However, the value of the capabilities approach is to move beyond the more traditional egalitarian focus on resource distribution, where resources are recognised as being valuable only where people can turn these resources into functions. People should be treated fairly by society and be given choices that respect and promote the equal worth of all persons.

Emerging Issues

Equality and human rights protections across the UK continue to be undermined by the various 'austerity' measures taken in response to the 2008 economic recession. Public sector cuts and welfare reform have had a disproportionate effect on women, disabled people and many other disadvantaged and marginalised groups.

At the time of writing, the application of the Equality Act continues to be undermined by failure to enact key provisions on the gender pay gap, to address socio-economic inequalities and the power of employment tribunals. The Equality and Human Rights Commission's budget has been significantly reduced and its powers restricted. At the same time the Conservative government attacks on the Human Rights Act and the threat of withdrawing from the European Convention on Human Rights are serious concerns for the protection of rights across the UK. The proposal to replace the Human Rights Act with a British Bill of Rights will most likely be a regressive move concerning rights protection in the UK.

There are some examples of divergent practice towards human rights protection across the nations of the UK. The devolved Welsh Assembly has increased protections around children's human rights. Northern Ireland has been developing a Northern Irish Bill of Rights as promised in the Belfast (Good Friday) Agreement; however, it has still not been enacted. Scotland has launched a National Action Plan for Human Rights, which aims to close the gap between human rights legal protection and realisation on the ground.

Guide to Further Sources

There are a number of textbooks that look at human rights as a social science concern. A good starting place might be M. Freeman (2002), *Human Rights: An Interdisciplinary Approach*, Cambridge: Polity Press, or R. Morgan and B. Turner (eds) (2009), *Interpreting Human Rights: Social Science Perspectives*, London: Routledge. On equalities, there are a wide range of books to choose from. A good starting place might be S. White (2007), *Equality*, Cambridge: Polity Press. R. Drake (2001), *The Principles of Social Policy*, Basingstoke: Palgrave, offers contributions to debates on equality, justice, freedom and rights, while A. Coffey (2004), *Reconceptualising Social Policy: Sociological Perspectives on Contemporary Social Policy*, Maidenhead: Open University Press, reflects in ch. 5 on the relationship between equality and difference debates within social policy. Squires has made a critical contribution to debates on equality policy through her work on

mainstreaming; see, for example, J. Squires (2005), 'Is mainstreaming transformative?: Theorizing mainstreaming in the context of diversity and deliberation', *Social Politics: International Studies in Gender, State and Society*, 12:3, 366–88. A. Hosie and M. Lamb (2013), 'Human rights and social policy: challenges and opportunities for social research and its use as evidence in the protection and promotion of human rights in Scotland', *Social Policy and Society*, 12:2, 191–203, explores the valuable contribution that social policy research can make to the promotion and protection of human rights

A number of texts are now available on the capabilities approach, including A. Sen (2009), *The Idea of Justice*, Cambridge, MA: Harvard University Press; M. Nussbaum (2000), *Women and Human Development: The Capabilities Approach*, Cambridge: Cambridge University Press; and M. Nussbaum (1999), *Sex and Social Justice*, Oxford: Oxford University Press. For more practical application of the capabilities approach in the modern policy context, see T. Burchardt and P. Vizard (2007), *Definition of Equality and Framework for Measurement: Final Recommendations of the Equalities Review Steering Group on Measurement*, CASE Paper 120, London School of Economics; and Equalities Review (2007), *Fairness and Freedom: The Final Report of the Equalities Review*, London: Cabinet Office. Finally, N. Fraser (2008), *Adding Insult to Injury: Nancy Fraser Debates her Critics*, London: Verso, is an excellent source to explore recognition and redistribution as critical debates within social justice.

Web sources: Equality and Human Rights Commission, www.equalityhumanrights.com; Northern Ireland Human Rights Commission, www.nihrc.org; Northern Ireland Equalities Commission, www.equalityni.org/site/default.asp?secid= home; Scottish Human Rights Commission, www.scottishhumanrights.com; Government Equalities Office (UK government), www.equalities.gov.uk; Information on the Equality Act 2010, www.equalities.gov.uk/equality_bill.aspx; Information on European NHRIs and Equality Bodies, fra.europa.eu/sites/default/files/fra_uploads/816-NHRI_en.pdf; United Nations Human Rights information, www.un.org/en/rights; Council of Europe Commissioner for Human Rights, www.coe.int/en/web/commissioner/home; Equality and Diversity Forum collection of essays discussing 'Beyond 2015: shaping the future of equality, human rights and social justice', www .edf.org.uk/blog/wp-content/uploads/2015/05/ EDF_Beyond_2015_PDF.pdf.

Review and Assignment Questions

1 How and why does economic austerity impact on human rights and equality?
2 Some have been critical of the move to a single equalities focus. What reasons might people give for this critique and what possible reasons might be given for promoting a single equality focus?
3 Nancy Fraser argues that a just society relies on both recognition and redistribution. What are the key features of each? Why are both important? Can both be achieved?
4 How might the capabilities approach be turned into a practical tool to promote equalities and protect human rights? What are the limitations of this tool?
5 You work for a local authority and have been tasked with providing a report on the likely human rights and equality impacts of a new social policy. Your report should outline: how and when you would consider human rights and equality in your planning and how you would ensure the meaningful participation of the local community in its development.

Visit the book companion site at www.wiley.com/ go/alcocksocialpolicy to make use of the resources designed to accompany the textbook. There you will find chapter-specific guides to further resources, including governmental, international, thinktank, pressure groups and relevant journal sources. You will also find a glossary based on *The Blackwell Dictionary of Social Policy*, help sheets, guidance on managing assignments in social policy and career advice.

6

Efficiency, Equity and Choice

Carol Propper

Overview

- Economic analysis begins from the assumption of scarcity – we cannot have everything we want. So people and society must make choices.
- The appropriate cost of these choices to society is the opportunity cost – the resources forgone if the choice is made.
- Economic efficiency means making the most of scarce resources. Economic efficiency occurs when the opportunity cost of using resources in a particular activity is equal to the sum of everyone's marginal benefits from that activity.
- Efficiency is not the only goal. Other goals include fairness and choice. These goals may clash with efficiency.
- Economists see markets and choice as one way of delivering efficiency and responsiveness in public services.

Introduction

Economic ideas and concepts are widely used in public policy. The domain of social policy is no exception: 'effective' and 'efficient' are adjectives frequently cited by politicians and policymakers as goals for those responsible for delivering public services. Yet the ideas of economics are considerably more than buzz words. Economic analysis provides a framework that can, and is, used to analyse questions about behaviour as diverse as worker participation in unions, the relative welfare of nations, the tendency of bureaucracies to grow, the behaviour of politicians or why increasing wealth does not appear to bring us happiness.

The Student's Companion to Social Policy, Fifth Edition. Edited by Pete Alcock, Tina Haux, Margaret May and Sharon Wright.

Terms such as efficiency and effectiveness have a rather more precise meaning within economics than when used by politicians or policymakers. Economists see efficiency, equity and (sometimes) choice as ends – and ends that may be achieved through a number of possible means. These means include the market, the state and a mixed economy.

Scarcity and Choice

Economic analysis begins from a single fact: we cannot have everything we want. We live in a world of scarcity. This is obvious in the case of the homeless, but it applies equally to the carer who works part-time and would like to have more time to devote either to her work or to the person she cares for, or to the rich rock star who goes on giving concerts in order to buy yet one more Caribbean island. It equally applies to governments, which have a larger budget than an individual but can never spend as much on health services or education as the voters would wish.

Faced with scarcity, be it of money or time, people must make choices. To make a choice, we balance the benefits of having more of something against the costs of having less of something else. Because resources are finite, in making choices we face costs. Whatever we choose to do, we could have done something else. So, for example, the carer with limited time can choose between working more or looking after the person she cares for. Or a society that invests in building roads uses up time and material that could be devoted to providing hospital facilities. Economists use the term 'opportunity cost' to emphasise that making choices in the face of scarcity implies a cost. The opportunity cost of any action is the best alternative forgone. So, if building a hospital is viewed by society as the next best thing to building a road, the cost of building a hospital is the opportunity cost of building a road.

In many situations the price paid for the use of a resource is the opportunity cost. So, if a road costs £1 million to build, then if the cost of the materials and labour used in road construction were the same as those for the construction of something else, £1 million is its opportunity cost. But market prices do not always measure opportunity costs and nor are all opportunity costs faced by an individual the result of their own choices. For example, when you cannot get on to a train at busy times of day, you bear the cost of the choice made by all the other people who did get on the train. This is not a price that is quoted by the market and nor it is one that the other people on the train take into account when they get onto it.

Efficiency

Efficiency has a specific meaning in economics. When deciding how much of a good or service should be produced we need to take into account that having the good or service gives rise to both benefits and costs, and how those benefits and the costs vary with the amount that is produced. In general, benefits are desirable and costs are to be avoided. Given this, it would seem sensible to choose that amount of the good at which the difference between total benefits and total costs is largest. When society has selected this amount of the good and allocated resources of production accordingly, economists call this the efficient level of output of this good, or, alternatively, say that there is an efficient allocation of resources in production of this good.

In determining the level of output that is efficient, we need to take into account both the benefits from the good and the opportunity costs of producing it. As an example I consider the consumption and production of something simple – ice cream. But the analytical framework can be equally applied to hospitals, schools, social work services and nuclear power stations.

Benefits of consumption

We would expect the benefits from eating ice cream to vary according to the amount eaten. In general, for someone who likes ice cream we would expect the total benefit to rise the more that is eaten. However, this total benefit may not rise proportionately with each mouthful consumed. Let us consider the first spoonful. If the eater is really hungry, the first spoonful will give considerable satisfaction. But as the amount eaten is increased the satisfaction derived from each additional spoonful will begin to fall. By and large, we would expect to find that the benefit derived from each additional spoonful falls the more that has been consumed. If we define the last spoonful as the marginal spoonful, we can say that the marginal benefit falls as the quantity of ice cream eaten increases. Either you become full or, because variety is nice, you would rather eat something else.

This analysis can be applied to society as a whole. Defining society's benefits as the sum of the benefits received by all individuals from ice cream, we can add up across all individuals to get the total social benefit. Similarly, we can add up each person's marginal benefit at each amount of ice cream eaten to get the marginal social benefit. This is the increase in total social benefit as we increase society's consumption by one unit. We assume that we can add up the benefits received by different people. Often we can do this easily because benefits are measured in a single unit, say pounds. But in some cases there may be measurement problems; for example, when it is

hard to value a good, or when £1,000 is worth much more to one person than another.

Both the total social benefit and the marginal social benefit can be drawn on a graph. Figure 6.1 shows the total social benefit from ice cream consumption. The amount of ice cream consumed is on the horizontal axis and the benefit from this in pounds is on the vertical axis. Total social benefit rises as consumption increases, but it rises at a falling rate. It rises at a falling rate precisely because the marginal social benefit of consumption falls as more ice cream is eaten.

Figure 6.2 shows this marginal social benefit of ice cream consumption. The total amount consumed is on the horizontal axis and is measured in the same units as in Figure 6.1. On the vertical axis we show the value in pounds of the marginal benefit. The marginal benefit curve slopes downwards from left to right, showing that the marginal social benefit falls as consumption of ice cream increases.

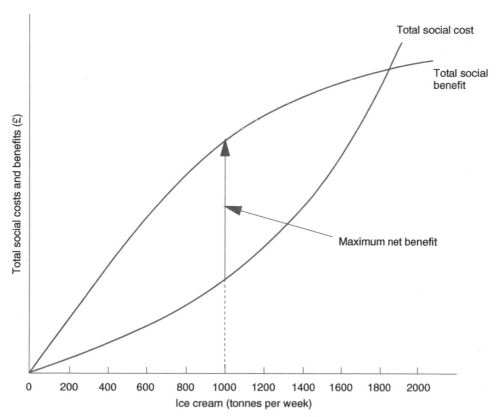

Figure 6.1 The total social benefit from ice cream consumption.

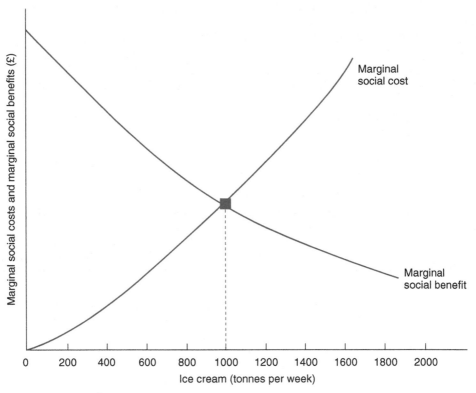

Figure 6.2 The marginal social benefit of ice cream consumption.

Costs of production

To determine the efficient level of production and consumption of ice cream we also need to consider the costs of production. Typically, the more of a good that is produced the more costly it is to produce. So total costs increase with production. However, what is required to establish efficiency is the cost of producing an extra unit of output, known as the marginal cost. Studies of production generally show that there is a level of production beyond which it becomes increasingly costly to expand output. This could be for a variety of reasons: firms may have to pay overtime or use less productive machinery, or the costs of coordinating production or delivery rise as the amount of good produced rises. So the marginal cost of production increases as output increases.

Assuming that ice cream production has the same pattern, we can add up the total costs of production across all producers. This will be the total social cost. We can also add up all the marginal costs to obtain the marginal social cost

for each unit of output. The total social cost of Figure 6.1 shows the way that total social cost rises with output of ice cream. The corresponding marginal social cost of production is shown in Figure 6.2.

The efficient level of output

We can use the information on how social benefits and social costs of ice cream consumption and production vary with output to identify that level of output at which the difference between total social benefits and total social costs (net social benefit) is at a maximum. This is the efficient level of output. From Figure 6.1, we can identify this as at 1,000 tonnes per week. Looking at Figure 6.2, we can see that this is the point at which marginal social benefits equal marginal social costs. This is no coincidence. As long as the marginal social cost is below the marginal social benefit, society will gain by producing and consuming more ice cream. Conversely, if the marginal social benefit is below the marginal social cost, society would do better by putting its resources to other uses and consuming and producing less ice cream. Only when the marginal social benefit is equal to the marginal social cost will it be impossible to increase net social benefits.

The analysis of the efficient amount of ice cream output is relevant to all goods and services. So we can define the socially efficient output of hospitals, home helps, education or cars in exactly the same way. We may have more problems in measuring the benefits and costs, but the principle remains the same: the socially efficient amount of the good or service is produced at the point where the marginal cost and benefit are equal.

An efficient level of production is thus a desirable end: if all goods are produced in their efficient quantities then net social benefit cannot be increased by reallocating resources. Conversely, if the level of production is not efficient, then net social benefits can be increased by producing more (or less) of one good and less (or more) of at least one other. Given that resources are always finite, efficiency is thus an important social objective.

Efficiency and effectiveness

Although efficiency and effectiveness are often used synonymously by policymakers, they are different. Effectiveness means producing something in the best possible way technically, and is sometimes called technical efficiency. We can check whether a production is technically efficient by seeing whether, given the current technology, more output could be produced from the present inputs. As an example, consider the delivery of meals on wheels by one person with one van. One service might visit houses by order of number. If all the even houses are on one side of the street and all the odd numbers on the other, this will mean crossing the road between each delivery. This is likely to be less technically efficient than delivering meals to all the odd numbered houses and then to all the even ones.

Efficiency goes further than (and encompasses) effectiveness. To know whether a production process is efficient we must first check that it is effective. Then, we have to see whether its current technology produces the output in a cheaper way than the alternatives. This requires looking at the prices of inputs, whereas effectiveness does not. So

in our example it may be that once costs are taken into account, it might be found that it is better to change the amount spent, and so to employ two people and one van. Then, we must check that consumers cannot make themselves better off by choosing to buy other goods. Finally, we must check that all the costs and benefits involved have been taken into account. This is known as checking that there are no external costs and benefits. In the train example given above, there were external costs when the train was crowded – the costs imposed by train users on others. In some activities, for example, smoking cigarettes or the use of fuels that pollute the atmosphere, these external costs may be large and may dwarf the private costs.

So before we can say that something is efficient we must first ensure that it is effective; hence, the drive towards effectiveness in the use of scarce medical resources, for example. However, just because a production method is effective, it does not mean it is efficient. We need to know the costs and the benefits of the service and of alternatives to know that. For many areas of social policy, we are still at the stage of establishing effectiveness and not efficiency.

Efficiency versus Other Goals

Equity

Even though efficiency is a desirable end it is not the only one. An efficient outcome is not necessarily a fair or equitable one. An efficient output is one for which the sum of all individuals' marginal valuations equals the marginal social costs of production. But each individual's valuation of a good or service – and so the sum of these valuations – will depend on the resources he or she has. So the efficient level of production will be defined in relation to the existing distribution of resources. If initial resources are distributed in a way that is judged as unfair, there is no reason why an efficient allocation of those resources should be fair.

An example may make this clearer. Suppose there are only two members of society, Ms A and Ms B. Given their initial resources, their likes and dislikes, and the production methods available to them, the efficient level of production of ice cream is four tubs per week. These tubs could all go to Ms A, or all to Ms B or they could share them equally. Each of these divisions of the total production is possible, but not all will be judged as fair or equitable. On the other hand, if each received only one tub, this allocation might be judged as fair, but it is not efficient. It is not efficient because we know that the efficient level of production is four tubs. If only two tubs were produced, net social benefit would be increased by producing more and in so doing we could make both Ms A and Ms B better off.

There are many possible definitions of equity or fairness – for example, minimum standards or equal distribution for all – but we do not discuss them here. The points to note are: first, that efficiency is not the same as fairness; second, that there is often a trade-off between the two (a fair allocation may be one that is not efficient); third, that efficiency embodies a value judgement just as definitions of fairness do. The value judgement underlying the definition of efficiency is that some distribution of income (often the existing one) is legitimate.

Choice

Choice is seen as an important mechanism by economists. By making choices, individuals can indicate their valuations of goods and services. If valuations are known, then the production of those services that have greater net (marginal) value will be increased and the production of others will be decreased, and so the outcome will be more efficient. Choice is often linked to competition: competition is one means by which individuals can exercise choices. To see this, consider the case where there is no competition in the supply of a service because there is only one supplier. In this case, individuals cannot choose the type of service they prefer as there is only one on offer.

Of course, there are costs to making choices – individuals have to decide which product they prefer and this will mean finding out about each possible option. In some circumstances, it could be the case that very small differences between goods do not merit the costs of trying to choose between them. In others, the amount of information required to make informed choices may be very high. It has sometimes been argued, for example, that the level of medical knowledge required to make informed choices in healthcare is too large for individuals to make good choices. The same argument has been advanced in debates

about giving greater choice in pension arrangements. However, in general, more choice is judged to be better than less.

In the field of social policy, where choice has often been limited, increasing choice – and the allied goal of increasing responsiveness of suppliers to users' wishes – is viewed as an important goal. From an economics perspective this is viewed as a move in the right direction. However, this does not mean that the benefits of increasing choice necessarily outweigh the costs. This will depend on the particular service.

The Means of Delivering Efficiency and Choice

All societies have had methods of trying to get the most out of limited resources. In large-scale societies, two dominant mechanisms of allocation have been used. These are allocation by the government and allocation by the market. Under the former system (the so-called command economies), planning and administration were used to decide what and how goods should be produced, and to whom they should be allocated. Under the latter, allocation decisions are made by the decisions of large numbers of individuals and private firms.

Markets are seen as desirable by economists since – in the absence of market failure – they will lead to an efficient allocation of resources without the need for coordination mechanisms and the costs of planning. In practice, of course, not all decisions in a market system are made by individuals, and not all ownership is private. Government has a large role in all market economies. However, the market mechanism currently has dominance: command economies have largely abandoned their structures in favour of freer markets.

Issues for Public Service Delivery

In the provision of public services, choice and competition have been introduced into systems where allocation was by means of administrative decision. Politicians from the left and the right have seen choice as a way of allowing more responsiveness; for example, giving parents choice in where their child goes to school or health service users the right to choose where they get medical care. In a range of public services competition in supply has been introduced as a means of increasing choice, responsiveness and efficiency. So private firms collect garbage, build houses for low-income tenants and run prisons. Private suppliers compete with the public sector to provide care for the mentally handicapped, and not-for-profit public education providers compete for contracts to provide education. In some countries – Canada is one – healthcare is financed by the state but provision is private. Thirty years ago these arrangements would have been seen in the UK as the wrong way to provide services; today, many go without comment.

On the other hand, in the provision of public services there is still considerable debate about the role of the private sector as a provider, the role of individual choice and for competition between suppliers. Research findings make it clear that the precise institutional arrangements of choice and competition in public services matters: a reform that works well in one context cannot be transposed without adaptation to another. Nevertheless, if choice and efficiency are important goals, market mechanisms have their uses in welfare services as in other parts of the economy.

Guide to Further Sources

J. Le Grand, C. Propper and S. Smith (2008), *The Economics of Social Problems*, 4th edn, Basingstoke: Palgrave, provides an economic analysis of social policy issues and assumes no previous knowledge of economics. A more advanced textbook, designed for those already studying economics, is N. Barr (2004), *The Economics of the Welfare State*, 4th edn, Oxford: Oxford University Press. For a book also aimed at economics students which discusses these issues in a US context, see J. Stiglitz (2000), *Economics of the Public Sector*, 3rd edn, New York: W. W. Norton. A non-technical review of a range of issues in the economics of the provision of public services is provided in P. Grout and M. Stevens (eds) (2003), 'Financing and managing public services', *Oxford Review of Economic Policy*, 19:2, 213–34. For a

discussion of the role of economic motivation in the behaviour of those who provide public services, see J. Le Grand (2005), *Motivation, Agency, and Public Policy: Of Knights and Knaves, Pawns and Queen*, Oxford: Oxford University Press. For an analysis of the economics of health, see S. Morris, N. Devlin and D. Parkin (2007), *Economic Analysis in Health Care*, Chichester: John Wiley and Sons.

Review and Assignment Questions

1 The concepts of social cost and social benefit involve the summation of individual benefits and costs. Explain why. What problems does this procedure pose?

2 'The specification of an efficient allocation of resources, unlike the definition of an equitable distribution, does not involve value judgements.' Do you agree?

3 Explain the concept of opportunity costs and how it relates to an efficient allocation of a good or service. Give examples where the private opportunity cost of an activity does not equal the social opportunity cost. In these cases, what tools may be used to make the private opportunity cost equal the social cost?

4 Explain why technical effectiveness is not the same thing as efficiency. Which is more difficult to achieve in your view?

5 Explain why economists value choice. Give examples of policies to improve choice in the provision of at least two public services. What are the advantages and disadvantages of increasing choice in the provision of public services?

Visit the book companion site at www.wiley.com/go/alcocksocialpolicy to make use of the resources designed to accompany the textbook. There you will find chapter-specific guides to further resources, including governmental, international, thinktank, pressure groups and relevant journal sources. You will also find a glossary based on *The Blackwell Dictionary of Social Policy*, help sheets, guidance on managing assignments in social policy and career advice.

7

Citizenship

Peter Dwyer

Overview

- Citizenship is fundamentally concerned with relationships between the individual and the communities that they inhabit.
- Debates about rights and responsibilities and the relationship between them are central to competing visions of citizenship.
- Citizenship implies membership of various forms of community, which in turn opens up linked issues of inclusion and exclusion.
- Liberal and Communitarian traditions of thought offer contrasting conceptions of citizenship and the ideal society.
- A new more conditional and constrained vision of contemporary social citizenship is being mapped out within, and beyond, the UK.

Defining Citizenship: Three Common Elements

In common with many ideas in social policy, citizenship remains a contentious notion that is subject to much philosophical and political debate. It is used in a range of contexts, by a multitude of commentators, and as such it is difficult to offer a simple precise and universally accepted definition of the term. However, three core aspects central to competing visions of citizenship can be identified.

- First, citizenship is fundamentally concerned with the relationship between individuals and the communities they inhabit. In contemporary society, membership of a national community, that is, a defined nation-state,

The Student's Companion to Social Policy, Fifth Edition. Edited by Pete Alcock, Tina Haux, Margaret May and Sharon Wright.
© 2016 John Wiley & Sons, Ltd. Published 2016 by John Wiley & Sons, Ltd.

remains a key, though not the only gateway to enjoyment of the rights associated with citizenship.

- Second, notions of citizenship imply that, alongside rights, citizens are also the bearers of certain responsibilities.
- Third, by invoking membership of a community, citizenship opens up allied questions related to inclusion and exclusion.

Exclusion from citizenship has both internal and external dimensions. Internal exclusion occurs when aspects of difference such as gender, ethnicity and disability, etc. are constructed and articulated in ways that deny certain individuals who are otherwise legally regarded as citizens, access to their full rights and responsibilities (see Lister's 2003 discussion of gendered citizenship). External exclusion occurs when noncitizens from beyond the bordered communities that citizenship promotes and sustains are denied citizenship status. Formal, *legal* inclusion, brought about by possession of an appropriate passport, is routinely a prerequisite of citizenship; however, full and effective citizenship also requires that citizens are equally able to actively participate in the *political* and *social* life of the community in which they are members. Citizenship then is concerned with a number of important, interlocking relationships, most notably, the connections between individuals and the communities in which they live. As a minimum, contemporary citizenship promises civil, political and social rights. It also implies certain responsibilities, including engaging in paid work or undertaking other socially valued activities such as unpaid care work, and respecting the rights of

fellow citizens. In turn, such responsibilities open up important questions about the ways in which citizenship rights should perhaps be linked to responsibilities.

Rights, Responsibilities and Competing Visions of Citizenship

Political philosophy matters when considering citizenship. A useful starting point is a comparison between broadly Communitarian and Liberal visions of citizenship. This rather crude distinction can be defended because implicit in these two competing normative frameworks are opposing views on the relative importance of the 'individual' and the 'community', and also whether the rights or responsibilities of citizens are assigned primary importance. Linked to this later point is a significant disagreement between Communitarians and Liberals about the extent to which an individual citizen's enjoyment of their rights should be linked to prior acceptance of wider communal responsibilities Table 7.1 highlights their key differences in respect of citizenship.

The Communitarian approach to citizenship has its roots in the civic republicanism that gave rise to the earliest forms of citizenship in the city-states of ancient Greece. Good citizenship in these smaller early communities demanded that, as citizens, all free men (citizenship did not extend to women or slaves) accept a common commitment to actively engage in the civic duties of government and live responsibly according to the shared values and rules of the *polis* (city). Today, Communitarianism similarly stresses the social embeddedness of human beings and the

Table 7.1 Communitarianism and Liberalism: contrasting visions of citizenship.

Dimension	Communitarianism	Liberalism
Primacy afforded to:	Community	Individual
Citizenship conceived as:	'Practice'	'Status'
Prioritises:	Collective responsibilities and duties	Individual rights and entitlements
Citizenship implies:	Particular and conditional privileges reserved for active, responsible citizens	Universal and largely unconditional rights passively enjoyed by all citizens

importance of community in enabling the development of shared values and a collective commitment to others. Communities are seen as constitutive of who we are able to become and vital in nurturing our capacity to be 'good citizens'. Therefore, our responsibilities to the community should take precedence over individual rights and preferences. Communitarians view citizenship as a 'practice' that prioritises duty and obligation above and beyond any rights that citizenship may bestow. They believe that it is only in recognising and practising our wider communal responsibilities that we can truly become citizens.

Early Liberal thinking on citizenship is associated with seventeenth- and eighteenth-century classical Liberal theorists such as John Locke, Adam Smith and, subsequently, John Stuart Mill's in the nineteenth century. Classic Liberal ideas emerged as a challenge to the old feudal order which asserted the divine right of the monarch, as the head of state, to exercise arbitrary power over their subjects. Linked to the development of capitalism and the emergence of the nation-state, early Liberalism asserted each individual's right to liberty (freedom from the interference and rule of an overbearing monarch or state), alongside basic equality before the law and the right to own property acquired by fair means through market transactions and the rule of law. These early ideas remain central to Liberal notions of citizenship, which stress the paramount importance of citizenship as a 'status' that bestows largely unconditional rights and entitlements on individual citizens. Plant neatly sums up the core differences in approach of these two traditions, see Box 7.1.

Although these are two long-established approaches they retain a relevance as they have been influential in contemporary debates about citizenship rights and responsibilities. Neo-liberal thinkers (see Chapter 9) have long drawn on classic Liberal thinking to endorse a notion of citizenship that guarantees only the civil and political rights they see as necessary for a functioning free market, together with a minimal welfare state restricted to the minority of poor citizens unable to meet their welfare needs through market mechanisms; an approach that has subsequently underpinned the views of prominent New Right thinkers such as Murray and Mead. Alongside

> **Box 7.1** Plant on Liberalism and Communitarianism
>
> The first [*Liberalism*] sees citizenship as a status that is not fundamentally altered by the virtue (or lack of it) of the individual: it does not ask whether the citizen is making a recognised contribution to society . . . You should thus be able, as a citizen, to claim benefits even if you are not discharging what others may regard as your proper obligations to society . . . The second [*Communitarianism*] and alternative view, places much less emphasis on rights, and focuses instead on obligation, virtue and contribution. In this view citizenship is not a kind of pre-existing status, but rather something that is achieved by contributing to the life of a society. The ideas of reciprocity and contribution are at the heart of this concept of citizenship: individuals do not and cannot have a right to the resources of society unless they contribute to the development of that society through work or other socially valued activities, if they are in a position to do so. (Plant, 1998: 30)

this 'New Communitarians', such as Etzioni, have been influential in persuading governments to introduce a more constrained and contingent notion of social citizenship in which access to basic, publicly provided, welfare entitlements become dependent on citizens first agreeing to meet particular compulsory duties or patterns of responsible individual agency/behaviour. This conflicts with the largely unconditional and social liberal approach to citizenship as outlined by T. H. Marshall in his much discussed 1949 lecture.

The Importance of Social Rights for Citizenship

The core components of Marshall's approach to citizenship are set out in Box 7.2. In his 1949 lecture 'Citizenship and Social Class', Marshall set out a social liberal or social democratic theory of

Box 7.2 Citizenship as envisaged by T. H. Marshall

A definition of citizenship

Citizenship is a status bestowed upon those who are full members of a community. All those who possess the status are equal with respect to the rights and duties with which that status is endowed. There is no universal principle that determines what those rights and duties shall be, but societies in which citizenship is a developing institution create an image of an ideal of citizenship against which achievement can be measured and towards which aspiration can be directed (p. 18).

Three rights elements: civil (legal), political and social

The civil element is composed of the rights necessary for individual freedom – liberty of the person, freedom of speech, thought and faith, the right to own property and to conclude valid contracts, and the right to justice. The last is of a different order from the others, because it is the right to defend and assert all one's rights on terms of equality with others and by due process of law . . . By the political element I mean the right to participate in the exercise of political power, as a member of a body invested with political authority or as an elector of the members of such a body . . . By the social element I mean the whole range from the right to a modicum of economic welfare and security, to the right to share to the full in the social heritage and to live the civilised life according to the standards prevailing in society (p. 8).

Equality of status

What matters is that there is a general enrichment of the concrete substance of civilised life, a general reduction of risk and insecurity, an equalisation between the more and less fortunate at all levels . . . Equalisation is not so much between classes as between individuals within a population which is now treated for this purpose as though it were one class. Equality of status is more important than equality of income (p. 33).

Rights and responsibilities

If citizenship is invoked in defence of rights, the corresponding duties of citizenship cannot be ignored . . . the duty to pay taxes and insurance contributions . . . Education and military service are also compulsory. The other duties are vague, and are included in the general obligation to live the life of a good citizen, giving such service as can promote the welfare of the community . . . Of paramount importance is the duty to work . . .
  The essential duty is not to have a job and hold it, since that is relatively simple in conditions of full employment, but to put one's heart and soul into one's job and work hard (pp. 41–6).

(Marshall, 1949, 1992; page numbers refer to the 1992 reprint of the 1949 lecture)

citizenship that asserted the importance of an additional set of social rights, which sit alongside the civil and political rights seen as fundamental by earlier classic Liberal theorists. These three linked elements of civil, political and social rights are deemed to be universal in the sense that the 'equality of status' implied by citizenship should guarantee equal access to them for all who are citizens. For Marshall, citizenship rights are embedded in developing social institutions and material conditions. Writing in the immediate

post-war period, he argued that the establishment of the institutions of the post-war welfare state, for the first time, enabled all citizens to enjoy substantive social rights to healthcare, housing, social security and such like. In particular, it is the addition of a substantive set of social rights, and the importance that Marshall attributes to these rights to welfare, that makes Marshall's contribution to the citizenship debate distinctive. By including social rights alongside civil and political rights, Marshall's conceptualisation of citizenship makes some measure of autonomy possible for a large number of individuals in modern capitalist market societies. For many, particularly marginalised groups, social rights should ensure that citizenship becomes a substantive status. Whereas civil and political rights are about ensuring the liberty of citizens, that is, 'freedom from' the exercise of arbitrary power, social rights guarantee a limited measure of material equality and offer all citizens, regardless of their class position, some 'freedom to' meet their needs independent of the paid labour market.

According to Marshall, the 'equality of status' that existed between each individual citizen in terms of common rights and duties would ensure that citizenship as an institution reduced some of the inequalities of individual conditions generated by the continuing operation of a class system within a capitalist market economy. Marshall's citizenship is clearly a vision of society in which the enrichment of the universal status of citizenship is combined with the recognition and stabilisation of certain status differentials, largely through educational training and achievement, which are then consolidated by awarding different levels of monetary income tied to a stratified occupational hierarchy. In short, market-generated class-based inequalities are held in check by the promotion of social citizenship. He believed that individuals will tolerate certain social inequalities provided that such inequalities are generally accepted as legitimate. He was clearly aware of the limits of his social liberal approach to citizenship, noting in a later work that it attempted to combine an expansion of the progressive egalitarian rights of citizenship with the continuation of a capitalist economic system that generates inequality. It would be wrong to attribute a more radical agenda to Marshall. His citizenship theory fits comfortably within the social liberal/democratic tradition, which seeks to emphasise equality of opportunity and simultaneously make tolerable continuing inequality of outcome by the promotion of universally held rights.

Marshall is clear that the status of citizenship involved membership of a national community and that each citizen could expect specific rights from a (nation) state and in return he expected that individual citizens would be willing to accept certain responsibilities and duties. His consideration of the duties that citizenship entails is brief, perhaps because he optimistically believed that all citizens shared his values and would simply accept them without question. Nonetheless, he clearly states that the primary duty of each citizen is to work hard in order to contribute to their own individual well-being and the collective rights to welfare available to them and others as citizens.

Marshall's theory has been the subject of much subsequent debate and to many criticisms. He has been accused of not properly considering the financial cost implications of the extensive social rights he envisaged and criticised for the contradictory tension at the heart of his definition of social rights. Many scholars have noted the inherently limited universality and exclusive assumptions, language and outlook that underpin his thinking in relation to dimensions of difference such as gender, disability and ethnicity. Others view his theory as optimistic, outdated and flawed in terms of both its Anglocentric focus and its historical account of the sequential development of citizenship rights. Neo-Marxists on the left believe that the system of 'welfare capitalism' that Marshall proposed is not radical enough to bring about meaningful equality and a fairer society. Right-wing critiques have attempted to undermine the legitimacy of providing with citizens access to extensive and unconditional social rights and have, arguably, been more successful in changing the content and character of contemporary social citizenship.

Conditional and Constrained: Twenty-first-Century Social Citizenship

Marshall and other social liberal or social democratic theorists, such as Titmuss, were influential in setting out a vision of social citizenship in the post-war period that emphasised the fundamental importance of largely unconditional social rights and universal citizenship, with individuals meeting their responsibilities through a shared sense of collective duty. They wished to ensure that public welfare would lessen class-based inequalities and foster a sense of social solidarity between citizens, and were dismissive of explanations of poverty based on individual failings or inappropriate individual behaviour. Today, such rights-based visions of social citizenship have been challenged by both neo-Liberal influenced New Right thinkers and intrinsically conservative New Communitarian commentators, who view unconditional entitlement to public welfare benefits and services as entrenching and sustaining the inactivity of a morally corrupt and welfare-dependent 'underclass'.

In an attempt to counter such 'passivity', contemporary social citizenship has been reframed around the twin logics of conditional entitlement and individualised responsibility, whereby a citizen's right to claim welfare is increasingly linked to prior contribution through paid work and specified responsible behaviour. Only those who 'take charge' of their own lives are seen as responsible, 'active' citizens worthy of support. The welfare rights of the 'irresponsible' who cannot, or will not, meet certain state-endorsed standards of behaviour are increasingly subject to reduction or removal through the application of benefit sanctions or loss of entitlement.

In the last three decades conditionality has been an increasing feature of much UK welfare policy initiated by successive UK Conservative, Labour and the Coalition administrations. Building on Conservative legislation such as the Jobseekers Act 1995 and the Housing Act 1996, increased conditionality, under the unequivocal mantra of 'no rights without responsibilities', became a central part of New Labour's 'Third Way' (see Chapter 20) welfare reforms in social security, the management of anti-social behaviour and, to a lesser extent, healthcare and education. Previously exempt groups such as lone parents and disabled people found themselves having to attend work-focused interviews or face sanctions as the remit of conditional welfare was extended beyond recipients of unemployment benefits to other 'inactive' groups. Changes instigated under the Welfare Reform Act 2007 and the introduction of the Employment and Support Allowance (ESA) have since seen thousands of disabled people either re-categorised as fit for work and/or subject to benefit sanctions.

On assuming power in 2010, the Conservative/Liberal Coalition introduced further policies to deliver on its promise of 'intensified, personalised and extended conditionality', while simultaneously prioritising a reduction in the public finances deficit triggered by the 2008 global financial crisis. The Work Programme and Mandatory Work Activity was introduced in 2011 for long-term Jobseeker's Allowance (JSA) recipients. Alongside a new, more robust and extended sanctions regime for existing JSA and ESA claimants, Prime Minister David Cameron hailed the Welfare Reform Act 2012, which initiated a benefits cap of £26,000 and Universal Credit (see emerging issues below), as the 'biggest welfare revolution in over 60 years' and 'a new law [that] will mark the end of the culture that said a life on benefits was an acceptable alternative to work'.

Emerging Issues

Looking forward, two issues related specifically to UK citizenship require comment. First, by extending the use of sanctions to low-paid workers (and their partners) in receipt of in-work benefits for the first time, the introduction of Universal Credit heralds a step change in the application of conditionality. The willingness of future governments to rigorously pursue this policy remains largely untested, but it may in time be seen as a step too far by some. Second, following the 2014 Scottish independence referendum, discussions about the devolution of further aspects of welfare policy to the Scottish Government are ongoing. The extent of the transfer of powers is not yet decided, but it is possible that in future social citizenship may take divergent paths within the constituent nations of the UK.

More generally, the content and scope of citizenship remain open to contestation and redefinition by citizens and their elected representatives. However, neo-Liberal and New Communitarian-inspired notions of duty, reciprocity, individual responsibility and contribution appear to dominate mainstream political and public debate. Increasingly, they inform policy in the UK, much of Europe, the USA, Australia and elsewhere. The development of more residual and conditional welfare states remains the most likely future outcome of ongoing reforms.

Guide to Further Sources

P. Dwyer (2010), *Understanding Social Citizenship*, Bristol: Policy Press, provides more detailed discussion of the approaches, debates and issues outlined in this chapter. S. L. Greer (ed.) (2009), *Devolution and Social Citizenship in the UK*, Bristol: Policy Press, offers a critical debate of T. H Marshall alongside a consideration of the implications of devolution in the UK for social citizenship.

P. Taylor-Gooby (2010), *Reframing Social Citizenship*, Oxford: Oxford University Press, provides an interesting account of the restructuring of welfare states based on an analysis of international evidence. R. Lister (2003), *Citizenship: Feminist Perspectives*, 2nd edn, Basingstoke: Palgrave, provides a good discussion of the gendered nature of citizenship.

R. Plant (1998), 'So you want to be a citizen?' *New Statesman*, 6 February 1998, 30–2, is a good summary of different approaches to being a citizen. Marshall's 1949 lecture on citizenship is republished as 'Citizenship and social class', in Part 1 of T. H. Marshall and T. Bottomore (1992), *Citizenship and Social Class*, London: Pluto Press.

The website of a major ESRC project exploring welfare conditionality and behaviour change can be found at: www.welfarecondtionality.ac.uk. It contains a range of publications and resources.

Review and Assignment Questions

1 How would you define citizenship?
2 What are the key differences between broadly Liberal and Communitarian visions of citizenship?
3 In light of its many subsequent critics, does T. H. Marshall's theory of citizenship retain any contemporary relevance?
4 Why might T. H. Marshall's definition of social citizenship be seen as contradictory?
5 Discuss the extent to which a more conditional and constrained notion of social citizenship is being been mapped out in the UK.

Visit the book companion site at www.wiley.com/go/alcocksocialpolicy to make use of the resources designed to accompany the textbook. There you will find chapter-specific guides to further resources, including governmental, international, thinktank, pressure groups and relevant journal sources. You will also find a glossary based on *The Blackwell Dictionary of Social Policy*, help sheets, guidance on managing assignments in social policy and career advice.

8

Changing Behaviour

Jessica Pykett

■■■

Overview

■ Whilst governments have always been implicated in shaping the behaviour of citizens, a more explicit governmental agenda of 'behaviour change' has emerged recently.

■ Novel insights from behavioural economics, psychology, marketing and design disciplines have been influential in developing this emerging policy agenda.

■ Behaviour change policies are founded on a conception of the human subject.

■ Policy initiatives and nudges have been developed via experimental trials which have often been centrally organised by special behavioural insight units of national governments.

■ The behaviour change agenda raises important political and ethical issues.

■■■

Introduction

Much social policy research necessarily focuses on the design of welfare systems, the effectiveness of these systems in meeting the needs of citizens, and delivering the outcomes of social policy in terms of ensuring the health, wealth and well-being of national populations. As a complement to this focus, there has been a long-running interest amongst social researchers in the behaviour of citizens, and in governmental efforts to shape and influence their conduct. Some of this work has attended to particular spheres in which directing citizen behaviour can significantly shape social welfare; for example, the state education system, public health promotion and programmes targeting 'anti-social' behaviour.

The Student's Companion to Social Policy, Fifth Edition. Edited by Pete Alcock, Tina Haux, Margaret May and Sharon Wright.
© 2016 John Wiley & Sons, Ltd. Published 2016 by John Wiley & Sons, Ltd.

More recently, however, there has been a groundswell of interest in social policies that are explicitly aimed at changing the behaviour of citizens, cutting across almost any sector of social policy (including health, benefits, pensions, personal finances, education, environmental and consumer behaviours). A suite of policy initiatives, experiments and programmes have emerged in countries such as Australia, Denmark, France, the Netherlands, Norway, Singapore and the USA – dubbed 'behaviour change' policies (Jones et al., 2013).

Changing Understandings of Behaviour

A number of important intellectual and academic developments within the behavioural sciences have directly informed the emergence of this distinct behaviour change agenda in public policy. Most influential amongst these is behavioural economics. This branch of economics bloomed in the USA in the 1970s, but came to public prominence much later, when two key authors won the Nobel Prize for economics in 2002. Kahneman (who won along with his co-author Smith) was the first person with a PhD in psychology to be awarded this economics prize, marking a pivotal moment in the acceptance of behavioural, human-centred approaches no longer abstracted from the messy realities of the human psyche. Whilst there have been many other influential research areas that have shaped the behaviour-change agenda, including social psychology, design thinking and social marketing (see Box 8.1), what they share is a commitment to understanding the complexities, inconsistencies and vulnerabilities of observable human behaviour in the real world as opposed to via economic models.

Unlike the self-determining and profit-maximising model of *rational economic man*, behavioural economics instead forwarded the proposition that human behaviour is far from rational, is governed by mental shortcuts or 'rules of thumb' and is context-dependent, reliant on incomplete knowledge and prone to errors. Behavioural economics has enjoyed a boom period buoyed by the publication of a swathe of popular economics and psychology books during the 2000s on the nature of human decision-

> ### Box 8.1　Intellectual Influences on the Behaviour-Change Agenda
>
> ■ Behavioural economics.
> ■ Behavioural psychology.
> ■ Cognitive design.
> ■ Engineering psychology.
> ■ Ethology.
> ■ Intuitive judgement theory.
> ■ Material psychology.
> ■ Neuroeconomics.
> ■ Neuropsychology preference theory.
> ■ Psychographics.
> ■ Social cognition.
> ■ Social influence theory.
> ■ Social marketing.
> ■ Theories of affect.
> ■ Time preference theories.
> ■ User-centred design.
> ■ Visual perception theory.
>
> (from Jones et al., 2013: 43)

making, our essential irrationality and our often self-defeating nature. This has had a wide-ranging impact on both popular cultural understandings of ourselves and on public policy initiatives that seek to 'go with the grain' of what we now know about certain habituated patterns of human behaviour and errors in judgement – for instance, our propensity to prioritise short-term gratification over long-term gain, or the tendency to mistake recent/prominent events with frequent ones (such as a disproportionate fear of flying based on news reports of tragic accidents rather than actual safety rates).

One of the key implications of this post-rational and psychologically informed model of human behaviour and decision-making is that it has opened up new pathways for behavioural forms of government intervention. If our observable behaviours can be understood and modelled from a psychological perspective, then our social policies, regulatory environments and economic systems can be designed much more effectively. This contention is explored in detail by behavioural economist Richard Thaler and legal scholar Cass Sunstein, whose book *Nudge: Improving Decisions about Health, Wealth and Happiness*

Box 8.2 Spelling out NUDGES

iNcentives Understanding mappings Defaults Give feedback Expect error Structure choices

(2008) is credited with popularising behavioural economics in conjunction with a political programme known as 'libertarian paternalism'.

Libertarian paternalism describes the capacity of governments (and indeed any public, private or other organisation) to shape people's decisions not through coercion or mandatory regulation, but through more indirectly intervening in what they call the 'choice architectures' in which people make these decisions. This can mean rearranging the immediate spaces in which people make decisions – for instance, designing the layout of the school canteen or the supermarket to encourage healthy eating. It can also take the form of designing administrative arrangements to make wiser, more sustainable and welfare-enhancing options the easiest to pursue – as in the example of automatic enrolment in pensions saving schemes or presumed consent for organ donation.

Box 8.3 Modes of Operation of Libertarian Paternalism

- Non-conscious priming.
- Intelligent assignment.
- Presumed consent.
- Mandated choices.
- Anchoring.
- Culture change.
- Channelling factors.
- Collaborative filtering.
- Disclosure.
- Feedback.
- Self-registered control strategies.
- Peer-to-peer pressure.
- Norm formation.
- Choice editing.
- Default positions.

(from Jones et al., 2013: 43)

Thaler and Sunstein's claims for a political philosophy, which at once guarantee individual freedom *and* yet enhance welfare paternalistically, are of course the subject of much debate. However, they are not just the musings of academics. Richard Thaler acted in an advisory capacity to the UK Government, whilst Sunstein became head of the US Government's Office of Information and Regulatory Affairs in 2009 (or, as Thaler liked to call him, the 'Nudger-in-Chief').

There are several techniques, policy levers, programmes and initiatives associated with these new understandings of behaviour (see Box 8.3). Some of these methods are informed by behavioural economics, others are more discretely psychological in character, and some are techniques that have a longer history within the marketing and design fields.

Experimenting with Behaviour Change

The UK has become known as an influential incubator for policy experiments informed by the political philosophy of libertarian paternalism, and by a more general enthusiasm for initiatives aimed at changing citizens' behaviour. To be true to the schema for libertarian paternalism, citizens must be aware of these initiatives and their behaviour must only be shaped in ways which are in their own best interests, in terms decided by them. To this point, libertarian paternalism seems to have enjoyed wide, cross-party appeal. Under Labour, the Cabinet Office's Strategy Unit began thinking about developing a distinct governmental programme of behaviour change during the late 1990s and early 2000s, and other government departments were also developing similar strategies to embed behavioural techniques into policy design.

Under the Coalition Government, *Nudge* was established as something of a blueprint for effective policy design. It was invoked, perhaps most notably, in the justification of new social marketing methodologies in public health promotion, which would be less 'nagging' and paternalistic, and by implication, more liberal. At the same time, the Cabinet Office set up a specific Behavioural Insights Team, quickly dubbed the 'Nudge Unit'. This team included key civil service and thinktank

> **Box 8.4** Examples of Trials run by the BIT since 2010
>
> - Improving adult literacy and numeracy.
> - Redesigning energy performance certificates.
> - Encouraging people through targeted messaging to sign the organ donation register.
> - Investigating the link between the way in which advice is given to small business and their economic success.
> - Improving compliance with tax demand letters.
> - Redesigning contact and correspondence with claimants of Job Seekers' Allowance to encourage active commitment and motivation to finding work.
> - Research on the incidence and circumstances of mobile phone theft in England and Wales.

personnel who had a long-running interest in promoting behavioural change, including David Halpern – a former adviser to Tony Blair and previously director of research at the Institute for Government. In a joint venture between the Cabinet Office and Institute for Government, Halpern co-authored the MINDSPACE report (Dolan et al., 2010), which outlined nine core behavioural insights (Messenger, Incentives, Norms, Defaults, Salience, Priming, Affect, Commitments, Ego) to act as a guide to effectiveness for policymakers.

The work of the Behavioural Insights Team (BIT, now a social purpose company) included advising other national governments as well as developing randomised control trials (see Box 8.4). The BIT have since developed the EAST (Easy, Attractive, Simple and Timely) framework for integrating behavioural insights into public policy. Amongst its many behavioural devices or techniques are the use of social norms, setting defaults in administrative procedures, simplifying messages or attracting attention in communications, designing effective incentives and harnessing individuals' personal commitments to change their conduct.

A Global Policy Movement

A rapid web-based survey of the influence of the behavioural sciences in different national contexts uncovers a number of countries in which the ideas found in *Nudge* have had a direct impact. For the purposes of this chapter, it is more illuminating to leave aside the much more diffuse influence of psychology on governmental apparatus, as well as the impact of behaviourally savvy marketing and communications methods on all manner of governmental and non-governmental public health bodies, non-governmental organisations, environmental campaign movements and so on. Instead, the chapter identifies specific examples where nation-states have adopted the principles of libertarian paternalism and have directly promoted behaviour change as a core goal for policy design.

In France, a number of strategic reports were published by the central government around 2010 in which the possibilities for nudges (here combining insights from behavioural economics with the new discipline of neuroeconomics) in the realms of pro-environmental behaviour and public health promotion were outlined. In the Netherlands, several ministries and a civil service training thinktank have explored the possibilities for developing nudge techniques to combat obesity and CO_2 omissions. In the USA, in 2014, the White House established a central initiative for Social and Behavioral Sciences, labelled the 'Nudge Squad' by the media.

In many cases, it has been through invited seminars and advice provided by *Nudge*'s co-author, Richard Thaler, that these governments have been inspired to change their own thinking on the role of government intervention as 'choice architects'. This emphasis on choice architecture echoes a longer-running trajectory which social policy scholars have been at the forefront of identifying and analysing – that is, a move towards the personalisation of public services and the evolution of government authorities towards being arbiters and facilitators of that choice.

In some cases, however, it is possible to discern an even more explicit policy movement associated with the behaviour-change agenda. In Australia, for instance, staff from the UK have been seconded to the New South Wales government, and have been influential in setting up behaviour-change experiments in Victoria. They have also strong relationships with the Singapore Government, where the Ministry of Manpower set up a Behavioural Insights and Design Unit in 2014.

At both more global scales and more devolved scales of governance, behaviour-change strategies have been notable in institutions such as the OECD, World Bank, the European Commission and the World Economic Forum. Within the UK's devolved nations, behaviour change has been integrated into the work of the Welsh Government's Sustainable Futures Division on pro-environmental behaviour, and EU funding worth £1million has been invested in research to boost business productivity and improve organisational practices. In Scotland, meanwhile, behaviour-change initiatives on low-carbon living, sustainable consumption and in public health promotion have been evaluated by the Scottish Government.

These organisations and national governments have also experimented with behaviour-change methods and evaluated various initiatives. More significantly, such experiments mark the heralding in of new forms of expertise and influence on public policy, which have the overall goal of achieving policy efficiency, of making policies based on using behavioural evidence and design thinking in order to establish *what works.*

Challenging Behavioural Government

It may seem overly simplistic to clump together a diverse range of social policy initiatives under the rubric of behaviour change. So, too, it is important not to overemphasise the impact of a sometimes disparate set of behaviour-change initiatives with sometimes modest outcomes. However, it is clear that there is more than policy experimentation at stake in the evolution of these specific governing practices, and that these forms of behavioural governance are enjoying global appeal amongst political elites. Nevertheless, academic critics have sought to qualify and interrogate the political, ethical and democratic stakes within the behaviour-change agenda.

It is, of course, possible to evaluate behaviour-change initiatives on the basis of relatively straightforward democratic concerns, such as the potential of using psychological knowledge to manipulate people's decisions. For its proponents, this issue is easily rejected, since the libertarian paternalist framework that underpins nudging is only libertarian if people are free to choose from a range of options. But it is still crucial to monitor nudges for their transparency, openness and the opportunities they provide or deny consent at a conscious level of engagement, if behaviour change approaches are to meet this high aspiration to maintain and even increase individual freedom.

And yet, in equating choice with freedom in the way that Thaler and Sunstein and their supporters have tended to do, substantive issues of freedom can be obscured in the ready adoption of interventions aimed at shaping people's error-prone capacities for highly individualised and choice-focused forms of decision-making. It is partly for this reason that John and colleagues have charted an alternative to nudge-based policies through invoking 'Think' strategies for behavioural change (John et al., 2011). Where libertarian paternalism offers the means to govern free choosers, theirs is an attempt to bring active citizenship back as the core ideal for government.

Their experimental research trials on issues such as increasing registration for organ donation and promoting recycling sought to *both* build nudges into information aimed at persuading participants to change their behaviour, *and* to provide them with opportunities to publicly debate the decisions with which they were faced. Whilst in some of their trials, nudges without this more open public thinking were decidedly more effective in terms of changing people's behaviours, the authors did not conclude that 'what worked' was therefore the best policy option. Instead, they maintained a critique of solely using behavioural insights in public policy based in their commitment to ensuring that substantively free public discussion and deliberation could take place on the issues in question.

An alternative critique focuses on the cumulative impact of these developing behavioural forms of governance in terms of the role that an emerging 'psychological state' might play in shaping our popular cultural understandings of our sense of self or subjectivity, as well as its role in managing populations at different scales (Jones et al., 2013). This type of critical analysis is inspired by Foucault's concepts of biopower and governmentality.

Biopower refers to the way in which 'life itself' becomes a target of governance and often state intervention, by which both an individual and a population's capacity to take charge of themselves – including psyche and body – provides the means to exercise power. It is a type of power that operates *through* rather than *despite* freedom of choice. *Governmentality* similarly emphasises how modern power has become much less coercive, centralised and paternalistic. It is curiously both more diffuse and yet also much more intense in nature than any kind of mandatory regulation. It is a form of power that shapes the environmental conditions in which people act, behave and decide, in ways that might well be described as libertarian. However, its freedom-enhancing and often non-interventionist qualities do not make it any less effective as a form of regulatory power. Indeed, it is often precisely by non-intervention, by acting on the field of possibilities of citizens' action, that governmental power is practised in ways that are highly attractive within neo-Liberal political contexts.

Conclusion

Social policy research provides a useful framework to evaluate the effectiveness, ethics and potential for citizen (dis)empowerment within the behaviour-change agenda. It has helped us to investigate the historical trajectories of specific kinds of disciplinary knowledge (for example, behavioural economics or social psychology) in order to understand better their deployment as a foundation for setting out 'what works'. It has drawn attention to the often selective nature of these knowledges in terms of the account of human nature offered. Finally, it has re-situated the behaviour-change agenda within real spaces, outlining the particular policy networks, institutional arrangements, events, social relationships and political programmes which have laid out the circumstances within it has flourished. This has served to re-position such policy experiments, as well as the populations they target, as historically and geographically specific, and to provide much

needed political, economic and cultural context to what appears to be governments' recent eagerness to embrace the quite particular findings of behavioural science research in designing effective policies.

Emerging Issues

With the ongoing successes of the UK's BIT and new units emerging onto the policy scene in several countries and at global policy levels, the groundswell of enthusiasm for behavioural governance looks set to continue. Against this backdrop, there is a pressing need to subject policy experiments to proper democratic scrutiny and to offer a broader range of perspectives on how to judge their effectiveness than are currently on offer. The establishment of randomised control trials as the gold standard in assessing what works in public policy, buoyed by the UK Government's investment in 'What Works' networks of evidence centres severely narrows just what counts as research evidence fit for informing and impacting policymakers. This risks de-politicising the very act of making policies and has significant implications for who takes responsibility for political decision-making, especially where 'what works' and 'what should be done' are the matter of substantial public and scientific debate.

There are new forms of data and evidence that may also become highly influential in shaping the kinds of psychological and behavioural knowledge available to behavioural science and behavioural insights policy units in the future. New technologies that collate intimate, personal, emotional, sensory and biophysical data online via social media, and often geo-located in specific spaces are developing apace. These technologies associated with the 'quantified self' movement and the 'Internet of Me' will widen the scope for behavioural forms of self-government individually, en masse and in real time and space. Such data will likely prove valuable (commercially and politically) in understanding and shaping human behaviour. However, difficult questions are also raised with regard to the ownership of behavioural data and the role of commercial organisations in providing behavioural evidence consultancy. In sum, they signify the extension of behavioural change beyond state-led injunctions aimed at the avoidance of harm and towards a much more diffuse but intensive management of new forms of selfhood.

Guide to Further Sources

Two edited collections outline a range of public policy sectors in which the behavioural sciences have had explicit influence: A. Oliver (2013), *Behavioural Public Policy*, Cambridge: Cambridge University Press, and E. Shafir (2013), *The Behavioural Foundations of Public Policy*, Princeton: Princeton University Press. Both are broadly enthusiastic accounts of the value of taking a much more empirically evidence-based approach to policy.

Other books offer critical appraisals of the behaviour-change agenda and libertarian paternalism. P. John, S. Cotterill, L. Richardson, A. Moseley, G. Stoker, C. Wales and G. Smith (2011), *Nudge, Nudge, Think, Think*, London: Bloomsbury, reports on behavioural policy experimentation that builds in public deliberation. R. Jones, M. Whitehead and J. Pykett (2013), *Changing Behaviours. On the Rise of the Psychological State*, Cheltenham: Edward Elgar, presents empirical data and policy analysis on the influence of behavioural economics on UK-based policy networks, and offers an introduction to Foucauldian critiques of behaviour change. J. Le Grand and B. New (2015), *Government Paternalism: Nanny State or Helpful Friend?*, Princeton: Princeton University Press, scrutinises the circumstances under which paternalism might be justified in light of the mistrust of individual citizens' capacity for rational judgement.

Finally, it is always worth reading for yourself sources aimed at directly shaping policy design and strategy. Three key texts are: P. Dolan, M. Hallsworth, D. Halpern, D. King and I. Vlaev (2010), *MINDSPACE. Influencing Behaviour through Public Policy*, London: Institute for Government and Cabinet Office; O. Service, M. Hallsworth, D. Halpern, F. Algate, R. Gallagher, S. Nguyen, S. Ruda, M. Sanders, with M. Pelenur, A. Gyani, H. Harper, J. Reinhard and E. Kirkman (2014), *EAST: Four Simple Ways to Apply Behavioural Insights*, London: Behavioural Insights Team; and, of course, R. Thaler and C. Sunstein (2008), *Nudge: Improving Decisions about Health, Wealth and Happiness*, London: Yale University Press.

Review and Assignment Questions

1   What vision of the human subject or self is forwarded by contemporary behavioural science?
2   How have behaviour-change policies emerged and spread in different national contexts through specific policy networks?
3   How and why are behaviour-change policies aligned with the particular political philosophy of libertarian paternalism?
4   What principal critiques have been levelled at behaviour-change policies?
5   The behaviour-change policies associated with libertarian paternalism are said to be designed to be freedom-enhancing; on what basis are critics concerned about their significance as tools of behavioural governance?

Visit the book companion site at www.wiley.com/go/alcocksocialpolicy to make use of the resources designed to accompany the textbook. There you will find chapter-specific guides to further resources, including governmental, international, thinktank, pressure groups and relevant journal sources. You will also find a glossary based on *The Blackwell Dictionary of Social Policy*, help sheets, guidance on managing assignments in social policy and career advice.

PART II
Key Perspectives

9

Neo-Liberalism

Nick Ellison

Overview

- Neo-Liberal ideas pose a significant challenge for supporters of extensive systems of public welfare.
- Neo-Liberalism has its roots in classical Liberal thinking and in the writings of Adam Smith in particular.
- Late-twentieth-century neo-Liberalism is closely associated with the work of Friedman and Hayek, based on 'negative liberty' and the role of free market.
- Neo-Liberals want to cut back public welfare systems, to eliminate bureaucratic waste, reduce taxation and allow greater choice through private service provision.
- Neo-Liberal thinking contains critical flaws. The conception of 'negative liberty' is unduly restricted and the faith in pure market solutions may be misplaced.

The Neo-Liberal Challenge

Neo-Liberal ideas challenge those who believe that the state has a central role to play in the organisation and delivery of 'welfare' in economically developed societies. Why? Because neo-Liberals fundamentally question the need for the majority of publicly funded, state-delivered or state-regulated institutions that, taken together, comprise a 'welfare state'. As they developed from the 1960s onwards, the core beliefs and principles of neo-Liberalism are best understood as a concerted attack on the comprehensive systems of social protection that emerged in Western Europe and the UK in the immediate post-war period, as well as on socialist and social democratic assumptions

The Student's Companion to Social Policy, Fifth Edition. Edited by Pete Alcock, Tina Haux, Margaret May and Sharon Wright.
© 2016 John Wiley & Sons, Ltd. Published 2016 by John Wiley & Sons, Ltd.

about the importance of social equality and social justice that underpinned them.

Two important arguments stand out. First, neo-Liberals believe that nation-states were undermined economically during the post-war period (roughly 1945–80) because governments diverted resources away from productive, entrepreneurial firms and individuals operating in the free market to the systematic state-based protection of vulnerable sections of their populations. The high taxation required to sustain levels of welfare provision that went beyond a basic 'safety-net' for the worst off reduced the scope for private sector investment. Second, neo-Liberals argue that comprehensive social protection does not work anyway. For one thing, public money is wasted on vast welfare bureaucracies that appear keener to preserve their own budgets than to provide a good level and choice of services; for another, welfare recipients tend to become 'welfare dependent' and so fail to act as responsible individuals earning in the marketplace and looking after themselves and their families.

These claims about the damaging effects of state welfare will be examined below. It is worth noting here, however, that, whether or not neo-Liberal ideas are considered valid, they force those who engage with them to think hard about their own values and beliefs. How 'responsible' should individuals be for their own welfare and well-being? How far should the state intervene to support the lives of those who, for whatever reason, struggle to support themselves? Conversely, should the free market and the individual freedom that neo-Liberals closely associate with it be regarded as the key organising principles of human societies? A brief historical survey of classical Liberalism and its contemporary – neo-Liberal – variant will show how perennial these questions are and how relevant they remain to modern social policy.

From Classical Liberalism to Neo-Liberalism ´

The roots of neo-Liberalism lie in the particular understandings of the nature of the free market and individual freedom developed by Liberal political economists in the late eighteenth and nineteenth centuries. Although writing in very different circumstances to his modern-day counterparts, Adam Smith (1723–90) is regarded as the founding figure of an approach to political economy that considers the free market to be the main organising feature of society, and believes state intervention in market activities to be inherently destructive. Smith argued that the market can secure individual *and* social welfare, and, most importantly, human liberty. It creates these benefits in his view because, paradoxically, individuals' self-interested pursuit of wealth naturally leads to *collective* prosperity. Simply put, the selfish desire to prosper and make a profit is constrained by market competition because free competition among producers inevitably leads to falling prices and thus a 'natural' balance between supply and demand. As long as this self-correcting mechanism is allowed to function essentially unhindered, prosperity is assured. Indeed, for Smith, interference in the marketplace is only justifiable on the grounds that its free operation is being protected and preserved. A legal framework for market operations is important, for instance, as is the provision of certain public goods like law and order, and public health.

These basic principles were endorsed and extended by successive generations of liberal thinkers in the Victorian era – with one interesting twist. While Smith and early Victorian thinkers such as David Ricardo were primarily concerned with the role of the free market and the place of free individuals within it, their later Victorian counterparts took the further step of elevating this economic individualism into a political creed that stressed the virtues of individual responsibility, hard work and 'self-help'. As Heywood (2012: 53) has noted, Samuel Smiles' popular volume *Self-Help* (1859) 'begins by reiterating the well-tried maxim that "Heaven helps those who help themselves"'.

These ideals of individual liberty, the free market and a minimal state, with the added element of self-help, make up the classical liberal legacy. Neo-Liberals like Friedrich von Hayek and Milton Friedman writing in the post-war period more or less reproduced these ideas in their own thinking – but enhanced particular aspects in their critique of the failings of twentieth-century state collectivism embodied in the 'Keynesian welfare state'.

Box 9.1 Key Principles

- *Human liberty*: individuals are free to act as they choose providing that their actions are consistent with the liberty of others.
- *A competitive market economy*: kept as free as possible from state interference.
- *Preservation of the rule of law*: a constitutional framework that limits state

powers and institutionalises rules of property and contract.
- *Minimal public provision*: applying only to those goods like public health that markets cannot efficiently provide.
- *'Safety-net' security*: for those who are unable to work in the marketplace.

Late-Twentieth-Century Neo-Liberalism

Friedman is best known for his commitment to limited government and the conviction that individuals' natural initiative and drive can be released only if they are allowed to compete freely in the marketplace (Friedman, 1962). He was particularly critical of Keynesian economic policies designed to stimulate consumer demand in periods of economic recession because the government borrowing that they entailed fuelled inflation. Friedman argued that governments should restrict their activities to controlling the amount of money in the economy at any time – expanding or contracting supply depending on the balance of inflationary and deflationary tendencies, but otherwise keeping taxes and spending low so as not to distort market outcomes.

Hayek's ideas pushed beyond economics into a developed neo-Liberal political philosophy. The free market and minimal state were cornerstones of this perspective, but Hayek also built on the ideal of human liberty proposed by Smith and others. In particular, he used the concept of 'negative freedom' to underpin an approach to politics and society that proved particularly influential for a generation of neo-Liberal thinkers that emerged in the late 1970s and 1980s in the UK and USA. For Hayek (1960: 12), freedom meant 'independence of the arbitrary will of another'. Individuals were 'free' as long as they were not coerced into decisions or actions that they would not otherwise take. Indeed, like Smith, the only form of 'coercion' that Hayek countenanced was from a minimal state dedicated to ensuring, through an agreed impersonal legal framework, that private

individuals could not arbitrarily limit others' actions and choices.

This understanding of liberty is 'negative' because it argues that individuals should be free *from* constraints – what individuals do with their freedom is a private matter. Hayek believed that human liberty and the free market, working through a process of 'catallaxy', would create a natural, spontaneous socio-economic order more efficient and less coercive than the interventionist systems produced by Keynesian social democracy. Attempts to interfere with this natural order, however well meaning, would increase coercion and reduce liberty. Hayek (1960: 385) was especially critical of efforts to 'limit the effects of accident' through policies designed to produce greater 'social justice', arguing that policymakers and others could not conceivably possess the necessary levels of information to ensure a better distribution of justice than that achieved in the marketplace – indeed, it was a 'conceit' to try. This conviction that the organisation of society should approximate to the 'natural order' produced by the market inspired the neo-Liberal attack on state welfare in the 1970s and 1980s.

Neo-Liberalism and Welfare

For neo-Liberals, 'welfare states' with their large, complex public welfare bureaucracies are inherently coercive. Coercion comes through monopolistic state provision of social services, which has the effect of 'squeezing out' private and voluntary alternatives, thus limiting both consumer choice and the freedom of individuals to supply welfare goods and services. The fact that most people in

Box 9.2 Two Concepts and Five Remedies

Two concepts

- *Bureaucratic over-supply*: public servants will devise budget-maximising strategies to increase salaries and prestige rather than dispense high-quality services to service users.
- *State coercion*: state welfare services are monopolistic and therefore restrict choice.

Five remedies

- *Reduction of state welfare provision*: reduced state activity will allow private and voluntary organisations to enter the welfare marketplace, cutting the costs of public sector bureaucracy.

- *Greater choice of services*: new service providers will allow welfare consumers greater choice of provision.
- *Negative income tax*: the state should subsidise low earnings through a negative income tax (NIT) to ensure continued participation in the labour market.
- *Safety-net welfare*: individuals should be encouraged to insure against risk. The poorest will need public support, but income should be provided at subsistence level and services delivered through voucher schemes wherever possible.
- *Tax cuts*: savings from the closure of monopolistic state bureaucracies should be returned to individual earners through tax cuts.

the UK have to obtain medical care from the state-run National Health Service and education from state comprehensive schools constrains choice, according to neo-Liberals, and thus restricts human liberty.

In addition to the problem of state coercion, neo-Liberal thinkers like Seldon and Minford in the UK, and Public Choice economists such as Niskanen and Tullock in the USA, have argued that civil servants have an interest in expanding the size of their budgets 'because their salaries and frills of office vary directly with the size of the budgets they administer' (Seldon, 1987: 7). This tendency is compounded by politicians, who collude with budget maximisation strategies because they believe that voters respond positively to public spending on key services. Unfortunately, according to neo-Liberal thinkers, politicians are less keen on imposing the taxes required to pay for these services, with the result that 'bureaucratic oversupply' inevitably leads to unmanageable public-sector deficits and budget crises.

Taken together, monopolistic behaviour that crowds out alternative service providers and civil servants' tendencies to protect their own budgets are perhaps the worst evils of state welfare for neo-Liberals. However, Seldon lists a number of other features that exacerbate the problem. For example, the high taxation required to fund extensive public welfare systems depresses incentives and therefore reduces risk-taking in the marketplace. Again, owing to lack of competition, state-supplied services tend to neglect quality, while public sector employers and (unionised) employees can be resistant to change, thereby compromising innovation in terms of both choice and quality of service. Finally, Seldon makes the point that the real losers in the welfare game are the poor. Low-income groups lack the resources to contest bureaucratic decisions and pay a higher proportion of their earnings in taxation to fund poor-quality services. Moreover, as Murray (1984) argues, lack of choice leads to welfare dependency and failures of personal responsibility because families on low incomes are not encouraged to take active decisions about the goods and services they require, or to budget to meet their costs.

What policies do neo-Liberals recommend to reduce the size of the state and 'manage' welfare? Minford (1991) maintains that the waste associated with monopolistic provision and oversupply can be reduced through privatisation strategies, which would widen individual choice and encourage individuals to understand that many services should be paid for. In his view, the state should guarantee only a minimal 'safety-net' for the poorest, provided through a Negative Income Tax (NIT) to subsidise low wages and maintain work incentives. This system would replace costly means-testing with effectively one 'payment' covering housing costs and other recognised needs associated with, for instance, family size. Elsewhere, health and education services would have to be 'paid for' by vouchers, which could be exchanged at surgeries and schools of choice. For Minford, there would be no extra help for vulnerable groups such as retired people, who should have made provision for their old age during their working life. Echoing Murray's views, support for single parents should be minimal because 'there is a trade-off . . . between alleviating distress and encouraging the conditions for more distress' (Minford, 1991: 79). Finally, in true neo-Liberal fashion, savings made from the reduction of state welfare services would be handed to individuals in the form of tax cuts so they can use a greater proportion of their earnings to buy services of their choice.

Neo-Liberalism and Welfare: A Critique

Although neo-Liberal arguments about the size, power and expense of state welfare systems can appear compelling, they have certain drawbacks. Four key criticisms question the core assumptions that underpin the neo-Liberal approach. First, might it be that the definition of human liberty employed by Hayek and others is too narrow? It focuses exclusively on *individuals* and, as mentioned, is conceived negatively as 'freedom from' constraint. This understanding dismisses a 'positive' conception of liberty cast in terms of various social groups' 'freedom to' enhance their potential and prospects. Women, disabled people and minority ethnic populations, for example, typically have less access to resources and suffer from greater discrimination than others. To offset these disadvantages, it may be that they need to pursue specific political objectives and demand particular policies that can increase their *collective* opportunities, thus adding to the liberties of individual members.

Second, as Plant (1990) points out, neo-Liberals do not distinguish between 'freedom' and 'ability'. The free market distributes income and resources neither fairly nor equally, and those with less earning power and few other advantages have less *ability* to use their liberty than wealthier individuals. Lacking access to particular goods (the best education and healthcare) they are not in a position to make the most of their notional freedom.

Third, state institutions are not necessarily more coercive than their private sector counterparts. *Any* organisation can be insensitive to the needs of its 'customers' – and state welfare agencies are certainly no exception. Nevertheless, private sector service providers can also 'coerce' consumers by creating price cartels, thus restricting choice, or by providing 'selective information' about the benefits of their products. In each case, providers are able to circumvent the supposedly price-reducing environment of the competitive market. Arguably, too, state institutions can at least be called to account through the democratic process if service provision is unsatisfactory. Where neo-Liberal objections about bureaucratic oversupply are concerned, critics argue that high-level executives and managers in the private sector appear to be rather more successful than their public sector counterparts at expanding salaries and budgets.

Finally, on taxation and incentives, comparative analysis suggests that expectations about tax levels vary greatly in different countries. The USA and the UK favour low taxation on the grounds that it stimulates entrepreneurial behaviour and encourages personal responsibility. Scandinavian countries, however, despite some adjustments in

---

Box 9.3 Four Criticisms

Neo-liberals fail to:

- appreciate the potential of 'positive' freedom;
- distinguish between freedom and 'ability';
- appreciate that privately run institutions can also act coercively;
- understand that the socio-cultural dimensions of welfare are important.

recent years, tax highly and provide comprehensive social services as a basic citizenship right. High tax rates and an extensive welfare state do not appear to have reduced Swedish economic competitiveness or created unsustainably high levels of welfare dependency. Might it be that attitudes to taxation, incentives and responsibility have a socio-cultural dimension, which influences individuals' decision-making and the kind of rationality they deploy?

Neo-Liberalism in the Twenty-first Century

Neo-Liberal thought has undoubtedly had a major impact on social and economic policies in countries like the UK, the USA, Australia and certain parts of Europe, and will continue to do so. Over the past thirty-five years, UK governments have broadly accepted the free market as the principal system of resource allocation for the economy. Even during the New Labour years (1997–2010), when the party's 'social justice agenda' saw a dramatic expansion of spending on core public services and efforts to reduce the effects of social exclusion, enthusiasm for market solutions remained intact. Like their Conservative predecessors in the 1980s and 1990s, New Labour mimicked market behaviour by creating 'internal markets' within publicly funded services like the NHS. Moreover, 'welfare' certainly got tougher, with more conditions attached to benefit receipt, more means-testing and greater official endorsement for the view that salvation for all but the most vulnerable groups lies in finding paid employment in the marketplace. These policies were tightened yet further by the 2010–15 Conservative-led Coalition government. For example, spending on benefits for working-age adults and for children has fallen by around £7 billion since 2010, the suggestion being that the government has pursued a typically neo-Liberal anti-big-state, anti-dependency welfare agenda.

Despite the apparently neo-Liberal zeitgeist, however, it is important to be clear that even governments supposedly dedicated to market solutions struggle to push their neo-Liberal ideals too far for at least two reasons. First, 'politics' persistently interferes with 'markets' and, in consequence, political parties need to be responsive to the demands of key voter populations. Spending plans have to be adapted accordingly. In the UK, the Conservatives' reliance on the pensioner vote, for example, meant that the Coalition government increased public spending in this area by roughly £7 billion over the course of the 2010–15 parliament. Very differently, in southern European countries such as Greece and Spain, unpopular neo-Liberal-inspired austerity measures have provoked serious political unrest that threatens to destabilise these market-friendly economic strategies. Second – and paradoxically – it appears that a strong central state is required to sustain and advance and neo Liberal economic policies. The bail-out of the banks following the 2007–8 financial crisis is clearly one case where governments were compelled to step in to stabilise markets. Again, serial privatisations in the UK and elsewhere have required strong central direction and continuing state involvement, first to break up the public sector and then to control and regulate private corporations – nowhere is this clearer than in the transport and energy sectors.

Does this apparent reliance on the state mean that neo-Liberal ideas have little purchase in political actuality? By no means: if neo-Liberal ideas have clearly not been implemented by governments in any pure form, they have nevertheless provided the sustained *ideological* support required to ensure that demands for greater equality and social justice are understood *as subordinate to* market needs. Neo-Liberalism remained the dominant theme underlying the austerity proposals of Conservatives in the 2015 election, and the new government is committed to implementing continued downward pressure on public spending and direct taxation, including £12 billion of, unspecified, cuts in the social security budget, and a commitment to legislate to prevent future increases in income tax rates.

Guide to Further Sources

The 'classic' economic case for the free market and limited government is made by M. Friedman (1962), *Capitalism and Freedom*, Chicago: Chicago University Press. For a more philosophical account of neo-Liberal ideas, see F. Hayek (1960), *The Constitution of Liberty*, London: Routledge. Essential reading for an understanding of the neo-Liberal approach to state welfare is P. Minford (1991), 'The role of the social services: a view from the New Right', in M. Loney et al. (eds), *The State or the Market: Politics and Welfare in Contemporary Britain*, London: Sage, 70–83. See also A. Seldon (1987), *The New Economics, Study Guide No. 2*, London: Libertarian Alliance. C. Murray (1984), *Losing Ground*, New York: Basic Books, provides a view from the USA.

The best short critique of neo-Liberalism is R. Plant (1990), *Citizenship and Rights in Thatcher's Britain: Two Views, R. Plant and N. Barry*, London: IEA. For an overview of liberal ideas see A. Heywood (2012), *Political Ideologies: An Introduction*, 5th edn, Basingstoke: Palgrave.

Key neo-Liberal thinktanks can be found at: www.adamsmith.org; www.cps.org.uk; www.iea.org.uk. Policy Exchange is a centre-right thinktank sympathetic to neo-Liberal ideas, www.policyexchange.org.uk. The Conservatives' long-term economic plan can be found at: www.conservatives.com/Plan.aspx.

Review and Assignment Questions

1 What are the key components of neo-Liberal thought?

2 How do the ideas of Friedman and Hayek build upon Adam Smith's understanding of liberal political economy?

3 What are the key elements of the neo-Liberal critique of state welfare systems?

4 What are the main criticisms of neo-Liberal ideas about welfare? How convincing are they?

5 How influential have neo-Liberal ideas about welfare been over the past thirty years?

Visit the book companion site at www.wiley.com/go/alcocksocialpolicy to make use of the resources designed to accompany the textbook. There you will find chapter-specific guides to further resources, including governmental, international, thinktank, pressure groups and relevant journal sources. You will also find a glossary based on *The Blackwell Dictionary of Social Policy*, help sheets, guidance on managing assignments in social policy and career advice.

10

The Conservative Tradition

Hugh Bochel

Overview

- Conservatism can be hard to define, having historically been seen as being more about broad beliefs than specific political positions.
- During the 1920s and 1930s a number of Conservative politicians sought to encourage the party to be more supportive of a greater role for the state in the economy and social reform.
- Following their return to government at the 1951 general election, the Conservatives maintained, and in some respects developed, the welfare state.
- By the 1970s, the balance of power within the party shifted to the right, and the Thatcher and Major governments sought to roll back the frontiers of the state.
- From 2005, David Cameron sought to give the party a broader appeal, but the policies of the Coalition and Conservative governments aimed to reduce public expenditure and the size and role of the state.

Conservatism

Conservatism has often been seen as difficult to define, for, as Norton has noted, 'There is no single corpus of Conservative dogma, no particular text which Conservatives can hold aloft as representing the basis of their beliefs . . . [And] This in itself says something about the nature of British Conservatism' (Norton, 1996: 68). Indeed, many writers argue that rather than being a theory of society, Conservatism is a disposition. This may help to explain why for much of the twentieth century the Conservative Party was widely characterised as pragmatic in relation to ideas and policies, with its emphasis being on winning and exercising power, rather than on ideology.

The Student's Companion to Social Policy, Fifth Edition. Edited by Pete Alcock, Tina Haux, Margaret May and Sharon Wright.
© 2016 John Wiley & Sons, Ltd. Published 2016 by John Wiley & Sons, Ltd.

Box 10.1 Conservative Outlook and Beliefs

- A view of society as organic, as more than the sum of its individual parts, and as developing slowly and naturally, so that radical reform is often seen as potentially problematic; an acceptance of gradual change, but a scepticism about reforms that emerge from what may be passing fashions.
- A commitment to the ownership of property by individuals, with property seen as providing freedom and social stability.
- Support for the free market economy and a belief in the importance of market forces in wealth creation, with government intervention seen as inefficient, monopolistic and damaging to individual freedom.
- A view that the wealthy have obligations, including to assist those who are less fortunate, for example, through voluntary charity or through supporting a degree of social reform by the state.
- A belief that people are imperfect, and that there is a need for authority, a strong state and strong government to maintain law and order.
- A belief in the union of the United Kingdom, and key political institutions such as parliament and the monarchy.
- A willingness to be pragmatic and compromise, when necessary, including on these underlying beliefs.

Nevertheless, it is possible to identify a Conservative outlook and Conservative beliefs; see Box 10.1.

While it is possible to identify many different strands of thinking within Conservatism, those that are most widely seen as influential from the second half of the twentieth century are One Nation Conservatism and neo-Liberalism. Although some would argue that it draws upon and reflects a long strand of Conservatism, including the ideas of Disraeli and Baldwin, One Nation Conservatism is most associated with the One Nation Group of Conservative backbench MPs, which was formed in 1950, and with the policies pursued by the Conservative governments of 1950–64, which were generally supportive of the welfare state and the mixed economy. On the other hand, as discussed in more detail in Chapter 9, neo-Liberalism argues that the state should play only a very limited role in economic and social affairs, seeing the market as a better way of providing and distributing goods and services.

The Development of Conservative Ideas and Politics

The Conservative Party grew out of the Tory Party, which had its origins in the seventeenth century and supported the monarchy, the Church of England, and the rights and interests of landowners. Toryism, and later Conservatism, tended to oppose the ideas that emerged from the Enlightenment from the late seventeenth to the early nineteenth centuries, and many of the changes associated with industrialisation. The French Revolution of 1789, and ideas associated with it, such as those of liberty, equality and fraternity, were opposed by conservative thinkers who felt deeply uncomfortable at the nature and scale of such change. For Edmund Burke and others, utopian political visions were doomed to fail because they worked against human nature, because change should come about through the organic development of society rather than through revolution, and because they contradicted the traditional framework of obligations and entitlements that they saw as underpinning British society.

Conservatism sought to maintain the economic, political and social order against these pressures for change. Yet Conservatism was also able to accept change, and flexibility and pragmatism continued to be key aspects of Conservatism, albeit with a preference for gradual rather than radical reform. As the franchise was widened in the nineteenth century, Conservatism had to develop a new basis of support, becoming identified with the interests of property, and thus much of business, rather than simply landed property, and even seeking support from the working classes through the introduction of a degree of social reform. In the 1840s, Peel's government introduced income tax as a temporary measure, creating a shift from indirect to direct taxation, and repealed the Corn Laws; under Disraeli in the 1870s, the Conservatives became the 'national party', associated with patriotism and a strong defence and foreign policy, but also displayed some early signs of a willingness to accept social reforms; and in the 1890s, Joseph Chamberlain and the Liberal Unionists sought to make the Conservatives the party of social reform, although with only limited success.

Conservatism and Social Reform

By the early twentieth century the Conservative Party was facing the challenges of Liberal collectivism and the growing strength of the Labour movement. It opposed most of the social reforms that were introduced by the Liberal governments from 1905 to 1915. However, when the party was in power for much of the 1920s and 1930s, the paternalistic tradition and the pragmatic nature of Conservatism were obvious, particularly with the Baldwin government of 1924–9 having the avowed aim of reconciling the bitter differences in the country. The Conservatives therefore maintained the basic structures introduced by the Liberals, and indeed expanded some provision, including pensions and unemployment and health insurance, and encouraged local authorities to develop hospital provision. However, unemployment remained high in many parts of the country, and the government made extensive use of means-testing. A strong element of concern over public morals also became evident within the Conservative Party at this time.

During the Second World War, Churchill's Conservative-led Coalition government introduced the 1944 Education Act, with the intention of improving educational opportunities for all, the 1945 Family Allowances Act, and published plans for major improvements in healthcare and social security. The Conservatives opposed some of the key proposals of the Beveridge Report during the 1945 general election campaign, but retained a generally positive approach to social and economic intervention, including a commitment to high levels of employment, and promises

to build at least 220,000 homes in the first two years in office, to develop a compulsory National Insurance scheme, and to create a comprehensive health service with no one excluded from treatment because of an inability to pay. However, when Labour swept to victory in 1945, some more progressive Conservatives called for a clearer statement of principles and a clearer vision for the party in the post-war era.

In 1950, a group of nine backbench MPs formed the One Nation Group, the publications and ideas of which have frequently been seen as underpinning the Conservatives' approach to social policy through the 1950s and into the 1960s. The extent to which this was actually the case, and to which there was a consensus between the political parties on the future of the welfare state from 1951 to 1979, is perhaps debatable (see Chapter 18), but, as with the Liberal reforms of the early twentieth century, the Conservatives, particularly under Macmillan's premiership, maintained a commitment to full employment, an incomes policy and social welfare, including developing further some parts of the welfare state.

However, when Macmillan resigned as prime minister on health grounds in 1963, and with the Conservative Party's defeat at the 1964 general election, the strength of the One Nation strand within the party was arguably in decline, leaving the door open for the growing influence of neo-Liberal thinking.

Conservatism and Neo-Liberalism

While the Heath government of 1970–4 saw some shifts in emphasis towards the free market policies associated with neo-Liberalism, the pressures caused by high levels of unemployment saw these abandoned, and it was not until 1976, when Margaret Thatcher became leader of the Conservative Party, that power within the party moved markedly in favour of the 'New Right' wing and their neo-Liberal views, including on free market economics and the responsibility of individuals and families for their own welfare (see also Chapter 9).

This was a period when the Conservative Party sought to 'roll back' some elements of the expansion of the state that had taken place since the end of the Second World War, but at the same time to try and ensure that when government did act, it would be able to do so effectively. The concern was therefore with smaller, although not necessarily weaker, government, and a greater role for the market and market forces. Although 'Thatcherism' was, in some respects, complex and even contradictory, there were a number of ideas which were visible across government activities during the period from 1979 to 1997, some of which have continued to impact upon Conservative Party policies up to the Cameron government.

Drawing upon neo-Liberal ideas, from 1979 there was an emphasis upon:

- Monetarism: the idea of tackling inflation through controlling the money supply, rather than trying directly to limit price and wage increases was fundamental to Thatcherism, although the Thatcher governments frequently missed their money supply targets, and later played down the idea. Monetarism has also been credited with substantially increasing unemployment during the 1980s, although this in itself might have had some impact on reducing inflation.
- Privatisation and competition: the Thatcher governments' preference for the market was illustrated by the privatisation of state-owned industries and utilities (including electricity, gas and telecommunications), and the sale of council houses, often at substantial discounts, to tenants. Compulsory competitive tendering was introduced for many ancillary services, such as hospital cleaning and laundry provision. Even where it was not possible to introduce private sector providers the Conservatives sought to create market-type systems, such as 'parental choice' of schools, and a split between 'purchasers' and 'providers' in healthcare.
- Trade union reform: through a series of Acts between 1979 and 1990 the rights of trade unions were gradually restricted, making collective action through unions much more difficult. At the same time, the government also sought not to become openly involved in trying to resolve disputes.
- Reforming government: despite having come to office committed to reducing the number of quangos, the Thatcher governments shifted responsibility for many of the functions of central government to semi-autonomous agencies. Although intended to strengthen the position of managers and increase efficiency, these changes also led to a blurring of accountability. In addition, controls were introduced limiting the ability of local authorities to raise taxation (initially household rates, later the community charge ('poll tax') and then council tax, which also made them much more dependent on grants from central government.
- Cutting tax: Thatcher and her supporters believed that high taxation was damaging to entrepreneurialism and the economy, and sought to reduce the levels of taxation, including through the use of receipts from privatisation and revenue from North Sea oil, although the emphasis was primarily upon cutting income tax, whilst VAT, which is paid by everyone regardless of their income, was increased.

While the Thatcher governments made significant changes in some areas of social policy, the extent of real cuts and change in the welfare state should not be overstated. In addition, despite the anti-state and anti-public expenditure rhetoric, the Thatcher governments were not particularly successful at cutting public expenditure, in part because high levels of unemployment led to higher expenditure on welfare benefits. Indeed, while in many respects the Thatcher governments did mark a significant break with what had gone before, including being more conviction-led and ideologically driven, at the same time they also displayed a significant degree of pragmatism.

Searching for Direction

Following Margaret Thatcher's resignation in 1990, John Major won the 1992 general election and continued with broadly similar approaches to social policy, albeit with a Conservative Party that was deeply divided, particularly over Europe. If part of Thatcher's legacy was to leave the traditionally pragmatic Conservative Party more ideologically driven than it ever had been, the election of the Labour Party (then branded as 'New Labour') in 1997, under the leadership of Tony

Blair, posed new challenges for the Conservative Party that took many years for it to respond to successfully. Labour's shift towards the political centre ground from the mid-1990s, its apparent control over the political agenda, and the Conservatives' attachment to Thatcherism, meant that it was hard for the Conservatives to develop a new identity and approach to policies. In particular, the party's commitment to tax cuts was difficult to square with the public's apparent desire at that time for increased expenditure on public services.

Major's successor, William Hague, arguably tried to follow Blair by 'modernising' the Conservatives in a fashion similar to that which had created 'New Labour'. He also sought to reach out to potential supporters with a more liberal line on some social issues, including gender, race and sexuality. However, the Conservatives remained committed to privatisation and tax cuts, and failed to convince the public that public services were safe in their hands. Ultimately, his period as leader was characterised by attempts to consolidate the party's core support, including hardening its line on Europe.

Hague was followed as Conservative leader by Iain Duncan-Smith, whose leadership followed a broadly similar pattern, with attempts to be more socially inclusive, to be more positive about public services, and to recognise the party's past shortcomings. Like Hague, these attempts failed to generate widespread support within the party and he resigned in late 2003. However, Duncan-Smith's vision of 'compassionate Conservatism' did find an audience among some new, young, Conservative MPs who would eventually come to prominence under David Cameron.

The next Conservative leader was a former Home Secretary, Michael Howard, whose leadership was seen by many as something of a return to the Thatcher and Major era, and which saw little by way of policy development.

Conservatism under David Cameron

David Cameron became Conservative leader in December 2005. Almost immediately he sought to move the Conservatives towards the centre ground, arguing that economic stability should take precedence over tax cuts, that the Conservatives would support action to promote social justice and combat poverty, and that the party should reach out beyond its core support. In his early years as leader, despite a relative absence of policy development, Cameron attempted to change public perceptions of the Conservatives, including through a number of symbolic shifts, such as his statement in 2006 that 'there is such a thing as society, it's just not the same thing as the state', deliberately designed to set Cameron apart from Margaret Thatcher's famous claim that 'there is no such thing as society'.

In opposition, the Conservatives drew significantly on the work of the Centre for Social Justice, established by the former party leader, Iain Duncan-Smith, including its reports on *Breakdown Britain* and *Breakthough Britain*. The idea that society was 'broken', whether applied to poverty, family breakdown or problems with public services, became a major theme for Cameron and the Conservatives in the run up to the 2010 general election, as did the view that to respond to this situation there was a need for a smaller state, with some of its functions being replaced by charities, community organisations and social enterprises, encompassed for Cameron in the term the 'Big Society'.

Following the inconclusive general election of 2010, the Coalition government between the Conservatives and Liberal Democrats was strongly driven by the desire to cut public expenditure, at least in part with the aim of reducing the public deficit following the financial crisis of 2007–8 (see also Chapter 21), but also for ideological reasons. This, unsurprisingly, carried over into the Conservative government elected in 2015. Under both governments, while the NHS budget was to some extent protected from cuts, there were significant implications for other areas of social policy, with particularly large cuts in spending on social security, excluding pensions, and in housing. In addition, other policy preferences appeared to move back towards more neo-Liberal approaches, including the introduction of further conditionality in the benefits system, the preference for markets and the greater involvement of the private sector, social enterprises and local and community organisations, including in the NHS.

Emerging Issues

The policies of the Coalition government, and those on which the Conservatives fought the 2015 general election, help to highlight the challenges that continue to face the Conservative Party. The depth of cuts in spending on other services, the calls for a smaller state and for greater private, third sector and citizen involvement in the delivery of services, can clearly be seen as echoing many of the neo-Liberal-influenced policies of the 1980s and 1990s. On the other hand, the commitment to maintaining expenditure on front-line services in schools and the NHS, and on supporting pensioners, suggested that, whether for ideological or pragmatic electoral reasons, the Conservatives were unable or unwilling to apply such significant change directly across all parts of the welfare state. Critics, of course, would point out that the Conservatives' plans for deep cuts in future public expenditure, as laid out in the 2014 budget and their 2015 manifesto, would necessitate further and even more substantial change that would inevitably alter the welfare state beyond recognition.

For the Conservative Party, the period following 2010 saw a further challenge in the continuing growth of the United Kingdom Independence Party (UKIP), which won 12.6 per cent of the vote at the 2015 general election, meaning that for the first time it potentially faced a major electoral challenge from the political right, and indeed one that reflected at least some of the core beliefs of conservatism outlined at the start of this chapter. In some respects, therefore, arguments over the future of conservatism remained unresolved.

Guide to Further Sources

T. Bale (2010), *The Conservative Party: From Thatcher to Cameron*, Cambridge: Polity Press, is a thorough and interesting consideration of the Conservative Party and its problems from the end of the Thatcher period to the emergence of David Cameron as leader. H. Bochel and M. Powell (eds) (2016), *The UK Coalition Government and Social Policy*, Bristol: Policy Press, reflects on social policy under the Coalition government, including the influence of Conservative ideas. J. Charmley (2008), *A History of Conservative Politics Since*

1830, 2nd edn, Basingstoke: Palgrave, provides a useful history of the Conservatives from Peel's leadership in the 1830s to David Cameron's election to the leadership in 2005. It highlights both the ideas and the individuals that have contributed to the party's development through almost two centuries.

K. Hickson (ed.) (2005), *The Political Thought of the Conservative Party since 1945*, Basingstoke: Palgrave, contains a number of chapters which consider the traditional ideological positions associated with the party, and others which focus on particular themes, such as social morality and inequality. P. King (20122), *The New Politics: Liberal Conservatism or Same Old Tories?* Bristol: Policy Press, examines the extent to which the Conservative Party, and the Coalition government, under David Cameron, represented a new politics in Britain, and whether Cameron's 'progressive conservatism' represented a distinctive break from the party's past. P. Norton (ed.) (1996), *The Conservative Party*, Hemel Hempstead: Prentice Hall/Harvester Wheatsheaf, although somewhat dated, many of the chapters, particularly in Part I, continue to provide valuable analyses of British Conservatism.

The website of the Conservative Party, at: www.conservatives.com, provides access to a wide range of information on the party, particularly of a contemporary nature. In addition, the websites of right-leaning thinktanks also contain a variety of information and publications, such as www.adamsmith.org, www.centreforsocialjustice .org.uk, www.civitas.org.uk, www.cps.org.uk, www.iea.org.uk, www.policyexchange.org.uk and www.reform.co.uk.

Review and Assignment Questions

1 Can you identify the significant shifts in Conservative approaches to the welfare state since 1945?

2 Why do neo-Liberal and One Nation Conservatives take different approaches to the role of state welfare?

3 How visible are One Nation and neo-Liberal views in the policies adopted by the Conservatives since 2010?

4 To what extent are the elements of the Conservative disposition, outlined at the start of

this chapter, evident in contemporary Conservative social policies?

5 In what ways and for what reasons might 'pure' neo-Liberals criticise the social policies of the Thatcher and Cameron governments?

Visit the book companion site at www.wiley.com/go/alcocksocialpolicy to make use of the resources designed to accompany the textbook. There you will find chapter-specific guides to further resources, including governmental, international, thinktank, pressure groups and relevant journal sources. You will also find a glossary based on *The Blackwell Dictionary of Social Policy*, help sheets, guidance on managing assignments in social policy and career advice.

11

Social Democracy

Robert M. Page

Overview

- The political doctrine of social democracy originated in northern Europe in the latter part of the nineteenth century.
- There has been ongoing debate about what constitute the defining elements of social democracy.
- In the British context it is more common to refer to the closely related doctrine of democratic socialism rather than social democracy.
- Social democratic welfare states have developed most strongly in Nordic societies such as Sweden.
- Following frequent adaptations, the electoral appeal of social democracy appears to be in decline.

Historic Roots

The roots of social democracy can be traced back to developments in northern Europe during the latter part of the nineteenth century, most notably in Germany. In 1863, Ferdinand Lassalle founded the General German Workers Association (ADAV), which campaigned for political reform and for improvements in the living conditions of the working class. The ADAV eventually merged with the German Social Democratic Labour Party (SDAP) to form the German Socialist Labour Party in 1875. This new manifesto of the combined organisation, the so-called Gotha programme (which was drafted by the key theorists Bernstein and Kautsky and subsequently critiqued by Marx), attempted to reconcile reformist and revolutionary strands of socialist thought. Those

The Student's Companion to Social Policy, Fifth Edition. Edited by Pete Alcock, Tina Haux, Margaret May and Sharon Wright.
© 2016 John Wiley & Sons, Ltd. Published 2016 by John Wiley & Sons, Ltd.

in the former camp believed that the immediate focus should be on social reforms, such as the right to vote, enhanced trade union rights and the abolition of child labour, while the latter believed that revolutionary change was the only effective way to achieve transformative economic and social change. This tension between reformers and revolutionaries became more marked over time. By the end of the nineteenth century, the influential social democratic revisionist Eduard Bernstein challenged the Marxist contention that revolutionary change was inevitable because of the downward pressure that capitalism placed on working-class living standards. Bernstein's belief in the resilience and adaptation of capitalism led him to press for progressive, democratic cross-class alliances to secure social reforms to curb market excesses rather than waiting fruitlessly for capitalism to self-destruct. The dissolution of the Second International (a federation of socialist parties and trade unions established in Paris in 1889) in 1916 led to a clear divide between revolutionary-inclined Communist parties and reform-minded social democratic parties which occurred at the end of the First World War.

While social democratic political participation increased in a number of European countries during the inter-war period, it was in the second half of the twentieth century that this doctrine rose to prominence when many western European governments pursued interventionist economic and social policies which were designed to enhance living standards and provide improved forms of social protection. The social democratic ascendancy began to recede, however, in the mid-1970s amid growing concerns as to whether this approach remained viable in the light of changing economic and social circumstances.

What is Social Democracy?

Social democracy, like many political doctrines, defies easy definition. The fluidity of the term leaves it prone to differing interpretations and nuances. As Gamble and Wright (1999: 2) note, social democracy 'is not a particular historical programme or political party or interest group, or even an unchanging set of values. As a political movement its only fixed point is its constant search to build and sustain political majorities for reforms of economic and social institutions which counter injustice and reduce inequality'.

All social democrats are committed to maximising personal freedom for all, which is deemed to require positive action on the part of an elected government to ensure that individual liberty is not undermined by the adverse effects of unregulated free market activity, the lack of an adequate income or healthcare, or the denial of educational opportunities. Second, and relatedly, social democrats are strong advocates of democracy, believing this to be the best means for reconciling the conflicts that will inevitably arise in any society through peaceful means. The political process is seen as vital for engendering the broad degree of solidarism and cooperation needed for communities and nations to flourish.

Social democrats tend to differ, however, in relation to other features of a 'good' society or the optimal ways of reconciling personal freedom with social justice. Those on the liberal wing of social democracy tend to display less utopian zeal, believing that it is better to focus on small-scale advances that avoid the threats to both personal freedom and to the democratic process to which more expansive, transformative approaches can give rise. Liberal social democrats tend to hold more positive attitudes towards the market, provided that they are properly regulated, and they are more receptive to the use of innovative, non-state methods to resolve contemporary problems. In contrast, those on the socialist wing of the social democratic movement tend to be less enamoured by capitalism, believing it to be inherently unstable and in need of tight regulation and control. Their greater commitment to equality of outcome also leads them to favour more extensive constraints on personal freedom if these can be shown to have broader social advantages. Socialist social democrats are more deeply wedded to values such as universalism, have greater confidence in the benevolent power of state action, and are keen to ensure that an extensive public realm is protected from unwarranted incursions from market influences.

Social Democracy: The British Context

The term social democracy has had less resonance in Britain than in other parts of Europe. Although a distinctive Social Democratic Party was founded in 1981 by four ex-Labour ministers (Roy Jenkins, David Owen, Shirley Williams, Bill Rodgers) in response to what they perceived to be a leftward drift within the Labour Party, this could not be said to be indicative of a re-run of the earlier European battles between reformers and revolutionaries in the late nineteenth and early twentieth centuries.

In the British context, it is the related doctrine of democratic socialism that has been the dominant force in centre-left politics. Within this more 'capitalist sceptic' tradition ethical and Fabian socialists have, since the late nineteenth century, debated the role the state can play in taming the market. According to ethical socialists, the operation of capitalism, underpinned by a legal system that permits wealthy property owners to exploit and control the poor, was both unfair and immoral. To counter such exploitation, they called for increased collective action and social reform in order to create a better society. The Fabian socialists (whose founding members included Sidney and Beatrice Webb and George Bernard Shaw) also favoured state collectivism and social reform.

Although the Fabians shared the concerns of their ethical compatriots in terms of the dehumanising impact of capitalism, their main focus was on the inefficiency and waste of this mode of production. Like the Marxists, the Fabians believed that capitalism was prone to crisis and that it would inevitably be superseded by a more efficient planned economy. Unlike the Marxists, who contended that the abolition of capitalism would necessitate violent revolutionary insurrection, the Fabians argued that democratically elected, reform-minded governments would be able to transform unjust and inefficient economic and social arrangements. Fabianism underpinned the approach to economic and social adopted by the 1945–51 Labour governments. Planning and nationalisation were seen as key means of constraining the power of capital in the economic sphere, while the welfare state would serve to protect citizens from its negative impacts in the social sphere.

It is open to question whether the Attlee governments were fully committed to the establishment of a transformative egalitarian society – a socialist commonwealth. Their unwillingness or inability to devise an effective blueprint for change certainly casts doubt on the extent of their transformative vision. Following the Labour Party's electoral defeat in 1951, this issue was brought out into the open as so-called revisionists began to sketch out an economic and social strategy intended to humanise rather than to abolish capitalism. For example, in his seminal text *The Future of Socialism*, Anthony Crosland argued that post-war Britain should no longer be regarded as an 'unreconstructed capitalist society' (1956: 57). He contended that capitalist power and control had become diluted by the advance of democracy, by the increasing level of state intervention, and by growing trade union influence and the emergence of a more autonomous, socially responsive managerial class. For Crosland, these developments meant that different means could now be used to create a more equal society. Unlike socialist 'fundamentalists' such as Bevan, Crosland believed that more extensive forms of public ownership were no longer required for the establishment of a socialist society. Economic interventionism to secure higher levels of growth to fund an expanded welfare state was now seen as a more appropriate egalitarian strategy.

The Labour Party's gradual acceptance of revisionism is often seen as signalling the decisive shift from a *transformative* democratic socialist strategy to a *reformist* social democratic approach. Indeed, it has been suggested that a cross-party 'social democratic' consensus took firm root in Britain between 1945 and 1979, a period in which successive Labour and Conservative administrations accepted the need for high levels of employment, a mixed economy and a welfare state. While the existence of such a welfare consensus remains a matter of dispute, there is more general agreement that such an accord, real or invented, ended with the election of Thatcher's neo-Liberal-inclined government in 1979. New Labour's subsequent attempt (1997–2010) to pursue what they termed a 'modernised' social democratic strategy that sought to harness the dynamism of the free market with a socially just welfare strategy was regarded by some critics not as a further phase of socialist revisionism, but rather as an accommodation with the tenets of neo-Liberalism.

Social Democratic Welfare States

Social democrats in Britain and Europe have been closely involved with, and highly supportive of, the welfare state. State action to protect and promote the welfare of citizens, irrespective of labour market participation, has been a hallmark of social democratic societies. In conjunction with economic interventionism and an active labour market policy, the welfare state is seen as a key means of providing security and opportunity for all citizens, enhancing equality and fostering social solidarity. The elasticity of the term social democracy has given rise to diverse forms of welfare arrangements. Liberal social democrats, with their emphasis on 'progressive' outcomes, have accepted that it is possible to tackle injustice and pursue equality by diverse configurations of public, private, voluntary and informal provision. This has led to a focus on 'progressive' outcomes rather than adherence to a particular principle (universalism), method (public provision) or 'form' of government (national rather than local). Socialist social democrats, in contrast, have tended to be more wedded to the principle of universalism, state provision and a more uniform pattern of service delivery.

One of the main problems faced by liberal social democrats is their difficulty in distinguishing their approach from, say, that of early twentieth-century New Liberals or One Nation Conservatives (see Chapter 10). Indeed, one leading exponent of regime theory, Gøsta Esping-Andersen, has made a case for defining the constituent features of a social democratic welfare state more precisely. In his seminal book, *The Three Worlds of Welfare Capitalism* (1990), he contends that a social democratic welfare regime is characterised by de-commodified, comprehensive, universal state welfare services provided on the basis of citizenship, with relatively minor contributions from the private, voluntary and informal sectors. This calls into question the ethos of some of the welfare policies pursued by supposedly social democratic governments in recent decades. The 'traditional' social democratic regimes identified by Esping-Andersen have tended to flourish in the Nordic countries.

Sweden

Sweden has come to be regarded as exemplar of a social democratic welfare state. This stems from the fact that the Social Democratic Party has been in power in Sweden in its own right or in coalition for lengthy periods of time since first coming to

office in 1932 (it has only been out of power during 1976–82, 1991–94 and 2006–14). The party's long-standing electoral success has been linked to their decision to secure a broad coalition of support based on a cross-class electoral appeal. Per Albin Hansson, who was the leader of the Swedish Social Democratic Party from 1928 to 1946, adopted the term 'the People's Home' to emphasise his party's commitment to govern in an inclusive way so that the values of equality, selflessness and cooperation could take root in society as they would in an 'ideal' family. The achievement of this goal required the removal of class differences, the establishment of universal social services and industrial democracy.

Although the Swedish Social Democrats were aware of the exploitative nature of capitalism, they believed it could be reformed through purposeful government action and by enlisting the cooperation of industrialists and property owners. Crucially, they sought to use political influence, rather than measures such as nationalisation, to regulate and control the market economy. This led one influential American journalist, Marquis Childs, to assert in a book titled *Sweden: The Middle Way* (1936) that the Swedish Social Democrats were pursuing a path midway between the free market form of capitalism that flourished in the United States and the centrally planned economic system that had developed in the Soviet Union.

By the late 1930s, the Social Democratic 'middle way' had begun to take root in Swedish society. Under the Saltsjöbaden accord of 1938, employers and trade unionists entered into an agreement to work cooperatively, so that economic productivity and worker prosperity could be enhanced without recourse to damaging industrial disputes. Although the government was not 'formally' involved in these industrial agreements, it played a major role in creating a macroeconomic climate conducive to full employment, and pressed ahead with active labour market policies that enabled workers to move from declining industries to those that were prospering. The government also took active steps to develop high-quality social welfare provision and to ensure that income was distributed in a more equitable way.

From 1945 to the early 1970s, the key features of the Swedish social democratic welfare 'model' were established. Full employment, universal state welfare provision, industrial democracy, a solidaristic wage policy (designed by the two leading economists Rehn and Meidner) and an active labour market programme became defining features of Swedish society. The development of high-quality day-care facilities, which formed part of this process, enhanced gender equality by providing all parents with opportunities to combine child rearing and paid work.

From the late 1970s onwards, the Swedish social democratic welfare state came under increasing scrutiny. The expansion of the welfare state stalled in the wake of lower growth, inflationary wage settlements, increasing oil prices, higher unemployment and growing budget deficits. In the 1980s, some pragmatic cutbacks in welfare expenditure were deemed necessary to revitalise the economy. By the 1990s, more stringent reforms were put in place as Sweden struggled to cope with severe international financial pressures occasioned by its decision to deregulate its financial markets in the mid-1980s. The notion that welfare spending might need to be reduced rather than increased during an economic downturn led, for example, to cuts in the level of unemployment insurance in the 1990s as well as to a dilution of the party's historic commitment to full employment and egalitarian wage structures. While some social democrats defended such measures on the grounds that they were compatible with the pragmatic 'revisionism' that lay at the heart of their political doctrine, others feared that such compromises reflected an undue eagerness to adapt to the growing influence of neo-Liberal ideas and practices.

Debates about the commitment to universalism and the encroachment of non-state provision into the public realm remain topical issues within Swedish social democracy. The gradual dilution of universalism whereby, for example, entitlements to unemployment benefits and pensions have become more closely linked to individual contribution records and choices can be seen as undermining social solidarism. The same observation can be levelled at the growth in non-state welfare, which has been promoted by some revisionist social democrats as a way of responding to a heightened sense of individualism and increased diversity in Swedish society. Publicly funded private providers have gained significant footholds in secondary schooling, healthcare and social care. While such moves have been welcomed by more prosperous middle-class service users who value more exclusive tailored services, this has disadvantaged lower income citizens who have been forced to contend with declining state service levels and higher user charges.

Emerging Issues: An Uncertain Future?

One of the major critiques levelled at social democracy is that it is a doctrine better suited to the second half of the twentieth century rather than the twenty-first century. The primacy that social democrats accord to democratic state action as an effective bulwark against the inequities arising from a dynamic capitalist economic system is seen as being particularly suited to an era in which it was still possible for governments to provide effective macroeconomic management, oversee steady economic growth and provide welfare protection to a culturally homogeneous citizenry. In a rapidly changing environment in which global economic forces and neo-Liberal ideology have limited the ability of nation-states to pursue autonomous state action and where demographic shifts, increased diversity and individualism have made it more difficult to sustain universal welfare arrangements, the social democratic message appears to have lost its former potency. In an effort to remedy this situation, some have called for a reaffirmation of traditional social democratic beliefs and practice, while others have called for more radical reappraisals of the social democratic message not least to stem the long-term decline in electoral support.

Finally, the current electoral fragility of social democracy is reflected in the decision of the German Social Democrats to enter into a Grand Coalition government with their right-wing 'rivals' the CDU (albeit as a junior partner) following the 2013 general election. In Scandinavia, the Swedish Social Democrats returned to office in 2015, but only after securing centre-right opposition party agreement to a political pact designed to stem the growing political 'threat' of the far right anti-immigrant Sweden Democrat Party. In Denmark, the social democratic-led minority government of Thorning-Schmidt was replaced by a Liberal (Venstre) minority administration committed to tougher immigration laws and lower taxes following the general election of June 2015.

Guide to Further Sources

There are a number of excellent guides to understanding the development and practice of social democracy. These include Gøsta Esping-Andersen (1990), *The Three Worlds of Welfare Capitalism*, Cambridge: Polity Press; D. Sassoon (1996), *One Hundred Years of Socialism*, London, I. B. Tauris, a magisterial overview of developments in socialist and social democratic thought and practice; and S Berman (2006), *The Primacy of Politics*, Cambridge: Cambridge University Press, a lucid account of the impact of social democracy in twentieth-century Europe. N. Brandal, Ø. Bratberg and D. Einar Thorsen (2013), *The Nordic Model of Social Democracy*, Basingstoke: Palgrave, is also highly recommended. M. Newman (2005), *Socialism: A Very Short Introduction*, Oxford: Oxford University Press, provides a concise overview of social democracy within a broader socialist context.

Useful accounts of developments in social democratic social policy in Sweden can be found in Marquis Childs (1936), *Sweden: The Middle Way*, New Haven, CT: Yale University Press; H. Mattsson and S-O. Wallenstein (eds) (2010), *Swedish Modernism: Architecture, Consumption and the Welfare State*, London: Black Dog; and B. Larsson, M. Letell and H. Thorn (eds) (2012), *Transformations of the Swedish Welfare State*, Basingstoke: Palgrave.

A. Crosland (1956), *The Future of Socialism*, London: Jonathan Cape (republished in 2006 by Constable), is widely regarded as the most significant contribution to British post-war social democratic thought. Anthony Giddens has published a number of influential texts on modern social democracy thinking, including A. Giddens (1998), *The Third Way: The Renewal of Social Democracy*, Cambridge: Polity Press. P. Diamond and R. Liddle (2009), *Beyond New Labour: The Future of Social Democracy in Britain*, London: Politicos, have reviewed the future of social democracy. Other influential texts on social democracy include A. Gamble and A. Wright (1999), *The New Social Democracy*, Oxford: Blackwell; C. Pierson (2001), *Hard Choices: Social Democracy in the 21st Century*, Cambridge: Polity Press; T. Fitzpatrick (2003), *After the New Social Democracy*, Manchester: Manchester University Press; and T. Wright (2010), *Where Next? The Challenge for Centre-Left Politics*, London: IPPR. A spirited defence of social democracy is provided by T. Judt (2009), *Ill Fares the Land*, London: Allen Lane.

The *Social Europe Journal* provides topical discussions on developments in European social democracy. Policy Network, a British-based think-tank, seeks to promote debate and discussion relating to social democratic economic and social policy (www.policy-network.net). The Friedrich Ebert Foundation, which was established in 1925 and now has offices throughout the world, promotes discussion and debate on social democracy. It has published a reader on social democracy which can be found at: library.fes.de/pdf-files/iez/07077.pdf. The Foundation has also produced a YouTube video on social democracy, which can be found at: www.youtube.com/watch?v=OvJ8YDma7Wk.

Review and Assignment Questions

1   What are the key points of difference between reform-minded and revolutionary socialists?
2   Is it possible to make clear distinctions between the doctrines of democratic socialism and social democracy?
3   Why has it proved to be so difficult to provide a clear-cut definition of social democracy?
4   What are the distinguishing features of a social democratic welfare state?
5   How would you make the case for the continuing relevance of social democracy in the twenty-first century?

Visit the book companion site at www.wiley.com/go/alcocksocialpolicy to make use of the resources designed to accompany the textbook. There you will find chapter-specific guides to further resources, including governmental, international, thinktank, pressure groups and relevant journal sources. You will also find a glossary based on *The Blackwell Dictionary of Social Policy*, help sheets, guidance on managing assignments in social policy and career advice.

12

The Socialist Perspective

Hartley Dean

Overview

The socialist perspective on social policy:

- Argues that capitalism as a social and economic system is inimical to human well-being.
- Regards the welfare state as an ambiguous phenomenon that has benefited disadvantaged and working-class people, while also subjecting them to social control in the interests of capitalism.
- Has nonetheless played a role in the development of social policy in capitalist societies.
- Has informed past attempts to establish 'communist' social and economic systems with different approaches to welfare provision.
- Represents a significant critique of particular relevance to our understanding of social inequality and the practical development of alternative social policies.

Socialism as Critique

Elements of socialist thinking may be traced back to a variety of sources, from the Bible to the seventeenth-century English Levellers. But socialism is best understood, like liberalism, as one of the principal 'meta-narratives' of the post-eighteenth-century Enlightenment era. While liberalism champions individual freedom, socialism champions social equality. Socialism emerged in western Europe as a political critique of the capitalist economic system and its social consequences.

The Student's Companion to Social Policy, Fifth Edition. Edited by Pete Alcock, Tina Haux, Margaret May and Sharon Wright.
© 2016 John Wiley & Sons, Ltd. Published 2016 by John Wiley & Sons, Ltd.

Essential tenets

Socialism as a creed is humanistic, collectivist and egalitarian. Modern socialism articulated itself in opposition to industrial capitalism: its dehumanising effects, its individualistic competitive ethos and the ways in which it exacerbated social inequality. Early socialists were utopians who drew upon religious authority or ethical argument for their beliefs, as indeed some do today. But the writings of Karl Marx (1818–83) offered a brand of 'scientific' socialism that crystallised its essential tenets. His central insight is that control over the natural, physical, technological and financial resources required for the maintenance of life determines the structure of society. Human history has been a story of struggles between dominant and oppressed classes and, under capitalism – the most recent stage in human history – the mass of humanity has become alienated from the productive process by which it sustains its own existence. Capitalism, however, contains the seeds of its own destruction, because the oppressed class under capitalism (the working class) will in time be able to seize control of the state apparatus established by the dominant class (the capitalist class). Socialism, therefore, is the project by which workers' control will be exercised, leading in time to a classless or communist society in which human needs can be fully realised and properly satisfied. Marx did not offer a blueprint for a classless society. Nor was he a theorist of the welfare state, which did not exist in his lifetime. He offered an analysis of capitalism's unjust and contradictory nature and of the relations of social and economic power on which it was founded.

The capitalist welfare state did not emerge until the twentieth century. Certain of its proponents and supporters subscribed to some kind of socialism. From a socialist perspective, however, there are various ways in which we can interpret the role of the welfare state as it has in practice developed. We can distil these into three kinds of explanation: the instrumentalist, the structural-logical and the neo-Marxist. These explanations overlap in some respects and they all contend that the capitalist welfare state remains a capitalist institution rather than the outcome of a socialist transformation.

Instrumentalist critiques

Some critics interpret literally the claim that the state behaves as the managing committee of the capitalist class. The welfare state in capitalist countries ultimately serves the interests of the capitalist, not the working class. The key positions in government and administration are held by people from relatively privileged backgrounds or those who have an underlying allegiance to 'the establishment' and/or the status quo. The welfare state, by implication, is a conspiracy against the working class.

According to this explanation, the shape and nature of the welfare state are deliberately contrived to accord with the economic requirements of capital. The welfare state has become both the handmaiden of capitalism and its henchman. Through health and education policies, the state ensures an orderly supply of workers for industry and commerce, so reducing the costs of reproducing labour power. Through a range of social services the state ensures that the costs of the weak and vulnerable do not fall on industry. Through social security and labour market policies the state manages those workers who are unemployed or temporarily unproductive. The welfare state has not hastened capitalism's demise but smoothed over its contradictions and helped to sustain it.

Structural-logical critiques

A different line of reasoning is that the functioning of the state under capitalism is not a cunning conspiracy so much as a consequence of capitalism's structural constraints or immanent logic. The state behaves like a managing committee only in a metaphorical sense. It is not necessarily a willing handmaiden or henchman. It has a degree of autonomy. And yet well-meaning reformers remain, in part at least, captive creatures of circumstance. In the last instance, it is economic imperatives that determine the outcomes of social policy. This happens because in order to survive the state must acknowledge certain priorities over which it has no control. For example, it must maximise economic growth, protect profits and maintain social order. In liberal democracies economics trumps politics. It is deterministic or functionalist argument.

A more abstract variation is that the essential form of the welfare state is derived from or mirrors the unequal relations of power that characterise capitalist market relations. So, just as the exploitative nature of the relationship between capital and labour is obscured through the legal fiction of the individual wage bargain, so the disciplinary nature of the state's relationship to its citizens is obscured by the way welfare goods and services appear as a form of 'social wage' or democratic settlement. Social welfare reforms are one-sided compromises driven by economic imperatives, and the beneficiaries of such reform are ideologically manipulated in the interests of capital so they cannot see the true nature of their oppression. This gloomy scenario is brightened through the ideas of thinkers, such as Gramsci, who argued that not everyone is hoodwinked by capitalist ideology, nor are they necessarily persuaded by the inevitability of capitalism's logic. Part of the socialist project has to do with whose ideological interpretations of the world will dominate. Drawing on this insight, social policy can be understood not as the inevitable outcome of capitalist structures, but as a distillation of the class forces in play within an enduring political struggle. Socialism can act as a counter-hegemonic force.

Neo-Marxist critiques

Finally, there is a group of academics who in the 1970s brought together elements of the above critiques to produce a distinctive overarching 'neo-Marxist' critique. In a critical review Klein (1993) dubbed this 'O'Goffe's tale'. The epithet captured the names of three of the most prominent contributors to the neo-Marxist critique: James O'Connor, Ian Gough and Claus Offe. The essence of O'Goffe's tale is that the welfare state has proved to be an ambiguous phenomenon, since it exhibits two kinds of contradiction.

First, while the welfare state has brought real benefits to the working class and the most disadvantaged members of capitalist society, it has also played a part in repressing or controlling them. The welfare state succeeded in increasing social consumption and living standards, but capital benefited more than labour, while poverty and inequality persisted. State welfare enhanced the productivity of labour, while minimising the adverse social consequences of the capitalist economic system. It regulated both the quantity and the quality of labour power. The development of state welfare played a necessary part in constituting the modern wage labourer and by according popular legitimacy to capitalism. It also subjected the working class to new forms of administrative scrutiny and normative control – through, for example, compulsory education and the conditions that attach to the receipt of many welfare benefits.

The second kind of contradiction was that the stabilising influence which the welfare state had brought to capitalism would be fiscally and politically unsustainable. Capitalism could neither survive without having a welfare state nor endure the costs and implications of having one. To an extent, this prophecy has been borne out since in times of crisis capitalist countries seek to 'roll back' their welfare states and to shift the responsibility and costs of welfare provision from the public to the private sector, from the state to the individual or, in effect, from capital to labour. At the same time, many poorer countries have been persuaded in their pursuit of capitalist economic development to establish no more than limited state welfare provision.

Socialism as Practice

Socialism is concerned not only to critique capitalism conceptually, but to challenge it politically. There are anarchistic and libertarian socialists who have envisioned a society in which human welfare would be achieved though mutuality and cooperation, without any kind of state intervention. However, we shall concern ourselves with two strands within the socialist perspective that have sought practically to *harness* state power as a means of promoting human welfare: the gradualist and the revolutionary.

Gradualist socialism

The emergence of the capitalist welfare state is attributable, in part at least, to the effects of class struggle. Class agitation and the growth of the labour movement in capitalist societies were significant factors in the way in which – from the end of the nineteenth century onwards – state social welfare provision developed, although how this played itself out differed between countries. Socialism played a key part in helping to mobilise the working-class movement. Some socialists saw this mobilisation as a step towards the overthrow of capitalism. Others saw it as transition to socialism by stealth. This was the position of Fabian socialists (who were an early influence within the British Labour Party).

Gradualist socialist politicians, such as Anthony Crosland, argued that the development of a mixed economy and the policies of a Labour government in the post-Second World War period were such that by the 1960s a country like Britain was no longer a capitalist society in the original sense. However, it can also be argued that social liberalism was probably a stronger force than gradualist socialism in the creation of the modern welfare state. 'Enlightened' capitalists were prepared not only to concede some of the demands advanced by organised labour, but to promote measures that would compensate for the foreseeable failures and correct the inherent instabilities of free-market capitalism. The extension of state welfare, therefore, was implicated in the transition from industrial to post-industrial or 'advanced' capitalism in which both the state and the market play a role.

As capitalism changed, Fabianism was effectively absorbed into the social democratic tradition (see Chapter 11), which is resigned to further improving capitalism, not gradually superseding it; to the progressive amelioration by state intervention of the adverse effects of market forces. The distinction between socialism and social democracy is not necessarily evident from the names by which political parties and organisations call themselves. For example, the Party of European Socialists (with thirty-two affiliated parties) and the reformed Socialist International (with 170) include a mixture of parties from across the world which describe themselves variously as 'socialist', 'social democratic' or 'labour' parties, but whose shared objectives are at most gradualist and more social democratic than socialist in essence.

Revolutionary socialism

Revolutionary socialism aims to overturn capitalism not by gradually transforming the state, but by taking command of it so it may properly serve the interests of the oppressed and working class.

Marx's contention was that if this were achieved the state would in time 'wither away' as a truly classless society emerged. There were in the course of the twentieth century examples of socialist revolutions – most notably in Russia in 1917 and China in 1949. The societies that resulted were called 'communist' regimes, despite the fact that in none of them did the state wither away. On the contrary, what characterised such societies was a highly centralised and enduring form of state planning. The countries in which socialist revolutions occurred were not at the time fully industrialised capitalist countries and revolution was pursued not so much by the organised working class as by vanguard activists. The programmes the activists adopted were informed by visions of human progress. The social and economic arrangements they wanted would be based not on the wastefulness of unfettered competition, but on rational planning and cooperation. The intention was to maximise human welfare.

Even supporters of the socialist perspective admit that such examples of 'actually existing' socialism turned out to be a failure. Not only did 'communist' regimes never reach the stage when universal human welfare could be assured without state intervention, but in many instances the socialist project was cruelly stripped of its essential humanity. Initially, under the Soviet system, for example, citizens were guaranteed work with state enterprises that offered a range of social benefits as well as wages. Prices were subsidised. Housing, education, healthcare and pensions were all provided. However, the standard and nature of provision were such that it often failed to satisfy human need. The ruthless idealism of the original revolutionary activists, however beneficent in intent, was 'top-down' and authoritarian. The Stalinist era that succeeded the Bolshevik revolution became brutal and totalitarian. Additionally, it may be argued that socialism should be an international project since it is impossible to establish socialism in just one country or group of countries: in an interconnected world, dominated by capitalist modes of economic production and by global markets, systems such as that in the former Soviet Union and China have ended up functioning not as state socialism, but as centrally regulated state capitalism. Alternatively, one tiny socialist country, Cuba, with its impressive health and education systems, has suffered reduced living standards because, until very recently, its capitalist neighbours would not trade with it.

The Death of Socialism?

It has been suggested that socialism is now dead: that the historic 'Cold War' between socialism and capitalism has ended with a global victory for capitalism. Towards the end of the twentieth century we witnessed the collapse of Soviet communism. 'Post-communist' countries have now largely transformed themselves into capitalist welfare states. Communist China has adopted market-based reforms and is evolving broadly 'Western'-style social policies (see Chapter 67). We have, supposedly, entered a post-modern age in which the meta-narratives of liberalism and socialism have been superseded (see Chapter 15).

There are two questions that the socialist perspective must now address. The first has to do with the nature of social class and the unfashionable notion of 'class struggle'; the second with the global nature of capitalism and the scope for anti-capitalist social policies.

Class versus identity?

The concept of class has been central to the socialist perspective. But as we pass from the industrial age to an information age the nature of class structures in capitalist societies has been changing. And as we pass from the age of cultural modernity to an age of post-modernity we have become preoccupied with issues of identity, not class.

Throughout the capitalist world the 'traditional' manual working class has been declining in size. In a 'high-tech' global environment, with increasingly flexible labour market requirements, the class divisions within post-industrial societies are complex, but there is a trend for such societies to become more unequal as the gap between rich and poor increases (see Chapter 30). There is an incontrovertible and enduring association between people's socio-economic status and their life chances. From a socialist perspective conceptualising the class divide requires some sophistication, but the concept is, or ought to be, as meaningful as ever it was. Contemporary socialist theorists argue that, while there are those in capitalist societies who occupy anomalous or

ambiguous class positions, there is still a fundamental distinction to be drawn between the many who sell their labour (whether it be manual, technical or intellectual) in order to live and the few who own or control a significant amount of capital.

If, despite this, the idea of class has lost salience, this is in part because a new politics of identity has tended to displace the old politics of class. The past few decades have witnessed the emergence of new social movements, which address issues hitherto neglected in class-based struggles over the distribution of power and resources. These movements address human rights, global poverty and ecological issues, but significantly they also include second-wave feminism, the black power and anti-racist movements and, for example, movements of disabled people, older people, gays and lesbians. The struggles these movements promoted are not about material redistribution, but 'parity of recognition' (Fraser, 1997). They are concerned with social injustices arising from social divisions other than class. None of this necessarily precludes the possibility of alliances between movements and the combination of different struggles. Feminist socialism and eco-socialism, for example, now provide their own distinctive strands within the socialist perspective. What the socialist perspective emphasises is the extent to which the social injustices inherent to capitalism can exacerbate or fuel all kinds of oppression.

Emerging Issues

As an intellectual critique the socialist perspective plainly is not dead. Nor is it necessarily dead in any practical sense. As long as anywhere in the world there is active resistance to capitalism, socialism is more than an atavistic curiosity. The end of the twentieth century witnessed the beginning of an amorphous global movement opposed to economic globalisation. This began with a series of spectacular protests mounted at meetings of the World Trade Organization and various G8 summits. Meanwhile, the World Social Forum, founded in 2001 as a counterweight to the pro-globalisation World Economic Forum, brought together an eclectic mixture of political groups, social movements and non-governmental bodies, who attempted to articulate demands for a more inclusive form of globalisation, rather than a world shaped by capitalist market forces. In the ensuing years there have also been, for example, electoral successes in several Latin American countries for left-leaning presidential candidates, most notably the late Hugo Chavez, who declared a Bolivarian socialist revolution in Venezuela. More recently, during and after the global financial crisis of 2007–8, the anti-capitalist movement found a new manifestation through *Occupy*, a loose network of campaign groups in various cities around the world, seeking to mobilise popular resentment at the gross inequality of a world divided between the richest 1 per cent and the 99 per cent who constitute 'the people'. The influence of this populist brand of anti-capitalism has most recently been captured in new political parties, including Syriza in Greece and, most recently, Podemos in Spain, which have effectively harnessed popular resentment at the imposed austerity resulting from the financial crisis.

Though anti-capitalist in their demands, these disparate movements and parties can be ideologically ambivalent (Hardt and Negri, 2012). They are not traditionally socialist. Nor do these movements necessarily focus on social policy matters. Nevertheless, many of their active members are socialists and some of the ideas by which they are informed are socialist in provenance. Amongst their disparate demands are such things as universal basic income, progressive and radically redistributive forms of taxation, widespread reduction in working hours and the defence of public services, none of which by themselves would be sufficient to achieve socialism, but which together amount to a fundamental challenge to capitalism (Callinicos, 2003). To that extent, they engage with the central question raised by the socialist perspective on social policy, namely, are the short-term interests of capitalism compatible with the long-term needs of humanity.

Guide to Further Sources

For accessible general introductions, see T. Benn (1980), *Arguments for Socialism*, Harmondsworth: Penguin, and G. Cohen (2009), *Why Not Socialism?*, Princeton: Princeton University Press. For reflections on emergent anti-capitalist movements, see M. Hardt and A. Negri (2012), *Declaration*, ebook, Berkley, California, and A. Callinicos (2003), *Anti-Capitalist Manifesto*, Cambridge: Polity Press.

For introductions to classic neo-Marxist thinkers, see V. George and R. Page (eds) (1995), *Modern Thinkers on Welfare*, Hemel Hempstead: Prentice Hall. For a critique of neo-Marxism, see R. Klein (1993), 'O'Goffe's tale', in C. Jones (ed.), *New Perspectives on the Welfare State in Europe*, London: Routledge. For a socialist social policy text: I. Ferguson, M. Lavalette and G. Mooney (2002), *Rethinking Welfare: A Critical Perspective*, London: Sage. For a contrasting 'post-socialist' account, see N. Fraser (1997), *Justice Interruptus: Critical Reflections on the Post-Socialist Condition*, London: Routledge.

Potentially relevant websites include the Socialist International at: www.socialistinternational.org; the Party of European Socialists, www.pes.org; the World Social Forum, www.worldsocialforum.org; *Red Pepper Magazine*, www.redpepper.org.uk; the London *Occupy* group, www.occupylondon.org.uk.

Review and Assignment Questions

1 What are the defining characteristics of the socialist perspective?
2 In what ways does the socialist perspective interpret the role of the welfare state?
3 To what extent has socialism been a practical influence on the development of social policy?
4 Where does the difference between socialism and social democracy lie?
5 What relevance, if any, does the socialist perspective have today?

Visit the book companion site at www.wiley.com/go/alcocksocialpolicy to make use of the resources designed to accompany the textbook. There you will find chapter-specific guides to further resources, including governmental, international, thinktank, pressure groups and relevant journal sources. You will also find a glossary based on *The Blackwell Dictionary of Social Policy*, help sheets, guidance on managing assignments in social policy and career advice.

13

Feminist Perspectives

Shona Hunter

Overview

- The welfare state, its policies and practices construct are simultaneously constructed through gender inequalities.
- Feminists have used women's experiences to challenge what is understood by welfare to include the cultural and intimate spheres.
- Recent focus on the concept of care has informed the development of a feminist political ethic of care.
- More differentiated approaches to feminist social policy analysis includes issues of masculinity and relations of power.
- Feminists interact with mainstream political structures to fight for gender inequality. However, there are complexities and costs in this.

Feminist Questions

What does it mean to have a feminist perspective on welfare and social policy? There are a vast and changing range of contested responses to this question. Liberal, welfare, socialist, Marxist and postmodern feminisms (to name a few) approach this question differently. Each is concerned in different ways about women's equality, their agency, gender relations and social justice, and how these are achieved enabled or hindered through the arrangement of welfare.

Liberal feminism, advocating the equal participation of women in the public sphere, has a long history dating back as far as Mary Wollstonecraft's *A Vindication of the Rights of*

The Student's Companion to Social Policy, Fifth Edition. Edited by Pete Alcock, Tina Haux, Margaret May and Sharon Wright.

Women published in 1792. Its influence is still seen in policies for equal employment rights, including equal pay, and in anti-discrimination legislation. In contrast to liberal feminism is welfare feminism's concern to improve the lives of women in the private sphere, as wives and mothers. Forwarded by a range of social reformers such as Beatrice Webb in the early 1900s, Eleanor Rathbone in the 1930s, it can even be seen in Beveridge's 1945 welfare reforms. By the 1970s, however, radical, Marxist and socialist feminists were critical of the connection between women's public and private disempowerment and the assumption as to the existence of natural, biological differences between men and women. Their arguments were around the important role of welfare in maintaining the subordination of women in the home which served to support the broader material and ideological needs of labour. Thus, the gendered division of welfare was viewed as an important means of reproducing class relations and maintaining the social stability necessary for the smooth running of capitalist labour relations.

These feminist debates show the complexities of understanding gendered inequalities; where being treated the same as men causes a problem for women because of the neglect of their specific needs (as mothers, for example), but being treated differently on the basis of an assumed women's specificity can lock women into unequal and dependent relations with men and constitutes the source of their inequality.

Later, in the 1980s and 1990s, post-modern feminists critiqued the universalising and generalising nature of earlier debates over sameness and difference. Their aim is to think about the *differential* relationships of various groups of older, black, disabled and heterosexual women to welfare arrangements and their varying material and social consequences. This sort of approach emphasises the dynamic, changing and contradictory processes of welfare and its *changing gendered relations* between men and women, rather than assuming universally disempowering consequences of social policies for women.

At their most radical feminist analyses have the potential to expose and transform how we understand the very notions of welfare and the state as gendered. That is, how the state is both defined through and defining of broader social and cultural formations of gender. The key issue here is not to measure levels of gendered inequality (though this is part of an analysis), but to explore how the social and cultural categories of gender (being a woman or a man) come to be understood and constructed through the institutions, practices and policies of the welfare state. Feminists have used women's lived experiences and agency as household heads, (hetero)sexually active partners, caregivers and abortion seekers, to include matters of divorce, birth, and care for parents and in-laws as well as for children in definitions of welfare. This has expanded definitions of welfare to include families and the informal sphere as well as states and markets.

Taken as a whole feminist analyses seek to recognise the multidimensionality of women's experiences as structured through macro institutional disadvantages, but explore how women's agency is also supported and contested at the subjective, symbolic and emotional levels within families, kinship and organisational contexts. Together these analyses bring into question whether liberal models of welfare can ever enable gendered equality when they rely on models of risk which do not consider the cultural and emotional costs incurred in welfare citizenship.

Women Workers and Carers

Despite debates over the appropriate breadth of feminist concerns in welfare, the substantive focus of much work has tended to be on women's contradictory positioning as providers and receivers of welfare – that is, the marginality of women's concerns within welfare, coupled with their centrality to its formal and informal provision.

The post-war welfare settlement in the UK was built upon the male breadwinner model, rooted in the principle of cohabitation based on a family wage system, where benefits were paid to men for the support of their wives and children. Thus, where a woman cohabited with a man her benefits were withdrawn. This system created, supported and maintained a structured dependency between men and women.

Even when women occupied public roles within state bureaucracies, their positioning often reflected the private distribution of women's work, with women occupying lower ranks, providing domestic functions within health, child care and personal services. One example of where this division has been most marked is within nursing, a traditionally gendered profession where women fulfil the care role in public, but within a hierarchically ordered division of medical labour and where nursing management continues to be dominated by men.

Feminist analysis coming in particular from the USA, identified important variations on this male breadwinner model, highlighting maternalist as well as paternalist roots to social policies. Whilst women in the USA lacked formal political power to shape welfare, they exerted considerable agency at key points in the early stages of welfare development through grassroots organisations and effective lobbying. This meant that even in a context of minimal state-managed and funded welfare provision like the USA, these groups successfully pressed for maternal child welfare benefits, such as mother's pensions (an early form of child welfare benefit) and other protective labour legislation.

Shifts from the male breadwinner to the 'adult worker model' of welfare are related to the rise of dual-earner families in western contexts. Also known as the citizen-worker model, this adult worker model moves some way to equalising women's position vis-à-vis men in terms of treating them as economically independent, for example, through the individual basis for national insurance and income taxation since the 1970s.

By the late 1990s, feminists had capitalised on discourses around 'social investment' to argue for the positive contribution of care and the caring role within welfare and society as a whole. So-called 'social investment states' developed more gender inclusive 'citizen-worker-carer' models directed towards investment in children and young people as the future of economic stability and growth, resulting in more child-, family- and mother-friendly policy. The Scandinavian welfare states are often considered to be the most advanced in these terms, with child-friendly, work–life balance policies such as paid parental leave, including a period of at least one month's leave reserved for new fathers dubbed the 'daddy quota'.

In the UK the New Labour Government pursued similar policies, such as:

- the National Care Strategy committing to the universal right to child care;
- the National Carer's Strategy for those providing various forms of home care;
- Sure Start support for parents and family, and more generous parental leave rights.

However, there are ongoing feminist concerns around the ways in which these arrangements can continue to disadvantage women if, as in the more gender neutral versions such as the USA, there is a failure to recognise the already gendered starting points for women and men workers which impact on ability to benefit from these policies. For example, men's take-up of caring responsibilities is structurally discouraged within a working context where women's work is lower paid than men's. This material discouragement is often accompanied by cultural antithesis to male involvement in child care.

More ambitious feminist interventions around the social investment state have sought to develop a political ethics of care to challenge established ways of conceptualising welfare citizenship through economic or intergenerational contracts of market and welfare systems. In the UK, research into Care, Values and the Future of Welfare sought to capitalise on a renewed interest in the concept of care to argue for care for the self and for the other as meaningful activities in their own right and regardless of their value in supporting the future labour market. This concept of care is used to rethink collective human agency as rooted in interdependence, challenging individualist models of social responsibility. This sort of approach begins to fulfil the promise of more radical feminist critiques around the nature of human values and how these values are supported or denigrated through welfare systems. It considers the value of paid work and caring activities together (see Box 13.1).

Box 13.1 A Political Ethic of Care

A political ethic of care reconsiders (Williams, 2002):

- The unequal distribution of time and space between the activities of personal care, other care and paid work, valuing all three as crucial to work/life.
- Differences in social relationships of care, rooted in historical formations of power, identity.

- Intimacy as broader than the traditional heteronormative family to cover the role of kith as well as kin in the form of friends, lovers, step-families, etc.
- Inclusive diversity to include multiple identities which create forms of belonging which cross-cut family, community and nation.
- User voice as a core component of trust within the identification of welfare needs.

Gender Relations and Masculinities

These developments in feminist theorising on social policy, along with movement towards a 'universal caregiver' model of welfare, serve as a reminder of the ways in which gender in social policy is as much about men as it is about women. The rise in explicit interest in men and masculinities within social policy is manifest in a number of ways in terms of concern over men's relations to education, violence, health and social exclusion, but in particular through a focus on father's fatherhood. Critique of monolithic hegemonic masculinity in favour of understanding multiple masculinities highlights the way male breadwinner models of welfare created hegemonic oppressive, but ultimately unattainable, ways of being a man, as much as it created problematic conflations between women, care and the home.

Debates over men's health, such as their higher mortality rates, including suicide, and particular forms of ill-health, relate these phenomena to certain 'inappropriate' or risky masculine behaviours, for example, the reluctance to seek medical help or an apparent propensity to violence. Another prominent debate since the late 1990s has been over the disproportionately lower educational attainment of boys, with a variety of measures created within schools to encourage boys' participation in learning. A focus on fathers and fatherhood has been prompted by concerns to stem this educational (and broader social) exclusion of boys, for instance:

- asking schools to send children's reports to fathers who live outside the family home;
- a drive to encourage fathers to read to their children;
- training for professionals who work with children to communicate with fathers;
- the promotion of childcare services to black and ethnic minority fathers.

However, the tendency to focus on children and fathers can be at the expense of a broader analysis of the complex gendered dynamics of violence, power and care within families. It can reproduce the invisibility of mothers and motherhood. This neglect risks the reproduction of women's disempowerment within the home through the provision of formal services.

Feminist Intersections

Feminists have long been concerned with the interconnections between, gender, class and race. Williams's (1989) ground-breaking analysis of the UK welfare state as part of a racially structured patriarchal capitalism in which women were central to the reproduction of nation as well as family demonstrates the uneven and contradictory progress of post-war welfare for different groups of women. For example, the opening up of higher education in the 1960s benefited largely white middle-class women. Whilst the post-war NHS improved general health of women, it had done this less so for working-class and black women.

This analysis paved the way for a more differentiated and critical feminist analysis of welfare in the UK and other contexts, one that takes account of the struggles of a range of welfare users, social movements and activists. Other UK-focused critiques, such as Carabine's intervention 'Constructing women' and Morris's '"Us" and "them"?', show how mainstream feminist analysis continued to rely on heterosexual assumptions as to the primacy of mothering and the separation of women and dependent people.

This emphasis on differentiation within the category of woman built on debates from within the feminist movement around the reproduction of racism, heterosexism, ablism and so on. It highlights the ways in which multiple social relations produce differential experiences of disadvantage within welfare and how different groups of women may require different support and policy in order to meet differing needs. Perhaps most importantly, emphasis on difference and differentiation serves to highlight the ways in which women can be simultaneously vulnerable and empowered within the organisation of welfare through their multiple identities. For example, a black woman worker suffering institutional discrimination blocking career progression as a black person may benefit as a woman worker who is a mother from child care services provided by that same organisation, designed to enable women's career progression. Differential analysis poses challenges around how to provide for women's sometimes competing needs, and puts into question the possibility of broader feminist collective challenges to welfare services.

Gender mainstreaming policies, first developed at European Union level, seek to respond to many of these complexities. They recognise the lack of gender neutrality in normative welfare systems and the advantages accrued to a white middle-class (masculine) norm, and aim to correct this bias, rather than to prescribe ad hoc piecemeal measures aiming to develop women's position. They also dovetail the feminist language of intersectionalities and multiple social difference, using the notion of human diversity as a way of considering how normative welfare systems exclude a broad range of people, including some white men. However, feminists have also criticised the way mainstreaming and diversity policies have been co-opted to serve individualistic rather than collective ends.

Feminists in Public Policy and Activism

Despite their marginality within formal public policy mechanisms feminists have long played an important role in the public sphere. This contribution as activists and more recently as public intellectuals within policymaking is evidenced by the introduction of gender mainstreaming. Even within the more paternalist context of UK welfare, feminist activism's challenging of women's economic dependency on men had early success with the introduction of family allowances payable directly to women at the same time as the introduction of Beveridge's family wage. Later, the Women's Family Allowance Campaign defeated the Conservative government's 1972 tax credit proposals which would have removed this form of direct payment to women, replacing it with an indirect payment to the working father through tax breaks within the wage packet. The Women's Budget Group has also been actively scrutinising the budgets of UK governments since the early 1990s; and the Fawcett Society, named after its founder the Dame Millicent Garrett Fawcett, has adopted a liberal campaigning role for women's equality for well over a hundred years.

Much of feminism's ability to influence social policy has depended on its ability to impact on the broader social and cultural relations through which policy is established. Equal opportunities policies, the Equal Pay and Sex Discrimination Acts and the establishment of the Equal Opportunities Commission (EOC) are all important elements of this broader cultural shift in the UK. Increasing opportunities for women to occupy positions within formal political institutions are an important dimension to women's influence.

Milestones in women's political visibility in the UK have been the introduction of a Minister for Women in 1997 (Minister for Women and Equality since 2014) and the establishment of the Women and Equality Unit in 2001. However, there is considerable feminist ambivalence around these sorts of mainstream political engagements as a 'politics of women without feminists', arguing that engagement with formal systems tends to be confined to certain, largely white, middle-class women.

Emerging Issues: Post-Feminism, Human Rights and the Impact of Austerity

The last ten or so years have seen debate about our entry into an era of 'post-feminism', where the core arguments of feminism have become irrelevant. This debate turns on two ideas: that women's increasing visibility in public life attests to the success of struggles for gender equality; and that this success has even, in some circumstances, been at the disadvantage of men and boys. Other developments related to mainstreaming have created a move away from the specificities of women's concerns. The EOC, like its counterpart the Commission for Racial Equality, has been collapsed into the newly established Equality and Human Rights Commission (EHRC). Ostensibly created in order to integrate intersectional analysis of multiple inequality, there is an absence of a strong feminist agenda within the EHRC which has been a concern to feminist campaigners. It remains to be seen how the human rights agenda adopted by the commission will play out in relation to broader feminist concerns (see Chapter 5). The Coalition government has been ambivalent at best to the Commission's agenda, setting up an Independent Steering Group to review the Equalities Act's key mainstreaming measure – the Public Sector Equality Duty – only two years after its implementation. The full recommended review is pending post-election.

Fears over the material effects of Coalition and Conservative government austerity policies on women have been largely founded. Post-austerity politics has hit women hard, with 74 per cent of cuts to tax credits, benefits and pensions being taken from women's incomes, mirroring pre-existing gendered inequality and putting women and children at risk of deeper and sustained poverty. Flagship policies like the new Universal Credit have been especially regressive, reversing hard fought for aspects of women's financial independence. Other policies like the introduction of a 'bedroom tax' have impacted women's ability to find independent housing on leaving the family

unit. Government commitments to tackle domestic violence have worked in tension with other aspects of its agenda. On the up side, the last five years have seen lively feminist debate around the role and visibility of women in public life, fuelled by the rise of Twitter and social media, and supported by a new cadre of openly feminist women MPs in government and opposition ranks. However, concerns over increasing violence and hostility towards women remain, as do concerns over their potentially increasing role as 'shock absorbers' for the impact of public austerity.

Guide to Further Sources

There are a range of textbooks and edited collections which forward feminist analysis of social policy, including F. Williams (1989), *Social Policy: A Critical Introduction*, Cambridge: Polity Press, and G. Pascall (1999), *Social Policy: A Feminist Analysis*, 2nd edn, London: Routledge. S. Watson and L. Doyal (1999), *Engendering Social Policy*, Maidenhead: Open University Press, explicitly focuses on gendered social relations adopting a more postmodern difference focused analysis. Other books consider key social policy ideas from a feminist perspective, for example, R. Lister (2003), *Citizenship: Feminist Perspectives*, 2nd edn, Basingstoke: Palgrave. F. Williams (2002), 'The presence of feminism in the future of welfare', *Economy and Society*, 31:4, 502–19, is a good introduction to ideas around a political ethic of care.

There are also a range of relevant feminist journals, in particular, *Social Politics: International Studies in Gender, State and Society*. *Critical Social Policy* remains a key source for current feminist debate in welfare and is a good means to explore feminism's development within the social policy. J. Carabine (1992), 'Constructing women: women's sexuality and social policy', *Critical Social Policy*, 12:34, 23–37, and J. Morris (1991), '"Us" and "them"? Feminist research community care and disability', *Critical Social Policy*, 11:33, 22–39, are good examples of critique moving forward internal feminist debate over gendered difference and its relationship to social policy.

Used critically the web hosts a vast range of relevant feminist resources. The Fawcett Society website, www.fawcettsociety.org.uk, provides an up-to-date sense of liberal feminist campaigning on equality, including research reports and facts and figures. The fword is a webzine, including a wide range of contemporary feminist debate and resources from a range of feminist perspectives, www.thefword.org.uk/index.

Review and Assignment Questions

1 How is it that social policies disadvantage as well as advantage women?
2 What are the key points of contention between different feminist approaches to social policy analysis?
3 In what ways does the idea of multiple social relations impact on feminist social policy analysis, and what are the benefits and the challenges?
4 Why introduce an analysis of men and masculinities into a feminist analysis of social policy, and what does this add to an understanding of gender relations?
5 Consider the role of feminism in social policy; how far can it be argued that feminism has been successful in achieving its concerns to achieve gender equality in social policy provision?

Visit the book companion site at www.wiley.com/go/alcocksocialpolicy to make use of the resources designed to accompany the textbook. There you will find chapter-specific guides to further resources, including governmental, international, thinktank, pressure groups and relevant journal sources. You will also find a glossary based on *The Blackwell Dictionary of Social Policy*, help sheets, guidance on managing assignments in social policy and career advice.

14

Social Movements

Louisa Parks

Overview

- Definitions of social movements have shifted over time, but are now understood to encompass conflict with an identified opponent, collective identity and a composition relying on informal networks of people and organisations.
- Social movements can demand recognition for a group in society that was not previously recognised or valued.
- Social movements engage in contentious claims-making, using demonstrations, protests or other attention-grabbing strategies, often combined with media-oriented strategies and advocacy work.
- Social movements do not always secure their short-term goals, but may have more impact over the longer term.
- Recent challenges include how social movements act in an online age and how they have changed in a context of global financial crisis.

What is a Social Movement?

Social movements have played an important part in the histories of most countries in the world. In western Europe, they played a critical role in the development of states by voicing the demands of people to steadily centralising authorities and ultimately wresting rights from them in return for duties fulfilled. Understanding why social movements should matter to students of social policy today means we must first take the time to think through what a social movement is – how can we define a social movement? Definitions of movements have shifted over time and can be read

The Student's Companion to Social Policy, Fifth Edition. Edited by Pete Alcock, Tina Haux, Margaret May and Sharon Wright.
© 2016 John Wiley & Sons, Ltd. Published 2016 by John Wiley & Sons, Ltd.

as the products of the times in which they emerged. The first discussions of movements came about between the two world wars during the rise of fascism, and linked social movements to mass hysteria. Later, the labour movement and demands for the redistribution of wealth were seen to epitomise the idea of the social movement. In the late 1960s, the rise of the women's and gay rights movements among others saw definitions linked to identity politics. It is worth noting that as understandings of the goals and definitions of social movements have evolved, so have theories seeking to explain their various aspects.

Today, scholars have identified a number of features that together are considered to define a social movement (della Porta and Diani, 2006).

- Social movements are in conflict with some opponent. This trait refers both to how social movements *act*, for example, by holding demonstrations and protests of many different kinds, and to whom social movements *address*, which may be a government, a business, an international organisation or any number of other actors.
- Social movements are made up of informal networks. We may think of a range of organisations as linked to social movements, but these organisations are only *components* of a social movement. Movements involve individuals and groups, but they do this informally – there is no 'membership list' for the environmental movement, for example, though many environmental activists may also be members of groups such as Greenpeace or Friends of the Earth.
- Social movements display a collective identity. The individuals who turn up to protest feel obliged to do so because of a common cause – for example, students protesting about university fees share the student identity, and the understanding that fees are unfair.

These three characteristics are also mutually reinforcing – each strengthens the others. Social movements have also been found to act in what Sidney Tarrow calls 'cycles of contention': movements move through stages of formation and contention (such as protest), and then enter more latent phases where new organisations may be created (this is known as institutionalisation) or,

in some cases, sections of the movement may take up violent tactics (this in known as radicalisation). To give some examples, the mobilisation against section 28, introduced in late 1987 to the UK Local Government Bill to prohibit 'promoting homosexuality by teaching or by publishing material', prompted the formation of the gay rights group Stonewall. The civil rights movement in Northern Ireland and its brutal suppression in what is known as 'Bloody Sunday' in January 1972, on the other hand, was the genesis of the violent Provisional Irish Republican Army.

Social Movements and the Definition of Groups in Society

The importance of social movements in relation to social policy formation is rooted in how the movements seek to define groups in societies. The central aims of many social movements in the past have been based on this ability to secure recognition and full inclusion of a certain group within a society's definition of citizenship. Before turning to some examples of such movements, some exploration of citizenship is necessary to clarify this line of thought. The liberal view – which has had a strong influence in the UK – sees citizenship as formed of bundles of rights (and, of course, the duties that accompany them). T. H. Marshall, an influential writer on liberal citizenship, saw a special role for social movements in the development of rights. In a nutshell, social movements are catalysts for change in this view: the demands made by social movements can lead to the accordance of rights to newly recognised groups in society or indeed the formation and normalisation of new bundles of rights.

This is the case for the example Marshall draws on – the labour movement. Writing in 1950, Marshall saw the efforts of the labour (or trade union) movement as necessary for securing the rights of 'industrial citizenship', including, for example, sick pay and better working conditions. Moving back in time, the suffragette and suffragist movements can also be understood in this way. Campaigning for universal suffrage was essentially a demand for women to be fully included in the definition of citizenship, of which the right to vote is an essential part. Extending this logic to later movements secures further evidence for the importance of social movements in this vein.

The movements of the 1960s onwards have been described as 'identity movements', and sit well with this view of movements as catalysts for change through the definition of societal groups. The US civil rights movement is a clear-cut example of a demand to be included in the definition of citizenship, but also inspired a wave of social movements that can also be seen in this light. The 'second-wave' women's movement flourished in the wake of the civil rights movement and sought – among other things – the end of discrimination against women; the gay rights movement that also grew in this same late 1960s wave of movements had similar goals.

Nevertheless, it should be noted that these social movements not only sought recognition from authorities, but first and foremost worked to create positive identities for groups previously seen in negative ways. Indeed, new theories of social movements were developed as a direct result of the late 1960s protest wave. While previous theory (known as 'resource mobilisation theory', and linked, as already mentioned, to the importance of the labour movement) saw social movements as externally oriented, rational actors seeking the redistribution of goods, these new movements inspired new social movement theory, which saw an equally important goal of movements in the elaboration and defence of specific identities.

How far can this understanding of social movements as delineators of new groups in society apply today? One important characteristic of more recent social movements is their tendency to cross borders. Although social movements have often been international (the historic movement to abolish slavery, for example), movements today not only tackle international issues, but have sought to define citizenship at the global level. One such example can be easily read in this way: the global justice movement came to the world's notice with the 'Battle for Seattle' protests staged against meetings of the World Trade Organization in 1999 and followed its cycle of contention with ever larger protests directed at various international meetings in following years.

Though often labelled in the media as the 'no global' or 'anti-globalisation' movement, what activists prefer to call the global justice movement (against what is seen as a neo-Liberal globalisation

agenda) is a clear call to extend citizenship rights to the global level: the Charter of Principles adopted at the World Social Forum in Porto Alegre in 2001, for example, makes explicit reference to universal human rights. Still more recently, similar discourses of global citizenship, again in the context of contestation of the power of multinational business, can be read into the *Occupy* movement's slogan of 'we the 99%'. More classic examples of social movements as claims for the recognition of citizens have also abounded in recent years in the social movements of what has come to be known as the 'Arab Spring'. These movements, beginning in Tunisia, also serve to underline an important point brought to bear by scholars of social movements: it may be useful think of social movements as falling on a continuum from reform to revolution. For students of social policy, the role of movements in securing reform is perhaps most interesting – nevertheless, we should bear in mind that social movements do have the potential to grow and effect much more radical change.

Social Movements and the Emergence of Social Policy

How then do social movements actually exert any influence over policymaking? As should be clear from the previous discussion of definitions of social movements, they do not field candidates for elections and cannot therefore influence policy directly through the ballot box – though they may have indirect effects on elections, as will be discussed below. The study of social movements has in fact been considered to fall into the category of 'politics between elections'. Social movements draw on a variety of strategies, known as a movement's *repertoire of contention*, to make their claims public, but the idea of conflict and contention is central. Given its lack of formal power, a social movement has a greater chance of influencing policymaking if it can threaten some kind of conflict.

This logic is most commonly linked to the social movement strategy of the protest march – a march shows that large numbers of people are unified behind a demand, and that they are willing to take action to voice that demand in a public way that may well carry risk. Though the risk factor depends greatly on the rules of the society where the protest march takes place, they are generally considered in the literature to be risky activities to take part in when compared with, for example, signing petitions or writing letters to elected representatives. For this reason social movements are understood as 'unconventional participation', whereas voting, and the like, is labelled 'conventional participation'.

In order to successfully mount the kind of protest march that grabs the attention of policymakers, a social movement must be able to mobilise its activists and other members of the public. This means that a movement must be organised enough not only to spread the word about a protest march, but also to convince as many people as possible that the claim is important enough to march about. A great deal of scholarly writing on social movements thus concentrates on mobilisation, but also on framing. Framing refers to how social movements speak about perceived problems in society in a way that convinces people of the importance of the problem, that names a particular enemy responsible for the problem, and inspires people to act on that problem by taking part in the movement's activities. Framing is crucial not only at the stage of mounting a protest, but also in ensuring that the demand outlasts a single protest event: problems must be framed in ways that make them salient if they are to see a prolonged wave of protest and, perhaps, some response from policymakers.

Although the protest march is the archetypal social movement tactic, a host of others are also employed. The protest march itself plays host to great variety – from the classic marches of trade unions to the carnival-like celebrations of gay pride marches. Other forms of protest fall under the umbrella of civil disobedience and include sit-ins and building occupations, which have evolved in more recent times into camps set up in public spaces. Other methods involve fewer people but are more spectacular: it is impossible to list all the possibilities here, but some examples include scaling buildings, infiltrating parliament to unfurl banners or individuals chaining themselves to trees. These kinds of tactic are particularly useful to understand how social movements may exert power through the media.

Though the shows of numbers and unity of protest marches may attract the attention of policymakers in government, they are unlikely to secure any influence without the intervening power of the media. The media may act not only to amplify the protest march through their coverage by giving voice to the social movement, but also to recruit new individuals to the cause, thus prolonging the movement. This is crucial: one protest march does not make a social movement. A groundswell of action over time is necessary for any influence to be had. In addition to contentious tactics, social movements are also likely to use a host of other more conventional means to make their claims public, such as press releases and conferences, briefing papers and advocacy (meeting with public authorities). Research on social movements has found that a combination of different kinds of tactic is needed to influence policy.

That a social movement will actually exert influence over policy is thus very far from given. Indeed, most social movements do not secure their immediate demands; for instance, the public may tire of a social movement, especially if large-scale protests persist and cause disruption or damage over any length of time, or if protests involve violence. Violence is also systematically over-reported in the media (since it is seen as more 'newsworthy'), meaning that a generally peaceful social movement can be damaged by media coverage rather than helped. The media may also misrepresent the movement in other ways, or provide more space to detractors of the movement. This is all assuming that a social movement has been able to mobilise sufficient activists in the first place – itself a difficult feat. With more recent global movements the difficulties linked to mobilisation and salient framing are compounded with the distances involved and resources required as well as language barriers. It is thus important to note that social movements often fail in terms of immediate claims. However, social movements may have an impact over a longer length of time – here we move again to the idea of the recognition of groups in society.

Analysing Social Movements and the Policy Process

Taking social movements into account in analyses of the policy process means paying attention to the input side of the policy equation: social movements may be among the voices in society demanding certain policies be changed or initiated. Showing how social movements may have impacted a certain policy is particularly difficult, however. This is because, as already discussed, the effects of social movements may be more obvious over the long term than over the short. Social movements may change the overarching norms or discourses of a society over time: that women are equal to men is now generally accepted and protected in law, and discrimination on the basis of race or sexuality is condemned. Without the women's, gay rights or the anti-racism movements it is hard to imagine how ideas that dominated before these movements might have been overcome.

In some cases, however, a social movement may mobilise over a certain policy. This was the case in the section 28 example mentioned earlier, a case that also serves to highlight the fact that social movements are more likely to mobilise and protest against a threat than they are to mobilise to make a specific policy demand. This means that while movements may set agendas in the long term, their campaigns may be more reactive in the short term. In purely analytical terms, then, it is difficult to prove the impact of social movements – many other actors in society will also be seeking to influence policymakers to act in different ways. Careful work teasing out the actions of different actors is needed to prove the impact of social movement campaigns on specific policies, a process that again becomes more complex when policies are formulated by international governmental organisations such as the European Union. Yet broader historical work has decisively proven the changes that social movements have wrought at the societal level.

Emerging Issues

Recent years have thrown up a host of fascinating issues and challenges in the field of social movement studies. Though not an 'emerging' issue, it should be noted that a continuing gap concerns work on social movements outside the global North; while many scholars have written on movements across the world, theories of social movements tend to be based on examples from Europe and the USA in particular – as is reflected in this chapter. More specific emerging issues that

have formed the subject of much recent work concern the global financial crisis and innovations in technology, respectively.

The advent of the global financial crisis more or less coincided with the winding down of the global justice movement – international summits are not longer marked by mass demonstrations as they were in the first decade of the twenty-first century. As the financial crisis translated into an austerity agenda of various cuts to public services in Europe in particular, a new movement, known as the *Occupy* movement in the English-speaking world and labelled the 'Indignados' (outraged) movement by media in the rest of Europe after the Spanish protests of May 2011, came to the fore. This movement was known for its occupations of squares and other public spaces, where protesters set up camps. In contrast to the international protests of the preceding global justice movement, the camps of *Occupy* reinforced their very local presence and field of action.

Scholars of social movements have explained this shift from the global level to the very local in different by complementary ways.

■ First, they argue, the threats to ordinary people posed by the cuts of the austerity agendas – particularly in European countries subject to 'bailouts' – manifest themselves locally. Thus, the movement in Spain is very active in preventing the repossession of homes, while the *Occupy* movement in the USA has bought up debt sold off cheaply by banks, subsequently clearing those that owed money.
■ Second, they argue that the preoccupation of national governments and international governmental organisations with propping up banks and the business sector more generally has left social movements with few opportunities to engage with these actors. Paradoxically, this has led many to dismiss the *Occupy* movement for having no 'demands'.

Another exciting area of new work on social movements concerns the online world. The Internet has provided movements with a new way of organising which came into focus during the 'Arab Spring', where sites such as Twitter and Facebook were important in diffusing information about protests as well as in some mobilisation efforts. The Internet has also become both a means and a subject of protest itself. As a means of protest, options stretch far beyond the possibilities offered by signing petitions (although these have had some impact). Many of the most spectacular uses have been linked to movements for the freedom of information and have been linked with individuals, thus mirroring the move of protest from the global to the local: Wikileaks and the 'whistle-blower' Edward Snowden come to mind here. The potential for individuals to have such profound impacts raises interesting questions for the field of social movement studies, where the importance of numbers and unity has been paramount. The Internet has also become the subject of contention, however. Digital rights and freedom of expression movements have mobilised over access to knowledge and against policies seen as restricting the freedom of the Internet.

Guide to Further Sources

Among the most comprehensive and in-depth texts for students interested in theoretical issues surrounding social movements is D. della Porta and M. Diani (2006), *Social Movements: An Introduction*, Oxford: Blackwell. For a broader and very readable overview focusing on an understanding of political movements as rational actors and particularly informative on cycles of contention, see S. Tarrow (2011), *Power in Movement*, Cambridge: Cambridge University Press, is a good choice. A good collection of key readings on different social movements and on concepts useful for their study is brought together in J. Goodwin and J. M. Jasper (eds) (2015), *The Social Movements Reader*, Oxford: Wiley-Blackwell. On social movements in Europe in particular, see C. Flesher Fominaya and L. Cox (eds) (2013), *Understanding European Movements*, Abingdon: Routledge.

Review and Assignment Questions

1 How can we define a social movement?
2 Name three social movements that fought for citizenship rights, and explain your selection of these.
3 What sort of tactics do social movements use?
4 How might social movements influence the formation of policy?
5 How important are social movements to democratic societies, and why?

Visit the book companion site at www.wiley.com/go/alcocksocialpolicy to make use of the resources designed to accompany the textbook. There you will find chapter-specific guides to further resources, including governmental, international, thinktank, pressure groups and relevant journal sources. You will also find a glossary based on *The Blackwell Dictionary of Social Policy*, help sheets, guidance on managing assignments in social policy and career advice.

15

Post-Modernist Perspectives

Tony Fitzpatrick

Overview

- Post-modernism articulates disillusionment with traditional social and political theories, one which makes room for new approaches and ways of thinking.
- Post-structuralism also departs radically from previous philosophies, though it is more theoretically and methodologically precise, drawing attention to the instabilities of identity and meaning.
- Post-modernism and post-structuralism have become established features of the intellectual landscape, but many have queried their importance or significance.
- They can appear distant from the 'bread-and-butter' issues of social policy, yet they articulate the changing social realities with which social policy must get to grips.
- Other social changes include increased attention to the concept of risk and its relevance to contemporary notions of citizenship and well-being.

Theories of the Post-Modern

Post-modernism was *the* intellectual fashion of the 1980s, and like all fashions it attracted zealous supporters and equally zealous critics. Yet post-modernism's legacy has confounded both sides. It did not sweep away traditional schools of thought, as its supporters had anticipated, yet nor has it proved to be an empty, transitional fad, as its critics had hoped. This is because, with its roots reaching far into the history of ideas, post-modernism reinvented some old themes within new social, political and cultural contexts. Therefore, whether we agree with post-modernism or not, we cannot ignore its recent influences. By the time social policy took an interest in post-modernism,

The Student's Companion to Social Policy, Fifth Edition. Edited by Pete Alcock, Tina Haux, Margaret May and Sharon Wright.
© 2016 John Wiley & Sons, Ltd. Published 2016 by John Wiley & Sons, Ltd.

the latter already nurtured the intellectual soil upon which the former depended.

The turn towards post-modernism was largely inspired by a disillusion with traditional forms of politics and social philosophy. The 'rediscovery' of Marxism in the 1960s inspired the left to believe that alternatives to consumer capitalism were both imaginable and achievable. By the 1970s, however, many activists and intellectuals had become disenchanted with Marxism and began to rethink the meaning of emancipation and progress.

Jean-François Lyotard contended that we can no longer cling to 'metanarratives'. A metanarrative is any system of thought that attempts to understand the social world within a single, all-encompassing critique. Marxism is one such 'grand narrative' in trying to explain all aspects of society in terms of material production and class struggle. This is like trying to step beyond the social world and understand it from the outside. But Lyotard, like Wittgenstein before him, insisted that there is no 'outside' to which we can ascend; since we are enmeshed within language there is no space beyond language that would enable us to map the world in its entirety. Therefore, knowledge must proceed from 'the inside', from within our language-using communities: knowledge is always contextualised and particular, rather than absolute and universal. Lyotard defines post-modernism as an 'incredulity towards metanarratives', and so a rejection of the view that emancipatory politics can rely upon a single explanatory model or system (see Box 15.1).

Jean Baudrillard goes even further. Marxism may have been appropriate in an age of production, but we now live in societies of signs and codes. Indeed, so ubiquitous are these signs and codes that they no longer symbolically represent reality; instead, the philosophical distinction between reality and representation has collapsed into a 'hyper-reality'. Whereas we could once distinguish between original objects and their copies, hyper-reality implies that only copies exist and no originating source for those copies is identifiable. Ours, then, is an age of simulations that endlessly refer only to other simulations. The infinite circularity of these self-references is what Baudrillard calls the simulacra: everything is a reproduction of other reproductions. Society implodes in on itself and we cannot liberate ourselves from the simulacra: ideologies of progress are just another form of seduction to the system of codes.

These ideas came under considerable attack from other theorists. Jürgen Habermas alleges that post-modernism is a philosophical justification for social and political conservatism. By taking progress to be impossible and undesirable, post-modernism resembles a conservative defence of the status quo. Habermas charges post-modernist theorists with depending upon the very philosophical premises and assumptions that they claim to have dispelled.

However, there are some who, while not supporting post-modernism per se, insist that its emergence and popularity reveal something very important about recent social change. Fredric Jameson describes post-modernism as 'the cultural logic of late capitalism' in that it accurately describes the fragmentation and heterogeneity of contemporary life. This is because of developments within capitalist production and consumption. Our cultures are pervaded by surfaces, hybrids, repackaging, parody, pastiche and spectacle because this is now the most effective way of valuing, circulating and consuming commodities. Capitalism dominates by seeming not to dominate, by fragmenting both itself and the objects it dominates. So, Jameson is insisting that post-modernism *can* be utilised by those committed to a progressive politics of the left.

Post-modernists reject the idea that values, judgements and principles can apply universally across space and time. For critics of post-modernism such as Christopher Norris, this leads inevitably to relativism, the idea that there are

---

Box 15.1 Lyotard

In contemporary society and culture – post-industrial society, post-modern culture – the question of legitimation of knowledge is formulated in different terms. The grand narrative has lost its credibility . . . regardless of whether it is a speculative narrative or a narrative of emancipation. (Jean-François Lyotard (1984), *The Post-modern Condition*, Manchester: Manchester University Press, 37)

Box 15.2 Post-Modernism

Post-modernists:

- reject universalism;
- believe truth to be contextual;
- abandon foundationalism and essentialism;
- avoid binary distinctions;
- support identity politics;
- celebrate irony and difference.

no universal standards of morality and truth. This, he argues, tempts post-modernists into intellectual absurdity, such as Baudrillard's 1991 claim that the Gulf War never happened.

However, as a defender of post-modernism, Richard Rorty argues that it is the futile search for absolute truth that creates relativism, so if we stop searching for that which is unobtainable then we can transcend the sterile distinction between universalism and relativism. This does not leave us unable to speak about truth; it means that truth is contextual, that is, dependent upon the frame within which truth-claims are made. As Chantal Mouffe observes, ideas are rooted within particular traditions and there is no 'God's eye view' which is external to all traditions.

Post-modernists also reject foundationalism and essentialism. Foundationalism is the notion that knowledge and belief are based upon secure foundations that can be discovered, for example, through science. Post-modernists argue that there are no such foundations as we can never fully justify any knowledge- or belief-claim. Understanding is always a matter of interpretation and interpretation is never complete. Essentialism is the idea that objects have essences that define and explain that object, for example, the essence of humans is 'human nature'. For post-modernists, though, all objects and their supposed essences are merely social constructs.

Post-modernists insist that we should avoid thinking in terms of binary distinctions, hierarchies and structures, for example, nature versus culture. Post-modern feminists like Judith Butler argue that this way of thinking reflects masculinist assumptions about the world – that the world is

divisible into parts, which relate to one another in relations of higher and lower, superior and inferior. For post-modernists there are no edges and peripheries or, rather, *everywhere* is an edge *and* a periphery! Instead, they prefer to emphasise the importance of centreless flows, fluidities, networks and webs.

Post-modernism is often taken to prefer a form of identity politics based around culture and the self. Oppression and discrimination is not just about a lack of resources, but also about a lack of recognition and status, about not being able to shape the norms that define and exclude you. Yet identity – of individuals, groups, societies – is never fixed, but is in a state of indeterminate flux, being constantly renegotiated and redefined. Identity implies not only 'resemblance to' but also 'difference from'.

Finally, post-modernism embodies a playful, ironic stance: post-modernists often refuse to take anything too seriously, including themselves! Yet, rather than being self-indulgent, this playfulness is meant to be a celebration of diversity, hybridity, difference and pluralism. For Rorty, philosophy is not the 'mirror of nature', but a means of devising new vocabularies and descriptions. Rather than debating which description is real our job is to assist each other in endlessly deconstructing and reconstructing our understanding of the social world. Solidarity, rather than truth, is the proper object of inquiry.

Post-Modernism and Social Policy

Many social policy theorists and researchers are quite critical towards post-modernism. For instance, if social policy is concerned with welfare, then we must be able to distinguish between higher and lower forms of well-being in making interpersonal, historical, cross-national and cross-cultural comparisons. Yet it is precisely these judgements that post-modernism might disallow. By embracing contextualism, anti-foundationalism and anti-essentialism, post-modernists undermine notions of truth and social progress and so efforts to create greater freedom, equality and community. But if these notions should *not* be dismissed – as their enduring popularity might suggest – then perhaps we should reject post-modern ideas because their political and social consequences are likely to be damaging.

Take one example. Social policy is arguably based upon the view that there is a human nature consisting of basic needs. The task of welfare systems is to enable those needs to be fulfilled. But if human nature is a modernist fiction, as post-modernists claim, and if needs are constructed through language rather than being natural, then the rationale of state welfare may be undermined. This is just one reason why some social policy commentators are very suspicious of post-modernism, accusing it of providing an intellectual justification of anti-welfare state politics.

Others, though, insist that post-modernism and social policy need not be so hostile. Traditionally, social policy has been concerned with class, that is, income and occupation. Yet, although our identities are undoubtedly constructed in terms of socio-economic relations, there may be other forms of relations that are also important: gender, ethnicity, sexuality, religion, disability, nationality, age. Therefore, social policy must take account of these additional categories and how they intersect. Yet this is where disagreement kicks in, for how should we weigh class against non-class divisions? For some, class is still of central importance and post-modernism is therefore an unwelcome distraction. For others, there has to be a more equitable balancing of class and non-class categories.

Nancy Fraser suggests that social justice requires both redistribution and recognition, not only material questions of distribution but also cultural questions of status and respect for different groups. If we place too much emphasis on economic justice and redistribution we may neglect the extent to which discrimination is about symbolic exclusions, the denial of status and disrespect. Conversely, if we place too much emphasis on cultural justice and recognition we potentially ignore the role which class continues to play in shaping social institutions and the distribution of opportunities and liberties. We need both. Therefore, by drawing attention to the importance and complexity of social identities, post-modernism has arguably performed an important service.

Another form of rapprochement between post-modern themes and social policy is outlined by Zygmunt Bauman. Bauman believes that we now live in a post-modern world, one that has been individualised, fragmented and, through the flows of globalisation, speeded up. Yet, in their rush to celebrate this, post-modernists themselves often neglect the role of deregulated, global capitalism in bringing about that state of affairs. Post-modern capitalism, says Bauman, empowers the wealthy by disempowering the poor. Collective systems of welfare – though also the victims of global capitalism – are the means by which we recognise our interdependency and reassert the importance of common values and needs.

The influence of post-modernism may also extend to the delivery of services. Social policy has been characterised by a debate between universalists and selectivists, with the former resisting the means-testing advocated by the latter. A post-modern slant on this debate suggests the provision should be universal but that, within this framework, there must be a greater sensitivity to the particular needs and demands of certain groups. For some, this will imply market-driven, consumerist forms of local empowerment. Yet a progressive post-modernism stresses the importance of non-market types of participative inclusion and deliberation.

So although some believe post-modernism and social policy to be irreconcilable opposites, others think that both contribute to our understanding of self and society.

Post-Structuralism

Post-structuralism agrees with post-modernism that we cannot transcend the traditions in which we are embedded. For post-structuralists, what we call reality is no more than a temporary effect of discourse and signification, with no stable reality beyond the play of language. Truth is therefore discursive, that is, there is no such thing as 'Truth', merely a series of truth-claims that have to be understood in terms of the subjectivities expressing them. What we call truth is just another face of power and there are no structures of reality lying beneath the social surface. Power has endless faces and there is no real one underpinning all the rest.

Michel Foucault focuses upon the conditions (the discourses) through which knowledge and ideas are generated. He sets out to understand discursive practices through a 'genealogical' approach that closely traces the history and operation of power within a number of institutional settings, for example, prisons, asylums, clinics. For

Box 15.3 Madness/Normality

The judges of normality are present everywhere. We are in the society of the teacher-judge, the doctor-judge, the educator-judge, the 'social worker'-judge; it is on them that the universal reign of the normative is based; and each individual, wherever he may find himself, subjects to it his body, his gestures, his behaviour, his aptitudes, his achievements. (Michel Foucault (1991), *Discipline and Punish*, Harmondsworth: Penguin, 304)

instance, in the nineteenth and twentieth centuries madness was medicalised, redefined as mental illnesses that require specialised treatment by medical practitioners eager to assert their influence. Other discourses, such as the religious emphasis upon mania, possession and exorcism, were thereby dispelled. Foucault analyses the extent to which medicalisation places the mentally ill in a new normative framework, which is not necessarily superior to any of the earlier discourses (such as the religious one). 'Madness' enables the rest of us to define ourselves as healthy and normal (see Box 15.3).

So Foucault identifies the 'panopticon' as the essential metaphor for all modern forms of discipline and normalisation. The panopticon was a design for a prison that would use the least number of prison officers to survey as many prisoners as possible. The prisoners would not know when they were being observed and so would need to act as if they were under constant surveillance. Using these ideas we can understand welfare systems as discourses, as the disciplinary mechanisms of normative surveillance. To be a subject is to be constantly policing oneself. Post-structuralism does not offer manifestos for welfare reform. Instead, it is a kind of 'spring-cleaning' exercise, a way of undermining our commonly held assumptions.

Many within the social policy community reject these ideas, however. If truth-claims dominate, if power is everywhere, what happens to the struggle for universal emancipation, progress and justice? Ironically, just as some Marxists interpret everyone as a representative of their class, so post-structuralists often treat agents merely as the embodied

spaces of discourses flowing in and around them. I may believe in progress and rationality *as* a white, Western, middle-class male, but that does not mean I hold those beliefs *because* I am a white, Western, middle-class male. Perhaps truth is not simply another face of power.

Yet Foucault has been highly influential, and, like post-modernism, post-structuralism has contributed to contemporary debates regarding identity, agency, governance, regulation and surveillance.

Risk Society

There are other theorists who, while believing that modernity has changed, do not allege that the modern period is over. Ulrich Beck argues that we have reached the beginning of a *second* modernity. The first modernity was an age of industrial progress where all political and social institutions were designed to generate 'goods' (welfare, economic growth) in a world that was taken to be stable, knowable and scientifically calculable. By contrast, the second modernity is a risk society characterised by the attempt to limit, manage and navigate a way through a series of 'bads', anxieties and hazards. For instance, nuclear and industrial pollution undermines the simple class hierarchies of the industrial order, affecting the ghettos of the rich as well as those of the poor (see Box 15.4).

One implication is that whereas state welfare was once thought of as a protection against collective risks, for example, through social insurance provision, the welfare state has now become a principal source of risk. Tony Giddens agrees with much of Beck's thesis and insists that welfare reform must be based upon a notion of 'positive welfare' in which people are equipped with the skills needed to navigate their way through the new social environments of insecurity, transforming risks-as-dangers into risks-as-opportunities.

Box 15.4 Risk Societies

. . . risk societies are *not* exactly class societies; their risk positions cannot be understood as class positions, or their conflicts as class conflicts. (Ulrich Beck (1992), *Risk Society*, London: Sage, 36)

The risk society idea has proved to be very influential, but has attracted many criticisms. Some reject the sociological assumptions upon which it is based. The contrast between the first and second modernities may be too crude and the suggestion that class structures have become less important has been condemned as naive. Also, Beck may neglect the extent to which risks have been produced politically by those opposed to welfare state capitalism.

Emerging Issues

All the ideas reviewed above deal with three main themes that show no sign of declining in importance. First, whether we should describe ourselves as still living in a period of modernity. Second, whether class is the main organising principle of contemporary society. Finally, how we should try to understand society and judge the best means of reforming it and its welfare institutions. Social policy debates in the twenty-first century continue to revolve around these themes and these new directions.

Guide to Further Sources

A comprehensive survey of the key figures in post-modernism is provided in H. Bertens and J. Natoli (2002), *Postmodernism*, Oxford: Blackwell. An excellent, comprehensive anthology of the greatest philosophers, which traces key debates about modernity across the centuries, can be found in L. E. Cahoone (2003), *From Modernism to Post-modernism: An Anthology*, Oxford: Blackwell. For useful and accessible discussions of post-modern-ism in relation to social policy, see J. Carter (ed.) (1998), *Postmodernity and the Fragmentation of Welfare*, London: Routledge; P. Leonard (1997), *Postmodern Welfare*, London: Sage; and J. Rodgers (2000), *From a Welfare State to a Welfare Society*, London: Macmillan.

Good introductions to post-structuralism include C. Belsey (2002), *Post-structuralism: A Very Short Introduction*, Oxford: Oxford University Press; A. Finlayson and J. Valentine (2002), *Politics and Post-Structuralism: An Intro-duction*, Edinburgh: Edinburgh University Press. For Foucault in relation to social work, see N. Mik-Meyer and K. Villardsen (2013), *Power and Wel-fare*, London: Routledge. Foucault is also central to S. Ball (2013), *Foucault, Power, and Education*, London: Routledge.

For a wide-ranging application of the risk society literature to questions of social and public policy, see D. Denney (ed.) (2009), *Living in Dangerous Times: Fear, Insecurity, Risk and Social Policy*, Oxford: Blackwell.

Web resources can be found at: EpistemeLinks, www.epistemelinks.com; Everything Post-modern, www.ebbflux.com/postmodern; Internet Modern History Sourcebook, http://www.fordham.edu; *Stanford Encyclopaedia of Philoso-phy*, plato.stanford.edu/entries/postmodernism.

Review and Assignment Questions

1 Can post-modernism inspire progressive forms of social critique?
2 Are 'needs', 'rights' and 'class' nothing more than constructs of language and discourse?
3 To what extent are our social identities cultural rather than material?
4 What are the disadvantages of using post-structuralist ideas to understand the signifi-cance for social policy of risks and of social movements?
5 What would a 'post-modern welfare state' look like?

Visit the book companion site at www.wiley.com/go/alcocksocialpolicy to make use of the resources designed to accompany the textbook. There you will find chapter-specific guides to further resources, including governmental, international, thinktank, pressure groups and relevant journal sources. You will also find a glossary based on *The Blackwell Dictionary of Social Policy*, help sheets, guidance on managing assignments in social policy and career advice.

PART III
Historical Context

16

Nineteenth-Century Beginnings

Bernard Harris

Overview

- During the nineteenth century, many people sought protection against the risks of poverty and poor health with the aid of their families, friends and communities, through charities and by joining mutual aid associations.
- The main form of statutory provision was the Poor Law. In England and Wales, the Poor Law Acts of 1597 and 1601 gave local parishes the power to introduce a compulsory levy, which was used to 'set the poor on work', support those who were unable to work and to provide apprenticeships for pauper children. Scotland possessed a much more rudimentary system of poor relief, and Ireland lacked any form of poor law before 1838.
- The English and Welsh Poor Laws, and the Scottish Poor Law, experienced significant changes during the nineteenth century. The Poor Law Amendment Act 1834 aimed to deter able-bodied men from seeking poor relief, whilst the Poor Law (Scotland) Act 1845 gave Scottish parishes the right to levy a compulsory rate for the first time. Able-bodied men were excluded altogether from the Scottish poor law system, but a more flexible attitude to welfare provision also became apparent during the final decades of the nineteenth century.
- The nineteenth century witnessed important developments with regard to the improvement of working conditions and the introduction of new housing standards, together with the provision of healthcare. Government grants to educational bodies were introduced in 1833, and school boards assumed responsibility for the provision of elementary schools after 1870. The first Public Health Act was passed in 1848, and local authorities intensified their efforts to improve the standard of public health from the 1870s.
- Despite considerable progress during the final part of the nineteenth century, there was also growing anxiety about the need for further reform, and this contributed to the introduction of the Liberal welfare reforms after 1906.

The Student's Companion to Social Policy, Fifth Edition. Edited by Pete Alcock, Tina Haux, Margaret May and Sharon Wright.
© 2016 John Wiley & Sons, Ltd. Published 2016 by John Wiley & Sons, Ltd.

All societies have social policies of some kind, even if the state plays only a minor role in welfare provision. However, nineteenth-century Britain witnessed a series of changes that had a major impact on the scale and scope of public activity. This chapter summarises these developments, whilst also recognising the role of other providers within the overall framework of a 'mixed economy of welfare'.

In the late eighteenth century, the vast majority of British people still lived in small towns and villages. It has been estimated that approximately 21 per cent of the population of Scotland and 30.9 per cent of the population of England and Wales lived in towns containing more than 5,000 inhabitants in 1801, but both these figures increased rapidly over the course of the next century. In 1901, 57.6 per cent of Scots lived in towns containing more than 5,000 inhabitants and 78 per cent of the population of England and Wales lived in towns containing more than 2,500 inhabitants. The total number of people in England, Scotland and Wales increased from 10.5 million to 37 million over the course of the century.

Throughout this period, families, friends and neighbours played a central role in meeting social needs. Many people also relied on the support of charities and mutual aid organisations, often providing local, spontaneous and independent support, which left little trace in official records. More institutional forms of charity also helped to build bridges between different social groups, creating an infrastructure of support for education and healthcare, developing different forms of housing provision, and giving financial and other kinds of support during periods of crisis. In Coventry, seven appeals for the relief of distress were launched between January 1837 and April 1860, and a national appeal was initiated in November 1860. The Lord Mayor of Manchester appealed on behalf of Lancashire cotton workers and their families in 1862, and the Lord Mayor of London issued emergency appeals in 1866 and 1886.

Historians have become increasingly interested in the role played by friendly societies and other mutual aid organisations in the development of a range of social protection schemes. The friendly society movement 'took off' during the mid-eighteenth century. Members paid money into a common fund in return for support during periods of sickness and old age and following their deaths. By the end of the nineteenth century, more than four million individuals (of whom the vast majority were male) belonged to a friendly society, whilst many others belonged to trade unions (many of which also offered welfare benefits), collecting societies (a specialised form of friendly society offering funeral benefits), cooperative societies, savings banks and building societies. However, despite these provisions, many people continued to rely on the assistance provided by public welfare authorities, such as the Poor Law, at different stages of their lives.

Poor Relief

Although several authors have argued that the development of state welfare was directly related to the process of industrialisation, the earliest form of statutory welfare in Britain predated the emergence of an industrial society by more than two centuries. The Poor Law Act 1572 instructed magistrates in England and Wales to establish the number of poor people in their areas and to tax local inhabitants to provide funds to support them. The Poor Law Acts 1597 and 1601 transferred responsibility to the churchwardens and overseers of each parish and made them responsible for 'setting the poor on work', maintaining those who were unable to work, and boarding out pauper children to become apprentices. The Scottish Poor Law Act 1574 also required parishes to support their poor, but made no provision for compulsory rating. This meant that the Scottish system became much more reliant on voluntary funding and the Church. Scottish legislation also differed from England's because it made no provision for the support of those needing employment.

These two factors help to explain the contrast between the different paths taken by the two Acts that shaped the development of the English and Scottish Poor Laws during the nineteenth century. In Scotland, despite evidence of widespread hardship, there was relatively little pressure for reform of the Poor Law before the 1840s. The immediate cause of reform was a split in the Church of Scotland, known as the Great Disruption, in 1843. This placed increasing financial pressure on the Church of Scotland and led it to support plans to give parishes the power to introduce a compulsory levy. However, even after the new powers were introduced in 1845, able-bodied men continued to be excluded from the poor relief system.

The reform of the Poor Law in England and Wales was preceded by a much longer and more heated debate over the relief of the able-bodied poor. Critics argued that the provision of relief had undermined work incentives, weakened social ties, encouraged population growth and exacerbated the hardship it was meant to prevent. In 1832, the Royal Commission on the Poor Laws drew a sharp distinction between *indigence* – 'the state of a person unable to labour, or unable to obtain, in return for his labour, the means of subsistence' – and *poverty*, which was 'the state of one who, in order to obtain a mere subsistence, is forced to have recourse to labour'. In order to deter members of the second group from seeking relief, it recommended the introduction of a 'workhouse test'. It argued that if relief was provided only within the confines of a 'well-regulated workhouse', this would deter those who were capable of supporting themselves from seeking relief.

The Poor Law Report provided the foundation for the Poor Law Amendment Act 1834. However, this Act did not compel Poor Law authorities to establish workhouses or to abandon the payment of 'outdoor relief' (that is, the provision of assistance to individuals outside a workhouse). Its most important innovation was the establishment of a central body, the Poor Law Commission, with the power to make and issue rules for the management of the poor throughout England and Wales, and to create combinations of Poor Law parishes, known as Poor Law Unions, to administer the poor law in each area. The Commission could only order Unions to construct workhouses if it obtained the written consent of a majority of the Poor Law Guardians, or the support of a majority of the ratepayers and property owners who were eligible to vote in Guardians' elections.

Historians have offered conflicting assessments of the Act's impact. Although many traditional Poor Law practices survived the advent of the 'New Poor Law', workhouses were constructed in most parts of the country and the vast majority of parishes had been reorganised into Poor Law Unions by the end of the 1850s. However, although the establishment of the New Poor Law led to a substantial reduction in the number of able-bodied male paupers, the Poor Law authorities continued to support large numbers of non-able-bodied men, as well as women and children, and the majority of these people received support outside the workhouse.

Whilst many people thought that the New Poor Law was too harsh and was failing in its duty to provide for the most vulnerable, others believed that the original principles of the 1834 reform had been diluted and that its deterrent functions were being undermined by 'indiscriminate' charity. In 1847, the Poor Law Commission was replaced by the Poor Law Board, and in 1869 the Board's president, Viscount Goschen, advised London's Poor Law authorities to work more closely with private charities and to restrict the flow of statutory relief. This policy continued when the Poor Law Board was itself replaced by the Local Government Board in 1871, and this led to what became known as the 'Crusade against Outdoor Relief'. The 'crusade' led to sharp reductions in the numbers of both male and female paupers throughout the decade.

However, despite the 'crusade', other evidence suggested that approaches to poverty were moving in a different direction. This was reflected in measures such as the use of income scales to identify parents who might qualify for the remittance of school fees following the introduction of compulsory education in different parts of England and Wales after 1870 and in Scotland after 1872; the removal of restrictions that prevented men who claimed outdoor medical relief from voting in parliamentary elections in 1885; the authorisation of public works schemes during periods of unemployment between 1886 and 1893; and the democratisation of Guardians' elections and the appointment of the Royal Commission on the Aged Poor in 1894. Attitudes to poverty were also shaped by the results of two major surveys of poverty in London and York between 1887 and 1901. Many of these developments contributed to the adoption of new approaches to the prevention and relief of poverty by the Liberal governments of 1906–14 (see Chapter 17).

Public Services

Although the Poor Laws provided the bedrock of public welfare services during the nineteenth century, the period also witnessed major developments in other aspects of the state's welfare role. These developments were reflected in the introduction of measures to regulate living and working conditions, as well as the establishment of new kinds of public service.

As we have already seen, the late eighteenth and early nineteenth centuries saw a significant increase in the scale of industrial employment, including the growth of factories and workshops. During the late eighteenth century, reformers such as Thomas Percival highlighted the conditions under which children were employed in these establishments, and this led to a series of attempts to regulate conditions of employment for children and, subsequently, for women and, eventually, men. The earliest Acts included the Health and Morals of Apprentices Act 1802 and the Factory Acts of 1819, 1820, 1825 and 1833, and they were followed by more wide-ranging legislation such as the Ten Hours Act 1847, the Factory Acts 1867 and 1874, and the Factory and Workshops Acts 1878 and 1901.

Local authorities acquired new powers to prosecute the owners of 'filthy and unwholesome' properties and to demolish 'ruinous or insanitary buildings' during the 1840s and 1850s. The Public Health Act 1848 allowed local Boards of Health to prohibit cellar dwellings, to regulate common lodging houses, to ensure that all new buildings were connected to sewers, and to make arrangements for the removal of 'nuisances', such as refuse piles and unclean privies, but its application to Scotland was blocked by medical disagreements over the causation of disease.

The Artizans' and Labourers' Dwellings Act 1868 and the Artizans' and Labourers' Dwellings Improvement Act 1875 gave local authorities the power to demolish insanitary dwellings, but little effort was made to provide affordable forms of replacement housing for displaced tenants. However, the Housing of the Working Classes Act 1890 allowed local authorities to construct new houses for more affluent workers and encouraged hopes that this would reduce the pressure of demand at the bottom of the housing market. Although the Act had relatively little effect on total housing stock before 1914, it anticipated the first large-scale experiments in council housing after 1919.

The nineteenth century also saw important changes in the development of medical services. The traditional divisions between physicians, surgeons and apothecaries became increasingly blurred, and a more unified medical profession began to emerge. At the start of the century, most people preferred to be treated in their own homes, but by the end of the century they were more likely to seek hospital care for more serious forms of treatment. In 1891, approximately 25 per cent of hospital beds were located in charitable or voluntary institutions, and the remainder were in the public sector. The majority of these were located in Poor Law infirmaries, but a growing number were housed in more specialised institutions administered by local authority public health committees.

As the number of people who lived in urban areas increased, many contemporaries feared that the pace of urbanisation and the concentration of health problems in towns would undermine the health of the population as a whole. In addition to the housing clauses already described, the Public Health Act 1848 led to the creation of the first central government health department, the General Board of Health, and gave it the power to examine the sanitary condition of any area where more than 10 per cent of ratepayers requested such an enquiry, or where the local death rate averaged more than twenty-three deaths per thousand living over a seven-year period. The General Board of Health was also empowered to create local Boards of Health if this seemed appropriate. However, it was not until much later in the century that many local authorities began to take concerted action to improve sanitary conditions. The expansion of public health activity after 1870 had many causes, including the provision of central government support for the appointment of local Medical Officers of Health from 1872.

The history of public health reform in Scotland followed a slightly different path, and was much more dependent on local initiative. Many of the earliest attempts at reform were spearheaded by the local police commissioners. However, the pace of reform accelerated during the 1860s, when major Improvement Acts were implemented in Glasgow and Edinburgh, and the first Public Health (Scotland) Act was passed in 1867. This Act was amended in 1871, 1875, 1882 and 1890, and further changes followed the establishment of the Scottish Local Government Board in 1894.

At the start of the nineteenth century, many observers were afraid that the expansion of educational opportunities would provoke unrest, and it was left to a number of religious societies, including the Non-Conformist British and Foreign Schools Society and the Church of England National Society, to take the lead in establishing new schools. In 1833, the government granted £20,000 to these societies to enable them to build more schools in northern England, and both the scale and scope of public educational funding expanded rapidly after 1840. During the 1860s, many commentators expressed concerns about the number of children who were not attending recognised elementary schools, and this led to the introduction of the Elementary Education Act 1870 and the Education (Scotland) Act 1872.

The new Acts aimed to 'fill the gaps' in the existing systems of voluntary education by creating School Boards in areas where the level of provision was deemed to be inadequate. The 1870 Act allowed School Boards to make school attendance compulsory for children between the ages of five and ten, but the 1872 Act went further and made attendance compulsory for all Scottish children between the ages of five and thirteen. The principle of compulsory education was extended to other parts of England and Wales in 1876 and 1880, but elementary school fees were only abolished in England and Wales in 1891 and in Scotland in 1899. The powers and duties of English and Welsh School Boards were transferred to Local Authority Education Committees in 1902, but School Boards remained in place in Scotland until 1918.

Emerging Issues

As this chapter has shown, the nineteenth century witnessed many important changes in welfare provision. At the start of the nineteenth century, the English and Scottish Poor Laws were very different, with the Scottish system relying much more heavily on support from the Church and private charity. The Scottish system also excluded able-bodied men altogether. Over the course of the next seventy years, the two systems became much more closely aligned, although significant differences remained. The Poor Law Amendment Act 1834 sought to deter able-bodied men from seeking poor relief in England and Wales, whilst the Poor Law (Scotland) Act 1845 allowed local parishes to introduce a compulsory levy to fund poor relief, but able-bodied men continued to be excluded. However, a more expansive attitude to the relief of poverty became apparent on both sides of the border from the 1870s onwards. The state's role also expanded in other ways. These included the introduction of a series of Acts to regulate the employment of women and children, establish minimum standards of health and safety at work, improve the quality of new housing, protect the population against the spread of disease and provide new educational services.

Although many Victorians welcomed these measures, they also approached the start of the new century with growing unease. During the 1880s and 1890s, surveys by two independent researchers, Charles Booth and Seebohm Rowntree, appeared to show that the extent of poverty was much greater than previously thought, and Rowntree's findings in particular helped to fuel concerns that a significant proportion of the working-class population was living below the standard of 'merely physical efficiency'. These fears were compounded by suggestions that the health of the population was being undermined by continuing urbanisation and by the high proportion of prospective army recruits who were rejected on grounds of physical unfitness. The established political parties – the Liberals and Conservatives – faced a growing challenge from an increasingly organised labour movement (the Labour Representation Committee was formed in 1900), and concern over Britain's failure to keep pace with the emerging economic powers of Germany and the United States continued to mount. Many of these anxieties were reflected in the background to the new welfare measures which the Liberal government introduced after 1906.

Guide to Further Sources

B. Harris (2004), *The Origins of the British Welfare State: Society, State and Social Welfare in England and Wales, 1800–1945*, Basingstoke: Palgrave, provides an introduction to the history of social policy in England, Scotland and Wales during the nineteenth century. Additional information has been derived from the following sources: T. M. Devine (2012), *The Scottish Nation: A Modern History*, Harmondsworth: Penguin; T. M. Devine and R. Mitchison (eds) (1988), *People and Society in Scotland, vol. 1: 1760–1830*, Edinburgh: John Donald; R. Floud, J. Humphries and P. Johnson (eds) (2014), *The Cambridge Economic History of Modern Britain, vol. 1: 1700–1870*, Cambridge: Cambridge University Press; and W. H. Fraser and R. J. Morris (eds) (1990), *People and Society in Scotland, vol. 2: 1830–1914*, Edinburgh: John Donald.

The following sources are also helpful: D. Fraser (2010), *The Evolution of the British Welfare State*, 4th edn, Basingstoke: Palgrave; P. Thane (1996), *The Foundations of the Welfare State*, 2nd edn, London: Longman. The development of social policy in nineteenth-century Ireland is discussed in chapter 1 of M. Considine and F. Dukelow (2009), *Irish Social Policy: A Critical Introduction*, Dublin: Gill & Macmillan.

Review and Assignment Questions

1   How important were charity and mutual aid in helping working-class people to support themselves during the nineteenth century?

2   Why, and to what extent, did the English and Scottish Poor Laws converge over the course of the nineteenth century?

3   How might we explain the growth of state intervention in *either* public health *or* education in Britain before 1900?

4   How did the development of social policy during the nineteenth century contribute to the origins of the modern welfare state, and what lessons, if any, should contemporary policymakers draw from nineteenth-century developments?

5   What were the major social challenges facing policymakers in England, Scotland and Wales during the nineteenth century?

Visit the book companion site at www.wiley.com/go/alcocksocialpolicy to make use of the resources designed to accompany the textbook. There you will find chapter-specific guides to further resources, including governmental, international, thinktank, pressure groups and relevant journal sources. You will also find a glossary based on *The Blackwell Dictionary of Social Policy*, help sheets, guidance on managing assignments in social policy and career advice.

17

The Liberal Era and the Growth of State Welfare

Noel Whiteside

███ █ █ ███ ███ █ ███ ███ █ ███ ███ █ ███ ███ █ ███ ███ █ ███ ███ █

Overview

- In the late nineteenth century, international economic competition and rising pauperism created fears about social degeneration and imperial decline.
- New social scientific and medical analyses created fresh debates on the causes (and prevention) of poverty.
- A more radical organised labour movement threatened the political hegemony of Britain's two-party system.
- The Liberal governments of 1906–14 introduced extensive, controversial legislation designed to promote the health of the rising generation and to organise urban labour markets.
- While in some respects prescient of the British welfare state of the late 1940s, the impact of this legislation was later undermined by industrial opposition and the mass unemployment of the inter-war years.

███ █ █ ███ ███ █ ███ ███ █ ███ ███ █ ███ ███ █ ███ ███ █ ███ ███ █

Changing Socio-political Contexts

In the late nineteenth century, social welfare issues began to emerge as national problems requiring national solutions. This modified laissez faire liberal sentiments and a Poor Law orthodoxy that understood poverty as a sign of personal moral inadequacy. Why did this happen? And why did the Liberals – the political party closely associated

The Student's Companion to Social Policy, Fifth Edition. Edited by Pete Alcock, Tina Haux, Margaret May and Sharon Wright.

with industrial interests and the free market economy – emerge as the champion of welfare reform? What were these reforms like and what did they set out to achieve? With hindsight, the period 1900–14 represents the zenith of Britain's imperial and industrial power. Extensive areas on global maps were tinged pink, the pound sterling was the main global trading currency and Britain's merchant marine dominated international commerce. With all this prosperity, it seems an odd time for poverty and its effects to attract state attention.

Yet Britain's manufacturing and commercial centres were causing increasing public concern. By 1900, Britain was no longer the sole industrial economy in the world. Domination of global trade had been easy when few countries were industrially developed. However, others were catching up; rivalry from the United States and particularly from imperial Germany threatened British supremacy. While the UK had been a world leader in the first and second industrial revolutions (based on water and steam power, respectively), it trailed others in the third, based on electricity and petrochemicals. German rates of growth outstripped Britain's own, industrialisation in Germany took place behind the safety of tariff barriers (while Britain remained committed to free trade) and, thanks to innovations in the realm of social insurance, poverty in Germany appeared far less problematic than it was in Britain. The promise that a free-market economy would create prosperity for all without government intervention was being drawn into question. In Germany, state policy actively protected and promoted industrialisation.

The example set by German social legislation proved influential. By 1900, Germany was Britain's chief industrial competitor and, of all European countries, the one whose urban and economic profile most closely matched Britain's own. Germany's state-sponsored social insurance protected against the risks of accident, ill health and old age. Introduced in the 1880s, this excited a mixture of admiration and hostility in Britain: admiration for the protection these schemes offered; hostility towards German authoritarianism and the heavy-handed bureaucracy that British critics assumed underpinned these measures. Germany, however, was not the only nation that attracted attention. Other countries offered alternative solutions. The German system of contributory old-age pensions was readily compared with

the New Zealand – and later Australian – schemes, which offered tax-based support to all elderly citizens. In the event, the latter examples were more significant in shaping Britain's Old Age Pensions Act 1908. Then, as now, measures adopted overseas informed discussion about possible British responses to social problems that threatened economic growth and social peace.

The 'Social Question' and the Threat of Economic Decline

Late nineteenth-century social investigations revealed the poverty dominating Britain's inner cities and reawakened fears of mass pauperism. Widespread destitution caused the number of paupers to increase, particularly in overcrowded and insalubrious inner city areas, where they added to the ratepayer's (local tax payer's) burdens. Thanks to the expansion of major industrial centres and the flight of the middle classes to the suburbs, inner city boroughs were unable to raise the local taxes (rates) required to meet their social obligations without pauperising yet more residents. Places like Poplar in East London (a notorious example) required loans from the Treasury to make ends meet – loans that could never be repaid. This mismatch between local needs and local financial resources proved one of the most compelling reasons to promote national solutions to welfare issues – leading eventually to a national welfare state.

The causes of destitution and the financial burden of pauperism forced attention onto an overstocked labour market. Under-employment, poor diet and overcrowded accommodation promoted disease and fostered economic inefficiency. The results were manifest in the numbers of casual or intermittent workers and domestic workers employed in 'sweated' (underpaid) occupations. During the economic slumps of 1884–7, 1888, 1892–5, the situation degenerated further. In the eyes of potential reformers, 'regular' workers thrown out of work had no more right to state support than the most hopeless casual. In hard times, the respectable man (and attention focused on the male breadwinner) would be forced to compete for work with those considered degenerate: the 'social riff-raff'. Insecure employment, poor diet and exposure to the 'rougher' end of the job market would eventually undermine both the willingness and capacity of the regular worker to hold down a proper job. Unemployment thus bred unemployability, added to the casual 'residuum' and damaged those with working skills essential for economic recovery. If treated like a pauper, the 'respectable' unemployed became 'pauperised'; demoralised and incapable of self-support. To prevent this cycle of impoverishment that threatened the working population, some social investigators started to advocate new types of state intervention – most notably for the elderly who could not work (and life expectancy was rising at this time).

This construction of the 'social question' fed fears of economic and imperial decline. Growing international competition fostered falling prices and lower profits; this, in turn, produced more aggressive management strategies designed to raise productivity and to cut labour costs. As a result, established modes of industrial relations – based on mutual understanding between employer and employed – deteriorated. In the 1880s and 1890s, the number of strikes grew as 'new', militant trade unions organised unskilled workers. The successful London Dock Strike of 1889 epitomised the shift from cooperation to confrontation which this climate invoked. For contemporary observers, these developments appeared to threaten Britain's economy and, with this, the security of Empire. First, strikes disrupted production and trade union resistance delayed the introduction of key technologies, damaging entrepreneurship and economic growth. Second, inner cities were breeding social and mental degenerates. Inefficient workers formed a growing burden on the industries they served and the communities in which they lived, thanks to their irregular working habits and perpetual reliance on poor relief. In brief, the free-market economy was not working in the manner its supporters suggested it should. The need for reform and state action was winning support on all sides of the political spectrum.

The Social Question: Diagnostics and Analysis

During this period, forms of social analysis and social investigation were changing with the development of social scientific methods. These were based on rather different premises from those that informed the Poor Law. The focus of concern shifted from individual failings towards environmental and social factors. Social classifications were established as the foundation for poverty analysis, based on the reasons for destitution such as unemployment, old age or infirmity.

Social scientists were not alone in creating a new diagnosis of the 'social question'. Eugenicists claimed inheritance explained much poverty through the reproduction of mental, moral and physical weaknesses. Eugenicists demanded that 'unfit' paupers be sterilised and that a couple's physical and mental capabilities be officially reviewed prior to marriage. Such ideas, later elaborated in Hitler's Germany, carried heavy racist overtones and appealed to imperial sentiment through references to quasi-Darwinian theories concerning 'the survival of the fittest'. Socially indiscriminate breeding, endemic in inner cities, threatened the pre-eminence of the British race, eugenicists argued. The solution lay in reversing middle-class population decline (who, thanks to Marie Stopes, could now control family size) and in reducing reproduction among the degenerate poor. This approach was vigorously opposed by left-wing Fabians, who argued that the causes of poverty should be professionally analysed and state services developed to address them: medical help for the sick, jobs for the unemployed, pensions for the elderly and so on. The poor law should be abolished; its indiscriminate approach was demoralising and served no socially constructive purpose.

The debates stimulated by such conflicting views were revealed in many official enquiries into causes of industrial unrest, of physical degeneration and of Poor Law problems that took place before 1914. Official investigations demonstrated rising concern about the welfare of the British population – embracing industrialists and defenders of Empire as well as philanthropists, Poor Law officials and the labour movement. How the issue was apprehended determined how it would be tackled – and it is to the political dimension of the question that we now turn.

The Social Question: Politics and Reform

Urban degeneration carried political consequences. Radical organisations, such as the Social

Democratic Federation (SDF), recruited extensively among the unemployed. In the 1880s and early 1890s, the SDF organised demonstrations in major British cities that degenerated into riots and looting. Socialist ideas also informed the strikes perpetrated by the 'new' trade union organisations; the Trades Union Congress (TUC) began to create its own reform agenda. In 1900, trade unions and socialist groups combined to form the Labour Representation Committee, later the Labour Party. Such developments threatened the political status quo, challenging both the main political parties.

By 1900, many philanthropists also recognised that poverty would not be solved through the medium of social casework and self-improvement, but required state intervention. Prominent politicians in the main political parties became convinced of the need for action. Following the near disaster of the Boer War (1899–1902), when potential military recruits had to be turned away as physically incapable of bearing arms, concern for physical, economic and general national efficiency reached new heights. Within the Conservative Party, Joseph Chamberlain had established a reform agenda, including the provision of extensive public works for the unemployed, to be funded by tariffs on imported goods. In the General Election of 1906, the Conservatives were heavily defeated as voters rallied in support of free trade and the Liberals. The new Labour Party did particularly well and subsequently sponsored private members' bills to help poor schoolchildren and to promote the right to work. If the 1906 new Liberal government was to retain the support of working-class voters, it had to produce its own programme of reform.

This was not easy; the Liberal Party was the natural base for industrial interests and supported classic liberal principles of minimal government. Conventional Liberals were neither natural allies of left-wing socialists nor would they support reforms that undermined Poor Law principles. State help for poor children, for example, contravened the basic tenet that fathers should be held responsible for the well-being of their families and that failure to provide should be punished by incarceration in the workhouse. From this perspective, provision of free medical care or school meals rewarded parental indolence and vice, and should be opposed. In consequence, the Liberal

programme did not go as far as some of its supporters would have liked. Such compromise, however, papered over divisions of principle that eventually tore the Liberal Party apart. After the First World War, the left turned to the Labour Party and the right to the Conservatives as the Liberals went into political decline.

Before 1914, however, this uneasy political alliance was sustained. In 1908, the Prime Minister, Campbell Bannerman, unexpectedly died and Asquith, the leader of the party's reforming wing, took over the premiership, supported by Lloyd George (a radical land reformer and future wartime prime minister (1916–24)) as Chancellor of the Exchequer. The young Winston Churchill became President of the Board of Trade (and in charge of labour market policy). This reforming alliance was augmented by the rise of civil servants of reforming persuasion in major Whitehall government departments. The agenda revolved around two main issues: the organisation of the labour market and the welfare of the next generation. Both invoked an increased role for the state.

High infant mortality and evidence of the impact of poor diet on physical and mental development presented to the Interdepartmental Committee on Physical Deterioration (1903–4) focused official attention on children. In 1904, the then Conservative government allowed Poor Law authorities to fund meals for poor children, but this pauperised the parents and take-up rates were very low. The first private member's bill sponsored by a backbench Labour MP in 1906 addressed the feeding of schoolchildren. Two years later, the Liberal government added compulsory school medical inspection (but not treatment) and legislation providing for trained health visitors, midwives and infant welfare centres. The object was to protect infant life by offering trained attendance at childbirth and professional instruction to new mothers on infant care. Thanks to internal political divisions, the Liberals made the provision of such services permissive, not obligatory. Local authorities could, if they wished, raise a rate to provide school meals or fund infant welfare; compulsion was only introduced after 1918.

The labour market attracted more concerted attention. The main objective was to concentrate work in the hands of the most efficient workers, to raise industrial efficiency and to promote economic growth. This required the separation of those who could not work regularly (due to age, incapacity or illness) from those who would not (the incorrigible idlers in Poor Law parlance) to offer support to the former and punitive correction to the latter. The agency for sorting the good from the bad was the labour exchange; promoted by the young William Beveridge. The idea of labour exchanges was directly adopted from German cities that Beveridge visited in 1907. The UK project was developed in his vision of a national network, linked by the latest technology (the telephone) to allow labour to be sent where required from any part of the country. Lloyd George piloted the first UK old age pensions through Parliament in 1908. Independent of the Poor Law and available to all over seventy on a means-tested basis, tax-funded supplementation to reduced income allowed women (widows, then, as now, the vast majority of aged poor) to claim in their own right

Finally, the National Insurance Act 1911 offered benefits to working people earning less than a stipulated minimum income per year. Part I of the Act provided health insurance, to be administered by the myriad voluntary friendly and collecting societies offering protection against sickness (see Chapter 16), and industrial insurance companies who had long sold life policies to the poor. Again inspired by German example following Lloyd George's visit to that country in 1908, a tripartite contribution from employer, employee and the state funded a weekly sickness payment and basic medical treatment for workers (but not their families). This aimed to remove another source of inefficient labour, to prevent the sick being forced, by threat of poverty, to continue working – thereby exacerbating their condition and becoming chronic (pauperised) cases. Unemployment insurance, Part II of the 1911 Act, covered workers in construction, shipbuilding, engineering and associated metal trades. It was compulsory, involved similar tripartite contributions and offered unemployment benefit for up to fifteen weeks per year. Long-term unemployment was not recognised; on exhausting benefit rights the claimant ceased to be 'unemployed' and rejoined the pauper class.

With hindsight, we can see how these reforms formed the antecedents of what later, extended and modified, became the welfare state, and their legacy is still discernible today. The trained midwives and health visitors, the protection of child health and nutrition are still public obligations. Although health insurance was replaced by the National Health Service, unemployment insurance cover was extended in 1920 and 1946: its principles are still just discernible in today's Jobseekers Allowance – albeit that this benefit also owes much to Poor Law precedent. Labour exchanges are the ancestors of current Jobcentre Plus offices and means-tested, tax-funded old age pensions are still with us. Above all, we can discern a shift away from local discretion in the provision of help to the poor and towards a national policy grounded on categories derived from social scientific precepts with rights to welfare that are not determined by destitution alone.

Far from being welcomed at the time, however, reform generated hostility. The costs of tax-funded pensions provoked a major budget crisis in 1911, led to a confrontation with the House of Lords and a constitutional change permanently reducing their Lordships' powers. While services for children were popular on the left, its breach of Poor Law principles provoked opposition from both Conservatives and traditional Liberals. Both sides of industry viewed labour market reform with distrust, hating compulsory insurance contributions and seeing labour exchanges as an unwelcome state intervention into private business. Trade unionists feared their use for breaking strikes. Even members of the Liberal Cabinet found the reforms distasteful. The President of the Local Government Board described the results as creating 'a race of paupers in a grovelling community ruled by uniformed prigs'; his opinion was hardly unique.

Aftermath

It remains to evaluate these initiatives: did they succeed in securing social harmony and prosperity? In general, historians have concluded that their impact was marginal – certainly well removed from their original objectives. The principal reason stemmed from the hostility they provoked, an opposition that reformers had been prone to ignore.

The First World War offered the chance for the advocates of central labour market coordination to prove their case. Total war required tight labour market controls, to prevent industrial conflict disrupting war production and to apportion scarce manpower according to war priorities. In the 'scientific' analysis of labour markets, policy solutions would be found and enforced by impartial administrators. The results were disastrous. Unofficial strike action rocketed; an attempted extension of unemployment insurance to all war workers collapsed as those covered refused to comply. Union leaders and management alike found Whitehall inefficient, uninformed and arbitrary. When the war ended in 1918, the trend towards central regulation of the labour market, visible before the war, was abruptly halted and, when peace was restored, was thrown into reverse.

Mass unemployment in old industrial centres in inter-war Britain undermined the logic of pre-war Liberal policy: far from rationalising the labour market, it became desirable to spread work among as many people as possible. Nor could unemployment benefits be confined to fifteen weeks per year. Instead, constant modifications allowed most unemployed men (but not women) to continue on benefit, creating 'the dole' on which long-term cases relied. As unemployment worsened during the slump years of the 1930s, ever stricter means tests were applied to contain public expenditure – stimulating the Hunger Marches and renewing debate about the association of poverty with deformity and disease. The experiences of this decade explain the huge acclaim that greeted the Beveridge Report in 1942, with its promises of total state protection 'from the cradle to the grave' (see Chapter 18).

Meanwhile, constraints on public expenditure took their toll in cuts to schools, school medical and meals services, local infant welfare, public sector salaries and the new housing programmes ('homes fit for heroes' promised by Lloyd George). In spite of wartime inflation, old age pensions were not raised, forcing older people to supplement their income with means-tested assistance. Then, as today, the solution to poverty was presumed to lie in reducing state intervention to allow the free market economy to create new prosperity and new jobs through economic growth. Then, as now, such growth was sporadic and failed to benefit all sectors of society. The birth of Keynesian economics, advocating the redistribution of wealth, underpinned the later creation of a welfare state. As Keynesian solutions are now repudiated, we seem destined to revisit those grim inter-war years.

Guide to Further Sources

Texts by Harris, Fraser and Thane cited at the end of Chapter 16 include sound accounts of the Liberal reforms (1906–14). A more detailed description can be found in J. R. Hay (1975), *Origins of the Liberal Welfare Reforms*, Basingstoke: Macmillan. More specialist texts include J. Harris (1971), *Unemployment: A Study of British Politics*, Oxford: Oxford University Press, and, for real enthusiasts who want to understand local government finance, A. Offer (1981), *Property and Politics 1870–1914*, Cambridge: Cambridge University Press. A detailed comparison of British and German welfare reforms can be found in E. P. Hennock (2007), *The Origins of the Welfare State in England and Germany, 1850–1914*, Cambridge: Cambridge University Press.

Review and Assignment Questions

1 How was 'the social question' in Britain understood in the early twentieth century?
2 What were the key welfare policies developed in the Liberal era?
3 How did new forms of social scientific knowledge inform Liberal welfare policies?
4 Were the Liberal governments' social policies socialist in intent, or were they capitalism's answer to the problems of capitalism?
5 Did the reforms of 1906–14 form the foundations of a welfare state?

Visit the book companion site at www.wiley.com/go/alcocksocialpolicy to make use of the resources designed to accompany the textbook. There you will find chapter-specific guides to further resources, including governmental, international, thinktank, pressure groups and relevant journal sources. You will also find a glossary based on *The Blackwell Dictionary of Social Policy*, help sheets, guidance on managing assignments in social policy and career advice.

18

The Modern Welfare State, 1940–74

Robert M. Page

Overview

- The Second World War proved to be a major factor in the growth of public support for more extensive forms of state welfare provision.
- The first post-war Labour government (1945–50) introduced major welfare reforms in areas such as social security and health. This government is commonly credited with 'creating' the modern welfare state.
- The Conservative Party developed a more 'progressive' approach towards the welfare state, first in opposition and then during thirteen years in government (1951–64).
- The Labour governments of 1964–70 adopted a revisionist social democratic approach to the welfare state. They found it difficult to emulate the achievements of the earlier Attlee governments not least because of adverse economic conditions.
- The Conservative government of Edward Heath (1970–4) attempted to 'modernise' the welfare state along less 'ideological', 'technocratic' lines.

The Second World War: The Catalyst for Change?

The impact of the Second World War is seen as having played a decisive role in the development of the post-war welfare state. Increased social solidarity, more positive public attitudes towards state action, and a desire to banish the spectre of inter-war poverty and unemployment paved the way to the election of a Labour government in 1945 that was committed to the establishment of a fairer society.

The Student's Companion to Social Policy, Fifth Edition. Edited by Pete Alcock, Tina Haux, Margaret May and Sharon Wright.
© 2016 John Wiley & Sons, Ltd. Published 2016 by John Wiley & Sons, Ltd.

The fact that the electorate placed their faith in the Labour Party led by Clement Attlee, rather than the victorious war leader Winston Churchill and the Conservatives, can be linked to Labour's enthusiastic support for social reform during their period as junior partners in the wartime coalition government from 1940 to 1945. The Conservatives did adopt a more positive approach in relation to economic and social policy on the home front following criticism of their lukewarm reaction to William Beveridge's influential *Report on Social Insurance and Allied Services* in 1942, which had pledged to confront the five giant evils in British society: disease, idleness, ignorance, squalor and want.

Under pressure from Labour members of the coalition, the Conservatives established a Ministry of Reconstruction in 1943 and published a series of White Papers proposing reforms in relation to family allowances (1942), unemployment (1944), social insurance (1944), health (1944) and housing (1945). Two major legislative changes were introduced; the Education Act 1944, which provided free, but diverse, forms of secondary education for all children up until the age of fifteen, and the Family Allowances Act 1945, which provided financial support for second and subsequent children (this was enacted by Churchill's Conservative caretaker administration in June 1945). Although commentators such as Addison (1977) have suggested that the coalition government should be credited with creating the modern welfare state, this accolade is usually awarded to the post-war Labour governments of Clement Attlee.

The Labour Governments and the Creation of the Welfare State, 1945–51

The first Labour government (1945–50) pressed ahead with its ambitious plans for a welfare state despite inauspicious economic circumstances. The decision by the United States to end the Lend-Lease credit agreement (which had been in operation since March 1941) in September 1945, as well as coal and power supply shortages during the early part of 1947 and a subsequent currency convertibility crisis later that year proved difficult to contend with. Nevertheless, by the end of their first term in government, Labour had created the welfare state, nationalised key industries,

introduced more extensive forms of economic regulation and persisted with a progressive tax system, which were all deemed to be necessary requirements for the establishment of a more equal and solidaristic society.

The introduction of a comprehensive social security system was one of Labour's most notable welfare initiatives. Under the universal National Insurance Act 1946 contributors were entitled to claim unemployment benefits, sickness benefits, dependants' allowances, maternity payments, retirement pensions and a death grant at time of need. Those ineligible for National Insurance benefits were provided with less generous means-tested allowances under the National Assistance Act 1948. Although Labour's reforms represented a significant step forward in meeting the needs of citizens, it was recognised that provision would need to be extended and improved in subsequent decades.

The National Health Service (which came into effect in 1948) is generally regarded as the finest achievement of the post-war Labour government. Aneurin Bevan's decision to nationalise the voluntary hospitals represented a major departure from previous coalition health policy. Bevan was criticised for granting too many concessions to the medical profession, most notably consultants, in his drive to establish a universal, comprehensive, tax-funded health service based on medical need rather than ability to pay. However, his supporters argued that his willingness to compromise ensured that his overarching goal of free, high-quality healthcare for all was achieved.

Labour's manifesto commitment to provide a 'good standard of accommodation' for all families proved difficult to deliver. Bevan, who had ministerial responsibility for housing as well as health, was faced with an unenviable task of meeting a high level of demand for homes at a time when half a million homes had been destroyed during the war, and when there was a peacetime shortage of both construction workers and building materials. By 1951, some one million new homes had been completed, which fell far short of the four million that had originally been envisaged. Bevan's critics argued that his ideological preference to grant local authorities, rather than the private sector, the lead role in providing high standard homes at affordable rents was a major reason for the subsequent shortfall in supply.

In the sphere of education, Labour's energies were directed to ensuring that the aims of the 1944 Education Act, based on a 'separate but equal' tripartite system of free, secondary schooling (grammar, technical and modern), in which children were allocated to schools on the basis of their skills and aptitudes rather than their social background, were successfully implemented. This 'pragmatic' approach proved disappointing to more radical thinkers within the party who believed that the government should have introduced comprehensive schooling, not least because of justifiable fears that working-class children would find it difficult to secure places at the elite grammar schools. Labour's reluctance to reform the 'public' (fee paying) schools, which continued to ensure that those from privileged backgrounds maintained a stranglehold on elite positions in British society, was also a source of disappointment for those on the egalitarian left of the party.

By the end of its first term in 1950, the Attlee government's democratic socialist 'crusade' had run out of steam. Labour appeared to have few ideas as to how to build on their first term initiatives. Consolidation, rather than further reform, seemed to be the order of the day. Although the party managed to secure a further term in office (their increased share of the vote only translated into a slender five-seat majority), a further election was called a year later at a time of internal party strife, balance of payments problems, growing industrial unrest and an oil supply crisis. Although Labour managed to secure a marginally higher proportion of the popular vote than their Conservative opponents (48.8 per cent against 48.1 per cent), it was the latter that were returned to office with a seventeen-seat majority.

Modern 'One Nation' Conservatism and the Welfare State, 1951–64

The Conservatives responded to their unexpected and sizeable defeat in the 1945 general election by making strenuous efforts to persuade the British public, not least through influential publications such as *The Industrial Strategy* (1947) and *The Right Road for Britain* (1949), that they were no longer a reactionary party who were unwilling to tackle poverty and unemployment, but rather a modern progressive party that supported an enhanced economic role for government and the welfare state.

A subsequent electoral setback in 1950 led to the formation of the One Nation Group (ONG), which included a number of newly elected MPs such as Iain Macleod, Enoch Powell and Edward Heath, who were to become influential figures in the party over the next twenty-five years. This broad-based grouping helped to map out a distinctive Conservative approach to the welfare state in which traditional party beliefs such as sound finance, efficiency, lower taxation, thrift, self-reliance, voluntarism and charitable activity were combined with increased support for economic interventionism and the welfare state.

In a highly influential pamphlet titled *One Nation. A Tory Approach to Social Problems*, the ONG sought to mark out a distinctive Conservative approach to the welfare state. Increased welfare expenditure should not, they argued, be used for egalitarian purposes or reach levels that threatened economic stability. Instead, state provision should be targeted at those in the greatest need (selectivity) rather than provided in profligate ways for all citizens (universalism).

Following their electoral success in 1951, the Conservatives' commitment to the welfare state was soon put to the test in the light of mounting economic pressures. The new Chancellor, R. A. Butler, declined to make any major cut backs in social spending so that he was in a strong position to refute Labour's claim that the Conservatives would dismantle the welfare state. His cost containment measures were restricted to paring back the school building programme and some additional NHS charges.

The government's commitment to build 300,000 new homes a year, which was achieved by 1953, was a key element in the party's social compact with the British public. By the time of the 1955 general election (in which the Conservatives increased their overall majority to 100 seats), the party was able to present itself as the one best able to deliver economic prosperity and opportunity as well as security for all citizens in the shape of an efficiently administered welfare state.

While stringent efforts were made by Treasury ministers to keep public spending under control, both the Eden (1955–7) and Macmillan (1957–63) governments were determined to balance the party's traditional quest for economic stability with their post-war commitment to the welfare state and full employment. This proved a far-from-straightforward task. In 1958, the then Chancellor Peter Thorneycroft and two junior colleagues resigned from the government after Macmillan and fellow cabinet members refused to sanction a range of welfare cuts deemed necessary to curb inflation and restore confidence in sterling.

During their lengthy period in office from 1951 to 1964, which their Labour opponents characterised as 'thirteen wasted years', the Conservatives bolstered their reputation as a party that could exercise effective stewardship over the welfare state whilst avoiding the egalitarian 'excesses' associated with previous or prospective Labour administrations. However, in the aftermath of a difficult period in government, which included a major ministerial reshuffle following a sensational by-election defeat at the hands of the Liberals in 1962, continued economic turbulence and the French veto on Britain's membership of the European Economic Community, and the infamous Profumo sex and spy scandal of 1963, it was Labour that electors choose to guide the nation's fortunes from 1964 to 1970.

Revisionist Labour and the Welfare State, 1964–70

By the time Labour returned to office in 1964, an internal 'truce' had been established between the democratic socialist and revisionist social democratic wings of the party. Under the leadership of Harold Wilson, the party now declared itself to be supportive of a planned, growth-oriented economic strategy based on modern scientific methods that would deliver the resources for further expansion of the welfare state. The incoming government recognised that a drastic overhaul of the social services was now necessary in order to deliver better education, improved housing at affordable prices, high-quality healthcare and enhanced living standards for pensioners and widows.

Labour's attempt to combine economic efficiency and social justice proved to be difficult to achieve in practice. The government was beset by a succession of economic crises, not least a humiliating currency devaluation in 1967, which made it difficult to achieve the growth levels deemed necessary to fund their ambitious plans for the welfare state. This resulted in a number of policy 'U'-turns, including delays in benefit increases, the postponement of the pledge to increase the school leaving age to sixteen and the re-imposition of prescription charges.

Although Labour presided over a number of progressive welfare reforms during their period in government, including less stigmatising social security procedures, the expansion of comprehensive schooling, higher NHS spending, increased housing supply and enhanced rights for tenants, these measures did little to satisfy the egalitarian aspirations of their core supporters. By the time of the 1970 general election, the government was even struggling to refute claims by the recently established Child Poverty Action Group (1965) that the position of the poorest groups in society had deteriorated, rather than improved, during Labour's period in office.

It should be noted, however, that the 1964–70 Labour government did oversee some transformative legislative changes which enhanced personal liberty. During Roy Jenkins' tenure as Home Secretary, capital punishment was abolished and major liberalising reforms were enacted in areas such as divorce, abortion, homosexuality, and stage and literary censorship. Although a number of these measures originated as Private Members' Bills, Jenkins played a key role in ensuring the passage of what proved to be contentious legislation.

The Conservatives and the Welfare State, 1970–4

Modernisation was also a key theme of the Conservative Party when, contrary to the predictions of many seasoned commentators, it returned to power under Edward Heath in 1970. Unlike Labour, the Conservative version of modernisation was not equated with further expansion of the welfare state. Rather, the aim was to improve efficiency, target support on those most in need, increase opportunity, enhance choice and improve service quality.

Although Heath favoured a pragmatic, evidence-based approach to economic and social policy, some of his Cabinet colleagues were persuaded that it was now time to reform the welfare state along neo-Liberal lines. A number of policy initiatives, such as the introduction of Family Income Supplement (FIS) in 1972, which provided additional means-tested income for low-earning families with dependant children, had a decidedly neo-Liberal provenance (see Chapters 9 and 47). Other measures of this kind included the introduction of tighter control over benefit fraud, higher 'market-level' council house rents and a less prominent role for the state in relation to retirement pensions.

In other spheres of social policy, however, it could be said that the 'One Nation' strand of Conservative thinking remained influential. The introduction of a new non-contributory 'disability' benefit (Attendance Allowance) in 1971, free nursery places for 50 per cent of three year olds and 90 per cent of four year olds, and the raising of the school leaving age to sixteen (1972) were all in keeping with this strand of Conservative thought.

Like the previous Labour government, the Conservative administration was beset by numerous economic problems. Its initial resolve to withhold state support from failing industries was quickly tested and reversed in the face of growing unemployment. Its trade union reforms proved to be unworkable and its decision to re-introduce statutory, rather than voluntary, price and income controls signalled a return to the forms of interventionism that it had originally sought to abandon. Industrial disputes with the National Union of Mineworkers proved to be particularly testing for the Health government. Although an earlier strike over pay was resolved in 1972, the failure to reach agreement following a subsequent dispute in 1973 led the government to introduce a 'state of emergency' for the fifth time in three years and then call a general election in February 1974 to resolve the question of 'who runs Britain?' After a close electoral contest it was Labour who eventually formed the next government, remaining in power until 1979 (see Chapter 19).

A Post-war Welfare Consensus or Settlement?

The Conservative Party's rapprochement with Labour's pioneering post-war welfare reforms during their period in office from 1951 to 1964 has led some commentators to suggest that a welfare consensus was forged between these two parties which was to last until the mid-1970s. Although both parties continued to highlight their distinctive social agendas, particularly during general election campaigns, the absence of significant policy divergence when either was in office was seen as indicative that an accord had been reached that the welfare state was now an integral and legitimate part of modern British society.

Anti-consensus critics argue, however, that the decision by a newly elected government to continue with the welfare agenda of a previous administration may not be a result of ideological conversion, but rather the upshot of unanticipated extraneous factors such as a downturn in the economy, insurmountable administrative problems or public hostility to a policy initiative. From this perspective, the compromises that parties make in office should not be interpreted as signalling, in the case of Labour, a retreat from its commitment to an expansive, egalitarian, universalistic welfare state or, in the case of the Conservatives, a willingness to jettison their belief in selectivity and the avoidance of egalitarian-inspired welfare initiatives. This has led to the notion of a 'settlement' being seen as a more apt descriptor of post-war developments in British social policy.

While there has been continuing debate about whether a welfare consensus or settlement could be said to have occurred in the post-1945 era, there is more general agreement that what Lowe (2005) has termed the 'classic welfare state' came under more concerted challenge from neo-Liberals in the turbulent economic and social circumstances of the 1970s.

Guide to Further Sources

There are a number of very useful accounts of the wartime coalition, including P. Addison (1977), *The Road to 1945*, London: Jonathan Cape; K. Jefferys (ed.) (1994), *War and Reform: British Politics during the Second World War*, Manchester: Manchester University Press; S. Brooke (1992), *Labour's War: The Labour Party and the Second World War*, Oxford: Clarendon Press.

M. Francis (1997), *Ideas and Policies Under Labour 1945–1951*, Manchester: Manchester University Press, is an extremely readable and accessible account of the post-war Attlee governments and provides extended commentary on social policy issues. Other wide-ranging accounts of the Attlee years are to be found in K. Morgan (1984), *Labour in Power, 1945–1951*, Oxford: Clarendon; P. Hennessy (1993), *Never Again: Britain 1945–1951*, Vintage: London; and S. Brooke (ed.) (1995), *Reform and Reconstruction: Britain after the War, 1945–51*, Manchester: Manchester University Press.

Texts by N. Timmins (2001), *The Five Giants: A Biography of the Welfare State*, 2nd edn, London: HarperCollins; R. Lowe (2005), *The Welfare State in Britain Since 1945*, 3rd edn, Basingstoke: Palgrave Macmillan; H. Glennerster (2007), *British Social Policy 1945 to the Present*, 3rd edn, Oxford: Blackwell; and R. Page (2007), *Revisiting the Welfare State*, Maidenhead: Open University Press, provide useful overviews of social policy issues and developments during the post-war era. P. Bridgen and R. Lowe (1998), *Welfare Policy Under the Conservatives 1951–1964*, London: Public Records Office, provides a forensic examination of Conservative social policy from the early 1950s to the end of the Douglas-Home government in 1964. H. Bochel (ed.) (2011), *The Conservative Party and Social Policy*, Bristol: Policy Press; and R. Page (2015), *Clear Blue Water? The Conservative Party and the Welfare State from 1940*, Bristol: Policy Policy, provide broad overviews of Conservative approaches to the welfare state from the start of the Second World War to the present day.

Accessible information about the post-war welfare state can be found on the following websites: www.bbc.co.uk/history; http://www.nationalarchives.gov.uk.

Review and Assignment Questions

1 Why do you think so much attention has been given to the impact of war on the development of the welfare state?
2 What were the most significant welfare achievements of the Labour governments from 1945 to 1950 and from 1964 to 1970?
3 What factors might have led the Conservatives to become more supportive of the welfare state between the late 1940s and the mid-1960s?
4 Were there clear signs that the Conservative government of 1970–4 had become less supportive of the post-war welfare state?
5 To what extent was there a welfare consensus or settlement between Labour and the Conservatives between 1945 and 1974?

Visit the book companion site at www.wiley.com/go/alcocksocialpolicy to make use of the resources designed to accompany the textbook. There you will find chapter-specific guides to further resources, including governmental, international, thinktank, pressure groups and relevant journal sources. You will also find a glossary based on *The Blackwell Dictionary of Social Policy*, help sheets, guidance on managing assignments in social policy and career advice.

19

Crisis, Retrenchment and the Impact of Neo-Liberalism, 1976–97

Howard Glennerster

Overview

- Neither 'economic crises' nor resulting 'retrenchments' in social spending are new either in the UK or in other countries. They can change the ideological climate within which policy is formed and can have a lasting impact.
- The neo-Liberal ideas that took root during the oil crisis of the mid-1970s have had a lasting influence pressed home by powerful private interests. They reasserted the efficacy of markets and the need to reduce the scale of the state. They persuaded governments to change their approach to social policy.
- The outcome, in the years under review here, was not to drastically reduce the *size* of the UK welfare state. Social policy spending continued to grow, albeit it at a slower pace. Neo-Liberal theorists failed to appreciate that many of the problems which they argued faced state welfare institutions faced their private alternatives to an even greater extent. Rolling back the state was not that simple.
- However, these ideas did prompt a major *restructuring* of welfare institutions worldwide, not least in the UK between 1979 and 1997.
    - Governments were convinced that it was necessary to limit working age benefits both in scale and duration.
    - Competition was introduced between state-run providers and new private entrants to welfare markets in the hope of improving welfare state efficiency.
    - Public service agencies were given output or achievement targets. Failing to reach them was publicised and punished.
- Neo-Liberal ideas that took root at this time remain a powerful influence on current policy.

The Student's Companion to Social Policy, Fifth Edition. Edited by Pete Alcock, Tina Haux, Margaret May and Sharon Wright.
© 2016 John Wiley & Sons, Ltd. Published 2016 by John Wiley & Sons, Ltd.

Neo-Liberal Theory and Economic Crisis

The immediate reason for the economic crisis in the mid-1970s lay in the decision of the oil producing countries to substantially raise the price of oil. But this came on top of a long-run acceleration in inflation in the UK. Other countries responded by restricting spending and imports. That led to a worldwide recession, not as big as 2007–8, but the first major crisis since the Second World War. The UK Labour government resisted such a response for a period, but one country cannot hold out against a worldwide trend. The UK faced a major balance of payments debt and the outflow of capital. Inflation rose to over 20 per cent a year. The government had to call on the International Monetary Fund for help. That required public spending cuts and wage restraint. But more significant in the long run was that this experience gave credence to the claims being made by many economists that British economic failure since the Second World War lay in Keynesian economics – using state funding to counter recessions, the excessive power of trade unions, the size of the welfare state and its erosion of the work ethic.

Mrs Thatcher, elected to lead the Conservatives in 1975, accepted that the Conservative Party had been guilty of following such post-war policies and vowed to reverse them.

The Labour government after 1976 went some way to accepting this diagnosis too. The new Labour Prime Minister, James Callaghan, gave a speech to the annual Labour Party Conference in 1976 arguing that full employment could not be restored by regularly boosting public expenditure. Public spending was to be cut. Trade unions would have to accept limits to wage increases. This provoked public sector strikes and the defeat of the government in 1979. That was to usher in a Conservative period of office that lasted until 1997.

The crisis was fertile ground for those who were challenging the 'post-war settlement', that is, government support for full employment, a universal safety net, and free and growing public services (see Chapter 18). American neo-Liberal writers, beginning with Milton Friedman (1962) and younger followers challenged the core belief that social welfare institutions had emerged in

response to revealed human need – child poverty, for example. Not so, claimed these authors:

- Those who press for extensions in social provision are merely seeking to advance their own monetary gain and power by increasing the size of their state agencies' budgets. Public employees and professionals are importantly driven by their own interests not that of their clients.
- Once established, albeit for good reasons, public sector institutions tend to become monopolies. They do not face competition from other schools or healthcare providers, for example. In consequence their employees can draw 'monopoly rents' by being lazier, more inefficient or incompetent than they would be if they faced competition. Public organisations are run in the interests of their employees not their users, Friedman claimed.
- Though cash benefits to those in need have a place in society, the rules that governed them had become too lax. Over the long term 'good behaviour'– the desire to work and marry – had been undermined. It was now possible to live without work or a partner and depend on the state. These changes in public behaviour had only taken root slowly, but after forty years of generous welfare states 'bad behaviour' was becoming the norm. Productivity gains are achieved in the marketplace by entrepreneurial companies. The financial gains are partly shared with their employees in higher wages. This drives up real wages across the economy. The need for public sector operators to sustain the quality of their labour force, aided by trade union pressure, means that public sector wages rise in line with those in the private sector over the long term. Public social services are incapable of achieving productivity gains, or not as fast. So the relative price of these services tends to rise. The faster productivity in the private sector grows, the faster the relative price of public sector services will grow. So taxes tend to rise and the tax-paying public will eventually revolt.
- Populations were living longer and birth rates declining so the tax burden falling on the working population was growing for this reason too. The tax claims on working families were leading to wage claims that attempted to pass on the tax burden to the employer and,

hence, eventually, onto the consumer. This was producing a vicious inflationary cycle and destroying 'productive' jobs. Taken together, this set of arguments amounted to a formidable critique of post-war social and economic policy. They were largely accepted by the incoming Conservative government of 1979. Any reader will find strong echoes in current Conservative reasoning.

Neo-Liberal Programme

Public spending cuts

In its first public spending White Paper in 1979, the new government declared that excessive public expenditure and public ownership were the main reasons for the UK's poor economic performance. Public spending was to be reduced as a share of total economic activity. This led to a review of all aspects of social spending.

One of the early measures of the new Conservative government was to stop increasing benefits annually in line with the earnings of the average worker (1982). Instead, benefits were to rise in line with prices. This meant they fell further and further behind wages. The theory was that this would force people to return to work faster, reduce supposed 'scrounging' and save money. In the long run it did do the latter on a large scale, but in the short run as unemployment was allowed to rise to 'cure' inflation the benefits bill rose. Much later the government began to take some tentative measures to introduce tougher sanctions on those who were not 'actively seeking work'. This was all to be taken further by later UK administrations: Labour (1997–2010, see Chapter 20), Conservative–Liberal Coalition (2010–15) and Conservative (see Chapter 21).

The government instituted a major review of social security and produced a proposal to abolish the New Labour initiated State Earnings Related Pension Scheme (SERPS) was proposed. That ran into considerable opposition and was retained, but was made less generous and individuals were encouraged to enter private pension schemes with tax advantages.

Privatisation

The then extensive nationalised industries dating from the immediate post-war period were privatised step by step: electricity, gas, coal, railways, buses and water. Tenants of council houses were given the right to buy their own dwellings at low prices depending on the length of time they had been living in them (1980).

Prime Minister Mrs Thatcher also toyed with the idea of privatising schools and hospitals along with many local authority services. In the end, she confined her major acts of social service privatisation to social care. Local authorities were encouraged to use privately run homes for older people, not employ staff in their own residential care services. In 1980, 65 per cent of all places in residential care were provided by local authorities. By 1997, the share had fallen to 20 per cent and has fallen further since. The same policy was adopted for services caring for people in their own homes.

Quasi-markets

Mrs Thatcher also wanted to develop private health insurance, subsidising it for older people, and funding healthcare by a mix of social and private insurance. She soon realised that this was a political step too far at that time and opted instead for a 'quasi-market' in health services. Hospitals were to compete for custom from local health authorities and general practitioners, who would receive their funds from the central exchequer. This major reform was launched in a White Paper published in 1989, and was driven through under her successor John Major and her health minister Kenneth Clarke. Hospitals, it was argued, instead of acting like sluggish monopolists, knowing they had a captive set of customers, would have to compete to gain contracts. Scotland, which always had some degree of independent action and legislative power in social policy, largely resisted these trends. After devolution they were reversed. Mrs Thatcher aimed to introduce state-funded 'school vouchers' for parents that could be cashed in at any school, state or private, as Milton Friedman had advocated. Here, again, she realised that this was too radical for that period and opted instead for increasing parents' power to choose between state schools. They would compete for pupils and once a pupil was accepted a sum of money would automatically follow paid by the local authority. Parents would be able to judge how well the school was doing by requiring all pupils in state schools to take tests based on a National Curriculum at 7, 11 and 14. Along with GCSE and A-levels, these results would be published nationally. These measures were introduced in the Education Reform Act 1988. A small scheme that helped parents who wanted to take up places in private schools was also introduced – the Assisted Places Scheme. It was ended after 1997.

These moves were never followed through in Scotland and were reversed after devolution (see Chapter 51). But the essence of the other measures has remained and indeed been extended in England (see Chapter 51).

Funding higher education

Loans were introduced to cover student maintenance costs (1990) – a partial implementation of an idea Milton Friedman had again advocated. Universities themselves, however, at first faced reduced funding for student places but, then, as more qualified school leavers had to be denied places, universities were told they could expand if they were willing to be paid much less for each additional student they took. They responded with what some saw as ill-judged enthusiasm. The numbers of students rose sharply and the resources available to teach each of them fell by about half in real terms between 1979 and 1996. This was interpreted by some as clear proof that universities, like any public bureaucracy, were more concerned about growing their overall budgets than the product they were producing!

What was Wrong with the Neo-Liberal Diagnosis?

Part of the attraction of the neo-Liberal diagnosis was that it contained elements of truth. Each of the criticisms advanced at the beginning of this chapter, which drew attention to worrying features of monopoly state provision, carried some weight. What they failed to do was subject the alternative market solutions to equally critical analysis.

A key persistent problem with the use of market forces in social policy is that people do not necessarily act rationally when faced with risks that may occur many years later. This is true of pensions and long-term care in old age. We call

this and other weaknesses the theory 'market failures' (see Chapters 35 and 40).

Moreover, what the neo-Liberal literature failed to mention was that the difficulties these critics saw facing state service funding applied even more strongly to human services in the private sector. Private services typically offer higher staffing standards than public tax-funded ones. That is their selling point. The relative price of those services has therefore risen faster than in the public sector since the 1980s.

Another difficulty was that rising life expectancy affected the funding of traditionally organised occupational private pension schemes too. They underestimated the rise in longevity even more gravely than the state had. So-called 'defined benefit schemes' gave employees the promise of a pension that was a proportion of their final or near final salary – 'half pay on retirement'. Employers found they could do this only if they put large additional supplements into their pension fund. Not surprisingly, most were reluctant to go on doing this. Most private employers began to close access to such schemes. They were replaced, if at all, by promises to contribute a given fixed sum to an employee's pension scheme – a 'defined contribution scheme'. If you lived longer than was expected when that contribution was made – well, too bad.

Faced with a collapse in public confidence in a failing private pensions market the state had to step in and underpin the declining role of private pension provision (see Chapter 60). This has led to an increase in state pension spending. Private healthcare alternatives to the NHS also failed to materialise and the state had to raise NHS spending once more after 1989.

There was some competition between state providers and some between state and private ones. This happened especially with the care of the elderly. Critics at the time argued that:

- There was actually little opportunity for new entrants or other state providers to enter local health or education markets.
- If they did enter, they would merely cream off the easy or cheap cases or the clever or easier to teach children.
- Competition would be about the wrong things – cutting standards or qualifications of staff to appear cheaper – services for older people being a particular case.

■ It would infuse public services with a competitive mentality and destroy the sense of social solidarity, altruistic and professional behaviour that should characterise welfare institutions. It could remove or reduce support for local institutions in which everyone felt they had a stake.

Emerging Issues

As a set of coherent arguments, however, neo-Liberalism was, and still is, a force to be reckoned with. It was the dominant framework underpinning much of the UK Conservative–Liberal Coalition government approach to social policy after 2010 (see Chapter 21). The 'reforms' to the NHS, schools policy, higher education and long–term care in *England* all bear the hallmarks of this strand of thought.

The major cuts in social spending carried through up to and beyond 2015 may have been triggered by the banking crisis, but in reducing the size of the state they conform to the main objective of this set of ideas. They try to portray 'welfare' as a set of handouts to workshy individuals not as an insurance policy against 'bad times' on which we all draw at some point in our lives (Hills, 2014).

A coherent and widely agreed set of alternatives to neo-Liberalism has not yet emerged. To do so would mean convincingly answering some or all of the following questions:

■ What are the best institutional models for delivering social welfare services?
  ■ a mix of public, private and not-for-profit agencies;
  ■ locally devolved and financed organisations run by local users;
  ■ organisations run on a not-for-profit basis by their professional staff competing for custom;
  ■ a market of private for-profit providers from whom state-supported users buy their services;
  ■ staying with the 'classic' welfare state model of the 1940s.
■ How do we best finance the growing demands for high-quality services for an ageing population?

■ simply raise more revenue from existing taxation;
■ introduce new forms of taxation linked to the social purposes for which the revenue is intended;
■ encourage people to insure themselves for the risks life brings;
■ are the answers different for different services?
■ Should cash benefits for those of working age be strictly curtailed and made dependent on accepting any work after a short period? How fair or realistic is this?
■ Should we make it clear to people that in future they are essentially on their own – the social safety net will be steadily withdrawn? If they do not like that option, they must pay significantly more in taxation of one kind or another.

Politicians do not seem prepared to offer these stark choices.

In the coming five years a range of issues are likely to emerge at the centre of political debate which strikingly parallel those in the period we have been discussing:

■ Are the scale of the cuts being carried through in the UK and other European countries fully justified by the 'crisis' or are they merely an excuse to carry through a long-held neo-Liberal agenda that did not get implemented in the 1980s?
■ What are the limits, if any, to the 'privatisation' of public services? Who will gain and who lose from such a policy?
■ Will electorates lose faith in the implied generational contract that welfare states embody?
■ How should those who care about that social contract respond?

Guide to Further Sources

Much of the theoretical literature is difficult for the non-economics student to follow, though the basic ideas are very simple. M. Friedman (1962), *Capitalism and Freedom*, Chicago: Chicago University Press, is, however, beautifully lucid. For a social policy endorsement of the case for choice and competition, see J. Le Grand

(2003), *Motivation, Agency and Public Policy: Of Knights and Knaves, Pawns and Queens*, Oxford: Oxford University Press.

The argument that welfare benefits undermine 'good behaviour' was influentially expressed in the work of the American, Lawrence Mead (1986), *Beyond Entitlement: The Social Obligation of Citizenship*, New York: Free Press.

I have described the interaction between these ideas and the social policy of this period in H. Glennerster (2007), *British Social Policy 1945 to the Present*, Oxford: Blackwell, chs 8 and 9.

For an account of the way the neo-Liberal prescription has been followed in different countries, see N. Ellison (2006), *The Transformation of Welfare States?*, London: Routledge; see especially the summary ch. 8.

For the long-term survival of ideas from this period, see C. Crouch (2011), *The Strange Non Death of Neo-Liberalism*, Cambridge: Polity. For a challenge to the notion that 'welfare' is mainly designed for a separate class of poor people, see J. Hills (2015), *Good Times Bad Times: The Welfare Myth of Them and Us*, Bristol: Policy Press.

Review and Assignment Questions

1 Why did neo-Liberal ideas flourish in the period 1979–97?
2 Outline the main impact of neo-Liberal ideas on broad direction of social policy in this period.
3 Take one area of social policy and consider in detail how far it was informed by key neo-Liberal ideas in the period 1979–97.
4 What elements of neo-Liberal thought have most to offer social policy, and why?
5 How far have neo-Liberal ideas from this period shaped later Conservative Party social policy?

Visit the book companion site at www.wiley.com/go/alcocksocialpolicy to make use of the resources designed to accompany the textbook. There you will find chapter-specific guides to further resources, including governmental, international, thinktank, pressure groups and relevant journal sources. You will also find a glossary based on *The Blackwell Dictionary of Social Policy*, help sheets, guidance on managing assignments in social policy and career advice.

20

Modernisation and the Third Way

Martin Powell

▪▫▪▫▪▪▫▪▪▫▪

Overview

■ It is difficult to define the 'Third Way', but it is best represented by the US Clinton Democratic (1992–2000) and UK Blair/Brown New Labour (1997–2010) administrations.

■ The Third Way can be examined in terms of discourse, values, policy goals and policy mechanisms.

■ The Third Way in practice shows a wide variety of new policy goals and mechanisms, which increasingly seem to draw upon neo-Liberalism.

■ In many areas, the rhetoric of the New Labour government was not matched by delivery, and so 'third order' or 'paradigmatic' change was limited.

■ The New Labour legacy is probably less than those of the Attlee Labour (1945) and Thatcher Conservative (1979) governments.

▪▫▪▫▪▪▫▪▪▫▪

Introduction

The 'Third Way' is now history, like previous 'third' or 'middle' ways associated with such diverse individuals as David Lloyd George and Harold Macmillan, and movements as different as Swedish social democracy and Italian Fascism. The 'New Labour' government that ruled the UK from 1997 to 2010 gave way to a Conservative–Liberal Democrat Coalition (2010–2015) with its own 'big idea' of the 'Big Society'.

The Third Way was generally associated with the writings of Anthony Giddens and the policies of the Democrat administrations of Bill Clinton in the USA (1992–2000) and of the New Labour government of Tony Blair in the UK. Giddens

The Student's Companion to Social Policy, Fifth Edition. Edited by Pete Alcock, Tina Haux, Margaret May and Sharon Wright.
© 2016 John Wiley & Sons, Ltd. Published 2016 by John Wiley & Sons, Ltd.

claimed that it was new and distinctive from both traditional social democracy (see Chapter 11) and from neo-Liberalism (see Chapter 9), but stressed that it is a renewed or modernised social democracy: a left-of-centre project. For a few years around the millennium 'Third Way' left or left-of-centre governments were in power in many countries in Europe. However, the left lost power in many countries such as Germany and Sweden, and the UK Blair government was a rare exception of a left party that remained in power for a long period. Blair was the longest serving Labour prime minister in British history (before being replaced by Gordon Brown in June 2007), and the New Labour government secured a historic third term, winning general elections in 1997, 2001 and 2005. During this period in office, New Labour attempted to 'modernise the welfare state' (but, as we shall see, many critics argued that the Third Way increasingly blurred with neo-Liberalism (see Chapters 9, 19 and 21).

This chapter provides a brief introduction into these large and complex debates. The first part examines the dimensions of the Third Way, arguing that it is useful to unpack the concept with a focus on discourse, values, policy goals and policy mechanisms. The second part discusses the broad features of the Third Way in practice, concentrating on the social policies of New Labour in England and UK social policy matters reserved to Westminster, such as welfare-to-work, social security and employment policy (as Chapters 22–25 show, there are some differences between the administrations in London, Cardiff and Edinburgh). The final part aims to sum up the New Labour legacy.

The Essence of the Third Way

Much has been written about the Third Way, but its essence remains unclear, with many critics dismissing it as vague and amorphous. The problem in examining the Third Way is that the term was used in very different senses. A number of commentators suggested broad characteristics or themes of the Third Way or new social democracy. However, this conflated different elements such as means and ends. As a simplifying learning device, it is useful to distil these out into separate discussions of

discourse, values, policy goals and policy means or mechanisms.

The Third Way generated a new discourse or a new political language. Clinton and Blair shared a number of key slogans or mantras, such as being 'tough on crime; tough on the causes of crime'; 'a hand up, not a hand out'; 'hard working families that play by the rules', and 'work is the best route out of poverty'. In addition to new phrases, there was a redefined language where old words had new meaning. For example, the Third Way vocabulary or 'NewLabourSpeak' includes terms such as 'full employment' and 'equality', but they have very different meanings to their traditional usage.

The new discourse did not simply consist of new terms, but also emphasised the relationship between them. The Third Way was a political discourse built out of elements from other political discourses to form, in Blair's term, political 'cross-dressing'. The language of the Third Way was a rhetoric of reconciliation, such as 'economic dynamism as well as social justice', 'enterprise as well as fairness'. They were not deemed antagonistic: while neo-Liberals pursued the former and traditional social democrats the latter, the Third Way delivered both. The more radical claim was of 'going beyond' or transcending such themes: it was not simply about managing the tension between the promotion of enterprise and the attack on poverty, but claiming that they were no longer in conflict. However, it does seem difficult to achieve a reconciliation of some terms such as inclusion and responsibility. New Labour appeared to dangle the carrot of inclusion in front of all, but also wielded a stick with which to beat the 'irresponsible'.

Some commentators have suggested a number of core values for the Third Way. These included 'community, opportunity, responsibility and accountability' (CORA) and 'responsibility, inclusion, opportunity' (RIO). However, the values of the Third Way remained problematic. This is mainly for two reasons. First, adequate understanding of values required more than one-word treatments; terms such as 'equality' as essentially contestable concepts, meaning different things to different people. It follows that values must be more clearly defined and linked with goals (see below).

Second, and linked, it is not clear whether the Third Way was concerned with 'old' values, new or redefined meanings of old values, or new values. The best known accounts argue the first position. For example, Blair claimed that the Third Way is concerned with the traditional values of social democracy. However, critics disputed that Blair's values – equal worth, opportunity for all, responsibility and community – adequately summed up traditional socialism in Britain. Moreover, some terms were redefined. For example, the old concern with equality of outcome and redistribution was diluted. A few 'new' values also appear to have been smuggled in. Positive mentions of terms such as entrepreneurship were rarely part of the vocabulary of traditional social democracy (see Chapters 9 and 11).

Blair claimed that policies flow from values. In this sense, goals or objectives may be seen as a more specific operationalisation of values. For example, 'equality' was often referred to as a value, but this may result in very different policy objectives, such as equality of opportunity or equality of outcomes. It follows that advocates of 'equality' might desire very different goals, such as a reduction of inequalities of income, wealth, health status and educational qualifications or merely that there must be an equal opportunity to enter a race with a large gap between rich prizes for the winners and nothing for the losers.

It was claimed that traditional values and goals must be achieved by new means. In some ways this had parallels with Croslandite revisionism, associated with the Labour politician and theorist Tony Crosland (Chapters 11 and 18), who separated the means and ends of socialism, suggesting that the Labour Party means of nationalisation was not the best way of achieving the end of equality. Similarly, the Third Way claimed that new times called for new policies. The world had changed and so the welfare state also had to change. However, new solutions were not based on outdated, dogmatic ideology. There was a new emphasis on evidence-based policymaking, with a key phrase of this new pragmatism being 'what works is what counts'.

Table 20.1 presents a necessarily rather stylised account of the Third Way that has been distilled from a variety of sources. It does run the risk of some rewriting of history, caricaturing the 'Old Left', the 'New Right' and the Third Way that has been a feature of both advocates and critics (see also Chapters 9–12).

The Third Way in Practice

This section develops some of the themes of policy goals and means from Table 20.1. New Labour emerged during the long period of opposition to the Conservative governments of 1979–97 (see Chapter 19). The Labour leader, John Smith, set up the Commission on Social Justice which flagged up many elements of the Third Way in its report of 1994. It rejected the approaches to social and economic policy of the 'Levellers' – the Old Left – and the 'Deregulators' – the New Right, and advocated the 'middle way' of 'Investor's

Table 20.1   Dimensions of the Third Way compared with Old Left and New Right.

Dimension	Old Left	Third Way	New Right
Approach	Leveller	Investor	Deregulator
Citizenship	Rights	Both rights and responsibilities	Responsibilities
Outcome	Equality	Inclusion	Inequality
Mixed economy of welfare	State	Public/private; civil society	Private
Mode	Command and control	Cooperation/partnership	Competition
Expenditure	High	Pragmatic	Low
Benefits	High	Low?	Low
Accountability	Central state/upwards	Both?	Market/downwards
Politics	Left	Left of centre/post-ideological	Right

Britain'. This approach featured much of the discourse which became central to New Labour: economic efficiency and social justice are different sides of the same coin; redistributing opportunities rather than just redistributing income; transforming the welfare state from a safety net in times of trouble to a springboard for economic opportunity; welfare should offer a hand-up not a hand-out; an active, preventive welfare state; paid work for a fair wage is the most secure and sustainable way out of poverty; and the balancing of rights and responsibilities. An Investor's welfare state is proactive, emphasising prevention and stressing causes rather than effects: attacking the causes of poverty rather than its symptoms, preventing poverty through education and training rather than simply compensating people in poverty.

New Labour probably set itself more targets than any previous British government. However, despite the claim of specific, measurable, accurate, relevant, timed (SMART) targets, many were vague and difficult to operationalise. In broad terms, it set targets on increasing educational qualifications, reducing child poverty and health inequality but not, crucially for 'Old Labour' critics, income equality. New Labour rejected a simple, fiscal equality to be achieved through the tax and benefit system. It claimed that it sought a more ambitious and dynamic redistribution of assets or endowments. In short, instead of compensating people for their poverty with benefit payments, it aimed to increase opportunities by increasing poor people's levels of health and education. Critics who argue that *all* New Labour's *aims* are less radical than Old Labour were wide of the mark. Old Labour would be proud of the child poverty and health inequality targets. However, they were long term, and were not met.

In terms of policy instruments, New Labour emphasised conditional or contractarian welfare. Rights were not 'dutiless', but tended to be given to those who fulfilled their obligations. The main obligations were connected with work, but others were concerned with housing and checking a baby's progress with a health professional. At the extreme, this can be seen as a change from a patterned to a process-driven distribution: distribution does not depend simply on people's need, but on their actions and behaviour.

Services were still largely financed by the state, but were increasingly delivered by private or voluntary bodies in a 'purchaser/provider split'. Rather than hierarchies or markets, coordination and collaboration through 'partnerships' or networks were stressed. New Labour ended the old 'class war' with private education and health providers, and worked with them through agreements or 'concordats' in which NHS patients were treated in private hospitals. The government encouraged new 'independent' (for-profit) centres to treat NHS patients, and allowed patients to choose a private hospital under its 'choose and book' scheme. Moreover, many hospitals and schools were built and run under a revamped Conservative Private Finance Initiative (PFI), which Labour had termed 'privatisation' in opposition. However, in some cases there was some 'privatisation of risk' where the state expected people to provide more of their own resources towards contingencies such as old age. Tax and service levels were pragmatic rather than dogmatic, with a tendency to prioritise services such as health and education that can be preventive in nature and increase human capital over reactive, passive, 'relief' cash benefits. Redistribution was 'for a purpose' and based more on endowments rather than in terms of transfer payments, although there has been some 'silent' or 'backdoor' fiscal redistribution especially to families with children.

Work was central to the Third Way. Key policy goals were seen in the slogans of 'work for those who can; security for those who cannot' and 'making work pay'. The Third Way stressed 'full employment', but this was to be achieved in terms of 'employability' through the 'supply-side' than by 'old'-style Keynesian demand management. Work was more 'flexible', with an increase in part-time and temporary employment. The Third Way's work-centred social policy had a mix of carrots and sticks. On the one hand, it emphasised carrots in the form of advice from case workers and investment in human capital. The slogan of 'making work pay' included a national minimum wage, in-work benefits of tax credits (or fiscal welfare) and making high-quality affordable child care available. On the other hand, critics argue that there was an element of US policy that tended to 'starve the poor back into work' through low or time-limited benefits.

Debates about universalism versus selectivity were not dogmatic. On the one hand, inclusion through universal services or civic welfare was stressed. On the other hand, there was increasing selectivity in cash benefits such as targeting on the poorest pensioners and new area-based policies.

The New Labour Legacy

It is difficult to examine the New Labour legacy for three main reasons. First, the Third Way was difficult to pin down, with the original 'Third Way' looking like more like a 'blurprint' than a 'blueprint', or indeed a 'Blairprint'. Second, it is difficult to find a clear analytical template. Third, it is probably a little too early to detect long-standing legacies.

Perhaps the clearest analytical template draws on the work of political scientist, Peter Hall, who set out three orders of change. The first order refers to the settings of instruments (for example, increase expenditure). Second order refers to change in instruments (for example, new institutions set up). Third order, or paradigm change, refers to change in settings, instruments and, more radically, to goals. However, one major problem with this framework is that it may stress discourse ('talking the talk'), but underplay results ('walking the walk'). In other words, it may emphasise 'symbolic politics'– words that succeed and policies that fail.

A number of commentaries appeared at the time of Blair's resignation. These were broadly positive on social policy, although some questioned the gaps between rhetoric and delivery, and between spending and results. It might be said that in terms of achievements, to use Tony Blair's own words, 'a lot done; a lot still to do' – an ambitious policy agenda has only partially been delivered. Like Bill Clinton, Blair campaigned in poetry but governed in prose. In his resignation speech, Blair claimed that 1997 was 'a moment for a new beginning, for sweeping away all the detritus of the past. Expectations were so high. Too high. Too high in a way for any of us. However, only one government since 1945 can say all of the following: more jobs, fewer unemployed, better health and education results, lower crime, and economic growth in every quarter' (in Powell, 2008: 259). Some of this changed with the brief and unhappy period of the Gordon Brown premiership (2007–10), which saw the scandal of MPs' expenses, a banking crisis, an economic crisis and the need to sharply reduce public expenditure

and the national debt. In short, boom turned to bust, and Brown was – in cricket terms – playing on the back foot. Brown's mistaken claim that he had 'saved the world' (not saved the banks – by a vast injection of public money) did not save his job as prime minister. There is some uncertainty among commentators about Brown's influence on social policy. Some see a partial return to some 'Old' Labour themes, while others detect a becalming of policy. However, it is difficult to see a distinctive Brownite agenda on social policy.

In terms of Hall's orders of change (above), there was much 'first-order change' (the settings of instruments), most notably a significant increase in public spending and employment after about the year 2000. There was also second-order change in terms of new instruments and institutions, most notably a 'snooze' of regulators (as they tended to sleep through vital warning signs in the NHS and in finance). There were potentially significant third-order changes, such as conditionality and welfare pluralism, shifts from public provision and responsibility, blurring of boundaries, and individual choice. However, with some important exceptions (such as the vast future 'mortgage' bill associated with the Private Finance Initiative), many of these were more significant in terms of rhetoric rather than delivery or impact. Probably the most important legacy is whether a government changes the political landscape for future governments, making it almost impossible to return to previous agendas. In this sense, there were probably few paradigmatic changes for three reasons. First, many of New Labour's themes built on earlier Conservative reforms (especially the later rather than the earlier years of New Labour). As former Conservative Prime Minister, John Major, put it in 1999: 'I did not appreciate at the time the extent to which Blair would appropriate Conservative language and steal their policies. The attractive candidate was to turn out to be a political kleptomaniac' (in Powell, 2008: 267). Second, while the differences between New Labour and the subsequent 'ConDem' government may not be highly significant, it is difficult to determine whether continuities relate to previous Labour or Conservative administrations (see Bochel and Powell, 2016). There is also the difficulty of the 'counterfactual': what Labour would have done if it had been re-elected in 2010 (compare Chapters 19 and 21). It would have cut public expenditure, although probably not as quickly and not as steeply. Third, there was no clear linear policy development over time as policy changed in a series of phases with some U-turns. There were many changes over time. If we had 'New Labour' and the 'Third Way' in 1997, perhaps we had in later years 'New New Labour'; 'Even Newer Labour', or the 'fourth way'. For example, New Labour initially stated that it wished to 'abolish' the market in the NHS, only to later reinstate a stronger market. However, two very broad trends involved the 'New Labour shuffle', a complex dance involving one step backward, and then two forward, towards markets and choice; and the 'New Labour ventriloquist', talking left but acting right.

Putting all these factors together, New Labour promises of 'welfare reform', 'world-class public services' and a 'modern welfare state' have only been partially delivered, resulting in an incomplete New Labour legacy. Blair's legacy is probably less far reaching than Attlee's (1945) or Thatcher's (1979), in the sense that their governments made it almost impossible to return to previous policies.

Emerging Issues

The influence of the Third Way in the future shape of British social policy is difficult to detect. There is clearly some shared ground between New Labour and the Coalition government of 2010–15. It is likely that elements such as 'active' and 'positive' welfare, consumerism, obligations and a more pluralist welfare state are here to stay, and it is very doubtful that there will be a return to the traditional social democratic welfare state. After their decisive defeat in the 2015 general election, the Labour Party appointed a new leader and deputy leader, and conducted a major review of its policies. Although the 'Third Way' term did not feature in the debate, the tension between (to oversimply) swinging left in an attempt to appeal to Scotland and swinging right in an attempt to appeal to England has some similarities with the period after Labour's decisive 1983 general election defeat, which led to the development of the Third Way. In the final analysis, when all the 'spin' has been stripped away, it is possible that millionaire bankers will derive more benefits from both the 'Third Way' and the 'Big Society' as compared with poorer people.

Guide to Further Reading

C. Arndt (2013), *The Electoral Consequences of Third Way Welfare State Reforms*, Amsterdam: Amsterdam University Press, examines four countries, with ch. 2 (theoretical background) and ch. 4 (UK) most useful.

T. Blair (1998), *The Third Way*, London: Fabian Society, gives the 'political' equivalent of Giddens' book.

H. Bochel and M. Powell (eds) (2016), *The UK Coalition Government and Social Policy*, Bristol: Policy Press, discusses the Coalition government, but includes some comparisons with the Third Way, and briefly explores the emerging social policies of the 2015 government.

A. Giddens (1998), *The Third Way*, Cambridge: Polity Press, is the influential original source written by the leading academic proponent of the Third Way.

J. Huo (2009), *Third Way Reforms: Social Democracy after the Golden Age*, Cambridge: Cambridge University Press, provides a comparative study of nine country experiences with Third Way reforms. Chapter 2 on 'Theorising the Third Way' and the material on Britain are particularly useful.

M. Powell (ed.) (2008), *Modernising the Welfare State: The Blair Legacy*, Bristol: Policy Press, this is the final part of the editor's 'New Labour trilogy' which examines the impact of New Labour up to Blair's resignation in 2007. M. Powell (2013), 'Third Way', in B. Greve (ed.), *The Routledge Handbook of the Welfare State*, London: Routledge, 202–12, updates the story to the end of the Labour government in 2010.

The 'Progressive Governance Network' advances 'centre-left' solutions through conferences and books, with the latest book (downloadable) based on a 2014 conference: www.policy-network.net/content/345/progressivegovernance.

Review and Assignment Questions

1   What do you understand by the 'Third Way'?
2   In what ways is the 'Third Way' a new and distinctive approach, which differs from both the 'Old Left' and the 'New Right'?

3 Examine how the 'orders of change' apply to individual services and benefits under New Labour.

4 How relevant are Third Way approaches to UK governments after 2015?

5 Critically discuss the extent to which social policies under New Labour (1997–2010) differed from those of the Conservative–Liberal Democrat Coalition (2010–15).

Visit the book companion site at www.wiley.com/go/alcocksocialpolicy to make use of the resources designed to accompany the textbook. There you will find chapter-specific guides to further resources, including governmental, international, thinktank, pressure groups and relevant journal sources. You will also find a glossary based on *The Blackwell Dictionary of Social Policy*, help sheets, guidance on managing assignments in social policy and career advice.

21

Austerity Politics

Jay Wiggan

Overview

■ The politics of austerity is related to, but not reducible to, the 2007–8 financial crisis. Disputes over austerity are embedded in competing ideological and political preferences regarding the appropriate relationship between the market, state and society.

■ In the UK this has manifested in disagreement over whether austerity is necessary at all and/or contestation over the means by which austerity policy should be enacted.

■ At the core of debates over austerity politics is the question of whether government should emphasise spending cuts or tax rises, and this inevitably raises distributional questions regarding who pays for and who is entitled to access specific welfare state services.

■ The UK Coalition government (2010–15) developed a simple, but compelling, austerity narrative that cut through competing economic theories and proposals by connecting their preferred policy to 'everyday' personal experience of money management and broader societal norms about individual self-reliance and social obligations.

■ The austerity narrative has legitimated a restructuring of the welfare state in line with neo-Liberal preferences, but is potentially threatened by the emergence of movements and political parties who oppose austerity and challenge the discursive narrative of austerity.

The Student's Companion to Social Policy, Fifth Edition. Edited by Pete Alcock, Tina Haux, Margaret May and Sharon Wright.
© 2016 John Wiley & Sons, Ltd. Published 2016 by John Wiley & Sons, Ltd.

Global Financial Crisis and 'Austerity'

In the wake of the global 2007–8 financial crisis governments and central banks in Europe, the USA and Asia coordinated the implementation of economic and social policy measures intended to stimulate stricken economies so as to prevent a severe recession turning into complete economic collapse. At the time it seemed the return of Keynesian economics, with governments willing to increase spending and/or reduce taxes and interest rates to sustain demand for goods and services and hence support employment, in the context of global economic downturn might herald a definitive break with the prevailing neo-Liberal political economy and usher in a new period of social democracy (see Chapters 9, 11 and 19). As we now know, the turn to Keynes (see Chapter 18) was a limited, pragmatic and temporary move to stabilise the global economy. As the immediate danger of collapse receded, the notion that the state and public spending could be a force for economic growth was rapidly displaced. Long-standing advocates of neo-Liberalism recovered their composure and launched a concerted campaign that successfully re-presented the miss-pricing of risk, market failure and a colossal banking crisis as a crisis of state solvency, originating in public spending. The re-location of the crisis from the private to the public sector via bank bailouts had, of course, rapidly increased public debt in the UK and in other states. This transformed political and public debate so that the parameters of policy narrowed to a focus of how governments should go about cutting public spending to reduce deficits and pay off their debts.

This chapter explores the politics of austerity through a focus on the UK. The first section clarifies what we mean by austerity. The second section outlines the shift from mild Keynesian stimulus under Labour (2008–10) to austerity and resurgent neo-Liberalism under the UK Coalition (2010–15). Section three considers how the Coalition sold this shift through the development of a simple, yet seductive, austerity narrative that taps into societal beliefs about personal responsibility and social obligation through reference to 'everyday' money management practices and popular concerns about 'worklessness'. The final section reflects on the potential fragility of austerity in the face of emergent opposition and the potential consequences.

The Theory of Austerity

The term austerity denotes the imposition of a period of public spending restraint or reduction and/or increase in taxes. The ostensible intention of austerity is to tackle the deficit and/or public debt (Box 21.1). Proponents of austerity regard high deficits as a source of instability as they contribute to public debt, and high levels of public debt as a percentage of Gross Domestic Product (GDP) are regarded as a drag on growth and a source of instability. It limits room for manoeuvre in an economic downturn and raises the cost of borrowing from investors who, regarding the state as a credit risk, demand higher interest rates. As a consequence, debt payments over time take up a growing portion of public expenditure.

Amongst contemporary proponents of austerity, spending cuts rather than tax rises have been favoured as the means to 'balance the books'. The 2010–15 UK Conservative–Liberal Coalition government, for example, achieved over 80 per cent of adjustment through spending cuts and only 20 per cent through tax rises (see below). Other UK

Box 21.1 Deficit and Public Debt

- The deficit refers to the annual difference between the revenue raised (for example, taxes, charges, licences, sale of assets) and the revenue spent by the state (for example, health services, education, pensions). The deficit is typically covered by borrowing money via sale of state-issued bonds that are purchased by, and provide an income stream to, investors.
- The public debt refers to the total accumulated stock of debt that is outstanding.

political parties, committed to alternative auster-ity packages, have proposed different spending reductions/tax increases (for example, Labour's proposed mansion tax rather than the Conserva-tive cuts to social security). Advocates of empha-sising public spending reductions argue that limiting the use of tax rises or greater borrowing signals to business and citizens that future levels of taxation will remain where they are or decline. Effectively the aim is to place a limit on the state's current and future claim on the income of business and citizens. The presumption is that, as these actors realise they are able to keep a greater portion of their resources to spend as they choose, this will generate the confidence necessary to stimulate the business investment and citizen consumption that will drive economic recovery. Policymakers aim to support this consolidation of public spending through monetary policy in an approach known as expansionary fiscal contrac-tion (Box 21.2).

As a policy prescription, the notion that a state should not spend more than it raises in revenue is intuitively appealing. Yet austerity is one of those 'common-sense' propositions whose assumptions are strongly contested.

Box 21.2 Expansionary Fiscal Contraction

- As austerity rules out fiscal policy as the means to restore economic growth, policymakers instead look to monetary policy (supply and cost of money/credit). A straightforward example is the reduction of interest rates to historic lows by the Bank of England, US Federal Reserve Bank and the European Central Bank.
- Through low interest rates central banks attempt to prevent debt defaults and offset fiscal contraction (spending cuts) by enabling business and consumers to borrow at cheaper rates for investment/consumption (hence, 'expansionary fiscal contrac-tion').

Challenges to the Theoretical Basis of Austerity

The underlying economics of austerity have been challenged by economists and other social scien-tists from outside (for example, Keynesian and more radical perspectives) the neo-Liberal tradi-tion where austerity finds its strongest contempo-rary champions. To simplify somewhat, opponents of austerity contend that public spend-ing reductions made in the midst of a recession, when business and citizens are already reigning in their spending and paying down their debts, removes the last pillar supporting economic demand. As austerity reduces expenditure on public services (including benefit payments), the collective demand for goods and services in the economy must also decline as the state purchases less from business directly (for example, services to the NHS) or indirectly (personal spending by people in receipt of tax credits or out-of-work benefits). The result is that business is again forced to reduce its outlays, making some staff unemployed. As this declining investment and consumption cascades through the economy, con-fidence collapses and rising unemployment places additional demands on the state. These must be financed either by raising taxes or by further spending cuts (at the risk of further constraining economic activity) or more borrowing to make up the difference. The latter creates a short-term rise in the deficit, which, of course, runs counter to the objectives of advocates of austerity.

For critics of austerity, however, expanding state borrowing in a crisis is not a problem as it leads to greater economic growth. The objection of austerity supporters to borrowing is misplaced and is an example of a fallacy of composition, whereby what may be desirable for an individual cannot simply be scaled up for society as a whole. In this case, the fallacy of composition associated with austerity is known as the paradox of thrift. So while it may be sensible for an individual citizen to save money and pay down debt in response to an economic crisis, this does not make sense when aggregated to a societal level. If all citizens, all business and the government seek to reduce spending at the same time, then economic demand collapses and recession deepens, because one person's spending is another person's income.

An alternative approach (see below) informed by Keynesian ideas advocates the reverse of the austerity position. Instead of cutting spending governments could use fiscal policy (borrowing to increase spending and cutting taxes) to drive economic expansion in the short term. Once the economy achieves sustained growth the state then begins to pay down the deficit and public debt, with the latter becoming less of a concern as it automatically shrinks as a proportion of GDP as the economy expands.

From Emergency Keynesianism to the Return of Neo-Liberalism

What was perhaps most striking about the imposition of austerity and its accompanying politics is that the financial crisis raised serious questions about the viability of neo-Liberal policy notions of self-correcting markets and minimal state intervention. Between 2008 and 2010, the UK Labour government under Gordon Brown briefly rediscovered Keynes and implemented a mild state stimulus package to prevent economic collapse. Spending on social security benefits was allowed to rise in response to declines in individual income resulting from unemployment or wage cuts (this is known as benefit payments functioning as an 'automatic stabiliser'), and introduced additional measures to encourage economic activity. These included targeted tax cuts (for example, Value Added Tax) and the car scrappage scheme (a £2,000 subsidy to individuals to exchange their old car for a new one). The aim was to prioritise economic stability, and once recovery had been 'locked in' to then pay down the deficit and public debt. Whilst Labour was committed to bringing about a reduction in state spending the key point is that this would occur once economic growth was accelerating, which is in line with the broad Keynesian position of paying down debt in the good times, while allowing increases in public spending and borrowing during downturns. Labour went into the 2010 general election proposing a ratio of 2:1 spending cuts to tax rises and a moderate pace of deficit reduction, with tighter spending beginning in 2011 to be complete by 2016–17. In contrast, the Conservative Party entered the 2010 general election campaign committed to a ratio of 4:1 spending cuts to tax rises

and a faster pace of tightening, beginning in 2010 with the deficit eliminated by 2015–16.

The Coalition government reaffirmed deficit reduction as the number one priority and that adjustment should fall mainly on reductions in spending, not tax increases. Continued economic instability and a conscious decision to slow the pace of austerity (an implicit concession to the Keynesian position to help growth) meant the original 2015–16 deficit target was missed and pushed back to 2018–19. The Coalition did successfully achieve their intended 4:1 ratio, with 82 per cent of consolidation by 2015 coming through reductions in public expenditure rather than tax rises. Public services have, therefore, experienced sustained retrenchment, though the extent and nature of this vary by policy sector (for example, health, education, social security, social care) and constituent country due to the degree of authority the governments in Scotland, Wales and Northern Ireland have to formulate their own policies and exercise control over spending (see Chapters 22–25).

To an extent the UK Coalition government's approach (2010–15) and the Conservative approach (2015–present) continue policies embarked upon by Labour, but also marks a step change in the opening up of public services to competition and intensification of benefit conditionality and erosion of entitlement to working age benefits (see Chapters 7, 47 and 56). The important point is that austerity has been utilised as a means for advancing long-standing neo-Liberal preferences for expansion of private sector involvement in public services and residualisation of social security for working age people. This is commensurate with pursuit of a long-term goal to shift expectations about what individuals can expect the state to provide and realising a leaner, more targeted, safety net welfare state.

The Austerity Narrative and the Legitimation of Welfare State Restructuring

Opponents of both austerity and welfare state restructuring have found themselves hampered by the discursive construction of austerity as the only 'credible' economic policy and as morally desirable. The UK Coalition government constructed a powerful, sophisticated (if simplistic) austerity narrative by weaving together threads concerning the supposed main challenges facing the UK. First, the financial crisis was reinterpreted so that it was transformed from being a problem of private sector banking practices and market failure, into a problem caused by extravagant, ineffective public spending by the state. Not only was spending viewed as excessive, but also it was presented as failing to solve the social problems it sought to rectify. Nowhere was this more clearly articulated than in the UK Coalition's identification of state spending on working age social security benefits as both contributing to, and resulting from, public spending (see Chapter 56).

In this sense, the austerity story is powerful not simply because it is conveyed by a coterie of elite politicians. The capacity to frame a policy issue so that interpretations of the problem and possible solutions align with and favour core ideological preferences cannot simply be imposed. It relies on the ability of political actors to connect their preferred story to particular threads of ideas, experiences and perceptions already held by the public. The analogy drawn by the Coalition between UK state deficits and public debt and individuals' credit card debts is an apposite example.

> It's like going on a spending binge with a credit card and having absolutely no idea how you are going to meet the interest. That is what Labour are about. They have learnt absolutely nothing in the past five years. It's still more borrowing, more spending, more debt (Prime Minister David Cameron, quoted in Mason, 4 January 2015)

Though misleading in the sense that an individual does not have the authority to levy taxes or issue the currency and cannot borrow at the same low interest rates as the UK, the use of the credit card analogy is politically astute. Research indicates the public interpret policy debates about debt and economic growth by drawing on personal experience. The credit card analogy works because it reworks a potentially complicated matter of economic policy as a 'big' version of personal finance embedding austerity in a morality tale about only spending what you can afford. Given that repayment of debts is viewed as a socially responsible obligation and individual indebtedness is difficult

to solve through more borrowing, the implication is that solving the deficit and debt require everyone (citizen and state) to tighten their belts and live within their means. So far the austerity narrative (Box 21.3) has proved a politically and economically seductive story with which to legitimate reforms. The question arises though as to whether the cumulative effect of year-on-year spending reductions and welfare state reform will begin to undermine public acquiescence to austerity.

Emerging Issues

In ruling out deficit financing and emphasising spending cuts over tax rises, the Coalition ensured that the immediate cost of austerity has been borne by those who tend to rely most heavily on public services and social transfers, especially working age claimants of out-of-work benefits. Given that expenditure on these benefits is less than half of total state spending on social security, the possibility of achieving substantial further savings from this area implies severe cuts and substantial restructuring of what the state offers to working age people.

The distributional effects of restructuring have already generated opposition by old (trades unions) and new (for example, Disabled People Against Cuts, Boycott Workfare and UK Uncut) social movements (see Chapter 14). Meanwhile, the electoral dynamics in Scotland, Wales and Northern Ireland, where the Conservative Party is a marginal electoral force, has created space for anti-austerity parties and ideas. Both the Scottish National Party and Plaid Cymru, for example, went into the 2015 general election articulating an anti-austerity narrative. If austerity measures persist, it may well deepen the emerging political divisions between Scotland, Wales, Northern Ireland and England, and pose a threat to the continuation of the UK as a single nation-state.

Guide to Further Sources

For an accessible overview of the history and contemporary relevance of the political economy of austerity, see M. Blyth (2013), *Austerity: The*

Box 21.3 Summary of the Austerity Narrative of the 2010–15 Coalition Government

Economic problem definition

■ Deficit and debt resulted from public spending that was too high under Labour.

■ Size of deficit/debt risk to economic credibility of UK.

■ Imperils capacity to attract investment and raises cost of borrowing.

■ Borrowing 'crowds' out business and consumer spending as they 'save' in anticipation of future tax rises. Cannot borrow your way out of debt (credit card analogy).

Moral problem

■ State was irresponsibly living beyond its means. Social obligation to now pay for the 'good times' of easy money. Borrowing more just adds to the debt, imposing burden on future generations.

■ Public spending masked underlying causes of social problems such as 'work-lessness and welfare dependency', which contributed to high spending.

■ State should minimise not maximise taxation, as money is that of individual/business.

Policy solution

■ Paying down deficit/debt protects credibility of UK state.

■ Reducing spending will restore confidence of business and consumers.

■ Economic and moral case for reforms that prevent 'welfare dependency'. The state must promote self-reliance through strengthened conditionality; benefit sanctions and curtailment of entitlements, and value of out-of-work benefits.

■ Labour's profligacy means scope for efficiencies and economic case for the state doing less overall and for innovation (markets) in public services to save money and improve effectiveness.

History of a Dangerous Idea, Oxford: Oxford University Press. More recently, an insightful analysis of the power of austerity and its consequences in the UK, Ireland and Spain is provided in S. Dellepiane-Avellaneda (2015), 'The political power of economic ideas: the case of "expansionary fiscal contractions"', *British Journal of Politics and International Relations*, 17:3, 391–418.

A good source of information on the details of social and economic policy under the Coalition government and its predecessor can be found in work regularly produced by the independent thinktank the Institute for Fiscal Studies. In particular, refer to C. Emmerson, P. Johnson and R. Joyce (2015), *The IFS Green Budget*, London: Institute for Fiscal Studies; A. Hood and D. Phillips (2015), *Benefit Spending and Reforms: The Coalition Government's Record*, IFS Briefing Note BN160, London: Institute for Fiscal Studies; Institute for Fiscal Studies (2010), *Election Briefing 2010 Summary*, London: Institute for Fiscal Studies.

The debate about austerity is often infused with comparisons to personal finance and half-truths, misdirection and confusion about the nature, scale and distributive function of various aspects of the welfare state. A good example of the use of personal finance as metaphor can be found in R. Mason (2015), 'Cameron says Tories' £25bn spending cuts are necessary and reasonable', *The Guardian*, 4 January. Accessible research into how the public interpret the austerity analogies deployed by political elites can be found in L. Stanley (2014), '"We're reaping what we sowed": everyday crisis narratives and acquiescence to the age of austerity', *New Political Economy*, 19:6, 895–917. For clarity on the size, scope and role of the UK welfare state and the problem with dichotomous categorisation by politicians and media of society into taxpayers and claimants, see J. Hills (2015), *Good Times, Bad Times: The Welfare Myth of Them and Us*, Bristol: Policy Press.

Review and Assignment Questions

1 What do we mean when we talk about austerity?
2 How does the politics of austerity policy construct cuts in public spending as both necessary and desirable?
3 Is the UK deficit and public debt comparable to the position of an individual who is heavily indebted to a credit card company?
4 Describe the paradox of thrift?
5 Critically discuss the implications of austerity politics for the welfare state.

Visit the book companion site at www.wiley.com/go/alcocksocialpolicy to make use of the resources designed to accompany the textbook. There you will find chapter-specific guides to further resources, including governmental, international, thinktank, pressure groups and relevant journal sources. You will also find a glossary based on *The Blackwell Dictionary of Social Policy*, help sheets, guidance on managing assignments in social policy and career advice.

PART IV

Devolution and Social Policy in the United Kingdom

22

Social Policy and Devolution

Richard Parry

■■

Overview

- ■ The United Kingdom is a unitary, London-centred state without a uniform system of territorial government that has made a political adjustment to the wishes of Scotland, Wales and Northern Ireland by devolving powers over many areas of social policy.
- ■ England still dominates in both scale and thinking, retains control over the tax–benefit system, but has not divided itself into regional political entities comparable to the devolved nations.
- ■ The devolved nations have taken some interesting policy initiatives, generally in the direction of a more universalist, more integrated and less privatised welfare state.
- ■ The current arrangements are politically and financially unstable, as evidenced by the Scottish independence referendum of 2014 and subsequent legislative proposals for more devolution.
- ■ Devolution within England is back on the agenda, but focusing on city regions earning the right to take powers on economic and social development.

■■

The UK is a strongly unitary state and lacks a clear concept of regional differences in social policy in terms of formation, implementation and content. The main source of difference is the status of Scotland, Wales and Northern Ireland within the UK, enjoying nationhood but not statehood and, since 1999, having their own devolved elected administrations with extensive powers over social policy. This chapter introduces chapters on Scotland, Wales and Northern

The Student's Companion to Social Policy, Fifth Edition. Edited by Pete Alcock, Tina Haux, Margaret May and Sharon Wright.
© 2016 John Wiley & Sons, Ltd. Published 2016 by John Wiley & Sons, Ltd.

Ireland (Chapters 23–25) by explaining the framework of government and public finances within which they operate, the reasons for differences between them, and the impact of recent political developments across the UK on them.

The Pattern of Devolution

The starting point is the dominance of England in the UK. It accounts for 85 per cent of the population, and London, its capital, is the centre of political, governmental, cultural and media activity. Britain has uniform welfare benefit rates and a lesser sense of systematic multi-level political structure than any country of comparable size. There is a tension in UK social policy between tolerating differences on grounds of diversity and choice, and distrusting them on grounds of uniform citizen rights not varying according to place of residence (in the British term, avoiding 'postcode lotteries') and transferable across nations on some notion of a 'social union'. All UK policy uses English practice and organisation as a reference point (following it or resisting it), while England lacks a stable identity distinct from 'Britain'.

Scotland, Wales and Northern Ireland have distinct historical traditions and political profiles:

■ Scotland was independent until 1707, and the Act of Union preserved its legal system, Presbyterian Church and local government. It had stronger traditions in education and medicine than did England, and became a UK leader in these fields.
■ Wales was never a defined independent state, but its linguistic and religious pattern was clearly different, and Welsh policies and institutions developed during the twentieth century.
■ Ireland had a separate parliament until 1801, then united with Great Britain but split in 1922 into an independent country (later the Republic of Ireland) and the six counties of Northern Ireland, which remained in the UK and until 1972 had a local parliament.

In all three nations many local services were run by departments of the UK government (the Scottish, Welsh and Northern Ireland offices).

The Labour government of 1997 created a law-making Scottish Parliament, a National Assembly for Wales administering and financing services within a framework of Westminster legislation, and a law-making Northern Ireland Assembly with a compulsory 'power-sharing' coalition in government. All were elected for four-year terms until 2011, but now have in effect five-year terms with elections one year after UK general elections, under proportional representation systems. Referendums approved the proposals by a strong majority in Scotland (74 per cent) and Northern Ireland (71 per cent), but a bare 50 per cent in Wales. Scotland also voted 63 per cent to give the Scottish Parliament limited powers to alter income tax. The new administrations assumed their powers in 1999, but Northern Ireland's was suspended from 2002 to 2007, and continues to show political instability.

Devolution to Scotland and Wales was the UK Labour government's creation and they dominated its first eight years, in coalition with the Liberal Democrats in Scotland throughout, and in Wales from 2000 to 2003. After the 2007 elections, in Scotland the pro-independence Scottish National Party (SNP) edged ahead of Labour in seats and votes and formed a minority administration. It was able to pass its budgets after deals with other parties, but not its proposal for a referendum on independence. In Wales, Labour secured a coalition deal with the nationalist Plaid Cymru, whose centrepiece was the promotion of a 'yes' vote in a referendum about giving the Welsh Assembly full law-making powers in devolved areas. This was secured in March 2011 with a 63 per cent yes vote on a 36 per cent turnout.

After the 2011 devolved elections, the presumption that the UK Government would be single-party (and so 'strong') and the devolved governments coalitions (and so 'weak') was reversed. Labour narrowly resumed single-party government in Wales, and in Scotland the SNP dramatically won an overall majority on 45 per cent of the vote. In the 2015 UK general election, the SNP increased its vote to 50 per cent and, under a first-past-the-post system, won fifty-six of the fifty-nine Scottish seats in the House of Commons, forty of which were taken from Labour. With the Conservatives strengthening their relative position in Wales (up from no seats in 1997 to eleven in 2015), both Labour and Conservative parliamentary parties at Westminster are heavily English with a small Welsh influence and see devolution through that similar lens.

UK devolution is severely 'asymmetrical' – it responds to circumstances and political pressures in each part of the country rather than proceeds from a uniform territorial framework of levels of government (as found in, for instance, the United States and Germany). Although there had been interest for decades in a regional elected level of government in England, this has severely been put into reverse. The North East was given the chance to have a weak elected assembly in 2004, but rejected it in a referendum 78 per cent to 22 per cent. Government offices in the regions and regional development agencies were abolished in 2010 and 2012, and a non-uniform structure of Local Enterprise Partnerships based on cities was substituted. Meanwhile, there is a debate in London, a diverse world city, about gaining policy discretion commensurate with the tax revenue it raises for the country of which it is the capital.

The Operation of the Devolved Administrations

The Scottish and Welsh governments (previously called the Scottish Executive and the Welsh Assembly Government) are descendants of the 'joined-up' former Scottish and Welsh Offices. Since 2007, the Scottish Government has no central departments as such, only groups of directorates serving ministers. Wales has non-statutory departments. In contrast, Northern Ireland departments have statutory existence as part of the power-sharing arrangements, with parties choosing which ones to take in proportion to their strength; the departments resemble the 'silos' found in Whitehall, with similarly tense relations between ministers. All three systems have permanent committees of elected members in the subject area of each minister that combine the functions of legislative scrutiny and policy investigation.

The three devolved nations use traditional UK legal forms in the organisation of social policy and have avoided English innovations such as elected mayors, free schools and commercialised health contracting. Scotland and Wales have integrated area Health Boards and have abandoned the trusts found in England; Northern Ireland has trusts, but they report in a non-competitive way to a single, integrated Health and Social Services Board. Local government in the three nations is much more neatly organised than it is in England, with single-tier authorities. Scotland and Northern Ireland have single police forces.

Spending Patterns within the United Kingdom

The UK's social policy has been underwritten by an implicit northwest-to-southeast gradient – Scotland, Wales, Northern Ireland and northern England were seen as relatively deprived and so could claim additional resources to deal with their problems. These justifications have eroded, and because house prices are lower and public sector health and education better serviced, the non-English nations may feel better off and rank high in subjective quality-of-life indices.

This provides the backdrop to the position on relative public spending (Table 22.1). Figures for 2012–13 reveal that Northern Ireland leads, at 18 per cent more social expenditure per head than the UK average, but the North East is ahead of Scotland and Wales. Housing differentials stand out, but public housing expenditure is very small. More important is Scotland's and Northern Ireland's advantage in health and education, which is more structural than needs-based. London spends more than the UK average (though in its eyes amply justified by the amount of tax revenue it brings in) and the more prosperous English regions are consistently at the bottom of the table.

With Scotland's income-tax raising powers not yet used, the devolved administrations have access only to the traditional sources of local finance, the council tax and business rates. Their money comes mainly from a block grant from the UK Government and they are bound by UK Treasury rules on public expenditure management and government accounting. Although there is freedom to choose spending priorities within the block grant, there is not the full political debate around choices on taxation and spending found in developed political systems.

The patterns reflect the 'Barnett Formula' used for apportioning expenditure to the nations both before and after devolution: put simply, the block grant changes year by year in step with changes in corresponding English expenditure. This avoids

Table 22.1   Spending per head on social policy, 2012–13.

Index: UK = 100	Total social	Social protection	Health	Education	Housing and community amenities
Northern Ireland	118	116	109	113	288
North East	110	112	111	101	137
Scotland	109	106	109	105	185
Wales	108	113	101	99	136
North West	106	107	110	99	85
London	102	95	104	116	129
Yorkshire and the Humber	100	100	102	102	81
West Midlands	100	101	100	101	75
South West	96	100	93	90	64
East Midlands	95	96	96	96	78
East	92	93	90	95	60
South East	89	90	89	90	64
UK average £	7,366	3,891	1,937	1,373	165

Source: calculated from HM Treasury, *Public Expenditure Statistical Analyses 2014* (Cm 8902, July 2014), Tables 9.15 and 9.16.

constant haggling over items and is meant to converge expenditure over time, because new money is apportioned on a population basis rather than on historic shares or after argument about relative need. The fact that the differentials are moving only slowly led to repeated calls for more fiscal autonomy for the devolved nations. The Scotland Act 2012 created the first new devolved tax, Land and Buildings Transactions Tax, which replaced Stamp Duty in April 2015, and from April 2016 will cut the block grant by the yield of 10 per cent on income tax and force the Scottish Parliament to fix an income tax rate to balance its books. These tax powers are on offer to Wales under the Wales Act 2014 and further UK proposals in February 2015. Northern Ireland has been offered some discretion on Air Passenger Duty and Corporation Tax to reflect its exposure to lower tax levels in the Irish Republic. This growth of 'fiscal federalism' sets ever-contracting parameters on the necessary uniformity and burden-sharing in the UK 'social union'.

The Pattern of Flexibility at the Devolved Level

An important justification for devolution is that it allows for flexibility and experimentation within

the UK. But in social policy the room for manoeuvre is not complete. There is basically a single UK framework for social security; Northern Ireland has different original legislation, but a parity of structure and rates, implemented only with great political difficulty in the case of the Welfare Reform Act 2012. Pre-devolution, education and housing legislation was largely the same in England and Wales, but different in Scotland and Northern Ireland (especially in the structure of school examinations in Scotland and denominational education in Northern Ireland). These latter two nations also had a distinct tradition in health within the common NHS 'brand' that has proved resilient, leaving open which 'nation' is being spoken about. Outside the area of cash benefits, social policy is largely devolved, exceptions include the health professions, abortion and drugs policy. But crime, justice, police and prisons in Wales have always been run on a common basis with England and are not devolved.

Since devolution, policy initiatives have tended to greater generosity, universalism and public provision. All three nations have abolished prescription charges. Scotland has abolished undergraduate tuition fees for Scottish (and non-UK EU) students at Scottish universities; Scotland has moved towards non-means-tested personal care for the elderly in assessed need in response to the

Royal Commission on Long-Term Care for the Elderly of 1999. Scotland's policy attracted much attention, but caps on the allowable fees and the need for local authority assessment of needs make it less free and universal than it might seem. Devolved nations have been at the forefront of concern that the proposed EU–US Transatlantic Trade and Investment Partnership (TTIP) might compromise the ability of governments to exclude private health and education providers from pursuing their business within state-run systems.

Devolution has brought into focus two long-standing themes: the uniformity of UK benefit structures that makes it hard to run ambitious devolved anti-poverty policies, and the ability of the three non-English nations to do things their own way with relative Westminster political indifference. Paradoxically, devolution policies that were meant to leave the territories to take local decisions have highlighted the occasions where the logic of their policymaking differs from that of the UK Government, and have called into question the historic expenditure advantage of Scotland, Wales and Northern Ireland.

Divergence in delivery structures has been more of a policy design choice than an adaptation to local circumstances, especially in health service organisation and the 'lifelong learning' area (skills training, higher and further education in terms of provision, financing and charging). The devolved administrations have tried to deal with the whole range of social and economic variables in their nations even when lacking powers to address them, as in the SNP government's fifteen 'national outcomes' set in 2007 that structured 'single outcome agreements' with local authorities. Equality provisions (gender, ethnicity, religious community, language) have been taken forward in all three devolved nations with a valuable thinking-through from first principles. But the devolved systems cannot resist UK changes on tax and benefit policy, especially the introduction of Universal Credit incorporating housing benefit. The 'bedroom tax' (the removal of the so-called 'spare room subsidy' for social housing tenants on housing benefit occupying dwellings deemed larger than necessary) was very controversial and small flexibilities were conceded to Scotland and Northern Ireland.

Another factor is the vulnerability of devolved social policy to UK spending cuts. The devolved systems can opt out of English policy changes, but any negative expenditure consequences of the changes are passed on to them. The direction of policy, starting with Scotland, is towards fiscal autonomy where tax levels must follow spending decisions even if it means higher taxes. This poses a threat to the divergent social policies that had in fact been more generous policies and to the stability of devolution as a mid-point between a unitary UK and independence for the nations.

Emerging Issues: The Scottish Independence Referendum and Beyond

What had seemed a durable structure of devolution lasted just fifteen years. The UK Government removed any legal doubt by authorising the Scottish Parliament to hold a referendum on independence by the end of 2104. In international terms, this facilitation of secession was remarkable, but followed the UK's approach towards Northern Ireland that its wish was only to allow its citizens to determine its own constitutional future. One UK motivation was a positive keenness to force the SNP into a straight single-question referendum without delay, thinking that a large 'No' majority was inevitable. In the end, the 'No' majority on 18 September 2014 was clear (55.3 per cent to 44.7 per cent), but the path towards it included a period of total panic ten days before when two opinion polls showed the 'Yes' side in the lead. This prompted 'The Vow', an agreement between three UK party leaders to reconcile by the end of November 2014 proposals for further devolved powers previously produced within their parties. After the referendum, the UK Government proposed a mechanism for this that was acceptable to the Scottish Government – an all-party commission chaired by Lord Smith of Kelvin, a widely admired non-partisan business leader, and serviced by officials seconded from Edinburgh as well as London.

The proposals that emerged from Smith – and the previous party positions from which they derived – reflected serious interest (and public support in surveys) in devolving taxes and benefits in the same way as public services. Bold proposals were in play from the parties. Last-minute negotiation, with the SNP more or less a spectator and the UK Government scared of unpicking conditionality and sanctions within the benefits system, confined the proposals to rates and thresholds of income tax on earnings, the housing elements of Universal Credit and disability benefits. The proposals were put into legal form by the UK Government in the Scotland Bill 2015. Much implementation work remains to be done, but grant transfers via the Barnett formula will fall, and tax revenue paid direct to the Scottish devolved system will rise (to around half its income), especially from the total transfer of income tax on earned income. The devolved system will, in effect, be cast adrift and have to pick up the bill for both policy generosity and weakness in tax receipts relative to England.

The effect of these policies is to put under strain the resilience of UK frameworks. A chronic problem is the so-called 'West Lothian question' (or 'EVEL' – English Votes for English Laws). MPs from Scotland, Wales and Northern Ireland sit at Westminster and can vote on England-only legislation in devolved fields. If there is not to be a separate English Parliament and Government, nor devolved English regional assemblies, this is hard to resolve. With their 2015 election victory, the Conservatives had the votes to force through changes in House of Commons Standing Orders to require consent to England-only (or England and Wales-only) provisions from the relevant group of MPs, but this will only be tested when a future UK Government may lack a majority in either or both of these groups.

The UK Conservative stratagem for English territorial government – 'city deals' of devolved spending power with the major conurbations – has made good progress only in the area where Manchester is dominant. From April 2016, the NHS budget in Greater Manchester was due to be brought under local control and so could (in theory) be merged with that for social care. This breaks with the UK principle, also maintained by choice in the devolved nations, that the NHS is not run by local politicians. The Cities and Local Government Devolution Bill 2015 would give powers to confer wide functions on 'mayoral combined authorities', but in many parts of England jealousies between cities or the absence of large cities makes the definition of such authorities an unresolved issue.

Scotland will continue to have a serious and realistic independence option for which much preparatory work was done in 2014. Wales and Northern Ireland 'slipstream' on Scotland, being offered more and more powers as long as they are prepared to pay for them – which is not necessarily an attractive offer, as these nations have always seen the UK connection as a recognition of their relative economic weakness and their need for subvention to provide UK standards of public service. The UK Conservative government has come to the point of pressing more tax-raising powers on the devolved nations to make them less of a demander of transfers from London. Although the SNP wants 'Full Fiscal Autonomy' (taking a control of all tax revenues in Scotland and paying a contribution to London for Scotland's share of non-devolved services), they are pragmatically cautious about the speed and manner with which this might be achieved short of independence.

Ironically, the devolution question has begun to turn into the English question. How far will English political interests tolerate divergent policies in the devolved nations that are not fully paid for by local political decisions? How far is diversity and solidarity within the UK valued and underwritten? How far down to localities and their political institutions should the devolution of discretion and spending capacity go? Might the UK centre force tax and spend responsibilities on to reluctant devolved systems? A political system that has never absorbed federal thinking is bound to find these questions difficult, especially when the spirit of the times is making it hard to use a generous welfare state as an instrument of territorial stabilisation.

Guide to Further Reading

The best source, a comprehensive and pioneering account, is D. Birrell (2009), *The Impact of Devolution on Social Policy*, Bristol: Policy Press.

Keeping up with post-devolution developments is not always easy: the best long-term work is by the Constitution Unit at University College London, which publishes quarterly monitoring reports available at: ucl.ac.uk/constitution-unit.

A good summary is in J. Adams and K. Schmueker (eds) (2010), *Devolution in Practice*

2010, London: Institute for Research on Public Policy.

An important comparative study is S. Greer (2005), *Territorial Politics and Health Policy*, Manchester: Manchester University Press.

Evidence submitted to the Smith Commission in 2014 by the UK and Scottish governments gives valuable analytical material on the practicalities of existing and further devolution; see: smith-commission.scot/resources/analysis.

Current commentary is provided by the University of Edinburgh's Centre on Constitutional Change at: www.futureukandscotland.ac.uk/blog.

Review and Assignment Questions

1 What areas of social policy have been devolved to Scotland, Wales and Northern Ireland?

2 What has been the effect of having nationalists in government since 2007?

3 What have been the extent of social policy divergences and innovations in the devolved nations?

4 How is devolution funded, and how may this change in future economic circumstances?

5 Discuss how far UK devolution in social policy can be made to work when England is such a dominant reference point.

Visit the book companion site at www.wiley.com/go/alcocksocialpolicy to make use of the resources designed to accompany the textbook. There you will find chapter-specific guides to further resources, including governmental, international, thinktank, pressure groups and relevant journal sources. You will also find a glossary based on *The Blackwell Dictionary of Social Policy*, help sheets, guidance on managing assignments in social policy and career advice.

23

Social Policy in Northern Ireland

Ann Marie Gray and Derek Birrell

▪▫▪▪▫▪▫▪▫▪▫▪▫▪▫▪▫▪▫▪▫▪▫▪▫▪▫▪▫▪▫▪▫▪▫▪▫▪▫▪▫▪

Overview

- Devolution in Northern Ireland, introduced in 1998, followed thirty years of violent conflict and the signing of a peace agreement. It has continued, but with some disruption.
- The Northern Ireland Government is unique in the UK in that it is a mandatory coalition.
- There are examples of divergence and convergence between social policies in Northern Ireland and other parts of the UK.
- The structure of government in Northern Ireland has led to impasse and delays in policymaking. It has been argued that, to a large extent, social policy has been based on pragmatism with little evidence of the values or principles that have been at the centre of debates in Scotland and Wales.
- More critical discussion of some social policy issues and changes to the structure and functioning of government may emerge as Northern Ireland seeks to address significant structural problems and the potential for further devolution.

▪▫▪▪▫▪▫▪▫▪▫▪▫▪▫▪▫▪▫▪▫▪▫▪▫▪▫▪▫▪▫▪▫▪▫▪▫▪▫▪▫▪

Introduction

The establishment of devolved government in Northern Ireland in 1998 followed the signing of a peace agreement after more than three decades of violent conflict between the two main communities in Northern Ireland. At the heart of the conflict was the constitutional position of Northern Ireland. For the unionist and mainly Protestant majority, the aim was to remain

The Student's Companion to Social Policy, Fifth Edition. Edited by Pete Alcock, Tina Haux, Margaret May and Sharon Wright.
© 2016 John Wiley & Sons, Ltd. Published 2016 by John Wiley & Sons, Ltd.

part of the United Kingdom, while the goal of the nationalist and republican, mainly Catholic minority was for unity with the Republic of Ireland. The outbreak of the conflict in the late 1960s led to the suspension of the then unionist-controlled devolved government in 1972, and Northern Ireland was to be governed by direct rule from Westminster until the restoration of devolution in 1998.

In a number of respects the operation of government in Northern Ireland is quite distinct from other parts of the UK. The system established in 1998 was to accommodate power-sharing between nationalist and unionist parties, and devolved government is therefore inextricably linked to the peace process. Elections to the Northern Ireland Assembly are conducted using a form of proportional representation. The number of seats each party has in the government Executive is based on the number of seats they hold in the Assembly. Since 2008, the Democratic Unionist Party (DUP) and Sinn Féin have been the two largest parties in the Assembly, and as such hold the First Minister's Office: the DUP's Peter Robinson held the title of First Minister until retiring in 2016, when he was replaced by Arlene Foster. Wilford (2010) has referred to the structure of government in Northern Ireland as a 'contrived model of governance' in that the Executive is a mandatory coalition made up of five political parties: the DUP, Sinn Féin, the Social Democratic and Labour Party (SDLP), the Official Unionist Party and the Alliance Party. All parties in the Executive have to reach consensus on policies. There is no provision for an opposition in the structures. Officially the principle of collective responsibility does not govern Executive decision-making and ministers commonly disagree with each other in public.

Most social policy responsibilities are devolved to the Northern Ireland Executive. Two categories of functions are not devolved: reserved matters that might be devolved in future, and excepted matters that will remain as Westminster responsibilities (see Table 23.1).

There are overlapping areas, with addressing child poverty and welfare reform being two examples. The Northern Ireland Executive is obliged to conform to the policy goals and targets set out in the Westminster Government's 2010 Child Poverty Act, but within this framework can develop its own child poverty strategy and initiatives to tackle it. The area of social security and benefits is complex, with the matter constitutionally devolved but funding being the direct responsibility of Westminster.

Table 23.1 Devolved, excepted and reserved responsibilities.

Devolved responsibilities	Excepted matters	Reserved matters
Health and social care	The constitution	Firearms and explosives
Education and youth services	International relations	Broadcasting
Justice and policing	Defence and national security	Import and export controls
Social security	Immigration and asylum	Navigation and civil aviation
Employment and skills	Elections	International trade and financial markets
Housing	UK-wide taxation	Financial services and pensions regulation
Transport	Currency	Minimum wage
Local government	Nuclear energy	Genetics
Culture and sport	International treaties	Data protection
Economic development	Human rights	Consumer rights
Pensions and child support	National Insurance	
Environment and planning		
Equal opportunities		
Agriculture		

International treaties and conventions also involve some overlap. Macro-economic policy is not devolved, economic development is but the area overlaps. While the Westminster Government is the 'state party' reporting to and accountable to the international bodies for progress on the implementation of the conventions, responsibility for domestic social policy mostly lies with the devolved administration. Where policies or actions have been found to contravene the obligations, as has been the case with abortion law in Northern Ireland, the Westminster Government can seem relatively powerless in the face of opposition from the devolved government.

Funding and Spending on Social Policy in Northern Ireland

Funding, in the form of a block grant, is allocated to the Northern Ireland Government, as in Scotland and Wales, through the Barnett Formula, in part a population-based formula. It reflects changes to spending allocated to public services in England. It is up to the Northern Ireland Executive to determine how the money is allocated. The largest allocation goes to health and social care, with almost half the block grant (of about £10 billion) allocated to this department. The Northern Ireland Executive has limited discretion to raise additional revenue through, for example, local and regional rates, but these amount to only about 4 per cent of total regional income. Across the UK public expenditure per capita has fallen, and while the three main political parties at Westminster have different priorities in terms of spending all are committed to further austerity, resulting in further cuts to public expenditure. In practical terms this means the money coming to the devolved administrations through the block grant will be reduced.

Social Policy Priorities in Northern Ireland: Convergence and Divergence

The study of social policy in Northern Ireland raises questions about parity and convergence and divergence. It might be expected that where

policymakers have the capacity to vary policy this would be the likely outcome as they seek to tailor policy to local needs and priorities. However, as this chapter shows, this is not straightforward, with a number of factors influencing approaches to social policy in Northern Ireland.

Some of the divergence from policy elsewhere in the UK is historical; for example, Northern Ireland's unique structurally integrated system of health and social care was established in 1972. Local government in Northern Ireland has had no significant social welfare responsibilities since the early 1970s, with housing, education and social care all being governed by quangos – appointed bodies. Other divergences have occurred since 1998.

In a number of respects social policy priorities in Northern Ireland are similar to those in other parts of the UK, including reducing inequalities in health, addressing educational under-achievement, developing more personalised models of care and getting more people into work. However, living standards in Northern Ireland have lagged behind the rest of the UK, and research in recent years has identified worrying trends. The Monitoring Poverty and Social Exclusion Report published by the Joseph Rowntree Foundation in 2014 showed that between 2010 and 2014 poverty rates worsened, household incomes declined and poverty among young adults (16–29 years) rose by eight percentage points. The employment rate is lower than the UK average due to higher rates of economic inactivity (the economic activity rate is 68 per cent compared with a UK average of 72 per cent). Long-term unemployment is a problem, with half of unemployed adults out of work for twelve months or more. Youth unemployment, as in the rest of the UK, is well above the average rate of unemployment. In Northern Ireland, these problems are accompanied by concerns about educational attainment. The 2011 Census shows that over 29 per cent of 16–64 year olds in Northern Ireland have no qualifications compared with 15 per cent in England and Wales. While the number of young people achieving A–C grades at GCSE level exceeds the UK average, this masks a problem of under-achievement. Northern Ireland also lags behind in some areas of social policy provision, including childcare provision and adult social care.

Under devolution there has not been the same emphasis on social policy in Northern Ireland as there has in Scotland and Wales, and Northern Ireland has not yet carved out what could be described as a uniquely Northern Ireland approach. There are some examples of convergence with policies elsewhere in the UK through 'policy copying' – where Northern Ireland has decided to directly copy a policy introduced in Scotland, Wales or England. For example, the decision to introduce free prescriptions was justified by reference to the same rationales used by ministers in Scotland and Wales, and Northern Ireland followed Wales and Scotland in introducing a children's commissioner, and Wales with a commissioner for older people. A number of inter-departmental high-level strategies on poverty, children and young people, older people and gender equality were developed, but not fully implemented. With separate executive departments, all but one headed by a single minister, the structure in Northern Ireland has been argued to impede a joined-up approach to policymaking. It has also contributed to what could be referred to as 'ministerial fiefdoms', with departmental ministers who make up the Northern Ireland Executive acting autonomously without any sense of collective responsibility.

An understanding of social policy in Northern Ireland requires some examination of the approach taken to policymaking and decisions within the Northern Ireland Executive. As explained earlier, the Northern Ireland Executive has to reach consensus on policy decisions. The period of devolution since 2008 has been marked by the failure of the coalition Executive to reach agreement on a number of major social policy issues, producing at times a policy impasse or serious delays. This has been evident at the most fundamental level, with the Programme for Government following the 2008 election only being agreed ten months into the mandate. Its content also indicated that agreement had been difficult to find on the detail, with the content being broad-based and mainly aspirational. The impasse on policy has included education issues, human rights and equality issues, and approaches to poverty and welfare reform. Northern Ireland has a system of education divided along religious lines and has maintained a system of grammar and secondary schools, never moving towards the comprehensive model adopted elsewhere in the UK. Academic selection has attracted controversy

over many years, and when the Sinn Féin Minister for Education abolished the 11+ examination in 2002 this was met with considerable resistance by grammar schools, and by unionists politicians in particular. No replacement method of transferring children from primary to secondary school could be agreed, and in the absence of this the grammar schools (all of which are state-funded) established their own entrance examinations, a situation which continues. A similar impasse occurred with regard to the advice that the Executive should provide to the Secretary of State for Northern Ireland with regard to a new Human Rights Bill for Northern Ireland (human rights is the responsibility of the Westminster Government). There was some support for the Bill to include social and economic rights, including from the Northern Ireland Human Rights Commission. However, the lack of consensus in the Executive resulted in it being abandoned.

The considerable delay over decisions about welfare reform from 2012 to 2015 illustrates some of the challenges created by the lack of consensus in the Northern Ireland coalition, and also by the overlapping responsibilities of the Westminster and Northern Ireland governments. While formally and constitutionally social security is a devolved matter, in practice social security is almost totally kept in parity with Great Britain (see Chapter 22). Resistance to introducing the same provisions as in the Westminster legislation came from a number of parties in the Executive. Sinn Féin expressed vocal opposition and initially argued that it would not support the policy. The DUP was broadly supportive of the principles underpinning welfare reform, but argued it would seek to ameliorate the impact on the most vulnerable. The DUP minister argued that some administrative flexibilities had been agreed with the Department for Work and Pensions, including that Universal Credit could be paid fortnightly rather than monthly as is the case in Great Britain, and that Housing Benefit will continue to be paid directly to landlords rather than to the claimant as is the case elsewhere. The impasse appeared to be resolved as part of the Stormont House agreement of December 2014, with the two main parties agreeing to implement the legislation but also committing to provide financial support for people who would lose money due to the welfare changes in Northern Ireland. The welfare reform debate showed that the scope for divergence from parity in social security matters was limited by financial considerations – as any additional spending would have to be met from the block grant allocated under the Barnett Formula, and also by the notion that Northern Ireland should remain in step with the rest of the UK with regard to social security benefits. What divergence there will be from welfare reform in Great Britain will be to the regulations rather than the legislation.

Reasons for the delay and impasse in policy-making lie partly in the fact that Northern Ireland processes for decision-making have built into them an extensive system of vetoes and blocking mechanisms to protect group interests. If there is not a consensus a vote can be taken, but any three members of the Executive Committee, out of twelve, can require the vote on a particular matter to have cross-community support. This effectively gives the two parties with over three members, the DUP and Sinn Féin, a veto over Executive decision-making. They are therefore not encouraged to engage in negotiation and bargaining to reach agreement on difficult and divisive issues. Legislation brought before the Assembly can also be blocked by a Petition of Concern signed by thirty members of the Northern Ireland Assembly. In reality, due to the number of seats they hold in the Assembly, it is mostly the two main largest parties who can use this. The use of these has become so extensive that it has been criticised for making the Northern Ireland Assembly dysfunctional.

It has been much easier for the Executive to reach agreement on what could be considered more populist measures, such as the decision to introduce free prescriptions, free travel for the over sixties, the decision not to introduce water charges in Northern Ireland and a cap on domestic rates. It also agreed to maintain university tuition fees at at £3,600, increasing to £3,805 in 2015/16. In these areas Northern Ireland would be considered to have more beneficial arrangements than England and Wales, although it has been argued that this has inhibited a more equitable distribution of resources from the better off to the more disadvantaged, a point reinforced by unanimous support from the parties within the Executive for a reduction in corporation tax. The rationale for the reduction in Corporation Tax, which has to be legislated for by the Westminster Government as an excepted matter, is to bring the Northern Irish

rate closer to that of the Irish Republic to attract inward investment, but the UK Treasury will make a cut in the block grant to offset some loss of revenue.

What Underpins Social Policy in Northern Ireland?

It could be argued that policymaking in Northern Ireland has been marked by pragmatism rather than by ideology, and that this is a product of the consensus required at executive level. There have not been the discussions about values and principles that have occurred in Scotland and Wales, and there is a notable absence of reference in policy documents to a conceptual and value basis for policy direction. Some decisions suggest a neo-Liberal approach to policymaking, such as the unwillingness to use the limited tax-raising powers open to the Assembly, the support for a reduction in Corporation Tax, and privatisation and outsourcing of some public services. The official positions of the parties in the Executive represent a wide range of political ideology. The SDLP is the sister organisation of the Labour Party; the Ulster Unionist Party (UUP) has close historic links with the British Conservative Party, the Alliance Party has fraternal relations with the Liberal Democrats; the DUP, fundamentalist in its social and religious beliefs, is the only Executive party to explicitly espouse neo-Liberal values; Sinn Féin describes itself as 'socialist'.

Social policy in Northern Ireland could also be said to be cautious and conservative. On occasion, the religious belief of individual parties and ministers has been argued to influence policy decisions. There has been a rather limited endorsement of equality legislation, with a sexual orientation strategy promised in the 2008 Programme for Government not published by 2015. In 2013, a Sinn Féin motion in support of marriage equality for gay couples supported by the Alliance Party, the SDLP and the Green Party, was defeated by fifty-three votes to forty-two when politicians from the DUP and the UUP voted against it. Considerable controversy and legal challenge has arisen from a decision by a DUP Minister of Health to support a permanent ban on gay men donating blood in Northern Ireland, even though this has been lifted in other parts of the UK. A decision by the Minister for Justice to consult on amending Northern Ireland's abortion law to allow very restricted access to abortion on the grounds of fatal foetal abnormality has met with opposition from some political parties and the churches in Northern Ireland.

Social policymaking in Northern Ireland has been described as a lowest common denominator approach as politicians avoid or fail to deal with controversial issues. Since 2008, the two main parties in the Executive have dominated decision-making, while the smaller parties have attempted to modify decisions in line with electoral commitments. Northern Ireland has lacked the influence that can come from independent thinktanks, and the entrenched position of the political parties on some issues has led to evidence being largely ignored. The tendency has been for Northern Ireland politicians to adopt an approach to social policy issues based on communal interests: looking at how particular social policies will be to the benefit of their own community in comparison with other communities.

Emerging Issues

It could be argued that since devolution was reintroduced in Northern Ireland in 1998, social policy has not been a priority. As devolution has not bridged common ground in what could be called 'legacy issues' – issues arising from a generation of violent conflict such as identity and territory – the constitutional issues have continued to dominate political debates. However, more critical debate about social policy has perhaps begun in the light of ongoing public expenditure cuts, discussions about welfare reform and major challenges facing the health and social care system.

There have been efforts to bring greater coherence to policy design and delivery; the Office of the First and Deputy First Minister has introduced a Delivering Social Change Programme primarily to tackle poverty and social exclusion, which aims to achieve more collaborative working across departments with a number of signature programmes, including on literacy, early years development and family support. Some measures contained in the Stormont House Agreement, reached in December 2014, seek to address some of the difficulties with policymaking. This includes commitments to reducing the number of government departments

to encourage joined up government, changing the operation of the Petition of Concern mechanism, and some arrangements to enable an official opposition. The Stormont House agreement also committed to the establishment of a civic advisory panel, which would consider key social, economic and social issues and advise the Executive. This may bring a different voice to policy debates.

There is potential for greater devolution arising from the Scottish Independence Referendum and subsequent developments. What might this mean for social policy in Northern Ireland? In the context of Scotland and Wales arguing for greater devolved powers, it is difficult to see Northern Ireland doing otherwise. To date, debates about welfare have not been integral to the constitutional debate in the way that they have been in Scotland, but a push for change may come from lobbying groups, the media and the Westminster Government. Policies announced by the Conservative government elected to the Westminster Parliament in 2015, especially those relating to further social security reforms, have given rise to calls for great divergence in all of the devolved countries of the UK. With Northern Ireland MLA s continuing to fail to agree legislation on the 2012 welfare reforms and with all of Northern Ireland's political parties represented at Westminster voting against the 2015 Welfare Reform Bill (Sinn Féin MPs do not take their seats in the Westminster Parliament), there are indications of increasing tension between Westminster and the devolved Assembly.

Guide to Further Sources

A discussion of social policy and devolution in the UK can be found in D. Birrell (2009), *The Impact of Devolution on Social Policy*, Bristol: Policy Press.

Discussion of social policy under devolution in Northern Ireland can be found in A. M. Gray and D. Birrell (2012), 'Coalition government in Northern Ireland: social policy and the lowest common denominator thesis', *Social Policy and Society*, 11:1, 15–25; and G. Horgan and A. M. Gray (2012), 'Devolution in Northern Ireland: a lost opportunity?', *Critical Social Policy*, 42:3, 467–78.

For discussion of the model of governance in Northern Ireland, see R. Wilford (2010), 'Northern Ireland: the politics of constraint', *Parliamentary Affairs*, 63:1, 134–55.

The Joseph Rowntree Foundation publishes regular Monitoring Poverty and Social Exclusion reports on England, Scotland, Wales and Northern Ireland; see, for example, Monitoring Poverty and Social Exclusion in Northern Ireland at: jrf.org.uk/publications/monitoring-poverty-and-social-exclusion-northern-ireland-2014.

Review and Assignment Questions

1   Why, and to what extent, has Northern Ireland been able to consider and make changes to the UK Coalition government's welfare reform policies?

2   How has the structure of government in Northern Ireland impacted on policymaking? What changes might help to address some of the difficulties?

3   Describe what is meant by the 'lowest common denominator approach' to social policymaking in Northern Ireland and provide examples of this.

4   What kind of ideologies have been reflected in social policies introduced in Northern Ireland?

5   There are continuing debates about the degree of divergence and convergence between social policy in the different parts of the UK. What would you consider to be the amount of divergence in Northern Ireland?

Visit the book companion site at www.wiley.com/go/alcocksocialpolicy to make use of the resources designed to accompany the textbook. There you will find chapter-specific guides to further resources, including governmental, international, thinktank, pressure groups and relevant journal sources. You will also find a glossary based on *The Blackwell Dictionary of Social Policy*, help sheets, guidance on managing assignments in social policy and career advice.

24

Social Policy in Scotland

Lynne Poole

■■

Overview

- Questions about Scottish social policy and devolution have increasingly become entwined.
- The debate around the division of social policy-related powers between the UK and Scottish governments is ongoing following the 'No' vote in the 2014 Referendum on Scottish Independence.
- Devolving social policy is not merely an administrative or technical issue – it involves debates about democracy, accountability, social justice and how best to meet welfare needs.
- The devolution process that has been underway since 1998 has produced welfare settlements that are limited, complex, unsustainable and unstable.
- Nevertheless, that process has opened up space for some significant Scottish social policy initiatives that mark a divergence from English policy in important ways.

■■

The 1998 Devolution Settlement in Scotland

Whilst policymaking in the UK has historically been Westminster/London-centric, some policy areas had already developed rather differently in Scotland *prior* to the passing of the 1998

Scotland Act, in part reflecting the guarantees made following the 1707 Act of Union regarding the independence of its civil society institutions, but also the struggles and negotiations between the nations of the UK and the centre of power that have emerged periodically since. Indeed, Scottish-specific legal, education and local

The Student's Companion to Social Policy, Fifth Edition. Edited by Pete Alcock, Tina Haux, Margaret May and Sharon Wright.
© 2016 John Wiley & Sons, Ltd. Published 2016 by John Wiley & Sons, Ltd.

government systems, along with the ongoing evolution of Scotland's own policy networks, communities and associations, resulted in the need for 'sister' social policy legislation to be passed that recognised and accommodated these differences. In this period, the Scottish Executive, in the form of the Scottish Office, played a key role in dealing with the tasks of administrative devolution that followed from these arrangements. This period was thus characterised by some institutional and organisational divergence as Scotland was empowered to shape its own approach to the pursuit of shared UK policy objectives. However, significant autonomy in some welfare areas also led to a clear divergence of *policy orientation* too, perhaps best illustrated by the setting up of the Kilbrandon Committee charged with considering provision in Scottish law for dealing with juveniles in need of care or protection who came before the courts. Its recommendations led to the introduction of Scotland's Children's Hearings System following the Social Work (Scotland) Act 1968 and a more welfarist approach to juvenile justice than that taken in England (see Chapter 55).

However, post-1979, the policymaking landscape was challenged significantly as successive Conservative governments adopted a more unilateral, partisan approach to policymaking, in some cases even abandoning the tradition of separate Scottish legislation. For example, the 1990 NHS and Community Care Act was applied, with few small exceptions, north *and* south of the border. This, coupled with the lack of Conservative Party representation in Scotland after 1979, fuelled calls not only for a Scottish Parliament but, in some quarters, for more radical constitutional and political change.

Subsequently, the 1998 Scotland Act, introduced by the first Labour government of 1997, sought to reconstruct a new settlement around the devolution of some additional powers – particularly relating to education, health and housing policy, along with social work and social care policy, criminal justice, policing and prisons policy – to a reconstituted law-making Scottish Parliament. The 1998 Act did not go so far as to provide for a radical transfer of powers in *all* areas of policymaking, with key powers being retained in Westminster, including

those over immigration and asylum policy, and the tax and benefit systems. However, this settlement can be seen as a bid by the government of the day to go some way to accommodating calls from Scotland for more control over its own affairs *without* radically altering the balance of power, impinging on the sovereignty of the Westminster Parliament or overturning the existing system of administrative devolution. Those social policy areas reserved to Westminster, resulting in the retention of a UK-wide framework for social security and taxation policy (with just one notable exception in relation to the 3p variation on income tax), perhaps best illustrate this; devolution encompassed only those areas where Scottish policy, institutional, organisational and systemic divergence was *already* in evidence. However, even here provision was made through the 'Sewel Convention' for Westminster to legislate within devolved areas with the consent of the Scottish Parliament.

Policy Divergence Since 1998

Before examining some of the tensions and limitations of post-1998 Scottish social policymaking, it is useful to outline some of the key ways in which that shifting policy terrain has impacted on the shape of Scottish social policy.

Obviously, in the reserved areas of social policy we see continued convergence, so a UK-wide framework for social security and taxation policy (the Scottish Parliament having never used the 3p variation on income tax power it had), as well as a single set of age-differentiated minimum wage levels was maintained. But in those areas where the Scottish Parliament has devolved responsibility there is now evidence of some significant policy divergence. Three key examples perhaps stand out:

Example 1: Health policy

The marketisation strategies embodied in the 1990 NHS and Community Care Act (see Chapter 49) had been resisted at the level of local implementation in Scotland, but with the devolved governance of the NHS came marked differences in the organisational structure and principles underpinning NHS Scotland policy too. These built on past patterns and traditions, bringing:

- an explicit rejection of the marketisation–managerialism–consumerisation nexus at the heart of successive NHS England reforms as the *primary* coordinating mechanism for healthcare (although significant inroads were made by the private sector, for example, through the use of private finance in capital rebuilding programmes);
- a reassertion of the principles of cooperation and collaboration with professional groups and public sector workers with the aim of better supporting work across the different tiers of the NHS, different groups of health professionals and the health and social care divide.

The explicit aim was to deliver national health improvement agendas, particularly a reduction in health inequalities, within the constraints of increasingly limited budgets and growing demand.

- Free prescription charges have also been phased in, in contrast to the situation in England where prescriptions are charged for, albeit with some exceptions.

Example 2: Higher education finance

In terms of meeting maintenance costs, the Scottish Government provides a mix of loans (through the Student Loans Company) plus non-repayable, means-tested bursaries to Scottish students. But successive Scottish governments have all refused to support tuition fees (up-front or deferred), opting in 2001 for a 'graduate endowment' paid by students from the April after their graduation (set at £2,000 for 2001/02) to help finance bursaries for poorer students, and abolishing even that contribution in 2008. On their re-election in 2011, this time as a majority government, the Scottish National Party (SNP) ruled out the return of both fees and the graduate endowment in the future, although the value of the bursary was reduced in 2013, with a parallel increase in the value of loans available to students.

Example 3: Personal care

The 'majority' recommendations of the UK-wide 1999 Sutherland Inquiry were adopted in Scotland, resulting in the universal provision of free long-term 'personal care' from 2002 onwards. This was financed out of the existing block grant as additional money from the Treasury to cover the costs was not made available. The then Labour UK Government had adopted the 'minority' recommendation, which meant payments for care in England based on the means-test.

Clearly, there was much more scope for Scottish particularism in some key areas of social policy-making following the 1998 Act. However, whilst the first of these examples of policy divergence helps to illustrate the limitations of that devolution settlement in relation to the complexities of the policymaking terrain, the second two highlight additional tensions, particularly around finance.

Social Policy in Scotland: The Settlement under Strain?

The nature of this social policy settlement created much ongoing debate as different commentators highlighted the different tensions embodied in the 1998 Act. For example, reserved and devolved areas are often related and interdependent in important ways, making for a complicated policy terrain. This makes the tackling of social problems in Scotland particularly challenging as many of the factors at play remained outside the direct control of the Scottish Government. This is illustrated by the example of persistent health inequalities. Research evidence strongly suggests that as a multi-faceted issue, action in relation to a whole range of factors and actors, including levels of poverty and deprivation, is required for an effective, adequate policy response. However, the Scottish Government still did not have control over all of the policy areas that impact on the production and reproduction of health inequalities. With fiscal and social security policy reserved to Westminster, along with the minimum wage, for example, the Treasury and the Department of Work and Pensions (DWP) can limit the power of Scottish Government to act, even where there is the political will and all levels of Scottish governance identify the issue as part of their core business agenda and have the capacity to play their part.

Another tension centres around the limitations placed on any Scottish Government as a result of the financing of the 1998 devolution settlement.

Given that the block grant does not take account of additional commitments made by the Scottish Government and the UK Treasury has been unwilling to finance increased welfare rights granted to Scottish, but not English residents (such as free university tuition and free personal care), money has to be found from the existing budget. This has led to some debate about the extent to which current social policy commitments involve a reallocation of scarce resources from other public services and user groups based on the Scottish Government's self-defined priorities, which is unsustainable in the longer term.

A third area of tension can be illustrated with reference to two of the social policy reforms that have formed part of the UK Coalition's austerity package, the introduction of Universal Credit and the 'under-occupancy charge' or 'spare-room subsidy' (often referred to as the 'bedroom tax'). Here argument focused on Scotland's inability to resist new benefits or benefit cuts that may not be supported by Scottish Government. For example, should the Scottish Government wish to offset reductions in Housing Benefit paid to claimants who are deemed to be under-occupying their dwelling, it can do so only by redirecting resources from elsewhere in the budget. This is what happened in 2013, although some again questioned the sustainability of such a response.

These tensions and limitations made for a politically and financially unstable settlement, creating further debate and pressure, both in Scotland where a democratic deficit was highlighted in a context of continued Conservative electoral failure, and in England and the other nations of the Union, where questions about the fairness of uneven citizenship rights across the UK emerged. Together with the growing electoral success of the SNP, these pressures fuelled a new push for change, with the election of an SNP majority Scottish Government in 2011 providing the final impetus for a referendum on the future of Scotland's place in the Union.

The Scottish Independence Referendum: Debates and Outcomes

In the Scottish Referendum of 18 September 2014 voters were asked to vote 'Yes' or 'No' to the question: 'Should Scotland be an independent country?'. Much of the debate centred around social policy issues in a context of the 2007–8 financial crisis and the politics of austerity that were being imposed by the UK Coalition government. Of key concern was the impact that cuts to benefits and tax credit support were having on child poverty levels and those who were unemployed and wholly dependent on benefits, as well as those in low paid, reduced hours, temporary and insecure work, who needed in-work benefits to survive. The presentation of these concerns often drew on the language of meeting needs, tackling inequality and granting fundamental social rights to *all* citizens, and suggested that current austerity policy limited the scope for delivering on these agendas.

Debate also hinged on whether or not there was increased scope for a more socially just use of resources in an independent Scotland, free of the UK Coalition (and future Conservative-led governments), and with the alternatives to a neo-Liberal Labour Party on offer in a more consultative policymaking and proportional, democratic Scottish environment (notwithstanding the ongoing democratic deficit increasingly recognised at local authority level). Under the 1998 settlement, any Scottish government committed to tackling inequalities in income and wealth, health, housing and debt, for example, had limited policy options given the reserved nature of taxation and social security policy, so was independence the best solution to that problem?

This aspect of the debate, in turn, connected to discussions around the affordability of Scottish independence and a Scottish welfare system (along with the welfare bureaucracy necessary to support it). Different sources of evidence were called upon as Scottish fiscal autonomy was pitched against the reinforcing of UK-wide social solidarity through the ongoing pooling of risks and resources as the best way to protect social rights and the poorest and most at risk in society.

Debate also emerged around the very nature of austerity politics (see Chapter 21): whether they represented a necessary, politically neutral, technical response to economic and fiscal crises or, in contrast, whether the drive for deficit reduction through the further undermining of the social contract embodied in the post-war welfare settlement was really an ideologically driven, regressive attack on income, the social wage and the very idea of 'social security', in the interests of capital accumulation and elite/establishment interests and to the detriment of ordinary citizens.

These debates were made more complex given the variables relating to the 2015 UK and 2016 Scottish elections, public opinion, the performance of the Scottish economy and Scottish media representations.

Towards a New Settlement?

Voting 'No' by a margin of 55.3 per cent to 44.7 per cent (on a 84.59 per cent turnout), Scotland was promised additional devolved powers. Following on from the recommendations of the Calman Commission on Scottish Devolution, the Scotland Act 2012 had already enabled the Scottish Parliament to vary the income tax rate by 10 per cent (up from 3 per cent) from 2016 onwards. But after the referendum, the newly constituted Smith Commission was charged with the task of further building on this legislation. The White Paper titled *Scotland in the United Kingdom: An Enduring Settlement* followed in January 2015 and contained draft clauses for future legislation focusing on two key areas:

■ Revenue raising: the UK-wide income tax system will remain, but Scotland will get *additional* powers to set income tax rates and *new* powers to set tax thresholds (or personal allowances) within that system. This gives the Scottish Government increased responsibility and autonomy over its tax and spend policies, although all income tax raised in Scotland will be met with a parallel and equal reduction in the Block Grant, which will still be determined by the Barnett Formula. This is to ensure the devolved Scottish budget bears the full costs of Scottish Government policy decisions that reduce revenues or increase expenditure, and benefit in full from those that increase revenues or reduce expenditure. Other important taxes, including corporation tax, remain reserved to Westminster.
■ Welfare benefits: pensions, unemployment-related benefits and Universal Credit will remain part of a UK social security system. Housing Benefit as a whole will also remain

reserved. The administration of the Work Programme is to be devolved, but the Scottish Government will not have the power to vary conditionality or sanctions policy, nor will it be empowered to link social security, labour market and economic development policies together effectively.

In essence, newly devolved responsibilities for cash benefits will incorporate those for some carers and people with disabilities – including Attendance Allowance, Carer's Allowance, Disability Living Allowance (DLA), Personal Independence Payments (PIP), Industrial Injuries, Disablement Allowance and Severe Disablement Allowance. But these account for a very small proportion of social security expenditure in Scotland. Indeed McEwan (CCC, 2014–15: 1) calculates that 'Around 87% of Scottish welfare spending, including pensions, child and family benefits, tax credits and almost all working-age benefits, will remain reserved to Westminster after the new settlement is implemented.'

Emerging Issues

This partial devolution of taxes and social security benefits will result in a division of responsibilities across parliaments that will further complicate what is an already complex policy/policymaking terrain. Any such system requires clarity regarding the principles on which the distribution of powers rests. However, this appears to be missing. The inconsistencies and anomalies that will result will have material consequences for people in need, as well as for any future Scottish Government. The latter would be unable to determine the nature and scope of programmes and entitlements, thus limiting its ability to address social problems. The new settlement being proposed will thus be politically unstable.

Another area of tension relates to the 'No Detriment' principle embodied in the proposed legislation, which states that where either a UK or Scottish Government makes a policy decision affecting the other, reimbursements or compensatory transfers will be used to redress the balance. Put another way, neither should suffer financially from the policy decisions of the other. However, how workable this is given the complex interactions of welfare services and benefits, both reserved and devolved, is questionable. For example, if a Scottish claimant has their benefit suspended by the DWP and consequently needs to use local support services, would the DWP be required to compensate the affected Scottish local authorities? Similarly, if Scottish employment polices worked to reduce the number claiming unemployment-related benefits would the UK Treasury make a compensatory transfer to the Scottish budget equal to cash benefit savings?

A further issue is the reserved nature of immigration and asylum policy. Decisions in this area affecting Scotland remain *outside* the Scottish Government's direct control, despite the particular needs of Scottish society.

In sum, the issues emerging from the 1998 devolution settlement have not been resolved. Of course, with more far-reaching powers there would be *no guarantees* of a Scottish-specific welfare system that breaks with recent English trends given that the outcomes of future Scottish elections cannot be known. But with the constraints embodied in the White Paper even the *potential* for change in key social policy areas is lost. Scottish social policy will continue to be significantly shaped by the UK Government.

Interestingly, the political landscape in Scotland has been transformed by the independence referendum debate. With an ascendant SNP, growing support for smaller players such as the Green Party, and a Scottish Labour Party failing to maintain its position, the nature and extent of the new welfare settlement being proposed by the UK Government will be subject to further contestation and challenge. Indeed, following the 2015 UK election, which resulted in a strong SNP presence at Westminster following the collapse of Labour and Liberal Democrat support in Scotland, the SNP – as the third biggest party in the UK, holding all bar three Scottish seats – has signalled its intention to win more comprehensive powers for the Scottish Parliament, suggesting that intense debate and struggle around the nature of future constitutional and welfare arrangements in Scotland will continue. Given that the SNP formed the Scottish Government for a third time after the 2016 Scottish elections, albeit a minority government, there will be continued pressure for a more far reaching settlement, although the strength of resistance to that should not be underestimated, not least because of the majority enjoyed by the current UK Conservative government, itself also now with more support in Scotland following the relative electoral success of the party there too.

In addition, crucial questions remain regarding the *use* of both existing powers and the greater fiscal and welfare autonomy that is now being offered to Scotland. The extent to which a reworking of the Scottish social contract is *possible* should there be the political will and public support for it makes for another interesting point of discussion. For example, a broad review of local government finances may open up a debate about the possibility of Scottish local authorities raising more of their own revenues and hence options for a broader, more progressive tax base, improvements in levels of public spending accountability, and delivering a more socially just agenda, closing the gap between Scottish Government rhetoric and reality. What *is* certain is that debates around social policy in Scotland will continue to be central to the question of Scotland's future place in both the UK and Europe.

Guide to Further Resources

D. Birrell (2009), *The Impact of Devolution on Social Policy*, Bristol: Policy Press, and S. L. Greer (ed.) (2009), *Devolution and Social Citizenship in the UK*, Bristol: Policy Press, provide comprehensive and engaging accounts of the first ten years of devolved social policy in Scotland.

G. Mooney and G. Scott (eds) (2012), *Social Justice and Social Policy in Scotland*, Bristol: Policy Press, is a valuable source providing critical discussions of a range of social welfare issues relating to social justice. J. McKendrick, G. Mooney, J. Dickie, G. Scott and P. Kelly (eds) (2014), *Poverty in Scotland 2014: The Independence Referendum and Beyond*, London/Glasgow: CPAG, focus on poverty and inequality in Scotland in the run up to the 2014 Referendum, with a view to informing the debate and exploring the potential futures of Scottish social policy. G. Mooney and G. Scott (2015), 'The 2014 Scottish Independence debate: questions of social welfare and social justice', *Journal of Poverty and Social Justice*, 23:1, special issue, examine the specific role of social welfare issues in the Referendum debate showing how they were entwined with questions relating to constitutional change, democracy and political accountability.

The Centre for Constitutional Change's (CCC) website (futureukandscotland.ac.uk) offers a breadth of academic research and analysis seeking to inform the Referendum debate and to analyse the post-referendum constitutional options, drawing on the work of scholars from largely Scottish universities.

For Professor Paul Spicker's response to the setting up of the Smith Commission (with links to his submission) and his individual assessment of the potential problems embodied in the subsequent White Paper; see: paulspicker.wordpress.com.

Publications from the Scottish Parliament are available on its website at: scotland.gov.uk.

Review and Assignment Questions

1 What were the main factors and actors that drove forward the demand for Scottish devolution in 1998?

2 In what ways has Scottish social policy diverged from social policy in England?

3 What are the proposals for the devolution of additional powers in Scotland?

4 What tensions and limitations can be identified in the new devolution settlement being proposed following the Smith Commission?

5 How might future Scottish governments, seeking to meet need, tackle inequalities and protect the social rights of all groups in Scottish society, deliver these agendas within the context of limited devolution arrangements?

Visit the book companion site at www.wiley.com/go/alcocksocialpolicy to make use of the resources designed to accompany the textbook. There you will find chapter-specific guides to further resources, including governmental, international, thinktank, pressure groups and relevant journal sources. You will also find a glossary based on *The Blackwell Dictionary of Social Policy*, help sheets, guidance on managing assignments in social policy and career advice.

25

Social Policy in Wales

Paul Chaney

Overview

- Devolution in Wales has undergone rapid and profound changes since 1999. Early policies were often minor, symbolic initiatives that lacked an enforcement mechanism. This has changed with a shift to a parliamentary mode of governing and the National Assembly for Wales' gaining of primary law-making powers in 2011.
- Social policy development in Wales is intimately linked to left party strength and one-party dominance (the Welsh Labour Party). This has seen a general rejection of private sector delivery of welfare and a social democratic, statist-orientation to policy across a breadth of policy areas, including health and education.
- Current 'devolved' social policymaking in Wales is characterised by three (conflicting) factors: greater scope for taking an original, innovative approach to policy issues following revised powers set out in the 2006 devolution statute; enduring tensions and frustrations as key aspects of welfare (such as social security are, as yet, non-devolved); and remedial action to address under-performance in public services.
- Social policymaking has been shaped by a political rhetoric around equity; universalism; equality of provision, access and opportunity; and 'a new set of citizenship rights'. A key issue is whether, in the face of austerity cuts, present and future governments can maintain this expansive vision of welfare and services whilst rejecting the use of newly gained income tax-raising powers and private sector input to services.
- It is clear that in the short to medium term Welsh devolution will see further major change as key issues are addressed, such as the limited policy scrutiny capacity of an under-sized sixty-member National Assembly, the need for a separate Welsh jurisdiction in the face of an increasingly distinct legal system, and potential devolution of further policy areas such as youth justice and policing.

The Student's Companion to Social Policy, Fifth Edition. Edited by Pete Alcock, Tina Haux, Margaret May and Sharon Wright.
© 2016 John Wiley & Sons, Ltd. Published 2016 by John Wiley & Sons, Ltd.

Introduction

Devolution in Wales continues to develop at a rapid pace with far-reaching implications for social policy and welfare. When it was created in 1999, the National Assembly for Wales was a comparatively weak body. It had limited powers over secondary legislation, and it suffered from an unwieldy structure based on political parties sharing responsibility for government. Moreover, its constitutional powers over social policy were piecemeal and intertwined with those of Westminster – meaning that it was often unclear who was responsible for what. The subsequent narrative is one of increasing powers and policy-making responsibilities. Since 1998, these changes have been set out in three Westminster Acts covering the constitutional arrangements for Wales, with a further one promised in the government's 2015 legislative programme. In 2006–7, the National Assembly was remodelled on parliamentary lines (with a clear distinction between the Welsh Government and opposition parties). More recently, the results of the overwhelming 'yes' vote in the 2011 referendum on devolving primary law-making powers to Wales are now becoming evident as the Welsh Government is routinely underpinning its policies with primary Welsh legislation (Acts of the National Assembly for Wales).

The most recent devolution statute, the Wales Act 2014, conferred significant tax-raising powers (including a proportion of income tax) to the National Assembly for Wales (the latter's use is subject to a referendum). The Welsh Revenue Authority is currently being created to deal with the Welsh Government's growing tax administration role involving the collection of landfill tax and a replacement for stamp duty, to be called the Welsh Land Transaction Tax. A further milestone has been the Westminster Government's current commitment to further major constitutional change; specifically, the move to a 'reserved powers' model of devolution (as in Scotland). This will greatly increase clarity and accountability by simply listing which policy- and law-making powers are 'reserved' to Westminster and devolving the remainder to the National Assembly. It should also be noted that prior to 1999, government in Wales had a poor record in relation to use of the Welsh language. Since then, reflecting provisions in the devolution statutes, the way that government and

policy- and law-making is conducted has changed – with a commitment to public administration in both Welsh and English; although critics argue more remains to be done to ensure full equality.

Public attitudes to devolution in Wales have also undergone a major shift. In 1997, 28 per cent of 18–35 year olds and 40 per cent of 36+ year olds were opposed to devolution. The devolution referendum of that year was passed by a margin of less than one percentage point (or 6,721 votes). More recent data show a significant change indicating that devolution has become the settled will of the Welsh people. Almost two-thirds (63.5 per cent) of people voted 'Yes' in the 2011 referendum on whether the National Assembly should have primary law-making powers. Opinion polls 2011–14 show a minority (just 10 per cent of people aged 10–35 years) said they wanted the National Assembly to be abolished. The overwhelming majority, almost three-quarters of adults, wanted the status quo (28 per cent), more devolved powers (37 per cent) or independence (5 per cent). Furthermore, over 60 per cent of respondents said the National Assembly should have most say over core areas of social policy, such as health and education, as well as over areas presently not devolved, such as law and order and policing. In under two decades it is fair to say that devolved governance in Wales has been transformed from a weak 'regional' Assembly to parliamentary arrangements with the same law-making and tax-raising responsibilities as enjoyed by similar bodies around the world. As noted, this shift has profound implications for social policy-making. The greater clarity in the governance arrangements promised in the 2015 Queen's Speech has political consequences, and means Welsh governments are less able to blame Westminster for unpopular or failing policies. The prospect of devolved tax-raising powers also means difficult spending decisions can no longer be dismissed as solely the fault of the UK Government.

Politics and Ideology

One of the biggest discontinuities introduced by devolution is the fact that social policy in Wales is linked to territorial party politics and five-yearly Welsh general elections to the National Assembly (using a semi-proportional voting system). It is a four-party system and differs significantly from the party politics at Westminster. This matters to policymaking because parties seek voters' support at the ballot box with manifesto commitments to policies specifically tailored to Welsh needs. This is a challenge for the two main state-wide parties (Labour and the Conservatives), because it can mean that they hold different policy positions in the devolved elections compared with UK general elections. Such contrasts have an ideological dimension. Most notably, the Welsh Labour Party has positioned itself as 'classic' rather than 'New' Labour (see Chapter 20), and is keen to espouse traditional socialist principles. The civic nationalist party Plaid Cymru is also a left-of-centre party concerned with advancing nationhood, identity and autonomy. Parties' electoral performance in devolved elections ultimately determines which policies are mandated. In this respect, Welsh politics are distinctive because of one-party dominance and left party strength. Unlike Scotland, since the introduction of the universal franchise voters have always returned a majority of left-of-centre MPs from Welsh constituencies – and the Conservatives have always fared worse in electoral terms in Wales than in England. Labour has been the dominant party in Wales since 1945 and devolution has not changed this. Welsh Labour has continuously held government office since the National Assembly was founded (albeit in an informal alliance with the Welsh Liberal Democrats in 2000–3 and in coalition with Plaid Cymru in 2007–11). Thus, the combination of territorial politics, contrasting party ideologies and devolved elections shapes social policymaking in Wales in ways that, as the following discussion reveals, may contrast to the approach followed elsewhere in the UK.

Education and Skills

Devolution has ushered in major changes with a development of an education system that is distinct from that over the border. In compulsory phase education a separate school curriculum has emerged reflecting the priorities set by the Welsh Government. Future major changes are afoot as the Welsh Government responds to two independent policy reviews published in 2015 ('Teaching

Tomorrow's Teachers' and 'Successful Futures' – popularly known as the Furlong and Donaldson Reviews); these are likely to transform teacher training, as well as the curriculum and assessment arrangements. For children aged 3–7 years a key component of the change seen to date is the Foundation Phase (introduced in 2011). It is a flagship policy that emphasises play, experimentation and 'learning by doing' in order to develop children's problem-solving skills. It is a significant departure from more traditional, competency-based teaching. Its recommended adult to pupil ratios are 1:8 (for children aged 3–5) and 1:15 (children aged 5–7). Notwithstanding mixed evidence on its initial implementation, the policy has generally been viewed in positive terms. However, comparative data covering pupils to 16 years show school education in Wales to be falling behind the rest of the UK in reading, maths and science (although other data show that pupils in Wales do better than elsewhere in cognitive measures such as forming ideas and reasoning). Critics argue a contributory factor to the lower performance was the Welsh Government's scrapping of school league tables in 2001 and Standard Assessment Tasks (SATS) tests in 2004. This reduced professional understanding of how pupils were progressing. It has subsequently been addressed by the introduction of National Reading and Numeracy Tests (2013–14). Devolution has also seen the introduction of a new qualification, the Welsh Baccalaureate. One of its aims has been to give parity to academic and vocational routes. Revised in 2015, the Welsh Baccalaureate is based on a Skills Challenge Certificate and Supporting Qualifications; its primary aim is to promote essential skills for employment. The overall narrative of post-devolution compulsory phase education can be summed up as the emergence of a distinctively Welsh system, a general rejection of private sector involvement in schooling, and a willingness to innovate (for example, Foundation Phase, Welsh Baccalaureate). This is coupled with remedial action (for example, National Reading and Numeracy Tests) to address shortcomings and mistakes made in the early years of devolution.

In post-compulsory phase education two policy developments stand out: the creation of *Coleg Cymraeg Cenedlaethol* (National Welsh-Medium College); and distinctive funding arrangements for Welsh higher education students. The former seeks to address lamentable past failings in the provision of Welsh-medium higher education through co-working between universities across Wales to develop Welsh-medium opportunities for students. Measures taken include the funding of Welsh-speaking lecturers, as well as undergraduate and postgraduate scholarships for Welsh-medium study. More generally, there are distinctive funding arrangements for all Welsh domiciled students, including the Welsh Government Learning grant. The amount students receive depends on household income. Students pay approximately £3,500 in tuition fees (compared with the maximum of £9,000 per annum in England), with the Welsh Government paying the rest (up to a current maximum of £5,161 per annum) wherever they choose to study in the UK.

Health and Social Care

Today health accounts for almost half the Welsh Government's budget (£15.3 billion in 2015–16). Spending per head on health doubled in Wales between 2000 and 2010, and over that period the total number of NHS Wales staff increased by a quarter. Published in 2005, the first Welsh Government Health Strategy included the flagship policy of free prescriptions, a measure that is still in place. However, the Welsh health service is still struggling to meet key targets set out in successive government health strategies, including those on waiting times, ambulance response times and access to diagnostic tests. Health provides further evidence of the ideological differences between Welsh and Westminster governments. This is illustrated by the early dismantling of the NHS internal market ('inherited' from the pre-devolution era), rejection of the Private Finance Initiative (used by Westminster governments) and continued support for state delivery of services. However, NHS Wales has not been immune to reorganisation. For example, in a major restructure seven large Welsh health boards were formed in 2009. Notwithstanding ongoing issues and challenges, in 2014 an influential study by the Nuffield Foundation concluded that there had been a significant improvement in the performance of the health system in Wales over the past two decades; including a reduction in long hospital waiting times and a sharp decline in

'amenable mortality' (in other words, deaths that could have been prevented through better healthcare).

Two examples can be used to illustrate how devolution is territorialising health policy. The first is the Human Transplantation (Wales) Act 2013. It is aimed at increasing the number of organs and tissues available for transplant. In contrast to practice elsewhere in the UK, on death individuals in Wales are presumed to have consented to their organs being used for transplantation unless they have opted out (in England, Scotland and Northern Ireland patients are presumed not to have consented unless they carry a donor card). A further example, is the Social Services and Wellbeing (Wales) Act 2014, the first time there has been completely separate social care legislation for Wales. It is an example of the redefinition of citizenship rights associated with devolution. This is because it places a duty on local authorities and local health boards to assess citizens' need for care and support in their area. It sets out specific provisions for children, adults in need and carers – and places an emphasis on promoting well-being. The result of this piece of legislation is to give people in Wales rights that sometimes differ from those enjoyed elsewhere in the UK.

Housing and Homelessness

Housing and homelessness provide examples of policy development at the devolved level designed to counter the perceived negative effects of Westminster welfare policies. For example, the 'right to buy' (RTB) was a flagship policy of the first Thatcher government at Westminster. It was introduced in 1980 and gave tenants of local authority housing the right to buy their homes at a discount proportional to the duration of their tenancy. Opponents have long attacked it as privatisation of a key aspect of the welfare state. In response, and reflecting the distinctive ideological orientation of policy and politics in Wales, the Welsh Government introduced the Housing (Wales) Measure 2011 to mitigate its impact by introducing a discount cap (£16,000, much lower than England at £75,000) and giving local authorities the right to apply to the Welsh Housing Minister to suspend the RTB completely in areas of high housing demand.

Whilst social security is a non-devolved matter, in order to mitigate the effects of the 'bedroom tax' (the reduction of Housing Benefit if you live in a housing association or council property that is deemed to have one or more spare bedrooms) the Welsh Government has allocated a new fund for social landlords to build one- and two-bedroom properties across Wales. However, some have argued that the policy has not been adequately funded to build enough new housing (just 357 units in the first phase) to fully offset the impact of the 'bedroom tax'. Such issues aside, the greater significance of this and the Right to Buy policy alluded to above, is that 'devolved' policymaking can shape people's experience of social security/ welfare changes made at Westminster, even if the Welsh Government lacks powers to directly veto such measures as far as they relate to Wales.

Homelessness policy has undergone significant change in the wake of devolution. Previously it was often shaped by England and Wales legislation. Under the provisions of the Housing (Wales) Act 2014, local housing authorities are under a legal duty to undertake homelessness reviews as well as to formulate and adopt a homelessness strategy. These measures are designed to place an emphasis on preventing homelessness, not least by providing accommodation and support for people before they become homeless. This aspect of policy provides a further example of the territorialisation of welfare rights. Specifically, the provisions of this policy mean that if a person threatened with homelessness and eligible for help applies to a local housing authority in Wales, the authority must ensure that 'suitable accommodation does not cease to be available for the applicant's occupation'. Specific provisions relate to different categories of people, including those leaving prison or youth detention, young people leaving care and people leaving the armed forces. In welfare terms, such policy development (re-)defines what the citizen can expect from the state in Wales and provides mechanisms for legal redress if public bodies fail in their duties.

Transport

Welsh transport policy has been hampered by limited legislative powers and shared policy competency with Westminster. Greater powers were conferred under the Transport (Wales) Act 2006, and subsequent Welsh Government strategies have emphasised the reduction of environmental impacts from transport, integrating local transport and improving access between settlements. An early flagship transport policy was the introduction of 'free' bus and local train travel in Wales for people aged 60+, as well as for disabled people and injured service personnel/veterans. The statist orientation of Welsh governments is reflected in three notable developments that can be seen as a form of 'quasi-nationalisation'. Cardiff Airport was taken into public ownership in 2013 with the aim of developing a base for tourism and economic growth and, in 2014, the transport minister established a not-for-dividend wholly-owned subsidiary company of the Welsh Government. This is part of the goal of achieving a more effective integrated transport system with a view that it could run the Welsh rail franchise when it is renewed in 2018. Moreover, since 2007, successive governments have extended state funding for a daily air service to improve access between north and south Wales.

Equality and Human Rights

It is something of a paradox in that equality of opportunity is technically a non-devolved issue. Yet the reality is that successive Welsh governments have developed a broad range of policies and legislation on equality and human rights. Again, the significance of this is the rise of different, legally enforceable citizenship rights over the way public bodies implement social policy in Wales. Thus, uniquely, the devolution statute places a duty on the Welsh Government to promote equality for all people in the exercise of all its functions (Government of Wales Act, 2006, s.77). Furthermore, 'devolved' public bodies have Wales-specific equality duties (under the Equality Act 2010 (Statutory Duties) (Wales) Regulations 2011). Inter alia, these require bodies to publish equality objectives, to involve those targeted in the objectives in preparing, publishing or reviewing a Strategic Equality Plan, and to publish an action plan to address the causes of any gender pay difference. In a further example, the Welsh Language (Wales) Measure 2011 places Wales-specific duties on public bodies delivering services in Wales. These include the requirement to 'promote or facilitate the use of the Welsh language, or to work towards ensuring that the Welsh language is treated no less favourably than the English language'. In addition, the Rights of Children and Young Persons (Wales) Measure 2011 places a duty on all Welsh Government ministers to have due regard to the substantive rights and obligations within the United Nations Convention on the Rights of the Child.

Emerging Issues

The party politics of Wales, notably one-party dominance by Welsh Labour – coupled with left-of-centre party strength (Labour, Plaid Cymru and the Welsh Liberal Democrats) – exerts a strong influence on the underlying ideology and aims of social policy in Wales. This has seen the general rejection of private sector involvement in public services (in contrast to practice in England). Instead, successive governments have developed state provision in line with a broadly socialist model of welfare. However, a key challenge for ministers will be to sustain this expansive vision of the state in the face of austerity cuts and the Welsh Government's stated opposition to using newly devolved income tax-raising powers to raise revenue. It is clear that the public sector and local government are facing significant restructuring over future years with a likely reduction in their size and capacity. This will inevitably affect their ability to deliver services. One potential solution is packaged in the political rhetoric of 'co-production'. This involves civil society organisations taking responsibility alongside the state for the design and delivery of some services. However, it is far from certain that this will compensate for the unprecedented scale of the likely cuts. Difficult questions remain about whether some of the policies and universal entitlements seen to date (for example, higher education student grants, free prescriptions, etc.) are sustainable over the longer term.

Overall, it is clear that devolution has transformed social policymaking in Wales. Yet constitutional reform is far from a finished 'project'. As noted, further major changes in the constitutional arrangements for Wales are likely in the near future. Some of these were set out in the recommendations of the UK Government Commission on Devolution. Published in 2014, its concluding report made wide-ranging recommendations on increasing the devolved policy responsibilities. For example, 'we conclude that policing should be devolved'; there should be 'the creation of a Welsh Criminal Justice Board'; 'the youth justice system should be devolved'; and there should be 'further devolution of powers on rail, ports, bus and taxi regulation, and speed and drink drive limits'. Importantly, the Commission recommended that 'there is also a case for further administrative devolution in the courts system and judiciary, particularly as the volume of Welsh law develops; and 'the size of the National Assembly should be increased so that it can perform its scrutiny role better'. Many, though not all, of the recommendations will be set out in the Wales Bill 2015. This will see key changes become law in 2016, including further devolution of transport (including responsibility for ports, taxi and bus regulation, and road speed limits); licensing for all onshore oil and gas exploration in Wales (including fracking); setting the law on elections (including whether 16- and 17-year-olds should vote in Welsh elections); and enshrining the permanence of the National Assembly for Wales in UK law and giving it the legal power to rename itself the Welsh Parliament.

Guide to Further Sources

D. Birrell (2009), *The Impact of Devolution on Social Policy*, Bristol: Policy Press; K. Blakemore and L. Warwick-Booth (2013), 'Devolution and social policy', in *Social Policy: An Introduction*, Buckingham: Open University Press, ch. 13; P. Chaney, T. Hall and A. Pithouse (2001), *New Governance – New Democracy?* Cardiff: University of Wales Press; P. Chaney and M. Drakeford (2004), 'The primacy of ideology: social policy and the first term of the National Assembly for Wales', *Social Policy Review*, 16, 211–43; P. Chaney (2011), *Equality and Public Policy: Exploring the Impact of Devolution in the UK*, Cardiff: University of Wales Press; J. Mitchell and A. Mitchell (2011), *Devolution in the UK*, Manchester: Manchester University Press; C. Williams (2011), *Social Policy for Social Welfare Practice in a Devolved Wales*, 2nd edn, Birmingham: Venture

Press; S. Wright (2014), 'Devolution and social policy', in H. Bochel and G. Daly (eds), *Social Policy*, London, Routledge, ch. 4.

Review and Assignment Questions

1 Devolution in Wales has developed rapidly since 1999. What have been the main changes and what do they mean for the way social policy is made?

2 What impact have one-party dominance (the Labour Party) and the left-of-centre orientation of Welsh politics had on the way policy is made in Wales?

3 What evidence is there that devolution has introduced distinctive, territorially specific policies in Wales?

4 To what extent has devolution in Wales been accompanied by new legal rights over the way services are delivered and social policy implemented?

5 How has devolution changed the way policy is made and is it delivering distinctive 'made in Wales' policies?

Visit the book companion site at www.wiley.com/go/alcocksocialpolicy to make use of the resources designed to accompany the textbook. There you will find chapter-specific guides to further resources, including governmental, international, thinktank, pressure groups and relevant journal sources. You will also find a glossary based on *The Blackwell Dictionary of Social Policy*, help sheets, guidance on managing assignments in social policy and career advice.

PART V
Contemporary Context and Challenges

26

The Demographic Challenge

Jane Falkingham and Athina Vlachantoni

Overview

- Changes in the size and composition of the population are the result of the combined effects of changes in mortality, fertility and migration. However, the most important driver behind population ageing is the decline in fertility rates.
- The key demographic changes in the UK over the last century include a declining fertility rate, a fluctuating but generally low mortality rate and the shift of the UK from a being country of emigration to country of predominantly inward immigration.
- The UK today can be described as an aged society, where the proportion of older people (aged 65 and over) increasingly represents a greater part of the total population.
- Changes in mortality, fertility and migration in the UK have been taking place alongside an increasing diversity in the ethnic composition of the population, and changes in family structures and living arrangements.
- Understanding demographic changes is a key part of designing and implementing social policies for a constantly changing population.

Population Change

A basic understanding of the drivers and consequences of population change is essential for all students of social policy. This is because demographic trends determine the number of children and other pupils requiring education, the composition of families requiring housing and social benefits, and the size of the current and future older population who will rely on pensions in later life. Demographic changes also impact upon the demand for, and supply of, health and social care, with

The Student's Companion to Social Policy, Fifth Edition. Edited by Pete Alcock, Tina Haux, Margaret May and Sharon Wright.
© 2016 John Wiley & Sons, Ltd. Published 2016 by John Wiley & Sons, Ltd.

improvements in mortality meaning more people will survive into old age. At the same time, changes in patterns of family formation and dissolution mean that older people may continue to live with a partner in later life, but more will also have experienced a divorce and may be estranged from their adult children and grandchildren.

However, the relationship between demography and social policy is not one way, as social policies may also impact on demography. For example, the introduction of sanitation into Britain's burgeoning cities during the nineteenth century contributed to the reduction of the death rate, whilst the introduction of midwives towards the end of the same century led to improvements in infant mortality (see Chapter 16). Today, family policies such as parental leave, child care and cash benefits can impact on women's employment and fertility behaviour, and international migration flows are directly regulated by migration policies. Here we explore recent changes in the key demographic variables of fertility, mortality and migration (see Box 26.1), as well as trends in marriage and divorce and their implications for changing family structures. All these changes are set in the context of an ageing population.

A Century of Population Change in the UK

The last century witnessed a transformation of the UK population. In 1901, the total population of the UK was 39.3 million; by 2001 it had reached 59 million, and in 2014 the population was estimated to be just over 64 million. In 1901, the total fertility rate, which is the average number of children a woman could expect to bear over her lifetime if current birth rate rates prevailed during her entire reproductive lifespan, was 3.5; by 2001 it was 1.7, and by 2014 had reached 1.9 children.

Similarly, in 1901 the average life expectancy in the UK for a man was 45 years and for a woman it was 48 years, but by 2001, this had increased by thirty years to 75 for men and 78 for women. Today, a new-born baby boy could expect to live 79 years and a new-born baby girl 83 years if mortality rates remain the same as they were in the UK throughout their lives. The improvement in mortality across the last hundred years is equivalent to three years in every decade of the twentieth century, or 3.6 months in every year, or 2.1 days in every week, or 7 hours in every day. The advance in survivorship should be seen as one of the greatest achievements of the twentieth century, but it also has important policy implications, which are discussed further below.

Figure 26.1 shows the annual number of births and deaths registered in the UK since 1901. There are several things to note in this figure. First, in all years (except 1976) births exceeded deaths, resulting in a positive rate of natural increase in the population. The gap between births and deaths shows the growth in the population, excluding migration. Second, the two baby boom cohorts following the end of the two world wars are clearly visible in the peaks in births 1920 and 1947, as is the more extended baby boom of the 1960s and the recent increase in births over the last decade. Finally, the peaks in deaths around the world wars are also visible. Over the century, the annual number of deaths has risen, reflecting the growth in the overall size of the population. The year-on-year trend has also become more stable as the impact of epidemics and infectious diseases has reduced.

Box 26.1   The Drivers of Population Change

The size and age structure of the population at any one time is determined by the population in the previous period plus births and minus deaths. If the population is an 'open' population, it is also important to take into account migration, adding the in-migrants and deducting the out-migrants.

The formula to calculate the population is known as the *balancing equation*, and is expressed as:

$$Pt2 = Pt1 + B - D + I - E$$

where:

Pt2 population at time t2
Pt1 population at time t1
B births
D deaths
I in-migration
E out-migration (or emigration)

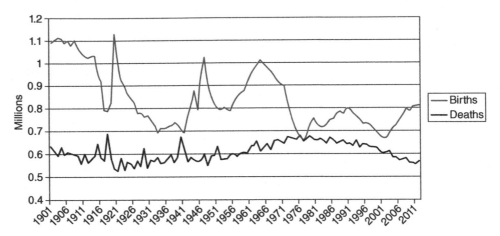

Figure 26.1 Births and deaths in the UK, 1901–2012.
Source: ONS Vital Statistics: population and health reference tables.

An Ageing Population

One of the main consequences of the changes in fertility and mortality across the last century has been a dramatic shift in the age structure of the population. Figure 26.2 shows the percentage of Britain's population aged 65 and over, and 85 and over. We can see that the share in the total population of those aged 65 and over has increased dramatically. In 1901, around 5 per cent of the population were aged 65 and over, by 1941 it had doubled to 10 per cent and by 1981 it had reached 15 per cent. This share has been fairly stable for the last thirty years.

However, over the next twenty years, we can expect to see a significant rise in the percentage of those aged 65 and over, as the baby boom cohorts (those born in the late 1950s to mid-1960s) begin to enter retirement. In 2021, 19 per cent of the population will be aged 65 and over, and this will rise to 23 per cent by 2031 and 25 per cent by 2041. The graph also indicates the ageing of the elderly population itself, reflecting an increase in the proportion of the 'oldest old'. The proportion of those aged 85 and over was only 0.2 per cent in 1901. Today, the 'oldest old' account for about 2.5 per cent of the total population, which numbers 1.5 million people, and by 2041, this will have more

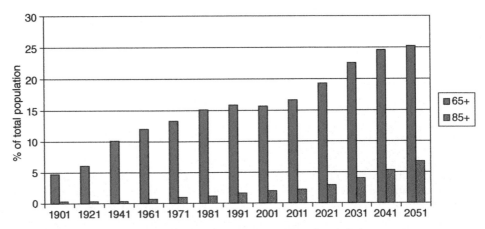

Figure 26.2 Proportion of Britain's population aged 65+ and 85+ (%), 1901–2051.
Source: 1901–2011: ONS Population Trends; 2021–51: ONS Population Projections 2012 based (principal projection).

than doubled, reaching 3.8 million – accounting for over 5 per cent of the total population.

How does a population age? It is important to distinguish between individual ageing and population ageing. Individuals age inevitably from birth to death, and can only become older. Although there is a debate about physiological ageing and slowing the pace of ageing, technology has not yet been successful in the quest to reverse the ageing process. In contrast to individual ageing, which can happen only in one direction, populations can become older or younger depending upon their age structure, that is, the share of the population in different age groups.

An ageing population is one where the proportion, rather than the absolute number, of older people is increasing (generally taken as those aged 65 and older). The age of a population is generally measured in one of three ways: the proportion of the population aged under 16; the proportion aged 65 or over; or the median age of the population. The UK today may be said to have an 'aged' rather than an 'ageing' population, in that a significant rise in the proportion of older people has already taken place.

The age structure of a population is determined by fertility, mortality and migration. The most important factor in determining the proportion of elderly people in the population is not the improvement in the ability to survive to older ages, but rather changes in the sizes of all age groups. More particularly, whether a national population is relatively young or old depends on the numbers of children born, because the level of fertility determines the numbers of people entering the population at its base. As such, high-fertility populations tend to include a larger proportion of children relative to adults of parental age, whilst low-fertility populations tend to have few children relative to current parents, who in turn are not numerous relative to their parents. Falling fertility leads to fewer younger people in the population and hence a rise in the proportion who are elderly. Thus, the main engine driving the ageing of the UK population has been the decline in births across the twentieth century.

However, that is not to say that mortality is unimportant. Improvements in mortality and increasing life expectancy lead to an increase in the proportion of people who can expect to survive to old age. Moreover, mortality decline at older ages is particularly important for the ageing of the elderly population, itself, that is the increase in the proportion of the 'oldest old'. The projected increase in the proportion of those aged 65 and over, and 85 and over, raises challenges for the design of social policies in the future, as older people will comprise a larger part of the total 'client' population of the welfare state (see Chapter 60).

These changes are taking place alongside other demographic and socio-economic changes affecting the quality of life of older people. In 2011, 9 per cent of people aged 65 and over were divorced compared with just 5 per cent a decade earlier, and 31 per cent were living alone. Although later life is not always synonymous with deteriorating health for older people, these changes have implications for the amount and kind of support older people can be expected to require in the future and for the organisation of long-term care provision (see Chapter 54).

Migration

Across the whole of the twentieth century more people emigrated from the UK than immigrated, with the net exodus from the UK being just over 15 million. Without this net out-migration, the growth in the size of the population would have been even higher. However, as we will see below, today the UK is a country of net in-migration. Figure 26.3 shows trends in international migration to and from the UK over the past two decades. Much has been written in the press concerning the increase in migration, particularly following the accession of the A8 countries (Czech Republic, Estonia, Hungary, Latvia, Lithuania, Poland, Slovakia, Slovenia) to the EU in 2004. The UK was only one of three European countries that fully opened their borders and labour markets to migrants from such countries.

However, although there was a clear rise in net migration in 2004–5, net migration was already at around 175,000 in the early 2000s. Moreover, through the decade significant numbers of people have continued to emigrate. Emigration peaked at over 425,000 in 2008, whilst immigration has fallen since 2010, reflecting the introduction of a points-based system (PBS) aimed at managing migration for work or study in the UK.

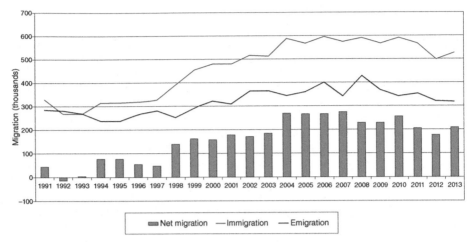

Figure 26.3 Long-term international migration, UK, 1991–2013.
Source: ONS, Long-term International Migration 2013, table 1.01 (2014).

Nevertheless, the numbers of people migrating to the UK has remained at over half a million a year. In 2013, there were around 210,000 more immigrants arriving than emigrants leaving, and migration accounted for 46 per cent of the overall increase in the size of the population, with the excess of births over deaths accounting for the other 54 per cent.

Some of the rise in births since 2001 shown in Figure 26.1 is due to the increase in the number of births to non-UK-born mothers. In 2000, 15.5 per cent of births were to non-UK-born mothers; by 2013 this had risen to 26.5 per cent. Poland, Pakistan and India were the three most common countries of birth for non-UK-born mothers in 2013. Both the rising birth rate and the growing share of births to non-UK-born mothers have

implications for the provision of school places and support for children with English as an additional language (EAL). Data from the 2013 School Census show that one in six primary school pupils in England and one in eight pupils at secondary schools do not have English as their first language.

An Increasingly Diverse Population

One outcome of extended periods of migration to the UK is the country's increasingly diverse ethnic composition. Figure 26.4 shows that in 2011 just over a fifth of all young people aged 15–19 in England were from a background other than White British.

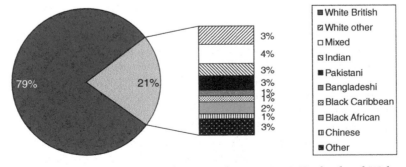

Figure 26.4 Ethnic composition of population aged 15–19, 2011, England and Wales.
Source: ONS 2011 Census.

The number of older people from a black and minority ethnic background is still relatively low. According to the 2011 Census, people from minority ethnic groups comprise less than 3 per cent of the total population aged 65 and over in Britain, and the largest minorities within this group are of an Irish, Indian, Black Caribbean or Pakistani origin. However, as the cohorts who came to Britain in the 1960s, 1970s and 1980s move through the life course and enter into retirement, this proportion will increase and service providers from all sectors will need to respond to a much more diverse older population.

Changing Patterns of Partnership and Family Formation

The last thirty years have seen significant changes in patterns of partnership and family formation. Figure 26.5 shows the percentage of women who have experienced various life course events according to the year of their birth. For example, amongst women born in 1943–7, 75 per cent had married by age 25, and this contrasts with (24 per cent of women born thirty years later, in 1973–7. Although the number of marriages has declined across successive birth cohorts, this does not indicate a rejection of partnership per se, as the

percentage of women cohabiting has increased. However, the rise in cohabitation has not been sufficient to offset the fall in marriage, and overall fewer young women are entering partnerships, and those that do tend to enter partnerships later.

Alongside the delay in partnership, the average (mean) age at childbirth has also increased steadily since the late 1960s. The delay in child bearing is clearly visible in Figure 26.5 with just 30 per cent of those women born in 1973–7 having had a child by age 25, compared with over half of women at the same age who were born in 1943–7. In 2013, the average age at first birth amongst women in England and Wales was 28.3 years compared with 23.7 years in 1970. It is, however, important to bear in mind that this is an average, and that the UK still has one of the highest teenage pregnancy rates in Europe. In 2012, there were 19.7 live births per thousand women aged under 20 in the UK compared with 12.6 births among the EU28. Across the EU28 in 2012, the birth rate among women aged 15–19 was lowest in Denmark (4.4), Slovenia (4.5) and the Netherlands (4.5). The highest birth rates were in Romania and Bulgaria at 39.4 and 42.6, respectively (Eurostat, 2014). In February 2010, the government published a policy document entitled *Teenage Pregnancy Strategy: Beyond 2010*, which set out a series of measures to tackle the high teenage pregnancy rate,

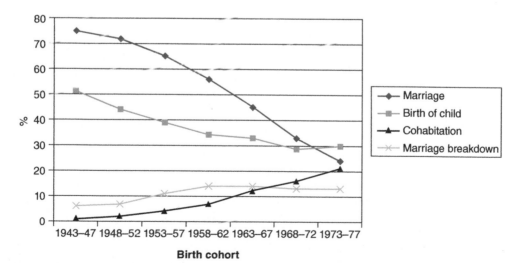

Figure 26.5   Percentage of women who have experienced various life events by age 25, by birth cohort.
Source: Adapted from figure 2.17 in ONS (2009) Social Trends 39.

including improving the quality of sex and relationship education in schools and increasing access to online advice.

The decline in marriage is reflected in the increasing proportion of children who, according to their birth certificate, are born outside a legal marital union. In the nineteenth century, the percentage of all births outside a marriage hovered at around 7 per cent. This rate persisted through the twentieth century, apart from a small rise during both world wars. However, since the 1970s there has been a consistent and steep increase, and, in 2013, 47 per cent of all children were born to parents who were not legally married.

Many parents do still go on to marry after the birth of a child, but the combination of declining marriage and increasing partnership breakdown has meant that the proportion of dependent children in the UK living with married parents has fallen from 72 per cent in 1997 to 63 per cent in 2014. In contrast, the proportion of dependent children living with cohabiting couples rose from 8 per cent to 14 per cent, whilst the proportion of dependent children living in lone parent families has remained relatively stable, increasing from 22 per cent to 23 per cent.

The number of dependent children living in different family types has implications both for the way in which services and benefits aimed at children are provided and for the future availability of informal care from kin. It is an open question whether children will be willing to provide care for a step-parent or for a natural parent that they may not have grown up with. Similarly, it is unclear whether women and men in mid-life will be willing to care for their ex-parent-in-laws.

Emerging Issues

Changes in the timing of demographic events such as partnership and childbirth, combined with an increasing average life expectancy, have resulted in a continuous restructuring of the life course into the future. For example, according to the latest projections by the ONS, one-third of all the children born in the UK in 2013 will live to celebrate their 100th birthday, and some experts think this figure could even rise to one in two. Such remarkable demographic changes have been taking place alongside other social and economic changes, for

example, the economic recession which started in 2008 has impacted on patterns of immigration into the UK, as a decrease in employment opportunities has forced many migrants to return to their home countries.

The extent of demographic changes over the last few decades has also meant that it has become more difficult to predict what kind of lifestyle, work, leisure and family roles individuals may be engaged in at a particular chronological age. Finally, we can expect the increasing diversity in the composition of the younger population in the UK, for example, the ethnic diversity of the teenage population described in Figure 26.4, to be reflected among the older population as this cohort moves through the life course.

One of the key questions facing policymakers is how to accommodate for these demographic changes in order to continue tackling social problems, satisfying social needs and maximising well-being across all age groups (see Chapter 3). A key part of designing social policies to take demographic changes into account is understanding population change, the various forms it takes, its dynamic nature and what it means in terms of policy implications.

Guide to Further Sources

An excellent source of information on the UK population and on families and households is the annual publication *Social Trends* published by the Office for National Statistics (ONS). Since 2010, *Social Trends* has been published online and is available at: www.statistics.gov.uk/socialtrends/stissue.

Another valuable source of data and commentary on demographic changes is the ONS. Its website, www.ons.gov.uk, includes current and historical population projections, as well as statistics on specific subject areas, such as life expectancy, living arrangements and the older population.

Other useful websites include the ESRC Centre for Population Change at: www.cpc.ac.uk.

Comparative data on countries in the European Union is available through the European Statistics (Eurostat) portal at: europa.eu/documentation/statistics-polls/index_en.htm, and useful comparative data and research findings on demographic trends in Europe can also be found on the website of the Population Europe partnership at: www.population-europe.eu. Finally, international comparative data are available from the United Nations Statistics Division at: unstats.un.org/unsd/demographic/default.htm, and the Population Reference Bureau at: www.prb.org, which is based in the USA but contains useful articles and resources on global trends.

Review and Assignment Questions

1   What are the key drivers of population change?
2   What have been the most important demographic changes in the UK over the last century?
3   What causes population ageing?
4   How can we measure population ageing?
5   What are the some of the implications for social policy of population change in general?

Visit the book companion site at www.wiley.com/go/alcocksocialpolicy to make use of the resources designed to accompany the textbook. There you will find chapter-specific guides to further resources, including governmental, international, thinktank, pressure groups and relevant journal sources. You will also find a glossary based on *The Blackwell Dictionary of Social Policy*, help sheets, guidance on managing assignments in social policy and career advice.

27

The Economic Context

Kevin Farnsworth and Zoë Irving

■■

Overview

■ The economy and social policy have a symbiotic relationship that has developed in tandem with the development of capitalism.

■ We can identify ways in which the needs of the economy and the needs of people combine, but there are also conflicting needs which are managed through the processes of political democracy.

■ Economic growth underpins the development and sustainability of social policy, but equally social policy is crucial to the achievement of economic growth.

■ Problems arise for the sustainability of social policy when there is a mismatch between the raising of tax revenues, the levels of spending promised by governments, and the extent to which a gap between these is closed through government borrowing.

■ Social policy played a key role in mitigating the social and economic effects of the 2008 financial crisis, but is also under threat as governments seek to reduce levels of spending and debt.

■■

The economy is an essential driver of social policy development and change. Throughout the twentieth century, from the 1930s Great Depression to the demands of post-war reconstruction in the 1940s, to the 1970s oil crisis, to the rise of the 'global economy' in the 1990s, periods of rapid economic transformation have been accompanied by significant shifts in welfare provision. The 2007–8 economic crisis may similarly be viewed in future as a watershed moment for welfare states

The Student's Companion to Social Policy, Fifth Edition. Edited by Pete Alcock, Tina Haux, Margaret May and Sharon Wright.
© 2016 John Wiley & Sons, Ltd. Published 2016 by John Wiley & Sons, Ltd.

in the twenty-first century. What is less often highlighted in discussions of the importance of the economy to social policy outcomes is the centrality of social policies in shaping of the economic context itself. Although at an abstract level social policies are based on different sets of principles to economic policies, ideas of social justice, for example, rather than a desire for efficiency, in practice it is often difficult to disentangle the social and economic elements.

The Needs of People and the Needs of the 'Economy'

Industrialisation and the rise of democracy in the seventeenth and eighteenth centuries saw the emergence of new social problems, but also the political means to address them. The development of capitalism, as an economic system, shaped social needs and the ways in which they are recognised and met, not least through social policies and the welfare state.

Economic and social needs go to the heart of the welfare state (see Part I). It can be argued that social policies that satisfy both social and economic needs will create the optimal conditions that enable labour (or citizens more broadly) and capital (business in general and individual businesses) to thrive and will help to reconcile otherwise competing needs and interests (Gough, 2000). This notion of *needs* suggests that there is some connection between the satisfaction of a given need or set of needs and the sustainability of both individual citizens and the whole system of capitalism. Without the satisfaction of these needs both harm to individuals and failure of the system will result. At the most basic level, the physiological needs of human beings as biological entities need to be satisfied, but, beyond this, if they are to *thrive*, they require the economic, political and social means of survival.

We might similarly argue that capitalism itself has institutional or systemic needs, including the particular needs of businesses operating within the system. In order to produce, trade and profit, businesses need a stable fiduciary system and a well-established rule of law, but they also require access to an adequate supply of willing and disciplined workers who are appropriately skilled, fit and healthy for work, with a good balance between

new entrants to the workplace and older, retirees. Individually, companies need to be able to extract ever-greater profits, through either greater production or lower costs. Thus, advanced economic needs generate growing dependence on the welfare state for health, education and social security provisions, as well as a range of social services that contribute to effective social reproduction. Although the needs of people and the needs of the economy are sometimes in harmony, there is also potential conflict, since need satisfaction makes demands on resources and the principles of distribution preferred by citizens and business interests are not necessarily shared. In addition, there are also conflicts of interest between both types of business in different sectors of the economy (manufacturing and services, for example) and the interests of particular businesses and those of wider macro-economic strategies (construction companies and the management of interest rates, for example). At the points of conflict, it is political democracy that determines whose needs can be privileged and how.

One way of viewing this complex relationship between social policy and the economic context, then, is as a continual struggle between 'politics' and 'markets'. From this perspective the people's representatives elected to government and the collective representation of workers through trade unions act as counter-forces to economic interests that reduce societal relations to simple matters of exchange for profit regardless of human values. Through processes of democratic government the political demands of social groups for the amelioration of their working and living conditions are articulated, negotiated and enacted through social policies such as the provision of pensions, unemployment benefits, healthcare and so on. The outcomes of these political struggles and the consequent power balances between governments (the state), employees (labour) and employers (capital) vary widely between countries according to their national histories, industrial make up and political systems, and can be distinguished as different 'varieties of capitalism'. This does not necessarily mean that labour interests promote the welfare state whilst employers oppose its development. Sometimes employers firmly support the expansion of particular social policies that are regarded as conducive to higher productivity or increasing competitiveness, for example.

Box 27.1 Competitiveness and the Welfare State

An important and ongoing question for social policy analysis is: does the welfare state increase or decrease national economic performance? If welfare states undermine economic growth, the economic (but not the social) arguments for them may be weakened. Although this is a disputed area, there is growing evidence to suggest that social policies are essential for stable and strong economic growth. This is because social policies help to increase employee productivity at the same time that they help to smooth out naturally occurring economic booms and slumps. These positive effects are recognised by social policy scholars and trade unionists, but also business interests acknowledge the importance of a range of welfare policies to a strong economy. In its most recent World Competitiveness Index, the World Economic Forum (otherwise known as the DAVOS group) stated that: 'Basic education increases the efficiency of each individual worker', 'higher education and training is crucial' and 'A healthy workforce is vital to a country's competitiveness and productivity'.

The Promises and Pursuit of Economic Growth

Although there is variation in the types of welfare state model that countries possess (see Part X), the strength or weakness of the economy – the total production of an economy divided by the total population (GDP per capita) – very much determines the scope of social policies. There are two key dimensions to the social policy boundaries set by economic circumstances.

■ First, in terms of economic preconditions, the emergence of a 'welfare state' can only occur in states that have reached positions of enduring economic stability and have established functioning systems of law and public administration, including having the means to fund public policies through taxation. This status allows the development of formal systems of provision – education, health and social security, for example, that promote welfare and support further economic advancement. In states that are limited by a lack of natural resources, conflict or environmental instability, for example, economic insecurity prevents the consolidation of these structures and social policy is restricted to programmes and interventions dependent on external loans from international financial organisations, aid packages and state revenues drawn from whatever goods the country can export.

■ Second, within states that have achieved enough stability to have established or 'institutionalised' systems of welfare provision, the economic context continues to determine the extent to which these systems can expand or shrink through the continuing availability and redistribution of the state's resources. The continuing availability of resources depends on the balance between demand for benefits and services (which increases over time) and the extent to which economic growth can be maintained to match rising demands. The continuing redistribution of resources depends, as noted above, on political decision-making in relation to questions of social justice.

Economic growth is the condition on which the sustainability of welfare states is assumed to depend because it represents an upward spiral of production and consumption that enables governments to balance their national accounts. Jobs are created, employment expanded, wages are paid allowing workers to buy goods and services, and tax revenue is generated, which allows governments to finance public expenditure. A lack of growth threatens the opposite effects – unemployment and under-employment, higher demand for state-funded benefits and services as people are less able to meet their basic needs, and at the same less revenue generated by taxation because fewer people are in work. In the twentieth century, how governments dealt with periods of low growth has shifted from strategies based on the economic theory of John Maynard Keynes (1883–1946), which were dominant from the 1930s, to those reflecting a return to neo-classical economic theories that shaped governments' economic management before the Great Depression.

Keynesian economic theory represented a critical break with existing economic orthodoxy because it stressed the importance of comprehensive welfare states to post-war growth models. It proposed that unemployment benefits would serve as powerful counter-cyclical spurs during periods of economic downturn. Better services would be funded through higher taxation, which, in turn, would be afforded through increasing productivity and increasing wages. The break with Keynesianism came in the 1970s, when falling growth and economic instability gave rise to neo-Liberal growth models. Neo-Liberal economics (see Chapter 9) regard economic freedom, limited state intervention and more residual social policies as the necessary ingredients for economic growth. Since the 1980s, neo-Liberal strategies have encouraged the 'liberalisation' of trade, reducing or removing what are regarded as barriers to competition and growth, high corporate taxation and national tariffs (import and export taxes), and employment laws, for example. In addition to the deregulation of economies however, neo-Liberal economics also have important consequences for the approach taken by governments to the role of social policy.

Taxation, Spending and Debt

The dominant (neo-Liberal) view since the 1980s has been that state intervention, and the taxation required to pay for it, stifles private sector investment, growth and profits, and thus ultimately undermines economic growth and national prosperity. The underlying assumption of neo-Liberalism is that the demand for more extensive public spending will continually increase for various reasons. Most importantly, drawing on libertarian and public choice arguments from previous times, neo-Liberals argue that governments will invariably face, but fail to satisfy, ever-growing demand for public services; politicians and civil servants will seek to promote their own interests within their own government departments; and, all the time, higher state expenditure will crowd out more efficient private sector investment, undermine choice and discourage hard work and self-sufficiency. Even the successes of welfare states such as increasing life expectancy will create further demand as ageing populations impose greater health and pensions costs. As Figure 27.1 shows, public spending has continued to increase, even in the face of financial crisis, and

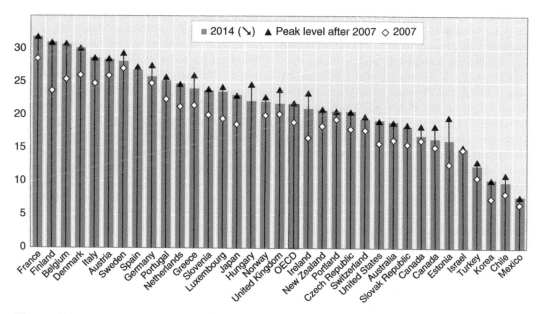

Figure 27.1 Public expenditure as a % of GDP, 2007, peak level after 2007, and 2014.
Source: OECD (2014), *Social Expenditure Update: social spending is falling in some countries, but in many others it remains at historically high levels. Insights from the OECD Social Expenditure database (SOCX)*, OECD, Paris, November.

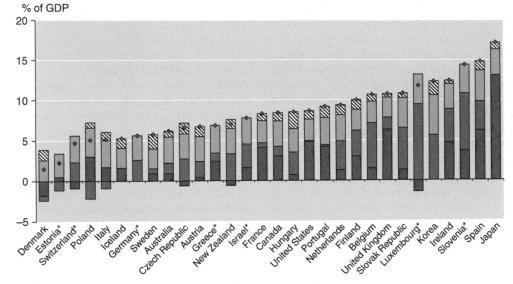

Figure 27.2 OECD projections of public spending requirements and the fiscal gap (assuming debt to GDP ratio of 60%) up to 2060.
Source: OECD (2014), 'Policy Challenges for the next 50 years', OECD Economic Paper No. 9, July 2014.

as Figure 27.2 shows, the pressures on public finances are likely to continue for decades to come.

One solution to increasing demand for public services and growing deficits is to raise taxation, but this is both economically and politically risky. Economically, increasing taxation risks dampening demand and diverting more resources away from the private sector. And politically, increasing taxation is a highly unpopular political exercise for any government. Personal taxation is not often welcomed by electorates, and corporate taxation is not welcomed by businesses, and is rendered less reliable in the context of global markets and the increasing incidence of corporate tax avoidance. Strong globalisation theorists argue that higher corporate taxes risk driving capital to other countries with less demanding tax regimes. In modern times, therefore, governments have tend to become more reliant on stealth taxes – including consumption taxes (such as VAT) – that are designed to maximise revenues and minimise popular and political resistance. Consumption taxes are also more regressive. The key battle in these exercises is in framing the principle of fairness, as a way to establish the political legitimacy of redistributive

outcomes in the context of where taxes are raised and where public money is spent (see Chapter 30).

Perceptions about the economic context, or what the market will tolerate in terms of state intervention, limit the redistributive ambitions of governments. With these constraints all governments will run fiscal deficits (some larger and more long term than others), and this gap between government revenue and spending is usually closed through government borrowing – the money borrowed becomes the 'national' or 'public debt'. Historically, states have always carried national debt, but it is only in the context of post-2008 financial crisis economics that 'debt' has gained such a level of political importance that reducing public expenditure through austerity measures has eclipsed all other welfare considerations.

Emerging Issues: Crisis, Austerity and the 'Burden' of Public Spending

The 2007–8 crisis and the subsequent national recessions, global economic slow-down and debt crises in the Eurozone countries have brought into sharp relief the ways in which social policy and economic concerns have become inextricably woven together within contemporary capitalism. Economic instability that stemmed from a crisis of housing finance in the US in 2007 continues to shape the possibilities but more importantly, the limitations, on social policy development in the future. Attempts to deal with the financial crisis and its aftermath in states such as the UK, US, Ireland, Greece, Cyprus, Iceland, Portugal and Spain have led to vast sums of money being injected into the banking system to ensure that both banks and the states themselves remain solvent. The cost of these bail-outs has added to existing national debt, on which interest payments must also be made.

Combined with the absence of economic growth, these pressures on state finances have motivated national governments, regional organisations such as the European Union (EU), and international organisations such as the International Monetary Fund (IMF) and the Organisation for Economic Cooperation and Development (OECD) to adopt the strategy of austerity as the

preferred means of rebalancing economies. Austerity, or in economic terms 'fiscal consolidation', requires that governments pursue deflationary policies that reduce public spending (as well as prices and wages), with the twin aims of reducing budget deficits and shifting resources from the public to the private sector, including both the financing and delivery of welfare services. The pursuit of austerity is undertaken in the belief that private enterprise rather than public investment is the key to economic growth. Post-crisis austerity is endemic in advanced economies and, as Figure 27.3 shows, since 2009, OECD countries have clearly preferred to opt for spending reduction rather than increases in taxation.

In understanding the relationship between social policy and the economic context, however, it is as important to recognise the need for social policy in creating and maintaining economic stability and growth as it is to consider the need for economic growth to support social policies. This recognition is particularly significant in determining the success (or failure) of austerity and the broader assumptions by which it is underpinned. Social policy serves key economic functions, as a

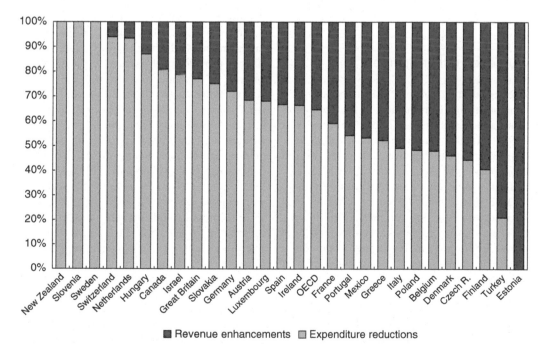

■ Revenue enhancements □ Expenditure reductions

Figure 27.3 Tackling fiscal imbalances: the ratio of tax increases to spending cuts since 2009. Source: OECD (2012), *Restoring Public Finances*, 2012 update, OECD, Paris.

form of regulation within economies and as a support for consumption, but beyond these it is also a tool for development. The efficiency of labour markets, for example, relies on social security protections and the existence of mass public education and training systems, as well as the provision of a vast range of caring services that enable high levels of participation in employment. Beyond these functions however, as the UN Research Institute for Social Development has argued, social policy is 'transformational', that is, it enables societies to progress rather than simply to grow their economies.

The fact that economics has a 'context' is something that is often lost in the world of theoretical economics, detached from its place in the real world. In this theoretical world, assumptions about individual and collective behaviours and their predictability underpin the value attributed to social spending and the kind of strategies that are proposed to maintain economic growth. For social policy analysis this is uncomfortable because the 'social' is rather unpredictable. For social policy in practice, the abstraction of economic theory is even less positive because it diminishes the human dimensions of production and exchange, and contributes to the continuing dominance of economic over social objectives.

Guide to Further Sources

The best starting point for students who want a straightforward introduction to the economics of social policy is by J. Le Grand, C. Propper and S. Smith (2008), *The Economics of Social Problems*, Basingstoke: Palgrave. N. Barr (2012), *The Economics of the Welfare State*, 5th edn, Oxford: Oxford University Press, provides a more detailed introduction to economic theory with detailed coverage of specific policy sectors, including health, education, benefits and pensions. Important cross-national comparative and global dimensions of the economic context are also addressed.

R. Skidelsky (2010), *Keynes, Return of the Master*, London: Penguin, is of interest in understanding who Keynes was as an economic theorist, what Keynesianism represents in terms of economic policy and why Keynes's work continues to matter even though the 1970s seemed to represent a fundamental rejection of the approach to economic management supported by his work. I. Gough (2000), *Global Capital, Human Needs and Social Policies*, Basingstoke, Palgrave, explores, through a collection of essays, the relationship between social and economic needs and the relationship between economic competition and the development of social policy.

For understanding the rise of 'austerity' as a dominant economic strategy both in the UK and internationally, M. Blyth (2011), *Austerity, The History of a Dangerous Idea*, Oxford: Oxford University Press, is a valuable analysis of the development and implementation of economic theory over time. The text is highly accessible to non-economists and tells a convincing story of how economic theories based on flawed assumptions are bound to fail.

W. Hutton (2015), *How Good We Can Be*, London: Little Brown, is the most recent in a series of books commenting on the development of the British economy within the context of domestic politics and international markets. Despite the problems of slow growth and high inequality, it argues that 'better' capitalism is possible with reforms in corporate governance and an economic strategy that recognises existing strengths.

The UK Office for Budget Responsibility (budgetresponsibility.org.uk) was established in 2010 to provide government with 'independent' analysis of taxation and spending to inform policymaking. The OBR produces many regular reports, including the *Economic and Fiscal Outlook* and the *Welfare Trends Report*, which provide statistics and commentary on the evolution of government finances and the place of social policies within these. Similarly, the Institute for Fiscal Studies (www.ifs.org.uk/publications) is also an authoritative 'thinktank' source for policy analysis and commentary focused on the role of taxation in policymaking. For accounts of policy activities, spending plans and economy-focused inquiries, the work of the UK Government's Treasury Committee is of interest, for example, its examination of impropriety within the banking system. The web pages of the Treasury Committee provide details of meetings, reports and other publications (www.parliament.uk/business/committees/committees-archive/treasury-committee).

Review and Assignment Questions

1 In what ways does social policy contribute to the achievement of economic growth?
2 To what extent does social policy reflect a politically achieved balance between the needs of the economy and the needs of people?
3 What is the relationship between taxation and government debt?
4 Does the 2008 global financial crisis represent a fundamental turning point for the sustainability of welfare states?
5 Outline the ways in which the economic context has constrained and enhanced the expansion of social policy in the twentieth and twenty-first centuries.

Visit the book companion site at www.wiley.com/go/alcocksocialpolicy to make use of the resources designed to accompany the textbook. There you will find chapter-specific guides to further resources, including governmental, international, thinktank, pressure groups and relevant journal sources. You will also find a glossary based on *The Blackwell Dictionary of Social Policy*, help sheets, guidance on managing assignments in social policy and career advice.

28

The Sustainability Challenge

Tony Fitzpatrick

Overview

- Since the 'fossil fuel era' cannot be maintained indefinitely, the principle of sustainability is becoming more important.
- There is a scientific consensus that climate change is occurring, is human-made and holds significant and urgent challenges to our societies.
- Those challenges are economic (the need for 'green growth'), political (the global coordination of efforts to reduce greenhouse gas emissions), and moral and cultural (to develop social values and habits that are sustainable).
- Social policies also face fundamental questions. Are our welfare systems able to cope with the new hazards and demands on public expenditure? Can they be adapted to ecological circumstances for which they were not originally designed?
- Efforts to address climate change have been very slow to commence.

Understanding Sustainability

Sustainability implies that you should not take out more than is put in. Think of a 'closed system'. If astronauts on a spaceship breathe oxygen at a greater rate than the vehicle can supply, then they will run out of air. Or imagine the inhabitants of an island. If people over-consume its resources, then eventually they will not have enough food to eat, water to drink or trees to burn for heating and

cooking. Sustainability therefore implies an equilibrium between the use of x and the renewal of x.

That balance also has to endure, since if something is described as sustainable this implies it is long term. It is not much comfort to the astronauts if their oxygen tanks might break down at any time because they are unreliable. That notion of security and stability is therefore important too. Say a damaged lifeboat accumulates three gallons of water per minute and the passengers manage to

The Student's Companion to Social Policy, Fifth Edition. Edited by Pete Alcock, Tina Haux, Margaret May and Sharon Wright.
© 2016 John Wiley & Sons, Ltd. Published 2016 by John Wiley & Sons, Ltd.

bail that amount of water back out of the boat every minute. But doing so requires all their time, energy and concentration. It would be a very stressful existence. They are not likely to stay afloat indefinitely, because they are in a precarious position with little margin for error. In short, sustainability has at least three key characteristics. It implies *balance, endurance* and *security*.

Humans have had to think carefully about sustainability for most of their time on Earth. If a hunter expended more calories tracking and killing his food than the food itself supplied, then he would begin to starve. Over the last two centuries, though, we have thought less and less about sustainability. This started to occur when we entered the fossil fuel era. Societies have long made use of coal and wood, of course. But once we learned how to extract and utilise the immense energy stored in oil and gas it looked like abundant energy would always be available. Industrialisation, urbanisation and modern affluence began at that point.

This had crucial effects on social values, priorities and goals. We began to think of ourselves as inhabiting 'open systems' in which there will always be more resources available. The astronauts can always have more oxygen sent up to them; the islanders can always migrate elsewhere. And if we can always find more resources, then planning for long-term security becomes less of a priority.

Such assumptions thus underpinned the development and organisation of modern societies. The global population has increased from 1 billion in 1800 to over 7 billion today – and it is set to hit 8 billion in 2024. Economic wealth has created material prosperity for many that would have been unimaginable to even the richest people of previous centuries. And we have become used to imagining that it can all go on forever; that there are no limits to growth, expansion, resource extraction and consumption.

Ecological Challenges

But this kind of faith has been challenged in recent decades. The Earth is itself a closed system. There is only so much pollution and waste we can discharge into it, and there are only so many resources that it can supply. In particular, it was increasingly clear from the 1960s onwards that what had previously been regarded as a sign of progress (the by-products of civilisation like smogs, polluted rivers, toxins, pesticides, oil spills, acid rain and population growth), in fact represented a considerable threat to it. This would later be joined by fears over the erosion of the ozone layer. And then in the late 1980s governments became aware of what scientists had been warning for years: the planet is warming due to the greenhouse gases (GHGs) we have been pouring into its climate. The most prevalent GHG is carbon dioxide (CO_2).

The scientific evidence for this has done nothing but accumulate ever since. Almost all climate scientists agree that (1) climate change is happening, and (2) this is because of human activities. In 2013–14, the Intergovernmental Panel on Climate Change (IPCC) produced what is the most thorough overview of the evidence to date. Some of its many conclusions are summarised in Box 28.1.

Box 28.1 Intergovernmental Panel on Climate Change

- GHGs have reached levels unprecedented in the last 800,000 years; a 40 per cent increase since pre-industrial times. In the North, 1983–2012 was probably the warmest thirty-year period of the last 1,400 years.
- By the next century the average global temperature will probably be higher than the 2°C of warming (above pre-industrial levels) that is widely regarded as the upper limit beyond which global warming becomes dangerously unmanageable.
- Arctic sea ice will continue to shrink.
- By 2100, sea levels are set to rise by 40–63 cm higher than they were at the end of the twentieth century. This will adversely affect coastal settlements.
- Thirty per cent of CO_2 increases have been absorbed by oceans, leading to greater acidity. The effects on marine life and ecosystems are vast, including the destruction of coral reefs and the reduced capacity for sea creatures to develop shells and skeletons.

Box 28.2   Mitigation and Adaptation

■ Mitigation implies reducing harms by, for instance, first slowing, then halting and eventually reversing global warming. CO_2 emissions have to peak, and then we have to remove those emissions from the oceans, land and atmosphere.

■ Adaptation implies trying to reduce the impacts of harms which we cannot avoid. Rising sea levels require better defences against flooding, for instance.

What are the effects on humans of all this likely to be? According to the IPCC, the health status of millions of people, especially in developing countries, is going to be affected through increases in malnutrition, diarrhoeal and infectious diseases, and cardio-respiratory diseases due to higher concentrations of ground-level ozone in cities. Increasing and disastrous incidents of hurricanes, floods, wildfires, droughts, deforestation, species extinction and heatwaves can be expected. These may well be joined by severely rising sea levels, ice sheet loss, mass species extinctions, larger and more frequent droughts and famines, rainforest collapse, coral reef devastation, acidic oceans and mass ecological migration as levels of potable water and crop yields decline. It is the poorest – those least responsible for creating the problem – who are most exposed and vulnerable to the effects of climate change.

Any effective response to the above has to involve both mitigation and adaptation (see Box 28.2). Mitigation and adaptation must often go together, however; and clearly any strategies we adopt have to recognise the interdependencies between nature and society.

Social Challenges

Many aspects of modern societies hinder proper understanding and appropriate action. We remain national actors, rather than global ones, who think and act across the short term, and find it difficult to respond to threats that can often seem quite abstract and far away. Four social challenges are particularly crucial.

The economic

What would a green economy look like? There are some who occupy a 'do nothing' position. Faith is here placed on human ingenuity, such as our capacity to develop new technologies that will 'engineer' climate-related problems out of existence. Some have faith in markets where green entrepreneurs will develop the industries and products we need to 'decarbonise' the economy. Others believe that the cure for tackling global warming could be worse than the ailment, arguing that economic growth will make our descendants rich enough to cope with any ecological deterioration.

But various economists have argued that, compared with the cost of doing nothing, the cost of taking effective action should amount to only a few percentages of global Gross Domestic Product (GDP) by the middle of this century. States and markets must work together to create 'green growth', though the longer we delay, the higher those eventual costs will be. And others go further, arguing that growth itself is a fundamentally flawed conceptualisation of real prosperity and well-being. We may need a 'steady state' economy. This basically means that there should be no depletion of resources that cannot be replaced and no emissions that cannot be absorbed. It implies a self-replenishing economy where we repair, recycle and reuse what we have, instead of constantly buying and throwing away. Growth is justified if, and only if, it is *sustainable growth*.

The political

But agreeing a strategy is one thing. Implementing it is another. Initiated in the 1990s, the Kyoto Protocol was an agreement for developed countries to cut their emissions by an average of 5.2 per cent below 1990 levels by 2008–12. Yet the USA and Australia did not even ratify the protocol until 2008! Furthermore, critics allege that initiatives such as the Emissions Trading Scheme and the Clean Development Mechanism allowed countries and firms to present themselves as achieving more than they have in fact achieved.

Arguments between developed and developing countries have also characterised international negotiations. The latter argue that since it is developed countries that are largely to blame for global warming, it is their responsibility to shoulder the burdens. But the former reply that developing countries now account for more than half of all GHGs; with many of those emissions coming from China, India and Brazil. So even if industrialised countries reduced their emissions to zero by 2040, total global emissions would still be higher than today!

Global discussions on what should replace Kyoto have been ongoing for years, culminating in a major conference in Paris in 2015. Yet the political dimension cannot simply be about inter-governmental regulations and environmental laws that most people, quite honestly, know little about. Environmentalism was a social movement before it was anything else. This means mobilising and facilitating grassroots initiatives and bottom-up actions through a range of non-governmental organisations, 'third sector' groups, peer-to-peer networks and community associations. Part of this is about influencing those who dominate the top-heavy, decision-making arenas across both private and public sectors. But it is also about encouraging a thriving, global civil society which instigates the changes that political and corporate elites frequently resist. 'Think global, act local' has long been the slogan of a movement determined to impel new, greener forms of citizenship.

The moral and cultural

How can we develop 'green citizens'? Clearly, a lot of action has to take place at local and national levels, but if we are to 'think global' then we need to develop cosmopolitan, post-national values and commitments. This is partly because of self-interest. In an interdependent world what happens thousands of miles away will probably affect us sooner or later. But it is also because we should be more humanitarian by acknowledging the needs of others as central to our well-being, regardless of self-interest.

Some of those others are separated from us in time. What we do now impacts upon the opportunities and constraints that future generations will encounter. But how far into the future do our obligations extend? And what kind of world do

we want to bequeath? And what about non-humans? Here, too, some of our duties to animals, vegetation and to the very biosphere itself is about self-interest. 'Greenspaces' not only absorb CO_2, disperse pollution and produce oxygen, but also are beneficial for physical and mental health. But some of it is about reconnecting nature and society in ways that the fossil fuel era has compelled us to neglect. Some philosophers argue that we have become too anthropocentric: too human-centred and forgetful of the extent to which because we inhabit an 'ecoweb' of life we have responsibilities to that web for its own sake, due to its inherent value.

Therefore, green citizenship is not just about new laws or taxes: it potentially raises profound questions that go to the heart of what it means to be human. There is one challenge left to consider.

Social policy

The welfare state is another offspring of the fossil fuel parent. Consider the two key roles it plays.

■ First, it affects the objectives and the organisation of the economy. In the Keynesian era social expenditure helped to stimulate demand and so create the conditions for full employment. In the 'neo-Liberal' era, state welfare has been used to encourage labour market flexibility and competition, for instance, fewer entitlements, more benefit conditions and greater means-testing. In both cases, the aim has been to encourage the kind of economic growth and material affluence which no longer appears sustainable.

■ Second, the welfare state affects the distribution of the wealth that is created by growth. Taxes, benefits and the provision of services make society more equal than it would otherwise be. But the degree to which society should be egalitarian is something about which left and right disagree. The former tend to stress universalism, collectivism, solidarity and distributive justice; the latter prefer selectivism, individualism, consumerism and market forces. But both approaches have taken continued economic growth for granted and neither has traditionally considered our obligations to the future or to the wider world (including to non-humans).

■ To what extent does the welfare state enable a transition to a green society?
■ Which aspects of state welfare are ecologically sustainable and which are not?
■ What social policy reforms must be implemented and with what degree of urgency?
■ How can those reforms be made to fit the broader economic, political, social-cultural and moral changes which are required?

The key questions we therefore need to ask are given in Box 28.3.

Climate change thus presents various challenges to contemporary welfare states. See Box 28.4.

Researchers tend to contrast interventionist approaches with market-dominated, neo-Liberal

Box 28.4 Challenges to Welfare States

■ New uncertainties and insecurities: including flood risks, drought risks and heat waves. The poorest are typically those most exposed to such hazards because they are most likely to experience them and, having few resources, lack the resilience to cope and recover from them.
■ New conflicts over resources: to reduce carbon emissions we need carbon taxes so that consumption is reduced. But such taxes are often regressive, that is, they hit the poorest hardest.
■ The need for new policy synergies: the costs arising from global warming – and the cost of implementing mitigation and adaptation strategies – place additional burdens on public spending. We must find ways to integrate ecological expenditure and social expenditure through new forms of investment.

ones. Many think that the former are best suited to the creation of a sustainable society because they seek to regulate and coordinate markets, shaping them to meet desirable public goals. Such nations – especially Scandinavian countries – are widely regarded as pioneers. That said, the more market-dominated UK also tends to score highly in green league tables. Why is this?

UK Government Policies

Part of the reason is that in the 1980s a concerted effort was made to change the UK economy, though addressing climate change itself was not an objective. The country shifted away from coal and towards gas as part of the government's attempt to de-industrialise Britain, that is, emphasising services (finance and banking, tourism, retail, consulting) rather than manufacturing industry.

By and large, the UK's approach has been one of 'ecological modernisation'. This means adapting existing institutions so that they meet environmental goals, rather than making any radical changes to society. In the field of social policy, this can mean a variety of things. See Box 28.5.

There are many other, more ambitious proposals which have been suggested as ways of addressing both social and ecological problems:

■ Ration cards could be given to every adult, giving them a set emissions allowance every year. If they exceed their allowance they would have to buy additional carbon credits.

Box 28.5 Ecological Modernisation

■ Encouraging healthier lifestyles and making healthcare more preventative.
■ Encouraging energy efficiencies, for example, through the retrofitting of houses such as the installing of solar panels.
■ Creating more sustainable urban densities by using land more effectively.
■ Creating sustainable transport systems.
■ Introducing carbon taxes.

But if they spend less than their allowance they could sell surplus credits to those who need to purchase them. Since the poorest are usually responsible for fewer GHG emissions than the more affluent, such a scheme could be redistributive. This would help to create the equalities which many think are necessary if the benefits and burdens of sustainability are to be shared equitably.

■ Local currency schemes are a way of encouraging local production and trade, enhancing communal sustainability and putting less pressure on national infrastructures and the international transport of energy, food and other consumables. It also enables scheme members to trade those skills which the formal labour market of waged work may undervalue. Such schemes are ways of trading time and so could assist in the growth of a 'post-employment' economy.

■ A land value tax (LVT) would help to address the problem of tax avoidance – rich people cannot hide the land they live on – and it would return to the community the value of the land which the community, rather than the landowner, has created. The revenue generated could be directed to low-income households, or to ecological schemes or to both.

However, to date the UK Government has done relatively little to implement even the less ambitious, but still important, ideas in Box 28.5.

Emerging Issues

A sustainable society would be one characterised by a balance between society and nature that is secure enough to endure across the long term. Getting from here to there implies: decreasing GHGs to the point where emissions are zero and we can begin to eliminate GHGs from the climate; reductions in pollution; greater reliance upon renewable resources and a wiser depletion of non-renewables. There is a sense in which if we create such a sustainable economy, social policies can then be left to do what – at their best – they have always done:

■ promote public goods, communal values and universal services to counteract the capitalist emphasis on self-interest, competition, profit and personal aspiration;

■ redistribute and equalise income, wealth, opportunities and life chances;

■ emphasise the importance of quality of life through social rights that counterbalance the 'commodified' cash nexus relationships of market forces.

Yet rather than regard social policies as subservient to economic policies, it may be that these features are precisely those that need to come to the foreground if a sustainable society is to be created. The Keynesian and the neo-Liberal eras both gave a great deal of emphasis to material prosperity as measured via GDP. The welfare state typically followed suit. The key questions are therefore these. Can the features of social policy outlined above be made to embody and serve the principle of sustainability: balance, endurance, security? If so, how might we reorder our priorities, practices and institutions so that green social policies and green economic policies can work together?

Guide to Further Sources

M. Cahill (2010), *Transport, Environment and Society*, Maidenhead: Open University Press, is a useful analysis of the contribution transport makes to GHG emissions and how sustainable transport systems might be devised that also effect social justice. J. Dryzek, R. Norgaard and D. Schlosberg (eds) (2011), *Oxford Handbook of Climate Change and Society*, Oxford: Oxford University Press, is a comprehensive overview of climate change from a diversity of perspectives: sociology, politics, philosophy, economics, public policy.

T. Fitzpatrick (ed.) (2011), *Understanding the Environment and Social Policy*, Bristol: Policy Press, is an edited collection that offers a wide-ranging introduction to those new to the subject. T. Fitzpatrick (2014), *Climate Change and Poverty*, Bristol: Policy Press, is an 'eco-social' account which examines poverty in terms of both social and natural resources across a range of domains: energy, food, housing, land, transport, waste, water and air. Whilst T. Fitzpatrick (ed.) (2014), *International Handbook on Social Policy and the Environment*, Cheltenham: Edward Elgar, provides a more specialised, advanced and in-depth collection of chapters from key experts in their field.

T. Jackson (2009), *Prosperity without Growth*, Abingdon: Earthscan, is an influential explanation of the implications of sustainability for economics, dealing with the need to 'decouple' GHG emissions from economic activity. C. Snell and G. Haq (2014), *The Short Guide to Environmental Policy*, Bristol: Policy Press, is a useful introduction to post-war British environmental policies. J. Urry (2011), *Climate Change and Society*, Cambridge: Polity Press, is an attempt to reintroduce sociology and social science to nature and the latter's implications for the future of both.

Review and Assignment Questions

1   How radical a change does the principle of sustainability represent to the traditional assumptions of social policy?

2   What are the most important obstacles hindering the development of social efforts to address climate change?

3   To what extent would a green society involve a radical break with existing social values, practices and organisation?

4   What are the main risks with which green social policies would have to deal?

5   How can we make significant progress towards a green welfare state?

Visit the book companion site at www.wiley.com/go/alcocksocialpolicy to make use of the resources designed to accompany the textbook. There you will find chapter-specific guides to further resources, including governmental, international, thinktank, pressure groups and relevant journal sources. You will also find a glossary based on *The Blackwell Dictionary of Social Policy*, help sheets, guidance on managing assignments in social policy and career advice.

29

The Role of Religion

Rana Jawad

Overview

- All world religions, including New Age religions, have teachings on the nature of happiness and well-being as well as selfless service.
- Religious bodies were the first providers of social welfare and remain so in many countries around the world.
- Mainstream accounts of the development of social policy in 'Western' societies have varied in the attention paid to the role of religion.
- Religion has a long-standing role in British public life and social policy, and has gained renewed vigour in England especially since the 1980s.
- Religious welfare organisations are becoming more involved in service delivery in the UK, re-opening debate about their relationship to the state.

Context

The role of religion in social policy can best be described as an 'old–new partnership', with the emphasis in this chapter being laid on 'old'. This is important for various reasons, but particularly since it:

- is a reminder of the extent to which social policy as an academic subject has often not

systematically recounted the way in which religious figures, values, voluntary groups, charities, political parties and institutions have influenced the development of social provision and welfare states across the world;
- helps to allay fears and suspicion regarding the apparent re-entry of religion into the public sphere both in the UK and elsewhere; and
- enables us to begin to see that social policy and religion share some core concerns and are

The Student's Companion to Social Policy, Fifth Edition. Edited by Pete Alcock, Tina Haux, Margaret May and Sharon Wright.
© 2016 John Wiley & Sons, Ltd. Published 2016 by John Wiley & Sons, Ltd.

built on similar foundations: both aspire towards an idea of the 'good society' and are underpinned by particular conceptions of human nature.

In short, the connections between religion and social policy are intrinsic, but also separate in large part because, particularly in sociological writing, social policy has come to symbolise the flagship enterprise of the modern secular nation-state dependent on science and human rationality for its flourishing. Religion in contrast often appears as a cultural leftover marked by conservativism and backwardness. There are, therefore, some very real cultural and material challenges for a constructive discussion of the role of religion in social policy, as will become clear in this chapter.

Social Welfare in the Five Main World Religions

As the sociologist Robert Wuthnow, in defining religion in his study *The Restructuring of American Religion* (1988), emphasised, it is deeply connected to social action. Like many others, he contends that religion has as much to do with a sense of belonging to a community and a drive to be socially engaged in society as it does with abstract moral beliefs and ideas. In this way, it is possible to argue that religious people and values have a natural role to play in public life and, indeed, to speak out against social injustices. Religion in effect need not be confined to the private sphere of life and can, and has, long played a key role in the development of social policy.

The five major world faiths of Hinduism, Buddhism, Judaism, Christianity and Islam command followers totalling more than half of the world's population (around 3 billion people). They also both underpinned the empirical studies that were a handmaiden to the emergence of sociology and social policy as disciplines in the early twentieth century and provide the most advanced forms of engagement with political mobilisation and poverty alleviation in history. These five religions are also the only ones to have penetrated formal state organs in many parts of the world, including, for instance, India, Iran, Israel and the UK. Although internally diverse, we will highlight here some of their key commonalities.

What is significant in the way in which religion and social policy have intertwined is that religiously inspired welfare has been championed not just by religious orders, but also by lay intellectuals, political activists and social reformers, such as members of the Christian Socialist movement and reformers like Seebhom Rowntree and William Beveridge in the UK (see Chapter 1), Mahatma Ghandi and Rammohan Roy in modern Hinduism, and Seyyed Qutub and Abdolkarim Soroush in reformist Islam. Historically and more recently examples of political mobilisation and social action by religious groups also abound elsewhere, for example, in the development of socialist strands of Protestantism and Sunni Islam in the nineteenth century, the establishment of the Hindu *gram seva* (village service) in India in the early 1900s, the Base communities of Latin America or the Catholic Church in the 1980s Solidarity Movement in Poland.

For these individuals and movements, as for many others historically and currently, the relevance of religious teachings to social welfare lies in their overarching concern with ethics (the rules that govern correct social relationships). These translate into basic values about human life, dignity, equality, social justice, property, honest communication, law and order. World religions do not immediately seek to prescribe what types of social structures and public institutions are needed for the good society. What they offer are moral standards for correct social relations that they see as the path to pleasing God and establishing a just social order. The *Ten Commandments* or *Decalogue* in Judaism, Christianity and Islam, and the skills required to live one's life according to the *dharma* as in Buddhism and Hinduism are key illustrations of this. Moreover, a common social welfare idea is that of (selfless) service. The main world faiths all incite believers to act selflessly and to help others in need as in the Christian story of the Good Samaritan; the Islamic injunctions to help orphans, the sick and the vulnerable, or to pay the obligatory tax of *zakat*; the Jewish emphasis on *g'millut chassadim*, which refers to selfless kindness and service, and *tikkum olam* (meaning repair the world); *seva* (service) and *dharma* in Hinduism as the key inspirations to fight against social injustice.

However, while the main world religions have clear injunctions about social and material well-being, the primary condition of welfare is found at the level of the individual's personal spiritual wellness. Hence, these religions do not necessarily like big government: they caution against the evils of earthly politics and the control of elite minorities over the masses. Nonetheless, certain strands of Christianity and Islam, for example, favour strong state control as the main guarantor of social equality and justice. In some cases, therefore, there is mistrust of the welfare state, and this explains the tension inherent in whether or not religious believers are to embrace or detach themselves from the material concerns of earthly life.

Religion, Spirituality and the Study of Social Policy

It follows, then, that religion might make very scant appearance in histories and theories of social policy. What has tended to be the case is that in practice discussion of its role in shaping social policy has fluctuated. It has also often been marked by variations in the analyses of welfare arrangements in Western societies and those elsewhere (see Part X). More particularly, as will be seen, in the post-Second World War era sociologically inspired accounts of the development of state welfare were influenced by studies that pointed to increased secularisation.

Putting it in very broad terms, until recently many academic authors tended to refer to religion as a social and political force in the medieval/post-medieval period, particularly in the European context. But from the time of the Enlightenment (eighteenth-century Europe), many argue that religion began to lose its grip on society as developments in science allowed mankind to take control of its destiny. Within this line of thinking, however, analysts varied in their view of the role played by religion in the development of social policy.

Social historians in the UK, for instance, pointed to its continued significance alongside other factors in promoting social legislation and the role of religious movements such as Evangelism in the nineteenth century or reformers like Rowntree and Beveridge in the first half of the last century. Arguably, though, religion was more central in America, continental and northern Europe, where historians have more readily highlighted its role in the development of social welfare. In the US, for instance, there is a rich literature on the role of voluntary religious groups and how their entrepreneurialism and free voting systems helped to develop social policy and democratic politics. European writers, too, cite the important role that state religions and established churches played, for example, in the Netherlands, Sweden and Germany, in fortifying governmental responses to social needs and problems.

Beyond these analyses though some historical accounts go as far as arguing that Catholic countries failed to develop the same kind of sophisticated welfare systems as certain Protestant ones because the Catholic Church was fiercely protective of its independence and continued to uphold the subsidiarity principle. This specified that responsibility for poverty lay outside state control, most notably within the family. Protestantism, on the other hand, emphasised the work ethic and was able to align itself more easily to the secular state and therefore to give way to its increased role in social welfare provision.

Indeed, until recently, much thinking thus posited religious welfare against modern state welfare. Most crucially, the post-Second World War years saw the growing influence of Modernisation Theory. In broad terms, this stated that societies were becoming increasingly secular with technological advancement. In consequence, religious welfare was being replaced by state welfare, since morality and social control were no longer the dominion of the church or temple with people now being able to provide rational solutions to make their lives better. In this view, social policy remained a moral endeavour, but its values came from humanist assumptions about social citizenship and social rights.

This notion of increasing secularisation reached its height in the 1960s and 1970s. It meant, as Gorski (2005) has argued, that in contrast to the study of so-called 'Third World' countries, in what amounted to a double standard Western academics paid only passing tribute to the role of religion in the development of the welfare state. Indeed, religious welfare was largely side-lined and, when considered, generally lumped with the voluntary sector with little or no critical discussion.

Recent years, however, have seen the emergence of a different approach to the study of the interaction between religion and social policy. In particular, it is now argued that established state religions continue to exercise power even in the supposed heartlands of secularity, northern and western Europe. Moreover, it appears that more people claim to be religious than in previous generations, while it is clear that tens of thousands of religiously inspired organisations operate around the world offering an array of social services from cash assistance to emergency relief, to education and healthcare. Religion has also entered the formal state apparatus, continuing to affect the design of social policies in countries from North America to the Far East. Rather than being a factor considered mainly in relation to 'Third World' policies, it is also now a major variable in sociological analyses of 'Western' societies, mainly for four major reasons:

- these societies have become multicultural, with religion playing a key role in the identity of significant proportions of their populations;
- cataclysmic events such as 9/11 mean that religion, especially Islam and the social integration of Muslims, is now seen as a government priority;
- the onward march of neo-Liberalism and cuts in state welfare have made it easier for religious groups to enter the social welfare scene as service providers;
- empirically, there is a cultural/spiritual turn in social science research that recognises the failure of money-metric analyses of poverty and a real need to respond to post-materialist understandings of human well-being.

What we find therefore is that world leaders such as Bill Clinton, George Bush and Tony Blair at the turn of this century actively opened the way for religious welfare associations and promoted religious freedoms through new legislation and welfare reforms, most notably Bush's Charitable Initiative Act in the US.

Critics, however, have been quick to highlight the threat that religious involvement in social welfare poses to social citizenship and civic values as the stakes run high over how best to sustain the ideals of social democracy. Faith-based schools are perhaps among the most hotly debated in this respect. But new empirical research is beginning to redefine and reconceptualise the contribution of religion to society and social provision, not least in the UK.

The UK Context

According to the 2011 census, 58 per cent of the British population consider themselves to be Christian and around 10 per cent are of other religions, primarily of immigrant origin. The Church of England, the Salvation Army and, increasingly, non-Christian groups such as Jewish Care, the Hindu Gujarati Society and Islamic Relief are now among the most active and largest religious social welfare providers in the country. Some of these organisations operate under contract with central or local government, or through various partnership arrangements with the latter, a process that has been hastened by the restructuring of the welfare state since the 1980s, considered elsewhere in this book.

Religion has, moreover, gained a new prominence in political debate and policy initiatives in other ways. In particular, whilst support for religious welfare had long been a feature of elements of both the two main UK political parties, it gained added momentum under Margaret Thatcher. Her policies, which some argue were religiously motivated, were staunchly anti-state and, as discussed in other chapters, opened the way for non-state, including religious, welfare initiatives. On Labour's side, Tony Blair's election in 1997 was a watershed for the re-entry of religion into British public life. In key speeches addressing the Christian Socialist Movement in 2001 and then Faith Works (the movement led by the Revd Steven Chalke, founder of one of the UK's most socially active Christian organisations, Oasis) in 2005, he seemed to embrace religious welfare as a kind of missing link in British social policy that tied the ends of the (new) political rhetoric of welfare pluralism, social capital, partnerships and community participation. This new policy direction was supported by influential writers such as Giddens, who began to argue that religious identity would help to fortify what was seen as the disintegrating moral fabric of British society. Indeed, in 2007, one minister, John Murphy, even observed that religious welfare would become a key plank of British social policy in the years to come.

Key aspects of the Coalition government's policies too owed much to the religious concerns of ministers such as the Conservative, Iain Duncan Smith. England, particularly its new discourse around the 'Big Society' with its emphasis on community and social capital, also seemed set to enhance the role of religious organisations in social policy. In practice, however, this was undermined by cuts in voluntary sector funding and was not pursued consistently (see Chapter 37). It was, however, reaffirmed by the Conservatives in the build up to their election in 2015, under whom the expanding welfare role of voluntary, including religious, organisations especially in England is continuing.

Recent policymakers thus see interest in religious welfare groups in three main ways as:

- providers of social welfare services, since they possess valuable resources such as buildings and volunteers;
- promoters of social cohesion, since the UK is now a multi-ethnic and multi-religious society;
- new actors in an ever-expanding network of stakeholder politics and democratic governance, particularly at local authority level.

Yet religious welfare politics remain very much in the making and are a source of contention, perhaps most notably in the case of the Church of England whose role as moral patron of the nation has increasingly been questioned. Since the publication of its report, *Faith in the City* in 1985, criticising the Thatcher government and highlighting the persistence of stark social inequalities and urban poverty, the Church of England has increasingly felt that its role is being marginalised as government funding moves towards multi-faith councils and forums. More recently, along with other religious organisations, it has though spoken out against the impact of the Coalition's austerity policies across the UK and pushed for the living wage to be made law. As the spread of food banks since 2010, many, like those of the Trussell Fund, with a Christian base or run by other faiths, also show that religious welfare organisations are in other ways at the forefront of bringing home the realities of contemporary British politics and rising social inequalities.

The social assistance offered by food banks and other services, however, also reflects a growing acceptance that faith-based groups are now part of the social policy landscape. It is thought, for instance, that their annual income is close to £5 billion, a figure nowhere near total state social expenditure in the UK, but still significant, and that they are providing considerable support for communities and individuals in need. Yet, though there is much grey literature, there are still many gaps in the depiction of this contribution.

Moreover, caution and even confusion still prevail; some religious groups remain suspicious of government, fearing that their prophetic mission and closeness to their local communities might be compromised if they are used instrumentally by the state as cheap and ready forms of welfare provision. In addition, many religious groups are small and lack the professional capacity to compete for government funding and take on more bureaucratic roles. Furthermore, on the part of policymakers there is an issue of 'religious literacy', broadly meaning that government officials lack knowledge about religious groups and the kind of values and language they use.

Emerging Issues

Debate over the role of religion and religious welfare organisations in social policy is likely to increase as the factors that have attracted recent attention continue to unfold. Interest in its role in the public sphere among policymakers and research-funding organisations is set to grow as concern over cataclysmic events such as 9/11 continue to reverberate, as is sociological debate over its place in late modern and, what some have called, post-materialist societies. Interest in the non-material aspects of people's well-being and issues such as spirituality, social cohesion and psycho-social interpretations of human well-being are also likely to feature more in policy development.

More specifically, the fundamental shifts in welfare provision in the UK, North America, much of Europe and the Antipodes that paved the way for the expanding role of religious organisations are likely to intensify. In the UK, this may well lead to attempts to fill the many gaps in our understanding of the services provided by religious welfare organisations and their scope and effectiveness. They will also, however, open up questions about the extent of support among both religious groups and the public for their role in social policy, whether as contracted deliverers of state services, complementary or supplementary providers, potential or actual substitutes or campaigners for policy change.

Guide to Further Sources

Stimulating overviews of the role of religion in the development of social policy in the UK are provided by M. Parker-Jenkins et al. (2005), *In Good Faith: Schools, Religion and Public Funding*, Surrey: Ashgate; F. Prochaska (2006), *Christianity and Social Service in Modern Britain: The Disinherited Spirit*, Oxford: Oxford University Press; and in Europe by K. Van Kersbergen and P. Manow (eds) (2009), *Religion, Class Coalitions and Welfare States*, Cambridge: Cambridge University Press. P. S. Gorski (2005), 'The return of the repressed: religion and the political unconsciousness of historical sociology', in J. Adams, E. Clemens and A. S. Orloff (eds), *Remaking Modernity: Politics, History and Sociology*, Durham, NC: Dale University Press, and A. Backstrom and G. Davie (eds) (2010), *Welfare and Religion in 21st Century Europe*, vol. 1, Surrey: Ashgate, offer further insights into the interplay between religion and social policy.

C. Milligan and D. Conradson (eds) (2006), *Landscapes of Voluntarism: New Spaces of Health, Welfare and Governance*, Bristol: Policy Press, includes several chapters on religion in the context of the voluntary sector. A. Dinham, R. Furbey and V. Lowndes (eds) (2009), *Faith in the Public Realm: Controversies, Policies and Practices*, Bristol: Policy Press, provides a good introduction to the key debates on the role of religion in the UK; and R. Jawad (2012) 'Serving the public or delivering social services? Religion and social welfare in the new British social policy landscape', *Journal of Poverty and Social Justice*, 20:1, 55–68, considers developments under the Coalition government. S. Furness and P. Gillingan (2010), *Religion, Belief and Social Work*, Bristol: Policy Press, offers an empirical analysis of the contribution of religion from the point of view social work, whilst many key issues can be explored via the Westminster Faith Debates website at: www.faithdebates .org.uk.

Review and Assignment Questions

1 How does religious welfare promote or hinder social policy?
2 Do faith schools pose a threat to citizenship?
3 Should religious welfare groups be considered as part of the larger category of voluntary sector organisations?
4 How has the secularisation thesis been challenged?
5 How might the study and practice of social policy benefit from greater appreciation of the role of religious welfare?

Visit the book companion site at www.wiley.com/ go/alcocksocialpolicy to make use of the resources designed to accompany the textbook. There you will find chapter-specific guides to further resources, including governmental, international, thinktank, pressure groups and relevant journal sources. You will also find a glossary based on *The Blackwell Dictionary of Social Policy*, help sheets, guidance on managing assignments in social policy and career advice.

30

The Distribution of Welfare

John Hills

Overview

- The distribution of resources is central to the provision of welfare, and distribution and redistribution take place through both state, and private and voluntary transfers.
- There is a range of different rationales underpinning the redistribution of resources to promote welfare.
- There are different ways of measuring distribution and its benefits. How it is paid for – and who pays – is very important in this.
- Much of the redistributive effect of welfare is as a sort of 'savings bank' transferring resources between different stages of people's own lives.
- However, redistribution also plays a significant 'Robin Hood' role benefiting poorer sections of society most, particularly once one allows for how it is paid for.

Distribution and Redistribution

Distribution is a central issue in the appraisal of social policies; for some, it is *the* central issue. Much of the justification advanced for social policy is about distribution: 'without a National Health Service providing free medical care, the poor could not afford treatment'; or 'the primary aim of social security is preventing poverty'.

Most of this chapter is about the distributional effects of government spending on welfare services. However, redistribution – and its measurement – are not only issues for government. For instance, governments, including in the UK, have attempted (not always very successfully) to enforce payments by absent parents (generally fathers) to parents 'with care' (usually mothers). Similarly, since 2012 employers (starting with the largest) have had to make a minimum contribution towards their employees' pensions, if the employee does not opt out of the pension scheme. Such payments

The Student's Companion to Social Policy, Fifth Edition. Edited by Pete Alcock, Tina Haux, Margaret May and Sharon Wright.
© 2016 John Wiley & Sons, Ltd. Published 2016 by John Wiley & Sons, Ltd.

made under state regulation can be important in distributional terms, but are outside the 'welfare state'.

Whether redistribution is occurring can depend on when you look at it. Under private insurance for, say, burglaries, a large number of people make annual payments (insurance premiums) to an insurance company, but only a small number receive payouts. After the event (*ex post*) there is redistribution from the (fortunate) many to the (unfortunate) few. But, looking at the position in advance (*ex ante*), not knowing who will be burgled, all pay in a premium equalling their risk of being burgled, multiplied by the size of the pay-out if this happens (plus the insurance company's costs and profits). In 'actuarial' terms there is no redistribution – people have arranged a certain small loss (the premium) rather than the risk of a much larger loss (being burgled without insurance).

Similarly, if you look at pension schemes over a single year, some people pay in contributions, while others receive pensions. On this 'snapshot', there is apparently redistribution from the former to the latter. But over a longer horizon, today's pensioners may simply get back what they paid in earlier. Redistribution is across their own life cycles, rather than between different people.

Assessing redistribution depends on the aims against which you measure services, and the picture obtained depends on decisions such as the time period used. The next section discusses the first of these issues, the aims of welfare services. The subsequent sections discuss the conceptual issues raised in trying to measure distributional effects, and illustrate some of the empirical findings on different bases.

Aims of Welfare Services

There is little consensus on the aims of social policy or of government intervention to provide or finance welfare services. For some, the primary aim of welfare services is redistribution from rich to poor. Whether the welfare state is successful therefore depends on which income groups benefit: do the rich use the NHS more than the poor, and are social security benefits 'targeted' on those with the lowest incomes? For others, this is only a part of the welfare state's rationale. Depending on political perspective, other aims will be more important (see Box 30.1); and the relative importance given to each aim affects not only the interpretation placed on particular findings, but also the appropriate kind of analysis.

Box 30.1   Potential Aims of Social Policy and 'Redistribution'

- *Vertical redistribution*: if the aim is redistribution from rich to poor, the crucial question is, which income groups benefit: since welfare services do not come from thin air, the important question may be which are the *net gainers* and *net losers*, after allowing for who pays the taxes that finance welfare provision. Allowing for both benefits and taxes in understanding distribution has become even more important since the UK Government started using 'tax credits' (which can count as reduced tax liabilities) instead of some cash benefits.

- *Horizontal redistribution on the basis of needs*: for many, relative incomes are not the only reason for receiving services. The NHS is there for people with particular medical needs: it should achieve 'horizontal redistribution' between people with similar incomes, but different medical needs.

- *Redistribution between different groups*: an aim might be redistribution between social groups defined other than by income; for instance, favouring particular groups to offset disadvantages elsewhere in the economy. Or the system might be intended to be non-discriminatory between groups. Either way, we may need to analyse distribution by dimensions such as social class, gender, ethnicity, age or age cohort (generation), or kind of area, rather than just income.

- *Insurance*: much of what the welfare state does is insurance against adversity. People 'pay in' through tax or national insurance contributions, but in return, if they are the ones who become ill or unemployed, the system is there to protect them. It does not make sense just to look at which individual happens to receive an expensive heart by-pass operation this year and present him or her as the main 'gainer' from the system. All benefit to the extent that they face a risk of needing such an operation. The system is best analysed in actuarial terms; that is, in terms of the extent someone would expect to benefit on average.

- *Efficiency justifications:* an extensive literature discusses how universal, compulsory and possibly state-provided systems can be cheaper or more efficient than the market left to itself for some activities, particularly core welfare services such as healthcare, unemployment insurance and education. Where this is the motivation for state provision one might not expect to see any redistribution between income or other groups. Services might be appraised according to the 'benefit principle' (how much do people receive in relation to what they pay?), and the absence of net redistribution would not be a sign of failure.

- *Life cycle smoothing:* most welfare services are unevenly spread over the life cycle. Education goes disproportionately to the young; healthcare and pensions to the old; while the taxes that finance them come mostly from the working generation. A snapshot picture of redistribution may be misleading – it would be better to compare how much people get out of the system over their whole lives, and how much they pay in.

- *Compensating for 'family failure':* many parents do, of course, meet their children's needs, and many higher-earning husbands do share their cash incomes equally with their lower-earning wives. But in other families this is not so – family members may not share equally. Where policies aim to counter this kind of problem, it may not be enough just to look at the distribution *between* families, we may also need to look at distribution between individuals; that is, *within* families as well.

- *External benefits:* finally, some services may be justified by 'external' or 'spill-over' benefits beyond those to the direct beneficiary. Promoting the education of even the relatively affluent may be in society's interests, if this produces a more dynamic economy for all. Appraisal of who gains ought to take account of such benefits (although in practice this is hard).

Conceptual Issues

There is no single measure of how welfare services are distributed. It depends on precisely what is measured, and apparently technical choices can make a great difference to the findings.

The counterfactual

To answer the question, 'how are welfare services distributed?' you have to add, 'compared with what?'. What is the 'counterfactual' situation with which you are comparing reality? A particular group may receive state medical services worth £3,000 per year. In one sense, this is how much they benefit. But if the medical services did not exist, what else would change? Government spending might be lower, and hence tax bills,

including their own. The net benefit, allowing for taxes, might be much less than £3,000 per year.

Knock-on effects may go further. In an economy with lower taxes, many other things might be different. Without the NHS, people would have to make other arrangements: private medical insurance, for instance. Britain without the NHS would differ in all sorts of ways from Britain with it, and, strictly, it is this hypothetical alternative country with which we ought to compare in order to measure the impact of having the NHS. In practice, this is very difficult – which limits the conclusiveness of most empirical studies.

Incidence

Closely related is the question of 'incidence': who *really* benefits from a service? Do children benefit from free education, or do their parents who would otherwise have to pay school fees? Are tenants of subsidised housing the true beneficiaries of the subsidies, or can employers attract labour to the area at lower wages than they would otherwise have to pay? In each case different assumptions about who really gains may be plausible and affect the findings.

Valuation

To look at the combined effects of different services, their values have to be added up in some way, most conveniently by putting a money value on them. But to do this requires a price for the services received. This is fine for cash benefits, but not for benefits that come as services 'in kind', such as the NHS or education. To know how much someone benefits from a service, you want to know how much it is worth *to them* – but you cannot usually observe this. Most studies use the *cost* to the state of providing the service. But 'value' and 'cost' are not necessarily the same. It may *cost* a great deal to provide people with a particular service, but if offered the choice they might prefer a smaller cash sum to spend how they like: the cost is higher than its value to the recipients. Conversely, collective provision may be much cheaper than private alternatives, so the value of the NHS, for instance, may be *greater* in terms of what people would otherwise have to pay privately than its cost to the taxpayer.

Distribution between which groups?

Comparing groups arranged according to some income measure is of obvious interest, but so may be looking at distribution between social classes, age groups, men and women, or ethnic groups. A related issue is the 'unit of analysis': households, families or individuals? A larger unit makes some things easier: we do not have to worry about how income is shared within the family or household. But it may mask what we are interested in: for instance, distribution between men and women. It may also affect how we classify different beneficiaries. The official Office for National Statistics (ONS) results described below examine the distribution of welfare benefits between *households*. In this analysis, a family with four children 'scores' the same as a single pensioner living alone – the

situation of six people is given the same weight as that of one person. Weighting each person equally would change the picture.

Distribution of what?

Depending on the question, different measures will be appropriate. We might be interested in gross public spending, or in net public spending after allowing for taxes financing services, or in gross public spending in relation to need. These can give apparently conflicting answers. NHS spending may be concentrated on the poor, but that may reflect their poor health. Allowing for differences in sickness rates, the distribution of NHS care in relation to need may not favour the poor after all.

Similarly, the gross benefits from a service may appear 'pro-rich'; that is, its absolute value to high-income households exceeds that to low-income households, say by 50 per cent. But if the tax that pays for the service is twice as much for rich households, the *combination* of the service and the tax may still be *redistributive*, in that the poorer households are net gainers and the richer ones net losers.

Time period

In a single week fewer people will receive a service than over a year. As services vary across the life cycle, a single year snapshot will differ from the picture across a whole lifetime. But available data relate to short time periods: there are no surveys tracking use of welfare services throughout people's whole lives. To answer questions about lifetime distribution requires hypothetical models – the results from which depend greatly on the assumptions fed into them.

Data problems

Finally, research in this area is based on sample surveys: whole-population surveys such as the Census do not ask the questions about incomes and service use required. Even the sample surveys may not be very specific, asking, for instance, whether someone has visited a GP recently, but not how long the consultation lasted, whether any expensive tests were done and so on. Results assume that GP visits are worth the same to all patients. But this may gloss over the point at issue: if GPs spend longer on appointments with middle-class patients – and are more likely to send them for further treatment – the distribution of medical services may be 'pro-rich', even if the number of GP consultations is constant between income groups.

Some Empirical Results

This section illustrates some of these issues by considering findings from empirical analysis, contrasting the gross distribution of welfare services to that of the taxes required to pay for them.

Figure 30.1 shows official ONS (2014) estimates of the average benefits in cash and kind from welfare services received by households in different income groups in the financial year 2012–13. Households are arranged in order of income, including cash benefits but after direct taxes like income tax, and allowing for the greater needs of bigger households (technically, 'equivalent net income'). The poorest tenth is on the left, the richest on the right.

On average, households with the bottom half of incomes received 1.9 times as much from cash benefits (including tax credits) as those with the top half. Means-tested benefits such as Income Support and Housing Benefit and tax credits are most concentrated on the poorest, but even 'universal' benefits such as the retirement pension are worth more to lower than to higher income households.

The figure also shows official estimates of the combined value of benefits in kind from the NHS, state education and housing subsidies. There are different ways of doing this, and answers will vary depending on things such as how the benefits of higher education for students living away from home are treated, or the way in which housing subsidies are calculated. Also, the assumption that people of the same age and gender use the health service equally is not necessarily correct: other characteristics affect service use too. However, even with adjustments for such issues, the general picture is similar: benefits in kind are less concentrated on the poor than cash benefits, but households at the bottom of the distribution receive considerably more than those at the top. On the ONS's estimates, these benefits in kind were worth an average of £7,400 for the poorest tenth of households in 2012–13, but only £4,700 for the richest tenth. On these estimates, the absolute value of welfare benefits and services is greatest for low-income households, and lower than average for high-income families. Taxation, by contrast, is greater in absolute terms for those with higher incomes (although it is not necessarily a greater proportion of income).

Most welfare spending is financed from general taxation, so it is hard to be precise about *which* taxes are paying for welfare: if state education were abolished, would it be income tax or VAT which

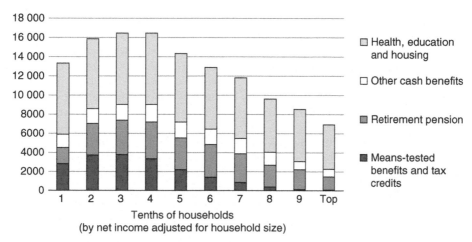

Figure 30.1   Welfare benefits and services by income group, 2012–13 (£).
Source: based on figures from ONS (2014).

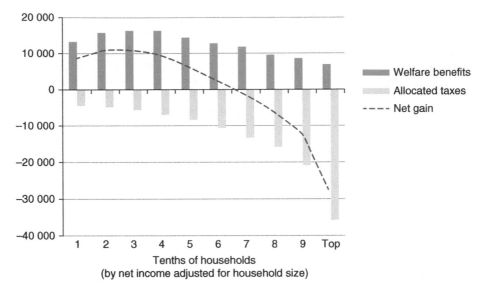

Figure 30.2 Benefits and allocated taxes by income group, 2012–13 (£).
Source: based on figures from ONS (2014).

would fall? Figure 30.2 compares the total of welfare benefits given in the previous figure with the ONS's estimates of the impact of national insurance contributions and an equal proportion (about 95 per cent in this year with a big budget deficit) of each other household tax to cover the remainder of welfare spending. For the bottom six-tenths of the distribution, benefits are higher than taxes and the figures suggest a net gain; for those in the top four groups (particularly the top two-tenths) taxes are higher, suggesting a net loss.

These results suggest that on a cross-sectional basis, the combination of welfare services and, on plausible assumptions, their financing is significantly redistributive from high- to low-income groups – although they say nothing about the scale of such gains in relation to 'need', such as for medical care.

However, it should also be remembered that redistribution also takes effect over the lifetime of individual citizens. Over their lives people both receive benefits and pay taxes. Those with higher lifetime incomes pay much more tax than those with low incomes. In effect, people finance some of the benefits they receive through their *own* lifetime tax payments. However, some people do not pay enough lifetime tax to pay for all of their benefits; they receive 'net lifetime benefits' from the system. These net lifetime benefits are paid for

by others who pay more than enough tax to finance their own benefits; they pay 'net lifetime taxes' into the system. Evidence on this lifetime redistribution suggests that on a lifetime basis the system does still redistribute from the 'lifetime rich' to the 'lifetime poor', but as it was in the 1980s and 1990s, nearly three-quarters of what the welfare state does is like a 'savings bank', and only a quarter is 'Robin Hood' redistribution between different people (see Hills, 2015a, ch. 3).

Emerging Issues

How welfare services are distributed has a major bearing on whether we judge them successful. The results presented above suggest that lower-income households receive more from the welfare state than they pay at any one time. As a corollary, policies to reduce the government budget deficit by cutting welfare services and benefits hit those in the bottom half of the distribution harder than those at the top; doing it through tax increases takes more from those with higher incomes in absolute terms (but much the same from all groups as a share of their income). The Coalition government of 2010–15 put most emphasis on spending cuts, with most analyses suggesting that losses through reduced benefits and services were a much greater share of income for those with lower than for most of those with higher incomes (Hills, 2015b; Reed and Portes, 2014; but see also HM Treasury, 2015).

Distribution between rich and poor is not the only issue though. As the population ages, and the retired population grows in size relative to the working age population, questions are being asked about whether the age groups are being treated fairly – and whether older 'baby boom' generations have done better out of the system than younger ones will do.

Guide to Further Sources

A wider discussion of the effects of the welfare state in redistributing income in a single year and across the life cycle and how to analyse them can be found in chapters 2 and 3 of J. Hills (2015a), *Good Times, Bad Times: The Welfare Myth of Them and Us*, Bristol: Policy Press.

Each year the Office for National Statistics publishes official estimates of the distributional effect of taxation and of a large part of public spending, including social security and welfare services. The figures in this chapter come from ONS (2014), *The Effects of Taxes and Benefits on Household Income, 2012/13*, at: www.ons.gov.uk/ons/taxonomy/index.html?nscl=Effects+of+Taxes+and+Benefits+on+Households)

The Institute for Fiscal Studies (www.ifs.org.uk) publishes regular analysis of the distributional effects and other effects of changes to tax and benefit policies, for instance, those of the Coalition government from 2010 to 2015 in its analysis published after the 2015 Budget in R. Joyce (2015), *Household Incomes: Trends and the Impact of Tax and Benefit Changes* at: www.ifs.org.uk/tools_and_resources/budget/502. The Treasury also publishes distributional analysis of its policies after each Budget and Autumn Statement. See, for instance, HM Treasury (2015), *Impact on Households: Distributional Analysis to Accompany Budget 2015*, London: HM Treasury, at: www.gov.uk/government/publications/budget-2015-documents. Differences in the precise assumptions made can make important differences to the conclusions reached.

For more general discussion of reforms in that period, including their distributional impact, see J. Hills (2015b), 'The Coalition's Policies towards

Cash Transfers', Social Policy in a Cold Climate Working Paper 11, London School of Economics, London, at: sticerd.lse.ac.uk/case/_new/publications/series.asp?prog=SPCCWP.

The distributional effects of cuts in both services and benefits on different groups in the population are discussed in H. Reed and J. Portes (2014), 'Cumulative Impact Assessment', EHRC Research Report 94, Equality and Human Rights Commission, London, at: www.equalityhumanrights.com/publication/research-report-94-cumulative-impact-assessment.

Review and Assignment Questions

1   Is its success in redistributing towards the poor the only, or even the main, criterion we should use in evaluating the impact of the welfare state?
2   Does it matter that some of those with middle or high incomes receive cash benefits and use services like the NHS and state education, as long as they pay in more for them through the tax system?
3   What does the distribution of who receives welfare benefits and services and who pays the taxes that pay for them tell us about how different ways of closing the public budget deficit would affect different groups?
4   If much of what the welfare state does is to act as a 'piggy bank', with people paying in at one point and benefiting later in their lives, is this a safe arrangement, if, for instance, younger generations decided that they no longer wanted to continue with as generous a system?
5   Who gains most, and who loses from the existence of the welfare state and how it is financed? How does the answer change depending on the time period looked at?

Visit the book companion site at www.wiley.com/go/alcocksocialpolicy to make use of the resources designed to accompany the textbook. There you will find chapter-specific guides to further resources, including governmental, international, thinktank, pressure groups and relevant journal sources. You will also find a glossary based on *The Blackwell Dictionary of Social Policy*, help sheets, guidance on managing assignments in social policy and career advice.

31

Divisions and Difference

Sharon Wright

Overview

- The study of the social divisions of welfare is concerned with understanding fundamental and enduring differences between social groups in their experiences of welfare provision and the type of outcomes they receive from it.
- Key divisions have been identified as existing between men and women, between disabled and non-disabled people, and between people of different socio-economic classes, ethnic groups, religions, nationalities, ages and sexualities.
- Social divisions can be complex and cross-cutting.
- Some social groups have distinct and identifiable welfare needs that are different from other categories of people.
- Class is an example of a social division that can influence welfare needs, access to resources and well-being outcome

Why Do Divisions and Differences Matter?

Processes of individualisation, mass consumption and the blurring of social boundaries can all contribute to give the impression that anyone can be anything. But how much choice do we really have in determining our own prospects? Can we choose freely to be who we want to be or are our life experiences and life chances already structured by forces beyond our individual control?

In order to understand contemporary social relations, it is important to note that unique individuals share aspects of their identities with other people. Shared characteristics can form the basis of group cohesion and a sense of inclusion.

The Student's Companion to Social Policy, Fifth Edition. Edited by Pete Alcock, Tina Haux, Margaret May and Sharon Wright.
© 2016 John Wiley & Sons, Ltd. Published 2016 by John Wiley & Sons, Ltd.

However, acknowledging that we belong to one group also involves highlighting that we are excluded from membership of certain other groups, for instance, as a white woman I am neither a black woman nor a white man. This leads us to the main argument of this chapter – that there are differences between social groups and that these differences can be significant and consequential, for instance:

- Globally you are more likely to experience poverty if you are a woman than a man.
- In the UK you could live up to ten years longer if you are a lawyer rather than a labourer.

These are examples of how experiences of well-being and life chances can be related to differences between social groups, which are mediated by social policies. These enduring social inequalities provide a radical challenge to popular misconceptions that self-belief and individual choices are capable of securing a long, healthy life and ensuring well-being. Contrary to the politicised emphasis on aspiration and behaviour, we do not live a social world where anyone can be anything – far from it. We live in societies that are structured by powerful constraints, stratified and deeply divided. On a global scale, the place, gender and socio-economic position we are born into determine to a large extent whether we will experience poverty or wealth. Ultimately, recognising that substantial, long-term divisions exist between different groups within society implies that these groups may have different interests and that these interests may be the source of conflict.

The study of the social divisions of welfare recognises the importance of understanding the different needs and experiences of social groups and argues that where these differences are fundamental and enduring, a division exists in society. The 'big three' social divisions that have received greatest attention in academic literature are class, gender and 'race' or ethnicity. Chronologically, class was the first category to receive sustained attention from social scientists, in the late nineteenth and early twentieth centuries. Much later, in the 1970s and 1980s, feminists and anti-racist writers became more prominent in identifying different social cleavages that had, until then, been largely ignored. This gave birth to

a new field of academic attention, the study of new social movements (see Chapter 14). Furthermore, a number of other divisions have been identified and explored more recently: disability, age, nationality, religion and sexuality.

This wider body of work is relevant for our discussion of social divisions in the sense that it sought to recognise and legitimise difference. In particular, it challenged the basic assumptions on which the welfare state had been built, such as the structure of families. It became necessary to acknowledge that lifestyles, relationships, family formations and the role of men and women had changed dramatically since the post-war period. This led to an increased awareness of issues of difference and the need to recognise the ways in which underlying policy assumptions impact differently on particular groups in society. For instance, the conditions for receiving access to council housing were found to be inherently racist because of their weighting towards those who had been resident in particular geographical areas for longest. Similarly, taxation arrangements (such as tax allowances in the past that were available only to married men) and inheritance laws assumed that long-term relationships were heterosexual, meaning that gay men, lesbian women and bisexual people were excluded from financial benefits and discriminated against in terms of joint claims on property or assets.

Thus, is it essential to recognise that policies that appear to be neutral can have differential impacts upon diverse categories of people. For example, welfare-to-work policies and programmes (such as the Work Programme; see Chapter 48) are presented as neutral in constructing paid work as the best way to provide for welfare needs. However, on closer inspection, we can see that compelling people who receive social security benefits to look for paid work may conflict with their other responsibilities, most significantly with caring roles. For example, in the UK, it is perfectly legitimate for a married woman to stay at home to bring up her own children if her partner is in well-paid employment. However, if the same woman was to split up from her partner, she would be required to look for a job in order to claim social security benefits, so her role as a full-time mother might be open to challenge (see Chapters 56 and 57).

Understanding Difference and Divisions

The experience of social divisions is related to differences between social groups. As we have already seen, each of us shares aspects of our identity with other people. The relationship between different groups is complex and variable. Social differences can (but do not always) lead to social divisions. At some points, one aspect of our group identity might be more important than others. On a rainy Saturday afternoon, for instance, being Scottish may matter more to a row of rugby spectators, as they watch their national team play against England, than being either male or female, or being working class or middle class.

However, Scottish national identity may have become much less important by 9 o'clock the following Monday morning when the rugby fans go back to their usual activities. Gender is likely to have a big influence on whether or not they are at home looking after children. For those who are in paid work, gender and class are likely to be related to the type of job they do, the amount of money they get paid for it and their potential future progression. Although the gender pay gap has narrowed, women still earn 9.4 per cent less than men (National Statistics, 2014). This example provides two insights. First, that it is impossible to make blanket assumptions about which aspects of group membership are most important to people's identities. Second, we can observe that people can belong to multiple groups and that social divisions may intersect or be cross-cutting. Ultimately, the differences between men and women or people of different classes, for instance, are of particular interest because they are related to their command of personal and collective resources, such as wealth, status and power. Since these are the means by which they can protect themselves from risks such as poverty, they bear a direct relationship to their means of meeting welfare needs.

Membership of some social categories may be dynamic, fluid or transitional, whilst membership of others may be more fixed. Clearly, for each individual, membership of some social groups is more fixed than others – people usually retain their gender throughout their life-time, but their age changes constantly, shifting through different phases of childhood, youth, adulthood and older age. It is interesting to consider how these multiple, and perhaps conflicting, social identities are negotiated, reconciled or changed. Each of us can exercise a degree of choice over membership of some social groups. We cannot choose the gender we are born with, but it is possible to change it. Similarly, we did not control the geographical place into which we were born, but we may (with access to resources) move to another town or country; we may choose to seek an alternative lifestyle, national citizenship or religion. However, such identity and status markers are often so deeply embedded that we would never consider exercising this choice.

On the other hand, we may experience a change that moves us against our will from one category to another, for example, a car accident could move us from non-disabled to disabled. So there is a complex relationship between the exercise of individual agency, or choice, and the impact of wider structural constraints. Although individuals can exercise some choice in decisions about their lives, they often do so within very powerful barriers. The value of a social divisions approach is that we can begin to understand some of the major axes of these structures of opportunity and constraint.

It is important not to over-simplify the issue of social divisions. In terms of social policy analysis, we are interested in how they affect well-being. Understanding divisions and difference is concerned with the role of the state, the market and the voluntary sector in creating, perpetuating, mediating or tempering the structures and processes that influence people's life experiences and life chances. Since social policies are designed to intervene in areas of well-being (such as health, income, housing or education), understanding how they impact differentially upon groups in divided societies is a crucially important task.

Studies of the social divisions of welfare have shown, essentially, that the costs and benefits of a welfare state are shared out unevenly between different groups of people. That is, the financial support (for example, social security for disabled people) and services (like healthcare) offered by the welfare state, as well as the costs of maintaining it (through paying taxes or charges), impact differentially on particular groups of people. Often this literature is based on an explicit or implicit argument that certain groups in society benefit unfairly from past and present welfare arrangements, whilst others are disadvantaged. People from more affluent socio-economic groups, for instance, can be shown to benefit more from services such as healthcare, but may pay proportionally less in some types of tax than their less affluent counterparts (however, this is a complex issue since the taxation burden and redistributive effects of welfare vary depending on how they are measured; see Chapter 30 for an analysis of this issue).

The following section uses the example of class to provide a more in-depth illustration of some of the key issues involved in analysing social divisions. Class was chosen as a case study because it is one of the most fundamental divisions in contemporary society. Also, unlike many of the other categories of division and difference, it is not explicitly investigated in greater depth elsewhere in this book (for example, for gender, see Chapters 5, 13 and 57; for 'race' and ethnicity, see Chapters 32 and 62; for age, see Chapters 58–60; for disability, see Chapter 61, and for religion and nationality, see Chapter 29).

Class: A Case Study of Divisions and Difference

Class presents an interesting example because, although it was the first social division to be recognised, it became commonly misunderstood and by the late 1990s was often overlooked. The work of classic theorists Karl Marx and Max Weber in the late nineteenth and early twentieth centuries was extremely influential in recognising deep divisions in societies. The main argument is that societies are stratified, or layered (like a wedding cake), with clear divisions between different social classes, which have largely separate and conflicting interests.

Marx believed the struggle between social classes would drive social change. Weber (although he accepted much of Marx's analysis) had a different view, holding that occupational classification would determine social status and life chances. Although societies have changed significantly since this body of work was written, these approaches continue to have relevance in their

recognition of class differences, and, more particularly, in Marx's analysis, class interests and conflicts. This leads us to a view of individuals who are connected to wider society through processes that are political and exploitative.

Perhaps it is partly *because* of this long history of class analysis – and the socialist or communist associations that it conjures up – that it became distinctly unfashionable to talk about class divisions in society. Some commentators even went as far as to announce the demise of class. However, the early twenty-first century has seen a revival of interest in class analysis.

Popular perceptions of class seem to be influenced by the life stories of celebrities such as David Beckham, J. K. Rowling or Lord Alan Sugar. Each of these individuals has tales of building massive personal wealth from humble beginnings – playing football at school, writing in a café or selling vegetables out of the back of a van. However, these extraordinary triumphs of personal talent over adversity, leading to multi-millionaire status, are exactly that – extraordinary and individual. The reason they are so newsworthy is that they are exceptional. Most people living in Britain retain the social class they were born into, much the same as a century ago. Where social mobility between classes does occur, it is generally at the boundaries between them, rather than the extremes of rags to riches. Social mobility (improving social status) is lower in the UK than in many comparable counties and is falling, meaning that it is less likely now than before that young people will have better prospects than their parents. Since inequality is also rising, the gaps between those born into wealth or poverty are also widening.

Thus, it is possible to identify distinct social classes (see below for further discussion on how this is done in practice) and it is evident that these classes are considerably cohesive. The next question to think about is: do the interests of different classes coincide or conflict? Furthermore, how do processes of inclusion and exclusion operate to reinforce positions of advantage and disadvantage? There are no easy answers to these questions, but it is worth considering, for instance, the ways in which class divisions are reproduced over generations through subtle processes of inclusion and exclusion. For example, during the transition from childhood to adulthood, young people experience a series of opportunities and constraints as they make important life decisions such as when to leave school, what sort of job to get and whether or not to go to university.

Class-based analysis also provides a fruitful basis for reflection on the welfare state. On the one hand, it is interesting to consider the role class interests played in the development of state welfare. For instance, one explanation for increased state intervention in the nineteenth and early twentieth centuries and the establishment of the post-war welfare state in the UK and elsewhere (see Chapters 16–18 and 63) is that it was a response to 'pressure from below' as working-class people (who previously had no vote) demanded that their welfare needs be met. On the other hand, more than half a century later, we could ask questions about why the welfare state has not made more of a difference in addressing class-based inequalities in health, education or in eradicating poverty. Class is, therefore, very much alive as a major social division.

Socio-economic classification

The precise definition of class and what it means to people, however, is the source of much debate and research. In the UK, socio-economic class is defined and measured officially using the National Statistics Socio-Economic Classification (NS-SEC).

This classification is based on occupation, taking into account the status and size of the organisation, the type of occupation and the status of the job (for example, routine or professional, lower supervisory or higher managerial), and is used in official surveys to capture a sense of the social and economic position of UK residents.

More recent sociological work (Savage et al., 2013) has argued for a rethink of the definition and measurement of class in the UK to include social and cultural preferences and resources, as well as occupation and financial resources. This used data from a national survey and that generated by the BBC's online 'Great British Class Survey' to reflect on changes to class structures. The research found that, although there was still evidence of traditional middle and working classes, there were new classes that did not easily fit within the existing categories (see Table 31.1). Instead, evidence was found of seven categories (see Table 31.2), including the new ones of 'new affluent workers', 'emerging service class' and the 'precariat' (with low

Table 31.1 UK National Statistics Socio-Economic Classification.

1	Higher managerial, administrative and professional occupations:
	1.1 large employers and higher managerial and administrative occupations;
	1.2 higher professional occupations.
2	Lower managerial, administrative and professional occupations
3	Intermediate occupations
4	Small employers and own account workers
5	Lower supervisory and technical occupations
6	Semi-routine occupations
7	Routine occupations
8	Never worked and long-term unemployed

Source: ONS (2015).

levels of economic, social and cultural resources, associated with insecure work).

The idea of a 'precariat' class was first mooted by Standing (2011), who argued that processes of globalisation have created insecurity and precariousness in the prospects of working life for a large swathe of society. A subsequent range of analysts have expanded on this notion, drawing attention to the proliferation of insecure forms of employment, such as casual, zero-hours, short hours or temporary jobs that offer uncertainty and low or variable pay to employees. Standing argues that this is dangerous because it is associated with social unrest and mass protests.

Another related and important debate is about how to categorise people who are not in paid

Table 31.2 Latent classes in Britain.

1	Elite
2	Established middle class
3	Technical middle class
4	New affluent workers
5	Traditional working class
6	Emergent service workers
7	Precariat

Source: Savage et al. (2013: 230). Office for National Statistics (2015), at: www.ons.gov.uk/ons/guide-method/classifications/current-standard-classifications/soc2010/soc2010-volume-3-ns-sec--rebased-on-soc2010--user-manual/index.html.

employment. The idea of a distinct class of non-workers can be traced back to Marx, who identified a group below labourers that he called the '*lumpenproletariat*'. More recently, however, the analysis of this type of group has been heavily politicised in highly controversial debates about whether or not an 'underclass' exists. This issue is not, therefore, simply a matter of statistical classification. The term 'underclass' was coined by an American academic, Charles Murray, who argued that a separate and dangerous group of poor people existed, whose behaviour presented a threat to the moral fabric of society. Murray's work has been discredited in a number of ways. The research methods that he used to reach his conclusion have been exposed as deeply flawed. Furthermore, his work has been interpreted as politically motivated and biased by right-wing values and beliefs about how other people behave. Most seriously, the idea of an 'underclass' has been seen as offensive, particularly in relation to its racist undertones.

Although the 'underclass' label remains popular with politicians and the media, it has been viewed by social scientists as an unacceptable way of conceptualising issues of class difference and poverty. Instead, many academics prefer to consider people who have very low incomes as 'living in poverty' or 'experiencing social exclusion' (see Chapter 33). This has the advantage of moving the analysis away from considering only individual behaviour (or exercising 'agency') to incorporating wider structural causes, such as worldwide economic recession, for understanding phenomena such as unemployment. We must also remember that 'non-workers' cannot be used as a definition for a class that is associated with poverty, since it would also include a range of people who do not have jobs but nonetheless have incomes or assets from other sources (for example, rich land-owners).

Emerging Issues

Understanding how differences between social groups affect well-being is an essential part of understanding how societies operate and how social policies affect our everyday lives. There are major differences between individuals and groups of people in relation to their life chances

and life experiences. The first category to be identified by theorists was class. From the 1970s onwards, gender, 'race' and ethnicity were also identified as key divisions. More recently, growing attention has been paid to inequalities that relate to age, religion, nationality, sexuality, health and disability. Researchers and campaigners have argued that diversity needs to be recognised as legitimate in the design of social policies. Challenges remain for policymakers in balancing the recognition of diversity with the provision of fair policies that produce equitable outcomes. For students and analysts of social policies, social divisions are an important way in which major axes of inclusion and exclusion can be understood.

Guide to Further Sources

G. Payne (2013), *Social Divisions*, 3rd edn, Basingstoke: Palgrave, is an indispensable introduction to the issues addressed in this chapter. An engaging account of why class differences matter can be found in O. Jones (2012), *Chavs: The Demonization of the Working Class*, London: Verso; and G. Standing (2011), *The Precariat: The New Dangerous Class*, London: Bloomsbury Academic, and G. Standing (2014), *A Precariat Charter*, London: Bloomsbury Academic, provide thought-provoking insights into current debates.

For definitions and measurements of class, see M. Savage, F. Devine, N. Cunningham, M. Taylor, Y. Li, J. Hjellbrekke, B. Le Roux, S. Friedman and A. Miles (2013), 'A new model of social class? Findings from the BBC's Great British Class Survey Experiment', *Sociology*, 47:2, 219–50; Great British class calculator at: www.bbc.com/news/magazine-22000973; and Office for National Statistics (2015), at: www.ons.gov.uk/ons/guide-method/classifications/current-standard-classifications/soc2010/soc2010-volume-3-ns-sec--rebased-on-soc2010--user-manual/index.html.

Review and Assignment Questions

1   In which ways are societies divided and why is this important for understanding welfare needs?

2 Choose one example of a social division (e.g. gender, race/ethnicity, class, ethnicity, disability). What differences exist for that group in relation to:
   a. the type and extent of their welfare needs;
   b. the type of services that exist to meet needs;
   c. the outcomes of these services?
3 What is class and why is it important for understanding welfare systems?
4 Why do politicians continue to use the term 'underclass' when it has been discredited by researchers?

5 How do social divisions of welfare operate to advantage or disadvantage certain groups?

Visit the book companion site at www.wiley.com/go/alcocksocialpolicy to make use of the resources designed to accompany the textbook. There you will find chapter-specific guides to further resources, including governmental, international, thinktank, pressure groups and relevant journal sources. You will also find a glossary based on *The Blackwell Dictionary of Social Policy*, help sheets, guidance on managing assignments in social policy and career advice.

32

'Race', Minority Ethnic Groups and Social Welfare

Lucinda Platt

░■

Overview

- Racialised perceptions and historical experiences of marginalisation inform our understanding of who constitute the UK's minority ethnic groups.
- Minority groups differ in average age, employment, income, region of settlement. Differences within as well across groups are also substantial.
- Social policy can impact ethnic minorities directly through immigration and race relations policies and indirectly through, for example, social security, housing and employment policies.
- Younger age profiles and greater risks of unemployment and poverty mean minority groups are disproportionately affected by policies relating to children, families and poverty reduction.
- Minority groups will constitute a larger proportion of the future population of western countries. Their current welfare therefore has long-run consequences.

░■

'Race', Ethnicity and Classification

Defining ethnic minority groups

Who belongs to the ethnic majority or an ethnic minority is a complex and contested question. Conceptual distinctions based on sociological theories of race and ethnicities translate only approximately into popular understandings or the categories that countries use for monitoring or measurement. While it is recognised that races do not exist in any meaningful biological sense, the

The Student's Companion to Social Policy, Fifth Edition. Edited by Pete Alcock, Tina Haux, Margaret May and Sharon Wright.
© 2016 John Wiley & Sons, Ltd. Published 2016 by John Wiley & Sons, Ltd.

language of race is embedded within both popular discourse and policy, and people act as if it has meaning, including through racism. *Racism* is behaviour that uses physical markers of difference such as skin colour as the basis of assumed inferiority and as a justification for hostility and unfavourable treatment. *Racialisation* is the process by which a dominant group comes to construct others as 'races', based on particular characteristics (typically phenotype, but also potentially other characteristics such as other physical features, accent, national or regional origins, religion, and so on). The racialised group is then ascribed a common social position and assumed common (negatively valued) attributes.

In the UK and Europe the terminology of ethnic groups is widely used by researchers and policymakers instead of that of 'race'. *Ethnicity* is a self-conscious and claimed identity that is shared with others on the basis of belief in common descent, and may be linked to country of origin, language, religion or customs. It may also be shaped by experiences of colonisation or migration. Ethnicity assumes a notion of a group to which belonging is asserted, even if such belonging stems in part from prior processes of ascription by the dominant population. Everyone in principle belongs to an ethnic group, and hence it is inaccurate to conflate ethnicity with minority ethnicity. Nevertheless, ethnicity is often regarded as being salient predominantly for those of minority ethnicity and, typically, for those of non-white ethnicity: dominant groups often only perceive the ethnicity of others, while regarding themselves as not ethnically marked.

Race and ethnicity continue to be linked conceptually, since ethnic minority groups are typically racialised and subject to racism. Cultural racism is also argued to stem from the allocation of individuals to groups that are assumed to be culturally, rather than necessarily phenotypically (that is, in terms of skin colour) distinct. Increasingly, such cultural distinctiveness is linked to religious affiliation, and in particular Islam, rather than national origins, although it is typically at the intersection of religious affiliation with ethnic origins (and 'colour') that cultural racism plays out.

The UK classification and policy focus has tended to be on non-white ethnic minorities, further demonstrating the conflation of notions of 'race' and ethnicity. Colour-based racism within society and within service provision was regarded as the primary challenge for policy development

and delivery. However, the boundaries of 'whiteness' are themselves malleable and recent research on migration from eastern Europe to the UK has highlighted how these groups have become 'racialised'. The long-standing disadvantage of the Irish also attests to prior historical periods in which common-sense understandings of 'race' based on a white–non-white divide cannot account for explicit processes of differentiation and marginalisation of certain 'white' groups.

Ethnic group classification in England and Wales

In the UK, ethnicity was first measured in the national censuses in 1991. Due to differences in census data collection across the constituent countries of the UK, the classification for England and Wales has developed slightly differently from that implemented in Scotland and Northern Ireland. Since the vast majority of the UK's minority groups live in England and Wales, for simplicity most of the illustrations used in this chapter will be restricted to these jurisdictions. Table 32.1 shows the evolution of classifications for the 1991, 2001 and 2011 censuses. Key changes introduced after 1991 were the introduction of recognition of white minorities and the development of 'mixed' categories to enable respondents to express dual heritages. The order of the groups also changed.

Table 32.1 also shows the population proportion of each group in 2011 (see too Chapter 26). According to 2011 UK census figures, minorities (that is, all those not in the first category of White English/Welsh/Scottish, etc.) made up 19.5 per cent of the population of England and Wales. The proportion of non-white minorities increased to its 2011 figure of around 14 per cent from around 6.5 per cent in 1991.

The UK's ethnic groups have distinct age profiles, which informs their interaction with social policy (Figure 32.1; see too Chapter 26). White UK and White Irish and to a lesser extent Black Caribbeans have substantial shares aged 60+, and therefore are more likely receive pensions and be heavier users of health and social care. The other groups are younger, with large shares of children among Pakistani, Bangladeshi and Black African groups, and with the growing numbers of 'mixed' heritage being predominantly children. One in five (21 per cent) under-15s is from one

Table 32.1 Census ethnic group categories in England and Wales 1991–2011.

1991	2001	2011
White	*White*	*White*
	British	English/Welsh/Scottish/Northern Irish/ British (80.5%)
	Irish	Irish (0.9%)
		Gypsy or Traveller (0.1%)
	Any other White background	Any other White background (4.4%)
Black-Caribbean	*Mixed*	*Mixed/multiple ethnic groups*
Black-African	White and Black Caribbean	White and Black Caribbean (0.8%)
Black-Other	White and Black African	White and Black African (0.3%)
Indian	White and Asian	White and Asian (0.6%)
Pakistani	Any other Mixed background	Any other Mixed/multiple ethnic background (0.5%)
Bangladeshi	*Asian or Asian British*	*Asian/Asian British*
Chinese	Indian	Indian (2.5%)
Any other ethnic group	Pakistani	Pakistani (2.0%)
	Bangladeshi	Bangladeshi (0.8%)
		Chinese (0.7%)
	Any other Asian background	Any other Asian background (1.5%)
	Black or Black British	*Black/African/Caribbean/Black British*
	Caribbean	African (1.8%)
	African	Caribbean (1.1%)
	Any other Black background	Any other Black/African/Caribbean background (0.5%)
	Chinese or other ethnic group	*Other ethnic group*
	Chinese	Arab (0.4%)
	Any other	Any other ethnic group (0.6%)

Source: Office for National Statistics (ONS). The 'other' categories allowed a write-in response. In 1991, an additional category of 'Other Asian' was constructed from write-in responses and was reported in statistical outputs.

of the non-white minority groups: they thus form a substantial share of those in school and are impacted by education and family policies (see Chapters 51 and 57). The overall population share of minorities will clearly increase as they grow up, regardless of migration policy.

Ethnic minorities and social policy

A key aim of the census classification – and the collection of data on ethnic group more generally – is to identify inequalities, monitor changes over time and to inform policies to address these inequalities. Two forms of policy can impact the experience of minority ethnic groups: targeted and untargeted. Immigration (see Chapter 62) and race relations policies are policies directly targeted on minority groups, whether their access to national citizenship and the graduated rights of non-citizens, or redress for unequal treatment. Social policies can also be targeted to provide particular support, for example, with job search or through translation and interpretation to help access services. However, non-targeted policies designed for the population as a whole also impact different ethnic groups to a lesser or greater degree.

As mentioned, age structure affects exposure to and use of specific areas of social policy. But groups' more or less disadvantaged position also informs the extent to which they are greater or heavier users of particular social policy domains, such as income-related benefits, disability benefits, social housing and so on. Both the design of policies and the extent to which they are more or

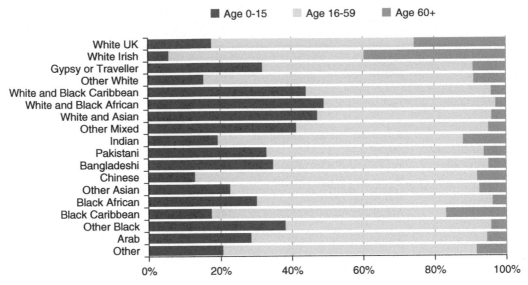

Figure 32.1 Age profiles of the ethnic groups in England and Wales, 2011.
Source: ONS 2011 Census. Drawn by author from table DC2101EW.

less generous can therefore mitigate or exacerbate inequalities between groups. This makes the chapters in Parts VIII and IX of this volume relevant to the social welfare of ethnic minorities. For reasons of space, this chapter focuses only on employment and income (see also Chapters 47 and 48). First, the next section provides some broader context.

Social Policy, Social Welfare and Ethnic Minority Groups

Immigration and ethnicity paradigms and policy regimes

Two different paradigms structure the relationship of states to their ethnic minorities. What I term the *immigrant paradigm* is typically concerned with the individual-level characteristics of immigrants (and their descendants) that may 'explain' their disadvantage relative to the majority population. A substantial degree of attention is paid, under this paradigm, to fluency in the destination society country: language as a key individual characteristic is assumed to impact employment and pay, and which immigrants (and their children) should be expected to master. The *ethnicity paradigm* by contrast focuses on ethnic groups as a whole, with the

primary focus being structural factors that limit opportunities and restrict equal participation, and the appropriate identification and elimination of discrimination.

While both paradigms operate side by side to some degree, whichever is dominant will tend to inform policies specifically focused on minority groups. For example, while some countries have placed more emphasis on assimilation to national norms and learning the language of the destination country as a route to citizenship, others have taken a multicultural stance, facilitating cultural maintenance.

The UK initially went down the more 'multicultural route' and had an early emphasis on anti-discrimination legislation. But approaches intersect in complex ways to form 'immigration regimes': Joppke (1999) characterised the UK as 'externally exclusive but internally inclusive', with restrictive control of access to the country, but an emphasis on equality of treatment once resident. Thus, increasingly restrictive controls on entry from 1962 onwards were accompanied by the introduction of equalities legislation as early as 1965, followed by more comprehensive statements on the illegality of direct and indirect discrimination in the 1976 Race Relations Act, still long before that implemented by other countries or required by the EU (see Chapter 62).

Distinctive 'immigration regimes' across European countries have, however, shown substantial convergence over time in terms of both rights and restrictions. Broader developments have also transformed the relationship of states to their (minority) populations. For example, conditionality of social security benefits and an emphasis on 'welfare to work' (see Chapter 56), and the expansion of the EU to twenty-eight countries by 2013 (see Chapter 46), with EU transnational citizenship premised primarily on free movement for the purposes of paid work both changed policies towards non-EU immigration and reinforced the emphasis on employment as fundamental to participation.

Minority groups' and migration histories

The contemporary position of minority groups in the UK continues to be influenced by different histories of migration. Figure 32.2 illustrates the timing of arrival of those from selected countries of birth that approximate to some of the main Census ethnic group categories. While Poles are overwhelmingly 'new' arrivals, even more so than Nigerians, Caribbeans, specifically those born in Jamaica, and Irish nationals arrived primarily in the early post-war migration period. Bangladeshis and Pakistanis have a more intermediate profile,

while Indians are represented by both old and new flows.

The extent to which timing of arrival related to particular phases of deindustrialisation, alongside the specific skills and resources that groups brought with them resulted in different patterns of settlement and occupational concentration among immigrants. Despite substantial educational attainment and upward mobility, this has had consequences for differentiated experiences across subsequent generations.

Minority groups continue to have very different spatial distributions and (somewhat relatedly) occupational concentrations. For example, 58 per cent of Black Africans and Black Caribbeans and 50 per cent of Bangladeshis lived in London in 2011 compared with 14 per cent of the total population of England and Wales. Twenty per cent of Pakistanis lived in each of the West Midlands and Yorkshire, compared with 10 and 9 per cent of the England and Wales population, respectively. In terms of occupation, in 2011, over a quarter of Bangladeshis and Chinese were working in accommodation and food services, compared with 5 per cent of the majority population; while over a quarter of Black Africans were working in human health and social work occupations compared with 12 per cent of the majority.

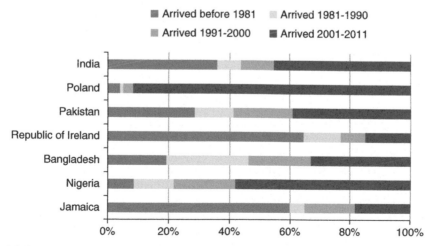

Figure 32.2 Time of arrival in the UK, by country of origin, selected countries, England and Wales, 2011.
Source: ONS. Drawn by author from 2011 Census table DC2804EWr.

Ethnic Minority Groups and Social Welfare

Employment

Employment and unemployment rates of working age adults show substantial differences across ethnic groups (Figure 32.3). A wealth of research from both the UK and Europe demonstrates that such differences are not specific to the first (immigrant generation), nor can they be fully accounted for by differences in age, educational attainment or occupational sector, even if these all play some role. The remaining gap, described as an 'ethnic penalty', can be attributed, at least in part, to discrimination. Those in work face pay gaps, which, while they again stem in part from regional and occupational differences, again leave an unexplained element, likely to reflect employment discrimination that persists despite race relations legislation. The 'Other White' ethnic group had typically shown substantial advantage in pay and employment, but the earnings of Eastern Europeans are highly concentrated close to the level of the minimum wage, transforming the profile of this 'group'.

Unemployment rates are particularly high for some groups of men, notably Black Caribbeans and Black Africans. The full age range covered in Figure 32.3 disguises some of the more extreme disadvantage: while young people's employment was a particular casualty of the 2008 recession, unemployment rates among young Black men at the end of 2014 remained double those of young white men (32 per cent compared with 16 per cent). In the years to 2008, employment differentials had shown some signs of declining, partly as a result of clear targets to close the gaps, and corresponding policy initiatives that also 'made work pay'. However, these gains were not sustained.

Turning to women, interest has tended to focus more on differences in economic activity, with steadily increasing expectations that women, regardless of their family situation, will participate in the labour market (see Chapter 57). In a buoyant economy and with concerted measures to support working families with children that characterised the first decade of this century, this may have seemed a reasonable expectation, though participation rates of Pakistani and Bangladeshi women remained relatively low. In times of recession, more limited employment opportunities, particularly for those with less employment experience, may restrict moves out of economic activity and into work. The activity rates of Black Caribbean and Black African women have typically been high, even though these are groups with high rates of lone parenthood, which tends to reduce participation. But they still face disproportionate unemployment risks.

Income

The combination of higher unemployment and inactivity risks pay penalties in employment, and families often with one rather than two earners resulting in higher risks of low income and (child) poverty across minority groups. This is compounded by demographic structure and policies that are more punitive towards families with young children, those of working age and those living in areas of high housing costs. Figure 32.4 shows that all minority groups faced higher poverty rates than the majority, in some cases more than twice as high.

Over the first decade of this century child poverty rates declined substantially among those groups with the highest rates (particularly Pakistanis, Bangladeshi and Black African children). This reflects the impact of policies intended to increase the incomes of low-income families (see Chapters 57 and 58). However, changes in policy since 2010 have hit families with young children particularly hard (see Chapter 33).

Figure 32.4 shows that above-average poverty risks were also experienced by those 'successful' minority groups, such as Chinese and Indian who tend to command high rates of pay on average and relatively high average incomes. This draws attention to inequality – and polarisation – within ethnic groups as well as between them. Widening income inequalities are well documented for the UK and elsewhere. It is clear that such income inequalities are also experienced *within* particular sub-populations. Discussion of disadvantaged 'groups', premised on average experience (as in this chapter), while important in highlighting areas for concern, may therefore not well represent the experience of many from those groups. Instead of commonality of experience within ethnic categories, individuals' social welfare is likely to be highly dependent on how that intersects with

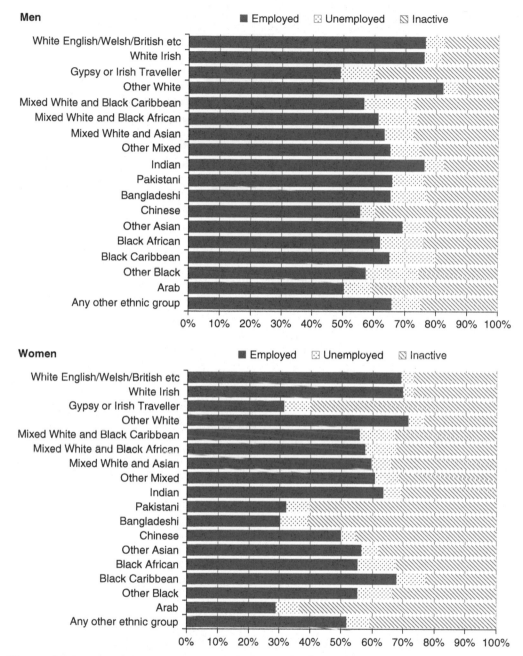

Figure 32.3 Employment status of men and women aged 16–64 by ethnic group, England and Wales, 2011.
Source: ONS. Drawn by author from Census table BD0076.

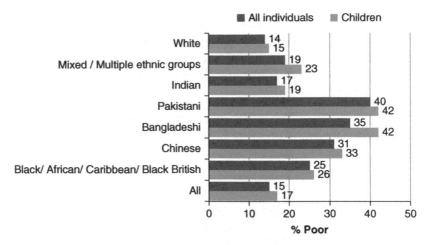

Figure 32.4 Risks of poverty of all individuals and children by ethnic group, UK, 2013–14 (from three-year average).
Source: Households Below Average Incomes 1994/5–2013/14. Drawn by author from tables 3.5db and 4.5db. Poverty is measured as the proportion of those below 60 per cent of median equivalised household income before housing costs; and rates are three-year averages except for 'All' figures.

class position, prior family resources and potential to realise upward mobility.

Emerging Issues

Key issues for the future social welfare of ethnic minority populations include changes in composition as new – and newly racialised – groups such as Eastern Europeans comprise a larger proportion of the population and increasingly settle and have children. In the face of their current often low-paid and marginal employment position, questions remain as to whether they will follow the pattern of earlier White migrant groups, with economic integration over time, ceasing to be distinguished as separate groups in the second and subsequent generations, or whether their current minoritised status will persist.

The differential effects of the 2008 recession on young people, combined with the much higher risks of unemployment for young minorities even compared with young majority group members, raises questions about long-term effects. Even in recovery there is a risk of substantial long-term 'scarring' for those who suffered most from the labour market impacts of the recession.

The post-2015 cuts to social security benefits are likely to have disproportionate effects on minority groups, particularly those with young children and who face labour market disadvantage. We are still to see the long-term effects of these changes and how they affect subsequent life chances. On the other hand, if investment in education is maintained, it could mitigate some of these impacts, given recent evidence that suggests that many minority groups are using education to achieve upward mobility from disadvantaged origins.

These are important considerations for those looking ahead to what the nation will look like over the next fifty years.

Guide to Further Sources

J. Burton, A. Nandi and L. Platt (2010), 'Measuring ethnicity: challenges and opportunities for survey research', *Ethnic & Racial Studies*, 33:8, 1332–49, provide an overview of conceptualisations of race and ethnicity and the implications for measurement categories. I. Shutes (2016), 'Citizenship and migration', in H. Dean and L. Platt (eds), *Social Advantage and Disadvantage*, Oxford: Oxford University Press, offers a detailed and accessible account of migration patterns and differentiated migration statuses. K. Burrell (2010), 'Staying, returning, working and living: key themes in current academic research undertaken in the UK on migration movements from eastern Europe', *Social Identities*, 16:3, 297–308, summarises the explosion of research since 2004 on westward migration from eastern Europe.

C. Joppke (1999), *Immigration and the Nation-State: The United States, Germany, and Great Britain*, Oxford: Oxford University Press, provides an insightful early consideration of particular immigration 'regimes'. A. Nandi and L. Platt (2010), *Ethnic Minority Women's Poverty and Economic Well-Being*, London: Government Equalities Office, demonstrates income inequality within and between ethnic groups, taking a gender perspective. I. Law (2009), 'Racism, ethnicity, migration and social security', in J. Millar (ed.), *Understanding Social Security*, 2nd edn, Bristol: Policy Press, describes the complex ways in which minority status intersects with social security policies. The 'Social Policy in a Cold Climate' research programme gives detailed information on recent policy development and its consequences, including breakdowns by ethnic group, see at: www.sticerd.lse.ac.uk/case/_new/research/Social_Policy_in_a_Cold_Climate.asp; and the Joseph Rowntree Foundation has commissioned a range of research poverty and ethnicity, see at: www.jrf.org.uk/topic/poverty-and-ethnicity.

Review and Assignment Questions

1   Who are the UK's ethnic groups?
2   What are the key features of policy relating to minority ethnic groups?
3   In what ways do general policies intersect with race and ethnicity?
4   Why do employment rates differ across groups?
5   Do ethnic minorities require targeted social policies? Discuss in relation to poverty or employment.

Visit the book companion site at www.wiley.com/go/alcocksocialpolicy to make use of the resources designed to accompany the textbook. There you will find chapter-specific guides to further resources, including governmental, international, thinktank, pressure groups and relevant journal sources. You will also find a glossary based on *The Blackwell Dictionary of Social Policy*, help sheets, guidance on managing assignments in social policy and career advice.

33

Poverty and Social Exclusion

Pete Alcock

Overview

- Poverty has always been a major concern for social policy researchers and policymakers.
- Academics and policymakers disagree about how to define and measure poverty.
- Definition and measurement have been extended to include the problem of social exclusion.
- Poverty and social exclusion are complex multi-dimensional problems, and more sophisticated definitions and measures have been developed to explore them.
- Recent evidence reveals that levels of poverty and social exclusion have remained high in the UK and have been growing in recent years.

Poverty and Social Policy

The problem of poverty has been a key concern of social policy throughout its development. Some of the earliest policy measures introduced in the UK were concerned with it, including in particular the Poor Laws, which can be traced back to the beginning of the seventeenth century and provided the core of social policy provision throughout the nineteenth and early twentieth centuries (see Chapter 16). Poverty has also always been a major focus for academic analysis and research. Some of the earliest social policy research in the

UK, and indeed in the world, sought to define and to measure the extent of poverty in the late nineteenth century in London (Charles Booth) and York (Seebohm Rowntree).

Poverty has been at the centre of social policy in part because it provides a bridge between academic debate and policy action. Starting with Booth and Rowntree, analysts have been concerned to define and measure poverty not merely as an academic exercise, but also because of a belief that, if poverty did exist, then policymakers would be obliged to do something about it. This is because poverty is a policy problem – an *unacceptable* state of

The Student's Companion to Social Policy, Fifth Edition. Edited by Pete Alcock, Tina Haux, Margaret May and Sharon Wright.
© 2016 John Wiley & Sons, Ltd. Published 2016 by John Wiley & Sons, Ltd.

affairs that requires some form of policy response. Debate about, and evidence of, poverty therefore not only is an academic issue but also 'drives' policy development.

There has also, however, been much debate, and disagreement, about exactly what poverty is and how we should seek to define and measure it; and this is linked to its role as a policy driver. The different ways in which we define and measure poverty, and the differing extent of the problem that we therefore reveal, will lead to different demands for policy action, and different forms of policy response. The definition and measurement of poverty are bound up with the policy response to it.

Defining Poverty

The question of how to define poverty is thus at the heart of policy debate and academic analysis; and it is a question to which there is no simple or agreed answer. Academics and policymakers disagree about how to define poverty, in large part because they disagree about what to do about it too. This

was captured most revealingly by the Secretary of State for Social Security in the Thatcher government of the late 1980s, John Moore, who sought to dismiss academic research that had pointed to a growing problem of poverty in the country:

> The evidence of improving living standards over this century is dramatic, and it is incontrovertible. When the pressure groups say that one-third of the population is living in poverty, they cannot be saying that one-third of people are living below the draconian subsistence levels used by Booth and Rowntree. (Moore, speech to Greater London Area CPC, 11 May 1989)

In the 1980s, the Conservative government did not believe that specific policies were needed to combat poverty beyond the well-established provision of social security benefits; and their argument that by the standards of the nineteenth century few people were poor meant that there was no need for further policy action.

At the heart of this controversy is a distinction between what are referred to as absolute and relative definitions of poverty (see Box 33.1).

Box 33.1　Absolute and Relative Poverty

■ Absolute poverty is the idea that being in poverty means being without the essentials of life, and it is sometimes referred to as subsistence poverty. It is often associated with the early research of Booth and Rowntree, who were concerned to identify a subsistence level based on the cost of necessities and then to measure the numbers of people with household incomes below this level, and hence unable to provide for themselves and their families. However, in practice what is essential for life varies according to where and when one is living; and, indeed, when Rowntree repeated his research later on in the twentieth century he extended his list of essential items (see Alcock, 2006, ch. 5). Despite Moore's assertion, most commentators do accept that the 'draconian' levels of the nineteenth century are not a valid basis for determining what it means to be poor over a hundred years later.

■ Relative poverty takes up this notion of changes in the determination of poverty levels over time and place. It has been associated in particular with the work of Townsend, who in the 1950s and 1960s developed a new definition and measurement of poverty linking income to social security benefit levels, which showed that, despite general increases in affluence and improved social security protection, a significant proportion of the UK population did not have enough to achieve the living conditions 'customary' in society. According to this approach, as overall living standards rise so too does the notion of what it means to be poor, so that any definition of poverty will be relative to the average standard of living of all within society. This is sometimes taken to be some proportion of average income levels, which, as we shall see, has become widely used as a poverty level in the UK and across many other developed countries.

Defining poverty by reference to average incomes is nevertheless a potentially circular approach. It would suggest that however much incomes rise a fixed proportion of a country's population would always be poor; and it was just this illogical relativism that Moore was seeking to attack in 1989. What it means to be poor may change over time; but there must be more to the definition of poverty than simply the proportion of average income received.

Income is only an indirect measure of poverty in any event, of course. It is what we are able to buy with our income that determines our actual standard of living. This was recognised by Townsend, who sought to identify indicators that could be used to ascertain whether someone was going without essential items of living. It has since been taken further by a range of different researchers, who have sought to develop the *indicators of poverty* approach, including the use of national surveys to identify those items that a majority of the population think to be essential for modern life and then measure the numbers unable to afford most or all of these, as discussed below.

Deprivation and Exclusion

In developing his relative approach poverty, therefore, Townsend was aware that maintaining a customary standard of living involved more than just having a sufficiently high income. He recognised that people's health, housing and working conditions would also affect living standards, and yet these might be determined by factors beyond current income levels. Townsend discussed these other dimensions of deprivation in the report of his major research on poverty (*Poverty in the United Kingdom*, Penguin, 1979) and argued that it was this notion of deprivation, rather than simply income poverty, that better captured the problem of an inadequate standard of living in modern society.

In the mid-1980s, the contributors to a Child Poverty Action Group (CPAG) publication (Golding, 1986) took up this broader approach and drew attention to an increasingly wide range of other aspects of life that could lead to deprivation for those excluded from them. These included information and communication technology, banking and financial services, and leisure activities, all of which are now readily recognisable as essential elements of modern life. The CPAG book was called *Excluding the Poor*, and it highlighted the notion of exclusion from social activities as an important element of the problem of poverty. It is not just what we *have*, but what we *do* (or do *not* do) that can be a problem in society; and it is this notion of social exclusion that has come to accompany poverty as a broader conceptualisation of this key driver of social policy.

Social exclusion has become a more central feature of UK academic and policy debate in part because of the influence of European policymaking, where it had for some time been a target of EU initiatives However, in 1997 a publicly funded research centre, the Centre for the Analysis of Social Exclusion (CASE) was established in the UK at the LSE. Here the researchers (Hills et al., 2002) developed the idea of exclusion as non-participation in key social activities such as:

- *Consumption*: purchasing of goods and services.
- *Production*: participating in economically or socially valuable activity.
- *Political engagement*: involvement in local or national decision-making.
- *Social interaction*: with family, friends and communities.

This expanded the approach developed in the CPAG book back in the 1980s; and led the researchers to focus their attention on a range of different ways of measuring social exclusion using both quantitative and qualitative approaches, which revealed that the experience of exclusion varied over time and place, with different people experiencing different dimensions of the problem at different times.

The broader approach was also taken up by the Labour government after 1998 through the establishment of a special Social Exclusion Unit reporting directly to the Cabinet Office, though it was later downgraded to a Taskforce. The unit was intended not to combat all the different aspects of exclusion mentioned above, but to focus action on a small number of key policy priorities, such as rough sleeping, school exclusion and teenage pregnancy. The hope was that it would influence policymaking across government departments; however, in this it had limited success, and in 2010 the Coalition government abolished it.

Measuring Poverty and Social Exclusion

Researchers have tried to develop some way of measuring the broader concept of social exclusion, taking account of some of the different dimensions involved. The Joseph Rowntree Foundation and the New Policy Institute, for instance, have supported research for over a decade on a list of indicators linked to different dimensions of money, housing, work, benefits and services (MacInnes et al., 2014). However, the complex and changing information that these multiple measures provide do not make it easy to establish general levels of poverty and social exclusion or track changes in them.

A more sophisticated attempt to do this has been developed in the research led by Gordon on 'Poverty and Social Exclusion' (PSE). This is based on a series of surveys of the population which ask them to identify what they thought were indicators of need, and then counted the numbers of people lacking significant numbers of these because they cannot afford to pay for them. The most recent survey was conducted in 2012 and its results (discussed in Mack and Lansley, 2015) are summarised in Box 33.2.

There was similar support for more general lifestyle indicators, such as visits to family members, leisure activities and (for children) places to study and play.

In 1983, the survey showed 14 per cent of the population lacked three or more of these basic necessities. By 2012, this had more than doubled

---

Box 33.2 Poverty and Social Exclusion Surveys

Over 90 per cent of people agreed on three top indicators of exclusion for adults:

- adequate heating,
- a damp-free home,
- two meals a day.

And four for children:

- a warm winter coat.
- fresh fruit or vegetables once a day.
- new, properly fitting shoes.
- three meals a day.

---

to 33 per cent. In 2012, almost 18 million people could not afford adequate housing; around 14 million could not afford one or more essential household goods; and 4 million children went without two or more items of need – twice the number in 1999.

Although depressing, the picture that these more sophisticated measures of poverty and social exclusion reveal is a rather complex one. However, there is sometimes a need for simple summary measures; and this is to some extent recognised by both academics and policymakers. There are therefore also some simpler (proxy) measures of poverty and social exclusion that are widely employed by researchers and politicians, which provide important evidence of the scale of the problem.

Most important here is the data on income levels produced annually in the 'Households Below Average Income' (HBAI) report, available on the DWP website. This uses a measure of poverty based on those households with an income below 60 per cent of median average income (that is, the mid-point in the income distribution), which is calculated for households both before and after taking account of their housing costs, as these are generally a significant proportion of expenditure over which households have little control. This is a widely cited measure. It is incorporated into the official definition of child poverty, discussed below, and is also utilised in many other developed countries, in particular across the EU.

On the latest figures, from 2013 to 2014, 9.6 million households (15 per cent) were poor before taking account of housing costs and 13.2 million (21 per cent) after this. For children the picture was gloomier with 2.3 million (17 per cent) poor before housing costs and 3.7 million (28 per cent) after. These are high levels of poverty, at least by this income measure; and children are particularly badly affected with over a quarter in relative poverty. The HBAI figures also include information about the differing risk of poverty for different social groups, including those with disabilities and ethnic minorities, and for different geographical regions.

Of course the explanations for these patterns are complex, and Hills and his colleagues explore some of them in his work on inequality. Nonetheless, the figures revealed that the proportions of people in poverty on this low-income measure had remained high since the 1980s, with only some improvement in the early 2000s. This led the

Labour government under Tony Blair to make the problem of child poverty a particular policy target, with a promise to eradicate it by 2020; a commitment enshrined in legislation in the Child Poverty Act 2010 (see too Chapter 57).

The Act also developed a more extensive official definition of child poverty drawing on both income and deprivation measures. It included:

- Relative low income: the proportion of children in household below 60 per cent median income before housing costs.
- Absolute low income: the proportion below 60 per cent at 2010–11 levels, adjusted for price inflation.
- Low income and material deprivation: the proportion below 70 per cent median income and in material deprivation.
- Persistent poverty: the proportion below 60 per cent for at least three out of the last four years.

However, what the recent HBAI figures reveals is that the target of eradicating child poverty by 2020 will be a demanding one. Despite the development of tax credits and the benefit increases introduced under Labour, the interim goal of halving it by 2010 was not met. Further movement will be likely to require policy changes that go some way beyond these. Yet Child Benefit and Child Tax Credits were cutback under the Coalition government; and further reductions are planned by the Conservative government elected in 2015 as part of their plans to cut £12 billion from the social security budget (see Chapter 47).

Emerging Issues

Despite the limited impact of Labour's attempt to eradicate child poverty and to tackle the wider problems of social exclusion, there was a strong policy commitment to anti-poverty policy and the promotion of a reduction in social exclusion as core public policy goals, represented in the creation of the Social Exclusion Unit. In opposition, the Conservatives were critical of Labour's record, however, and argued that despite increased government expenditure it had not succeeded in mending what they called 'Broken Britain'.

The Coalition government therefore abandoned Labour's initiatives, like the exclusion taskforce, and sought to shift the focus of policy development. Its primary policy commitment was the removal of the public sector deficit, and this meant widespread cuts in public expenditure. In particular, it instigated extensive cuts in spending on welfare benefits, with Child Benefit being frozen and means-tested, tax credits scaled back and unemployment benefit levels held below inflation, all of which have increased the pressures on households in poverty (see Chapters 21 and 47).

These trends will also continue under the Conservatives, who, while not formally abandoning Labour's 2020 child poverty target, plan to repeal the 2010 Act and replace it with a redefinition of child poverty, arguing that this is not primarily a function of low income, but rather the result of wider failures in individual and family responses to social problems. The focus will shift to factors such as the proportion of children living in workless households and the levels of educational attainment by school pupils, along with other measures based on family breakdown, debt and addiction.

As the evidence above suggests, levels of poverty and social exclusion have remained high in the UK. They also compare unfavourably with some other EU nations such as France and the Netherlands, and in 2009 the UK was only just above the EU average for the proportion of low income households. Others have higher levels, for instance, Italy and Greece, as do countries beyond Europe, such as Japan or the US.

To a significant extent, of course, poverty and social exclusion are major problems in all countries across the world. This is much more serious when developing countries are taken into account, however, in particular those in Africa and the Indian subcontinent. Here poverty and exclusion are much more pressing, with millions in Africa facing starvation and early death.

Poverty and social exclusion are therefore international – or rather global – problems (see, too, Chapters 70 and 71). This was brought into stark relief by the 'Make Poverty History' campaign in 2005, which sought to put pressure on the developed nations to make commitments to relieve poverty in Africa and elsewhere. This did lead to some promises to increase international aid for developing countries and to 'write-off' debts and trade deficits where these were preventing future economic development; and, in its Millennium

Goals 2000, the United Nations (UN) included a range of targets, including halving extreme poverty by 2015 – though in practice little progress has been made on many of these. International agencies such as the UN Development Programme, the World Health Organization and the World Bank have also become instrumental in implementing a range of international programmes to combat poverty and promote economic development across the world.

There is an increasing recognition amongst leading politicians and policymakers that poverty and social exclusion are global, and not just national, problems; and that concerted international action will be needed to address these – although the extent of the commitment and resources required, and the time taken to achieve significant results may not be fully appreciated by many. The scale of this international challenge has also now been explored by academic researchers, notably by Townsend, who went on to write about the need to combat 'World Poverty'. The future policy climate for poverty and social exclusion is therefore likely increasingly to become an international one, within which national government can only play a limited role.

Guide to Further Sources

The most comprehensive general book on research and policy on poverty and social exclusion is P. Alcock (2006), *Understanding Poverty*, 3rd edn, Basingstoke: Palgrave. R. Lister (2004), *Poverty*, Cambridge: Polity Press, provides a convincing explanation of why poverty is a problem and how we should respond to it, as does P. Spicker (2007), *The Idea of Poverty*, Bristol: Policy Press. Different dimensions of poverty and exclusion are discussed by the contributors to T. Ridge and S. Wright (eds) (2008), *Understanding Inequality, Poverty and Wealth: Policies and Prospects*, Bristol: Policy Press.

An overview of trends in levels of wealth, poverty and inequality is provided by J. Hills, F. Bastagli, F. Cowell, H. Glennerster, E. Karagiannaki and A. McKnight (2013), *Wealth in the UK: Distribution, Accumulation and Policy*, Oxford: Oxford University Press. T. MacInnes, H. Aldridge, S. Bushe, A. Tinson and T. Barryborn (2014), *Monitoring Poverty and Social Exclusion 2014*, York: JR Foundation/New Policy Institute, report on the latest data on their list of indicators.

Early discussion of the dimensions of social exclusion can be found in P Golding (ed.) (1986), *Excluding the Poor*, London: CPAG; and a summary of the early CASE research can be found in J. Hills, J. Le Grand and D. Piachaud (eds) (2002), *Understanding Social Exclusion*, Oxford: Oxford University Press. The most recent PSE survey evidence is discussed in J. Mack and S. Lansley (2105), *Breadline Britain: The Rise of Mass Poverty*, London: One World Books.

Government websites are important sources of official policy and research reports, in particular the Department for Work and Pensions at: www.dwp.gov.uk. The findings of the PSE survey can be access on their website at: www.poverty.ac.uk.

The Joseph Rowntree Foundation website, www.jrf.org.uk, contains copies of their many research reports in the area. The CPAG site, www.cpag.org.uk, includes information on campaigning activity, policy briefings and summaries of recent statistics.

Review and Assignment Questions

1 Why has research on poverty been so important to the development of academic social policy?
2 What is the difference between *absolute* and *relative* poverty?
3 How do the Poverty and Social Exclusion surveys seek to define and measure social exclusion?
4 Why did the Labour government identify child poverty as a policy target, and how successful have we been in eradicating it?
5 To what extent does poverty remain primarily a problem of inadequate income?

Visit the book companion site at www.wiley.com/go/alcocksocialpolicy to make use of the resources designed to accompany the textbook. There you will find chapter-specific guides to further resources, including governmental, international, thinktank, pressure groups and relevant journal sources. You will also find a glossary based on *The Blackwell Dictionary of Social Policy*, help sheets, guidance on managing assignments in social policy and career advice.

PART VI
Welfare Production and Provision

34

State Welfare

Catherine Bochel

■■

Overview

- ■ The role of the state in the provision of welfare grew markedly for much of the twentieth century, yet its extent and form have always been a matter of contention.
- ■ There have been major debates about the balance between public, commercial, voluntary and informal provision and the relationships between and responsibilities of individuals and the state, and these have been reflected in the approaches of governments.
- ■ From the late 1970s, Conservative governments sought to reduce the scope of state provision and make the public sector more similar to the commercial sector in its operation.
- ■ Between 1997 and 2010, Labour were much more accepting of the state's role in welfare, and public expenditure grew significantly.
- ■ The policies of the Coalition from 2010, and from 2015 the Conservative, government implied major changes in the size and role of the state.

■■

Defining the State

The modern state is complex and made up of diverse elements. It is difficult to define in simple terms. There are many views and conceptions of 'the state'. For example, some have seen it as providing protection and security; for some, the term has connotations of secrecy and control; for others, it is the power of the state and the ways in which this is exercised that is of greatest importance. While views of the state are varied and may contribute to our understanding of the state and

The Student's Companion to Social Policy, Fifth Edition. Edited by Pete Alcock, Tina Haux, Margaret May and Sharon Wright.
© 2016 John Wiley & Sons, Ltd. Published 2016 by John Wiley & Sons, Ltd.

its relationships with other entities, space requirements necessitate a more focused approach here. Suffice it to say, one of the most important reasons for studying the state is that it has enormous influence over our lives, and thus the relationships between the state and society and the state and individuals form a key underlying dimension to much of this discussion.

The state and the mixed economy of welfare

In social policy the term 'welfare state' is widely used. Given this appears to imply that the bulk of welfare is provided by the state, an impression perhaps reinforced by the fact that some services used by much of the population, such as healthcare and education, are widely associated with the public sector, it is perhaps unsurprising that there is a widespread belief that the state is the dominant institution in the provision of welfare services.

However, this is no longer the case, if indeed it ever was (see Part III). Welfare services are paid for and provided by a variety of different means, including individuals themselves and organisations from the public, commercial, voluntary and informal sectors. There is therefore a plurality of providers in areas such as healthcare and education, and even more so in relation to services such as child care, housing and pensions, a situation often referred to as 'the mixed economy of welfare'.

One of the major debates in social policy over recent decades has been about the relative sizes and roles of the different sectors, including that of the state in both funding and providing welfare. The balance of responsibility for service provision has changed markedly over time, and we can see, for example, a shift from a growth in state provision from 1945 to the mid-1970s to a greater role for the commercial, voluntary and informal sectors from the 1980s onwards. Increasingly, from the late 1990s 'state' welfare services have been provided by or in partnership with organisations from these sectors, and from 2010 many of the policies of the Coalition and Conservative governments were aimed at 'non-state' providers taking on an enhanced role, particularly in England, while reductions in public expenditure also implied a significant shrinkage in the size and role of the public sector.

Analysing the state

Although there are many approaches to describing and analysing the state, one is to view it as a sovereign institution – exercising legitimate power and recognised as doing so by other states – the government of which comprises a range of institutions through which laws and policies are developed and implemented (although even here the growth of supranational organisations, such as the European Union, raises questions about the degree of sovereignty; see Chapters 46 and 71).

There are also different views of the state that can be used to help us to understand the ways in which state power is exercised. For example, in liberal democracies, pluralist theory suggests power is widely distributed and that many groups and organisations are able to influence policy. In contrast, other perspectives, such as those from elite and Marxist approaches, suggest it is more restricted.

Given the difficulties of defining and analysing the state, and the particular focus of this chapter, it is perhaps appropriate to focus on the functions of 'government' in respect of state welfare. In the UK, the institutions that comprise government include:

- Central government: the Westminster Parliament, the Prime Minister, the Cabinet and central government departments. Within these it is possible to distinguish between, for example, the Treasury, which is responsible for managing public expenditure across the UK, and 'spending departments', such as those responsible for services like pensions and benefits in the UK or, education, training and skills and healthcare in England and the devolved administrations. It is also possible to make further distinctions, for example, between departments that largely play a policymaking role, setting the direction and frameworks for services that are delivered by other organisations, and those that are more involved in the direct delivery of services such as healthcare, the state pension and other benefits.
- The Scottish Parliament, the National Assembly for Wales and the Northern Ireland Assembly, each of which is able to exercise differing levels of power over welfare policy and provision within their jurisdictions (see Part IV).

■ Local government, which traditionally had a central role in the direct delivery of services, but whose powers since the 1980s have been dispersed. As a result of this, many services that were once delivered by local government are now delivered by other sectors (see Chapter 45).

■ A wide range of agencies at each tier of government, variously referred to as quasi-autonomous non-governmental organisations (quangos), non-departmental public bodies (NDPBs), committees of experts, 'Next Steps' agencies and extra-governmental organisations (EGOs). These perform some of the functions of government, but at 'arm's length' from the departments to which they are responsible. Whilst incoming governments frequently seek to reduce the number of such bodies, and they are susceptible to reorganisation and renaming, they remain both useful and significant. Devolution has also seen differential use across the UK. Examples from early 2015 include the Equality and Human Rights Commission and the Northern Ireland Human Rights Commission, the Education Funding Agency and Homes and Communities Agency in England, Skills Development Scotland, the Higher Education Funding Council for Wales and the Social Security Agency (Northern Ireland).

not funded or delivered by the state, but elements of it are regulated by the state, and in some cases the state will purchase particular services for public patients. These examples can be repeated across the range of welfare services and provision. Clearly, therefore, there is enormous complexity in the mixed economy of welfare.

The discussion above, together with the numbers and types of bodies involved, serves to provide some indication of the complexity of the role of the state in relation to the production and delivery of welfare. There is considerable debate as to what the role of the state should be. For example, some argue that the number of roles and functions of the state are now so great that it has reached the point where it can no longer undertake all of them successfully, and that it is necessary to get a range of other organisations involved in service delivery and administration. Some believe that a large state apparatus is inefficient, bureaucratic and unresponsive to the needs of its citizens, and reduces freedom and choice. Others argue that the state should retain much of its role, but that it needs to be more efficient and effective in fulfilling it. And yet others suggest that there is scope for further expansion of the role of the state in social policy, particularly in relation to reducing inequalities. All of these arguments are reflected not only here, but in other chapters in this book and in wider debates in society.

State Involvement in Welfare

It is also possible to analyse the state in terms of the functions that it performs, such as defence, the collection of taxation, the delivery of services and regulation. As is apparent from the discussion above, and other chapters in this book, state involvement in welfare happens in different ways (Box 34.1).

Given the variety of roles that the state plays in relation to social policy, and the existence of a mixed economy of welfare, it is unsurprising that it is possible to identify a whole range of different permutations of state involvement. For example, education can be commercially delivered and funded by individuals, delivered and funded by a mix of non-state and public bodies, or solely publicly funded and delivered. In the case of what in the UK is termed private healthcare, provision is

The Changing Role of the State

As the historical development of the welfare state is considered elsewhere in this book (see Part III and Chapter 42), the intention here is to provide a guide to the main changes and developments in the role of the state since 1979.

From 1979, the Conservatives, influenced by New Right thinking, pursued a strategy of reducing the state's role in welfare. There was an emphasis on 'managerialism' and, in the belief that introducing private sector business methods into the public sector could make it more efficient, from 1988 a range of different policy instruments, often termed 'the new public management', were introduced (see Chapter 43). These included the greater use of markets, such as privatisation (for example, sales of council houses); compulsory competitive tendering (such as cleaning services

Box 34.1 The Main State Functions in Welfare

- *Policymaking and the passage of legislation*: the state plays an important role in formulating policy in many areas, in central government, the devolved administrations and local government, with the two higher tiers also being able, in some circumstances, to direct local authorities or other agencies to implement their policies. State institutions, legislation and policies also provide the framework within which services are delivered.

- *Funding*: central government funds the great bulk of state welfare. It does this in a variety of ways, including as a direct provider of services, such as the NHS; through direct financial assistance to individuals, as with the state pension and Child Benefit; and indirectly through local government, 'arms-length' agencies, and commercial or voluntary sector providers, whether this is through grants or contracts for service provision. In addition, the state provides fiscal support for some people through tax relief, tax credits and other forms of assistance, such as free or subsidised prescriptions.

- *Delivery*: as is apparent from above, the state plays a major role in the funding of welfare services, such as the NHS, state education and large areas of social care, and in determining the form that they take, although responsibility for some services is channelled through local government or non-state providers.

- *Enabling*: since the 1980s the state has developed its role in enabling or overseeing service delivery by commercial and voluntary organisations rather than providing services itself.

- *Coordination and collaboration*: have become increasingly important in the delivery of welfare services, and across all tiers of government there has been an emphasis on bringing a range of organisations from different sectors together to respond to issues and deliver services in a way that is intended to be more flexible and comprehensive than would be achieved through agencies working alone or in competition with each other.

- *Regulation and direction*: recent years have also seen a much greater awareness of the regulatory role of the state, and this has been apparent in relation to social policy. Examples of regulatory bodies from early 2015 include the Care Quality Commission, responsible for registering, inspecting and reporting on the provision of health and social care services; the Office for Standards in Education, Children's Services and Skills (OFSTED), responsible for regulating services that care for children and young people, and those providing education and skills in England, and their equivalents elsewhere in the UK, such as Healthcare Improvement Scotland and the Care Council for Wales; and the Financial Conduct Authority, responsible for regulating firms and advisers in the financial services industry throughout the UK.

in hospitals); the introduction of market-type mechanisms into provision (for example, in health and education); the development of a view of the state as an enabler rather than as a provider of welfare services, with greater provision by the commercial and voluntary sectors and by individuals themselves; and the devolution of non-essential functions, such as policy implementation and service delivery, previously undertaken by central and local government to non-departmental bodies, Next Steps agencies and other organisations. Over time, such developments resulted in a more fragmented and complex organisation and delivery of services, while there was little agreement among commentators about their success or their social impacts.

Under Labour, from 1997, there were a number of sometimes overlapping or even contradictory elements to the relationship between the state and welfare. The state as an enabler was expanded, greater use was made of non-statutory agencies as service deliverers, and partnerships were seen as a way of utilising the perceived strengths of the commercial and voluntary sectors for social ends. The efficient and effective delivery of public services was seen as paramount, and to this end there was increased use of a variety of mechanisms for regulation, audit and inspection (see Chapters 43 and 44). Public expenditure in some areas of state provision, notably social protection, education and the NHS, was increased, and Labour also expanded indirect 'fiscal welfare', particularly through tax credits aimed at lower-income groups. The relationship between the state and individuals was seen as one where citizens' rights were matched by responsibilities. This was reflected, for example, in relation to work and benefits, where there were debates over conditionalities and how best to encourage individuals who failed to meet their responsibilities to do so (see Chapter 56).

The devolution settlements for Northern Ireland, Scotland and Wales created the possibility for increasingly different approaches to state involvement in welfare across the UK, with, for example, the Scottish Executive's decision in 2000 to provide personal care free for older people, that of the Welsh Assembly to abolish prescription charges from April 2007, and different approaches to tuition fees for higher education (see Part IV).

Under the Coalition government of 2010–15, there was an emphasis on reducing public expenditure. Whilst this was in part a response to the fiscal deficit arising from the financial crisis of 2007–8, for many in the government there was an ideological impetus for a smaller role for the state. The idea of a substantial shift from 'big government' to 'Big Society' was also a key element of the Prime Minister, David Cameron's vision and of other Conservatives. This was underpinned by a belief that there was too much government intrusion into people's lives, that the state's role in welfare had grown too large, and that the welfare state had become inefficient, wasteful and overly bureaucratic. This view was close to that of some Liberal Democrats, who sought to apply some of the ideas of economic liberalism to parts of social provision.

The election of the Conservative government in 2015 saw a restatement of many of these ideas, with proposals for further major cuts in public spending. In addition to cuts in public expenditure (falling from 42.3 per cent of GDP in 2010–11 to a target of 38.7 per cent in 2015–16) under the Coalition, it sought to save a further £30 billion, including £12 billion from the social security budget.

This, in combination with the perceived failings of the welfare state and, in England, a desire for greater provision by the voluntary sector, social enterprises and local communities, and a new relationship between individuals and the state, implied a significant reduction, or even residualisation, of the state in many areas, although like the Coalition government, the Conservatives committed themselves to maintaining or increasing expenditure on the NHS and school-age education. Although Cameron's idea of a 'Big Society' replacing much of the role of the state failed to gain widespread support under the Coalition, it again featured in the Conservative manifesto in 2015. More generally, the Coalition and Conservative governments sought to open up the public sector in England to a greater range of providers, for example, allowing schools to become academies, answering directly to Whitehall rather than to local councils, and creating 'free' schools to be run by parents or other organisations, and giving commercial and voluntary providers a greater role in the NHS.

Emerging Issues

The relationships between individuals, society and the state have been central to the development of social policy over the past three decades. The New Right's influence on the Conservative governments during the 1980s and 1990s was reflected in attempts to reduce the role and size of the state and an emphasis upon individuals providing for themselves and their families. While there were echoes of this in some areas of social policy under Labour, an emphasis on individuals' rights and responsibilities and citizen participation and involvement in decision-making were key dimensions of its approach and there was also a clear commitment to state welfare, and particularly state funding of welfare.

From 2010, the Coalition and Conservative governments placed particular emphasis on reducing and reshaping the state's role, with, in England, greater responsibility being placed on individuals, community groups, voluntary organisations and social enterprises as part of the 'Big Society', and an expansion of non-state providers in the public sector. Whilst a range of ideas were initially discussed, including the mutualisation of services, the promotion of multiple and diverse providers and the freeing up of bodies from state control, the primary driver for change was arguably reductions in public expenditure, particularly for social security and local government, although there was significant pressure for savings in education and the NHS.

The nature and balance of the mixed economy of welfare appear set to continue to be a central feature of social policy, and arguments about the form and extent of the state's role that is appropriate for different sectors will remain contentious, as highlighted by the Conservatives' aim of further cutting public expenditure.

In addition, at least in part because of the changes introduced by successive governments, including the fragmentation of systems of welfare provision and the consequent need for greater regulation and new methods of coordination, relationships between central government and the variety of providers, from all sectors, have become considerably more complex. The challenges associated with establishing a clear overview of what is happening, and in exercising control over those responsible for policy implementation, mean that accountability and regulation are therefore likely to remain key issues (see Chapter 44). Moreover, as the powers and political control of the UK's legislative bodies change over time, the prospects for greater divergence in social policy are likely to increase further.

Guide to Further Sources

H. Bochel and M. Powell (eds) (2016), *The UK Coalition Government and Social Policy*, Bristol: Policy Press, looks specifically at developments since 2010, while M. Powell (ed.) (2008), *Modernising the Welfare State: The Blair Legacy*, Bristol: Policy Press, reflects on the preceding Labour governments. J. Hills (2014), *Good Times, Bad Times: The Welfare Myth of Them and Us*, Bristol: Policy Press, looks at how, over a lifetime, we all

benefit from the welfare state. C. Hay, M. Lister and D. Marsh (eds) (2006), *The State: Theories and Issues*, Basingstoke: Palgrave Macmillan, considers a range of perspectives about the state from pluralism through to governance and globalisation. A different and detailed approach to some of the issues considered in this chapter is taken by T. Bovaird and E. Loffler (eds) (2009), *Public Management and Governance*, London: Routledge, which, for example, includes chapters on partnership working and the size and scope of the public sector. C. Pierson, F. G. Castles and I. K. Naumann (eds) (2103), *The Welfare State Reader*, Cambridge: Polity, covers a wide range of perspectives, debates and challenges to the welfare state.

HM Treasury (www.gov.uk/government/organisations/hm-treasury) is a good source of statistical information and other publications, while the Institute for Fiscal Studies (www.ifs.org.uk) produces authoritative work which can differ from the views of governments.

Review and Assignment Questions

1 To what extent is the state the principal source of welfare provision in contemporary society?
2 How has the role of the state in the provision of welfare changed since 1979?
3 Why might the relationship between and responsibilities of individuals and the state be so contestable for social policies?
4 What should the role of the state be in a mixed economy of welfare?
5 What do you see as the key issues facing the development of state welfare over the next decade, and how do you think these might best be tackled?

Visit the book companion site at www.wiley.com/go/alcocksocialpolicy to make use of the resources designed to accompany the textbook. There you will find chapter-specific guides to further resources, including governmental, international, thinktank, pressure groups and relevant journal sources. You will also find a glossary based on *The Blackwell Dictionary of Social Policy*, help sheets, guidance on managing assignments in social policy and career advice.

35

Commercial Welfare

Chris Holden

Overview

- Many different kinds of for-profit companies are involved in welfare delivery.
- The extent and type of state welfare activity play a key role in determining the scope for commercial welfare services in advanced welfare states.
- Recent reforms in advanced welfare states have led to a 'blurring of the boundaries' between the public and private sectors.
- The more the provision of welfare services relies on markets and non-state providers, the more important regulation of these becomes in the pursuit of social policy goals.

Markets and Businesses in Welfare

Commercial welfare involves the sale and purchase of welfare services and products in markets of one kind or another. The sellers of these services are usually aiming to make a profit for their owners, although not-for-profit providers such as voluntary organisations, provident associations (which are also technically non-profit-making) or social enterprises (which reinvest profits in the organisation or the community) may also be involved in welfare markets. All these types of providers, however, must usually try to maximise their income if they are to remain competitive. The consumers of these services are individuals, although the payers may be the individuals themselves (or their families) (see Chapter 40), insurance companies (with the contributions to the insurance plan paid by the individuals or their employers; see Chapter 36) or state agencies. In principle, services necessary for the satisfaction of

The Student's Companion to Social Policy, Fifth Edition. Edited by Pete Alcock, Tina Haux, Margaret May and Sharon Wright.
© 2016 John Wiley & Sons, Ltd. Published 2016 by John Wiley & Sons, Ltd.

human welfare needs may be sold and bought in markets in the same way as any household item. There are two key reasons, however, why welfare services should be distinguished from other goods and services.

The first is that welfare services are by definition so important for the meeting of basic human needs that governments often decide they should take action to ensure that all their citizens have access to at least a certain minimum level of these. If governments did not take such action, many of their citizens would not be able to afford to meet their basic needs, leading to huge inequalities. In countries like the UK during the course of the twentieth century, this often took the form of direct provision by state agencies, as well as state funding and regulation of services (see Chapter 34). Direct state provision was often seen as the best way of ensuring that services would be provided to the degree and standard the government thought necessary. In health services, for example, private provision was pushed to the margins by the creation of the National Health Service (NHS) in the UK, which is funded from general taxation and free to citizens at the point of use. However, governments have increasingly begun to question the idea that the state itself must be the provider of welfare services if the needs of their citizens are to be met.

The second key reason why welfare services should be distinguished from other goods and services is that the market often does not provide them efficiently (see Chapters 6 and 40). There are many reasons why this is the case. Deciding what kind of healthcare you need, for example, is not the same as choosing a new television, and you are much more dependent on the knowledge of professionals. Therefore, even if markets and for-profit providers are to play a role in the delivery of welfare services, they need to be carefully regulated to ensure they help to meet the goals of social policy.

In most countries, commercial provision of welfare services such as health and social care, child care, education, pensions, other financial products and, of course, housing, has always continued to exist wherever firms can make a profit. However, in advanced welfare states, the extent and type of state welfare provision have

tended to be the largest factor determining the scope for commercial provision. The less state provision there has been, the more scope there has been for other providers. Nevertheless, in many countries (including the UK) there have always been firms that have benefited from payments by the state to provide services on behalf of the government, and since the 1980s their number has grown considerably as a result of government policies. Furthermore, firms that produce goods such as medicines that are crucial for the delivery of welfare services have also benefited hugely from state funding.

Where state provision or funding of services is low, the size and shape of the market are largely determined by the degree of effective demand, that is, how much people are willing and can afford to pay for services. Since people will not necessarily have the money to pay 'out of pocket' for support when they need it, this tends to encourage the development of commercial insurance schemes. In countries like the UK with tax-funded health services, for example, insurance has tended to be taken out by those whose employers pay for it as an above-wage benefit (see Chapter 36), or those who are relatively better off and can afford to pay, for instance, to be treated more quickly or in pleasanter surroundings than those provided by the public system.

There are, in fact, a large number of different types of for-profit firms involved in some way in the delivery of welfare services (see Box 35.1). Any of these may be entirely privately owned by one or two individuals or a small number of investors, or they may be 'public' in the sense of being listed on the stock exchange so that people may buy shares in them. They range from home tutors, individual owners of care homes, day-care centres and other small businesses to huge transnational corporations (TNCs). Currently, most transnational firms are those that produce welfare-related *goods* such as pharmaceuticals, but as the provision of welfare *services* by businesses increases, these firms too are likely to become more transnational and international trade in welfare services between countries is likely to increase. Such developments will need careful study if the goals of social policy are to be safeguarded and advanced.

As well as those performing the different roles in the delivery of welfare described in Box 35.1, a

Box 35.1 Types of For-Profit Firms in Welfare Delivery

- Firms that provide welfare services directly to the public, including health and social care, child care, education and many other services. These are the most important type of firm for social policy.
- Firms that produce goods that are indispensable to the delivery of welfare services, such as medicines and educational materials. These type of firms have been somewhat neglected in the study of social policy, but their behaviour often has important implications for welfare outcomes.
- Firms that supply services to the organisations (state and non-state) that directly provide welfare services. For example, all hospitals, whether they are run by state agencies or businesses, rely on companies that distribute medicines to them, clean their premises and provide catering services to their patients

and staff. Firms in this category may also provide consultancy or management services to direct providers by, for example, taking over the management of a state-owned school or hospital where the existing management is deemed to have failed.
- Firms that provide insurance or financial services such as health and disability insurance, pensions or mortgages.
- Firms that are involved in the design, building and maintenance of the premises from which welfares services are provided, such as hospitals and schools, as well as prisons and the construction of houses. This type of firm has become much more important in Britain in recent years as a consequence of the Private Finance Initiative (PFI).
- Firms that, whatever their business, provide some form of occupational welfare services to their own employees.

variety of firms whose core business activities may have little or nothing to do with the direct provision of welfare may also exert influence on social policy. For example, firms may participate less directly in the management of state welfare services through various types of boards or sponsorship deals, as with academy schools in England. They might also take political action, such as lobbying politicians about social policy issues, in order to protect or advance their interests.

We can see then that there has always been a huge range of firms involved in some way in the delivery of welfare, often deriving a large portion of their income from the government by selling goods or services as inputs to state providers, as well as selling these goods and services directly to the public for private payment. The most important type for the meeting of social policy goals is the direct providers of services. In the UK, the most rapid growth in the involvement of commercial firms in welfare delivery in recent years has been among these.

Government Policy and Welfare Markets

We have said that the extent and type of government welfare activity are the most important factors determining the scope for commercial welfare in advanced welfare states. The *type* of government activity is particularly important, since governments may choose to pay companies to provide welfare services or mandate other organisations to administer services, rather than provide them itself. Government-mandated social insurance schemes are one example of this. So, for example, many European countries have social health insurance schemes, whereby citizens (or their employers on their behalf) pay into independent funds that are regulated by the government and pay for their healthcare when they need it (see Chapter 65). The government in these countries usually pays contributions for those who cannot afford to do so for themselves, so that everyone has access to a minimum level of healthcare. This set-up often means citizens can choose to access the services of non-state providers as well as public ones, and have their bills paid by the social insurance fund. In this way, commercial and other providers make their money not simply from private payments (either private insurance or out-of-pocket), but from payments by government-mandated insurance funds. Government activity in the pursuit of social policy goals may therefore support rather than inhibit commercial providers, depending on the form it takes.

In the United States, where the welfare state is less extensive than in most other high-income countries, but where many citizens can afford to pay for their needs, commercial welfare is more developed than in any other country (see Chapter 66). There is therefore a huge market in health and other services, with large chains of for-profit hospitals, for example. Inequalities in access to welfare services are consequently also much greater than in most other high-income countries, since not everyone can afford to pay for the services they need.

Even here, however, the government provides some support for its poorest citizens, with a government-funded health insurance service, Medicaid, for the poor and a similar scheme, Medicare, for older and disabled people. Healthcare legislation enacted by President Obama in 2010 is likely to extend support for those on lower incomes still further. People making use of Medicaid or Medicare may be treated by commercial providers just as other patients are, but the provider will claim back the cost of the service from the government scheme.

As already discussed, in countries like the UK, where services such as healthcare have mainly been provided by the state since the end of the Second World War, there has been less opportunity for commercial welfare. However, since the 1980s, that has begun to change for two reasons. First, there has been a relative shift towards individuals taking responsibility for their own needs, so that people cannot rely on the state for their pension, for example, but must make their own provision through occupational or personal private pension schemes. Second, there has been a relative shift towards the state paying private companies to provide services that it used to provide itself.

This second change has involved the introduction of 'quasi-markets' into welfare services that

were previously provided almost exclusively by state agencies. Reforms to the NHS are a good example of how these changes have provided more opportunities for commercial providers. As Prime Minister, Margaret Thatcher introduced an 'internal market' into the NHS, whereby purchasing of services was separated from their provision. This involved hospitals and other services (the providers) being reorganised into independent trusts, which would then provide services under contract to health authorities and 'fund-holding' GPs (the purchasers). At this point there was very little purchasing of services from the private sector, but NHS trusts were expected to behave more like independent businesses 'selling' their services to the purchasers, hence the term 'internal market' (see Chapters 34 and 49).

However, the purchaser–provider split was also introduced into social care services such as residential, nursing and domiciliary care for older people, with local authority social service departments as the purchasers and a 'mixed economy' of commercial, voluntary and state agencies as the providers. Here the market was not 'internal', but involved external for-profit providers, who soon dominated provision. Large transnational corporations moved into this new market alongside smaller businesses, making much of their profit providing care services under contract to local authorities.

The purchaser–provider split was thought by Thatcher to allow more choice for service users and to be more efficient than state-provided services, even though it involved extra costs in administering contracts. This new 'mixed economy of care' eventually became the model for public services adopted in England by the Labour governments of 1997–2010. Commercial providers were invited into the NHS system alongside NHS trusts, under contract to Primary Care Trusts (PCTs), the new NHS purchasers for England. The Coalition government of 2010–15 (and its Conservative successor) took these reforms even further by replacing PCTs with GP-led Clinical Commissioning Groups and widening the scope for business involvement in the English NHS. More widely, and controversially, it also further promoted the outsourcing of other services to non-state providers, including contracting companies to manage its 'welfare to work' programme and test claims for some benefits. The devolved administrations of Scotland and Wales, however, have been less keen on market mechanisms; although across the UK the advent of 'personalisation' in social care entails a greater use of non-state providers (see Part IV and Chapter 54).

The increasing involvement of commercial firms in welfare has also included new ways of commissioning welfare facilities such as schools and hospitals, through schemes such as the Private Finance Initiative (PFI). PFI involves for-profit consortiums financing and maintaining, as well as building, such facilities. It has been controversial because it means that these are then owned by the consortium for a period of twenty to thirty years, with welfare agencies such as NHS trusts locked into inflexible long-term leases which may not be cost-effective, despite the declared intention of making government procurement more efficient.

Equity, Quality and the State

Bringing businesses into the heart of the welfare state in these ways has led to a 'blurring of the boundaries' between the public and private sectors. This has both led and reflected a more general drift among policymakers across the developed world towards the view that the state should 'row less and steer more'. In other words, the pursuance of social policy goals does not necessarily require the state to directly provide services; rather, it is the role of the government to ensure that these goals are met through whatever means seem effective. In this view, it may be better for the government to pay for other agencies and organisations to provide the services, including for-profit companies, or simply oblige its citizens to make adequate provision for themselves, by paying into pension funds, for example (see Chapter 40). However, it is not enough for the government to fund the services or make sure citizens pay for themselves; where companies are providing services primarily in the pursuit of profit, it needs to think carefully about two additional issues if it is to 'steer' services effectively.

First, where it funds non-state provision, it needs to think about the kinds of behaviour that are encouraged by the payment system. Any kind of payment system creates its own incentives to behave in a certain way. For-profit providers, voluntary organisations and autonomous public agencies such as foundation hospital trusts will all tend to act in ways that maximise their income, even if other goals are also important to them. Markets, including the 'quasi-markets' created by governments, are premised upon and encourage this very fact. So the government needs to design its payment systems very carefully in order to try to incentivise companies to act in the optimum way. It also needs to specify its contracts with providers very clearly so that they know what is expected of them.

Second, it needs to make sure that it regulates providers properly. This means the government must create a set of rules within which all providers must operate, monitor adherence to these and apply sanctions where they are contravened. Different types of regulatory 'instruments' may be needed to ensure that different policy goals are met (see Chapter 44). For example, governments usually want to ensure that certain minimum quality standards are met. In a hierarchically organised service that is directly provided by a state agency, they can do this at least partly through the agency's internal management structure. However, where services are provided by others, they need to set up special regulatory agencies whose job it is to monitor the quality of services, and take effective action where standards are not met. This means they must specify clearly the standards which are expected to be met, how they will be monitored and what action may be taken towards those organisations that fail to meet them.

Perhaps the biggest concern about the use of markets in welfare though is their impact upon equity. The principle of equity is at the heart of the welfare state, and markets may have profound implications for both equitable access to services and for equitable outcomes. Markets are based upon competition and responsiveness to incentives rather than the encouragement of a public service ethos, and will therefore tend to change the nature of the welfare system. Careful thought therefore needs to be given to what the goals of social policy should be, and what are the most appropriate means to achieve them.

Emerging Issues

These issues of equity, quality and regulation are of the utmost importance, given that all the major UK political parties have accepted a significant role for non-state providers of welfare services, though business involvement has been promoted more in England than elsewhere (see Part IV). Equity issues have become especially important in the context of the austerity policies that have been put in place since the 2008 financial crisis (see Chapter 21). Government bail-outs of failing private sector banks led to a massive public borrowing deficit, to which governments subsequently responded by cutting public services ever more deeply. Such extensive cuts to public sector spending are likely to force even more people to rely on services purchased individually in the market, with those who cannot afford to pay suffering the most.

Furthermore, in the context of an increasingly liberalised and integrated world economy, welfare markets themselves are likely to become increasingly internationalised, with an ever greater movement across national borders of welfare-related firms, practitioners and service users. Such developments have the potential to enhance the sharing of knowledge and skills between countries, but also make regulation of services even more difficult, and have potentially even greater implications for equity, both within countries and between them. Additionally, the more these services are traded across national borders, the more they are likely to become subject to international trade and investment agreements (see Chapter 71). Such agreements are complicated, but they increasingly constrain the social policies that national governments are able to pursue, whilst giving more power to private corporations.

Guide to Further Sources

M. Powell (ed.) (2007), *Understanding the Mixed Economy of Welfare*, Bristol: Policy Press, contains several chapters looking at different aspects of the mixed economy of welfare. K. Farnsworth and C. Holden (2006), 'The business–social policy nexus: corporate power and corporate inputs into social policy', *Journal of Social Policy*, 35:3, 473–94, provides a useful way of classifying types of corporate inputs into social policy, while K. Farnsworth (2004), *Corporate Power and Social Policy in a Global Economy: British Welfare Under the Influence*, Bristol: Policy Press, looks in more detail at how corporations can act politically to influence social policy.

Processes of international trade, including the implications of trade and investment agreements for social policy, are examined in C. Holden (2014), 'International trade and welfare', in N. Yeates (ed.), *Understanding Global Social Policy*, Bristol: Policy Press. The main issues relating to international trade in health services, as an example of how welfare services can be traded across borders, are outlined in R. Smith, R. Chanda and V. Tangcharoensathien (2009), 'Trade in health-related services', *The Lancet*, 373:9663. The World Health Organization has a number of resources related to trade and health, see at: www.who.int/trade/trade_and_health/en. C. Holden (2009), 'Exporting public–private partnerships in health-care: export strategy and policy transfer', *Policy Studies*, 30:3, 313–32, provides an overview of the PFI and analyses Britain's 'healthcare industrial strategy'.

Review and Assignment Questions

1 What distinguishes commercial providers of welfare services from voluntary and state organisations?
2 What different types of for-profit firms might play a role in the delivery of welfare services?
3 Why have governments since the 1980s chosen to introduce a greater role for non-state providers in the delivery of welfare services?
4 What is meant by the term 'row less and steer more'?
5 Assess the potential benefits and problems that might arise from a greater role for commercial providers in the delivery of welfare services and make recommendations for government policy based upon your analysis.

Visit the book companion site at www.wiley .com/go/alcocksocialpolicy to make use of the resources designed to accompany the textbook. There you will find chapter-specific guides to further resources, including governmental, international, thinktank, pressure groups and relevant journal sources. You will also find a glossary based on *The Blackwell Dictionary of Social Policy*, help sheets, guidance on managing assignments in social policy and career advice.

36

Occupational Welfare

Edward Brunsdon and Margaret May

Overview

- Occupational or workplace welfare consists of mandatory and voluntary benefits provided through employment.
- While mandatory benefits are instigated through government/EU laws and regulations, voluntary provision is initiated by individual employers.
- Some voluntary schemes are designed to enhance or replace aspects of UK statutory welfare; others are unilateral arrangements developed by organisations specifically for their employees.
- Throughout the history of occupational welfare, there have been major inequities in the benefits supplied and to whom, both within and between organisations.
- Recent years have seen conflicting revisions to these disparities.

Context

Whilst there have been individual UK research programmes addressing aspects of the production and consumption of occupational welfare over the last decade, detailed investigations mapping its supply and distribution, funding and costs have still to be undertaken. This is something of a disappointment not simply because of its central role in the domestic welfare mix (Titmuss first drew attention to its relevance in the 1950s), but also because of the missed opportunities for detailed international comparisons at organisational, industry, sector and national levels. In the United States and Japan, for instance, occupational welfare has long been pivotal to the

The Student's Companion to Social Policy, Fifth Edition. Edited by Pete Alcock, Tina Haux, Margaret May and Sharon Wright.
© 2016 John Wiley & Sons, Ltd. Published 2016 by John Wiley & Sons, Ltd.

'employee proposition' and social protection generally. With the retrenchment of state welfare, it is also growing in importance in many European countries.

So why has it attracted so little attention in the UK? One argument is that it is because the subject matter is considered to have limited impact on overall provision. Much more likely, however, is that researchers have been discouraged by the difficulties of accessing primary or good quality secondary data, particularly from businesses. Employee benefits are an important element of remuneration packages, and organisations in competitive environments do not always want to disclose what they offer to recruit and retain staff. In spite of such obstacles, however, analysts who persevere with their investigations, often through indirect sources, have come to appreciate just how much these benefits contribute to the UK welfare mix and therefore why they are worthy of consideration.

What is 'Occupational Welfare'?

For an area with such a small research portfolio, studies of workplace provision have produced surprising differences of definition. Whilst there is general acceptance that it describes welfare supplied through employment and includes both mandatory and voluntary benefits wholly or partially funded, delivered and/or managed by employers, there is no agreement as to the range of provision it includes. There are basically two schools of thought, those who favour a 'narrow' definition and those supporting a 'broad' formulation.

Narrow definitions limit provision to employer-sponsored benefits whose purpose is construed as meeting the same or similar needs as state welfare. Broad conceptions, by contrast, cover all mandatory and voluntary non-wage benefits in cash and kind supplied to employees by virtue of their status, performance, record or recognised needs. For reasons explained elsewhere, the current authors favour this broad viewpoint as a more accurate conception. It means a more diverse and more intricate research domain encompassing not only interventions geared to complementing or replacing public provision, but

also bespoke measures that are organisationally instigated and independent of any state link.

A Brief Historical Overview

Three main agencies have contributed to the development and configuration of UK occupational welfare over the last two hundred years: employers (and employer representative bodies); trade unions (and through them employees); and governments. Though analytically discrete, historically their influence has been complex, with the grounds for their initiatives changing over time and in importance, and each frequently supporting but also capable of opposing specific options.

Individual employers and employers bodies

With little mandatory intervention beyond health and safety, individual employers were key to the nature and level of workplace welfare in the nineteenth and early twentieth centuries. The main drive for provision came from larger enterprises. In some instances this was based on a combination of philanthropic and business grounds, as in the case of the housing and social facilities built by Lever and Cadbury for their workers; in others, it was simply to gain economic advantage. The gas and railway companies, for example, provided pensions, housing and hospitals primarily as a way of attracting and retaining staff.

As the twentieth century progressed, companies grew and the grounds for workplace provision widened. During the First World War, employers were encouraged by government to boost output and limit absenteeism and turnover by improving health and safety, engaging specialist welfare staff and providing services such as canteens and rest rooms. The inter-war years saw the growth of the employers' industrial welfare movement that, whilst it did little to allay the hostile industrial relations of the 1920s, promoted company welfare through pensions, sick pay schemes, life insurance and on-site healthcare. Income enhancement and replacement benefits were, however, typically restricted to supervisory, clerical and managerial staff. The Second World War saw another concerted effort to expand benefits coverage, again to sustain productivity. Further growth and variation occurred in the post-war years as employee welfare developed alongside state provision and new benefits such as housing subsidies, company cars and other pay substitutes and supplements began to feature in remuneration packages.

There were a number of different reasons for these enhancements. The continuation of the pre-war shift to larger firms and new industries necessitated more formal human resource strategies, a process hastened by the entry of overseas businesses into the UK (many of whom brought their own workplace welfare practices). Tight labour markets also placed a new value on benefits that employers felt bought allegiance and eased technological change. They became particularly important as a way of rewarding staff in the 1970s by circumventing restrictive incomes policies.

Whilst coverage remained concentrated in larger commercial organisations and public services, in the 1980s and 1990s the range of provision was further modified through the arrival of American and Japanese companies and their vision of occupational welfare as part of corporate strategy. For UK establishments adopting their philosophy, workplace benefits added strategic and operational value not only in terms of recruitment, retention, staff performance and exit management, but in greater control of the labour process and curbing the financial losses associated with ill health and absenteeism. There was, in other words, a strong business case for treating this provision as core activity and a valuable investment.

This viewpoint continued post-millennium, although the economic slump of 2001–2 forced many commercial employers to review their benefits and seek ways of maximising what they offered whilst restricting costs. In particular, it contributed to a widespread switch from defined benefit to defined contribution pensions (see Chapter 60), and, more broadly, to the adoption of salary sacrifice schemes and the re-negotiation of voluntary benefit packages. Public sector provision was largely insulated from these pressures but, as discussed later, this was only temporary.

Trade unions

Trade union views of occupational welfare showed significant variation over the two hundred years. In the late nineteenth and early twentieth centuries, for instance, unions generally opposed pensions and health insurance arrangements provided by employers, viewing them as a threat to wage levels and the similar schemes they and friendly societies offered. It was also clear that some employers, particularly in industries such as mining and gas, were using workplace welfare to pre-empt unionisation and secure acceptance of hazardous working conditions. However, mandatory changes to health and safety along with the acceptance of unions' negotiating entitlements in many industries between the wars, led them to increasingly press for workplace benefits.

Whilst reserving the right to oppose particular interventions, they generally sought to protect and, where possible, improve what was becoming an important element of some members' remuneration. Benefits became a key negotiating tool in collective bargaining particularly:

- where they were not legally or contractually provided and thus could be withdrawn by employers;
- in response to changing work practices; and
- as a means of offsetting low pay rises.

With the steep fall in commercial sector membership from the mid-1980s, however, union influence on provision became more focused on the public sector and, in the prevailing economic conditions of the first years of this century, increasingly geared to protecting existing benefit levels rather than their enhancement. They did, however, engage in a range of cross-sector campaigns to raise awareness of the differing needs of a varying and ageing workforce.

Government

UK governments of varying political hues contributed to the development of workplace welfare through different combinations of:

- mandatory interventions;
- fiscal incentives and subsidies; and
- promotional activities.

Mandatory interventions stretch back to nine-teenth-century health and safety legislation addressing issues in particular industries or work groups. These were replaced by broader national legislation in the twentieth and twenty-first centuries (latterly through EU measures) that spread beyond risk protection to more general employment conditions. The twentieth century also saw the use of tax reliefs and subsidies as incentives or ways of cushioning the expense of implementation or delivery. In the latter half of the century, in particular, governments used both legislation and taxation to change the course and cost of benefits such as sick pay, family-related leave, paid holidays, child-care, pensions and company cars, revisions that were not uniformly welcomed by employers or unions.

Urging employers to adopt/develop welfare initiatives through promotional activities led to more consensual growth. Whether underwritten by fiscal incentives or simply supported through the dissemination of good practice, governments towards the end of the twentieth and in the first few years of this century recognised that employer-sponsored benefits had multiple potential advantages. They could:

- provide a cost-effective supplement to existing state welfare services or, in some instances, an active replacement;
- boost employee performance, productivity and engagement;
- enhance employment levels (through reduced absenteeism and turnover), thus cutting sickness benefit and unemployment costs;
- respond to the welfare issues posed by an ageing workforce; and
- contribute to wider social well-being through the benefits they offered employees' families.

The Blair and Brown administrations saw work-place provision as central to their bid to modernise the UK economy and welfare system, boosting market participation, improving productivity and meeting the challenges of globalisation. Legislative and fiscal support for family-friendly practices, including leave arrangements and child-care vouchers were considered integral elements of this strategy, along with the promotion of 'work-life balance,' and 'flexi-working' and

employer provision of a widening array of pre-ventive health, lifestyle and 'wellness' benefits.

Recent Developments in Provision

By the time the Coalition came to power, occupa-tional welfare had evolved into an extremely complex array of benefits that included financial support, social and healthcare, education and training, housing, transport, leisure facilities, con-cierge services and opportunities for community participation (see Table 36.1 for a more detailed breakdown).

Largely because non-mandatory benefits had always been at the behest of employers and not all employers were prepared to invest, there were marked inequities in distribution. These included disparities between sectors, with national and local government organisations more munificent and more inclusive than those in the commercial or third sectors. Within both the latter, larger employers tended to supply custom-built schemes for their staff, while many small- and medium-sized enterprises provided nothing at all. Specifi-cally, in the commercial sector there were also disparities by industry with capital-intensive man-ufacturing, finance, professional services and high-end retailing investing more heavily in pro-grammes. Within all three sectors, but notably the commercial sector, there were also differences in the range and level of benefits offered to different groups within the same organisation based on status, performance and record.

Recent years have seen conflicting revisions to these inequities. There have been some upward adjustments through mandatory changes and large employers responding to both fiscal incen-tives and workforce needs by enhancing their commissioned schemes. But there were also sig-nificant countervailing economic pressures in the wake of the 2007–8 banking crisis and subsequent recession, leading to a number of employers cut-ting or trimming some of their more expensive benefits. In the face of burgeoning government deficits, the five-year austerity programme imple-mented by the UK Coalition government from 2010 followed a similar pattern restricting expen-diture on non-contracted provision for public sector employees.

Table 36.1 Contemporary forms of UK voluntary and mandatory occupational welfare.

Type of provision	Examples
Financial support	Occupational pensions (retirement, survivors, ill-health retirement). Statutory social security contributions. Mandatory and above-mandatory pay substitutes (e.g., sickness and redundancy payments, paid maternity, paternity and adoption leave). Voluntary pay substitutes (e.g., maternity and child-care grants, life, critical illness, disability, personal accident insurance and death in service). Voluntary pay supplements (e.g., professional indemnity insurance, interest-free loans, affinity benefits). Corporate savings plans. Employee share schemes and long-term incentive schemes. Individual loans.
Social care	Mandatory and above-mandatory leave entitlements (e.g., for holidays, parents, carers, civic duties, bereavement). Flexible/homeworking. Voluntary support services (e.g., counselling, pre-school, school-age and adult care, work–life balance and pre-/post-retirement services, lifestyle benefits, debt advice).
Healthcare	Mandatory and above-mandatory safety measures. Voluntary health insurances (e.g., private medical insurance, dental and optical cover and cash plans). Voluntary preventive services (e.g., wellness, health education, health promotion, screening, flu jabs, fitness schemes, stress management, diagnostic and referral services). Voluntary rehabilitation services (e.g., for those with ongoing physical and mental health problems, continuing or re-entering employment).
Education and training	Mandatory and extra-mandatory health and safety and young workers' training. Employer-provided training. Employer support (e.g., study leave (paid), sabbaticals (paid/unpaid), professional subscriptions, coaching/mentoring programmes for professional/personal development, children's education). Financial and pension education.
Housing	Employer-provided accommodation. Voluntary financial assistance (e.g., with mortgage/rent, relocation costs, insurance).
Transport	Company cars. Voluntary financial assistance (e.g., with car purchase/lease, congestion charges, rail tickets, driving lessons, tax, fuel, insurance). Cycle-to-work scheme loans.
Leisure	Organisational recreational facilities (e.g., sports grounds, social clubs). Voluntary support (e.g., for attendance at sports/social events, Christmas lunches, company theatre/concert trips).
Concierge services	Voluntary provision (e.g.. information and referral services, cafeterias, meal allowances/vouchers, domestic services).
Community participation	Support for employees' community activities (e.g., school governorships, committee work, fund-raising, mentoring and secondments).

The most far-reaching cross-sector changes occurred in financial support, specifically, the restructuring of existing occupational pensions and the launch of a new employment-based mandatory retirement saving scheme. Growing concern over falling occupational pensions' coverage at a time of increasing longevity had led the previous Labour administrations to adopt the Turner Commission's proposals for auto-enrolment into pension schemes (see Chapters 40, 47 and 60). Under the 2008 Pensions Act, all employers had a duty to ensure workers in Great Britain over twenty-two and under state pension age who were earning more than £5,035 joined a retirement savings plan. Staff could opt out, but employers had to provide the opportunity whether through the new National Employment Savings Trust (NEST) or an approved vehicle providing equivalent or better benefits. Although tax supported, these were to be largely funded by compulsory employer and employee contributions and phased in between 2012 and 2017, starting with large organisations.

The Coalition reviewed these reforms in the context of the recession, making a number of adjustments, including extending implementation to 2018, phasing in the level of employer contributions and increasing the income threshold to £10,000 in the tax year 2015–16. It also adopted other elements of Labour's vision, abolishing the default retirement age and extending working lives by raising women's state pension age to sixty-five by 2018 (and for both men and women to sixty-six by 2020). Perhaps more controversially, it introduced the 2014 Taxation of Pensions Act, which introduced greater flexibility in the ways occupational schemes could be managed and savings drawn down.

Alongside these mandatory amendments, it continued Labour's work of negotiating changes to existing public sector pension schemes, eventually reaching agreement with most unions to switch employees away from final-salary to more economical career-average arrangements.

Employer initiatives in financial support brought a variety of other changes. To meet what their competitors were supplying more large organisations offered above-statutory sick, maternity and paternity pay and redundancy packages; large businesses included long-term incentive and share plans for executives and other key staff.

Most, however, also found it necessary to contain expenditure on the popular 'risk' insurances such as death-in-service/life assurance, critical illness and personal accident cover, and many also reduced the options of loans and affinity benefits.

The economic pressures forcing restraint in financial support also drove changes to other forms of voluntary provision. Employers pursued a policy of offering a wider range of benefits whilst looking to control outlay. They were able to do this by cutting some of the more expensive and/or under-used options, re-negotiating premiums with suppliers, switching to co-funding (with employees), introducing cost-capping and extending the use of salary-sacrifice schemes. Increased choice in healthcare, for instance, saw an expansion of preventive healthcare services addressing common mental health disorders (e.g., stress and anxiety), wider use of health education and health screening, and individualised schemes for illness management and rehabilitative care. Cost limitations were largely imposed through the re-negotiation of supplier premiums and co-funding.

Budgetary concerns also played a key role in the development of social care. Some employers extended holiday entitlements – typically by adding service-related leave – others reduced above-statutory leave for new starters. There was a steady development of support networks for employees balancing work with child/elder care responsibilities and an expansion in flexible working schemes, but restrictions on expenditure for outsourced Employee Assistance Programmes. Within the latter, however, there was growth in particular services, notably, counselling, debt advice and retirement planning.

Few employers retained workplace nurseries because of their expense, but child-care vouchers remained popular with both staff and organisations in spite of reductions in tax relief for higher-rate taxpayers in 2011. On the government agenda, however, were plans to replace voucher schemes for newly registered parents with a state tax-free childcare scheme in 2015 (subsequently postponed until 2017), which it felt would be more beneficial to employees paying basic-rate tax. The changes would, however, impact negatively on employers who could no longer make savings through salary sacrifice arrangements. The Coalition also revamped another family-friendly benefit by replacing the 2010 Additional Paternity Leave and Paternity Pay Regulations with Shared Parental Leave in 2015. This allowed parents and partners to choose more flexible arrangements for sharing maternity/paternity leave and pay.

The tension between benefits development and budgeting took a different tack in education and training. Mandatory obligations flowed through health and safety legislation generating financial requirements for linked training. The bulk of provision, however, involved voluntary initiatives giving organisations a level of control over costs. Sponsored learning ranged from apprenticeships and first-level vocational qualifications (overseen in strategy and funding by the different UK national governments) to higher apprenticeships, postgraduate and professional vocational training (see Chapter 52).

In addition to provision purchased from educational institutions, employers were also encouraged to address skills shortages by creating their own courses. Whilst still working in partnership with further and higher education institutions, these generally took the form of flexible, part-time and online modules often taught in-house and with accreditation for relevant work-based activities. This customised approach was championed by the Coalition through its Employer Ownership Pilot scheme rolled out in England from 2012. It was seen as responsive to the changing needs and life conditions of staff, offering a cheaper unit cost for employers and, potentially, an opportunity to spread constrained funds across a wider number of employees.

Housing, transport, leisure and concierge services saw less balanced approaches to their budgets. In the case of housing, there were reductions in allowances (sometimes by not meeting the rising costs) for relocation and household insurance premiums, cuts in the number and size of loans available for mortgages but increased assistance with rental deposits. With transport, it involved switching from outright purchase to contract hire for company cars or to employee ownership schemes through 'green car' salary sacrifice arrangements. Sports event attendance was largely expunged as an unaffordable benefit, luncheon vouchers and meal allowances were allowed to decline in value, while other concierge services chiefly became a benefit for executives only.

Emerging Issues

Although there are signs of economic recovery which may encourage government to introduce further mandatory and fiscal changes, it is doubtful whether many organisations with workplace schemes will expand their voluntary provision or those without adopt welfare initiatives in the near future. More likely is a period of review followed by piecemeal adjustments to non-contractual provision. In the public and third sectors, where equity and social inclusion hold some value, such changes can be expected to affect all or most employees. In the private sector, companies are more likely to calculate what they can afford and couple this with where they might invest to provide maximum business advantage. In other words, they could well reinforce existing inequities by rewarding managers and high performers rather than those in low-waged jobs.

Guide to Further Sources

The issues raised here are explored more fully in R. M. Titmuss (1958), *Essays on the Welfare State*, London: Allen & Unwin; E. Brunsdon and M. May (forthcoming), *Workplace Welfare in the UK: An Exploratory Analysis*; E. Brunsdon and M. May (2007), 'Occupational welfare', in M. Powell (ed.), *Understanding the Mixed Economy of Welfare*, Bristol: Policy Press; and K. Farnsworth (2013), 'Occupational welfare', in B. Greve (ed.), *The Routledge Handbook of the Welfare State*, Abingdon: Routledge. Mandatory and voluntary UK initiatives can be tracked through the magazine *Employee Benefits*.

Review and Assignment Questions

1   What are the main differences between 'mandatory' and 'voluntary' occupational provision?
2   Why do some employers invest in occupational welfare and others not?
3   What are the costs and benefits of occupational welfare?
4   On what grounds, if any, can the current inequities in occupational provision be justified?

5 As the employee benefits officer for a large UK company, write a short report for your finance director explaining why your organisation should invest in preventive healthcare initiatives.

Visit the book companion site at www.wiley.com/go/alcocksocialpolicy to make use of the resources designed to accompany the textbook. There you will find chapter-specific guides to further resources, including governmental, international, thinktank, pressure groups and relevant journal sources. You will also find a glossary based on *The Blackwell Dictionary of Social Policy*, help sheets, guidance on managing assignments in social policy and career advice.

37

Voluntary Welfare

Jeremy Kendall

Overview

- ■ 'Voluntary welfare' is nurtured and delivered through a plethora of organisations situated between the market and the state.
- ■ The scope, scale, structure and diversity of these organisations have been captured in empirical work and theoretical accounts.
- ■ Deepening interest in social capital has reinforced interest in their role in social, political and economic life.
- ■ Volunteering, typically mediated by voluntary bodies, is increasingly understood as involving a range of motivations and social structures.
- ■ Voluntary organisations' growing proximity to the state has been hotly debated.

Context

'Voluntary welfare' involves an extraordinary range of organisations which are components of neither the state nor the market, contributing crucially to the well-being of individuals and communities. The result is that social needs that would otherwise be ignored and unfulfilled are recognised and met in multifarious ways. The extent and range of this sector are extraordinary, ranging from local providers of care for children and vulnerable older people, to housing associations and the Child Poverty Action Group operating at regional and national levels, and CAFOD and Oxfam on the international stage.

As the above examples indicate, voluntary welfare may be organised through legally recognised charities, but also involves groups without this status, including numerous small and 'micro' associations which are not charitable, and companies limited by guarantee as well as community interest companies at the larger end of the scale.

The Student's Companion to Social Policy, Fifth Edition. Edited by Pete Alcock, Tina Haux, Margaret May and Sharon Wright.
© 2016 John Wiley & Sons, Ltd. Published 2016 by John Wiley & Sons, Ltd.

Historically, and contrary to some predictions by contemporaries, rather than contracting with the establishment of the welfare state, voluntary action expanded alongside it. From the 1970s, this development was increasingly acknowledged by policymakers, supported by governmental grants and also marked by the increasing use of paid staff. This process gathered momentum under the Conservative administrations of 1979–97, which, as part of their attempt to 'roll back' state welfare, increased state funding and promoted both the work of voluntary agencies and volunteering. In a new development, however, funding, especially in social care, was increasingly based on the use of contracts rather than grants and geared towards pre-specified services.

From 1997, Labour continued the practice of supporting voluntary agencies to deliver public services in social care and other fields, increasingly expressed as a process of 'commissioning' to emphasise that a particular service was being purchased. But it also sought to develop a strategic 'partnership' with the sector as a whole, in welfare and beyond, including investing in various measures to further voluntary activity more generally.

Indeed, the growth in government interest in and support for the sector was such that, in effect, it became 'mainstreamed' (Kendall, 2003). In England, the main focus of this chapter, this heightened attention can be seen as clearing the ground for some of the 'Big Society' policies of the 2010–15 Coalition government. But now there is less emphasis on a 'partnership' with the sector as such and more a hope and expectation that it will get on with delivering public services alongside commercial operators in the context of enormous contractions in public sector budgets. As a result, funding has generally needed to shift significantly away from the state towards fundraising and market transactions.

Why have we witnessed this 'rediscovery' of voluntary welfare? Latterly, in the climate of the austerity since the economic crisis of 2007–8 the search for cuts in public spending has been one ingredient. But, as we have seen, this phenomenon long pre-dates the crisis situation and more positive reasons have gained momentum over a much longer period. In particular, beliefs have developed in political and policy circles that these organisations can be not only cost-effective, but also more responsible, more sensitive to a range of social needs, and better positioned to generate social capital and encourage social enterprise than others.

Some of these beliefs are well founded, others less so. But they make political sense against the backdrop of a loss of faith in market and state solutions, with voluntary activity increasingly being promoted as a necessary additional ingredient for the supposedly exhausted narrow models of 'statism' for the political left and 'market dogma' for the right. In this sense, it partly finds support for what it is not, as well as reflecting what it can demonstrably achieve.

Definitional Issues

Some writers have suggested these organisations and activities are so varied and diverse and now blur into the state and the market in so many ways in terms of relationships and transactions that we should not refer to a '*sector*' at all. However, this observation would also hold for the worlds of business and the state. It is reasonable to use such a term, therefore, as long as we remain aware of this variety, and utilise it as shorthand to keep this space of welfare activity in focus.

What then are its shared characteristics? An influential international approach defines into the 'voluntary sector' *formally organised* entities which:

- are constitutionally/legally separate from the state and business;
- cannot distribute surpluses ('profits') freely to owners; and
- demonstrably benefit from some degree of voluntarism (uncoerced giving) of money ('donations') or time ('volunteering').

Once we have identified our overall domain in this way, we can then usefully contrast organisations within it in a number of ways to support the development of theory, and to provide heuristic frames of reference. In particular, a distinction is often drawn between different kinds of voluntary organisation according to their *functions and activities*, distinguishing between service delivery, campaigning, expressive and community-building/development roles. Some organisations specialise, essentially focusing on one of these. But many groups combine some or all of these roles because this is judged to be the best way for them to make an impact on behalf of those whose needs they are seeking to meet or represent.

Other classifications may categorise organisations according to differences in their values, norms and motivations – typically in line with particular normative assumptions that some are healthier for civil society than others. We can also differentiate them in terms of their governance/control/rights distribution, their size and the scope of their operations, and their resource base (financial and human).

In addition, contrasts may also be drawn between *tertiary associations*, that is, passive, 'armchair' or 'cheque book' membership-based bodies, and *secondary associations*, with demonstrably active memberships and apparently vibrant cultures of participation, reciprocity and networking. (Family and friendship circles being 'primary' forms of association.)

It can also be helpful to analyse organisations according to the area or *policy field* in which they operate. An 'international classification of non-profit organisations' has been specially developed to capture the relevant fields of operation within welfare, including Personal Social Services (social care), Health, and Development & Housing, alongside other areas such as Culture & Recreation and Environmental Action. There is also a category for sacramental religion, of relevance in the English case, although less empirically significant than in the US and some continental European countries (see Chapter 29).

Theoretical Issues

Over the past three to four decades, our knowledge of the empirical features of voluntary welfare in England and beyond has grown dramatically. At the same time, conceptual development and theory-building has proceeded, trying to address questions such as: why a 'third or voluntary sector' is needed alongside the market and the state in developed capitalist economies, how these organisations function, behave and contribute to social policies, and how they affect not only economic productivity but political performance.

In tackling these questions a leading role has been taken by economic theorists. Building on long-standing notions of *market failure* (see Chapter 40), one approach advanced from the mid-1970s views voluntary organisations as a response to the inability of both markets and states to provide collective goods (services where benefits cannot be limited purely to paying customers, and in which one person's consumption does not completely exclude that of other people).

Another, *contract failure* theory, was developed in the 1980s. This emphasised how the sector can be perceived as a trustworthy response to information problems, when funders are separate from users and users are vulnerable and unable to evaluate quality. The suggestion here is that since these agencies, by definition, have no shareholders expecting to reap financial gain, they avoid incentives to profiteer by cutting corners on services at the expense of users. Thirdly, on the supply side, the crucial role of *ideological (including religious and political) entrepreneurs* in starting and sustaining such organisations was also highlighted in the 1980s.

This theorising has been criticised on varying grounds, particularly on the basis that it is unable to explain changes over time or conceptualise patterns of cooperation (rather than substitution) between the voluntary and other sectors. It has also been challenged for focusing on service delivery, neglecting other roles and the ways in which the sector engages in socio-political processes beyond market transactions.

Looking at these criticisms, analysts such as Evers have emphasised a *welfare mix approach* and the tensions between market-, state- and community-driven logics. In similar vein, Salamon and Anheier have posited a *social origins framework* (see Anheier, 2014), pointing to how interactions with powerful political institutions at important moments of policy design profoundly shape the national space provided for these organisations, and fundamentally determine the roles they are positioned to play in welfare systems.

Complementing these analyses, the concept of *social capital* is now widely used, particularly the formulation popularised by Robert Putnam. This idea is concerned not only with welfare service delivery, but also with more general ties, habits, relationships and interactions in communities. These function better, it is claimed, when involving trust, reciprocity, stability and respect. Moreover, as the words 'social capital' indicate, these relations of trust and norms of reciprocity are viewed as functioning not just in relation to social life, but also to the productivity of the economy and in supporting basic democratic norms. This favourable understanding has been important in catalysing social science interest in the sector and, as will be seen below, has boosted the support for it across the political spectrum highlighted earlier.

Organised voluntarism, taken here as explained earlier to mean giving of money or time not directly constrained by state coercion or market imperatives and outside the informal sector (see Chapter 38), is an important element in some of these theories. Arguably, it should be fundamental to any attempt to study the interplay between the voluntary sector and social policy. However, as state engagement with it has expanded and public funding grown, especially in support of larger organisations, private donations have fallen proportionately, becoming relatively limited resources. Hence, the main way voluntarism is now manifested is through *unpaid labour*, which, despite the growth in the sector's paid workforce noted earlier, remains a key resource.

So, why do people volunteer? In the immediate post-war era it was widely seen as a manifestation of altruism, as distinct from the self-interest fostered by the market. But a much more sophisticated, multi-dimensional understanding of the drivers to commit time voluntarily has now emerged. Recognised motivations for volunteering mix altruism and self-interest, and include:

- improving 'social capital', intentionally or incidentally;
- developing human capital, bringing benefits both for individuals and the wider society in terms of training and experience of value in people's working lives;
- 'intrinsic' satisfaction from engaging in volunteering and the associated processes of relationship-building with others;
- 'extrinsic' satisfaction from the results of volunteering; and
- psychological benefits, including enhanced self-esteem and respect.

State policies and funding programmes seeking to foster volunteering may in practice, directly or indirectly, both affect people's interest and boost or impede organisations' strategies for recruiting and retaining volunteers. But social policy interventions can also shape interest in volunteering in other ways. Educational experiences and the policies that govern them, for instance, influence individual's perceptions of their aptitudes, abilities and understandings of the world and affect their basic dispositions to volunteer. Significantly, too, attitudes towards volunteering are systematically linked to ethnicity, gender and social class; while paid work, caring and other commitments also affect the extent to which people engage in volunteering.

Emerging issues

As indicated at the outset, the Coalition government of 2010–15 sought to encourage the development of the voluntary sector in England, but with a strong emphasis on independent funding and as part of a drive to dismantle state provision. In particular, it connected voluntary welfare with its overarching 'Big Society' agenda, hostile to the state and seeking to weaken it for both ideological and economic reasons in the context of austerity. In practice its enthusiasm for framing its policy with this notion ebbed and flowed during its period of office. But, as its manifesto indicated, the idea was revived by the Conservative administration elected in 2015, as part of its strategy to reform and reshape welfare.

Numerous commentators have dismissed the 'Big Society' construct as meaningless and existing purely as tactical cover to justify otherwise unimaginable cuts in public welfare (see Chapter 21). But at the most basic level it does seem to have content, even if its critics do not like its claims, asserting in novel language the proposition that voluntary action can only really flourish if 'Big Government' is downscaled. So it defines society as necessarily opposed to the state, which is then by definition equated in blanket fashion with inauthentic activity, excessive bureaucracy, inflexibility in policy implementation, and undue intervention and 'interference'.

So, weaving together these claims about the dysfunctionality of the state with the dominant policy discourse on the imperative to restrict welfare spending (due to the condition of the economy in a climate of austerity), a central idea for both the Coalition and the ensuing Conservative administrations has been to restrict the flow of public funds into social programmes. The voluntary sector, with scaled down state funding, has supposedly been encouraged to 'fill the gap' alongside provision by commercial for-profit companies. This involves abandoning an idea central to the theorists and architects of the post-war welfare state, including Marshall, Titmuss and Beveridge, that the state is well placed to directly foster social development (see Chapter 18).

Under the Coalition, we witnessed a large-scale withdrawal of state financial support along these lines, and, in England, a dramatically accelerated shift towards market-style commissioning and procurement in those situations where public funding continues to support voluntary agencies. Reports from research and infrastructure bodies have sought to demonstrate and problematise these emerging patterns. In multiple ways they have pointed to the extent to which the new funding environment, characterised by rigidity and insensitivity, appears to be undermining many organisations' modus operandi.

Moreover, when state funding has been withdrawn, leaving needs unmet and vulnerable communities exposed, there is no evidence that the sector has been able to 'fill the gap'. This seems to be because it often lacks the financial wherewithal, the skills and resources, the general infrastructure capacity, and perhaps sometimes the motivation to do so, while at the same time the market is failing.

Overall, the combination of these latest policy developments with the more generous legacy of mainstreaming inherited from Labour has resulted in a fragmented and variegated landscape that has been interpreted very differently according to analysts' theoretical predilections. Radical writers (often drawing on Marx's socio-economic analysis and some influenced by the Foucauldian tradition), as well as those on the right in principle hostile to state intervention in all its forms (see Chapters 9 and 12) have emphasised potential distortions to voluntary organisations' values and missions, and threats to the sector's ability to behave autonomously. At the extreme, they are said to be not only weakened but subverted. However, as stressed earlier, there are necessarily severe limits to generalisation and those working with more pragmatic approaches point to variation in experiences.

Against this backdrop, we can highlight two key questions for policy analysis:

■ First, in terms of front-line implementation, to what extent does the current policy environment help or hinder voluntary organisations as they seek to meet social needs and protect the interests of vulnerable people? Here rhetorical acknowledgement has now reached saturation point, and it is important to look beyond routinised claims of policy supportiveness to assess the extent to which they are being accompanied by actual deeds. An overriding concern is what may happen to those organisations that have been significant players in addressing social problems when state funding is scaled back or withdrawn, and resources from the market or the sector itself are hard or impossible to mobilise. The research to date has tended to be negative on these issues, so an ongoing, very close watch will need to be kept on how the situation evolves in the years ahead.

■ Second, are the relevant social policies developing in a balanced way more generally? Are institutions and relations forming that respect the variety of functions and roles identified above and facilitate the multiple activities of organisations varying by size, field and focus? Again, the overriding impression from research hitherto is far from encouraging. A key challenge for social policy research therefore is to continue to address the issue of whether the ongoing drive to expand the sector's role in public service delivery does not undermine its other roles, especially in relation to campaigning, community development and the building of healthy social and political relationships, particularly at the local level where most voluntary action is concentrated

Guide to Further Sources

H. K. Anheier (2014), *Nonprofit Organizations: Theory, Management, Policy*, 2nd edn, London: Routledge, is a wide-ranging, thought-provoking study for relatively advanced students by a leading comparative analyst. S. Bridge, B. Murtag and K. O'Neill (2015), *Understanding the Social Economy and the Third Sector*, 2nd edn, Basingstoke: Palgrave Macmillan, is less theoretical but brings together a range of different approaches; and R. Putnam (2002), *Democracies in Flux*, Oxford: Oxford University Press, provides an accessible and helpful edited collection of Putnam's thinking on social capital.

T. Clark with A. Heath (2014), *Hard Times: The Divisive Toll of the Economic Slump*, New Haven, CT: Yale University Press, offers the best overview of the relationship between austerity and social policy in the UK and US in recent years. It is important here due to its forensic examination of claims about the 'social recession' which take into account how this relates to the practices of voluntary welfare.

Michael Edwards has done important work in assembling both an authoritative edited overview volume covering civil society and the place of voluntary organisations within it, and in presenting his own analysis of the literature in a readable volume, see M. Edwards (ed.) (2011), *The Oxford Handbook of Civil Society*, Oxford: Oxford University Press, and M. Edwards (2014), *Civil Society*, 3rd edn, Cambridge: Polity.

J. Kendall (2003), *The Voluntary Sector: Comparative Perspectives in the UK*, London: Routledge, remains the most systematic and up-to-date analytical account on the UK with a focus on the situation in England, whilst the National Council for Voluntary Organisations is the main co-coordinating and infrastructure agency within the English voluntary sector. Its website at: www.ncvo-vol.org.uk can be useful for policy and research materials, but is seen by some as being insufficiently challenging of the recent direction of policy, including the National Coalition for Independent Action (www.independentaction .net). The best recent assessments of the effects of the 'Big Society' agenda can be found by starting with Civic Exchange publications, at: www .civilexchange.org.uk.

Useful starting points for exploring the often different developments in the devolved administrations (see Part IV) are the websites of the main 'umbrella' bodies: the Northern Ireland Council for Voluntary Action at: www.nicva.org.uk; the Scottish Council for Voluntary Action at: www .scva.org.uk; and the Wales Council for Voluntary Action at: www.wcva.org.uk. More widely, an extensive range of briefings, research papers and other publications can be found on the Third Sector Research Centre's website at: www.tsrc .ac.uk.

Review and Assignment Questions

1 Why are contemporary politicians and social policymakers so enthusiastic about voluntary welfare?

2 What are the most significant impacts of voluntary action?

3 Why do people volunteer for voluntary organisations?

4 Can and should this sector 'fill the gap' left by a withdrawing state?

5 How does voluntary welfare contribute to social policy in a modern capitalist democracy?

Visit the book companion site at www.wiley.com/ go/alcocksocialpolicy to make use of the resources designed to accompany the textbook. There you will find chapter-specific guides to further resources, including governmental, international, thinktank, pressure groups and relevant journal sources. You will also find a glossary based on *The Blackwell Dictionary of Social Policy*, help sheets, guidance on managing assignments in social policy and career advice.

38

Informal Welfare

Linda Pickard

Overview

- Informal or unpaid care is support provided for family members or friends, because of long-term physical/mental ill health or disability, or problems related to old age.
- In the context of demographic ageing, there is increasing emphasis on unpaid care in UK social policy.
- There is gender inequality in unpaid care provision, with women more likely to provide care than men.
- Unpaid care and employment are a key dilemma for policymakers.
- There is evidence of a growing unpaid 'care gap', and there may need to be a shift from unpaid care to paid services in future.

Informal Welfare and Unpaid Care

The most important source of welfare for disabled and older people in the UK is informal care provided by families and friends. It has been estimated that carers who look after relatives or friends in the UK are saving the country £119 billion a year, more than the cost of the NHS. Various terms are used to describe this form of welfare, including 'informal' and 'unpaid' care. This chapter will mainly use the term 'unpaid care', which is defined as looking after family members, friends, neighbours or others because of long-term physical or mental ill health or disability, or problems related to old age.

Unpaid care has been given increasing emphasis in social policy in the UK in the last twenty-five years or so. This has primarily been associated with policies emphasising care in the community

The Student's Companion to Social Policy, Fifth Edition. Edited by Pete Alcock, Tina Haux, Margaret May and Sharon Wright.
© 2016 John Wiley & Sons, Ltd. Published 2016 by John Wiley & Sons, Ltd.

since, in this country, these policies rely heavily on unpaid care (see Chapter 54). The emphasis on unpaid care has also arisen in the context of the growing numbers of older people, many of whom rely exclusively on families or friends for support.

Characteristics of Unpaid Carers

The 2001 Census asked people if they provided unpaid care and the question was repeated in 2011. The latest Census figures show that there are 6.5 million carers in the UK, 5.4 million in England, 0.5 million in Scotland, 0.4 million in Wales and 0.2 million in Northern Ireland. Carers constitute 10 per cent of the population in England, 9 per cent in Scotland and 12 per cent in Wales and Northern Ireland. The numbers of carers in the UK have increased, rising from nearly 6 million in 2001 to 6.5 million in 2011.

Unpaid carers are not a homogeneous group. A distinction can be drawn between 'informal helping' and 'heavily involved caring'. It is heavily involved carers who are most likely to need support. Heavily involved carers are often defined in terms of long hours of caring. Of the 6.5 million carers in the UK, the 2011 Census shows that

nearly 2.5 million provide care for twenty or more hours a week and 1.5 million for fifty or more hours a week. Carers providing care for twenty or more hours a week have increased since 2001, rising from nearly 1.9 million to nearly 2.5 million in 2011.

There is inequality in the gender provision of unpaid care, and women are more likely to provide unpaid care than men (see Figure 38.1). In England, women make up 58 per cent of all carers. There are 3.1 million women providing unpaid care in England, compared with 2.3 million men. Nearly 12 per cent of women in England provide unpaid care, compared with approximately 9 per cent of men. The gender inequality in caring has made it an issue of particular interest to feminists in social policy, and relates to wider issues around family policy and unpaid care for children (see also Chapters 57 and 58).

Care provision is most common among people in mid-life (see Figure 38.1). The peak age for women to provide care is at ages fifty-five to fifty-nine years, while for men it is sixty to sixty-four. People caring in mid-life are usually caring for their parents/parents-in-law, providing 'intergenerational care' for older people. However, there are also increasing numbers of older people who

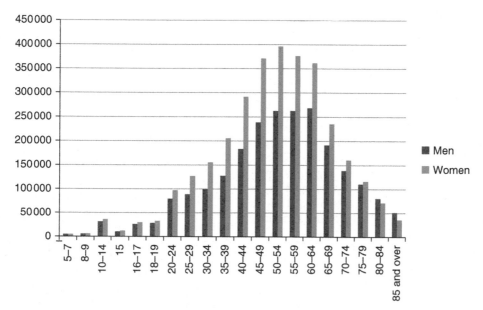

Figure 38.1 Numbers providing unpaid care by gender and age, England, 2011.
Source: 2011 Census.

themselves provide care. In England, there are approximately three-quarters of a million carers aged seventy years and over. Older carers are usually living with, and caring for, a partner, providing 'spouse care' often for another older person.

Key Issues Around Unpaid Care

The health of unpaid carers

There is a great deal of evidence that caring can damage the health of carers, particularly their psychological health. The 2011 Census shows that, in England, 29 per cent of adult carers aged twenty-five years and over say that they are themselves not in good health (defined as fair, bad or very bad health). The proportion is higher where care is provided for long hours or where the carer is aged sixty-five years and over. The majority (59 per cent) of older carers aged sixty-five and over caring for twenty hours a week or more are not in good health and may themselves be in need of support.

Working and caring

Most unpaid carers are of 'working age' (aged sixteen to sixty-four). According to the 2011 Census, there are approximately 4.1 million carers of working age in England, 2.3 million of whom are in paid employment. However, caring can have a negative effect on employment. A key threshold at which carers in England are 'at risk' of leaving employment occurs when care is provided for ten or more hours a week, a lower threshold than previously thought. Approximately 315,000 unpaid carers of working age in England, predominantly women, are estimated to have left employment to provide care. The public expenditure costs of carers leaving employment are at least a billion pounds a year, based on the costs of Carer's Allowance (see below) and lost tax revenues on forgone incomes (National Institute for Health Research, School for Social Care Research (NIHR SSCR), 2012).

Carers from Black and minority ethnic backgrounds

People in the UK from some minority ethnic backgrounds are more likely to provide long hours of unpaid care than people from White backgrounds. In particular, people from Asian backgrounds are more likely to provide care for twenty or more hours a week, compared with those from all other ethnic backgrounds, with the differences particularly marked at younger age groups. These differences in provision of caring for long hours are likely to be related partly to differences in family and household structure, partly to cultural expectations about the role of women and adult children in care-giving, and partly to the difficulties the people cared for often experience in accessing culturally acceptable services. Minority ethnic populations are ageing in the UK, and the increasing participation of minority ethnic women in the labour market is placing strains on family support systems.

Care by children and young people

The 2011 Census shows that in England there are approximately 165,000 children and young people under the age of eighteen who provide unpaid care, nearly 35,000 of whom care for twenty or more hours a week, an overall increase since 2001 when 139,000 children and young people provided unpaid care. Provision of care for long hours by children and young people affects their education and therefore their life chances. And there is increasing recognition in government policy that they should be protected from 'inappropriate' or 'excessive' caring (see recent Carers' Strategies, described below), although there is also a view that any provision of unpaid care is inappropriate for children and young people.

Social Policy for Unpaid Carers

Models of unpaid care in policy

It has been suggested that there are four models, or 'ideal types', of response of policymakers to carers (Box 38.1). In the UK, the predominant reality is that carers are taken for granted by the state and treated as a free resource ('*carers as resources*'). Since 1999, however, there have been explicit government policies around carers, set out in a series of Carers Strategies for England, with similar provisions elsewhere in the UK. All are essentially concerned with ensuring the continuation of caring and sustaining the well-being of carers.

Box 38.1 Policy Models of Unpaid Care

'*Carers as resources*': Reflects the predominant reality of social care in the UK. Carers are taken for granted by the state and treated as a *free resource*.

'*Carers as co-workers*': Policy aims to work alongside carers. Carers are seen as co-workers, or 'expert care partners', in a joint care enterprise. Carers are treated *instrumentally* and social policy only intervenes to support carers to ensure the continuance of care-giving.

'*Carers as co-clients*': Carers are regarded as clients in need of help in their own right. Carers' interests and well-being are valued outcomes per se, and support is provided aimed at making caring easier for carers to manage.

'*Superseded carer*': The aim is not to support the care-giving relationship, but to transcend or supersede it. The focus is on both the carer and cared-for. The aim is to intervene in ways that result in cared-for people no longer having to rely on a carer.

Source: based on J. Twigg (1992), 'Carers in the service system', in J. Twigg (ed.), *Carers: Research and Practice*, London: HMSO.

Policies therefore combine an instrumental concern with ensuring care-giving continues to be provided ('*carers as co-workers*') and a concern with the interests of carers per se ('*carers as co-clients*'). Short-term breaks from caring are emphasised as a cost-effective mechanism for enabling carers to continue to care for longer periods. There has been much less concern with *superseding* or replacing carers and, with a recent exception (discussed below), government policies across the UK have been concerned with avoiding the substitution of unpaid care with paid services.

Carers' assessments

As a result of legislation passed since 1986, social services departments in local authorities (also called councils) in England have certain statutory duties regarding carers' assessments, and adult social care falls within the statutory remit of the 152 Councils with Adult Social Services Responsibilities (Box 38.2). The Carers (Recognition and Services) Act 1995 (which applied in England, Wales and Scotland) gave carers the right to request an assessment if they provided a substantial amount of care on a regular basis and the local authority was carrying out an assessment of the cared-for person. This right was extended by the Carers and Disabled Children Act 2000, which

Box 38.2 Policy Timeline for Carers in England*

1995 Carers (Recognition and Services) Act
1999 National Strategy for Carers
2000 Carers and Disabled Children Act
2004 Carers (Equal Opportunities) Act
2008 Revised National Strategy for Carers
2010 Next Steps for the Carers Strategy
2014 Care Act
2014 Carers Strategy: Second National Action Plan 2014–2016

*Health and social services were devolved in 1999, but some of these measures have a wider application and/or are paralleled elsewhere in the UK.

introduced a free-standing right to a carer's assessment in England and Wales, with parallel legislation elsewhere. These Acts operated alongside each other and, in England and Wales, both were amended by the Carers (Equal Opportunities) Act 2004, which introduced a requirement that any assessment must include consideration of whether the carer worked or wished to work.

However, in England this legislation for carers' assessments was criticised by the Law Commission in 2011 as fragmented, overlapping and confusing for local authorities and carers alike, and it was recommended that the duties to assess a carer should be consolidated into a single duty. In addition, the Commission criticised specific aspects of the legislation, in particular, the 'substantial and regular test', which it described as unclear, confusing and complex. It recommended this test be removed and all carers providing care to another person should be entitled to an assessment, where the carer appears to be in need.

The government accepted many of the Law Commission's recommendations. The Care Act 2014 created a single duty for local authorities in England to undertake a carer's assessment. This replaced the existing law, and removed the requirement that the carer must be providing a substantial amount of care on a regular basis. The implication is that the criteria for carers' assessments are broadened and more carers are now able to access assessments. Moreover, the Care Act also introduced a new duty on local authorities to provide support to meet carers' needs, and assessments are a gateway to this new legal right to support for carers. The government is planning an increase of £25 million a year in England to finance the costs of additional carers' assessments arising from the new legislation, and an extra £150 million a year to finance the increase in carer support services, although these sums have been criticised as far too small (Pickard et al., 2015).

Breaks from caring

A key element of governmental Carers Strategies across the UK is the provision of breaks from caregiving to help carers continue caring. In England, the 1999 National Strategy for Carers introduced the Carers Special Grant, providing £140 million over three years for local authorities to develop services to give carers a break. The 2008 Carers Strategy included an increase of £150 million in the amount available for breaks, and in 2010, the Coalition government pledged £400 million additional funding over four years in England. The 2014 National Action Plan indicates that the Better Care Fund includes £130 million in NHS funding for carers' breaks in 2015–16. However,

the amounts governments have committed to carers' breaks over the years have been criticised as too small. Even the latest figure of £130 million for 2015–16 does not signal a major change in support structures when shared between 152 councils in England.

Support for working carers

In England, over the last twenty-five years, there has been an emphasis in government policy on enabling people to combine unpaid care and employment The main focus of policy relating to working carers here and elsewhere in the UK, as in other countries, has primarily been on 'flexible working' as part of a work–life balance agenda, and since 2014, under the implementation of the Children and Families Act, all employees in the UK have a right to request flexible working from their employer. However, carers have no entitlement to an extended period of leave to care, or to pay during that leave (although they may be able to claim Carer's Allowance if they have no other income; see below).

As well as an emphasis on flexible working, in England there is increasingly an emphasis on 'replacement care' to support working carers. This term was initially used in government policy around carers and employment in the 2008 Carers Strategy, which included a commitment to fund 'replacement care' for those participating in approved training, in order to help them re-enter the labour market. In the 2010 Carers Strategy, there was a new emphasis on developing social care markets partly to meet carers' needs for 'replacement care' to enable them to continue to work. This approach went further than previous policy because it implied *ongoing* support for working carers, rather than temporary support to help re-entry to the labour market.

The increasing emphasis on 'replacement care' is an important development because it represents a marked change from previous government policies. Earlier governments – and the devolved administrations – had rejected any notion of replacing, or substituting, unpaid care with paid services. In terms of the typology of carers in the service system, an emphasis on 'replacement care' is consistent with the *superseded carer* model (Box 38.1). It is important to note, however, that the 2010 Carers Strategy saw 'replacement care' as taking the form of services that would be provided through 'social care markets', whereas others would argue that more *publicly funded* 'replacement care' is likely to be needed.

Financial help for carers

Financial support for unpaid care across the UK primarily takes the form of Carer's Allowance, a cash benefit paid to people caring for long hours. It is paid to carers who provide unpaid care for at least thirty-five hours a week, earn less than a small amount (£110 a week in 2015–16), are not in full-time education and look after someone who receives a qualifying disability benefit. Carer's Allowance is based on a social security model of payments for care and is regarded by the Department for Work and Pensions as a compensation for loss of earnings, not as a wage for caring. There were over 675,000 recipients in the UK in 2014 and UK expenditure on the allowance was approximately £2.1 billion in 2013–14. Carer's Allowance has long been the subject of criticism in the social policy literature, primarily because of its low level, poor coverage of heavily committed carers, complexity, and failure to facilitate employment and caring.

Emerging Issues

The growing 'care gap'

Population ageing in the UK and other more economically developed countries means that there will be an unprecedented rise in need for long-term care in the next two decades. However, there is considerable uncertainty over the future supply of unpaid care. Research by Pickard (2015) shows that the supply of unpaid care to older people with disabilities by their adult children in England is unlikely to keep pace with demand in future (Figure 38.2). By 2032, there is projected to be a shortfall of 160,000 care-givers in England. Demand for unpaid care will begin to exceed supply by 2017, and the unpaid 'care gap' will grow rapidly from then onwards. An important driver of the care gap is that the numbers of older

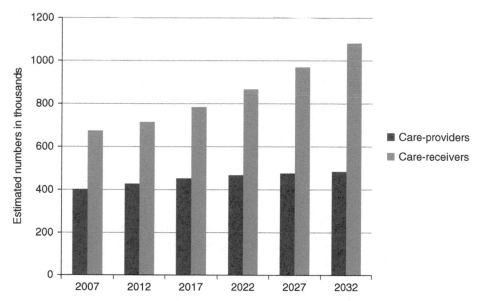

Figure 38.2 The growing care gap: supply of unpaid care provided by adult children for 20 or more hours a week to their older parents ('care-providers') and demand for unpaid care by older people with disabilities from their children ('care-receivers'), England, 2007–32.
Source: based on L. Pickard (2015), 'A growing care gap? The supply of unpaid care for older people by their adult children in England to 2032', *Ageing & Society*, 35:1, 96–123, available at: eprints.lse.ac.uk/51955.

people, especially the oldest old, are rising faster than the numbers in the younger generation (see too Chapter 26).

Policy dilemma around caring and working

In addition, in the context of population ageing, there is increasingly a dilemma around unpaid care and employment. Need for care is rising and many governments are keen to support the provision of unpaid care to meet this need. At the same time, partly to reduce the publicly funded costs of pensions, governments are extending working lives and encouraging older workers to continue in employment. However, older people of working age are those who are most likely to provide unpaid care, and unpaid care is often incompatible with employment. In this context, helping carers to combine caring with paid work is becoming a key policy objective in many countries, including the UK. In England, as we have seen, there is increasingly an emphasis on 'replacement care' for working carers to enable them to continue to work. It seems likely that this type of policy will be needed to a much greater extent in future, if the dilemma around unpaid care and employment is to be resolved.

Implications for long-term care policy

Both the growing care gap and the dilemma around unpaid care and employment raise wider issues for long-term care policy. If the care gap is to be filled in future, and if working carers are to be supported, then it is likely that more paid services will need to be provided. This suggests that there will need to be a shift from unpaid to paid care and that long-term care systems will need to reduce reliance on unpaid care. In England, this raises questions about the reforms of the long-term care system, introduced under the Care Act 2014, which are unlikely to reduce reliance on unpaid care (Pickard, 2015). If long-term care policy is to reduce reliance on unpaid care, there needs to be greater use of universal long-term care systems. These determine eligibility primarily on the basis of disability and tend to be less reliant on unpaid care. In England, a number of proposals for a more universal social care system have been put forward over the last fifteen years or so, including

recommendations for free personal care by the Royal Commission on Long Term Care in 1999 and proposals for a National Care Service by the Labour government in 2010. Similar issues are also being raised regarding long-term care funding provisions elsewhere in the UK (see Part IV). Ultimately, it is only with a more universal long-term care system that there is likely to be protection in future from the care gap and from the dilemma around unpaid care and employment.

Guide to Further Sources

2011 Census information on unpaid care in England and Wales is available at: www.nomisweb.co.uk/census/2011/data_finder; on Scotland at: www.scotlandscensus.gov.uk/documents/censusresults/release2a/healthboard/KS301SCa_HB.pdf; and on Northern Ireland at: www.niassembly.gov.uk/globalassets/documents/raise/publications/2013/general/3013.pdf.

Findings from research on working and caring in England are reported by the NIHR SSCR (2012), at: sscr.nihr.ac.uk/PDF/Findings/Findings_10_carers-employment_web.pdf.

A critical evaluation of care by children can be found in S. Becker, C. Dearden and J. Aldridge (2001), 'Children's labour of love? Young carers and care work', in P. Mizen, C. Pole and A. Bolton (eds), *Hidden Hands. International Perspectives on Children's Work and Labour*, Brighton: Falmer Press. An evaluation of the 2014 Care Act can be found in L. Pickard, D. King and M. Knapp (2015), 'The "visibility" of unpaid care in England', *Journal of Social Work*, doi: 10.1177/1468017315569645.

Review and Assignment Questions

1   Why is unpaid care of particular interest to feminists in social policy?

2   Should children and young people under the age of eighteen years provide unpaid care to disabled family members, such as their parents?

3   How would you characterise the approach to policy on unpaid carers adopted by successive

governments in the countries of the UK in recent years?

4 Why is there uncertainty over the future supply of unpaid care in the next two decades?

5 There is a dilemma for governments concerning policies around unpaid care and employment. Describe this dilemma and explain its likely causes, with particular reference to the UK or one of its constituent countries.

Visit the book companion site at www.wiley.com/go/alcocksocialpolicy to make use of the resources designed to accompany the textbook. There you will find chapter-specific guides to further resources, including governmental, international, thinktank, pressure groups and relevant journal sources. You will also find a glossary based on *The Blackwell Dictionary of Social Policy*, help sheets, guidance on managing assignments in social policy and career advice.

39

Welfare Users and Social Policy

Catherine Needham

Overview

- The welfare state was based on a passive view of welfare, but from the 1970s people increasingly campaigned to play a more active role in welfare services.
- From 1979, successive governments made it easier for people to be active consumers.
- In the era of 'austerity politics', this citizen-consumer model is changing to one in which people are expected to play a role as 'co-producers', shaping and producing services.
- Many users of welfare services are dissatisfied with the roles that governments expect them to play and demand a more active role based on citizenship.

Context

The welfare state that emerged in the UK after the Second World War was based in a society very different to that of twenty-first-century Britain. Immigration levels were low, few women worked, most men undertook manual labour, and could expect only a short retirement prior to death. In what was in some ways a more overt class system than exists today, there was an expectation of deference towards people in professional roles. The ways in which people talked about and treated users of welfare services reflected that world. Those who needed social security benefits because of sustained periods of unemployment or social care services because of disability or frailty were to be pitied and looked after in the welfare state safety net. These were not the active citizens who were accessing universal health and education services as a matter of entitlement, regardless of financial wealth. They were the people who had somehow failed to take the opportunities offered in post-war Britain, and had fallen into poverty as a result. Services were designed around principles of

The Student's Companion to Social Policy, Fifth Edition. Edited by Pete Alcock, Tina Haux, Margaret May and Sharon Wright.

professional gatekeeping rather than user accessibility or choice.

Disabled people and people with mental health problems were separated from their families and sent to large residential institutions, with rigid and sometimes abusive regimes. Families who lost their homes risked being split up rather than rehoused together. The combination of needs-testing ('why do you need this service?') and means-testing ('can you afford to support yourself?') which accompanied the allocation of most welfare benefits meant people had to share intimate details of their personal and professional lives with social workers, housing officers and unemployment centre staff.

Strivers and Shirkers

As Britain started to change socially in the 1960s, so too did the passive and deferential culture surrounding welfare services. Rising affluence created a more independent and assertive youth culture; demand for labour encouraged more women into the workforce, as well as stimulating mass immigration from the UK's former colonies. Life expectancy increased. In the 1970s, a movement that came to be known as the 'New Left' criticised the tendency of welfare state professionals to police and discipline the working class. The failure of standardised services to respond to the diverse needs of women, ethnic minorities and people with disabilities was also highlighted. Feminists objected to the assumption that the relevant unit was the family rather than the individual. A more participatory style of democracy was gaining support from new social movements, emphasising a need for the users of services to play a greater role in their design and operation (see Chapters 13, 14 and 61).

However, whilst the campaigns of the New Left made their mark on some inner cities, the end of the 1970s saw the triumph of the New Right with the election of Margaret Thatcher's Conservative government (see Chapter 19). One of the key items on Thatcher's agenda was to shrink state spending on welfare and to stigmatise those who remained dependent on the state. Rather than responding more fully to the needs of a more diverse society and using participatory and local forms of democracy to promote active welfare citizens, the

Conservatives prized the individual consumer, reliant on market rather than political power. New opportunities were provided for individuals to exit state dependence through home ownership and share-holding. Those who remained using public services were offered new 'charters' by the Major government (1992–7), in an attempt to mimic the consumer choice and control of the private sector. Business leaders were brought in to advise government on how it could better meet the needs of the public service customer. Patients in the National Health Service were given the choice of which hospital to go to for treatment, and patient satisfaction surveys became an important measure of success. There was an assumption that the mechanisms of choice and user feedback, dominant in private sector consumer markets, could be a stimulus for quality in public services.

However, as in the post-war era, much of this consumer rhetoric was oriented towards the in-work citizen, utilising health and education services for their family, but not requiring welfare support. Groups of welfare recipients – lone parents and asylum seekers, for example – were the subject of stigma rather than new charter rights. This distinction between the successful citizen-consumer and the failed welfare user has remained a theme of British welfare policy since that time, even as a succession of Conservative, Labour and Coalition governments have come and gone. Each in its way has attempted to cut the welfare budget and to stigmatise welfare users – although each has been much more successful in the second of these goals than the first.

The Labour governments of 1997–2010 continued to prize the citizen-consumer, creating more opportunities for users of public services to exercise choice. However, it was very much framed as a reciprocal arrangement, in which greater choice and control were the reward for people taking more responsibility for their lives. Their welfare to work (WTW) policies were based on a range of strategies which made welfare rights increasingly subject to return to work pressures. For example, lone parents were a focus of the reforms, with a carrot of childcare and a stick of reduced benefit to get people back into the workplace (see Chapters 47 and 56).

The Coalition government of 2010–15 further intensified this agenda, with a very explicit contrast between 'strivers and shirkers' (that is, those who work hard and those who do not). A benefits cap was introduced, due to the concerns of government ministers that it was not right for people receiving state benefits to be better off than people in work. There seemed little awareness that it was only people with large families in high-cost areas of the country that ever received the high sums that appeared to shock the tabloid newspapers. Nor was their concern much about the implications of the benefit cap on child poverty levels, and how it might intensify the problems associated with the so-called 'Troubled Families' which the government was supporting through other initiatives.

People with disabilities were also increasingly subject to the shirker label, as new eligibility tests for disability support appeared to find that a very large proportion of the people who had been claiming state financial support were in fact capable of working. Many of these decisions were reversed on appeal, and high-profile deaths of people who had been found 'fit to work' by the assessors led to high levels of criticism of the policy.

The devolution reforms instigated by Labour meant that the changes discussed here, and the reframing of the citizen as a consumer of welfare services, was a much more explicitly English rather than a UK-wide agenda. Governments in Wales and Scotland in particular were wary of the marketising forms on offer in England, and of the notion of consumer power as the route for citizen empowerment and service improvement (see Part IV).

Co-producers

The 'austerity politics' of the second decade of the twenty-first century (see Chapter 21) seemed to leave behind some of the citizen-consumer rhetoric and reinvent the ideal welfare user as a 'co-producer'. Whilst consumers sit at the end of a production line of services developed by the state, the co-producer is supposed to be actively involved in the production of those services. For example, citizens play a role in recycling waste, reporting crime and submitting tax returns. Health and education services can function only if pupils are engaged with learning and if patients take medicines as directed. In relation to welfare

services, people must be actively engaged in searching for jobs and in volunteering to run community activities in their localities so as to reduce the need for state services.

This agenda can be linked to the 'Big Society'. As discussed in other chapters, David Cameron began his period as Prime Minister in 2010 by talking about the need for a 'Big Society'. Communities and individuals were expected to do more for themselves and be less reliant on state support. Although it was put forward as the Conservative's 'big idea' for government, there was some cynicism about the political agenda behind this label and a feeling that it was being used as a cover for cuts in services, and the term seemed to have been largely abandoned only to be revived in the Conservative's 2015 election manifesto.

However, the idea of the citizen as an active participant rather than a passive consumer has much broader appeal. It involves recognition of the expertise individuals and communities can bring to tackling entrenched issues. For this reason, it has been warmly embraced by the Scottish and Welsh governments, both of which have explicitly endorsed co-production in their reform of public services (see Part IV). It is also part of a broader shift towards asset-based approaches in public services, which draw on the idea that all people and communities have assets (skills, time, relationships and spaces, for example), and should not always be talked about in terms of their deficits (illness, isolation, crime, poverty).

One example of the way in which a more co-productive approach has changed services is in the Expert Patient programme promoted in England. Here people with long-term health conditions take on a peer support role for other people with the same illness, recognising the expertise that comes from managing a condition over the long term. The Experts by Experience programme, run in England by the Care Quality Commission (CQC), also offers a much more active role for service users (see Box 39.1)

Within research undertaken by government and by universities it has again become increasingly common to involve people who use services as partners in the research. In this way, rather than always being the target of research initiatives and policy changes, service users are being asked to play a role in shaping what questions are asked and

Box 39.1 Experts by Experience

The CQC, which regulates standards in health and social care services in England, has recruited a group of people who use services to be 'Experts by Experience'. These people, who take part in inspections and advise on CQC policy, are those with experience of using health and social care services or of being a carer of someone in the health and social care system.

Box 39.2 The Social Model of Disability

The Social Model of Disability was developed in the 1980s, and has powerfully reshaped notions of disability. It is based on the idea that disability is not an individual problem or 'tragedy', but something that is imposed on people by a society that does not allow them access to the spaces and entitlements of full citizenship. Rather than 'fixing' the bodies of disabled people, it is necessary to fix society so as to remove disabling barriers.

how they are asked. This is indicative of a broader shift away from assuming that the only valid form of knowledge comes from professional expertise, recognising instead the validity of expertise that comes from the lived experience of living with poverty, disability or a mental health problem.

Taking Control

As the previous sections have indicated, the evolution of the welfare state since 1945 has seen the user of welfare services asked to play many different roles, depending on political agendas and financial cycles. From being passive recipients of professionally mandated services, they have been asked to become consumers and then co-producers.

However, it is important to recognise that many welfare service users have not simply been content to be blown about by the prevailing political climate, but have been active as self-advocates, challenging what the welfare state has given them. Within mental health services, for example, the user and survivor movement has challenged dominant psychiatric models of normalisation. Within disability services, the social model of disability (see Box 39.2 and Chapter 61) triggered more inclusive and person-centred models of support. Family carers have successfully campaigned to get recognition of their contribution through the work of organisations such as Carers UK and the Princess Royal Trust for Carers. For these campaigners, a key ambition has been to reshape the value and identities associated with, for example, having a learning disability, using mental health services or caring for a

spouse with dementia. Campaigns for improved support have been contingent on accepting that people must be recognised as full citizens with legitimate claims on public spaces and resources, rather than people with a deficiency who must be hidden away in homes or disability services.

The social movements emerging from disability campaigns have been effective in pressing for political change, using disruptive tactics where necessary (see Chapters 14 and 61). Campaigners for disability rights in the 1990s, for example, chained themselves to buses to protest about the lack of access to public transport. Some groups have been willing to work closely with the state to achieve change, and many disability charities have taken on roles as service delivery organisations. Others have resisted this co-option by the state, feeling that they can work best as advocates of change if they remain distanced from government.

An example of a campaign by people with disabilities that led to large-scale policy change is direct payments. A direct payment is a cash allocation from the state that enables frail older people, people with disabilities and people with mental health problems to manage their own care needs and purchase appropriate services. Such payments were illegal under the terms of the 1948 National Assistance Act, but sustained campaigning by disability organisations, particularly the commissioning of research demonstrating the potential cost-savings of direct payments, eventually led to a change in the law in the mid-1990s (see Chapter 61).

Personal budgets, which include direct payments, are now a mainstream approach in adult and children's services across the UK. If people are eligible for social care services (that is, they meet a needs-test and a means-test), they will be able to take the money as a direct payment (or ask someone else to manage the budget for them (see Chapter 54)). Monies can be spent in any way that meets an approved outcome, and many local authorities are encouraging users to be creative in how funds are spent. Service users can choose to employ a personal assistant and/or to spend money outside the formal care sector. For example, people have opted to take a holiday at Centre Parcs rather than going to a 'respite' facility offered by the local authority – or have taken out a Sky TV package rather than spending the money on going along to an older people's day centre.

Such changes are somewhat controversial. Many disability campaigners have argued that it is appropriate and cost-effective to spend money on what people with disabilities know will improve their well-being. Critics argue that it is not the job of the state to pay for perks such as Sky TV, and that it is unfair to do so for some people when it is not available to the broader population. It has also been argued that individualised financial allocations re-establish people as consumers and contribute to the closure of shared collective spaces such as day centres. Isolating people in their own homes and making them bear the risks of making 'bad' choices, is seen by some people as a very inadequate form of empowerment. However, for those whose lives have been improved through the freedoms provided by direct payments, such arguments are mistaking an idealised future for the possibility of real incremental improvements now.

These controversies get to the heart of the balance between the rights and responsibilities of welfare users, and the entitlements of the individual versus the community. One of the achievements of disability campaigners was to reject the dualism of individualism versus collectivism, and argue that collective expressions of identity needed to be accompanied by improvements in individual access to person-centred support. Centres for Independent Living were user-controlled initiatives which campaigned for both improved support and were spaces to marshal collective campaigns. Many of the early advocates for personalised approaches to social care came from this collective movement, and they continue to argue for personalisation to be located in a discourse in which citizenship and personhood are the basis for a legitimate collective voice in reshaping services – not a top-down tool for isolating people as consumers of care.

Emerging Issues

The future is likely to bring a further intensification of the trends identified here. Austerity is putting enormous strain on social care services, housing availability and secure employment, and successive governments are likely to deal with this by further stigmatising and marginalising welfare users rather than tackling any of the underlying causes of welfare dependence.

Individualised forms of funding such as direct payments and personal health budgets have caught the imagination of a range of political parties and look likely to be a continuing feature of the welfare landscape. As outlined above, these can be controversial. They also produce some new dilemmas: can users of welfare services make better spending choices than professionals and the state? What happens if users make bad choices: does the state still have a responsibility to step in and look after them?

The likelihood of greater devolution means that it will become more difficult to generalise about even England, let alone the United Kingdom. The Greater Manchester deal for devolved health spending and regional autonomy, announced in 2015, is symbolic of the extent to which Scottish, Welsh and Northern Irish devolution have created pressures for more local control in England (see Chapter 45). Such changes have the potential to energise local citizens, able to hold city regional governments accountable for the quality and range of public services in their area. But they also fracture the sense of a shared political community across the UK, in which citizens in one part enjoy the same services as those in another. The English media has been very hostile in the past to the idea of a 'postcode lottery' in public services, where people on one side of a local border get different services to their neighbours on the other side. It remains unclear whether welfare users will embrace diversity as citizens of a locality, or will prefer to be consumers asserting an entitlement to a standardised product in Bradford as well as in Brighton.

Guide to Further Sources

For an account of unemployment and poverty in 'austerity Britain', see T. Shildrick, R. MacDonald, C. Webster and K. Garthwaite (2012), *Poverty and Insecurity: Life in Low-pay, No-pay Britain*, Bristol: Policy Press. A set of short articles looking at recent welfare policy and likely future scenarios for welfare state change is provided by L. Foster, A. Brunton, C. Deeming and T. Haux (eds) (2015), *In Defence of Welfare II*, Bristol: Policy Press. The British Social Attitudes series provides a useful overview of how public attitudes to users of welfare services have changed. See A. Park, J. Curtice and C. Bryson (eds) (2014), *British Social Attitudes: The 31st Report*, London: Sage.

J. Clarke, J. Newman, N. Smith, E. Vidler and E. Westmarland (2007), *Creating Citizen-Consumers*, London: Sage, is based on research that explores relationships between public services and the public in the context of health services, social care services and policing. A European perspective on active citizenship can be found in J. E. Newman and E. Tonkens (eds) (2011), *Active Citizenship in Europe*, Amsterdam: University of Amsterdam Press. For a discussion of the advantages and disadvantages of personalisation and direct payments, see C. Needham and J. Glasby (eds) (2014), *Debates in Personalisation*, Bristol: Policy Press.

Relevant websites for social movements include Disability Rights at: www.disabilityrightsuk.org,

and the National Survivor User Network at: www.nsun.org.uk. The Spartacus Network is a coalition of disability groups and campaigners protesting against cuts in disability benefits; see: www.spartacusnetwork.org.uk.

Review and Assignment Questions

1 Why have users of welfare services (such as social security benefits and social care services) been stigmatised more than users of education and health services?

2 What does it mean to be a co-producer of public services?

3 What are the arguments for and against the use of direct payments for people with disabilities?

4 Why has the social model of disability been so significant in relation to disability rights?

5 Why might some people with disabilities be unwilling to work closely with the state to improve social care services?

Visit the book companion site at www.wiley.com/go/alcocksocialpolicy to make use of the resources designed to accompany the textbook. There you will find chapter-specific guides to further resources, including governmental, international, thinktank, pressure groups and relevant journal sources. You will also find a glossary based on *The Blackwell Dictionary of Social Policy*, help sheets, guidance on managing assignments in social policy and career advice.

40

Paying for Welfare

Howard Glennerster

Overview

- Some of the reasons why we have come to pay for many of the most important things in life through collective state funding lie in the economic theory of market failure.
- Another reason lies in the way needs vary across the life cycle, making welfare in many ways an intergenerational bargain.
- Nevertheless, many basic needs are paid for privately both in the form of money purchases and in time spent by carers and family members.
- Governments are trying to find new ways to respond to the challenge of an ageing population with growing needs.
- There will always be limits to welfare agencies' budgets, but how those limits are decided and how these resources are and should be rationed are becoming more contentious than ever.

Who Pays Matters

None of the ideals discussed elsewhere in this volume are attainable unless the means to achieve them are financed. Who pays and how are of central importance in social policy. If we have a generous set of public services, yet we pay for them by imposing heavy taxes on the poor, we are not helping but crippling them.

How do we ensure that no one, including our own family members, falls below a minimum acceptable standard of living? How do we ensure that all citizens, including our future selves, have access to an adequate diet, shelter, education and

The Student's Companion to Social Policy, Fifth Edition. Edited by Pete Alcock, Tina Haux, Margaret May and Sharon Wright.
© 2016 John Wiley & Sons, Ltd. Published 2016 by John Wiley & Sons, Ltd.

standard of healthcare? How can we achieve the ideals, especially during periods of unexpected personal disaster – the bad as well as the good times?

Market failure

There is, at first sight, no reason why we should not buy these services ourselves or take out private insurance to cover us in the bad times. Some economists argue precisely that. There are, however, some basic characteristics of human needs and the services that meet them that suggest they are not well suited to the market place. There is a large body of economic theory devoted to discussing this (Barr, 2012). We cannot buy clean air in bottles and consume it as a private product. If the air is clean, it will be enjoyed by the whole population. This 'non-excludability' is characteristic of what economists call a 'public' or 'social' good. Nevertheless, public goods are not 'free'. We pay the costs of clean air regulations in the price of goods produced in the factories that have to install filters or burn smokeless fuels.

While some aspects of social policy concern the production of pure public goods which cannot be produced without state action, much of social policy is not like that. We can buy medical care if we have the money. But we may make inefficient choices as private consumers since the information we need to buy medical care may not be available or readily understandable by us. There is an imbalance of information between seller and buyer. Economists call this a problem of 'information failure'.

Furthermore, the service we may want to buy may be needed a long time ahead. Most people are not good at doing that. How many young people spend time worrying about how to pay for their time in an old person's home? Pensions are another, slightly different, example. People put off taking action even if they know that theoretically they should take one out. That kind of market failure, studied by the new breed of behavioural economists, helped to inform the work of the 2004 UK Pensions Commission.

Notions of market failure, information failure and 'behavioural failure' help to explain why, even in a world largely driven by market exchange, many human services are paid for through collective means of funding – taxes, social insurance

contributions or through the state compelling individual action. The state requires us to take out third-party car accident insurance. This reasoning is not driven by the motive of being nice to poor people. The argument for state intervention is that it is more efficient in these special cases.

A savings bank

We collectively pay for such services for another, if linked, reason. Many things we need, education for our children, a new home for a growing family, long-term healthcare in early life cannot be financed at the time we need them. A child's education is very expensive relative to a young family's earnings. Only if a family has rich parents, a secure inheritance or a relatively secure asset such as a house will banks lend the money to pay bills now. So, overwhelmingly, what the welfare state is doing is acting as a gigantic national savings bank. Even a rich family will get back *five-sixths* of what they pay in taxes in the form of state benefits and free services at different stages of their lives (see Chapter 30 and Hills, 2015).

Countries vary in the extent to which their voters are prepared to share these lifetime risks. Voters in the Scandinavian countries and France have been prepared to pay over half their incomes to support a generous set of public services. That support may be waning, but the UK in 2014 was twentieth in the OECD ranking of expected government revenue expressed as a share of total national income. Reasons that lie behind these persistent differences are an interesting topic for comparative study (see Chapters 63 and 65).

Who Pays?

Despite a natural focus on tax-funded social services in this volume, many services that come within social policy's concern are paid for directly out of individuals' own earnings, savings or private borrowing. Government may tax some individuals less heavily to encourage private saving for retirement, house purchase or giving to charity. Economists call these flows 'tax expenditures'. Titmuss in his *Essays on the Welfare State* (1958) called them 'fiscal welfare' (see Chapter 41). Firms may enrol their employees in their own pension schemes, though few do so today outside the public sector. But employers may contribute to an independent pension scheme matching, or partly matching, their employees' contributions. They are now required by law to offer this option. Titmuss (ibid.) called this *occupational welfare* (see Chapter 36).

Colleagues have calculated how much we spend in total on each of these kinds of 'welfare' and how this has changed (Burchardt, Hills and Propper, 1999; Edmiston, 2011). They included spending on education, healthcare, housing, income maintenance, pensions, personal social services and long-term care. It turns out that over two-fifths of the nation's income (42.3 per cent in 2007–8 and probably more today) is being devoted to these purposes publicly and privately funded. (Notice this does not include the value of *time* that individuals devote to caring.) That share of the national cake has risen from a third in 1979–80. Much of that rise has come about because of the increase in *'pure private activity'* as these authors categorise it. That means individuals purchasing private services where the state has no involvement either in subsidising it or in determining how the money is allocated. That share amounted to about 13 per cent of GDP in 2007–8 compared with 8 per cent in 1979–80.

Fiscal welfare has also changed in the past thirty years. Tax subsidies to private pension schemes rose, but the substantial tax relief on housing mortgages was abolished in 2000. Overall, this led to a decline in 'fiscal welfare'. Perhaps surprisingly after the impact of Mrs Thatcher's term in office, the public funding of publicly provided services still constitutes just under half of all welfare activity today, down only slightly on 1977 when it was just over half. Overall, the share of GDP devoted to welfare activity financed by the *taxpayer* has grown steadily over the past century. It has only recently declined in the face of the 'austerity measures' taken by the UK Coalition government (see Figure 40.1).

What Level of Government Is Responsible?

Unusually among advanced industrialised countries, the UK relies overwhelmingly on taxes raised by the central Westminster Government to finance every aspect of government activity, including welfare. Less than 5 per cent of government activity is funded out of revenue raised by local government. The Coalition government in England capped what local government can raise in Council Tax. This policy is equivalent to running a 100 per cent central tax regime, as my colleague Tony Travers has argued. It is absolutely unique internationally. Among similar economies only the Netherlands raises less locally, and it is a much smaller country. Even France, which has a reputation for being a centralised state, raises 13 per cent of its taxes locally. Where Westminster has devolved legislative and administrative power over welfare to legislatures in Scotland, Wales and Northern Ireland, it has still raised nearly all the taxes needed to fund these services. It then allocates cash on a formula basis to these devolved assemblies (see Part IV). They pass this money on to their local authorities and health agencies on the basis of other formulae. Scotland has ended up gaining more cash per head for its services than English regions for reasons that are hotly disputed.

The devolving of statutory powers to subnational parliaments with minimal taxing powers has been storing up trouble ever since devolution was introduced in 2000. The Scottish Parliament has had limited power to vary the national income tax rate, but has never used it. In the wake of the referendum on Scottish independence, the whole basis of funding services in the devolved regions of the UK and, indeed, the funding of local government in England is under review (see Part IV). The principle that devolved administrative powers should go hand in hand with devolved taxing powers is at last gaining greater support. The same is true of local government. But some areas and regions have poorer and older populations, and the principle that any person in the UK should have the right to the same health and education as other citizens is also widely supported. Here is a crucial debate where the finance of social policy is taking centre stage and is a central concern for the Conservative government elected in 2015.

Who Decides How Much?

Her Majesty's Treasury is the central government department responsible for advising the Cabinet on how much money should be allocated to public

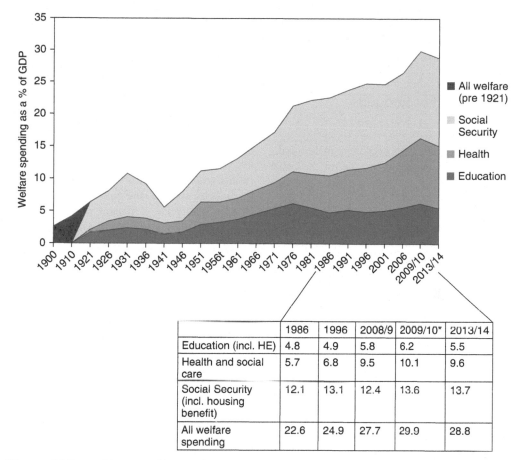

	1986	1996	2008/9	2009/10*	2013/14
Education (incl. HE)	4.8	4.9	5.8	6.2	5.5
Health and social care	5.7	6.8	9.5	10.1	9.6
Social Security (incl. housing benefit)	12.1	13.1	12.4	13.6	13.7
All welfare spending	22.6	24.9	27.7	29.9	28.8

Figure 40.1   Welfare spending* in the UK, 1900–2014.

*This includes the old Poor Law, modern social security, housing benefit and its predecessors. From 1987 some small items are included from agencies like the criminal justice system. They formed 0.5% of GDP in 1987. Social care spending has been removed from the official figures on social protection and added to healthcare for consistency with previous figures. Housing capital is excluded. Education includes public spending on higher education but excludes fee income.

†Maximum recession impact year.

Sources: H. Glennerster (2007), *British Social Policy: 1945 to the Present*, 3rd edn, Oxford: Blackwell; HM Treasury Public Expenditure Statistical Analysis 2014.

programmes. It masterminds the complex round of negotiations between it and the English spending departments. That determines how much is to be made available for the health services, schools or national defence for a period of years. The process is now called the 'Comprehensive Spending Review'. It also determines, in a way that is moderated by something called the 'Barnett Formula', how much Scotland and other devolved legislatures gain (see Chapter 22).

The final outcome of these negotiations is agreed by Cabinet and published in considerable detail. For example, the Review undertaken at the beginning of the 2010 Coalition government set the limits for public spending up to 2014–15. It was revised and extended up to 2015–16 in 2013. These documents embodied the 'austerity' strategy followed by the Coalition. Before that there had been Comprehensive Spending Reviews in 1998, 2000, 2002, 2004 and 2007, but the practice goes back in one form or another to the early 1960s. A long period of growth in the share of our national income taken by social policy was reversed after 2010 (see Figure 40.1).

Required or Encouraged Behaviour

Government can seek to encourage private individuals to act in ways that provide for their own welfare – to buy a house or save for their own pension – with tax reliefs or tax subsidies, as we have seen. But building on more recent work in behavioural economics, the Pension Commission (2005) suggested introducing another kind of incentive to get people to save for their own retirement. Evidence from other countries suggested that if employees are automatically opted into a pension scheme most people will not take steps to opt out. That would be more likely to be true if employers were required to contribute and government too. That line of reasoning was accepted first by the then Labour government and has been followed by the Coalition and now underpins the pension regime in the UK (see Chapters 36, 47 and 60).

Insured Against Catastrophe

Another principle has been adopted as practical policy in the past five years – that people should bear the costs of their own care up to a level at which these costs become 'catastrophic' – unreasonable or impossible for any family to meet. Asked to advise on better ways of paying for social care in England, the Dilnot Commission (Commission on Funding Care and Support, 2011) suggested families should be expected to save enough or insure themselves so as to be able to pay for a period of care most of us can expect to need. Only when our life-time spending has passed a 'reasonable' level, or if we are poor, should the state step in. The government decided this limit should be a cumulative total of £75,000 at 2015 prices. This is an example of a new principle – 'shared' payments – part individual and part collective (Glennerster, 2013), though, as yet, long-term care support differs in the rest of the UK (see Part IV).

Vouchers and Quasi-vouchers

Some economists argue that organisations such as schools or hospitals would work better if users had some sanction over them if they performed badly or not in the way the user wanted. Individuals should have the chance to move their custom giving them 'exit power' (see Chapter 19). Economists have suggested that users be given the equivalent of a piece of paper of a given value that people can cash in for the services they are entitled to at any school or care home they choose. In England schools and hospitals do now get paid for each pupil or patient who is treated at a set rate. This may be called a 'quasi-voucher' arrangement.

Giving

Individuals give large sums of money and time to voluntary organisations and to public statutory ones such as hospitals. Giving cash to a charity attracts tax relief. Giving time does not. In his classic study of blood donation, *The Gift Relationship* (1970), Titmuss showed how giving blood to the National Blood Transfusion Service without compensation was a tangible example of individuals contributing to a larger social whole and enriching that society in the process, but also turned out to be efficient. The donors had no incentive to lie about their medical history and the danger of introducing infected blood into the system. Better screening devices may have reduced the force of that argument, but the social gain from a system that encourages altruistic behaviour has not. Feminist writers (see Chapter 13) have made us much more aware of the scale of giving that takes place within the family when women, and to a lesser extent men, undertake caring tasks.

Rationing

Where services are free prices cannot rise to choke off demand and, hence, equate supply and demand. That is a major advantage in services like healthcare. But the result is that service providers have to set priorities and ration care for those in most urgent need. As is also discussed in

Chapter 7, rationing may take the form of rules and entitlements to benefit, or judgements made by professional staff working to fixed budgets. Rationing of scarce social policy resources thus takes place as part of a whole range of decisions, from fairly explicit judgements made by the Cabinet about what each service should receive and explicit allocations based on some publicly agreed formula to local health services or local councils and schools. But these explicit and public allocations are followed by less explicit judgements about which child in a class or which social work client gets most of the professional worker's attention (Glennerster, 2009). These are more difficult to monitor or discuss.

Emerging Issues

How to pay for our public services has become a central political issue and will grow in importance:

- The economic consequences of the 'great recession' will be here for years to come. Bigger national debts have been built up that will have to be repaid and interest payments made on them using tax revenue that might have been used for other purposes.
- We are living longer and the much larger numbers of those born just after the Second World War are now retiring and will soon be reaching ages when the cost of their healthcare will rise sharply.
- Expectations of what we mean by a 'good service' are rising.
- Climate change will make new demands on the public purse.
- Taken together these imply either higher taxes or other ways to pay for social services.

But:

- Societies are becoming more unequal, with living standards for the average person stagnant or declining.
- Hence, there is a natural reluctance by electorates to vote for higher taxes.
- Rich and wealthy people and companies seem able to escape their responsibility to pay.

So the demands for more social policy action are growing, but our capacity to pay and our willingness to pay are declining. Few politicians seem prepared to face these issues. In particular:

- Distinct from the 'how much' question is the question 'who pays'?
  - Should the older population pay more? It has been shielded from many of the recent cuts.
  - How far can the rich pay more?
  - Should wealth be taxed more and income less?
- How far should responsibility for funding services be devolved from Westminster? The Scottish independence vote has pushed this question up the agenda.
- Should local services be funded to a larger extent from local taxes? If so, what taxes?
- Or does equality of access to equally good services require national funding? If so, which 'nation'?

Guide to Further Sources

H. Glennerster (2009), *Understanding the Finance of Welfare: What Welfare Costs and How to Pay for It*, Bristol: Policy Press, summarises the economic literature in simple terms, describes and critiques the practical ways in which social services receive their funding in the United Kingdom. It also includes comparative material. For a fuller coverage of the underpinning economic theory, see N. Barr (2012), *Economics of the Welfare State*, Oxford: Oxford University Press.

J. Hills (2015), *Good Times, Bad Times: The Welfare Myth of Them and Us*, Bristol: Policy Press, shows how far the welfare state acts as a life-time savings bank for both the relatively well off and the poor. T. Burchardt, J. Hills and C. Propper (1999), *Private Welfare and Public Policy*, York: Joseph Rowntree Foundation, presents a framework to think about 'privatisation'. Recent trends in public and private funding are tracked in D. Edmiston (2011), 'The Shifting Balance of Private and Public Welfare Activity in the United Kingdom, 1979 to 2007', CASE Paper 155,

London: London School of Economics, Centre for Analysis of Social Exclusion.

The thinking behind the change in pension finance can be found in the Pensions Commission First Report (2004), *Pensions: Challenges and Choices*, London: Stationery Office, and Second Report (2005), *A New Pensions Settlement for the Twenty-First Century*, London: Stationery Office. The dilemmas of funding public services in a period of austerity are discussed by H. Glennerster (2013), 'Financing future welfare states: a new partnership model?', and C. Hood (2013), 'Reflections on public service reform in a cold fiscal climate', in S. Griffiths, H. Krippin and G. Stoker (eds), *Public Services: A New Reform Agenda*, London: Bloomsbury. The appendices, oral and written evidence for the all-party House of Lords Select Committee on Public Service and Demographic Change Report, Session 2012–13, *Ready for Ageing?* HL Paper 140, London: Stationery Office, provide a rich source for considering the consequences of an ageing population.

HM Treasury's medium-term limits to government spending are set out in regular Comprehensive Spending Reviews. Actual spending figures and long-term trends are reported annually in *Public Expenditure Statistical Analyses*, see at: www.hm-treasury.gov.uk.

The Institute for Fiscal Studies regularly reviews fiscal and spending issues see: www.ifs.org.uk.

Review and Assignment Questions

1 How should we respond to the growing needs and opportunities offered by an ageing population? Prepare evidence for a House of Commons Committee focusing on how we might pay for an ageing population.
2 How far should the funding of different social services be devolved to Scotland, Wales, Northern Ireland and English local government? Prepare a paper for a pressure group representing service users in a service of your choice.
3 Write an article for a popular newspaper to convince its readers that 'welfare' is not just funding the 'workshy'.
4 Brief an incoming Treasury minister on possible priorities for public expenditure in the coming five years.
5 Can we afford a welfare state anymore? If so how should we pay for it?

Visit the book companion site at www.wiley.com/go/alcocksocialpolicy to make use of the resources designed to accompany the textbook. There you will find chapter-specific guides to further resources, including governmental, international, thinktank, pressure groups and relevant journal sources. You will also find a glossary based on *The Blackwell Dictionary of Social Policy*, help sheets, guidance on managing assignments in social policy and career advice.

41

Taxation and Welfare

Stuart Adam and Barra Roantree

Overview

- Taxation plays an important role in society, with policy driven by multiple and, at times, conflicting aims.
- It is important to distinguish the legal or formal incidence of a tax from its economic or effective incidence.
- Neutrality is a useful benchmark against which to judge tax policy, but is not always desirable.
- A trade-off exists between redistributing resources from better- to less well-off individuals and maintaining incentives for individuals to increase their income.
- Increasing international mobility of tax bases poses a challenge for tax policy.

Introduction

One pound in every three earned in the UK economy is taken in tax. Taking that share of national income cannot fail to have large impacts on society, both reducing people's incomes and affecting how they behave. And the similar amounts of government spending that taxes pay for will also have huge effects.

Taxation has three main purposes:

- The primary purpose is to raise revenue, to finance government spending on public services and social security benefits.
- A second aim is redistribution, for example, to reduce the gap between rich and poor. When raising revenue the government must decide how much should come from different sections of society.

The Student's Companion to Social Policy, Fifth Edition. Edited by Pete Alcock, Tina Haux, Margaret May and Sharon Wright.
© 2016 John Wiley & Sons, Ltd. Published 2016 by John Wiley & Sons, Ltd.

■ The third aim is to change people's behaviour. While a natural starting point might be to try to minimise the extent to which taxes interfere with how people would otherwise choose to live, sometimes governments use taxation actively to try to influence behaviour.

These three aims are linked. For example, taxation redistributes resources both directly, by taking money from those taxed, and indirectly, through the social security benefits and public services it finances.

They can also be in tension. The more successfully a tax on a harmful activity discourages it, the less revenue it will raise. The more the government tries to redistribute from rich to poor, the less incentive there is for the poor to become rich, and the less income and wealth there will be to tax.

The UK Tax System

Taxes in the UK raised an estimated £622 billion, one-third of national income, in 2015–16; equivalent to roughly £11,700 for every adult or £9,600 per person. This tax take is middling by international standards: lower than in most west European and Scandinavian countries, but higher than is typical in Eastern Europe, North America, Ireland, Japan and Australia.

Tax policy is set mainly by HM Treasury (see Chapter 40) and administered by HM Revenue and Customs. Local authorities and the devolved governments of Northern Ireland, Wales and (especially) Scotland also have some tax-raising powers, which are being expanded (see Part IV).

Income tax is levied on earnings from employment, self-employment and other income, such as income from property and certain benefits. By default income from savings is also taxed, although various special treatments mean large amounts can be saved tax-free in forms such as pensions, Individual Savings Accounts (ISAs), people's main homes and, since 2016, ordinary bank accounts.

Each individual (before 1990, married couples were assessed jointly) has a tax-free personal allowance; income above this is taxed at a basic rate or, above certain thresholds, at one or more higher rates. For most employees, tax on their earnings is deducted by employers, but those with more complicated tax affairs must submit annual self-assessment tax returns.

National Insurance contributions (NICs) act like a tax on earnings, but their payment entitles individuals to certain ('contributory') social security benefits (see Chapter 47). In practice, however, contributions paid and benefits received now bear little relation to each other, so while there are arguments to be made for a genuine social insurance scheme, NICs are in effect a second income tax. But unlike income tax, they are charged only on earnings from employment and paid by both employees and employers, with the self-employed paying lower rates.

While NICs are levied only on earnings, there are other taxes aimed specifically at savings and wealth. *Capital gains tax* is levied on increases in the value of assets from when they are bought to when they are sold, while *inheritance tax* is charged on wealth passed on at (or shortly before) death, though there are major exemptions from each of these taxes which severely limit the revenue they raise. *Stamp duties* are charged each time certain assets (essentially land, property and company shares) are bought and sold, though it is hard to see why assets that change hands more often should be taxed more heavily. *Council tax*, levied annually on the value of residential properties (in England and Scotland, their value in 1991), partly funds local services and is Britain's only significant local tax, though while its level is set by individual local authorities, its structure is determined by central and devolved governments.

Corporation tax is levied on company profits; that is, revenue less costs such as wages, materials and interest on loans. Firms are also liable for *business rates*, levied on the value of business premises much like council tax is for housing (though rates are set by central and devolved governments, not locally).

Indirect taxes are added to the price of goods and services, rather than taken out of people's incomes. By far the biggest is *value added tax (VAT)*, charged at 20 per cent on sales of most goods and services, though not on most food, housing, books, children's clothes and some other goods, and at a reduced rate of 5 per cent on domestic fuel and power.

Other indirect taxes are levied on specific goods and services, mostly those considered harmful in some way. The biggest are *excise duties*

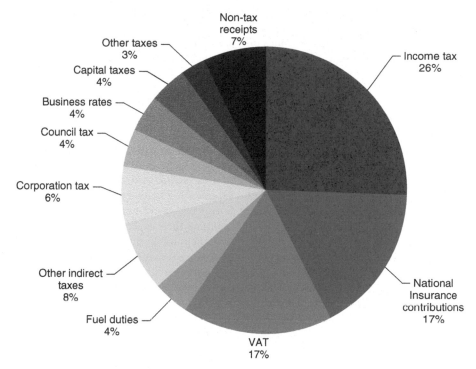

Figure 41.1   Composition of UK government revenue, 2015–16.
Source: Office for Budget Responsibility, *Economic and Fiscal Outlook December 2014*, at: budget-responsibility.org.uk/economic-fiscal-outlook-december-2014.

on petrol and diesel, though there are also taxes on vehicle purchase and ownership, alcohol, tobacco and flights, and a number of smaller environmental taxes.

Income tax, NICs and VAT together account for about 60 per cent of government revenue (see Figure 41.1). Compared with other developed countries, the UK raises slightly less than is typical through social security contributions and slightly more through property taxation, but is well within the normal range.

Key Concepts and Debates

Incidence

Tax scholars distinguish the *legal* or *formal incidence* of a tax, which asks who is legally liable to pay it, from its *economic* or *effective incidence*, which asks who is ultimately made worse off by it. The two are often different; for example, sales taxes are usually levied on the firms making sales,

but few doubt that in practice much of the tax is passed on to customers in higher prices.

Indeed, in the long run the formal incidence of a tax should be irrelevant to the effective incidence. Buyers care about the total amount they must pay, sellers about the amount they receive – irrespective of how much is made up of tax. So, if a tax is formally levied on the seller rather than the buyer, we would expect the price to rise correspondingly so that buyers pay, and sellers receive, the same amounts as before. In the short run, however, the legal incidence of a tax can matter, because that determines who pays the tax on the next day and it can take time for prices and wages – the mechanisms by which effective incidence is passed on – to adjust.

Since the formal incidence of a tax does not (in the long run) affect its effective incidence, it can be chosen to minimise administrative costs, and for that reason many taxes are formally incident on firms. But the effective incidence can never be on firms. Firms are legal entities, not real people who can be made better or worse off. The ultimate burden must be felt by its owners, employees or customers (through lower profits, lower wages or higher prices) or some combination. The idea of businesses paying their 'fair share' of tax is therefore difficult to make sense of without investigating which people are ultimately paying it.

In practice the incidence of taxes is usually shared rather than falling entirely on one party. As a rule, it will fall more on those less able to substitute other things for the taxed activity.

Neutrality

Neutrality in tax design means treating similar activities similarly. In general, neutral taxation will tend to be simpler, avoid discriminating unfairly between people doing similar activities and help to minimise distortions to people's behaviour.

Departing from neutrality requires drawing a boundary between the differently taxed activities. Since there are often grey areas, such boundaries can be difficult to define and police, especially when taxpayers have an incentive to 'dress up' their activities so that they fall on the more favourably taxed side. The resulting legislation often becomes highly complex.

Neutrality is a useful benchmark against which to judge real-world tax policy, but it is not always desirable. Sometimes there will be good reasons for interfering with people's freely chosen decisions. Obvious examples include discouraging damaging activities, such as pollution or smoking, or encouraging beneficial activities, such as R&D or pension saving. But as well as assessing the merits of these policy objectives in their own right, any advantages of departing from neutrality must be weighed against the complexity and unfairness that can arise in the grey areas. Policy for the mainstream cannot always be allowed to depend on borderline cases, but the hurdle for departing from neutrality should be high.

Redistribution and incentives

Chapter 30 showed (under some incidence assumptions) that higher-income groups pay more in tax, especially net of benefits, at a given point in time – at least in cash terms. A *progressive* (*regressive*) tax, or – more importantly – tax system, is one that takes a larger (smaller) percentage of income from those with higher incomes.

But it is important to consider the time horizon over which progressivity is assessed. For example, VAT looks regressive as a percentage of current income, because at any given point in time, low-income households typically spend a lot (and therefore pay a lot of VAT) relative to their incomes. But households cannot spend more than their income indefinitely. Over a lifetime, income and expenditure must be equal (except for bequests given and received, and the possibility of dying in debt); households spending a lot relative to their income at any given point are often those experiencing temporarily low income and either borrowing or running down their savings to maintain their expenditure at a level more befitting their lifetime resources. VAT paid over a lifetime is roughly proportional to lifetime income/expenditure – indeed, slightly progressive as items subject to zero or reduced rates of VAT are disproportionately consumed by the lifetime-poor. If only snapshot data are available, measuring VAT as a proportion of current expenditure (rather than income) gives a better guide to its underlying distributional effects.

Taxation creates financial rewards and penalties for behaving in certain ways, especially where it departs from neutrality. These incentives depend on the whole tax and benefit system. Disincentives to work, for example, are created not only by income taxes, but also by withdrawal of means-tested benefits, and also by indirect taxes: since the attractiveness of working presumably depends on the quantity of goods and services that can be purchased with net earnings, a tax that reduces earnings should have the same effect as one that increases prices.

Incentives are undoubtedly one – though far from the only – factor influencing people's decisions in all sorts of areas: whether and how hard to work, when to leave education or to retire, what to buy, how much to save and in what form, and how to run one's business, among many others.

But some groups, and some kinds of behaviour, respond much more than others to incentives. There is a large economics literature attempting to estimate the size of these responses, but it is difficult. Implicit or explicit disagreement about the likely effect of policy changes on behaviour underlies many debates about tax and welfare. Crudely, the political right tend to emphasise the dangers of discouraging work, reducing international competitiveness and so on, while the left tend to view these as less important relative to the benefits of redistribution, public services and so on. This is partly a debate about political priorities and values – maximising the size of the pie versus sharing it more equally, for example – but it is also a debate about how far sharing the pie more equally would reduce its size.

Taxation of income, expenditure and saving

The choice between taxing income and taxing expenditure is often misunderstood. As we have seen, the widespread perceptions that expenditure taxation is regressive and that it does not weaken work incentives are both misconceptions. In fact, the main difference between taxing income and expenditure lies in the taxation of saving; after all, expenditure is income minus the net amount saved.

This is not the same as the choice between direct and indirect taxation. Indirect taxes can easily vary between goods and services – taxing alcohol heavily and children's clothes lightly, for example – in a way that direct taxes cannot; whereas direct taxes can vary according to people's total resources (through higher rates of income tax, for example) in a way that indirect taxes cannot.

But it would be quite possible to levy a direct tax on people's total expenditure rather than their total income, simply by subtracting their net saving from their income (to calculate expenditure) before applying a progressive schedule (complete with tax-free allowance and higher rates) to the resulting figure.

It is appealing to tax all income the same, whether it comes from earnings or from savings. But saving merely defers consumption from today to tomorrow, and it is also appealing to levy the same tax whether I spend my money today or tomorrow. Taxing saving has the (possibly undesirable) effect of discouraging it, while not taxing savings income creates an incentive to dress up earned income as savings income (a strategy sometimes adopted by owner-managers of businesses, who can take profits out of the company as dividends instead of paying themselves a salary).

Governments everywhere wrestle with this dilemma, and policy often ends up as a messy compromise that both discourages saving to some degree and allows a degree of avoidance. The Mirrlees Review proposed one solution: taxing income from all sources in full, but giving an allowance for the amount saved and invested (irrespective of the income it generates) to avoid discouraging saving.

Tax reliefs and 'fiscal welfare'

Governments offer tax reliefs to support particular groups or activities. There are over 1,000 in the UK, ranging from income tax reliefs for saving and charitable donations, to reduced rates of VAT on domestic energy and children's car seats. Most are tiny in revenue terms, but the biggest cost many billions of pounds. Titmuss (1958) introduced the term 'fiscal welfare' to highlight the fact that many personal tax reliefs fulfil a similar function to government spending on social security benefits or public services. Recently, corporate tax reliefs (along with grants and subsidies) have begun to attract attention under the label of 'corporate welfare'.

Many reliefs are justified; for example, costs of generating taxable income should be tax deductible to avoid discouraging high-cost high-return activities more than equally valuable low-cost low-return activities. But it is sometimes questionable whether tax reliefs are the best tool to support particular activities; for example, whether an activity should be encouraged more among those facing higher tax rates. As Titmuss emphasised, fiscal welfare tends to favour those with higher incomes.

Each relief should be considered on its own merits. But as Sinfield (2013) has highlighted, fiscal welfare has low visibility and is little discussed, and is sometimes preferred because tax reductions are deemed more politically appealing than extra spending rather than because they are more suited to the task at hand.

Hypothecation

Hypothecation – the earmarking of particular tax revenues for particular areas of spending – has strong attractions. People may be less unhappy about paying a tax if they think the money is going to a worthy cause. And there is something intuitively appealing about, say, the revenue from alcohol and tobacco taxation being used to pay for public health programmes.

Yet economists and governments have tended to oppose hypothecation. One reason is that not all taxes can be hypothecated to the most popular causes. If some taxes are going to pay for health-care and education, others must be paying for less inspiring projects such as local government administration and legal defence of suspected criminals.

More fundamentally, there is rarely a good reason to make levels of spending on a particular area depend on revenue from a particular tax: if, say, income tax revenue fell because of a recession, it is not clear we would want to reduce health or education spending by the same amount. And hypothecation that does not impose a binding spending constraint is at best meaningless and arguably misleading, deceiving voters into think-ing their tax payments control government spend-ing in a way that in reality they do not.

Evasion and avoidance

Compliance with laws governing taxation has become an important political issue. There is a crucial distinction between tax evasion and tax avoidance: that of legality. *Evasion* is the use of illegal means to reduce tax liability – making a false declaration on a tax return, for example – whereas *avoidance* is the reduction of liability through legal channels – for example, setting up a company so that self-employment income (sub-ject to income tax) can be relabelled as profits (subject to corporation tax). If uncovered, evasion can be punished through fines or imprisonment; it is essentially a function of enforcement. Avoid-ance, on the other hand, is a function of the tax base – that is, the definition of what is taxable, which may leave scope to shift activities into less highly taxed forms.

Taxation and citizenship

For some social policy analysts, public concern over perceived injustices in taxation – especially evasion and avoidance – risks undermining the perceived legitimacy of the system and people's sense of a civic duty to pay taxes. Others have likewise argued that the links between citizenship and tax-paying are obscured by a 'disconnect' between public discussions of the burden of taxa-tion and of the benefits and services it finances. Hypothecation is one controversial suggestion for how to strengthen the link. The language of 'fiscal

welfare' is another attempt to change the terms of a debate in which benefit claimants are frequently contrasted to taxpayers despite the fact that many also pay income tax and all pay indirect taxes.

Emerging Issues

Governments face an increasing challenge over how to respond to the growing concentration of income. Those at the very top of the income distribution have seen their incomes race away over recent decades: between 1978 and 2012, the share of net income received by the top 1 per cent of households more than doubled from 3 per cent to 7 per cent. Governments may want to respond by increasing taxes on the better off and alleviating the burden on the less fortunate.

But another consequence of increased inequality is that government revenue is already quite reliant on a small number of well-off taxpayers. For exam-ple, in 2014–15, a quarter of all income tax revenue came from just 0.5 per cent of the adult population (about 250,000 individuals). This reliance leaves the public finances vulnerable to changes in the behav-iour of a small group who are considerably more mobile and responsive to tax changes than the rest of the population. Balancing distributional goals against risks to the public finances from relying on a small number of extremely well-off individuals is not a straightforward matter.

Mobility of high net-worth individuals and their incomes is one example of a broader chal-lenge: the changing nature of the global economy is making tax bases harder to pin down. Whether we think of levying VAT on sales or corporation tax on profits, it is harder to tax digital services such as music streaming than physical goods that are manufactured and sold in easily identifiable places.

Globalisation and technological change are not new and, contrary to some predictions, have not so far prevented governments from raising large amounts of tax revenue. Yet the challenge is none-theless real and constantly evolving. Countries can respond unilaterally, but international coopera-tion is crucial and multilateral steps are being taken, including increasing information exchange, making more demands of low-tax jurisdictions, and reforming the rules for taxing cross-border activities. Much depends on how successful these are and how they are taken forward.

Closer to home, the UK Government needs to manage the devolution of tax-setting powers referred to earlier. Tax policy is an important part of the ongoing debate on the UK's constitutional future.

Guide to Further Sources

Facts and figures about many aspects of the UK tax system are gathered on official web pages at: www.gov.uk/government/organisations/hm-revenue-customs/about/statistics, and on the Fiscal Facts pages of the Institute for Fiscal Studies' website at: www.ifs.org.uk/tools_and_resources/fiscal_facts. The best source of international comparisons is the Organisation for Economic Co-operation and Development at: www.oecd.org/tax/tax-policy.

Mirrlees et al. (2011), *Tax by Design: The Mirrlees Review* (available at: www.ifs.org.uk/publications/mirrleesreview), is a comprehensive and authoritative modern analysis of tax policy. J. Kay and M. King (1990), *The British Tax System* (available at: www.ifs.org.uk/docs/kay_king.pdf), is an older but excellent and very readable analysis.

Debates on fiscal welfare can be found in R. M. Titmuss (1958), 'The social division of welfare: some reflections on a search for equity', in *Essays on the Welfare State*, London: Allen & Unwin; and A. Sinfield (2013), 'Fiscal welfare', in Greve, B. (ed.), *The Routledge Handbook of the Welfare State*, London: Routledge

Review and Assignment Questions

1 In what ways can taxation affect well-being?
2 What trade-offs do policymakers face in setting tax rates?
3 Should tax policy be used to encourage or discourage certain behaviours?
4 Should particular taxes be earmarked for specific purposes?
5 How could the UK tax system better support social policy?

Visit the book companion site at www.wiley.com/go/alcocksocialpolicy to make use of the resources designed to accompany the textbook. There you will find chapter-specific guides to further resources, including governmental, international, thinktank, pressure groups and relevant journal sources. You will also find a glossary based on *The Blackwell Dictionary of Social Policy*, help sheets, guidance on managing assignments in social policy and career advice.

PART VII
Welfare Governance

42

The Policy Process

Hugh Bochel

░▓░

Overview

- Studying the policy process can add to our understanding of the ways in which policies are made and implemented, the reasons particular policies are or are not adopted and how power is exercised.
- For social policy a consideration of the relationship between power and inequalities is also important.
- A wide range of models and policies can be used to analyse the policy process.
- The approaches taken by different governments to policymaking and implementation can impact upon the types of policies that emerge.
- In recent years there has been a growing awareness of the complexity of the social world and new ways of analysing and understanding the policy process have been developed.

░▓░

Context

The term 'policy process' is used to describe the ways in which policies are made (or not made), implemented and evaluated. This process is 'political' in the broadest sense of the term, in that it can involve a wide range of actors and processes, and, importantly for social policy, is ultimately concerned with the ways in which power is distributed and exercised and by whom. This is often linked to debates about the state, democracy and the distribution of resources, with, for example, views differing about whether there is a pluralistic distribution of power with widespread opportunities for participation by the public and organised interests, or whether policymaking is slanted towards or dominated by

The Student's Companion to Social Policy, Fifth Edition. Edited by Pete Alcock, Tina Haux, Margaret May and Sharon Wright.
© 2016 John Wiley & Sons, Ltd. Published 2016 by John Wiley & Sons, Ltd.

Box 42.1　Types of Policy Analysis

Analyses of policy:

- are concerned with seeking to understand policy;
- may focus on policy content, describing and explaining how and why particular policies were developed and implemented, and assessing their impact, as is the case with much academic work;
- often involve consideration of policy outputs, for example, seeking to explain the particular distribution of resources.

Analyses for policy may involve:

- process advocacy: seeking to improve the systems of policymaking and implementation; or
- policy advocacy: using analysis to provide support for a particular idea or choice in the policy process, as may be the case with the work of thinktanks.

certain interests or groups. Similarly, we can (and perhaps should) consider not only the decisions and actions of governments, but also which alternatives are excluded from consideration and debate, and what the reasons for this might be. These are of crucial importance in enabling us to understand how and why social policies are developed.

The examination of the policy process is often described as '*policy analysis*', but there are many different types of policy analysis. These can be broadly, although somewhat artificially, divided into analyses *of* policy and analyses *for* policy (Box 42.1).

A range of models can be applied to specific policies and policy areas to gain a better understanding of the role and power of different groups in the policy process, and the motivations behind particular actions and inactions. However, it is important to recognise that while some models may seek to be prescriptive, policymakers themselves rarely set out to use a particular model in developing policies, so that models are generally best seen as tools for analysis.

Perspectives on the Policy Process

While we use the term 'policy' frequently in our everyday language, we do so in many different ways. For example, we may use it to describe the decisions of government, formal authorisations such as through legislation, fields of activity (education policy, pensions policy), specific programmes, and the outputs and outcomes of government actions. At the same time, policies, and the policy process, are continually interacting with and are affected by other factors, cultural, economic, social and political, as well as other policies. We therefore need to be aware of the environment in which policies are made and implemented.

Stagist and dynamic approaches

The policy process is often described and discussed in relation to a series of stages. This approach, with its depiction of a static, segmented process, is rather misleading. An alternative view would be one that sees it as dynamic and continuous, with overlap between the stages, a constantly changing environment and feedback, which in turn affects policy development (for example, when evaluations highlight weaknesses that need to be addressed and that then impact on the refinement of existing policies or the development of new ones). While traditional views of decision-making reflected the stagist approach, seeing politicians as making decisions that were then implemented by others, the dynamic, continuous model fits more closely with perspectives that highlight the continued influence of decision-makers in policy implementation and also the input of those who deliver policies on their formulation.

Despite its weaknesses, breaking down the policy process into stages, most frequently those outlined in Box 42.2, can help us to understand it.

Policy formulation

The initial 'stage' is usually seen as being that of 'formulation', when a policy idea is developed. To have a chance of becoming a policy, an idea has to get on to the agenda of policymakers. This might happen through the development of ideas by

Box 42.2   Stages in the Policy Process

■   Formulation
■   Implementation
■   Evaluation

This is sometimes broken down further, as with HM Treasury's ROAMEF model, which incorporates a circular process to reflect the cyclical nature of policymaking:

■   Rationale
■   Objectives
■   Appraisal
■   Monitoring
■   Evaluation
■   Feedback

bodies, such as political parties, thinktanks or the media; as responses to perceived problems, such as poverty or crime; or to particular challenges or demands, such as the pressures of an ageing population on healthcare or pensions provision. It is at this stage that pressure groups and the media are often seen as being able to exercise influence by bringing issues and ideas to the attention of policymakers.

However, while some have argued that in pluralistic liberal democratic societies there should be opportunities for a wide range of groups and interests to have input into policymaking, in practice agenda-setting is often skewed towards those with the greatest power, so that some ideas may never reach the agenda. The exclusion of some issues from discussion is sometimes referred to as a 'policy silence' or a 'non-decision', and illustrates that the ability to set the agenda is a fundamental way in which power is exercised.

Once an idea is on the agenda of decision-makers, it is then subject to discussion and development. Writing in the 1940s and 1950s, Herbert Simon suggested a 'rational' model, intended to improve decision-making. He argued that, ideally, all possible policy options would be considered before the most suitable to achieve the aims of the policy would be selected. Such an approach, is, however, generally unrealistic, as policymakers

are normally operating in the context of policies that have existed before, as well as within financial and administrative boundaries, while the time and resources required to explore all options would themselves be likely to be prohibitive.

Policymakers may therefore more usefully be seen as adopting a more limited approach, sometimes referred to as 'bounded rationality', taking account of factors such as existing policies and limitations on resources, and choosing from a more restricted range of options. Nevertheless, in some circumstances we can see policymakers adopt approaches that reflect Simon's arguments, for example, as happens with the use of experts for enquiries and reviews as part of policy development.

However, it can be argued that much government policy builds upon what has existed previously and often develops only in small steps. The idea of *incrementalism* is closely associated with the work of Charles Lindblom, who suggested that policymaking is a process whereby policymakers cope with problems as they arise, and that they tend to stick with the manageable and familiar, with new policies often differing only marginally from old policies.

He argued that incrementalism ('muddling through') is therefore a more realistic model of policymaking than rationalism. Critics have argued that such an approach may be essentially conservative, and that by focusing on short-term change it risks ignoring fundamental issues or major policy challenges, which could mean, for example, that disadvantaged groups could continue to lose out in favour of only small moves from the status quo. However, it can also be argued that while incrementalism may appear to work against radical policy change, a series of small steps can, over time, result in major change to policy.

The challenge of responding to new issues and demands, and the apparently increasing complexity and uncertainty of the contemporary world are, perhaps, some of the reasons why policymakers seek to learn lessons from other states, sometimes referred to as 'policy transfer' (see Chapters 63 and 64). Looking to other countries to see if they have any policies that can be transferred is popular with governments as it can provide a short-cut in policy creation. It has been argued, for example, that the 1997 Labour government drew upon the experiences of Australia and the United States in developing its welfare reform policies, while during the Coalition government the Conservatives drew upon examples from Sweden and the United States for 'free' schools. However, there are dangers in inappropriate transfer and a failure to take into account the differences between countries, with the Child Support Agency, introduced by the Conservatives in 1993 and drawing upon the experiences of the United States, often being seen as an example of policy failure.

Policy implementation

Implementation is often seen as following formulation in the policy process, although, as noted earlier, such divisions are arguably artificial. Governments have a variety of resources available to them, such as 'authority', including the law, financial, organisation and the provision of information, and can use these 'policy instruments' in a wide variety of ways and combinations. Those that they select may not only be chosen for their effectiveness, but also, for example, reflect other policy pressures or power relations.

Actors from different tiers of government, and from different sectors, public, commercial and voluntary, may be involved in policy implementation. The extent to which a policy is successfully implemented will be affected by many factors, including the clarity of the policy itself, the number and type of organisations involved, and the availability of appropriate resources. For example, if one body is responsible for implementation, then, in theory, it should be more straightforward than if successful implementation depends upon a number of autonomous organisations, which may have different aims, values and resources, and which may even be in competition with each other. In such instances, with high degrees of complexity, the potential for a policy to be only partially implemented increases.

'Implementation deficit' is often associated with top-down approaches to policymaking. These see policy as made by those at the top of a hierarchical structure, with those at 'street level', such as doctors, housing officials, the police or teachers, having no say in policy formulation and simply implementing policies without question. However, this is an artificial divide between not only stages, but also different actors within the policy process. Those who deliver services on the ground also have an interest in ensuring that appropriate and workable policies are introduced,

and are, for example, frequently able to exercise a degree of discretion and thus impact upon the ways in which policies are implemented.

Top-down approaches may therefore fail to recognise that policies are likely to be dependent upon a variety of agencies and individuals for successful implementation, and that policymaking is often more of a two-way process, with flows up and down, rather than the one-way system that the top-down model implies. Some argue that a more realistic and successful approach would be to take into account those who policy will affect and those who will be responsible for implementing it. From this perspective, good policymaking would start at the bottom and work upwards. In recent times a variety of other approaches, such as those focusing on policy networks, have also helped to highlight the complexity of policymaking and implementation and the interdependence of many actors in the policy process. Finally, it is worth noting that not all policies are actually implemented, with governments sometimes making policy statements, or even passing pieces of legislation, that are not put into practice.

Policy evaluation

Evaluation is often seen as the final stage, when the success or otherwise of a policy is assessed. Together with monitoring during the implementation of a policy or programme, it is generally seen as an integral part of the policy process which may lead to changes to existing policies or to the development of new policies. This view clearly relates to the idea of a dynamic, continuous policy process.

Recent developments and approaches

Approaching the policy process from a different perspective, recent years have seen greater attention paid to different levels of analysis, such as the macro, meso and micro used by Hudson and Lowe (2009). Analysis at the macro level is concerned with the broad themes and issues that shape the overall contexts within which policies are made and implemented, with 'globalisation' being a widely used example. However, there is not necessarily any consensus on if and how these shape policies and outcomes. The meso level comes between the micro and the macro, and considers how policies are made, how problems are put on (or kept off) the policy agenda, and the institutional arrangements within which policies are defined and implemented. Finally, the micro level directs our attention to the impact of individuals, whether politicians or civil servants, professionals providing a service, or the users of services.

Analyses have also recognised the greater complexity of politics and society, particularly the perceived need of governments to work with a wide range of other organisations and interests if they are to implement policies successfully. In many respects these run in tandem with other intellectual and political debates, including over the shift from government to governance, the extent, and likely impacts, of globalisation, technological change, and the growing awareness of 'risk', both for individuals and for the state, and its implications for policymaking and implementation, all of which feed into the literature on the policy process. Developments in recent decades have also meant that there is now more awareness of the multiple levels of government involved in making and implementing policies, including local, devolved, national and supranational tiers (see Part IV and Chapters 45, 46 and 71).

There are many other models and concepts that can be used to analyse policymaking, implementation and evaluation (see 'Further Sources'). However, perhaps one area that remains somewhat neglected is the consideration of why certain groups, such as children, some black and minority ethnic groups, and perhaps poorer people, tend to be able to exercise less power than others.

Governments and the Policy Process since 1979

The approaches taken to policymaking and implementation are likely to impact on the shape of the policies that emerge. As discussed in other chapters, the Conservative governments of 1979–97 were strongly influenced by ideas about individual responsibility and a preference for markets rather than the state, and this affected their approaches to policymaking and implementation.

For example, there was an emphasis on managerialism, performance measurement, competition and privatisation in the public sector in an attempt to improve efficiency and responsiveness to consumers, and a variety of implementation and delivery functions that had previously been undertaken by central and local government were devolved to quangos and non-departmental public bodies while allowing the centre to retain control over policy formulation. Broadly similar developments in other countries were seen, associated with what has widely been considered as a shift from 'government' to 'governance', with a move away from states taking full responsibility for policies towards the adoption of forms of provision based on networks with some degree of regulation by governments.

Under Labour from 1997 to 2010, considerable effort was put into attempts to 'improve' many aspects of the policy process, from formulation through delivery and evaluation. This made terms such as 'evidence-based' (perhaps more accurately 'evidence-informed') policymaking and 'joined up' approaches a common part of the social policy lexicon. At the same time, there was an emphasis on 'partnership' rather than competition between agencies in the implementation of policy and the achievement of the government's objectives, a development that was particularly noticeable in many areas of social policy.

However, while attempts to develop 'better' policymaking may be desirable, it is important not to understate the importance of values in determining policies, and to recognise that the aims and outcomes of policies will almost inevitably be contested. Policymaking is inevitably political, and values and value conflicts will therefore be part of the policy process, so that highly technocratic approaches, or indeed market approaches, risk depoliticising and legitimising decisions about the distribution of resources. Improvements to the policy process should therefore arguably aim to improve the quality of political interaction, rather than to replace it.

Labour also introduced a number of constitutional and structural changes that had implications for policymaking and implementation, including devolution to Northern Ireland, Scotland and Wales (see Part IV), increasing further the scope for a greater variety of approaches to policymaking (and to policies) within the UK, and the incorporation of the European Convention on Human Rights into UK law through the Human Rights Act 1988, enabling those who feel their rights have been infringed to pursue their grievances in the domestic courts.

Like its predecessors, the Coalition government formed in 2010 brought with it certain preferences which were likely to be translated into the policy process, particularly in England, most of which were, unsurprisingly, carried over into the Conservative administration elected in 2015. These included a preference for a smaller state and greater involvement by citizens, the commercial and voluntary sectors in the delivery of services, echoing in many respects the approaches taken by the Conservative governments of the 1980s and 1990s. In addition, the emphasis from 2010 on reducing the deficit and, in particular, cutting public expenditure both provided justification for and reinforced the need for such policy developments.

Emerging Issues

In recent decades there has been something of a shift from government to governance, but also a much greater awareness of and, perhaps, an increase in complexity and risk in relation to the policy process. For example, there has been a growing awareness of the need for governments to work with a wide range of agencies and interests to successfully implement social policies. As a result, it is hard now to envisage ways in which simple policies can be devised to deliver clear-cut outcomes.

In addition, as events in the relatively recent past have demonstrated, particularly at the global level, such as in relation to global warming or the financial crisis of 2007–8 and attempts to recover from it, governments may appear relatively weak, although there are also counter-arguments that suggest that nation-states remain of major importance in making policy choices (see Chapter 27). There have also been debates over the extent to which policies in different states may be converging over time (perhaps because many now experience similar pressures, or use similar policy instruments or as a result of greater use of policy transfer). However, there is no consensus on the extent of such a development, or even if it is occurring at all.

Guide to Further Sources

H. Bochel and S. Duncan (eds) (2007), *Making Policy in Theory and Practice*, Bristol: Policy Press,

combines academic and practitioner perspectives in an examination of approaches to the policy process under the Labour governments from 1997. A. Dodds (2013), *Comparative Public Policy*, Basingstoke: Palgrave Macmillan, provides a useful introduction to policymaking, including some areas of social policy, against a comparative framework.

B. Hogwood and L. Gunn (1984), *Policy Analysis for the Real World*, Oxford: Oxford University Press, despite its age continues to provide a useful introduction to policy analysis, covering a range of key issues in an approach that remains relevant. J. Hudson and S. Lowe (2009), *Understanding the Policy Process*, 2nd edn, Bristol: Policy Press, draws upon and highlights a wide range of perspectives to help us understand how change occurs in social policy, focusing in particular on analysis at the macro, meso and micro levels.

M. Hill (2013), *The Public Policy Process*, 6th edn, Harlow: Pearson, offers a good discussion and critique of theoretical and practical approaches. Giving an accessible overview of many aspects of policymaking and implementation, it draws upon social policy for many examples. W. Parsons (1995), *Public Policy: An Introduction to the Theory and Practice of Policy Analysis*, Aldershot: Edward Elgar, provides comprehensive coverage of the development of the study of the policy process and incorporates discussion and critiques of a wide range of perspectives.

The Green Book (www.gov.uk/government/publications/the-green-book-appraisal-and-evaluation-in-central-governent) and the Magenta Book (www.gov.uk/government/publications/the-magenta-book) provide a central government perspective on some aspects of the policy process, particularly evaluation.

Review and Assignment Questions

1   Why might 'top-down' approaches to policy implementation appeal to decision-makers, but prove not to be straightforward in practice?

2   How might the views of some groups be excluded from the policy agenda?

3   In what ways might shifts in power from Westminster to the devolved administrations of Northern Ireland, Scotland and Wales and to the European Union affect policymaking and implementation in the United Kingdom?

4   Why might the use of 'evidence' and 'expertise' sometimes be problematic in policymaking?

5   Discuss, with examples, social policies under governments since 1997 that might be said to reflect 'rational' or 'incremental' approaches to policymaking.

Visit the book companion site at www.wiley.com/go/alcocksocialpolicy to make use of the resources designed to accompany the textbook. There you will find chapter-specific guides to further resources, including governmental, international, thinktank, pressure groups and relevant journal sources. You will also find a glossary based on *The Blackwell Dictionary of Social Policy*, help sheets, guidance on managing assignments in social policy and career advice.

43

Managing and Delivering Welfare

Ian Greener

Overview

- There has been a huge change in the way we manage and deliver welfare services since the 1980s.
- The emergence of the 'new public management' (NPM) saw an increased emphasis on performance management and techniques from private sector management being brought into public management.
- At the same time as the NPM appeared, the boundaries between public and private sector management were also blurred.
- In the 2010s ideas that were central to NPM appear to be under question.
- Looking forward, we need to embrace psychological and other research giving us a richer view of organisational life, while accepting that some form of public management is necessary.

The Villains of Welfare Services?

In popular dramas and films, we see heroic doctors, nurses and firefighters, inspiring teachers and even sometimes university lecturers, but seldom is anything good portrayed about the managers of those services. The opposite is often the case – managers are seen stopping clinicians and teachers from doing their jobs by imposing rules and demanding budget cuts. They are the villains of the welfare state.

But a moment's thought moves us past these well-worn clichés. Most of us do not like the idea of being managed very much or may roll our eyes when our institutions start talking about 'strategy', but at the same get frustrated when things become

The Student's Companion to Social Policy, Fifth Edition. Edited by Pete Alcock, Tina Haux, Margaret May and Sharon Wright.
© 2016 John Wiley & Sons, Ltd. Published 2016 by John Wiley & Sons, Ltd.

disorganised and we end up seemingly having to do others' work as well as our own. Most welfare services are complicated – schools require massive levels of coordination to get students and teachers in the right places at the right times (which is why timetabling takes up such a lot of time), and benefit systems often need us to check eligibility against a range of criteria, as well as to make complex calculations that transfer billions of pounds from governments to households.

From OPA to NPM

The academic literature on the organisation and management of public services is often portrayed as showing a movement from what was termed the 'old public administration' (OPA) to the 'new public management' (NPM), with that shift occurring during the 1980s. The OPA placed public service professionals in the predominant role, with the 'administrators' of those services portrayed as supporting public professionals and dealing with any problems that occurred in a rather reactive way. Public professionals were sometimes accused of overlooking the needs of their service users and paying little attention to the standard of the service they offered. It is important to say that not all public services were like this – some did a remarkable job, and others did not correspond to this stereotype. But from an era where things are now very different, the combination of administration, lack of measurement and professional-dominated services appears somewhat anachronistic.

During the 1980s, things began to change. The governments of the US and UK especially called upon their public services to become more business-like and customer-focused, often calling in private-sector managers to come up with recommendations on how things could be improved. Improvements in information technology allowed data about public services to begin to be gathered on a far greater scale and in a timelier manner, allowing league tables to be drawn up. This, in turn, meant someone had to be held accountable for the performance of their organisation, and administrators turned into managers, directors and chief executives. Public services were made to compete for contracts with alternative

Table 43.1 The old public administration and the new public management.

OPA	NPM
Equity and fairness: everyone treated equally.	Differentiated service in line with customer need.
Public provision.	Mixed provision (public, commercial, voluntary/not-for-profit).
Hierarchy, rules.	Entrepreneurship, flexibility.
Standardised employment.	Flexible terms of employment and performance management.
Democratic accountability.	Market accountability.
Professional-led.	Manager-led.

commercial and voluntary sector service providers rather than having effective monopolies over service provision, on the grounds that competition would drive up standards and improve service user responsiveness. These changes combined to form the NPM (see Table 43.1).

These changes meant the professionals who had formerly been pre-eminent found themselves under increased scrutiny. Even though it is a cliché, as we discussed above, that public managers can easily be portrayed as blocking public professionals from doing their jobs, there is an element of truth here – the former did invoke efficiency as a goal for public services in a way that had not previously been the case. Equally, the increased measurement of data in just about every area of public services meant professionals found themselves having to account for their work in new ways.

Some public professionals responded to the challenge of the NPM by taking on managerial responsibilities themselves. However, they often appear to have struggled in these roles, finding it difficult to uphold both managerial and professional identities, especially where the two came into conflict and they were required to challenge their professional peers. There are instances of successful public managers from professional backgrounds, but balancing the two often seems to have been extremely difficult.

Public Management in the 2000s

As we entered the 2000s, it had become technologically possible to extend the measurement and monitoring of welfare services so that they could be monitored against standards. This had a number of effects. First, performance management became far more quantitative and target-based, with politicians making promises to the public for their improvement at election time. This had the potential to make politicians more accountable and more rigorous news programmes began to run 'fact-check' bulletins when politicians made claims about how well they were doing.

But it also had downsides – politicians, aware that they were being held under greater scrutiny, put increased pressure on welfare managers to show improvements in measures where they had been promised. Waiting times for services had to be reduced or outputs increased.

This increase in measurement sometimes led to welfare managers suffering from 'target focus', where they placed a greater emphasis on the aspects of their service that were being quantifiably measured than those where such measures were less important or did not exist. Where the performance measures captured the most important aspects of the service, this was sensible, but welfare service performance is often difficult to capture and it is often difficult to come up with reliable measures. Do we measure schools on how well their students do in exams, or is education about helping young people become responsible and informed citizens that can participate in public life (and, if so, how would we measure that)?

Equally, we know at least some welfare managers, faced by pressures to show improvements in the measures they were being judged upon, 'gamed' the system by managing the measures rather than actually improving services. Some hospital managers admitted patients within the specified target time, but put them on trolleys because beds were not available, and so, seemed to have 'hit the target but missed the point'. Some managers went further, and simply found ways of lying in their statistical returns to government (see Table 43.2).

There are some areas of welfare where performance management has seemed to work well. This seems most often to occur where targets are not imposed by politicians or managers, but, instead, agreed in collaboration with those who will be responsible for achieving them, and the targets themselves are shown to be based on achieving a need or goal that is generally agreed to be either necessary or evidence-based. Doctors, for example, are more likely to change their practices where they can see they are aiming at a target that is based on good clinical evidence. However, the pressures on politicians to make promises based on hitting specific targets, which is then passed onto managers and front-line workers, means that achieving agreement about targets, and working as a team to achieve them, still appears to be the exception rather than the rule.

Table 43.2   Some of the problems of performance management.

Ratchet effects	Targets are set at a level based on the previous year's performance, so managers deliberately under-perform to get undemanding targets.
Threshold effects	A uniform target is set which applies to everyone, giving no incentive for high achievement against it.
Output distortion	The manipulation of reported results: managers manage statistics rather than services and no real service improvement occurs.
Fraud	Deliberate misreporting of results: entering of inaccurate records into systems to make it look like targets are being hit (extreme version of output distortion).
Continually changing targets	Targets are changed every year, so it is impossible to see if progress is actually being made against them.
Targets perceived as political rather than designed to improve services	Politicians make promises which public managers believe distort their priorities, leading to them 'gaming' the system in the ways described above (arbitrary reductions in waiting times, for example).

Markets for Public Services

If targets and performance management have been one strategy for trying to improve the delivery of welfare services, a second and related approach has come through the increased use of market mechanisms. As is also discussed in other chapters, the use of quasi-, public or internal markets has had at least three phases. In the 1980s, the 'contracting out' of services was an attempt to pass non-essential services, such as cleaning, out of the public sector to commercial contractors to try and improve economy and efficiency, and to get public managers to focus on the job of delivering their service rather than worrying about issues that were not seen as being 'core' to their delivery.

In the 1990s, public services were then encouraged to compete with one another for contracts, as 'purchaser–provider splits' were put in place, in which contractual relationships were introduced to more closely monitor how well services were being delivered, with the potential threat of moving to other public providers on efficiency grounds, or should services be possibly delivered better by other public providers that might be available.

In the 2000s, the market-based approach was extended further by allowing non-public providers to enter the market for services more fully on the grounds that the increased competition would drive up standards and increase efficiency. Some services led the way, with social care, for example, being extensively privatised in the 1980s, while others lagged behind, with higher education still having very little private provision even in the 2010s.

The problem with much of the market-driven attempts at reform in the 1990s and 2000s is that they appear to rest on assumptions from economic theory regarding how markets should work rather than research showing how they work in practice. The idea of introducing contracts for public services was meant to make suppliers of such services compete with one another to drive up their quality or to reduce their costs.

However, whereas 'contracting out' services such as cleaning may well have reduced their costs, it may also have reduced the quality of the service offered or made the services available only on the terms explicitly stated in their contracts. Hospitals especially appear to have struggled with contracting-out cleaning services, and given the problems they have had in addressing and controlling infections such as MRSA, it is perhaps questionable whether services such as cleaning were 'non-core' or as straightforward as they were once thought to be.

Market-based reorganisations designed to offer the users of public services more choice again sound simple in principle – the public choose the best services for them, and the providers who are chosen are rewarded by receiving funding proportional to the number of people who have chosen them. In this viewpoint, it does not matter whether public services are provided by public, commercial or voluntary organisations, what matters is that they are doing a good job and are paid as such. Managers, and the staff responsible for delivering the services, have an incentive to provide good service to the public to make sure they keep getting chosen.

Again, however, it is not quite as simple as this. First, we need the public to be able to tell which service is the best one for them, and this requires people to make a careful and sensible choice. Many people are reluctant to change who provides their welfare service away from the one they know because they believe changing will be too much work or too risky, or there may be other sensible reasons – in the case of healthcare, for example, there may be only one or two hospitals in most cities and so, without travelling much further, the scope for meaningful choice is limited. Equally, it may well be that choice between different providers of services is entirely the wrong way to think about the service – in the case of train travel, most people book trains that run at the time they wish to travel rather than being particularly conscious of which company is actually operating them.

In addition, approaches to organising welfare services based around markets have yet to answer the question of what we do when non-public providers suffer business failure or decide to exit the market. In these circumstances, where a private train company or a private provider of healthcare decide they no longer wish to offer a service, then there is a frantic attempt to find another provider to cover the gap left in the market, and this may involve effectively nationalising (bringing the service back into the public sector) it. If the guarantee of service provision appears to depend in many cases on it being publicly owned, then this leads to the question of why we are making the provision of such services non-public in the first place, and whether they might be better run as wholly public services.

Crises in Public Delivery

What is also very noticeable is that there have been a series of problems in public service delivery that have emerged in the 2000s and 2010s. These have varied from failures to deal with severe natural phenomenon, including the New Orleans flooding, where the minimal state-based protection and welfare systems seem to have failed almost entirely, through to social care failings at Winterbourne View in Bristol, where staff were recorded abusing vulnerable residents, to the breakdown of the provision of care in the NHS at Stafford Hospital, to the PIP case outlined in Box 43.1.

These crises do seem to have some common features – the necessity of public provision remaining in place in order to deal with extreme events (New Orleans) or the failure of private organisations (PIP, Winterbourne View), or problems with the use of targets focusing the minds of those delivering care on measures rather than the actual care (Winterbourne View, Stafford Hospital), and the sense that neither public nor private provision intrinsically safeguards those receiving services from abuse (Winterbourne View, Stafford Hospital) – what we need are systems that actually care for people.

Emerging Issues

Critics of the NPM might now regard it as having been decisively undermined. Performance management systems have been extensively 'gamed', the use of private provision has not always worked out well, and private providers of welfare services have withdrawn from public delivery when the going gets too tough financially for them. But still the NPM appears to dominate the thinking of all our major political parties, and is certainly at the centre of the 2015 UK Conservative government's thinking, when perhaps we need public management of a different kind.

Looking forward, a good place to begin is to look at research that investigates how people

---

Box 43.1   The PIP Breast Implant Scandal

PIP was a French company that sold silicon implants for use in medical treatment. It was liquidated in 2010 when it was found to be using cheaper industrial-grade silicon rather than medical-grade silicon.

The extent to which the PIP implants might cause the women (in the case of breast implants) who had received them problems was uncertain, with the UK medical 'watchdog' suggesting the 'rupture' rate might be 5 per cent (as compared with 1 per cent for medical implants), but with no firm figures available. Women had received implants for cosmetic reasons, as well as after mastectomies.

In the UK there were an estimated 30,000–40,000 affected women. Large private treatment centres appeared unwilling or unable to deal with the problem themselves, and the

NHS offered privately treated women the opportunity to be examined and to have their implants removed if they were found to be defective, but not to be replaced. NHS-treated women were offered replacements if necessary.

As a result of the lack of response of many private clinics to replace the faulty implants they had sold, the NHS Medical Director promised to examine whether the cosmetic surgery industry needed to be more effectively regulated. Many of the women treated privately were left needing to find the funds for replacements, as well as requiring further surgery.

The case asks deep questions about what happens when private providers of health treatments fail – is it left to the public sector to deal with the resulting mess?

actually behave in organisational settings, and which does not regard them as either 'knights' (who always do the right thing), or 'knaves' (who always try and to the right thing for them and them alone). More recent research takes a more nuanced view, and tries to explain behaviour in terms of both intrinsic (doing the job for its own sake) and extrinsic (doing the job for reward) perspectives, and looks for organisational systems that harness intrinsic motivation to achieve organisational goals. The argument is that we can improve public delivery where we harness people's intrinsic motivation to improve public services. Work in this area has positive suggestions for how public services might be improved, including extending our trust to public professionals and public managers to do a good job, but such thinking goes very much against the grain of the still predominant NPM.

What we need to do, above all, is to stop looking for simple solutions to complex problems. Many public services work with the most vulnerable people in society, who have complex needs, and providing services to them needs us to stop trying to look for one-size-fits-all answers, and instead both to embrace the complexity involved in delivering services to them and begin to trust those delivering the services, with reasonable supervision, to do a good job. In an era where ghosts of the likes of a serial-killing GP still haunt us, this might seem an odd claim. But unless we learn to trust our welfare professionals again, we will not be able to harness their intrinsic motivation to do their work well and to deliver the best possible services. Of course, we need to manage our public services – but that does not mean that we have to measure every aspect of everything that goes on in them to the point where staff stop thinking about the service they are providing and only about the targets with which we demand they comply.

Guide to Further Sources

One of the classic first analyses of the NPM is provided by C. Hood (1991), 'A public management for all seasons?', *Public Administration*, 69:1, 3–19, while one of the key books on the transformation of public management is that by J. Clarke

and J. Newman (1997), *The Managerial State*, London: Sage.

M. Barber (2007), *Instruction to Deliver: Tony Blair, the Public Services and the Challenge of Achieving Targets*, London: Portoco's Publishing, written by the head of Tony Blair's 'Delivery Unit', provides insights into how government and public management changed in the 2000s. C. Hood (2006), 'Gaming in Targetworld: the targets approach to managing British public services', *Public Administration Review*, 66:4, 515–21, is one of the best-written accounts of why performance managmeent goes wrong. An interesting collection that presents a very different view of management to that of the NPM can be found in B. Frey and M. Osterloh (eds) (2001), *Successful Management by Motivation: Balancing Intrinsic and Extrnsic Incentives*, London: Springer.

The paradoxes of trying to reform welfare services can be explored through the strong collection in H. Margretts and C. Hood (eds) (2012), *Paradoxes of Modernization: Unintended Consequences of Public Policy Reform*, Oxford: Oxford University Press, and M. Powell and R. Miller (2014), 'Framing privatisation in the English National Health Service', *Journal of Social Policy*, 43:3, 575–94, provides perhaps the clearest explanation of what 'privatisation' means in the context of welfare services.

Review and Assignment Questions

1 What are the main differences between the OPA and NPM?

2 If managers are so essential for public services, why are they so often cast as 'villains'?

3 What are the main problems from which the NPM has suffered since the 1990s?

4 Give two examples of public service failure since the 2000s. What do these failures tell us about the pressures welfare services have faced?

5 One of the main challenges facing public managers is that public services often have professional groups (such as doctors or town planners), whose cooperation they need in order to deliver the services to the public. What do you think are the challenges involved

in trying to manage professionals who know more about the service they offer than you (as a public service manager) may do?

Visit the book companion site at www.wiley.com/go/alcocksocialpolicy to make use of the resources designed to accompany the textbook. There you will find chapter-specific guides to further resources, including governmental, international, thinktank, pressure groups and relevant journal sources. You will also find a glossary based on *The Blackwell Dictionary of Social Policy*, help sheets, guidance on managing assignments in social policy and career advice.

44

Accountability for Welfare

Jackie Gulland

Overview

- Accountability for welfare is about how organisations *account* for their actions.
- Accountability is about *counting*, but also about *narrating*.
- Accountability is a *relational* term and operates *on many* levels.
- While it is important that organisations should be accountable for their actions, mechanisms for accountability also carry disadvantages.
- Accountability is not neutral: it is a normative concept, closely related to issues of power and political priorities.

What is Accountability for Welfare?

When we read about scandals relating to failed or expensive policies or stories about people who have died or suffered harm while in the care of public services, the first call is for someone to be held 'to account'. Accountability is perceived to be a good thing, but these calls rarely consider the many tensions involved. Accountability is a normative concept, carrying underlying assumptions about how policies should operate.

Accountability is best considered as a *relational* term, concerning the interaction of state actors, commercial and voluntary organisations, service users and citizens. Bovens et al. (2014) remind us that although accountability appears to be about counting facts, it is also about 'storytelling', using numbers and 'facts' to explain how something happened and why. Accountability raises questions about wider issues of power and political priorities, which we will return to below.

The Student's Companion to Social Policy, Fifth Edition. Edited by Pete Alcock, Tina Haux, Margaret May and Sharon Wright.
© 2016 John Wiley & Sons, Ltd. Published 2016 by John Wiley & Sons, Ltd.

Social policy analysts approach the question of accountability by looking at:

- *What* kind of things should be accounted for?
- *Who* should be held accountable?
- To *whom* should they be held accountable?
- What *mechanisms* are available for ensuring accountability?

What Kind of Things Should be Accounted For?

Accountability for finances

Accountability in the public sector has focused primarily on finances. The idea of an 'accountant' as someone who checks financial records is related to this. We can see examples of financial accountability in the National Audit Office, which scrutinises the public spending of the Westminster Government. Other bodies (see Guide to Further Sources) are responsible for the financial auditing of local government and in the devolved administrations. These audit bodies were originally concerned with scrutinising the accuracy of records of how public money was collected and spent. However, since the 1980s, financial accountability bodies have extended their remit to looking at whether public agencies provide quality services which represent 'value for money'. This extension of their role expands the concept beyond the apparently objective activities of checking that money has not been mis-spent or used for the wrong purpose into much more contested areas of policy priorities. The increasing use of non-state providers in the delivery of public services, discussed elsewhere in this volume, has further broadened their role and that of other accountability bodies.

Meeting policy goals

As well as ensuring money has been well spent and services are of an acceptable standard, it is reasonable to expect publicly funded services to do what policymakers intend them to do. This is another difficult area, as policies may be in conflict with each other. For example, a general policy of cutting public expenditure may be in conflict with one of improving services. On a wider level, governments may have broad policies promoting equality and human rights which come into conflict with other priorities on public spending or on security. Local authorities and service providers also have a range of policy goals which come into conflict with each other. This means that being accountable for meeting policy goals is not an easy task and is a highly political endeavour.

Avoidance of risk

Accountability comes to the fore when things go wrong. When a child dies under local authority supervision, a hospital is found to have a history of medical mishaps, a policy 'fails' to meet its objectives or budgets are massively overspent, there are demands for improved accountability. This can lead public bodies to become focused on the avoidance of risk, skewing policy priorities in directions led by media scandals.

Who Should be Held Accountable?

In order to understand accountability we have to know who (or what body) is expected to account for their actions. The simplest way to think about this is in a hierarchy, with politicians at the top. As our democratically elected representatives, we expect that politicians, particularly government ministers, should be accountable for the actions of government. However, this is not always simple, since day-to-day decisions, as well as broader policy actions, are delegated to senior officials, service managers and front-line staff. Ensuring a hierarchy of accountability so that those at the top can be held responsible for the actions of those at the bottom is a complex and time-consuming activity.

This complexity is increased in a system of multi-level governance where devolved and local authorities are responsible for many public services. Other policy decisions are affected by the actions of supranational bodies such as the European Union (see Chapter 46). This 'hollowing out of the state', along with the practice of outsourcing much of welfare provision to third-party providers from the voluntary and commercial sectors (see Chapters 35 and 37), as well as 'arm's length' government agencies, has challenged hierarchical notions of accountability.

Whatever the level of governance, there is a question about the extent to which front-line service staff are expected to be accountable for their own actions. This varies depending on the nature of the service and the professional status of staff. For example, we would expect different levels of individual accountability from professionals such as teachers and doctors than we would from support workers such as cleaners and receptionists.

Some have argued that accountability does not stop at the front-line of service provision, with an increased focus on the responsibilities of service users and the community. Examples of user accountability include the requirement that benefit claimants account for their efforts to look for work, that parents take responsibility for their children's education and that health service users take greater responsibility for managing their own health. In these cases, service users have to *account* for their behaviour in order to qualify for services (see Chapter 39).

Accountability to Whom?

The third aspect of accountability that we have to consider is to whom service providers must be accountable. We can conceive of accountability as circular, where the agency or public body is in the centre and spokes of accountability radiate out, upwards to parliament, elected representatives, courts and supra-national bodies, sideways to colleagues, professional organisations and networks and downwards to the electorate, service users and other interest groups (see Figure 44.1)

Bovens (2007) has described this as 'the problem of many eyes'. This circle of accountability shows how tensions arise depending on where in the circle actors are situated. The upper and lower parts of the circle represent different levels of power, where the higher levels are considered to be more powerful and the lower levels, less powerful. When looking at mechanisms of accountability we can see that different mechanisms are aimed at different parts of this circle. The effectiveness and importance of each mechanism vary depending on the priority given to different parts of the circle.

Most notions of accountability assume that the beneficiary is ultimately the 'public'. Sociologists describe the concept of many 'publics' which can represent both individual and collective interests. The public consists of both the electorate who, in

Figure 44.1 Accountability as circular.

theory, have democratic control over elected bodies, and people who are directly affected by public services, some of whom are not able to participate in elections (for example, children, those without citizenship status), and those who may have the right to vote but are unable or unwilling to use it because of other structural disadvantages.

Politicians often talk about accountability to tax payers, but people experience publicly funded services in many ways: as service users, potential service users or their relatives, as employees and business operators, and as members of the community in which services operate. Service use is not always voluntary. People's interests in the provision and cost of services will be very different depending on their perspective. Their relationship with services will also be differentiated according to their gender, ethnic origin, age and any health problems or disabilities. The concept of 'the public' is not straightforward.

Mechanisms for Accountability

Bovens (2007) describes the process of accountability as having three stages:

- the person held accountable must feel an obligation (formal or informal) to account for his or her conduct;
- second, any information provided must be capable of interrogation or questioning; and
- finally, the people to whom the account is made must be able to pass judgement on the account, by accepting it or denouncing it with appropriate consequences, for example, democratic mechanisms, fines, disciplinary action, removal of government contracts or informal action such as negative exposure in the press.

Democratic mechanisms

The first stop of accountability is often considered to be to parliaments or other elected bodies. In a democracy elected politicians should know what is being done in their name and should be able to make changes to policies or practices which appear to be too expensive or not working well. Elected representatives, in turn, expect to be held accountable to their electorate. This applies to Westminster politicians, representatives in

devolved administrations, local councillors and other bodies where representatives are elected. The theory is that elected representatives are accountable to their electorate and so the electorate can remove them from power if they are unhappy with their activities. In recent years attempts have been made to make bodies more accountable by having more locally elected representatives. However, democratic mechanisms rely on accountability to the 'public', which as we have seen is a contested concept.

Legal mechanisms

Courts can be used to call public service providers to account if they are perceived to fail to meet legal requirements. Courts can hear claims for personal injury if someone is injured or dies as the result of medical negligence, for example. *Judicial review* is another legal mechanism that can be used to call public bodies to account if they are alleged to have failed to meet certain standards of administrative law, for example, that they have not complied with legislation, have been too restrictive in the use of discretionary powers, acted 'unreasonably' or taken action beyond their powers.

The grounds for judicial review are complex, and it is a technical and expensive processes. Despite this, actions for judicial review have mushroomed in the last thirty years and have led to some important decisions about the operation of public services, for example, in relation to housing homeless people, providing social care services and in relation to the rights of asylum seekers and prisoners. Public services are also governed by human rights considerations and can be held accountable to the European Court of Human Rights (see Chapter 5).

Related to courts, *public inquiries* are also legal mechanisms for accountability. Some are required by law, while others are set up in response to political or public demand after disasters or financial scandals. Public inquiries have been beset with problems relating to their independence, remit and powers, but continue to remain an important part of the accountability landscape.

Ombudsmen

Sometimes described as 'people's champions', ombudsmen have powers to investigate complaints about maladministration in public services. The first ombudsman in the UK was the Parliamentary Commissioner for Administration, set up in 1967 specifically to provide an additional measure of accountability to Parliament. This ombudsman investigates complaints about services that are the responsibility of the Westminster Parliament. Others investigate complaints about the devolved administrations and about local government in England. Ombudsmen have become increasingly prominent in dealing with problems with public services, seen by many as a cheaper and more user-friendly alternative to the courts.

Freedom of information

Freedom of information legislation, introduced from 2000 onwards, has opened up new avenues for accountability, leading to public debate about matters such as MPs' expenses.

It also has its limitations, however, and writers have criticised the prevailing culture of secrecy in public bodies as well as the complexities raised by the application of the legislation to privatised and outsourced public services.

Regulation, audit and inspection

Regulation, audit and inspection are mechanisms for accountability which have become particularly important since the transfer of many welfare services from the state to commercial and third-sector providers, discussed in other chapters. The increase in these mechanisms has been described as the growth of the 'regulatory state' or the 'audit explosion' (Power, 2007; see also Chapter 34).

Regulation involves the setting of rules or standards that services are expected to meet, and carries along with it sanctions if regulated bodies fail to meet these standards or follow the rules. Inspection often goes along with regulation, as inspectors are appointed to check that standards are being met. Inspection agencies include such bodies as Ofsted, which inspects schools in England, and its counterparts elsewhere in the UK. Some are both regulators and inspectors, while in other services the roles are separate. In order to have any power, regulation and inspection must carry the power to fine service providers for failing to meet standards, to make services change their

practices, to publicise poorly performing services, to remove government contracts and ultimately to close down services. Regulatory and inspection regimes also rely on information which can be considered by independent reviewers. The collection and assessment of information about the activities of public bodies is sometimes known as audit. Traditionally, audit concerned mainly financial activities, but in recent years has expanded to include issues such as service quality and value for money.

Professional mechanisms

Professionals such as doctors, nurses, teachers and social workers have traditionally relied on self-regulation and professional standards to provide accountability to their fellow professionals. The role of self-regulatory bodies is to use peer or elite knowledge to ensure that the standards of the profession are maintained. Pure self-regulation by the professions has come under increased pressure in recent years as trust in professionals has declined. Pressures have come from both the managerialist suspicion that professionals do not pay sufficient attention to value for money and from the user perspective that professionals do not take sufficient account of user views, combined with a small number of high-profile cases such as the murders committed by GP, Harold Shipman. This has led to a decline in self-regulation and an increase in independent or semi-independent regulatory bodies, covering wider areas of professional practice and including more lay members.

Market mechanisms

The market may not seem like an obvious form of accountability, but the outsourcing and privatisation of many welfare services relies on the market as a possible mechanism. The theory is that accountability is to the consumer or the purchaser in the market. Since consumer choice in market systems depends on information, choice can be supported by the use of such devices as league tables in health, education, etc. The use of league tables is closely linked to the expansion of regulation, audit and inspection, but the information needed for these mechanisms may be quite different from the information consumers want or need. Other market mechanisms, such as person-alisation and individual budgets in social care, turn service users into consumers, who, in theory, can hold suppliers to account by exercising greater choice (see Chapters 39 and 54).

User mechanisms

The role of service users in the provision of public services has been a growing feature of social policies, with a range of initiatives introduced to try and provide more user accountability. This can be pursued through the use of user panels or representatives on decision-making bodies and the expansion of personalisation and market-type mechanisms discussed above. Alongside these reforms, there has been a growth in the availability of complaints mechanisms to enable dissatisfied service users to voice their grievances. These are usually accompanied by a rhetoric that public services should learn from complaints. Although some complaints procedures have been effective in bringing problems to light, there is less evidence that public services use them as a mechanism for improving services generally.

Issues Arising from Accountability

Accountability and power

Accountability takes many different forms and is closely related to power. As the circular model of accountability shows, some of the people to whom public services should be accountable are more powerful than others. User movements have tried to increase the power of service users within this model by building into public services account-ability mechanisms that include those most directly affected. Critics have argued that much of this is just paying lip service to users and that it makes little difference because of the inherent power differences. Others have argued that increased citizen accountability at the expense of democratic accountability hands power to the more privileged in society, because they are more able to access information and pursue grievances and to participate in such things as the local management of schools and community services.

Costs of accountability

Despite the benefits of increased accountability, accountability also has negative consequences. Accountability mechanisms are expensive: public money is spent on record-keeping, audit, inspec-tion, courts and ombudsmen at the expense of direct provision of services. Alongside this, research has shown that organisations tend to react to increased monitoring by partaking in 'game playing', skewing their activities and their records to fit the requirements of the regulators, at the expense of priorities which may be more important. The benefits of increased accountabil-ity have to be weighed up against these costs.

Accountability and trust

Accountability is often thought of as being related to legitimacy and trust. Some writers have argued that accountability is more likely to be demanded where trust is low. If we generally trust state actors to get on with the job, we are less likely to demand accountability than if we do not trust them. Writ-ers have argued that the rise in demands for accountability in the last thirty years has gone hand in hand with falling public and political trust in the state. One concern of critics of the increase in accountability regimes is that increase in audit, inspection and regulation leads to a further decline in trust, which in turn leads to lower employee morale, a fall in professional responsibility and the stifling of creativity.

Accountability and democracy

Inherent to the explosion of different approaches to accountability is the relationship between the state and its citizens. As we have seen, citizens can relate to the state both in individual and collective ways. Managerialist and consumerist approaches to public services stress individual values and downplay collective values. Outsourcing of ser-vices and moves towards community-run services remove direct democratic control. Each time that central government has attempted to shift public services out of direct control, there has been a parallel move to increase regulation. This tension between direct control of services and increased centralisation through regulation is an intrinsic feature of accountability.

Emerging Issues

New governments coming to power have consistently called for changes to mechanisms for accountability, including reducing the number of unelected public bodies. This has proved to be difficult, highlighting some of the inherent contradictions in accountability, such as balancing cost, independence and democracy. The continuing focus on cost-cutting and privatisation of welfare services combined with personalisation in many areas of welfare policy means the complexity of accountability will increase. The growth of digital media has opened up new avenues for public accountability with the opportunity for both service users and the wider public to comment on service provision directly and for policy-makers to consult with the wider public about policy developments. While these mechanisms have potential for wider accountability, issues of access and power and the basic question of who should be accountable to whom and for what will continue to be important.

Guide to Further Sources

E. Ferlie, L. Lynn and C. Pollitt (eds) (2007) *The Oxford Handbook of Public Management*, Oxford: Oxford University Press, provides an overview of the issues from a management perspective and includes Boven's and Power's studies. M. Bovens, T. Schillemans and R. Goodin (eds) (2014), *The Oxford Handbook of Public Accountability*, Oxford: Oxford University Press, provides detailed chapters on accountability mechanisms across a wide range of public services and international issues.

Detailed discussion of the various mechanisms, including legal mechanisms, can be found in C. Harlow and R. Rawlings (2009), *Law and Administration*, 3rd edn, Cambridge: Cambridge University Press; M. Adler (ed.) (2010), *Administrative Justice in Context*, London, Hart; and J. Jowell and D. Oliver (eds) (2011), *The Changing Constitution*, 7th edn, Oxford: Oxford University Press. For discussion of the concept of 'publics', see N. Mahony, J. Newman and C. Barnett (eds) (2010), *Rethinking the Public: Innovations in Research, Theory and Politics*, Bristol: Policy Press.

For the major audit institutions at the time of writing, see at: www.nao.org.uk; (National Audit Office), and for the devolved governments www.audit-scotland.gov.uk; www.wao.gov.uk; www.niauditoffice.gov.uk.

For the main public sector ombudsmen, see at: www.ombudsman.org.uk (UK parliament and health in England); www.lgo.org.uk (English local government); www.spso.org.uk (Scotland); www.ombudsman-wales.org.uk (Wales); www.ni-ombudsman.org.uk (Northern Ireland).

Review and Assignment Questions

1 Think about a particular welfare service (for example, education, health, social care). In relation to this service, *who* should be held accountable? To *whom* should they be held accountable? What tensions arise between the needs of different groups?

2 In relation to a particular welfare service, what accountability mechanisms can you identify? How do these mechanisms overlap? Are any of them in conflict with each other?

3 What are the advantages and disadvantages of increasing accountability?

4 Identify any recent proposals for increasing accountability and/or cutting the costs of accountability. What implications do these proposals have for the issues raised in this chapter?

5 How do democratic and 'user'-focused accountability mechanisms conflict with each other? How could mechanisms be improved to take account of both?

Visit the book companion site at www.wiley.com/go/alcocksocialpolicy to make use of the resources designed to accompany the textbook. There you will find chapter-specific guides to further resources, including governmental, international, thinktank, pressure groups and relevant journal sources. You will also find a glossary based on *The Blackwell Dictionary of Social Policy*, help sheets, guidance on managing assignments in social policy and career advice.

45

Local Governance

Guy Daly and Howard Davis

◼◼◻◼◻◼◼◻◼◻◼◼◻◼◼◻◼◼◻◼◼◻◼◼◻◼◼◻◼◻◼◼◻◼◻◼◼◻

Overview

- ◼ The analysis of local provision involves the study of local government and local governance.
- ◼ Both are a key element of social policy formation and provision.
- ◼ Local government structures are subject to constant reorganisation and there is continuous tension between central and local concerns.
- ◼ The development of local government is best considered in terms of five stages, the latest involving major changes in its role and resources.
- ◼ These are presenting new challenges and questions about the configuration of local governance.

◼◼◻◼◻◼◼◻◼◻◼◼◻◼◼◻◼◼◻◼◼◻◼◼◻◼◼◻◼◻◼◼◻◼◻◼◼◻

The Development of Local Government and Local Governance

The 'local', however that is defined, has in the past and continues to help shape social policy and provision. As explored elsewhere in this text, social policy may be defined in a traditional Beveridgean manner with a focus on welfare services such as health and social care, education, housing, income maintenance and employment, or via a more expansive definition that also encompasses leisure, transport and the environment, or via more recent constructions that focus on community safety and social inclusion.

Whichever approach is used, local government and local governance are key parts of social policy and provision. These different terms – local government and local governance – are generally used to distinguish between elected local councils, on

The Student's Companion to Social Policy, Fifth Edition. Edited by Pete Alcock, Tina Haux, Margaret May and Sharon Wright.
© 2016 John Wiley & Sons, Ltd. Published 2016 by John Wiley & Sons, Ltd.

the one hand, and the wider range of local public service bodies, on the other.

Whilst Britain has a more centralised set of government and governance arrangements than many of its fellow European Union member states, the state at the centre legislates, cajoles and works alongside local, subnational and devolved (Scotland, Wales and Northern Ireland) policymaking and implementation structures (see Part IV). When one compares UK governmental structures with other European states, one notes that local government is constitutionally weaker, and at the same time, the units of local government are relatively large but have relatively fewer councillors per head.

What this means is, first, that in the UK local government's influence has tended to emanate from the scale and nature of its operations rather than through constitutional strength; and, second, that it is liable to and has experienced constant reorganisation and changes in its responsibilities, structures and governance arrangements that have become more complex and varied since devolution.

History is often an important influence on the way things are done and the structures and institutions that are in place. The government and governance of local communities are no exception. This history can be traced back for centuries. Present-day local government, however, really begins in the nineteenth century and has, in many ways, a strong connection with the progress of the industrial revolution. In particular, as urbanisation and industrialisation increased, the need for a wider range of services became more apparent.

Sanitation, elementary education, public health, law and order, and physical infrastructure were vital in building successful businesses and economies. In what might be seen as a period of enlightened self-interest by the local 'great and good', local public bodies increasingly took over service provision from commercial and charitable organisations.

Key dates include the Municipal Corporations Act 1835, the Poor Law Amendment Act 1834, the Local Government Acts 1888, 1894 and 1929 – and parallel legislation for London, Scotland, Wales and Ireland. By the time of the Second World War, local councils in most urban areas were responsible for, and running, most local

public services – literally from cradle to grave. In rural areas, this was less the case and provision far less developed.

Local governance within the post-Second World War consensus

The period from 1945 up until the election of the Thatcher Conservative government in 1979 is often described as a period of consensus across the major political parties, and this is arguably as true for local governance and local government as is it was for other social policy arenas. The period was one in which local government was a major partner in building the welfare state, reflected in a significant growth in local authorities' expenditure. In England and Wales councils had key responsibilities for providing:

- social housing;
- education;
- personal social services and social care for children and adults;
- community-based healthcare (transferred to the NHS in 1974);
- public health (transferred to the NHS in 1974);
- public protection – police and fire services, ambulances (transferred to the NHS in 1974), consumer protection.

Councils in Scotland had broadly similar responsibilities, but, from 1973 onwards, councils in Northern Ireland had a much narrower remit than others in the UK, with key functions such as education, social services and housing being transferred to Northern Ireland-wide public bodies.

Local governance and the New Right, 1979–97

During the 1970s, however, the consensual period of expansion and belief in state provision, including through local government, started to be questioned, and the advent of the Thatcher government in 1979 signalled the definitive break with the post-war consensus (see Chapter 19). Indeed, it can be argued that local government was one of the prime sites for New Right reforms in social policy. The ensuing approach to local government can be typified as:

- a period in the early 1980s of focusing on controlling local government expenditure;
- a period in the mid-1980s of restructuring with the abolition of the Greater London Council (GLC) and the metropolitan county councils – and shifts of responsibilities away from elected local government into government appointed local bodies ('quangos');
- a period in the mid- to late 1980s of challenging local authorities' role as the direct providers of services through privatisation and the encouragement of local authorities to be enablers of services rather than direct providers;
- a period in the early 1990s of new managerialist approaches, with, for example, the promotion of citizen's charters, league tables, inspection and audit.

All of local government's main services were affected, including.

- education: centralisation of control, including the weakening of local education authorities, the implementation of the national curriculum, local management of schools and the independence of further and higher education;
- housing: 'right to buy' schemes encouraged tenants to buy their council homes at a discount, transfer of whole estates through the creation of Housing Action Trusts, and, in the 1990s, the first large-scale stock transfer schemes;
- social care: promotion of local authority social services departments as enablers of residential and domiciliary care;
- introduction of competitive pressures into many services through compulsory competitive tendering (CCT) and the purchaser–provider split;
- the creation of Urban Development Corporations that took over key regeneration responsibilities.

All in all, the Thatcher–Major period of government has been depicted as one in which the local state began to be 'hollowed out' with the privatisation of certain responsibilities, the shift of some responsibilities to local quangos and increased central pressure on those services that remained.

Even so, it was not one of passive acquiescence by local government. On the contrary, perhaps in part as a response to the politics of the New Right, it saw the emergence of what has been described as the 'Urban Left' in local government. In a number of cities, for example, Liverpool, Sheffield, parts of London and the Greater London Council, Labour-controlled councils adopted radical left agendas, whether in relation to transport, housing, policing, education, jobs and services generally, multiculturalism or positive action for disabled persons' groups, and lesbian and gay groups. Local government was often the site of political dispute between the New Right and the left, epitomised by the fights over the 'poll tax'.

However, whilst the Conservative power-base in local government had been virtually wiped out by the time Labour came to power in 1997, much of the Urban Left's agenda was defeated by Conservative central government legislation. Paradoxically though, much of that agenda (for example, rights for disadvantaged groups) has nowadays been absorbed into mainstream social policy. What this also shows is the continual tension between central government and local governance bodies. On the one hand, the centre (whether the UK or devolved governments and parliaments) may wish for a universal policy and yet, because, for example, inequalities are not spatially uniform, at the local level particular solutions may be required to meet locally specific concerns.

Local governance and Labour, 1997–2010

Labour moved quickly to use the language and rhetoric of partnership between national and local government. It also soon repealed one of the most hated aspects of Conservative local government legislation – the obligation to subject local public services to open competition with the private sector (via CCT) – and replaced it with a new duty of continuous improvement.

Labour also established devolved administrations for Scotland and Wales and new arrangements for Northern Ireland, and transferred responsibility for overseeing local government in these jurisdictions (see Part IV). In England, however, it soon became apparent that, like its predecessor, Labour also had its doubts about local government. There was to be no return to old (pre-Conservative government) ways of working. There was to be no simple undoing of Conservative legislation affecting local government and local public services, and Labour quickly identified what it saw as a number of problems with local government as it stood.

Its agenda was two-pronged. On the one hand, there was a considerable investment in key services, along with an emphasis by central government on the important role of local government. However, at the same time, Labour also emphasised and enacted major programmes of reform in order to bring about its vision of a revitalised local government in England.

Whilst many aspects of its aspirations were widely shared, its solutions were not always so warmly embraced. Amongst the more controversial aspects were the requirements on councils to streamline their decision-making arrangements – leading to the separation of executive and representative roles among councillors. This led to the creation of local authority cabinets and executives, and the concentration of executive powers in fewer hands. A small number of English authorities moved to having directly elected executive mayors.

Legislation also gave Government new powers to act on service failures by local government and introduced the concept of inspection to all local government services. Whilst increasing the focus on service improvement, the inspection process did come at some cost. This led in time to moves towards more proportionate and risk-based approaches to inspection.

Localism and the UK Coalition government, 2010–15

On coming to power, the Coalition defined its priority for local government and local governance in England as 'localism'. But 'localism' was not simply to be equated with either place (in the geographical sense) or local government. It was seen as a means for pushing power downwards and outwards to the lowest possible level. This included communities acquiring the right to bid to run services and to save facilities at risk of closure. The government aimed to create a 'Big Society' – an empowered society where communities and voluntary action were to the fore – a 'Big Society' rather than a 'big state' (see Chapter 37).

At the same time, its overriding strategy heavily emphasised reducing the UK's budget deficit. Some of the reductions were passed on to the devolved bodies and administrations. In England, this led to huge cuts in funding for local government and local public services, resulting in big reductions in services and the numbers of people employed by local authorities and other public bodies. Local government faced particularly large proportionate cuts, with councils experiencing a fall in core central government funding of 40 per cent between 2010 and 2015. During the same period councils made £20 billion worth of savings.

By way of example, Coventry City Council's funding from central government fell from £214 million in 2010 to £135 million in 2015. And in Birmingham the City Council made cuts of £460 million between 2010 and 2015, and reduced its workforce from 20,000 in 2010 to 13,000 employees in 2014. At the time of writing, a further £360 million worth of cuts were expected to be needed by 2018, with the workforce falling to just 7,000. The scale and speed of cuts led the council's leader to say, in what became a well-known quote, 'this is the end of local government as we know it'. Thus, in England in particular a major legacy of the Coalition was the further hollowing out of local government and local public service provision, and a parallel increased expectation that individuals and communities look after themselves.

In addition, notwithstanding the discourse of 'localism', it often behaved in a very centralist manner. Local finance continued to be heavily controlled by central government. Government ministers also continued to express strong views publicly on the details of very local service provision, for example, the frequency of local bin collections, and to formally intervene in the operation of local councils through the sending in of commissioners and improvement boards.

At an operational level, education increasingly moved out of local government control, with social care for children and adults becoming the most high-profile area of local government responsibility in terms of spending levels, service sensitivity and reputational significance. Public health services, however, transferred back to local government control in 2013. At the same time, the day-to-day operation and provision of local public services were increasingly contracted out to, and delivered by, private-sector companies. Increasingly, local authorities and other local public services also moved to work more closer together, sharing services, officers and premises in order to offer seamless service delivery to the public and, essentially, to reduce costs.

In addition, the regional structures created by Labour were largely dismantled and gradually replaced by a complex series of enterprise partnerships, city regions and combined authorities at a subregional level – with powers and responsibilities varying widely. Attempts to force the major cities in England to have directly elected mayors, however, largely failed to gain momentum despite the Coalition strongly promoting it.

It is not easy to summarise the variations in policy during this period amongst and across the devolved administrations. There remain many similarities in approach, but in general they tended to adopt a less marketised approach. Local government responsibilities for education, social housing and social care in Wales and Scotland have been maintained – though in Scotland there has been a noticeable loss of other functions such as fire and police.

Local Government and Governance Structures

When it comes to local government structures, most of the UK population is served by so-called 'unitary' local authorities. This is where there is just one local authority for the particular local area, providing all or most local government services in that area. These authorities come in a variety of guises and varying titles, but all are responsible for overseeing the spectrum of local services – from street scene to libraries, from trading standards to care services.

An exception to this general rule applies in some parts of England, outside the main urban areas, where a two-tier local government system exists comprising a county council and a number of district councils. In these areas, the former is responsible for those services thought to need a larger scale for their operation such as social care and strategic planning. The district councils, on the other hand, have responsibilities for most local environmental services (such as refuse collection

and street cleaning), together with housing, leisure services and local development control.

All of the councils mentioned above are directly elected by local electors, whether they are in a unitary or two-tier setting. There are though some differences in electoral arrangements between different types of council.

In London, there exists in addition to the London local authorities (the London boroughs and the City of London Corporation) a directly elected regional authority – the Greater London Authority (GLA) – comprising an Assembly and a Mayor of London. The GLA is responsible for key London-wide functions such as public protection, transport and economic development.

One other tier of directly elected government that needs to be mentioned is the parish. Parish, town or community councils are a key link in the chain of local representation. In total, there are some 9,500 parish and town councils in England, some 730 community councils in Wales and some 1,200 community councils in Scotland. They do not exist in all areas – most notably being absent from the main urban areas, though this is beginning to change – and also have no equivalent in Northern Ireland. For the most part, they have powers rather than duties – acting as the voice of villages, small towns and neighbourhoods – and making that voice heard to other tiers of government as the occasion demands. They have few service delivery responsibilities.

Some important local services are not provided by elected local government at all. Key amongst them are most healthcare services – which are the responsibility of the various arms and parts of the National Health Service across the UK – and policing – which in, England and Wales, is the responsibility of directly elected Police and Crime Commissioners, and in Scotland and Northern Ireland the devolved administrations.

In order to overcome the fragmentation of local public services between local government and other bodies, there is an increasing emphasis on partnership working. In England under Labour a range of statutory partnerships aimed to bring together all the key local public service bodies in each local authority area – councils, police, health, etc. – to agree key common objectives and priorities for all the local public services in that area. Under the Coalition, the emphasis moved away from statutory partnerships to more voluntary arrangements based on local needs and wishes. However, whatever the political controlling forces, there is inevitably a need for some form of local governance, if not local government, arrangements.

Emerging Issues

As we have seen, local government and local public services remain important for the shaping and delivery of social policy. From the industrial revolution onwards, as well as during the period of establishing the post-war welfare state, and under successive governments since, local government has been expected to lead, coordinate and deliver elements of social policy.

However, across the UK issues remain around the need for local and subnational governance arrangements to engage more effectively with social policy agendas, including local inequalities and local needs. Ways of ensuring increased civic engagement and civic renewal – including the greater participation of citizens and service users in local decision-making – are likely to be areas of continuing focus and debate. This extends into questions of where the 'boundary' should properly fall between voluntary and community action and (local) state responsibility, in terms of both the staffing and funding of local services and facilities, especially in an era of continuing tight public finances.

The wider question of the adequacy or otherwise of the mechanisms for financing local government and local public services can also be expected to remain an area of differing views, not least because local government across the UK is financed from several sources – council tax (domestic rates in Northern Ireland), non-domestic rates, government grants, fees and charges for certain services, and loans – with government grants being key.

In addition, ongoing controversy can be anticipated concerning the effectiveness of local government and local governance structures and arrangements, including views on the effectiveness or otherwise of performance and accountability arrangements, and of alternative leadership structures such as elected police commissioners in England and Wales and, in England, greater numbers of directly elected mayors and new city and county regions.

Whatever the outcome of these particular debates, the scale and nature of local public services across the UK are such that there is still a need for local service delivery and local governance structures. The extent to which these should be accountable to local government and local electorates will remain a key area of political and policy debate.

Guide to Further Sources

A useful overview of the management and governance of public services can be found in T. Bovaird and E. Loffler (eds) (2015), *Public Management and Governance*, 3rd edn, London: Routledge. B. Denters and L. E. Rose (2005), *Comparing Local Governance: Trends and Developments*, Basingstoke: Palgrave Macmillan, is a good introductory text that compares local governance in the UK with several European countries, the US, Australia and New Zealand. C. Durose, S. Greaseley and L. Richarson (2009), *Changing Local Governance, Changing Citizens*, Bristol: Policy Press, is a useful exploration of the changing relationship between citizens and local decision-makers.

R. A. W. Rhodes (1988), *Beyond Westminster and Whitehall: Sub-Central Governments of Britain*, London: Unwin Hyman, remains a seminal text on the nature of the relationships between central government and local governance structures. J. Stewart (2000), *The Nature of British Local Government*, Basingstoke: Macmillan, is also a good source for capturing the historical underpinnings of British local government. D. Wilson and C. Game (eds) (2011), *Local Government in the United Kingdom*, 5th edn, Basingstoke: Palgrave Macmillan, offers a good general introduction.

Useful websites include www.local.gov.uk (the Local Government Association; there are equivalent sites for Scotland, Wales and Northern Ireland); www.gov.uk, a gateway portal for all public services and government departments.

Review and Assignment Questions

1   Which council or councils are responsible for overseeing what services in your locality?
2   What is the political complexion of your local council or councils, and what are the electoral arrangements?

3 What do you think could be done to increase participation in local elections, civic engagement and local decision-making?

4 What do you think are some of the advantages and disadvantages of directly elected mayors being in charge of local councils?

5 Discuss what roles and responsibilities you think elected local government across the UK should have in the future.

Visit the book companion site at www.wiley.com/go/alcocksocialpolicy to make use of the resources designed to accompany the textbook. There you will find chapter-specific guides to further resources, including governmental, international, thinktank, pressure groups and relevant journal sources. You will also find a glossary based on *The Blackwell Dictionary of Social Policy*, help sheets, guidance on managing assignments in social policy and career advice.

46

The European Union

Linda Hantrais

■■

Overview

- Social policy has been on the European agenda since the founding of the European Economic Community in 1957.
- The social dimension of the European Union (EU) has been primarily concerned with the social protection of workers.
- The EU has progressively extended its social policy competence and has introduced softer and more proactive instruments for policymaking and implementation.
- The relationship between EU and national-level governance is interactive, with national governments retaining responsibility for the content, organisation and delivery of social protection systems.
- In a context of population decline and ageing and the aftermath of economic recession, the EU faces important challenges to its social policy competence.

■■

The Development of the Union's Social Policy Remit

When it was established in 1957 with the signing of the Treaty of Rome, the European Economic Community (EEC) was essentially concerned with economic affairs. From the outset, however, it acquired a social policy remit to facilitate geographical and occupational mobility. Articles 117–128 on social policy in the Treaty advocated close cooperation between member states, particularly in training, employment, working conditions, social security and collective bargaining. They endorsed the equal pay principle, and provided for the harmonisation of social security measures to accommodate migrant workers, and the operation of a European Social

The Student's Companion to Social Policy, Fifth Edition. Edited by Pete Alcock, Tina Haux, Margaret May and Sharon Wright.
© 2016 John Wiley & Sons, Ltd. Published 2016 by John Wiley & Sons, Ltd.

Fund to support employment and re-employment programmes.

In the post-war context of rapid economic growth, the underlying objectives of European social policy were to avoid distortion of competition and to promote free movement of labour within the Community. Since the welfare systems of the founder member states were based largely on the insurance principle, unfair competition might arise if some countries levied higher social charges on employment, leading to social dumping as companies relocated to areas with lower labour costs. The functioning of the common market was expected to result automatically in social development, implying that the Community would not need to interfere directly with redistributive benefits.

The United Kingdom was not one of the six founding member states. Following accession in 1973, the British Government opposed Community action in social areas. At a time when economic growth was slowing down due to the oil crises, the belief in automatic social harmonisation was being called into question, stimulating interest in a more active approach to social reform. The 1974 resolution on a social action programme proposed that the Community should develop common objectives for national social policies, without standardising solutions to shared problems or removing responsibility for social policy from member states. The 1980s were marked by pressures to develop a 'social space', premised on social dialogue between trade unions and employers (the social partners), enabling them to agree objectives and establish a minimum platform of guaranteed social rights for workers, to be applied by individual member states to stimulate convergence.

The goal of harmonising social protection became more salient with the Single European Act 1986, and advancement of plans for economic and monetary union. The problem of agreeing even a minimum level of protection for workers was apparent in the negotiations leading to the 1989 Community Charter of the Fundamental Social Rights of Workers, which did not have force of law. The Charter's action programme recognised the importance of observing national diversity. By the 1990s, some convergence was occurring due to the common trend towards welfare retrenchment, made necessary by economic recession, and the shift towards mixed systems of welfare.

The British Government had sought to delay legislative progress on workers' rights, arguing that it would impinge on national sovereignty and adversely affect employment, resulting in the chapter on social affairs being relegated to a Protocol and Agreement on Social Policy appended to the Maastricht Treaty on European Union in 1993. The Treaty formalised the subsidiarity principle, thereby setting the tone for social legislation in later years. Subsidiarity means that the EU is empowered to act only if its aims can be more effectively achieved at European rather than national level, thereby constraining opportunities for concerted action among nations in the area of social protection.

Both the Maastricht Treaty and the Luxembourg summit in 1997 endorsed the priority given to employment, leading to the first employment guidelines. In the same year, Britain's Labour government signed up to the Agreement on Social Policy and the social chapter was incorporated into the Treaty of Amsterdam, thus lending social policy a stronger legal base, whereas the EU's competence in that area has remained a contentious and contested issue for the UK.

Each of the five successive waves of membership made harmonisation, or even convergence, of social policy provisions more difficult to achieve. The social protection systems of the six original EEC member states (Belgium, France, Federal Republic of Germany, Italy, Luxembourg, the Netherlands) were variants of the Bismarckian or continental model of welfare, based on the employment–insurance principle. The new member states in the 1970s (Denmark, Ireland, United Kingdom) subscribed to social protection systems funded from taxation and providing universal flat-rate coverage. The southern states that joined the Union in the early 1980s (Greece, Portugal, Spain) had less developed welfare systems, whereas the Nordic states (Finland, Sweden) that became members in 1995 shared features with Denmark, and Austria was closer to the German pattern. The two island states and eleven post-Soviet states that acceded to the EU in 2004, 2007 and 2013 (Bulgaria, Croatia, Cyprus, Czech Republic, Estonia, Hungary, Latvia, Lithuania, Malta, Poland, Romania, Slovakia, Slovenia) brought further variants of welfare systems.

Enlargement to the east stimulated the search for less formal approaches as an alternative to

Box 46.1 Mandate of the Commissioner for Employment, Social Affairs, Skills and Labour Mobility, 2014

- Contribute to the jobs, growth and investment package, prioritising the younger generation.
- Pursue the modernisation of labour markets and social protection systems, including the targets set in the Europe 2020 strategy in the fields of employment and social inclusion.
- Work on deepening Economic and Monetary Union and advancement of social dialogue at all levels.
- Promote free movement of workers, by improving conditions for geographic and professional mobility across Europe and recognition of qualifications.

- Develop the skills level of the European workforce, by promoting vocational training and lifelong learning, including a new European policy on legal migration to Europe to address skills shortages.
- Support forms of social innovation, and reinforce synergies with programmes such as Horizon 2020, to enrich national and EU policymaking.
- Ensure that employment and social considerations, including the impact of ageing and skills needs, are taken into account in all Commission proposals and activities.

harmonisation. A European social model was emerging; enshrined in the Charter of Fundamental Rights of the European Union agreed at the Nice Summit in 2000, it embodied citizenship rights and the core values that all member states were committed to pursue.

Faced with the growing threat of population ageing, a trend exacerbated as the baby-boom generation approached retirement age, the focus of EU social policy debates shifted following the Hampton Court Summit in 2005. In 2014, against a background of austerity in many member states, a new European Commission was instated. Its very broad social affairs mandate, summarised in Box 46.1, reflected the development of social policy over the years, while retaining the priority accorded to employment and labour mobility.

EU Social Policymaking Processes

Despite the relatively limited social policy remit in the founding treaties, after more than fifty years of operation, the EU has developed a multi-tiered system of governance, instituted under the Lisbon Treaty, which entered into force in 2009 (see Box 46.2).

Decision-making procedures have evolved to take account of expanding membership. To facilitate the passage of contentious legislation, the Single European Act introduced *qualified majority voting* (QMV) as an alternative to unanimous voting in the areas of health and safety at work, working conditions, information and consultation of workers, equality between men and women, and the integration of persons excluded from the labour market. The Amsterdam Treaty extended QMV to active employment measures. The Nice Treaty added anti-discrimination measures, mobility and specific action supporting economic and social cohesion, and introduced a re-weighting of votes to take account of population size. The Lisbon Treaty further extended QMV to measures combating climate change, energy security and emergency humanitarian aid, pending the implementation of double majority voting, but retained unanimous voting for any attempts at harmonisation in the field of social security and social protection.

The EU's legal sources include *primary legislation* in the form of treaties, and *secondary legislation*, ranging from regulations, directives and decisions, its most binding instruments, to recommendations, resolutions and opinions, which are advisory, or communications and memoranda,

Box 46.2 The EU's System of Governance

- The *Council* of the European Union (previously Council of Ministers), composed of heads of government of member states, meets twice a year to determine policy directions. As the principal governing body, it represents national interests and is responsible for decisions on laws to be applied across the EU. The Presidency of the Council rotates between member states every six months and is responsible for the functioning of the EU legislature. The Council appoints a full-time President of the European Union for a two-and-a-half year term by double majority voting, with the possibility of one renewal.

- As the executive branch of the European Union, the *Commission* formally initiates, implements and monitors European legislation. Under the Lisbon Treaty, each member state has one Commissioner. The European Parliament President elects the European Commission on a proposal from the Council for a period of five years. Commissioners are political appointees, but are expected to act independently of national interests. The directorates general are responsible for preparing proposals and working documents for consideration by the Council, thereby playing an important part in setting the EU's policy agenda. The Lisbon Treaty requires the Commission to monitor and report on the social situation – demographic trends, social policy development and employment data – and draw up guidelines for member states to assist them in drafting employment policies. In 2014, the Commission adopted a joined-up cross-sectoral approach enabling mainstreaming of the employment and social dimension in all policy areas.

- The *European Parliament* (EP), whose members are directly elected by citizens of member states every five years, has extensive budgetary and supervisory powers on a par with the Council for much EU legislation, although MEPs form political rather than national blocks. The EP cannot initiate bills, but it can decline to take up a position on a Commission proposal, and it can force the Commission to resign. To be elected, European Commissioners must successfully pass hearings at the EP.

- The *Court of Justice*, which sits in Luxembourg, is the EU's legal voice and the guardian of treaties and implementing legislation. Its main task is to ensure that legal instruments adopted at EU and national levels are compatible with European law. Through its interpretation of legislation, the court has built up a substantial and influential body of case law in the social area.

---

which signal initial thinking on an issue. Relatively few *regulations* apply in the social field, with the notable exception of coordination of social security arrangements for migrant workers and the Structural Funds. *Directives*, which set objectives for legislation, but leave individual states to select the most suitable form of implementation, have been used to considerable effect to promote equal treatment, and health and safety at work. *Recommendations* have played an important role in developing a framework for concerted action and convergence of social policies.

The *open method of coordination* (OMC), formally introduced as a means of intervention in employment policies at the Lisbon summit in 2000, offers a soft law alternative designed to encourage cooperation, exchange of best practice and agreement on common targets and guidelines for member states, supported in the case of employment and social exclusion by national action plans. OMC relies on regular monitoring of progress to meet the targets set, allowing member states to compare their efforts and learn from experience and good practice elsewhere.

Today, the EU has available a broad array of multi-layered and fragmented policymaking institutions, procedures and instruments, which have gradually extended its area of competence and authority. The policymaking process depends on the ability of national and supranational actors to cooperate in setting objectives, initiating, enacting and implementing legislation. The sharing of responsibility distinguishes European structures from those of most international organisations. As in federal states, the EU has to act for the greater good of its member states, while not encroaching too far into national sovereignty or infringing the subsidiarity principle. Whereas the EU has not secured full legitimacy as a supranational authority in the social policy field, the competence of member states has undoubtedly been eroded. A delicate balance has, therefore, to be struck between the interests of the different tiers of the EU's institutions, involving a complex process of negotiation and compromise, vested interests and trade-offs.

EU Social Policy Intervention

The Union's original objective of removing barriers to the free movement of labour served to justify an array of policies for coordinating social protection systems, supported by action programmes, networks and observatories to stimulate initiatives and monitor progress in the social field.

Rather than seeking to change national systems, action in the area *of education and training* focused initially on comparing the content and level of qualifications across the Community to stimulate transferability between member states. General directives were issued on the mutual recognition of the equivalence of diplomas. From the mid-1970s, the Commission initiated action programmes to develop vocational training, encourage mobility among students and young workers, and promote cooperation between education and industry. In the early twenty-first century, the Commission advocated investment in human resources through quality education and lifelong learning. Cooperation and support for member states are primary concerns in the Lisbon Treaty, while responsibility rests at national level for determining teaching content and the organisation of educational systems.

Several articles in the EEC Treaty were devoted to the improvement of *living and working conditions* as a means of equalising opportunities and promoting mobility. Particular attention was paid to health and safety at work, resulting in a large body of binding legislation. The introduction of QMV for health and safety legislation resulted in directives designed to ensure the physical protection of workers, including the protection of pregnant women, control the organisation of working time and expand action in the area of public health. Here, the Lisbon Treaty sought to complement national policies and combat cross-border threats to health.

In line with the priority given to employment policy and working conditions at EU level, and despite opposition from some member states – notably Denmark and the UK – wary of the possible impact on employment practices and equal opportunities, the Commission instigated legislation and set up action programmes to protect women as workers. The policies promoted include directives requiring equal pay for work of equal value, equal treatment and employment-related social insurance rights, and measures to reconcile occupational and family life. In the 1990s, gender mainstreaming was introduced to resolve persistent inequalities and, in 2010, the Commission adopted a Women's Charter committed to building a gender perspective into all its policies.

In the 1970s, the impact of economic recession, rising *unemployment* and demographic ageing became policy issues. The prospect of greater freedom of movement heightened concern about welfare tourism and the exporting of poverty between member states, if unemployed workers and their families crossed borders in search of more generous provision. The Commission funded a series of action programmes to combat poverty and social exclusion, and the Structural Funds were deployed to underpin regional policy by tackling the sources of economic disparities. The employment guidelines served as a major plank in the EU's strategy to combat labour market exclusion by improving employability through active policy measures, which remained high on the social policy agenda in the post-crisis economy of the 2010s.

Greater life expectancy created heavy demands on pension provision, health and care services. The Commission was required to monitor *provision for older and disabled people*, particularly with regard to maintenance and caring, arrangements for transferring the rights of mobile workers and pensioners, and the overall impact of policy on living standards. Communications published in

1999 and 2006 proposed strategies for strengthening solidarity and equity between the generations. By 2010, as the baby-boom generations reached retirement age, the main thrust of EU policy shifted to active and healthy ageing.

Despite the considerable body of legislation on freedom of movement, information about intra-European mobility suggests that migration between member states has remained relatively low, although enlargement to the east initially provoked an unprecedented westwards wave of internal migration from central and east European countries. Increasingly, attention has been paid to the challenges posed by *third-country migration* in coordinating national policies and in dealing with refugees and asylum seekers. The legitimacy of these concerns was formally recognised when the right to equality of opportunity and treatment, without distinction of race, colour, ethnicity, national origin, culture or religion was written into the Treaty of Amsterdam, and all discrimination on such grounds was outlawed in the Charter of Fundamental Rights. In recognition of the need for an EU policy on regular migration in addressing skills shortages, one of the Commissioners appointed in 2014 was given responsibility for Migration and Home Affairs.

While doubts may be expressed about the coherence of the EU's social policy remit, these examples illustrate how its institutions have developed a wide-ranging competence in social affairs to become a major, if contested, social policy actor. Despite the blocking tactics of some member states, a considerable body of legislation and practice – *acquis communautaire* – has been instituted, requiring compliance from national governments and constraining their domain of action. However, the changes incorporated in the EU's treaties, combined with the shift towards less binding forms of legislation in the social field, have tended to result in standards being sought that can realistically be achieved by the least advanced countries – the lowest common denominator – leaving individual member states with considerable discretion in policy implementation.

Emerging Issues

In the first two decades of this century, the treaties still formally recognised that member states should remain responsible for their own systems of social protection. The Commission was charged with promoting ever closer cooperation and monitoring progress towards common objectives using social performance assessments. It continued pursuing plans to 'modernise' social protection systems in response to socio-economic, demographic and climate change, while upholding the values embodied in the European social model by reinforcing intergenerational solidarity at the macro (societal) and micro (family) levels.

Although EU member states disagree about the extent of the Union's involvement in social policy or the form it should take, they broadly agree about the new pressures on welfare systems and the need to develop affordable and sustainable solutions. Population ageing, in combination with technological and structural change, raises questions about long-term old-age dependency, the conditions governing retirement age and pension rights, and the provision of health and social care in a context of changing family and household structures and gender relations. Persistently high levels of unemployment, particularly among young people, together with shortages of skilled labour present major challenges for social protection systems, education and training provision. The social impact of climate change was not made explicit in the remit of the new Commissioner for Climate Action and Energy in 2014, but the need is recognised for policies to manage the 'socio-ecological transition'.

The process of absorbing further enlargement to the east and the extension of the EU's sphere of influence was made more challenging in the 2000s by the global economic crises, particularly for the weakest of the nineteen Eurozone economies that were most in need of social reform. In an 'age of austerity', member states were struggling to ensure the financial viability and sustainability of their social protection systems, to contain the costs of providing high-quality services, to safeguard employment and promote social inclusion, while also being called upon to meet the humanitarian needs of growing numbers of refugees fleeing from conflict zones. Different mixes of solutions were being tried at national level, according to politico-economic circumstances: greater targeting of benefits, the tightening of eligibility criteria, greater emphasis on active welfare-to-work measures, the introduction of long-term social care insurance schemes, privatisation of services and promotion of a volunteering culture.

The need to find concerted responses to these new socio-economic challenges came at a time when the UK Government was renegotiating the terms of EU membership in an attempt to restore national sovereignty over social and employment legislation. Although much would depend on the outcome of both the negotiations and the referendum, proponents of 'Brexit' argued that, outside the EU, the UK would be in a position to review what they considered as the more onerous and controversial aspects of EU membership embodied in the social *acquis*, including the free movement of people, living and working conditions, and determining access to benefits and services for migrant workers, working-time arrangements, health and safety at work, social rights and gender equality issues.

Guide to Further Sources

L. Hantrais (2007), *Social Policy in the European Union*, 3rd edn, London and New York: Palgrave and St Martin's Press, analyses the development of the EU's social dimension. The European Commission's website provides regular updates on demographic trends, the social situation, social protection and employment at ec.europa.eu/social/; clear concise summaries of the main aspects of European legislation, policies and activities, covering education, training, youth and sport, employment and social policy, and public health at eur-lex.europa.eu/browse/summaries.

html; and annual updates on the provision of national social protection systems in MISSOC Comparative Tables at www.missoc.org.

Review and Assignment Questions

1 How has the relationship between economic and social policy evolved since the establishment of the EEC in 1957?
2 To what extent has the autonomy of national social protection systems been undermined by the growing EU social policy competence?
3 What has been the impact of different waves of enlargement on the EU social policy remit?
4 To what extent are national social policy models compatible with a European social model?
5 Assess the evidence for and against the European Union's growing social policy competence from the perspective of individual member states.

Visit the book companion site at www.wiley.com/go/alcocksocialpolicy to make use of the resources designed to accompany the textbook. There you will find chapter-specific guides to further resources, including governmental, international, thinktank, pressure groups and relevant journal sources. You will also find a glossary based on *The Blackwell Dictionary of Social Policy*, help sheets, guidance on managing assignments in social policy and career advice.

PART VIII
Welfare Domains

47

Income Maintenance and Social Security

Stephen McKay and Karen Rowlingson

Overview

- Social security represents just under one-third of all government spending – almost as much as spending on education and health combined. The largest group of benefit recipients are children (with over 12 million receiving child benefit, through their parents) and pensioners (around 13 million receiving state retirement pension).
- Definitions of social security vary from broad definitions encompassing all methods of securing an income to narrow definitions focusing on state systems of income maintenance.
- Social security systems vary in their aims. The UK system focuses on alleviating poverty, hence considerable reliance on means-tested provision. Continental European systems focus more on insurance-based systems and redistribution from rich to poor.
- State benefits are typically divided into *contributory benefits*, such as the state retirement pension; *means-tested benefits*, such as Income Support (and also tax credits); and contingent or *categorical benefits*, such as child benefit.
- There has been an emphasis from both Conservative (including Coalition) and Labour governments in the UK on individual responsibility rather than state provision. This is evident in recent reforms of pensions, disability benefit and child support.

The Student's Companion to Social Policy, Fifth Edition. Edited by Pete Alcock, Tina Haux, Margaret May and Sharon Wright.
© 2016 John Wiley & Sons, Ltd. Published 2016 by John Wiley & Sons, Ltd.

Introduction

The incomes of individuals and families come from several sources – from the private sector through wages/salaries, support from other family members, and often from the state in the form of cash benefits. The discussion of *social security* takes this as its starting point, sometimes looking broadly at the range of income sources, usually looking more narrowly at the role the state plays in maintaining incomes. Different welfare states play very different roles in income maintenance, from minimalist schemes existing only for the poor (if then), to comprehensive systems covering an extensive range of risks to income security, and involving significant redistribution.

The Importance of Social Security

This chapter provides an overview of social security in the UK. Most people spend much of their lives either receiving or paying for social security – often both at the same time. However, the system is far from simple and most of us understand very little about what it aims to do, how it operates and its effects. A number of facts illustrate the importance of the social security system in the UK:

- Government spending on social security benefits and tax credits in the UK in 2014–15 was around £200 billion per year – just under one-third of all government spending and almost as much as health and education spending combined. This represents over £6,000 each year for every family in the country.
- Some 60 per cent of UK families receive at least one social security benefit, with 21 per cent receiving an income-related (means-tested) benefit and 12 per cent a tax credit (FRS, 2012/13). Some 60 per cent of social tenants receive at least one means-tested benefit. Changes to tax credits in the 2015 summer budget may lead to reductions in these numbers.

The benefits responsible for the most spending are the State Retirement Pension, Income Support/Pension Credit, Housing Benefit, Child Benefit, Disability Living Allowance (becoming Personal Independent Payment for under-65s) and Employment and Support Allowance. Social security benefits are paid mostly from general taxes and from specific contributions for social security – which we know as National Insurance.

What is 'Social Security'?

Social security clearly plays a central role in people's lives. But what is meant by social security? There is no universally accepted neat definition of 'social security', and it may be defined in a number of ways.

Starting with the very widest definition, it is sometimes used to refer to all the ways people organise their lives in order to ensure access to an adequate income. This wide concept includes securing income from all sources such as earnings from employers and self-employment, financial help from charities, money from a family member and cash benefits from the state. If we take the widest definition, then the private sector is the foremost provider of income maintenance as earnings from employment and profits from self-employment are the chief source of income for most people of working age, and pensions in retirement are often based on such earnings.

A slightly narrower definition of social security would include all types of financial support, except those provided by the market system. In this way, reliance on the immediate or extended family would still be classed as helping to achieve social security. However, it is increasingly usual to adopt an even narrower definition, and to regard social security as those sources of immediate financial support provided by the state.

The definition of 'social security' as the system of cash benefits paid by the government to different individuals appears to be fairly simple and unproblematic. But it is inadequate not least because some 'benefits' are not paid for by the state, or need not be. For example, statutory sick pay used to be paid by government, but, whilst it remains a legal entitlement, it is now mostly a cost met by employers. There are also occupational schemes for sickness, widowhood and retirement that are similar to state benefits, and which have a similar function, but which are organised by employers. One could also envisage the government finding ways to 'privatise' what are currently state benefits, or instigating new compulsory private provision, perhaps for pensions.

So, both voluntary employer schemes, and some programmes mandated by government, may also be classed as social security – neither of which neatly fit the above definition.

Another rather grey area is the distinction between cash benefits, systems of tax allowances and, increasingly, 'tax credits', which are the responsibility of Her Majesty's Revenue and Customs (HMRC, formerly the Inland Revenue). Tax credits have become an increasingly important part of the 'social security' system. The government generally prefers to see them as standing apart from social security benefits – in particular, that they are designed for workers, rather than those not in work. There are, however, good reasons for seeing tax credits as very similar to social security benefits as there are important areas where tax credits and benefits perform similar roles. Indeed, the introduction of Universal Credit brings together tax credits and certain means-tested benefits into a single system.

For the reasons mentioned above, it is difficult to give a precise definition of social security, and different people/organisations will prefer different definitions. In this chapter, we take a fairly pragmatic approach, focusing on state systems of income maintenance – largely benefits (administered by the Department for Work and Pensions) and tax credits (administered by HMRC). The role of HMRC will, however, reduce as universal credit is enacted.

The Aims of Social Security

Having defined social security we now ask: what are the aims of the system? The answer is complex. Like elsewhere, the system in the UK has evolved over time and so is not what would be designed if policymakers were now starting from scratch. Furthermore, different parts of the system have different aims, and so it is not possible to identify a single or even main aim. With these reservations in mind, Box 47.1 lists some of the possible objectives of social security.

Within these general aims, the UK social security system has been designed to achieve the following:

- to maintain incentives for self-provision (through earning and saving);

- to keep take-up of benefits high;
- to counter possible fraud; and
- to ensure that administrative costs are low.

The aims of the UK system have traditionally been more limited than those of systems in Europe, if wider than in some parts of the rest of the English-speaking world. The importance of relieving poverty in the UK system explains the considerable reliance on *means-testing*. Receipt of means-tested benefits depends on a person or family having resources (typically income, and often savings) below a certain level in order to receive benefits. Means-testing is also common in America, New Zealand and Australia, but much less common elsewhere, especially in continental Europe where social security tends to be less centralised and more concerned with income maintenance and compensation (see Chapters 65 and 66).

An Overview of the Current System

The social security system today is a highly complex organism, which has evolved over time and which very few people understand in all its detail. For every possible generalisation about the system there are myriad caveats that need to be made. It is therefore difficult to give a brief overview without over-simplifying the system and therefore

---

Box 47.1 Possible Aims of Social Security

- Insuring against the risks of particular events in life, such as retirement, unemployment and sickness.
- Relieving poverty or low income.
- Redistributing resources across people's life-cycles, especially from working age to retirement.
- Redistributing resources from rich to poor.
- 'Compensating' for some types of extra cost (such as children, disability).
- Providing financial support when 'traditional' families break down.

possibly giving misleading information. Nevertheless, this chapter attempts to provide such a brief overview. There are various ways of classifying the different benefits in the UK system. For example, benefits can be categorised into two dichotomies: universal versus means-tested; contributory versus non-contributory. If we use the rules of entitlement as our yardstick, social security can be divided into three main components: contributory benefits (benefits which rely upon having paid contributions); means-tested benefits and tax credits (benefits which depend upon income); and contingent benefits (benefits which depend upon your position or category), as follows:

Contributory benefits

The main root for the current social security system lies in the Beveridge Report published in the early 1940s, although insurance-based and other benefits had been introduced well before this time. At the heart of the Beveridge approach – of contributory benefits or 'social insurance' – is the idea that people face a range of risks that might lead to severe reductions in living standards. These include the risk of unemployment, or being incapacitated and unable to work, or retiring or losing the main income-earner in a family. Some risks are rather uncommon, and relatively unrelated to economic circumstances, such as widowhood. Other risks, such as retirement, are much more widespread and predictable.

The main issues that arise with social insurance include:

- Why should the state provide this service, rather than private insurance? What relationship should there then be between state and private insurance?
- What risks should be covered?
- On what basis should contributions be made, or be deemed to be made?

Entitlement to social insurance benefits is based on having paid National Insurance contributions (which are paid by those in employment and the self-employed, above a low earnings threshold), and being in a risk covered by these benefits (such as unemployment or retirement). These benefits are individualised in that the earnings of a partner do not generally affect entitlement. The main benefit in this group is the State Retirement Pension. Other benefits are the contributory parts of Employment Support Allowance and contribution-based Jobseeker's Allowance (JSA).

Means-tested benefits/Tax Credits

Means-tested benefits generally bring up a person's or household's level of resources if it is deemed insufficient. The entitlement to means-tested depends generally on both income and savings. The four main examples in the UK system are Income Support (and Pension Credit for those older than pension age), Working Tax Credit, Housing Benefit and Council Tax Support. The first of these requires that people are not working more than sixteen hours, the second that they do, and for the other two the work situation does not matter. It is worth noting, however, that several of these (not Pension Credit for older people and Council Tax Support) are merging into the Universal Credit system that is in the process of being rolled out. Box 47.2 sets out some key points about this new system.

The system of benefits based on means-testing, particularly for those on low incomes, is sometimes known as 'social assistance'. In the UK, social assistance is almost synonymous with the benefit Income Support (and its equivalent for older people, Pension Credit), and income-based JSA for unemployed people. These benefits are paid to those whose income and savings are below defined levels, taking into account the size and type of family.

Countries differ a great deal in the extent of this type of provision. In Australia and New Zealand, almost all benefits include an element of 'means-testing' (see also Chapter 5 on social needs, social problems and social welfare). This does not mean that only the poorest may receive benefits – in some instances the aim is to exclude the richest rather than to include only the poorest. Child tax credit plays a similar role in the UK, with most families with children now entitled to it, and Child Benefit is removed from those families with one adult earning above £50,000 per year. In much of northern Europe, social assistance plays a much smaller role, picking up those not covered by the main social insurance system. In addition, they are often administered locally, with local organisations

Box 47.2 Universal Credit (UC)

- Before UC, there was a stark split between out-of-work means-tested benefits such as income support, and certain tax credits paid in-work, with a sharp division at sixteen hours of paid work per week.
- UC brings these together into a single system, removing some anomalies and disincentives to work.
- It is designed to replace JSA, Housing Benefit, Working Tax Credit, Child Tax Credit, Employment & Support Allowance and Income Support.
- It enacts ideas about a 'negative income tax' approach that have existed for decades.
- Associated changes – such as monthly payments and Housing Benefit direct to claimants – have caused particular controversy.

earns more than £50,000 per year. There are, moreover, certain tests of residence that must be satisfied. Disability benefits provide another example, where some elements are purely contingent and reflect neither means nor previous contributions.

It is worth emphasising that this division into three groups is something of a simplification of differences between benefits. Means-tested benefits do not just depend on financial resources; they tend to rely also on some combination of being in a particular situation or a particular family type. For example, able-bodied, single people may claim Income Support only if they meet conditions relating to being unemployed. And it is possible for certain sources of income to affect contributory benefits, for example, JSA and Employment Support Allowance (both contribution-based) can be reduced if a person receives income from a personal or occupational pension.

Alongside benefits for different groups, there are also benefits to help people meet specific extra costs of living. Housing Benefit helps people pay their rent if they are on a low income. The cost of this benefit has increased dramatically in the last three decades because there has been a deliberate policy shift from subsidising 'bricks and mortar' (in terms of low council rents) to subsidising individuals (by raising rents and paying benefit to those on low incomes). While low-paid renters can receive help, those with mortgages are mostly denied assistance with their housing costs. Those on low incomes can also receive help with their council tax.

having some discretion about the precise rules of entitlement.

Additional conditions are often attached to receiving social assistance. People of working age, without sole responsibility for caring for children or disabled adults, must be able to work, available for work and actively seeking work. In past times, they may have had to enter a workhouse to qualify.

Contingent benefits

These are sometimes referred to as categorical benefits or as non-means-tested and non-contributory. Entitlement depends on the existence of certain circumstances (or contingencies) such as having a child (Child Benefit) being disabled (Disability Living Allowance, Personal Independence Payment).

In the UK social security system, some benefits effectively recognise that certain groups of people face extra costs, which the state will share. The clearest example is benefits for dependent children and Child Benefit. There is no test of contributions. However, entitlement is removed where a parent

How Social Security is Delivered

In 2001, the Department of Social Security merged with parts of the Department for Employment and Skills to become the Department for Work and Pensions (DWP). This reinforced an increasing emphasis on 'work as the best form of welfare'. The new department increasingly differentiates those above and below working age, as well as those in paid work and those not. All those claiming benefits who are of working age but not in paid work are given a 'work-first' interview where issues about employment are discussed prior to a claim for financial support being dealt with.

Jobcentre Plus is the agency providing benefit and job-search services, while the service dealing with pensions and older people is the Pension Service. The Disability and Carers Service provides compensation for disabled people and their carers. The Child Maintenance Group within the DWP is responsible for the system of child support. Local authorities remain responsible for Housing Benefit and Council Tax Support.

Benefit Levels, Poverty and Adequacy

In the last twenty-five years, expenditure on benefits has risen. But increasing expenditure on benefits has not generally been fuelled by rises in the real levels of benefit, and indeed there is widespread evidence that benefit levels are not adequate to meet people's basic requirements. Beveridge initially aimed to set benefits at subsistence levels according to budget studies in the 1930s, but there is disagreement about whether he achieved this. Price inflation means that benefit levels have to be raised every year ('uprated') otherwise they are worth less in real terms. There is some evidence that both the initial levels of benefits and the uprating to prices in the 1940s were not set correctly. In more recent years, some benefits have been frozen and others have been linked to price inflation rather than to wage inflation (if it was higher). This means that benefit recipients have become increasingly worse off, relative to workers. Moreover, since the early 1980s more benefits have been brought within the scope of income tax, such as State Retirement Pensions, JSA and Incapacity Benefit, and this has affected the relative generosity of these benefits. The introduction of 'caps' on the amounts of benefit that may be received also restrict the entitlements of some families with large needs (see Chapter 53).

Benefits in Cash and In-Kind

In most cases the aims of social security are achieved by paying cash benefits. However, this need not be the case. Benefits could be provided 'in-kind', either through providing services or with vouchers that may be spent only on certain types of good. In the US, an important method of providing for poor families is through the Food Stamps programme (see Chapter 66). This pays out vouchers that must be exchanged for food. In the UK, receiving Income Support and some other benefits carries with it rights to some services at no charge, such as dental treatment, eye examinations and legal aid ('passported benefits').

The UK system developed along two lines: the national social security system generally provided cash benefits to cover some needs such as the need for food, clothes and money for bills; whereas other needs, particularly the need for social care, were covered by local social services departments that provided in-kind services.

Emerging Issues

The last twenty-five years have seen an increasing emphasis from all governments on individual responsibility rather than state provision. This trend looks set to continue, and the number of sanctions applied to benefit recipients has been on a rising trend. The 2010–15 Coalition government took the bold step of seeking major simplification for those of working age, creating a single benefit (Universal Credit) to subsume many existing benefits, and a Work Programme to replace a variety of welfare-to-work schemes. The Conservative government elected in 2015 is continuing with these policies.

The UK system continues to tread a neo-Liberal path towards minimal state support in favour of income maintenance through the labour market and individual savings. However, this approach appears doomed to fail to eradicate child poverty by 2020, as mandated by the 2010 Child Poverty Act, but which in 2015 was being reviewed for replacement with other measures (see Chapter 58 on children and child poverty).

One key change in the 2015 summer budget was to restrict means-tested benefits (and Universal Credit) to only two children for new claims from 2017. This represents a new and controversial way of limiting spending social security benefits.

Guide to Further Sources

It is best to start with J. Millar (ed.) (2009), *Understanding Social Security*, 2nd edn, Bristol:

Policy Press, an edited collection covering the key benefit groups and general issues in relation to social security. Its focus is the UK and it provides a user-friendly introduction to the main issues. R. Walker (2005), *Social Security and Welfare: Concepts and Comparisons*, Maidenhead: Open University Press, is aimed at those who already have a general understanding of the key issues. It focuses on the objectives and outcomes of social security systems through cross-national comparisons. Another useful introductory textbook (sadly out of print but in many libraries) is S. McKay and K. Rowlingson (1999), *Social Security in Britain* London: Macmillan. J. Hills (2014), *Good Times, Bad Times: The Welfare Myth of Them and Us*, Bristol: Policy Press, looks at the recipients of support of different kinds. N. Timmins (2001), *The Five Giants: A Biography of the Welfare State*, London: HarperCollins, provides more of the historical development.

Those wanting to keep up to date should read the *Journal of Poverty & Social Justice*, details online at: www.policypress.org.uk. The Institute for Fiscal Studies (www.ifs.org.uk) produces timely commentaries on reform from an economic perspective.

Review and Assignment Questions

1 What is the scope of social security?
2 What are the advantages and disadvantages of using means-tested support to alleviate poverty?
3 Is it better to provide people with either vouchers (such as Food Stamps in the US) or cash?
4 Is the wide variety of different benefits justified, or is a move to a 'Universal Credit' to be preferred?
5 Have changes in economic and social conditions rendered obsolete the Beveridge plan for the benefits system.

Visit the book companion site at www.wiley.com/go/alcocksocialpolicy to make use of the resources designed to accompany the textbook. There you will find chapter-specific guides to further resources, including governmental, international, thinktank, pressure groups and relevant journal sources. You will also find a glossary based on *The Blackwell Dictionary of Social Policy*, help sheets, guidance on managing assignments in social policy and career advice.

48

Employment

Adam Whitworth and Eleanor Carter

Overview

- The UK labour market and society have both changed radically in the post-war era, and paid work has become the key route for the satisfaction of citizenship obligations and the central policy instrument to securing resources and avoiding poverty.
- Key issues within the UK employment landscape from a social policy perspective are persistent structural unemployment (especially of the disabled), prevalence of in-work poverty, employment insecurity and underemployment.
- There is little prospect for radically reducing labour market inequalities and precariousness in the near to medium term, but, rather, a likelihood of continued spread and intensification of these trends.
- Since the 1990s, more stringent conditions have been placed on the unemployed in exchange for the receipt of out-of-work benefits. Work-related obligations have been ratcheted up and stretched to include traditionally 'inactive' groups, such as lone parents and disabled people.
- Universal Credit radically extends existing trends in the use of conditionality by extending surveillance and conditions to those in low-paid work for the first time, with significant implications for both the well-being of those in low-paid work and, more broadly, the storying of the 'deserving' and 'undeserving' poor.

The Student's Companion to Social Policy, Fifth Edition. Edited by Pete Alcock, Tina Haux, Margaret May and Sharon Wright.
© 2016 John Wiley & Sons, Ltd. Published 2016 by John Wiley & Sons, Ltd.

The Changing Nature of UK Employment Context: New Opportunities, New Risks

Around sixty years ago the work of T. H. Marshall outlined a model of citizenship in which citizens were said to possess a collection of various civil, political and social rights to welfare to enable them to enjoy a decent, socially acceptable standard of living – to be of 'equal social worth' and to 'live the life of a civilised being according to the standards prevailing in the society'. The reciprocity 'owed' by citizens in return for such rights – as the Blairite Third Way discourse would come to frame it around a half century later – is the obligation of employment. More precisely, Marshall's discussion in the mid-twentieth-century UK context focused on nuclear family structures where the obligation of men was to be in full-time work and where women were assumed to occupy care-giver roles in the household.

Fast-forward sixty years and both the economy and society are largely unrecognisable: expectations and realities around gender roles and family structure have been fundamentally shaken and many more women are in paid employment (see Chapter 57). Simultaneously, Marshall's view of full employment as an unproblematic economic

backdrop faded into a distant dream as structural unemployment – a fundamental long-term mismatch between labour supply and demand – has become the norm: in contrast to the rising post-war trend in female employment in the UK, 76 per cent of working-age men were employed in 2013 compared with 92 per cent in 1971. In terms of the transformation of that citizenship 'contract' – the delicate and ever-changing balance of rights and obligations that citizens owe and enjoy – paid work has become *the* key obligation of citizenship for virtually all adults. The shift from 'male breadwinner' to 'adult worker' model is one that policy-makers have also increasingly enforced via a gradually escalating regime of conditionality and sanctions (with receipt of social security increasingly made conditional on demonstrated willingness to work). The idea of paid work as a *right* of citizenship has faded away. However, paid employment remains an eligibility criteria for a number of social security benefits covering, for example, the risk of unemployment, sickness and maternity (see Chapter 47).

Current concerning features of the UK labour market can be understood as the manifestation of trends to *polarisation and precarity* afoot since the 1980s (see Box 48.1), which have served to

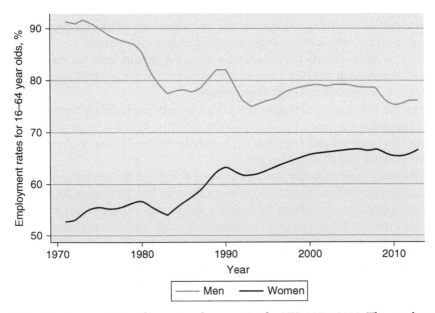

Figure 48.1 Employment rates for men and women in the UK, 1971–2013. The employment rate is the number in employment aged 16–64 as a percentage of all those aged 16–64. Source: ONS.

Box 48.1   Key Trends in the UK Labour Market

Polarisation occurs where the quantity of low- and high-skilled jobs expands, while middle-skilled jobs fall as a share of employment.

Goos and Manning (2003) describe the polarisation of UK employment into 'lovely' and 'lousy' jobs. Since the 1980s, there has been a growth in 'lousy' jobs (typically low-paying roles in the service sector), together with a large expansion of 'lovely' jobs (mainly professional and managerial positions in finance and business services). In parallel there has been a relative decline in mid-skill, mid-pay jobs.

Precarity and *precarious work* refer to employment that is poorly paid, insecure and unprotected. It is frequently associated with part-time or flexi-time employment, temporary and fixed-term work, all of which are linked in the way that they deviate from the 'standard' employment relationship (full-time, salaried, permanent and continuous work with one employer).

To capture this growing trend, Guy Standing (2011) uses the term 'precariat': a fusion of the adjective *precarious* and the noun *proletariat* to describe the growing numbers of people working precariously, moving in and out of a series of short-term, unstable jobs without long-term employment contracts and without stable occupational identities or careers.

fundamentally alter the shape and experience of the UK labour market. The institutions and governance of employment relationships have also altered profoundly. The quarter-century of trade union collapse (the proportion of the workforce in trade unions plummeted from around 55 per cent in 1980 to below 30 per cent in 2007) has reformulated the employer–employee dynamic, with employers now utilising a diverse and highly flexible array of more casualised employment contracts.

These trends give rise to specific concerns and create the terrain for social policy debate and potential policy intervention. Although the lucky few continue to enjoy secure, enjoyable and well-paid jobs (the top 10 per cent of workers in the UK have the same share of income as the entire bottom half of the workforce), significant labour market challenges are pervasive: for some unemployment is the problem; for others it is employment precarity and insecurity that is the concern; for others still, it is pay, hours or conditions that are problematic; whilst for virtually all the intensification of work has simply become the norm.

Employment as a Vehicle for Social Policy Goals: A Tool Fit for Purpose?

Paid work is widely associated with better mental and physical health, with the unemployed suffering negative well-being effects not just through loss of income, but also through the loss of social networks and the sense of purpose, control and identity that being in employment brings. Unemployment levels for certain social groups remains stubbornly high, and chief amongst these in the UK are young people and the disabled. Young adults (those aged 17–24) are nearly three times more likely to be unemployed than the rest of the working age population, yet it is for young adults where scarring effects of unemployment give rise to reduced future employment and earnings. Despite improvements over recent decades, the employment rate of disabled people remains around 30 percentage points below that of non-disabled people (46 per cent compared with 76 per cent), and over 2 million disabled adults continue to claim out-of-work benefits, a figure that has been stable at these levels for around twenty years (see Chapters 59 and 61).

At the same time, the well-being gains from paid work are known to vary according to the characteristics and quality of employment, as well as according to whether that employment is chosen voluntarily or instead mandated by employment activation programmes for the unemployed. If the full benefits of paid work are to be realised, particularly for those in weaker labour market positions, three key employment dimensions stand out as the locus for social policy interventions.

The first and most obvious dimension is pay. Just as paid work has moved to centre stage as the defining 'legitimate' activity in terms of citizenship

Box 48.2 National Minimum Wage: A Policy to 'Make Work Pay'?

The national minimum wage (NMW) is the minimum pay per hour almost all workers in the UK are entitled to by law. The minimum wage covers around one in ten workers, and in 2015 the adult rate (for over 20 s) was £6.70. The NMW was introduced in 1999 by the Labour government with the policy intention of 'making work pay' and narrowing the gap in wage inequality.

Importantly, the NMW (despite its rebadging as the 'National Living Wage' in the July 2015 Budget) remains wholly distinct from the 'living wage' understood by campaigners and academics, which looks in detail at the minimum income required for a range of household types to reach a minimum acceptable standard of living.

obligations, employment has also become the central poverty alleviation instrument across the UK political spectrum. However, this employment-centred poverty alleviation strategy presents serious – and seemingly growing – problems in the UK labour market context. In contrast to Marshall's mid-twentieth century account, the relationship between fulfilled obligations and adequate resources for socially 'normal' consumption and activities has over subsequent decades become stretched to the point of rupture. Talk of the 'squeezed middle' abounds, and towards the lower rungs of the employment ladder work long since ceased to deliver a life beyond poverty: one in six working adults are poor in the UK today, and around half of poor workers are doing forty or more hours of paid work per week despite the introduction of the National Minimum Wage (see Box 48.2).

A second dimension is *under-employment* – a situation of suboptimal employment as far as the individual is concerned and a reflection of a misallocation and under-utilisation of human resources. Under-employment is most commonly discussed in terms of workers being unable to secure as many hours of employment as they would like, but can be understood alternatively as workers not being able to make effective use of their skills at work, as being underpaid for their work, or as being under-stimulated, under-challenged or unable to progress their careers satisfactorily.

Around 3 million workers in the UK today can be described as under-employed on the basis of not having as many employment hours as they would like and this is a problem on the march, estimated to have increased by 1 million people between 2008 and 2012. The percentage of workers who have taken part-time jobs only because they were unable to find suitable full-time jobs

doubled from 10 per cent to 20 per cent over the same period, whilst the percentage of workers accepting a temporary job because they could not find a permanent one increased from 43 per cent in 2008 to a peak of almost 60 per cent in 2011. And whilst university fees rise, young graduates are increasingly likely to find work only in non-graduate roles.

A third dimension of concern relates to *employment insecurity and precarity*. Low paid, relatively insecure work has increasingly become a feature of the UK economy. The dichotomy between the 'deserving' and 'undeserving' poor is a long-standing one within British social policy, and recent UK governments of all political persuasions have worked hard to narrate discourses of the unemployed as 'undeserving scroungers' out of work due to their own behavioural limitations. Evidence consistently refutes notions of deviant moralities or cultures of worklessness amongst the unemployed, yet these narratives remain powerful in seeking to drive a clear wedge between those employed ('deserving') and those unemployed ('undeserving). From a policy perspective, however, the attempted construction of this strict binary unhelpfully conceals the significant problem of precarity within the labour market. In reality, the boundary between these two groups is a porous and dynamic one, particularly at the lower end of the labour market, with considerable movement over time into, and out of, work (and often back again). Around 70 per cent of new starts on Jobseeker's Allowance are repeat claims made by those who have left the benefit previously for employment, but who have subsequently fallen out of work. For the most part, the employed are not so different from the unemployed, especially amongst lower paid and less secure workers.

Poor quality work continues to undergo rapid change in the UK as it grows in relative size, spreads across the occupational spectrum and continues to intensify in its contractual casualisation. Zero hours contracts – just one manifestation of a much wider range of flexibilised employment contracts – have become normalised as employers seek to deliver maximum flexibility to themselves and minimal commitment to their employees. Between 2008 and 2014, total employment in the UK rose by around 900,000, of whom around 400,000 were employed on zero hours contracts. Given how quickly such hyper-flexibilised employment contracts are spreading throughout the UK it is clear why the issue has climbed towards the top of the political agenda.

Employment and Social Policy: Adding Ethical Considerations to Headline Economic Figures

Although aggregate economic statistics around GDP and jobs growth are important, even the most ardent neo-Liberals would agree that on their own they are inadequate as a measure of societal development. Stuart White's evaluative framework of 'fair reciprocity' raises important questions for the ethical acceptability of contemporary citizenship contracts which place paid work as the core duty and singular route to citizenship. Focusing on the 'reciprocity' of this contractualised relationship between citizens and state, the two-sided dynamic becomes central to evaluating the respective balance of rights/obligations. This raises important questions for the configuration of the work/welfare policy nexus:

1   Defining 'productive' contributions?
    Should a broader range of 'productive activities' be considered legitimate tasks for the satisfaction of one's citizenship obligations? Should citizens have a reasonable degree of input into the definition of those activities? For example, should unpaid care or voluntary work 'count' towards the satisfaction of one's citizenship obligations?
2   Achieving adequate resources in return?
    Should individuals receive a fair share of the social and economic product in return for fulfilling their citizenship obligations? Ought

those in low-paid work be able to escape poverty as a result of their efforts? Can we justly mandate the unemployed to work in jobs offering no escape from poverty?
3   Demanding obligations from all?
    Should *all* citizens be required to fulfil their citizenship obligations? Is it ethically acceptable for the 'idle rich' to live off capital or inheritance income?

The extent to which one wishes to elevate or dismiss such concerns naturally depends on the vision of social policy that one holds in terms of its underlying ideology, aims and objective. What is clear though is that the UK is a long way from satisfying such ethical conditions.

Policy Possibilities: Employment as Social Policy?

From a social policy perspective – where one is concerned not just with headline employment statistics, but more deeply with some consideration of the well being of individuals, families and communities – these multi-dimensional, and seemingly growing, ruptures between work and well-being represent a key problematic of the nature of the modern UK employment context.

The economic and political orthodoxy across recent decades presents *aggregate* macro-economic health as primate, with economic growth and job creation most commonly chased as a priority. Under an alternate framing, where social policy outcomes (for example, poverty, well-being, needs satisfaction) are priorities rather than economic goals, should economic policy instead become the servant of those social policy objectives, legitimising potentially quite radical interventions in the labour market on those grounds? If the latter, policies such as the creation of Living Wages and the regulation of contracts (banning or regulating zero hours contracts, for example) become a legitimate part of the social policy toolkit, otherwise not. In the late 1990s, the then Labour government under Tony Blair made some significant reforms to seek to improve people's experiences of, and rewards from, paid work: the creation of the National Minimum Wage and National Childcare Strategy; the commitment to eradicate child poverty; and the enhancement of in-work tax credits (and linked child-care subsidies) to better reward low-paid work. At the same time, all these progressive reforms can be understood to mediate and mitigate market outcomes rather than to fundamentally alter the nature of employment and the labour market.

If we consider the recent and likely future UK policy trajectory, then there is little sign of fundamental reform. Indeed, if anything the trends of polarisation and precarity seem to be continuing apace. The UK's weak employment legislation, weak union power, unemployment benefits with low financial values and strong conditionality requirements, and extensive opportunities for employment at relatively low wages are still held up by many as a positive example of how to develop and manage a highly flexible labour market. Over the last fifteen years, the momentum behind Labour's (themselves limited) reforms has gradually been lost, cut short or diluted. The value of child-care subsidies for the low paid has been cut as part of the Coalition's austerity measures and the real value of the National Minimum Wage has been eroded since 2008 as it has not kept pace with inflation. The Conservative government announced the new 'national living wage' in the July 2015 Budget, but this new emphasis on improved employment conditions is something of a red-herring given that the announced 'national living wage' is tied to no empirical assessment of how much is actually needed in order to live acceptably and was announced at the same time as severe cuts to in-work tax credits that for many households outweigh any gains made via the introduction of a 'national living wage'. The precarious and potentially exploitative nature of zero hours contracts also appears unlikely to be tackled in the medium term, with Conservative ministers increasingly describing these contractual forms as beneficial, flexible working arrangements for employees.

Emerging Issues

Looking at policies pursued by the UK Coalition government (2010–2015), Universal Credit (UC) – the flagship integration of out-of-work and in-work benefits and tax credits – emerges as perhaps the most telling signal of where the future lies (see also Chapter 47). This policy is continuing in its slow roll-out under the Conservative administration, but would likely have been maintained regardless of the outcome of the 2015 election. Cross-party support for the principle of simplifying and rationalising working age benefits means that criticism has been limited to technical and implementation concerns, with very limited critique of UC's more radical implications. Commitment to actively seek work has long been a condition for the receipt of unemployment benefits, and since the turn of the century this conditionality has gradually expanded in reach and depth to bring in more workless individuals (for example, disabled individuals and single parents); to demand more (a ratcheting up from mandatory work-focused interviews to mandatory job search to mandatory unpaid work placements); and to enforce these heightened demands with an increasingly severe sanctions regime.

Taking this 'creeping conditionality' to qualitatively new heights, however, UC for the first time extends the reach of conditionality to those *in work* as well as those out of work, mandating more employment hours and/or more pay for individuals inside working households in receipt of UC where the household is failing to earn beyond a set threshold (based around full-time employment at National Minimum Wage). Where decent work in Marshall's world was taken as the marker of citizenship obligations fulfilled, now even low-paid, poverty-inducing employment is no longer enough. For those struggling to get by in low-paid, insecure work, the message in the new world of UC is clear: policy is less inclined to seek to deliver a qualitative improvement in work prospects, pay or conditions, and it is at the door of workers and the unemployed where responsibility for improvement must lie. One of the frustrations of social policy analysts, but one of the enduring attractions of social policy, is that policy debates rest on ideologies, beliefs and gut feelings as well as on facts. The question to be answered, then, is this: is it the low-paid, insecure worker, the UK labour market or the UK's long-standing supply-side approach to welfare-to-work policy that is shirking?

Guide to Further Sources

On the citizenship debates, see T. H. Marshall and T. Bottomore (1992), *Citizenship and Social Class*, London: Pluto Press. On fair reciprocity, see

S. White and G. Cooke (2007), 'Taking responsibility: a fair welfare contract', in J. Bennett and G. Cooke (eds), *It's All About You: Citizen-centred Welfare*, London: IPPR.

On work and well-being, see G. Waddell and A. Burton (2006), *Is Work Good for Your Health and Well-being?*, London: Stationery Office; and P. Dolan, T. Peasgood and M. White (2008), 'Do we really know what makes us happy? A review of the economic literature on the factors associated with subjective wellbeing', *Journal of Economic Psychology*, 29, 94–122

On the impact on employment of the 2008 crisis and subsequent economic slowdown, see S. McKay and R. Smith (2014), 'The labour market before and after the recession', in *In Defence of Welfare II*, Social Policy Association.

On the storying of the unemployed, see J. Wiggan (2012), 'Telling stories of 21st century welfare: the UK Coalition government and the neo-liberal discourse of worklessness and dependency', *Critical Social Policy*, 32:3, 383–405; and T. Slater (2012), 'The myth of 'Broken Britain': welfare reform and the production of ignorance', *Antipode*, 46:4, 948–69.

On 'creeping conditionality', see P. Dwyer (2004), 'Creeping conditionality in the UK: from welfare rights to conditional entitlements?', *Canadian Journal of Sociology*, 29:2, 265–87; and A. Whitworth and J. Griggs (2013), 'Lone parents and welfare-to-work conditionality: necessary, just effective?', *Ethics and Social Welfare*, 7:2, 124–40. On Universal Credit specifically, see H. Dean (2012), 'The ethical deficit of the United Kingdom's proposed universal credit: pimping the precariat?' *Political Quarterly*, 83:2, 353–9.

On polarisation of the labour market, see M. Goos and A. Manning (2003), *Lousy and Lovely Jobs: The Rising Polarization of Work in Britain*, available at: eprints.lse.ac.uk/20002/1/Lousy_and_Lovely_Jobs_the_Rising_Polarization_of_Work_in_Britain.pdf.

On precarious work and the precariat, see G. Standing (2011), *The Precariat: The New Dangerous Class*, London: Bloomsbury.

Review and Assignment Questions

1 What have been the biggest changes to the nature of employment in the UK over the postwar period and what has caused these changes?

2 Should we seek to reshape job search requirements of the unemployed around the conditions of 'fair reciprocity'?

3 What policy interventions could be taken to improve the nature of employment in the UK?

4 Is it acceptable that people can work full-time and still be poor?

5 What are the key challenges regarding employment in the UK and what policy interventions could be implemented to respond to those challenges?

Visit the book companion site at www.wiley.com/go/alcocksocialpolicy to make use of the resources designed to accompany the textbook. There you will find chapter-specific guides to further resources, including governmental, international, thinktank, pressure groups and relevant journal sources. You will also find a glossary based on *The Blackwell Dictionary of Social Policy*, help sheets, guidance on managing assignments in social policy and career advice.

49

Healthcare

Rob Baggott

Overview

- Healthcare issues are prominent in most industrialised states. Healthcare takes up a large proportion of the taxpayer's money and attracts considerable media attention.
- The medical profession remains a powerful influence within the healthcare system, although the perspectives of patients, users and carers are increasingly acknowledged.
- Three main models of healthcare funding exist: tax-based, state insurance and private funding. The UK is largely a tax-based system. Large sums of money have been committed to the NHS in recent years, but financial problems and inequities in funding remain.
- There is increasing competition in health service provision with efforts to encourage the private and voluntary sector into the NHS 'market'.
- Renewed efforts have been made to encourage partnership working between the NHS, local government, voluntary groups and the private sector.

The Importance of Health and Healthcare

In modern societies, the state accepts much responsibility for the health of its citizens. This is reflected in the high level of public expenditure on health services in most industrialised countries. The state also takes steps to protect and promote the health of the public and prevent disease (see Chapter 50). Healthcare is not like most other goods and services. Supply tends to create demand. Hence, a technological

The Student's Companion to Social Policy, Fifth Edition. Edited by Pete Alcock, Tina Haux, Margaret May and Sharon Wright.

breakthrough – for example, a new breast cancer drug – generates demand from people who believe it will save their lives, even if this turns out to be misplaced. Moreover, people lack the specialised, technical knowledge needed to purchase health care appropriately. Furthermore, a healthcare market based on private purchasing power tends to discriminate against the very people that need treatment. Poorer people, people with disabilities, children and older people have the greatest health needs, but are the least able to afford private insurance or pay directly for care services.

In most industrialised societies, it is believed that healthcare is a promoter of social solidarity and citizenship, and should be regarded as a basic human right rather than a commodity. Although economic and social inequalities are tolerated, there is a strong feeling that good health should be available to all and that people's health should not be determined by their socio-economic circumstances or where they live.

At the time of writing, the annual UK NHS budget is over £130 billion a year and it employs 1.6 million people. The NHS is the fifth largest employer in the world (after Wal-Mart, McDonalds, the Chinese People's Liberation Army and Indian Railways). Health issues often attract media attention and are the subject of single-issue pressure group campaigns. Moreover, the policy arena is inhabited by powerful interest groups, such as the medical profession and healthcare businesses (for example, the drugs industry), which are highly skilled in influencing the political agenda. In addition, health issues are a major concern for voters and an important focus for party political debates.

What is Healthcare?

Healthcare is often divided into primary, secondary and tertiary care. Primary care is usually the first point of contact with health services and includes the care provided by GPs and other professionals in practices, clinics and community settings. Secondary care refers to the range of acute and specialist services provided by hospitals. Highly specialised services – known as tertiary services – deal with very complex and advanced conditions.

A further term, community healthcare, is used to cover a range of services provided in people's homes, local clinics and communities. It includes district nursing, health visitors, rehabilitation services and specialist services for managing long-term conditions (such as diabetes). Healthcare is increasingly provided in community settings and this is expected to grow further in the future.

Healthcare is often defined by the boundaries of professional work. The health professions, particularly the medical profession, are traditionally very powerful and have shaped services to reflect their own expertise and interests. As a result, services have developed in a paternalistic way. However, there are countervailing forces. A substantial amount of care is provided by informal carers, of which there are around 7 million in Britain. People also engage in self-help and self-medication (for example, buying medicines over-the-counter) and chronically ill people with long-term conditions increasingly self-manage their illnesses. Indeed, people with conditions such as asthma, arthritis and diabetes are increasingly acknowledged as 'expert patients', managing their health in partnership with professionals. Some patients are allocated individual budgets, initially for social care and now extending to healthcare. More generally, there is a greater emphasis nowadays on the perspectives and preferences of patients, users and carers. Successive governments have created local bodies to represent and articulate the views of patients, carers and the wider public. The latest embodiment of this is local healthwatch (overseen by a national body, Healthwatch England), established by the UK Coalition government (2010–15). Nonetheless, professions remain powerful both in individual clinical encounters and within the healthcare system. They can exert influence in many ways, including through control of information, shaping values and ideas about health and health care, and by directly influencing on health policymakers.

Funding Health Services

The amount of funding needed for future health services is obviously going to be be affected by the underlying health of the population. The level of lifestyle-related disease (see Chapter 50) is therefore of great concern. The growing elderly population is also likely to increase pressures on health budgets. The percentage of people aged over 65 is set to rise from under a fifth to almost a quarter of the population between 2010 and 2035. The population aged over 85 is expected to rise from 2 per cent to 5 per cent of the population in the same period. However, no one knows by how much spending will have to rise to meet additional demands. It is possible that tomorrow's elderly population may be fitter and healthier than previous generations, and will not need as much healthcare. Nonetheless, it is likely that additional social care and support will be needed as more people survive to a much older age. Another factor is new technology. Although this is likely to increase costs in the short term, new techniques can deliver greater cost-effectiveness in the long run. For example, endoscopy and 'keyhole surgery' have facilitated significant growth of day surgery, helping to reduce the cost of lengthy stays in hospital. Technologies to assist people with daily tasks and to monitor health remotely may also save money by enabling people with severe illness and disability to live independently in their homes.

In the 2000s, the Labour governments of Blair and Brown (1997–2010) granted large funding increases to the NHS. From being one of the cheapest healthcare systems in the industrialised world, the UK now spends just below the average for comparable countries (NHS plus private spending on healthcare has been around 9 per cent of GDP in recent years). The UK Coalition government ushered in an era of public sector austerity, while committing to above-inflation increases to the NHS. However, these increases have been very small and insufficient to meet increased demand. At the time of writing, NHS finances are in a poor state, with many NHS service providers in financial difficulty. It has been predicted that a £30 billion gap in the NHS budget could exist by 2021 (NHS England, 2013).

The UK Coalition government sought to reduce the gap between demand and resources by pay freezes, efficiency savings and promising some additional funds. The Labour Party joined the Conservative and Liberal parties in pledging

Box 49.1 Models of Healthcare Funding

There are three main models: tax-based, state insurance systems and private spending (including private insurance). In practice, systems draw on more than one source. The UK falls mainly in the first category, though a minority of the population – just over a tenth – have private health insurance. There are also co-payments – in the form of prescription charges, for example. Moreover, many people choose to pay directly for healthcare (such as alternative therapies, over-the-counter prescriptions and, in some cases, hospital treatment). Additional healthcare funding comes from charitable sources.

increases in funding. But the continuing shortage of funds has led some to consider other models of funding (see Box 49.1) and alternative sources of income for the NHS and care services (see Commission on the Future of Health and Social Care, 2014).

The allocation of funding within the NHS is also an important issue. Historically, budgets were allocated to health authorities on the basis of previous allocations adjusted for inflation. Following criticism that this did not reflect variations in health needs across the country, a formula was devised to set targets for fair funding of health services. This approach has since been revised on several occasions to link funding more closely to needs. Even so, considerable inequalities remain in access to treatment between different local areas and between different socio-economic groups. Notably, under the Health and Social Care Act 2012 (hereafter HSCA), the Secretary of State for Health and NHS bodies have a duty to reduce inequalities in health services.

There is also a persistent problem of unmet needs. Cases of people unable to access drugs and other treatments, often new and expensive therapies, are common in the media. However, such cases are not unique to the UK, or to tax-based healthcare systems. All healthcare systems have to prioritise and restrict treatments within the context of budgetary pressures.

Box 49.2 The NHS in Scotland, Wales and Northern Ireland

For many years, the NHS has been organised differently in Scotland, Wales and Northern Ireland. For example, Northern Ireland established integrated health and social care boards in the 1970s. Devolution encouraged further diversity. For example, all UK countries except England ended prescription charges. Scotland and Wales abolished local NHS trusts, bringing services under unified health boards. Scotland introduced free long-term personal care for elderly people. Important variations in how health services are managed and regulated are evident between the countries of the UK, and different performance management measures have been adopted. There has also been much less support outside England for extending private healthcare provision and increasing competition for NHS services.

Organisation, Planning and Commissioning

As noted in Box 49.2, there are important differences in NHS organisation and health policy across the different countries of the UK. The remainder of this chapter focuses on England, where regular reorganisations have been undertaken (Baggott, 2005; 2015). The current structure, following the UK Coalition government's Health and Social Care Act (HSCA) 2012, is described below.

The Secretary of State for Health, as the political head of the Department of Health, is accountable to Parliament for health policy and the NHS in England (and for UK-wide health matters). The Secretary of State has broad duties to promote a comprehensive health service designed to improve the physical and mental health of the people and to prevent, diagnose and treat illness, as well as specific duties (such as the inequalities duty already mentioned). The Secretary of State issues a Mandate setting out the key priorities for the NHS, and (subject to agreement with the Treasury) sets an overall budget. The Mandate is implemented by a separate body, NHS England, which oversees the commissioning of services, allocates resources to local commissioning bodies (Clinical Commissioning Groups (CCGs)), and directly commissions some services itself (such as specialised treatments, some public health services and primary care services). The CCGs, led by GPs and other clinicians and including lay members, are responsible for commissioning secondary hospital care, emergency and urgent care, mental health services and community health services for their local populations. These services are provided by a range of NHS trusts and Foundation Trusts (discussed further below) as well as by the independent sector (that is, the private 'for profit' sector and voluntary organisations).

Recent governments encouraged independent sector provision of NHS-funded services. The previous Labour government under Tony Blair established new independent sector treatment centres to deliver non-urgent surgical care on behalf of the NHS. It also allowed the independent sector to compete for other NHS clinical and support services. Commercial interests became heavily engaged in capital projects through the Private Finance Initiative, which involves building hospitals and running support services under long-term contracts (other similar schemes exist for primary care). The independent sector also secured contracts to provide primary care services, including 'out of hours' GP services. The private and voluntary health sectors were stimulated by measures to allow patients to choose where they would be treated, including independent as well as NHS providers. These policies were extended by the UK Coalition government. The HSCA gave the independent sector more opportunities to compete for NHS services. It explicitly creates an NHS provider market with competition rules enforced by regulatory bodies (including Monitor, the foundation trust regulatory body; see below).

In recent decades, the NHS in England has become more subject to market forces and competition. The Thatcher and Major governments presided over the introduction of an internal market in the NHS. This involved the identification of commissioners (GP fund-holders and health authorities) and providers (trusts) who would agree contracts to deliver healthcare. The Blair government abolished this market, but retained the division between service commissioners and providers. It later introduced Payment by Results (PbR), a system that remunerated service providers for volume of treatment provided. The UK Coalition extended this further by widening the scope for PbR and giving GPs a major role in commissioning services via CCGs.

Management and Regulation

Successive governments have sought to strengthen NHS management. This has taken the form of stronger line management, including tougher performance targets (such as reducing waiting times and reducing hospital infection rates) and 'top-down' performance assessment systems. The UK Coalition initially sought to reduce performance targets, abolishing some and downgrading others. However, it later reinstated some (such as hospital waiting time targets).

There have also been important reforms to NHS providers. In 2003, the Blair government created foundation trusts. Although remaining part of the NHS, these were promised greater autonomy in financial matters, and in organisation and management. They were also expected to involve local people and patients, and be more accountable to them. However, the local accountability of foundation trusts has been less than expected. Few people actually participate in foundation trust decisions, and senior managers and clinicians retain significant power. The autonomy of foundation trusts is also constrained. They are regulated by a national body (known as Monitor), which sets the terms on which they are established and can intervene if they fail to comply. They must also meet NHS standards as well as some national agreements (such as those on pay and conditions). The UK Coalition government sought to make all NHS trusts convert to foundation status. However, at the time of writing, a substantial proportion have not achieved this status and many of these are unlikely to ever become foundation trusts. Notably, the UK Coalition also increased the proportion of revenue that foundation trusts could generate from private sources (to 49 per cent), which led to fears about their future dependence on private income.

Despite the rhetoric about decentralising health services and giving more autonomy to local NHS bodies, there has been much centralisation.

Labour created a host of new national regulatory bodies. A key focus for these bodies was the improvement of quality and safety. They include the Care Quality Commission, responsible for monitoring, inspecting and regulating health and care services in order to ensure that they meet fundamental standards of quality and safety. Another important body is the National Institute for Health and Care Excellence (known as NICE), which provides guidance to the NHS in England and Wales on the cost-effectiveness of interventions in public health, healthcare and social care and develops quality standards and performance measures for these services.

The UK Coalition maintained a focus on improving the quality and safety of health and care services, galvanised by a series of high-profile service failures. In particular, the Francis Public Inquiry into Mid-Staffordshire NHS Trust revealed poor quality of care and maltreatment, a lack of care and compassion, weak leadership and governance, and an overwhelming focus on financial matters rather than care. The inquiry's recommendations aimed to make the NHS put care and compassion first, while strengthening leadership on quality and safety, and making it a more open and accountable organisation. The government responded with a raft of measures, including new statutory requirements forcing NHS organisations to be open about clinical mistakes, new criminal offences and penalties (for example, for wilfully neglecting or ill-treating patients), new fundamental standards of care, and a tougher system for inspecting and monitoring the quality of health and care services.

Partnerships

Effective healthcare depends heavily on other services, such as social care and housing. However, the relationship between the NHS and the providers of other care and health-related services has often been inadequate. This has arisen from poor systems of coordination and financial, organisational and cultural differences between the NHS and local government (and others, such as the voluntary and private sectors).

Many efforts have been made to address this problem, including joint planning and financial arrangements. Labour aimed to strengthen the statutory basis for cooperation between NHS and local authorities, including pooled budget arrangements between the NHS and local councils. A small number of areas experimented with care trusts, formal mergers of health and social care bodies. Other efforts included the formation of partnership bodies, joint appointments and the creation of integrated teams of staff drawn from the NHS and local authorities, closer working arrangements with the independent sector, and integrated planning and performance assessment systems.

If anything, the issue of integrating public health, healthcare and social care has become even more pressing in recent years. The UK Coalition introduced the Better Care Fund, a pooled budget for each local area (see Chapter 54). It also created new joint boards at local level, Health and Well-being Boards, with a range of responsibilities, including integration. The direction of travel appears to be to forge a much closer relationship between the NHS and local government (which now has additional responsibilities for public health; see Chapter 50) combined with greater devolution to the local level.

Emerging Issues

In 2015, the UK Coalition was replaced by a Conservative government with a small working majority. Despite its commitments to increase NHS spending in real terms by 2020 (by £8 billion), there are fears that this government will move towards a more market-oriented system of healthcare, with more private sector provision of services. For the moment, however, there is much continuity in NHS policy. So far, the Conservative government has redoubled efforts to extend '24/7' access to NHS services, proposed additional steps to improve efficiency and reduce costs, and announced some minor changes to regulatory and performance assessment systems.

The NHS, like other healthcare systems, is facing several key challenges, which will continue to shape the agenda, irrespective of which parties are in government.

First, to satisfy demands for health services while controlling costs, the NHS will continue to be under pressure. The focus on improving efficiency will continue. There will also be an even greater imperative to fund only interventions of proven effectiveness, and to restrict treatment to those who can benefit most.

Second, to respond more effectively to the preferences and views of users, carers and the wider public, it is acknowledged that health services should no longer be delivered in a paternalistic way. Indeed, people have a major contribution to make to the effective and efficient delivery of services by using them responsibly, taking some responsibility for their own health, and raising issues about quality and standards of services. However, as not all people have the same capacity and resources to exercise their preferences and make their views known, steps must be taken to ensure that efforts to involve people do not lead to greater inequalities.

Third, the modern health service (and the wider health and care system) includes many different organisations, public and private. The potential for fragmentation must be avoided. In particular, a more integrated system of health and care is needed, with a greater emphasis on prevention. Furthermore, it is particularly important that where commercial organisations are involved in providing services, they do not undermine the fundamental ethos of the health and care system.

Guide to Further Reading

For a general overview of post-war health policy, see R. Baggott (2005), *Health and Health Care in Britain*, Basingstoke: Palgrave. R. Baggott (2015), *Understanding Health Policy*, Bristol: Policy Press, analyses NHS policies and processes. The Francis Report (2013), *The Report of the Mid Staffordshire NHS Foundation Trust Public Inquiry*, London: Stationery Office, highlights the serious failings of the trust and the wider problems of the NHS, and makes key recommendations. The Commission on the Future of Health and Social Care in England (Barker Commission) (2014), *A New Settlement for Health and Social Care – Final Report*, London: King's Fund, explores future options for funding the health and social care system. NHS England (2013), *The NHS Belongs to the People: A Call to Action*, London, NHS England, and NHS England (2014), *Five Year Forward View*, London,

NHS England, set out the key challenges for the NHS and future plans.

Review and Assignment Questions

1 Why is healthcare a prominent political issue?
2 Why is it important for government to ensure equitable access to healthcare?
3 Should we spend more on healthcare? If so, how should these extra resources be generated?
4 Why are partnerships important in health and social care?

5 Does an increasing role for the independent sector in providing services funded by the NHS strengthen or weaken the NHS?

Visit the book companion site at www.wiley.com/go/alcocksocialpolicy to make use of the resources designed to accompany the textbook. There you will find chapter-specific guides to further resources, including governmental, international, thinktank, pressure groups and relevant journal sources. You will also find a glossary based on *The Blackwell Dictionary of Social Policy*, help sheets, guidance on managing assignments in social policy and career advice.

50

Public Health

Rob Baggott

Overview

- Public health has always been an important issue, but has lacked priority compared with treatment services.
- Key issues today include obesity, smoking, alcohol misuse and health inequalities.
- New Labour sought to prioritise public health and reduce health inequalities; although some targets were met, others were missed.
- The Coalition reformed the public health system in England, transferring responsibilities to local government, establishing health and well-being boards, and joint health and well-being strategies.
- Coalition policies and reforms faced criticism for not giving sufficient capacity and resources to the public health system, for being over-reliant on corporate responsibility, and failing to address the socio-economic roots of ill health.

What is Public Health?

According to Sir Donald Acheson, a former UK chief medical officer, public health is 'the science and art of preventing disease, prolonging life and promoting health through the organised efforts of society' (cited in Baggott, 2011: 4). Public health involves three areas of activity. *Health improvement*

(such as getting people to stop smoking cigarettes); *health protection* (for example, from infectious diseases like tuberculosis); and *health services* (to diagnose illness at an early stage and provide appropriate and timely treatment). The essence of public health, however, is that it involves more than the provision of good-quality treatment services. It is about preventing health problems before they manifest

The Student's Companion to Social Policy, Fifth Edition. Edited by Pete Alcock, Tina Haux, Margaret May and Sharon Wright.
© 2016 John Wiley & Sons, Ltd. Published 2016 by John Wiley & Sons, Ltd.

Box 50.1   Major Public Health Issues Today

Among the main public health issues facing the UK today are:

Obesity: an estimated 70,000 premature deaths in the UK are attributed to diet. Sixty-eight per cent of adult men and 57 per cent of women are overweight or obese. Over a quarter of children are also overweight or obese.

Smoking: over 100,000 premature deaths in the UK are associated with smoking tobacco. Over half a million hospital admissions are attributable to smoking in England and Wales alone.

Alcohol abuse: in the UK, alcohol is the leading preventable risk factor for death in the 15–49 age group. Alcohol abuse is the main cause of 326,000 hospital admissions a year in England alone. Nine million adults in England drink at levels detrimental to their health and 1.6 million are alcohol-dependent.

Health inequalities: health inequalities are a problem across the UK. For example, people living in deprived areas in England can expect to live seven years less than those from affluent areas. People in poorer areas also have fewer years of healthy life – around seventeen years less than those living in wealthier areas.

It should be noted that the UK is not alone in facing health problems related to lifestyles and social conditions. For example, tobacco is responsible for 6 million deaths every year worldwide. The UK has a comparatively better record in some areas (for example, smoking reduction), but does worse in others (for example, obesity).

(Sources: Marmot Review (2010); Public Health England (2014); Murray et al. (2013); BMA Smoking Statistics (bma.org.uk, last accessed 3 June 2015).)

themselves, and doing so by collective action, involving government, the voluntary and private sectors, communities and the public itself. Public health is all about 'focusing upstream', finding out what is causing health problems and intervening at the earliest possible opportunity. It reflects that well-known adage that prevention is better than cure. Box 50.1 contains some of the key public health issues affecting the UK today.

Why is Public Health Important?

Public health interventions are important because they address the causes of ill health. They can help to secure good health as a right, and promote the health of the whole community. As noted, health services are important to public health. But though the creation of a comprehensive, universal and largely free National Health Service (NHS) was a major public health advance, the NHS has been criticised for being primarily a sickness service. Since the 1970s, the growing importance of chronic and long-term illness (linked to lifestyles, the environment and socio-economic factors), coupled with the rising cost of health services,

led policymakers to take a greater interest in disease prevention and health improvement.

As will become clear, recent governments have identified prevention and health improvement as priorities. However, efforts in this direction have been limited in practice by several factors. First, governments fear unpopularity when making decisions about public health. Although occasionally some governments have been courageous, in general they are keen to avoid being labelled as the 'nanny state'. Second, the political forces in favour of public health interventions have been relatively weak compared with those that profit from ill health. Many of the main risk factors for disease today – obesity, alcohol and tobacco-related disease, for example – arise in part from profitable activities of large multinational corporations, who are skilled political operators. Third, there is a very strong institutional bias in favour of treatment services, which take the lion's share of health budgets. Fourth, orchestrating action on public health issues is usually far more complex than organising treatment services. This is because public health problems are often multifaceted and arise from a range of factors. Therefore, their resolution tends to involve a range of agencies. But

Box 50.2 Organisations that Might be Involved in a Local Alcohol Prevention Strategy

- police and criminal justice organisations;
- fire and rescue services;
- ambulance service;
- clinical commissioning groups;
- NHS primary care services;
- NHS mental health services;
- A&E departments;
- alcohol treatment services;
- universities, schools and colleges;
- probation services;
- social services;
- voluntary organisations;
- alcohol counselling services;
- local alcohol businesses (for example, supermarkets, off licences, pub, club and bar owners, other outlets selling alcohol, such as restaurants, and any local producers of alcohol);
- housing services;
- public health department;
- licensing department;
- mayor/cabinet/councillors.

these organisations often have different values, priorities, structures and processes. This impedes the high level of partnership working and coordination needed to respond to complex public health problems (Baggott, 2013). Box 50.2 illustrates the wide range of organisations that may be involved in a local alcohol misuse strategy, for example.

Public Health Systems in the UK

Scotland, Wales and Northern Ireland have their own distinct administrative structures for public health (see Baggott, 2013). Following devolution, they have also enjoyed greater freedom to set their own public health priorities. For example, Scotland introduced a smoking ban earlier than the rest of the UK and was the first to seek to introduce a minimum price for alcohol products (to discourage excessive consumption). Wales has

often been in the forefront of public health initiatives, and was the first part of the UK to develop its own national health promotion strategy. Public health has also been important in Northern Ireland, where successive health strategies have tried to tackle to socio-economic roots of ill health. The remainder of this chapter, however, focuses on recent public health policies in England.

Previous Labour Government and Public Health

The Labour governments of 1997–2010 stated that they wanted to prioritise public health and reduce health inequalities. A new post of Minister for Public Health was created. New public health agencies were established, including the Food Standards Agency and the Health Protection Agency. Two public health White Papers were published (in 1999 and 2004). In addition, strategic documents were produced on specific issues, such as smoking, alcohol, obesity, sexual health and health inequalities. These initiatives were reinforced by broader efforts to build stronger partnerships across agencies to improve services and outcomes (including health outcomes). The sheer volume of public health-related initiatives stemming from these strategies and reforms was immense (see Baggott, 2011, 2013).

Several themes can be identified across these various initiatives. First, there was an effort to incorporate health in decisions made by other government organisations, particularly at local level, and to some extent at regional and national level too. Experimental health action zones were introduced to promote local joint working on health. Sure Start programmes provided a basis for partnership working between health services, local government and the voluntary sector. Local strategic partnerships included NHS organisations (and others with health interests such as voluntary organisations), and the local area agreements they formulated contained health targets and indicators. Meanwhile, local authorities were given an expanded role in health, including new scrutiny powers, powers to improve health and well-being, and funding for partnership working to improve community health. Importantly, in 2007, local authorities and NHS primary care trusts were given a joint duty to assess their population's health needs (known as joint strategic needs assessment (JSNA)).

Second, the NHS was expected to take a more preventative approach. National service frameworks, setting out standards and models for services (for example, services for heart disease and for older people), emphasised prevention alongside care and treatment. NHS local plans were expected to follow suit and aim to improve health and reduce health inequalities. Public health criteria were included in performance management systems. This included national targets to reduce deaths from cancer, heart disease and stroke, suicides and accidents, alongside targets to reduce health inequalities and risk factors for ill health (such as smoking, alcohol-related hospital admissions and obesity). Although these targets were welcomed as key drivers for change, additional resources to support their aims were limited and short term. This restricted capacity for shifting the NHS towards prevention. Furthermore, while areas that performed poorly were identified and faced questions, in reality accountability for poor performance was weak. Public health targets were never considered as a 'must do' priority by senior NHS management and certainly not on a par with waiting time targets and financial indicators.

Third, great faith was placed in social marketing-style health promotion programmes. An expensive campaign (*Change4Life*) was launched in the last years of the Labour era. However, such schemes tend to be effective only when combined with effective regulation of risks in the environment, alongside high-quality community-based support for changing lifestyles. In some policy areas this did happen. There was an expansion of NHS smoking cessation programmes supporting people who wished to quit, coupled with the restrictions on smoking in public places, a ban on tobacco advertising and sponsorship, and a substantial rise in tobacco taxes. In contrast, health education messages about alcohol were undermined by increased availability (more outlets and longer hours), low prices and a lack of support services for people with drink problems. In other areas, policies were mixed. For example, with regard to food, nutrition and obesity, measures were passed to restrict advertisements of foods high in fat, salt and sugar to children. A salt reduction programme was agreed with industry partners, with some success. There were also

programmes to increase the consumption of healthy foods (such as fruit and vegetables, as in the 'Five a Day' scheme for schools). In addition, various programmes aimed to increase participation in physical exercise and sport. However, government was reluctant to adopt tougher regulatory interventions, such as higher taxes on unhealthy foods. It also failed to stop the closure of facilities that might improve physical activity levels (such as the sale of school playing fields).

Nonetheless, Labour had some successes. Deaths from heart and circulatory diseases fell by half, and cancer deaths by over a fifth, meeting official targets. Smoking rates fell in both adults and children. Suicide rates and accidental deaths fell, but short of government targets. Meanwhile, obesity increased in both adults and children. Alcohol continued to represent a serious public health problem as new evidence of the burden of alcohol problems on health services was revealed. The Labour government had mixed success in reducing health inequalities. Although it met one of its key targets, to reduce infant mortality rates, it failed to reduce inequalities in life expectancy between the most deprived areas and the average (by a target of 10 per cent). The gap actually grew by 7 per cent among men and more than double this percentage in women.

The Coalition and Public Health

The UK Coalition government (2010–15) proposed radical changes to the structure of the public health system. In 2013, statutory responsibilities for public health were transferred from the NHS to those local authorities already responsible for social services. These responsibilities included the commissioning of health promotion services (for example, health and lifestyle advice); services to support the prevention of illness (for example, smoking cessation services); and interventions to reduce health risks in the environment. Local authorities were given a new ring-fenced grant, worth around £2.8 billion annually, to help pay for these additional functions. In addition, local directors of public health (DPHs) and their teams were moved from the NHS to these local authorities.

To enable better coordination of public health, health services and social care strategies, and to promote closer integration of these services with each other, and with health- and care-related services such as housing, new local authority-based committees were created. These bodies, known as Health and Wellbeing Boards, include locally elected representatives, chief officers of children's services, adult social services and public health, representatives of NHS commissioning bodies, and local patient and public involvement bodies (local healthwatch; see Chapter 49). Health and well-being boards have statutory powers and responsibilities, including assessing population needs and formulating health and well-being strategies (which must be taken into account by health and social care commissioners).

Other important changes occurred at national level. A new national agency, Public Health England, was established as an executive agency of the Department of Health to undertake functions including monitoring health trends, providing expert advice and support, and overseeing the local public health system. In addition, a public health outcomes framework was outlined as a basis for measuring the impact of local authorities' policies and programmes.

The Coalition also introduced policies on improving healthy lifestyles, continuing policies established by the Labour government. It backed large-scale social marketing campaigns under the auspices of the *Change4Life* programme aimed at improving diet, increasing physical activity and reducing alcohol misuse. This was part of a broader initiative to 'nudge' people to adopt healthier lifestyles (and other socially responsible behaviours) through incentives and changes to social norms. In addition, the government endorsed 'responsibility deals', whereby businesses and other organisations would sign up to pledges to improve health (such as making food products low in saturated fat, sugar and salt more widely available).

There was much support for transferring public health responsibilities to local government (or, in fact, returning these functions, as local authorities had been responsible for public health until 1974). It was believed that local authorities would take a more strategic approach across different policy areas (for example, social services, children's services, leisure, planning and transport), and could coordinate services to improve public health. Local authorities were also seen as 'place shapers' bringing together local efforts to address problems (coordinating other agencies, such as the NHS, police and the voluntary sector). A further reason for increasing local authorities' role was that placing powers in the hands of elected representatives could strengthen democratic accountability for public health.

Criticism of the Coalition's Policies

In some quarters, it was feared that the transfer of public health functions to local government would further fragment some services. For example, in the new regime, commissioning responsibilities for sexual health services were confusingly divided between local authorities and various NHS commissioning bodies. There were also concerns about collaboration between local authorities in two-tier council areas (where important health-related functions such as environmental health and housing lay with district councils). Many county councils tried to address this by involving district councils in their public health strategies and initiatives.

Added to this were doubts about the capacity of local government to take on these responsibilities. There was concern about unfilled DPH posts (a year after the reforms were introduced one in six local authorities did not have a permanent appointee). Some feared that local authorities would divert public health resources to plug holes in other budgets, and there was some evidence of this. There was also concern that DPHs would lack influence within local government and might be prevented from speaking out on key public health issues, though to counter criticism, safeguards were introduced to strengthen their status.

The establishment of health and well-being boards was broadly welcomed, though their lack of formal powers and resources was noted (Humphries and Galea, 2013). Subsequently, they were given responsibility to oversee the Better Care Fund, a budget to promote integrated care (see Chapters 49 and 54). They were seen as bodies that could take on a bigger role in health and care commissioning in the future. In terms of accountability, most local authorities ensured that their health and well-being board was chaired by a senior local elected representative. Nonetheless, boards are still developing and it is recognised that they need to raise their profile and work more closely with communities and those who speak on their behalf, such as voluntary organisations and local healthwatch (Chapter 49).

On broader matters of policy, there was a strong feeling that the Coalition was too strongly influenced by vested interests. The responsibility deals were heavily criticised for allowing industries too much influence over policy. Meanwhile, corporate lobbying was held responsible for the removal of the Food Standards Agency's role in nutrition policy. This was also suspected as having a part in a 'U'-turn on setting a minimum unit alcohol price for England. For a while it appeared that tobacco policy might also be weakened. In the event, the Coalition backed key policies: the adoption of plain packaging of tobacco products and a ban on smoking in cars where children are present.

Another criticism of the Coalition's policy was that despite its acknowledgement of health inequalities (backed by new statutory responsibilities on the Secretary of State and other bodies), in reality little was done to address the underlying causes (Social Mobility and Child Poverty Commission, 2014). For example, the percentage of children in absolute poverty rose under the Coalition, and there was little progress on reducing relative child poverty. Also many Sure Start centres, which have a key role in improving the health and well-being of young children, had to reduce services for financial reasons and some were closed down (see Chapter 58).

Following the General Election of 2015, fears have been expressed that the Conservatives, now governing alone, may take the opportunity to reduce public health commitments. At the time of writing, the new government is consulting on a £200 million (7 per cent) cut to local public health budgets. Even so, the major public health problems described in this chapter will not simply go away. Indeed, there are already signs that the Conservative government is aware that much more needs to be done on some key public health issues, notably child obesity.

Emerging Issues

Debates on public health issues will continue, irrespective of which party is in office. But a few fundamental questions will set the context for these debates. First, given the rising demand for health services, how can the health system remain sustainable? The answer surely has to be that much more has to be invested in prevention, especially at an early stage. This poses uncomfortable questions about the balance of resources invested in prevention and treatment. Another further key issue concerns partnerships between agencies and organisations that can help to improve health. To a large extent, public health has to be a joint effort by all agencies concerned, and the key question is what more can be done to support and encourage this? A further issue concerns the balance of state and individual responsibilities. The 'nanny state' is not a useful term, and inhibits mature debate about where mutual responsibilities for health lie. Related to this are questions about the limited ability of governments to regulate public health. Although laws, taxes and other instruments of government are often vital, they cannot alone improve health. Efforts from citizens themselves are needed together with appropriate systems of support and information. Future public health policy will need to engage with people more effectively in order to harness the resources of the community itself.

Guide to Further Sources

R. Baggott (2011), *Public Health: Policy and Politics*, Basingstoke: Palgrave Macmillan, is a popular textbook on the subject of public health, focusing on the development and implementation of policies in the UK.

R. Baggott (2013), *Partnerships for Public Health and Wellbeing*, Basingstoke: Palgrave Macmillan, explores several aspects of partnership working in public health.

Department of Health (2010), *Healthy Lives, Healthy People: Our Strategy for Public Health in England*, London: Stationery Office, Cm 7985, sets out the Coalition's key policies on public health.

R. Humphries and A. Galea (2014), *Health and Wellbeing Boards: One Year On*, London, King's Fund, discusses the role of local health and wellbeing boards, the new bodies established to plan public health and coordinate local agencies.

C. Murray et al. (2013), 'UK health performance', *The Lancet*, 381:23, 997–1019.

Marmot Review (2010), *Fair Society: Healthy Lives*, London, Department of Health. This strategic review provides a clear insight into the problem and causes of health inequalities in England. It makes a series of recommendations about how to reduce health inequalities.

Public Health England (2014), *From Evidence into Action: Opportunities to Protect and Improve the Nation's Health*, London, Public Health England, sets out key public health challenges and how they can be addressed.

Social Mobility and Child Poverty Commission (2014), *State of the Nation 2014: Social Mobility and Child Poverty in Great Britain*, London, Social Mobility and Child Poverty Commission.

Review and Assignment Questions

1 What is public health? Why should it be a priority for government?

2 What were the main policies of the Labour governments on public health and how successful were they?

3 What were the main Coalition policies on public health?

4 What are the main criticisms of the Coalition's policies on public health?

5 Compare and contrast the public health policies of the Labour governments and the Coalition government.

Visit the book companion site at www.wiley.com/go/alcocksocialpolicy to make use of the resources designed to accompany the textbook. There you will find chapter-specific guides to further resources, including governmental, international, thinktank, pressure groups and relevant journal sources. You will also find a glossary based on *The Blackwell Dictionary of Social Policy*, help sheets, guidance on managing assignments in social policy and career advice.

51

Education in Schools

Anne West

Overview

- The school systems in the countries of the UK have differing legislative frameworks and policies. School structures, funding, curriculum and assessment vary.
- Market-oriented policies and school autonomy have a high profile in England, but not in the rest of the UK.
- Across the countries of the UK, there has been a focus on increasing the achievement levels of children from disadvantaged backgrounds. Approaches to tackle the attainment gap vary between countries with additional per pupil funding available for disadvantaged pupils in England and Wales.
- Across the UK, there is an entitlement to free part-time education for 3- and 4-year-old children and for disadvantaged 2-year-olds.

Context

The importance of education, particularly in terms of increasing human capital and economic competitiveness, is acknowledged at national and supranational levels. Education also plays a crucial role in terms of cognitive and skill development and personal and social development. It is significant for society more broadly given its role in socialisation, fostering social justice and enhancing social cohesion. This multiplicity of purposes and its compulsory nature mean that politicians and policymakers have traditionally given education a high priority.

This chapter is concerned with schooling in the UK. It focuses on England, but reference is made to other countries and in particular to Scotland. The first section presents a brief historical context and an overview of current school systems in the UK. The second section focuses on two current issues: market-oriented policies and school autonomy; and achievement levels and reducing the

The Student's Companion to Social Policy, Fifth Edition. Edited by Pete Alcock, Tina Haux, Margaret May and Sharon Wright.
© 2016 John Wiley & Sons, Ltd. Published 2016 by John Wiley & Sons, Ltd.

achievement gap between different groups of pupils. The final section concludes and highlights some emerging issues.

Schooling in the UK: Past and Present

Historical context

Different trajectories in educational provision have been followed in the countries of the UK, but the churches have historically played an important role. In England and Wales, the Elementary Education Act 1870 aimed to provide schools in order to fill the gaps in existing provision made by the church. Subsequently, the 1902 Education Act established local education authorities together with a system of secondary education. With the 1918 Education Act, fees for elementary schools were abolished and education became compulsory until the age of 14. In Northern Ireland, the school system, which developed along denominational grounds, goes back to the 1830s. In Scotland, legislation dating to the seventeenth century and before had established a parochial school system. This was extended from the 1830s until the 1872 Education (Scotland) Act created a Board of Education and education became the responsibility of local elected bodies with funding coming from the local property tax. Although fees were charged initially, free primary education was introduced in 1890, and in 1901, education became compulsory until the age of 14.

Introducing selection

In England and Wales, the 1944 Education Act set up a universal system of free, compulsory schooling from 5 to 15 years (raised to 16 in 1972). State-funded schooling continued to be provided by local authority and church schools. The 1944 Education Act did not prescribe the structure of secondary education, but enabled the implementation of a 'tripartite' system, comprising grammar schools, technical schools and 'secondary modern' schools for the remainder.

Following the introduction of a selective system in England, concerns emerged, as the main beneficiaries of grammar schools were the middle classes. During the 1960s, there was a policy shift, and in 1965 the Labour government requested local education authorities to submit plans for the introduction of comprehensive education. A broadly comprehensive ('all ability') system of education was eventually introduced across much of England and Wales and in Scotland, whilst in Northern Ireland a selective system was retained.

Focus on parental choice

Major changes in education policy took place under Conservative administrations (1979–97). Parental choice of school had a high political profile. In England and Wales, the 1980 Education Act enabled parents to express a preference for the school of their choice for their child; similar legislation was enacted in Northern Ireland. In Scotland, following the 1981 Education (Scotland) Act, parents had the right to nominate a school they wished their child to attend (make a 'placing request'), if they wanted him or her to attend a school other than the local school.

Subsequently, school diversity emerged, at least in theory, as a key policy issue in England, Wales and Scotland. Following the 1988 Education Reform Act in England and Wales, and the 1989 Self-Governing Schools etc. (Scotland) Act, schools could opt out of local authority control. They were then funded directly by the government and had more autonomy than previously. The majority of schools that opted out were in England – very few were in Wales and even fewer in Scotland. In England, there was further diversification, with fifteen independent city technology schools being set up, owned by not-for-profit bodies. Their capital funds were intended to be met by private sector sponsors, with revenue costs being met by the government via a funding agreement, a legally binding contract.

The arrival of league tables

In England and Wales, the 1988 Education Reform Act introduced formula funding, whereby individual school budgets were determined predominantly on the basis of the number of pupils on roll (a quasi-voucher system). Official school 'league tables' of public examination results were also published. Incentives were thus created for schools to maximise their income and their pupils' examination results via the newly created quasi-market (Le Grand and Bartlett, 1993). Underpinning the reforms was the view that parents would choose the 'best' schools for their child, based on the information available – in particular, examination results – and that the ensuing competition between schools would result in educational standards increasing.

Concerns were, however, raised about the crude nature of the published examination results. Because of the link between socio-economic background and attainment, schools with more advantaged intakes generally obtain higher results than those with less advantaged intakes. However, in terms of school quality, what is important is the value added by the school over and above social background factors. There were also concerns raised about 'cream-skimming' by certain schools, in the main church and grant-maintained schools (with control over admissions), selecting pupils likely to do well academically and enhance the school's league table position.

Private fee-charging and state-funded schools

In the UK, the vast majority of pupils of compulsory school age are educated in state-funded schools, although fewer in England (93 per cent) than in the other countries of the UK. The remainder are in private fee-charging schools, many of which are academically selective and require parents to pay high fees, thereby restricting access to these schools by those from poorer backgrounds.

The state-funded school systems in the UK vary. England and Wales have a similar legislative framework and that for Northern Ireland is also broadly similar. In Scotland, the legislative context is different, and some changes have also taken place since devolution.

Compulsory education begins at the age of 5, except in Northern Ireland when it begins at 4. Secondary school starts at 11 except in Scotland, when it starts at 12. Compulsory education ends at the age of 16, except in England when it ends at 18. Secondary education for 16–19-year olds is provided in schools, sixth-form colleges and further education colleges.

Primary schools cater for children of all abilities. However, at secondary level systems and structures differ. In Scotland and Wales, there is a comprehensive system. In England, the system is broadly comprehensive, although around 5 per cent of secondary schools are fully academically selective grammar schools. Further, a significant minority of nominally comprehensive schools, predominantly

those that control their own admissions, use a variety of different methods that are to some degree selective (for example, selecting a proportion of pupils on the basis of aptitude/ability in a subject area); and virtually all religious schools give priority to children on the basis of their religion (West et al., 2011). In Northern Ireland, there is an academically selective system with grammar schools and non-selective secondary schools.

Curriculum and assessment

The 1988 Education Reform Act introduced a national curriculum and programme of assessment in England and Wales, as did the 1989 Education Reform (Northern Ireland) Order 1989. In Scotland, the Curriculum for Excellence comprises curriculum guidelines for pupils aged from 3 to 18, but this is not prescribed by statute. In order to evaluate overall pupil attainment, there is a survey of a random sample of pupils, known as the Scottish Survey of Achievement.

Towards the end of secondary education there are public examinations across the UK; the age at which they are taken and the nature of the examinations both vary between countries (see Box 51.1). In England, performance tables ('league tables') are published by the government and in the media. Key indicators at the age of 16 years are the percentage of pupils achieving five or more

---

Box 51.1 Selected Public Examinations in the UK

England, Wales and Northern Ireland:

- GCSE examinations (or pre-vocational equivalent) taken in individual subjects by most pupils (16 years);
- GCE Advanced Subsidiary levels (17 years);
- GCE Advanced levels (18 years) (generally required for entry to higher education).

Scotland:

- National 4 and National 5 qualifications;
- Highers/Advanced Highers (generally required for entry to higher education).

GCSE passes at grades A* to C, and the percentage achieving the English Baccalaureate (EBacc), awarded to pupils who achieve a grade C or above in core academic subjects.

School management, governance and inspection

Local management of schools was introduced in England and Wales following the 1988 Education Reform Act (it was also introduced in Northern Ireland). Schools became responsible for deciding how the school budget from their local authority (which is determined largely on the basis of pupil numbers) should be spent. In Scotland, local authorities decide on the level of support to be given to schools. Local authorities distribute their agreed budgets to schools on a formula basis, with pupil roll being the main determinant measure used. Individual schools are responsible for managing their own day-to-day expenditure via devolved school management, but, unlike in England, the school's 'normal complement' of staff is paid by the local authority.

Governing bodies of schools that are maintained by local authorities in England, Wales and Northern Ireland include parents and representatives of the school and local community; they have a largely strategic role, including managing the school's budget. In Scotland, following the 2006 Scottish Schools (Parental Involvement) Act, parent councils replaced school boards, which have some similarities with school governing bodies; these are responsible for helping to improve the quality of education and to develop children's potential. Inspection bodies in each country have responsibility for ensuring that schools are providing an acceptable quality of education (see Box 51.2).

Box 51.2 School Inspection

England: Office for Standards in Office for Standards in Education, Children's Services and Skills (Ofsted);
Wales: Her Majesty's Inspectorate for Education and Training in Wales (Estyn);
Scotland: HM Inspectorate of Education (HMIE);
Northern Ireland: Education and Training Inspectorate (ETI)

Core Issues

Two current issues are of particular interest from a policy perspective. The first is market-oriented reforms and school autonomy, which are seen by the government as a means of raising overall educational standards. The second issue relates to reducing the achievement gap between different groups of pupils.

Market-oriented policies and school autonomy

Grant-maintained schools were abolished by the Labour government, which was in office from 1997 to 2010. In England and Wales, following the 1998 School Standards and Framework Act, their status changed, in the main to foundation schools, although some became voluntary schools. In Scotland, the 2000 Standards in Scotland's Schools etc. Act abolished self-governing status. Other aspects of policy in relation to choice and diversity have diverged, particularly since devolution. The divergence is clearest when England and Scotland are compared.

In England, market-oriented reforms have continued. Official school performance tables continue to be produced and published by the government and in the media. There has also been an increase in school diversity. A small number of new faith schools have also become part of the state-funded system. Most significantly, independent academies have been introduced. These were first introduced by the Labour government in the early 2000s and built on the city technology colleges programme. Under the Labour government, the main goal was to improve the quality of education in disadvantaged areas. Following the enactment of the 2010 Academies Act by the Conservative–Liberal Democrat Coalition government, local authority maintained schools were able to apply to convert to academy status and new free schools, a type of academy, could be set up. Academies are owned by not-for-profit trusts and have funding agreements (a legal contract) with the government, which provides revenue funding. Academies do not have to follow the national curriculum, teaching staff do not need to be qualified teachers, and the teachers' pay and conditions regulations do not need to be adhered to. Free schools, a type of academy, are not

Box 51.3 Academies and Free Schools

Academies are publicly funded independent schools. They do not have to follow the national curriculum and can set their own pay and conditions of employment for staff. They have to follow the same rules on admissions, special educational needs and exclusions as other state-funded schools. They receive their money direct from the government, not local authorities, and are run by an academy trust (which is not-for-profit); this employs the staff.

Free schools are 'all-ability' schools and cannot select pupils on the basis of ability (as grammar schools do). They can be set up by charities, independent schools, community and faith groups, teachers, parents and businesses.

Box 51.4 Comprehensive Schools in Scotland

No one in Scotland should be required to select a school to get the first rate education they deserve and are entitled to. Choice between schools in Scotland is no substitute for the universal excellence we seek and Scotland's communities demand. (Scottish Executive, *Ambitious, Excellent Schools*, 2004: 1).

mathematics and science have been broadly similar for England, Northern Ireland and Scotland, suggesting that the different education systems perform similarly even though their policies in relation to school choice and diversity differ; the results for Wales have been lower. This implies that other factors are responsible for differences in achievement.

academically selective and are set up by groups such as charities, parents and faith groups (see Box 51.3).

Legislation over time has sought to allay concerns about cream-skimming by schools; the 1998 School Standards and Framework Act and the 2006 Education and Inspections Act, along with a School Admissions Code, can be seen as an attempt to regulate what was initially a largely unregulated admissions system.

Whilst league tables and school diversity remain high on the political agenda in England, the situation in the other countries of the UK is different. No official school performance tables are published in Wales, Scotland or Northern Ireland. Moreover, in the case of Scotland, the 2000 Standards in Scotland's Schools etc. Act gave greater powers to local authorities in relation to restrict choice by refusing 'placing requests'. Significantly, there are no policies in place to increase parental choice of schools (see Box 51.4).

There are only limited data available comparing educational outcomes across the UK. However, the results of the Programme for International Student Assessment (PISA) organised by the Organisation for Economic Cooperation and Development (OECD) reveal that the mean scores for reading,

Achievement and reducing the gap

A major area of concern in England relates to differences in the levels of achievement of children from different social groups. The association between poverty and low educational achievement is an important and persistent concern. In England, pupils from low-income families perform less well, on average, in public examinations than do others.

There are also long-standing differences in terms of the achievement of girls and boys, with more girls than boys achieving five or more high grade (A^*–C) GCSEs (or equivalent), including English and maths at 16 years of age. Differences are also apparent outside the UK, with PISA results for 2012 revealing that in reading in almost all countries girls outperform boys. However, social attainment gaps are wide (DfE, 2012).

The evidence relating to the educational performance of children from different ethnic groups, most of whom live in England, is complex. More pupils of Chinese and Indian origin perform well in GCSE examinations than those from other groups. More generally, pupils classified as White achieve in line with the national level, whilst those from Black Caribbean and Pakistani backgrounds perform below the national level.

The overall differences are likely to be associated to a large extent with disadvantage. Other groups of children also fare poorly, in particular those with special educational needs and those in local authority care. The question arises as to how these achievement gaps are to be reduced.

In England, funding has traditionally been greater to local authorities with higher levels of disadvantage. In addition, the Conservative–Liberal Democrat government introduced a new 'pupil premium'. This is additional funding for publicly funded schools in England, the aim of which is to raise the attainment of pupils from disadvantaged backgrounds and to close the achievement gap. In 2014–15, schools received £1,300 for each pupil aged between 5 and 11, and £935 for each pupil between 11 and 16, registered as eligible for free school meals at any point in the previous six years.

In addition, there has been a UK-wide focus on the provision of free early education. There are benefits of high-quality pre-school educational provision to a range of cognitive outcomes. There is an entitlement to free part-time early education for 3- and 4-year-olds and there has been an extension to disadvantaged 2-year-olds. The details and implementation vary between the countries of the UK, but in all cases not-for-profit (voluntary) and for-profit private providers play a key role. The evidence suggests that quality is higher in certain types of provision – specifically nursery schools and integrated centres providing education and care; this is likely to be related to the differing staff qualifications, with those employing qualified teachers being more likely to provide higher quality provision.

Emerging Issues

Policy in relation to schools varies between the countries of the UK. However, there are common objectives in relation to increasing human capital and economic competitiveness, by improving overall attainment; and to reducing achievement gaps. The means by which these are to be achieved differ. In England, market-oriented policies and school autonomy are viewed by the government as being of key importance in terms of raising standards. In the other countries of the UK this is not the case.

The most striking difference between school-based education in England and the rest of the UK has been the development of the academies programme. By 2015, around two-thirds of secondary schools in England were academies, owned by not-for-profit trusts (not the local authority) and funded via a contract with central government. The Conservative government elected in May 2015 has a target to open at least 500 new free schools (see Box 51.3). The role of local authorities as providers of school-based education in England is set to decline further as academies and free schools increase in number (West, 2015).

As regards free early years provision, fifteen hours of free part-time education is available for all 3- and 4-year-olds and disadvantaged 2-year-olds across the UK. In England, the Conservative government is to legislate to make free childcare available for up to thirty hours a week for 3- and 4-year-olds whose parents are in employment.

Perhaps the most significant issue affecting school-based education is retrenchment and the increasing birth rate; there has been some protection for schools at least in England, but nevertheless budget reductions are likely. How these will affect provision remains to be seen.

Guide to Further Sources

UK government statistics relating to education in England can be found by searching for 'education statistics' at: www.gov.uk.

OECD PISA results for 2012 can be found at: www.oecd.org/pisa/keyfindings/pisa-2012-results.htm.

DfE (2012), 'PISA 2009: how does the social attainment gap in England compare with countries internationally?' London: DfE (dera.ioe.ac.uk/14208/1/DFE-RR206.pdf), provides an analysis of how the social attainment gap.

Scottish Executive (2004), *Ambitious, Excellent Schools: Our Agenda for Action*, sets out the reform agenda for Scotland's schools. A Curriculum for Excellence (2004), is central to this agenda: www.gov.scot/Publications/2004/11/20176/45852.

The Eurydice Network provides information on individual European education systems and

policies at: webgate.ec.europa.eu/fpfis/mwikis/
eurydice/index.php/Countries.

J. Le Grand and W. Bartlett (eds) (1993),
Quasi-Markets and Social Policy, Basingstoke:
Macmillan, discusses quasi-markets in different
policy areas, including schools.

A. West and E. Bailey (2013), 'The development of the academies programme: "privatising"
school-based education in England 1986–2013',
British Journal of Educational Studies, 61:2,
137–59, focuses on the transformation of
school-based education in England under the
Coalition government.

School selection and legislative changes are
addressed by A. West et al. (2011), 'Secondary
school admissions: impact of legislation on policy
and practice', *Oxford Review of Education*, 37:1,
1–20.

A. West (2015), 'Education policy and governance in England under the Coalition government
(2010–15): academies, the pupil premium and free
early education', *London Review of Education*
(eprints.lse.ac.uk/62528), focuses on policy
changes under the Coalition government.

Review and Assignment Questions

1   How do school systems across the UK vary?
2   What market-oriented policies have been
    implemented?
3   What approaches have been adopted to try
    and reduce achievement gaps between differ-
    ent groups of pupils?
4   Why is early education considered to be
    important?
5   How does the provision of school-based edu-
    cation vary between the countries of the UK?

Visit the book companion site at www.wiley.com/
go/alcocksocialpolicy to make use of the resources
designed to accompany the textbook. There you
will find chapter-specific guides to further
resources, including governmental, international,
thinktank, pressure groups and relevant journal
sources. You will also find a glossary based on *The
Blackwell Dictionary of Social Policy*, help sheets,
guidance on managing assignments in social
policy and career advice.

52

Lifelong Learning and Training

Claire Callender

Overview

- Lifelong learning includes people of all ages learning in a variety of contexts. It is an idea informing post-compulsory education and training policies, prompted by globalisation and labour market changes.
- These policies are important for economic growth and the well-being of society, but their economic objectives are prioritised.
- Policies focus on improving the skill levels and skills mix of the existing and future workforce so there is a balance in the supply of, and demand for, skilled labour.
- Since 1997, governments have tried to increase the supply of skilled workers by expanding post-compulsory education, encouraging greater participation, and getting people to take more and higher qualifications.
- The UK Coalition government expanded apprenticeships while at the same time cutting public expenditure on post-compulsory education, especially for adults. They have also shifted more of the costs of learning onto learners so more people have to pay for their learning.
- Participation in post-compulsory education remains unequal, with those from disadvantaged backgrounds in greatest need missing out. Educational inequality begets inequality and cumulates across the life cycle.

The Student's Companion to Social Policy, Fifth Edition. Edited by Pete Alcock, Tina Haux, Margaret May and Sharon Wright.
© 2016 John Wiley & Sons, Ltd. Published 2016 by John Wiley & Sons, Ltd.

Introduction

This chapter begins with an explanation of what lifelong learning is who provides it and why it came about. Next, it explores the ideas informing lifelong learning policies before discussing post-compulsory education policies in England, examining those aimed at improving the qualifications and skills of the future workforce, and those targeted at the current workforce. It concludes by highlighting some emerging issues.

What is Lifelong Learning?

At the heart of lifelong learning is the idea that learning should take place at all stages in a person's life, and should be embedded in people's lives. The learning can take place anywhere: in schools, colleges, universities, at work, at home or in the community. It focuses mainly on adults returning to organised learning rather than on the initial period of education (Schuller and Watson, 2009).

Lifelong learning requires a system of learning which gives everyone the chance to learn at all levels, whenever they need to learn rather than because they have reached a certain age. These opportunities need to cater for people with university degrees and those without any qualifications; those in highly skilled jobs wanting professional development, and people in unskilled jobs or without a job experiencing difficulties reading and writing; and people who have retired or just want to learn something new. This is a very different way of thinking about education and training, which is usually restricted to formal learning in specialised educational institutions, aimed mostly at young people. Lifelong learning is an *idea* informing and underpinning education and training policies. It captures an approach to a set of policies.

The policies most associated with lifelong learning traditionally focus on the period after the end of compulsory schooling or learning, which since 2015 is at age 18. This stage of education, post-18, is usually called post-compulsory education.

Varied organisations provide post-compulsory education: the state in further education colleges, higher education institutions and universities; the private and voluntary sector; and employers through work-based learning. Most takes place in further education colleges and universities, and

in the workplace. There is also a growing private market in adult learning.

Post-compulsory qualifications are usually higher than 'A' levels such as undergraduate and post-graduate degrees or certificates. However, for people who did not get 'A' levels while at school, or left without qualifications, their lifelong learning may entail taking lower-level qualifications. They may take vocational qualifications, which are work-related and involve learning practical skills and competencies aimed at preparing people for particular jobs, such as a plumber. In contrast, academic qualifications usually require learning about things that are unrelated to a specific job such as studying history. Some lifelong learning focuses on basic skills such as learning how to read, write and use information technology. Other lifelong learning may be undertaken purely for pleasure and may be irrelevant to someone's job or career aspirations. Not all lifelong learning leads to a qualification.

Unlike compulsory education, people do not have to engage in post-compulsory education and training, except for some professionals updating their skills. Individuals, rather than the state, take responsibility for their own education and training at this phase, except for the unemployed and the most disadvantaged where the state often intervenes. This raises issues about who should pay for it – the state, employers or individuals. Until 2010 and the cuts in public expenditure, most lifelong learning was funded by central government and taxpayers. Now more learners and their employers have to pay.

Why did Lifelong Learning Come About?

The early 1970s saw a global radical re-think about post-compulsory education and training with the emergence of the term 'lifelong learning' on the policy agenda. Why did this happen? The key drivers were globalisation and changes in the labour market. Together they help us to understand why lifelong learning policies were introduced, and the nature of these policies (Field, 2006).

Globalisation (see Chapter 71) has had a profound effect on Britain's economic and social policies, including education. Britain, as a result, has shifted towards a 'knowledge-economy' based on high skills and high knowledge work. Now knowledge rather than land, labour or capital is considered the most important factor shaping production and economic development. Therefore, skills and knowledge are essential for Britain's ability to compete in the global economy and to drive economic growth and economic recovery.

Globalisation, increasing competition between countries, and rapid scientific and technological advances also are leading to changes in the workplace, how work is organised and the nature of everyone's jobs. Few people today can expect to stay in the same job for life. Instead, they are likely to have more discontinuous and less secure work patterns over their lifetime, especially during an economic recession (see Chapter 48).

These developments affect the qualifications, skills and competencies workers need to perform their jobs, to keep them and to get new jobs. Over time, the number of unskilled jobs has shrunk, while skilled jobs needing higher level qualifications have grown. Some skills have become redundant while new skills have emerged (see Chapter 48). So many people will need to re-skill or up-skill. Consequently, their learning cannot be confined to one point in their lives, typically after leaving school. Often this learning will be part-time and fitted in around existing family and work commitments.

The Ideology of Lifelong Learning

Economic prosperity and social inclusion were key goals of the 1997–2010 Labour governments' social policies, especially in post-compulsory education. Labour believed that a successful knowledge economy depended on the creation and generation of technological improvement and innovation; and a well-educated, highly skilled and adaptable or flexible labour force.

For these Labour governments, skills were the key lever to improve workplace productivity. It recognised that education was the main route for increasing social mobility and social justice, while employment was a means of promoting social inclusion and tackling poverty. It was summed up by 'the more we learn: the more we earn'.

Labour's post-compulsory education policies had both economic and social goals, which brought together market principles and the idea of equality of opportunity. However, most of their lifelong learning policies were preoccupied with developing a more productive and efficient workforce – with the economic imperatives of lifelong learning. Their spending on lifelong learning was concentrated on those aged under 25.

The Conservative–Liberal Democratic Coalition government of 2010–15 similarly saw education and skills as the foundations for economic success, growth and recovery. They too thought that education and training were essential for ensuring people have jobs, earn wages and work productively. Just like their predecessor, the skill needs of the economy and of employers dominated the UK Coalition's policies, which focused on increasing the participation of 16–24 year olds in education, learning and employment, at the expense of older people. However, unlike Labour, the UK Coalition rarely discussed lifelong learning, thus squeezing lifelong learning off the policy agenda.

The economic climate in which the UK Coalition and Labour governments operated was very different. Because of the global recession, the UK Coalition cut public expenditure on post-compulsory education as part of its broader strategy to reduce the fiscal deficit and stimulate economic growth. The 2015 Conservative government is imposing further cuts. By contrast, under Labour public expenditure on post-compulsory education increased between 1997 and 2010.

The overall ideology and philosophy of the UK Coalition and Labour governments informing their post-compulsory education policies are also somewhat different. The UK Coalition and the 2015 Conservative government's vision is much more firmly rooted in neo-Liberal economics (see Chapter 6) and in the supremacy of the market, with a greater emphasis on consumer choice and provider competition.

Lifelong Learning, Training and Skills Policies

The overall objective of post-compulsory education and training policies is to balance the supply of, and demand for, skilled workers (OECD, 2012). These policies have to ensure the skill levels of the workforce meet employer needs, and the supply of skills reflects market demand. If these become out of kilter, two types of mismatches occur. First, skill shortages – when there are not enough appropriately skilled applicants for jobs. Second, skill gaps – when the existing workforce lacks the skills necessary to meet business needs. Skills policies, therefore, have to ensure that employers invest in their workforce, and that people invest in their own learning and skills. However, unlike many other European countries, England has very little post-compulsory vocational education and training, and relies on higher education to provide its skilled workforce.

Lifelong learning, training and skills policies can be divided into policies aimed at improving the skills of the *future* workforce, and those aimed at raising the skill levels of the *current* workforce.

Improving the Qualifications and Skills of the Future Workforce

Policies for 18–24 year olds

Educational attainment and qualification levels are used frequently as measures of the skills available in the population and the labour force. The thrust of policies targeted at those aged 18 to 24 are twofold. The first aim is to encourage more people to continue their studies in further or higher education, or undertake training so they have the qualifications and skills needed by the labour market and can get a job. The higher a person's level of education, the greater the likelihood that they will be employed.

The second aim of policies for 18–24 year olds is to help them make a successful transition into the labour market and into skilled employment, and this includes policies specifically aimed at young people not in education, employment or training (NEET) and the unemployed. However, youth unemployment is the highest it has ever been and it is getting harder for young people to find jobs.

By the end of 2014, half of all 18–24 year olds were employed, 31 per cent were in full-time education, 3 per cent were on government training schemes, while 16 per cent were NEET. Those most likely to be NEET left school without achieving five or more GCSEs grade A*–C and come from disadvantaged backgrounds; while being long-term NEET leads to lower lifetime employment, earnings and general life chances (OECD, 2014).

Over the past decade, there has been an increase in participation in full-time education among 18–24 year olds and a decrease in the proportion employed, especially after the 2008 economic downturn. The proportion of 18–24 year olds who are NEET rose between 2002 and 2012, but then began to fall slightly as the proportion who are in employment began to rise. There are similar trends across the OECD.

In OECD countries in 2013, the percentage of people in education was 87 per cent of 15–19 year olds, 46 per cent of 20–24 year olds and 16 per cent of 25–29 year olds. For those who are not in education (that is, 13 per cent of 15–19 year olds, 54 per cent of 20–24 year olds, and 84 per cent of 25–29 year olds), it is important to understand their situation in the labour market. Figure 52.1 shows that, on average, among all 20–24 year-olds, 36 per cent are not in education and employed, about 9 per cent are not in education and unemployed, and 9 per cent are not in education and inactive (that is, not employed and not looking actively for a job) (OECD, 2015).

Apprenticeships

Apprenticeships were the UK Coalition's flagship skills programme, which they positioned as a key policy to solve skill shortages and as an alternative to university. The 2015 Conservative government have pledged to expand apprenticeships targeted at young people and to give employers more control over apprenticeship courses.

Apprenticeships, available for those aged 16 and over, were paid jobs that incorporated on- and off-the-job training. Successful apprentices received a nationally recognised vocational qualification on completion of their contract, which had to last at least one year. The government paid a proportion of the training costs for apprentices, depending on their age, with remaining training costs normally covered by the employer.

In 2013–14, only about 5 per cent of all 16–24 year olds had started an apprenticeship in England compared with around 50 per cent in Germany (OECD, 2014). Consequently, apprenticeships were a route into employment for only a minority of young people, despite their growth under the UK Coalition.

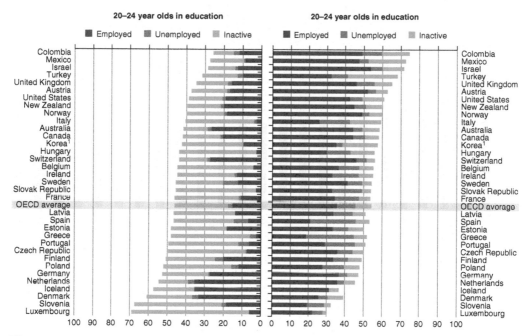

Figure 52.1 Distribution of 20–24 year olds in education/not in education, by work status, 2013. Source: OECD (2015), *Education at a Glance Interim Report*, Table 3.3, available at: www.oecd.org/education/eag-interim-report.htm, last accessed 21 May 2015.

Higher education

Governments see higher education (HE) and universities playing a major role in meeting the needs of the labour market, especially the growing demand for highly skilled workers. Over the last decade, the proportion of 17–30 year olds in the UK entering higher education for the first time has been rising, and in 2012–13 it was 43 per cent (OECD, 2014). Participation has remained high amongst young people studying full-time, but has fallen dramatically among older people studying part-time who combine studying with employment.

Despite the expansion of HE, access is unequal (Vignoles, 2013). There remain large differences in HE participation by social class, mainly because of students' prior educational attainment – how well they did in their GCSEs and 'A' levels. Young people from disadvantaged backgrounds tend to do less well in these exams than those from advantaged backgrounds. Consequently, they are three times less likely to enter HE, and six times less likely to go to the best universities. Labour's policies focused on widening HE participation, improving access to HE for the disadvantaged and combating

these inequalities. The UK Coalition policies' emphasised increasing social mobility and getting more disadvantaged young people into the best universities.

Another way of looking at these inequalities in access to HE is by examining the educational backgrounds of the parents of current students. As Figure 52.2 clearly shows, across the OECD, the likelihood of a student participating in tertiary/university education is far greater if their parents also attended higher education. More than half of 20–34 year olds in tertiary/university education have at least one parent with that level of education (56 per cent), and slightly more than a third (36 per cent) have at least one parent with upper secondary education as highest level of attainment. By contrast, the proportion of 20–34-year-old tertiary/university students whose parents have not completed an upper secondary education (equivalent to GCSEs) is small: about one tertiary/university student in ten has parents with below upper secondary education (9 per cent).

The growing importance of, and demand for, HE along with its expansion since the mid-1980s

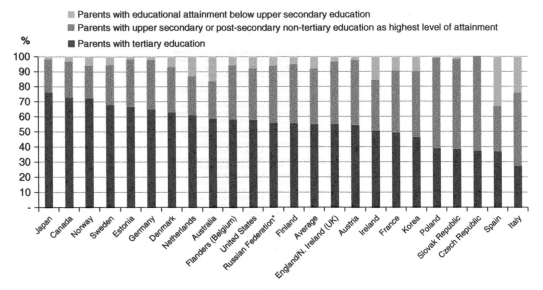

Figure 52.2 Proportion of 20–34 year olds in tertiary education, by parents' educational attainment, 2012.
Source: OECD (2014), *Education at a Glance*, derived from table A4.1a.

has increased its costs. Governments have tried to reduce costs and HE public expenditure by shifting more costs onto students and their families and away from government and taxpayers. They have done this by raising tuition fees. University graduates benefit by being more likely than those without a degree to have a job, especially a high-skilled and well-paid job. But society also benefits from more graduates (Brennan et al., 2013).

Labour first introduced tuition fees in England in 1998, and then increased them to a maximum of £3,000 a year in 2006. They provided students with subsidised income-contingent loans for their fees, repaid once students graduated. The UK Coalition also raised tuition fees in England to a maximum of £9,000 a year in 2012. Simultaneously, they withdrew most of the funding they gave universities for their undergraduate teaching, so courses were funded mainly through tuition fees paid by students. Once students, rather than the state, become responsible for paying for their HE, then HE becomes a private good and investment rather than a public good funded mainly by the state.

The UK Coalition also tried to create a quasi-market in HE with greater consumer choice and provider competition (Brown and Carasso, 2013). Yet there is very little variation in price as most universities charge the maximum tuition fee

allowed, although there is a growing private sector. The changes in fees and funding since 2010 may not have produced a functioning market, but they have certainly contributed towards managerialist behaviours and practices in universities and may be changing their values too.

HE remains free at the point of access because students get government loans to pay for their fees and living costs. However, there is growing concern about whether the system of student financial support, including loans, is financially sustainable because it is expensive and many students are unlikely to pay off their loans in full. Even so, the Conservative government is abolishing maintenance grants and replacing them with loans, in order to save money in the short term.

Improving the qualifications and skills of the existing workforce

The Labour government introduced the first ever national 'skills strategy' for adults with low-level or no qualifications and skills. It gave adults an entitlement to free education and training. However, the UK Coalition restricted this entitlement to people aged under 23. Older people now have to pay tuition fees, while some qualify for government-funded loans (24+ Advanced Learning Loans). These changes and large cuts in adult learning public expenditure put at risk the Further Education sector (Keep, 2015) and limit opportunities for lifelong learning. And these cuts are likely to continue under the new Conservative government.

There is unequal access to employer training, just like other forms of post-compulsory education. Low-skilled employees and those in lower status occupations receive measurably less training, as do older workers compared with younger workers, and employees in small- and medium-sized enterprises compared with those in large companies. Consequently, educational inequalities accumulate over people's lifetime (Janmaat and Green, 2013)

Emerging Issues

Whilst compulsory education is seen as failing to deliver the skilled workforce the economy needs and ensuring people are fit for work, governments will continue to use the post-compulsory sector as a means of redress. However, with very limited funds, there will be tensions about which groups and types of training should be prioritised; young or older people; those already with or without skills; those who work or who are unemployed; and the short-term skill needs of employers or longer-term needs of individuals. In future, the government is likely to fund less skill training and instead support employers and individuals as purchasers of skills. It has already pushed more of the costs of education and training onto individuals. It is questionable, however, if the HE funding reforms are financially sustainable in the longer term, which will lead to further reforms. Questions about the roles and responsibilities of individuals, the state and the private sector, including employers, in post-compulsory education provision and funding will continue well into the future (Keep, 2015).

Guide to Further Sources

R. Brown and H. Carasso (2013), *Everything for Sale? The Marketisation of UK Higher Education*, Abingdon: Routledge, analyses the 2010–15 Coalition government's reforms of higher education.

J. Brennan, N. Durazzi and T. Séné (2013), 'Things We Know and Don't Know about the Wider Benefits of Higher Education: A Review of the Recent Literature', BIS Research Paper No. 120, Department for Business, Innovation and Skills, London.

J. Field (2006), *Lifelong Learning and the New Educational Order*, Stoke-on-Trent: Trentham, explores lifelong learning at its peak, maps patterns of participation, evaluates the measures developed to promote lifelong learning, and assesses the prospects of achieving a viable learning society.

J. Janmaat and A. Green (2013), 'Skills inequality, adult learning and social cohesion in the United Kingdom, *British Journal of Educational Studies*, 61:1, 7–24.

E. Keep (2015), 'What does Skills Policy Look Like now the Money has Run Out?' ESRC Centre on Skills, Knowledge & Organisational Performance, Oxford University (www.skope.ox.ac.uk/?person=what-does-skills-policy-look-like-now-the-money-has-run-out), explores what the education and training system might look like in the future.

OECD (2014), *Education at a Glance OECD Indicators* (www.oecd.org/edu/Education-at-a-Glance-2014.pdf), provides a wealthy of data on education across all OECD countries

OECD (2012), *Better Skills, Better Jobs, Better Lives. A Strategic Approach to Skills Policies*, Paris: OECD, provides an integrated, cross-government strategic framework to help countries understand more about how to invest in skills.

T. Schuller and D. Watson (2009, *Learning Through Life: Inquiry into the Future of Lifelong Learning*, Leicester: National Institute of Adult and Continuing Education, presents an overview of the state of lifelong learning and how it should be reformed.

A. Vignoles (2013), 'Widening participation and social mobility', in C. Callender and P. Scott (eds) (2013), *Browne and Beyond: Modernizing English Higher Education*, London: Institute of Education Press, Bedford Way Papers, 112–29, explores the expansion of higher education and why there continues to be unequal access.

Review and Assignment Questions

1 Who should have access to lifelong learning?
2 Who should pay for post-compulsory education and training – the government and taxpayers or individual learners and employers?
3 Are post-compulsory education and training a private good or a public good?
4 Who should decide what post-compulsory education and training courses are available and to whom?
5 Is lifelong learning important and, if so, why?

Visit the book companion site at www.wiley.com/go/alcocksocialpolicy to make use of the resources designed to accompany the textbook. There you will find chapter-specific guides to further resources, including governmental, international, thinktank, pressure groups and relevant journal sources. You will also find a glossary based on *The Blackwell Dictionary of Social Policy*, help sheets, guidance on managing assignments in social policy and career advice.

53

Housing

David Mullins

Overview

- Housing policy plays an important role within welfare, but direct state provision is much less important than in health, education or social care.
- Between 1919 and 1979, council housing became a significant and desirable housing tenure. After 1979, it became residual, less subsidised and less popular.
- Housing tenure mix is changing; home ownership peaked in 2002, but has fallen since. Private renting expanded after 1995, overtaking social housing as the main rental tenure in 2012.
- After 1979, supply-side subsidies (for housing construction) were a key target for public expenditure reductions, but demand-side subsidies (to pay rents) grew significantly.
- Policies on homelessness and access to social housing once provided an important part of the social welfare net. Social protection has since been weakened by conditionality, local discretion, private provision with less security and higher rents not fully covered by benefits.
- Housing faced large public spending reductions after the 2008 global financial crisis. Supply-side subsidies fell by over 50 per cent under the Coalition government. Demand-side subsidies rose in aggregate due to increased claimants, but individual entitlements reduced.

The Student's Companion to Social Policy, Fifth Edition. Edited by Pete Alcock, Tina Haux, Margaret May and Sharon Wright.
© 2016 John Wiley & Sons, Ltd. Published 2016 by John Wiley & Sons, Ltd.

Context

Housing plays an important role in social policy and welfare. It involves the market, state and third sector and processes of production, exchange, ownership and control. Unlike some social policy fields, housing has never been a state monopoly, but responses to housing problems still involve a significant role for governments. From 1919 to 1979, council housing was the major mechanism for improving housing conditions in the UK. Since then, social housing has been part of the transfer of public services to third-sector organisations (housing associations). However, most housing continues to be provided in the market (through home ownership and private renting). Housing has been subject to fiscal, tax, subsidy and regulatory interventions by the state.

As direct state provision has declined, there has been an ongoing tension between market and community influences on housing. Housing policy and legislation have diverged at times (especially since 1997) between England, Scotland, Wales and Northern Ireland. This chapter focuses mainly on England; covering tenure changes, homelessness and access, the contemporary situation and emerging issues since the 2008 global financial crisis (GFC), under the Conservative-led Coalition government (2010–15) and since the 2015 general election.

The Historical Legacy

The origins of housing policy were responses to nineteenth-century industrialisation. Public health measures introduced in a market dominated by private landlordism were intended to control threats to the health of the whole population. Some attempts were made to meet housing needs by nineteenth century philanthropists (for example, Peabody and Guinness), but were insufficient. Before the First World War, supply-side subsidies were proposed for local authorities to build affordable housing for working-class families. War-time rent controls prevented exploitation, and the post-war pledge to provide 'homes fit for heroes' spawned council housing.

The key development in housing policy was the introduction, in 1919, of Exchequer subsidies for council housing. Over the next sixty years, local authorities had an expanding and pivotal role in the provision of housing. Over the same period, private renting declined and home ownership grew – more rapidly in some regions and for more affluent households.

The Second World War halted housing construction, and war-time damage to property left a serious housing deficit. This was addressed by cross-party support for a 'numbers game' to increase supply, including large-scale council building, since this was easier to plan than private construction. Nonetheless, housing was not fully part of the post-war welfare state because of the continued role of the market – there was no National Housing Service. Councils remained the key providers of social housing in a system dominated by private ownership. Housing has, therefore, been called the 'wobbly pillar' of welfare. However, Beveridge recognised 'squalor' as one of the five evils to be tackled: 'dealing with squalor means planning town and countryside and having many more and better homes' (Beveridge, 1943: 86). The post-war welfare state included stronger planning, a new towns programme and private rent controls. Local authorities and new towns received subsidies to build housing on an unprecedented scale.

Between 1919 and 1979, council housing and owner-occupation grew, while private renting faced long-term decline. Governments consistently encouraged home ownership, while private renting was stunted by rent control, slum clearance and incentives to sell dwellings to expand owner-occupation. More affluent groups bought their homes, and an attractive council sector was developed through supply-side subsidies with rents that people could afford, security and decent quality homes.

After 1970, the housing supply problem was seen as largely solved and political parties competed to champion home ownership. The 1979 Conservative government introduced the 'Right to Buy', resulting in over 2 million dwellings (out of 6.5 million) being sold to sitting tenants. Government's view of council housing had shifted. Significant building by local authorities was no longer supported, and smaller-scale funding for housing associations from 1974 only partly filled this gap. Deregulation of private renting and changes in housing finance accelerated the shift to a market-based system.

The last quarter of the twentieth century saw social housing transformed from state to third-sector provision. Housing associations (independent, non-profit bodies) became the preferred social housing providers. Stock transfers of rented homes to housing associations started in 1988, and by 1996 had overtaken 'Right to Buy' as the main mechanism reducing council housing. By 2012, over half of all local authorities had sold their housing stock to housing associations and were left with a strategic role. By 2012, only a quarter of social housing stock was still owned and managed by councils. The remainder was provided by housing associations and so-called 'arm's length management organisations'.

Privatisation has shifted the boundaries of the welfare state. Many affluent tenants bought their council dwellings under 'Right to Buy' with substantial discounts. While not in itself privatisation, stock transfer led to a social housing system more embedded in the market as housing associations' strategies were steered by business plans and loan covenants. Yet they remained subject to government regulation and finance rules.

Tenure Changes

A 'nation of private tenants' became by 1980 'a nation of home owners', but later these trends began to reverse as private renting grew again, while home ownership declined. These national patterns obscure considerable variation between the four UK jurisdictions, and enormous local differences, with some localities dominated by social housing or private renting and others by home ownership.

As tenures grew or declined, so their characteristics changed. By mid-century, the private rented sector comprised dilapidated stock housing a residual population of elderly long-term tenants and a more mixed, transient population. From the mid-1990s, this long-term decline was reversed. A number of complex changes were involved, including 'buy to let' investors saving for retirement, growing demand from 'generation rent', households 'priced out' of home ownership but ineligible for social housing and an increasing role played by private landlords housing low-income groups, including those accepted as homeless.

Home ownership and council housing had first developed to cater for young families, but later changed and diverged. The home ownership sector continues to house the most affluent sections of the population; however, it also houses poorer households including many older people. Home ownership was generally associated with wealth accumulation, but property values have sometimes fallen (for example, in the early 1990s and late 2000s). Access to mortgages for house purchase generally became easier until the GFC of 2008 that originated in high-risk loans to marginal purchasers. After the crisis more cautious lenders demanded higher deposits, thereby preventing potential first-time buyers from benefiting from historically low interest rates. Mortgage advances fell and the entry age for first-time purchase grew steadily. The proportion of (mainly younger) owners buying with a mortgage hit a post-war low, while (mainly older) outright owners increased.

Social housing (managed by councils and housing associations) contracted from housing nearly a third of all households in 1979, including some higher earners; and now caters mainly for low-income groups. Tenants are no longer predominantly young families, but include older people, people with long-term illnesses and disabilities, and lone-parent households. Rationing of access has left those with least bargaining power in the least desirable housing. Research on housing of minority ethnic groups evidences discriminatory outcomes of formal and informal rationing processes. These changes – with the poorest sections of the population becoming more concentrated in social rented housing and especially in the least attractive stock – have been referred to as residualisation. Concentrations of poverty and worklessness among social housing tenants have been constructed as a 'social problem'.

Homelessness and Access to Social Housing

Housing has formed an important part of the welfare safety net through homelessness legislation, access to social housing and housing benefits. Changing policies in these areas help to explain the changing composition of social housing. Council housing initially housed the better-off working class with stable incomes able to afford the rents; indeed, the first London council estate, the Boundary Estate (1897), housed hardly any of the inhabitants from the notorious Old Nichol slum it replaced because rents were too high and wages too insecure. In the 1930s, the emphasis on housing need increased, as for the first time residents affected by slum clearance had rehousing rights. Later, the 1977 Housing (Homeless Persons) Act provided access for vulnerable groups threatened with homelessness. Local discretion over lettings operates within statutory and regulatory guidance; the latter has increased in situations of shortage and in recognition of problems of discrimination and discretion. Homelessness is one of a number of 'reasonable preference' criteria defined by legislation regulating lettings. Local criteria such as residence points, 'sons and daughters' policies, and local lettings schemes have balanced local concerns (for example, for community sustainability) with housing need.

After 2000, the adoption of 'choice-based lettings schemes' placed an onus on applicants to bid for properties rather than wait for offers. Concerns about concentrations of 'worklessness' on housing estates led to policies favouring mixed-income communities, although this was hard to achieve through allocation policies alone. The 2010 government's proposals for 'a fairer future for social housing' included reducing security of tenure and increasing rents for new tenants, and giving local authorities and landlords greater flexibility in allocation policy. Changes introduced by the Localism Act 2011 allowed conditions to be imposed on new tenants (to seek work, training or volunteering), and there were further limits on eligibility of foreign nationals. Local discretion was also allowed on access to housing registers.

Research on homelessness has identified the risks faced by ordinary families of becoming homeless because of the operation of the housing market. Other risks relating to personal factors such as drug and alcohol problems, unemployment, ex-offending and military service have been significant among single homeless people. This led to initiatives to tackle 'street homelessness', to develop supported hostel accommodation as 'places of change' and pathways of support into housing and employment, including social enterprise solutions. These initiatives attempted to reduce the incidence of 'rough sleeping'. Rough sleeper counts in major cities generally declined between 1998 and 2009, but grew again after 2010 to over double their 2000 level.

Official figures for homelessness in England fell from a peak of 148,000 in 2003 to 49,000 in 2009, before rising again to 61,000 in 2013. The use of temporary accommodation fell from 95,000 to 53,000 between 2003 and 2009. This trend was associated with a 'prevention agenda', provision of 'housing options' advice and steering potentially homeless people into private renting. However, 70 per cent of households accepted as homeless continued to move into social housing.

The Localism Act 2011 introduced greater flexibility for English authorities to meet these homelessness duties through private-sector offers within their district and 'suitable' in terms of size, condition, location and affordability. This extended the previous government's direction, but applicants' agreement would no longer be required for 'suitable' offers. As rent caps on housing benefit began to bite (see below), there was a revival of an old trend of London local authorities 'exporting' homeless people to lower rent areas outside London, both for temporary accommodation and later in 'discharge' of duties to house accepted homeless households.

The Contemporary Housing Situation

There is a healthy scepticism within housing studies about how much impact governments and policy have on change in housing, which is largely driven by markets and global factors such as the 2008 GFC. Nevertheless, there have been significant changes to housing policy, spending and outcomes over the past twenty years that indicate the continued importance of policy.

The Labour administration (1997–2010) had begun its term with minimal change to policies inherited from the Conservatives. By 1997, there was no longer a major new-build programme of housing for general needs or for lower-income households, and the governance of housing was increasingly fragmented. Policy had shifted towards dismantling state intervention, relying on the private market to provide and funding this through welfare benefits. However, in the first decade of the millennium there were some changes of direction. The Communities Plan

(ODPM, 2003) sought to reverse under-investment in housing and regional divergence in economic performance and housing need. A ten-year
programme of stock transfer and area regeneration (including a National Strategy for Neighbourhood Renewal and a Housing Market Renewal
Areas programme) were cornerstones of the
Labour government's measures to improve housing conditions, provide 'decent homes' and
respond to failing housing markets. After the
2008 crisis, the Labour government supported a
'kickstart' programme to maintain construction,
shifting temporarily from housing for sale back to
rented housing. While this enabled much of the
planned social housing programme to proceed, it
could not prevent overall construction of new
homes in 2009 falling to the lowest level since
the 1920s.

The Conservative-led Coalition government
had a policy imperative to address the public
finances following the credit crisis, the bailing
out of the banks and Labour's counter-cyclical
investment. As in earlier crises, housing loomed
large in public spending reductions, but this time
there was greater attention to stemming the
growth of demand-side as well as cutting supply-side subsidies.

The 2010 Spending Review halved the housing
capital budget and a new investment framework
for 'affordable housing' was introduced. All new
social homes would be let at 'affordable rents' of up
to 80 per cent of market rents (compared with
55–75 per cent in 2007–8). Housing associations
were expected to fund new development by charging these higher rents for all new homes and some
relets, by investing their substantial surpluses and
reserves, and by subsidising development from
sales of existing assets and changes in tenure and
rents of existing properties. New tenants would
have 'flexible' (less secure) tenancies, which could
be reviewed every two years, to encourage those no
longer in need of subsidy to move on. By reducing
average subsidy to under 20 per cent of building
costs, and charging higher rents, the Coalition
government was for a time able to square the
circle of building more 'affordable homes' with
substantially less public subsidy.

Stemming the growth in demand-side subsidies through the housing benefit system promised
even greater savings – at £22 billion housing
benefit spend was three to four times greater

than the housing capital budget. For private tenants, housing benefits were capped in each area
and restricted to the bottom third of local market
rents. The most widely known benefit reduction in
the social housing sector was the so-called 'bedroom tax', known by the government as the 'spare
room supplement'. This restricted benefits to the
number of bedrooms a household was deemed to
require rather than actually occupied and forced
under-occupiers to either move or top up rent
from their own income. Caps were also placed on
the total welfare benefits paid to individual households, initially to £26,000, leading to severe problems for larger families in high rent areas. Single
people aged under 35 were restricted to a single-
room rent, requiring sharing unless benefits were
topped up from savings or other sources of
income. Housing benefit has been wrapped up
in a simpler Universal Credit scheme for low-
income households currently being rolled out (see
Chapter 47). Under Universal Credit, housing
benefit is paid to the claimant rather than to
landlords, forcing low-income households to
manage tight budgets or risk eviction.

The government's expectation was that caps
would place a downward pressure on private rents.
However, claimant numbers increased due to unmet
demand for social housing and increased use of the
private sector to meet homelessness duties. Many
London boroughs had very limited private rentals
within eligible benefit levels, raising several issues.
First, existing private tenants on benefit were forced
to move. Second, problems in finding temporary
accommodation for homeless households led to
'exports' to lower rent areas outside London. Meanwhile, higher rents for new social housing and relets
were inconsistent with containing housing benefit
(an issue finally acknowledged in the 2015 emergency budget; see below).

Under the Coalition government, regional
housing and planning infrastructure was dismantled, regional spatial strategies and housing targets
abandoned, and housing regulation substantially
reduced. New arrangements (neighbourhood
plans and community rights) were developed to
promote 'localism', but despite some growth in
'community-led housing' (for example, in the
'self-help housing' sector bringing empty homes
into use and in Community Land Trust start-ups)
this was generally a slow-burn policy. In contrast,
the social housing provisions in the Localism Act

led to less stable and secure communities, and did nothing to increase community influence on housing providers (housing associations continued to be exempt from the 'community right to manage').

Meanwhile, there was a new consensus about the emergence of a massive housing shortage as a result of under-investment in all sectors, and a deeper rooted concern about the reduction in home ownership. As well as re-invigorating 'Right to Buy', the Coalition developed a new government-backed initiative to stimulate housing demand. This 'Help to Buy' policy tackled the 'deposit gap' that had locked 'generation rent' out of home ownership after the GFC. This gap was tackled in several ways by providing 20 per cent equity loans or 30 per cent mortgage guarantees to enable 95 per cent mortgages for first-time buyers on properties of up to £600,000. This major new state-backed home ownership subsidy was one of the only housing budgets to increase under the Coalition, guaranteeing over £15 billion loan finance over the life of mortgages. There were also supply-side measures to stimulate house-building without regional housing targets, including a 'new homes bonus' – a five-year subsidy payable to local authorities towards local service costs, matching council tax receipts of each new home and easing of planning barriers to new development.

Emerging Issues

The 2015 general election campaign saw all the main parties proposing to boost housing supply to at least 200,000 a year. However, unlike the post-war numbers game, no parties showed any enthusiasm for new social housing. Indeed, the Conservative manifesto proposed to extend the Right to Buy to 2 million housing association tenants, with the costs of compensating associations and replacing lost rental homes to be met by forced sales of high-value council housing within their dwindling remaining stock. Other key manifesto commitments on housing included Labour's mansion tax on properties worth over £2 million and the Conservatives' proposal to remove inheritance tax for properties up to £1 million. Labour also proposed a registration scheme for private landlords.

In the event it was 'Right to Buy' and inheritance tax reductions rather than mansion tax and landlord registration that became part of the incoming government's housing agenda. However, soon after the election an emergency budget featured two housing surprises. In a reversal of four years of rent increases to fund new development, an annual 1 per cent rent reduction was imposed on housing associations for the next four years. The generous tax treatment of private landlords was partly reversed by plans to gradually reduce mortgage tax relief for buy-to-let landlords from April 2017. The Chancellor introduced the promised inheritance tax reductions in the budget, arguing 'the wish to pass something on to your children as most basic, human and natural aspiration there is'. However, the 2011 Dilnot Review cap on personal contributions to long-term care costs of £75,000 will not now be implemented before 2020, thereby eroding many inheritances.

For social housing, traditional advantages associated with security, affordability and decent conditions have been challenged by these recent policies. Welfare reductions remain at the heart of the new government's plans along with the shift to 'affordable housing' at 80 per cent market rents, with remaining social housing simply a 'springboard' to other tenures. Along with rising homelessness, rent reductions and the forthcoming 'Right to Buy' this forms a challenging agenda for housing associations. Despite growing market influences on them, they cannot simply be seen as independent private bodies. Government policies remain their key drivers.

Guide to Further Sources

Inside Housing provides weekly news and features. Academic journals include *Housing Studies*, *Housing Theory and Society*, *International Journal of Housing Policy* and *Journal of Housing and the Built Environment*.

W. Beveridge (1943), *Pillars of Security*, London: Allen & Unwin.

D. Mullins and A. Murie (2006), *Housing Policy in the UK*, Basingstoke: Macmillan, introduces housing policy in the UK, including historical developments, principal tenures and key policy issues.

D. Mullins and H. Pawson (2010), *After Council Housing. Britain's New Social Landlords*, Basingstoke: Palgrave Macmillan, reviews the causes and impacts of transferring council housing to housing associations.

P. Malpass (2005), *Housing and the Welfare State: The Development of Housing Policy in Britain*, Basingstoke: Palgrave Macmillan, is an account of the changing role of housing within the welfare state.

R. Tunstall (2015), *The Coalition's Record on Housing Policy, Spending and Outcomes 2010–15*, York: Centre for Housing Policy.

S. Wilcox (publishes annually), *UK Housing Review*, Chartered Institute of Housing and Centre for Housing Policy, University of York.

Review and Assignment Questions

1 Where does housing fit in the UK welfare state? How much influence do government policies have on housing in comparison with market drivers?

2 How do supply-side (construction subsidies) and demand-side (housing benefit) subsidies affect the roles of private landlords and social housing?

3 Is the stock transfer equivalent to privatisation?

4 How did 'localism' affect mainstream housing policies under the Coalition government?

5 What can governments do to increase housing supply and revive flagging home ownership markets? Where does 'Help to Buy' fit?

Visit the book companion site at www.wiley.com/go/alcocksocialpolicy to make use of the resources designed to accompany the textbook. There you will find chapter-specific guides to further resources, including governmental, international, thinktank, pressure groups and relevant journal sources. You will also find a glossary based on *The Blackwell Dictionary of Social Policy*, help sheets, guidance on managing assignments in social policy and career advice

54

Social Care

Jon Glasby

Overview

- Social care has a complex history, and current practice continues to be influenced in part by historic tensions around whether people are 'deserving' or 'undeserving' of assistance.
- Current services have struggled to cope with significant financial challenges, on the one hand and rising need and demand, on the other.
- Ongoing challenges include the need to develop a more preventative approach, the importance of integrated care and the need to personalise the care people receive.
- Despite its rhetoric, the Coalition government of 2010–15 arguably made little progress in each of these areas, and major tensions remain.

While most of this chapter focuses on general themes across the UK, specific policies and organisational names are typically those in England.

Context

In 1942, William Beveridge's report on *Social Insurance and Allied Services* set out a blueprint for post-war welfare services (see Chapter 18). One of the most quoted sections of the report is Beveridge's description of 'five giants', or social problems, which future services should seek to tackle. While these are couched in very 1940s language, they nevertheless map across to current social issues and even to some current government departments (see Table 54.1). Thus, as an example, a 1940s 'giant' such as 'want' becomes poverty or social exclusion and has traditionally fallen under

The Student's Companion to Social Policy, Fifth Edition. Edited by Pete Alcock, Tina Haux, Margaret May and Sharon Wright.
© 2016 John Wiley & Sons, Ltd. Published 2016 by John Wiley & Sons, Ltd.

Table 54.1 UK welfare services.

Beveridge's giants	Modern equivalent
Want	Social security
Disease	NHS
Ignorance	Education/lifelong learning
Squalor	Housing/regeneration
Idleness	Employment/leisure

the remit of the social security system. Although other chapters cover these various different services (see Chapters 47–55), a key gap in Table 54.1 is social care and social work. Is social care responding to a sixth giant that Beveridge failed to identify? Is it the glue that holds the other five together? Or is it a crisis service that works with people who fall through the gaps in other services?

Social care

Crucial to an understanding of social care is the distinction between several key terms, which are often used interchangeably. 'Social care' is an overall description for a range of services and workers who support both adults and children facing difficult changes in their lives. While this is a broad description, the focus has often been on providing practical support for a range of specific service user groups, including children at risk of abuse, frail older people, people with mental health problems, people with learning difficulties and disabled people. By the early twenty-first century there were some 1.6 million people using social care services, with some 1.4 million people working in the social care workforce. While this is more than the entire NHS workforce, social care staff are employed by some 30,000 public, private and voluntary agencies.

In contrast, 'social worker' is the name for trained professionals (the social care equivalent of doctors, nurses or teachers), who are now degree-trained, registered with a formal professional 'council' and governed by codes of professional conduct. Following the community reforms of 1990, adult social workers are typically responsible for assessing the needs of individuals, and arranging services to meet those needs from a range of social care providers from across the public, private and voluntary sectors. Many social workers have traditionally been employed in local authority 'social services

departments', although these have since been split into new children's and adults' services in England (see below for further discussion). Of the 1.4 million social care workforce, around 60,000 people are qualified social workers.

The History and Evolution of Social Care

While the history of social care is complex, a key contribution comes from a series of nineteenth-century voluntary organisations and philanthropists. Prior to this, much social support had been provided (as is still the case today) by families and local communities. In Tudor times, much of the assistance available was religious in nature and delivered via the monasteries. Following the dissolution of the monasteries and stimulated by rapid urbanisation and industrialisation, a number of more formal services began to develop via the now notorious Poor Law. While this included outdoor relief (payments to people in financial need), the main source of 'support' was typically the workhouse. Conditions were deliberately made as harsh as possible so as to ensure that only the most needy applied for state help (an approach known as 'the workhouse test' and the principle of 'less eligibility'). Over time, workhouses became increasingly focused on different groups of people, with different approaches emerging for the able-bodied poor (often seen as lazy and capable of supporting themselves) and for frail older people, people with mental health problems and people with learning difficulties (who were increasingly seen as not to blame for their plight and hence deserving of assistance).

During the latter part of the nineteenth century, two prominent voluntary organisations were important in developing new approaches to the alleviation of poverty and in pioneering many of the approaches that later became associated with modern social work:

■ The Charity Organisation Society (COS) was founded in response to a proliferation of almsgiving following the depression of the late 1860s. It promoted principles of 'scientific charity' – assessing those in need and providing charitable support only to those deemed deserving (with those deemed undeserving left to rely on the Poor Law and the work-house). In this way, COS hoped to coordinate the provision of financial support and to give individuals an incentive to be self-sufficient (guarding against the danger that generous support would only encourage the feckless and thriftless). In many ways, similar notions underpin current debates about whether or not to give to people begging on the street – does this support those in need or does it encourage people to be dependent on this form of assistance?

■ Founded in 1884 with the creation of Toynbee Hall in Whitechapel, the Settlement movement had considerable overlaps with COS (and the same individuals were often involved in both movements), but increasingly diverged over time. Settlements were colonies of educated people living in poor areas of large cities, with the dual purpose of using the education and privilege of 'settlers' to help the poor, but also of getting to know the poor as neighbours and, hence, understanding more about the nature of poverty. Over time, it became increasingly apparent to many settlers that poverty was not the result of individual failings, but the product of wider social forces. A number of settlers (for example, Clement Attlee and William Beveridge) later made significant contributions to the advent of a welfare state.

In many ways, these different perspectives continue to influence current practice. Whereas concepts such as 'care management' (see below for further discussion) focus on the assessment of individual need to ascertain entitlement to support, community development approaches focus much more on community empowerment and on the individual in a broader social context. Both movements were also influential in the development of early social work, collaborating with leading universities to help found early social work courses and provide placements for students.

Following the Second World War, an increasing amount of social work activity came to be subsumed within two local government departments: specialist children's departments and health and welfare departments. These were later combined into generic social services departments (SSDs) following the 1968 Seebohm Report. By bringing together a range of adult and children's social care services, Seebohm argued, there was scope to create a more comprehensive and coordinated approach, to attract greater resources, and to plan ahead to identify and meet the needs of a local area more effectively. SSDs were soon boosted by a growing national infrastructure, including a more unified system of social work education (advocated in various reports by Eileen Younghusband) and the creation of a new National Institute of Social Work Training (which was later subsumed into a new Social Care Institute for Excellence).

'Managing Care'

In many ways, this system was to remain intact until the late 1980s, when a review of community care services by Sir Roy Griffiths (managing director of Sainsbury supermarket) led to the 1990 NHS and Community Care Act. Henceforth, adult social workers were to be 'care managers', responsible for assessing individual need and arranging care packages from a combination of public, private and voluntary services. Consistent with the ideological commitments of the then Conservative government, this changed social workers into 'purchasers' rather than providers, and much of the new funding that accompanied the changes was to be spent in the independent sector.

Under the Labour governments of 1997–2010, much of this ethos remained, but with a growing emphasis on 'modernisation'. This modernisation was often portrayed as a 'third way' between the market-based ideology of the New Right and the public sector values of Labour. Unfortunately, such a concept tended to be better at defining what a 'third way' is not (that is, not the market and not the state) than what it is/could be, and the result was arguably a rather eclectic series of different policies and approaches. However, central to Labour's approach was an emphasis on:

■ Greater *choice and control*, with people using services having greater say over what they receive and how money is spent on their behalf. Perhaps the best example is the increasing role played by direct payments, with social care service users receiving the cash equivalent of directly provided services with which to purchase their own care or hire their own staff. From the mid-2000s, this was extended through the concept of a personal budget (an upfront allocation of money, thereby enabling the person and the worker to be more creative in deciding how best to meet need). This remains separate from any disability benefits paid to people by the social security system – although there may be scope for greater integration of separate funding streams in future.

- Greater *partnership working*, with health and social care in particular becoming increasingly inter-related over time. In 2000, this led to the announcement of a new form of organisation (in England) – the Care Trust – which was seen as a vehicle with which to integrate health and social care fully. While this model did not prove popular in practice, policy continued to stress the importance of joint working between health and social care.
- A stronger emphasis on *citizenship* and *social inclusion* (with a growing tendency – slow at first – to look beyond traditional health/social care to more universal services, and various attempts to tackle discrimination and promote human rights). As an example, the 2001 learning disability White Paper, *Valuing People*, stressed four overarching principles (rights, inclusion, choice and independence), viewing social care and health in terms of what they can contribute to the lives of people with learning disabilities rather than as an end in themselves.

In structural terms, the key change under New Labour was the abolition (in England) of generic SSDs, and the creation of new integrated services for children and for adults. Thus, new Directors of Children's Services became responsible for both education and children's social care, bringing together wider partners via Children's Trusts. Similarly, Directors of Adult Social Services were charged with developing partnerships with NHS colleagues and broader services, and often oversaw both adult social care and other services (such as housing, leisure or adult education) (see Chapter 49). In recognition of such changes, many English SSDs split into a Directorate of Children's Services and various configurations of adult care (termed 'Social Care and Health', 'Social Inclusion and Health', Social Care and Housing', 'Adults and Communities', etc.). Similar changes also took place elsewhere in the system, with English policy increasingly diverging between the Department of Health and the Department of Education. In many ways, this took social care back to pre-Seebohm days, though without necessarily stating why the need for generic SSDs, which Seebohm placed at the heart of his vision for social care, was now no longer relevant. In recent years, it has also been difficult for some of the national social care bodies to retain a generic approach to social care issues, with a series of more recent changes seemingly driven primarily by a need to reform child protection services rather than to develop social care and social work careers and values more generally.

Social Care under the UK Coalition

Since 2010, local government has struggled to cope with massive cuts in its funding coupled with rising need and demand. In children's services, an ongoing series of child protection scandals and allegations of service failures have continued to raise questions about the quality and future organisation of support. Many people would also argue that previous attempts to integrate social care and education have been unsuccessful, with a risk that social care and child protection become dominated by a more attainment-focused education sector. As a result, many authorities have begun to reintegrate their children's and adult services, with a single 'Director of People' role replacing separate directors of Adult Social Services and directors of Children's Services.

In adult social care, the Care Act 2014 primarily tidied up a messy legal framework. However, it also made some significant changes to the funding of long-term care and gave councils greater duties in terms of promoting well-being. While these were largely positive changes, the approach to funding long-term care was felt by many to be a sticking-plaster solution to much more fundamental problems. Moreover, draconian funding cuts are likely to mean that the reality for people in need is likely to differ significantly from the rhetoric of the Care Act. Also under the Coalition there was a renewed focus on developing more integrated care between different parts of the NHS and between health and social care – albeit that critics have suggested such terms are being used in a very loose way in a system that is more fragmented than it was prior to 2010. While personalisation is still a stated aspiration, there remain questions about the underlying motives of the government (with many concerned that the main aim may be to erode public service values and to implement severe cuts, rather than to promote citizenship). These themes and concerns are unlikely to change following the 2015 general election, and it is possible that providing extra funding for the NHS could lead to even more and even deeper cuts elsewhere, for example, in local government and hence in social care.

Emerging Issues

Always something of a crisis service for those in need, social care and social work have had a chequered history. While there has always been a need to support the most vulnerable in society, there has always been uncertainty over the best way to do this, from the different notions of poverty underpinning the voluntary action of the nineteenth century, to the different visions of Beveridge, Seebohm, Griffiths, the 1997–2010 Labour governments and the 2010–15 UK Coalition government. With increasing financial and demographic pressures, however, previous approaches are increasingly strained, and considerable uncertainty remains as to how best to refocus services towards a more preventative approach, secure added value through more effective inter-agency working and place the people who use services at the centre of decision-making. Whatever happens, history suggests that the imperative to support those most in need in society – be they adults or children – is unlikely to go away, and that some form of social support – whatever it is called and wherever it sits – seems as essential now as ever. This seems particularly the case following the 2010 and 2015 general elections, with the risk of rising need and less resources with which to work.

In the early twenty-first century, social care faces a series of challenges as it seeks to respond to a combination of social, economic and demographic changes. First and foremost, an ageing population, medical advances and changes in the availability of family support mean that there are more and more very frail older people in need of support, and a growing number of younger people with very profound and complex physical impairments and learning disabilities. With a very challenging financial context, fundamental change may be required to meet new demands, and a range of government policies emphasise the need to move from a system of crisis support to one based much more around prevention and promoting well-being. Quite how to do this in practice (and how to invest in long-term prevention whilst also continuing to meet the needs of those in crisis) remains unresolved. In recent years, this has also led to a growing debate about best to fund long-term care for frail older people – and the limited changes introduced as part of the 2014 Care Act are unlikely to prevent future public anxiety and political controversies over such a key issue.

Also linked is the increasing emphasis placed on partnership working or 'integrated care', with social care, health, education and other local services increasingly asked to work together to meet the needs of people with complex, cross-cutting needs. For all this seems like common sense, working with multiple partners and reconciling different priorities and cultures are extremely challenging. Questions also remain as to how much it costs to work in partnership, what outcomes this delivers in practice, and whether it is worth the time and energy involved. At the same time, structural changes in children's and in adult services in England have arguably left social care feeling very fragile and vulnerable, with a risk of being dominated by larger, better resourced and more publicly popular services (such as the NHS or education). Nor do structural changes seem to solve the problem – with practice in Northern Ireland still feeling very 'unintegrated' despite having had much more joined-up services, at least on paper, for many years.

Finally, the concepts of direct payments and personal budgets could represent a bold and radical challenge to current practice and to the current balance of power, heralding one of the most profound changes in social care since the advent of the Charity Organisation Society. Pioneered in adult social care, such concepts are also spreading to other sectors (such as health and some children's services), and so could become a more general organising principle for welfare services more generally. However, despite the initial value base of these approaches (very much focused on citizenship, choice and control), the reality in an era of austerity is that the same mechanisms could simply be used as a smokescreen for cuts and reductions in service. Similar risks also exist with regard to the 'well-being' agenda emphasised by the Care Act 2014. On the one hand, a number of commentators feel that current services focus too much on 'deficits' (what people cannot do for themselves), and do not do enough to value and build on people's 'assets' (things they can do, their strengths, their networks and their communities). While this could lead to a really exciting attempt to wrap formal support around existing social capital and community resources, the risk is that positive language is used to disguise dramatic funding reductions, and that the low-level services that are needed to help support existing community networks are the first to be cut.

As social care contemplates the period from 2015 to 2020, therefore, it has a number of underlying problems, some potentially positive tools with which to work – but also a lot to be concerned about.

Guide to Further Sources

Useful websites include the Social Care Institute for Excellence (www.scie.org.uk), a national body identifying and disseminating what works in social care in England, Wales and Northern Ireland; the College of Social Work (www.tcsw .org.uk), an independent national body representing the social work profession; and Community Care magazine (www.communitycare.co.uk), an online trade magazine for social care (children's and adult services).

Introductory reading includes J. Glasby (2012), *Understanding Health and Social Care*, 2nd edn, Bristol: Policy Press, an introductory textbook exploring the history, nature and current dilemmas of health and adult social care; M. Kellett (2011), *Children's Perspectives on Integrated Services*,

Basingstoke: Palgrave Macmillan, an introductory textbook on inter-agency children's services, emphasising a children's perspectives on recent reforms; R. Means, S. Richards and R. Smith (2008), *Community Care: Policy and Practice*, 4th edn, Basingstoke: Palgrave Macmillan, is an accessible history of community care services; C. Needham and J. Glasby (eds) (2014), *Debates in Personalisation*, Bristol: Policy Press, is an edited collection exploring different views on the nature and implications of personalisation; and M. Payne (2005), *The Origins of Social Work: Continuity and Change*, Basingstoke: Palgrave, provides a review of the history and evolution of social work.

Review and Assignment Questions

1 How can social care be encouraged to work effectively with other services (such as education or health) without losing its distinctive contribution and values?

2 How can services carry on meeting the needs of people in crisis whilst also trying to invest in longer-term preventative approaches?

3 What impact will personal budgets have on the nature and delivery of social care?

4 What impact will funding cuts have on adult social care, on workers and on people using services?

5 How fit for purpose does social care feel in the early twenty-first century, and what needs to change moving forwards?

Visit the book companion site at www.wiley.com/ go/alcocksocialpolicy to make use of the resources designed to accompany the textbook. There you will find chapter-specific guides to further resources, including governmental, international, thinktank, pressure groups and relevant journal sources. You will also find a glossary based on *The Blackwell Dictionary of Social Policy*, help sheets, guidance on managing assignments in social policy and career advice.

55

Criminal Justice

Tim Newburn

■■■

Overview

- Traditionally, criminal justice and penal policy have not been greatly studied by social policy scholars; this is now changing markedly.
- The main institutions of our 'modern' system of criminal justice came into being during the nineteenth and early twentieth centuries.
- A profound shift in emphasis away from welfare and rehabilitation occurred in the final three decades of the twentieth century.
- The dominant features of contemporary criminal justice have been punitiveness, politicisation and populism.
- The late twentieth century saw a remarkable growth in the use of imprisonment and other forms of penal surveillance.

■■■

Criminal Justice and Social Policy

In the main, scholars of social and public policy have tended to ignore the area of criminal justice. Compared with, say, health, education, welfare and culture, criminal justice has been relatively invisible. Yet, as Max Weber identified, the creation and maintenance of systems for protecting against the breakdown of internal social order are generally thought to be among the key characteristics and functions that define the modern nation-state. The period since the Second World War has seen a substantial increase in crime (though with a more recent down-turn) and a growing sense that this is one of the more pressing political and policy issues of the times.

The past two centuries or so have seen the progressive rationalisation and bureaucratisation

The Student's Companion to Social Policy, Fifth Edition. Edited by Pete Alcock, Tina Haux, Margaret May and Sharon Wright.
© 2016 John Wiley & Sons, Ltd. Published 2016 by John Wiley & Sons, Ltd.

of criminal justice and penal processes. From localised, community-based systems of policing and punishment, huge state-managed apparatuses, and vast bodies of laws, rules and regulations aimed at controlling crime have developed. The first thing to note is that there is no single system of criminal justice in the United Kingdom. There are three distinctive systems in England and Wales, in Scotland and in Northern Ireland. My focus here is primarily upon England and Wales. The criminal justice system is made up of the following major agencies and organisations:

- *Police:* forty-three constabularies in England and Wales (plus single forces in Scotland and Northern Ireland).
- *Crown Prosecution Service:* established in 1985 and currently administered in thirteen geographical areas.
- *Magistrates' Courts and the Crown Court:* the vast majority of cases (generally the less serious) are heard in Magistrates' Courts, whereas the more serious are heard in the Crown Court in front of judge and jury.
- *National Offender Management Service (NOMS):* an executive agency of the Ministry of Justice, which brings together HM Prison Service and the National Probation Service and community rehabilitation companies (which are responsible for the supervision of offenders in the community and the provision of reports to the criminal courts).
- *Crime and Disorder Reduction Partnerships/ Community Safety Partnerships:* established by the Crime and Disorder Act 1998, these are multi-agency partnerships involving representation from police, local authorities, probation, health and so forth, and are tasked with monitoring local crime problems, and publishing and overseeing plans for local crime reduction.

Patterns of Crime

Broadly speaking there are two main methods used for measuring and tracking trends in crime. One is taken from data collected routinely by law enforcement agencies concerning crimes reported by the public or otherwise coming to the attention of the authorities. In Britain, such data are collected by the police and are generally referred to as *recorded crime statistics.* The second uses survey methods to elicit information from a representative sample of the population about their experiences of crime – primarily as victims wherever this is the case – usually over the previous twelve months. In England and Wales, this is the Crime Survey for England and Wales (CSEW), first undertaken in 1981 and which has run intermittently since then, but is now an annual survey.

Both sources of data have their shortcomings. Recorded crime statistics can tell us little about those 'crimes' that are never reported to the police – estimated to be at least one-half of all offences. By contrast, the CSEW does not cover all crimes (including corporate or organised crime and 'victimless' crimes such as drugs possession). It is generally advisable to consult and compare both sources when attempting to understand and track levels and trends in crime.

It is widely believed that we live in times of unprecedented levels of crime. Whether such beliefs are accurate rather depends on the time-frame being utilised. It is certainly the case compared with, say, the 1940s, 1950s or 1960s that current levels of crime are very high. However, if we take a longer historical perspective, then there is rather reliable evidence to suggest that previous eras were characterised by very high levels of crime and disorder, even by contemporary standards. It appears to have been in the mid-1950s that crime began to increase markedly, with recorded crime rising by almost three-quarters between 1955 and 1960. Why might this be so? Well, one important point to note first is that this period saw a very substantial increase in the availability of mass market consumer goods, many of which were portable. Second, changes in the labour market saw a substantial increase in the proportion of women going out to work, with the consequence that houses were left empty for considerably longer periods than had previously been the case. Third, it is also likely that the police became more assiduous in their recording of crime during this period. As can be seen from Figure 55.1, crime continued to rise fairly markedly and consistently from that period on, all the way through to the mid-1990s when it began to fall.

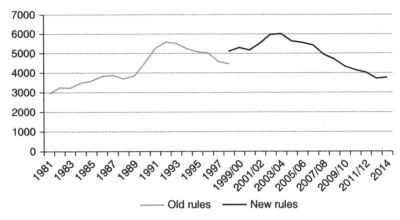

Figure 55.1   Overall recorded crime rate, England and Wales, 1981–2014.
Source: Criminal statistics, England and Wales (various), based on Flatley et al. (2010).

Figure 55.1 shows levels of recorded crime over the past three decades. Police-recorded crime data show crime rising relatively steadily during the 1980s and then increasing markedly from towards the end of the decade until 1992. From that point recorded crime rates declined until 1998–9 when new 'counting rules' (ways in which the police record crime) were introduced. As the gap between the two sets of 1998–9 figures illustrates, the new counting rules produced an immediate increase in the number of offences recorded and, thereafter, appear to show crime increasing again until 2003–4, whereupon crime begins to decline.

Data drawn from the various rounds of the Crime Survey in many ways match the general trend visible from police-recorded statistics in the 1980s and early 1990s, though they depart quite significantly in the period since the late 1990s. CSEW data, like police-recorded crime, show crime rising into the 1990s – in this case to 1995 – and then falling. By contrast with police-recorded crime, the downturn measured by the CSEW continues almost uninterrupted since 1995. Indeed, according to this measure, crime levels as measured by the CSEW were estimated to be at their lowest since the survey was introduced (see Figure 55.2).

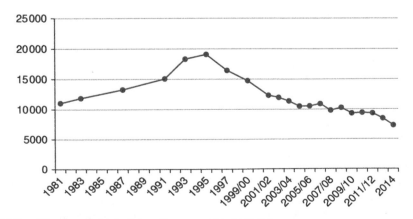

Figure 55.2   All crime, British Crime Survey, 1981–2013/14.
Source: Office for National Statistics (2014).

A Brief History of Criminal Justice

Though the death penalty was the focus of the penal system in medieval times, and levels of capital punishment were high, executions underwent something of a brief boom in the second half of the seventeenth century. Much of the eighteenth century was characterised by a search for viable secondary punishments. Transportation (whereby prisoners were taken by ship to serve their sentences in penal colonies, mainly in America and Australia) was the other major form of judicial punishment in Britain, and by the 1760s transportation to the colonies accounted for at least 70 per cent of all sentences at the Central Criminal Court in London. From this point on, however, transportation declined and the use of imprisonment began to grow.

The system of punishment in Victorian Britain differed quite significantly from that of the late eighteenth century. The use of the death penalty declined markedly throughout the 1800s, public ceremonies of execution ceased in 1868 and corporal punishment of adults was rare by the second half of the century. Put simply, imprisonment moved from being merely a repository for those awaiting trial, sentence or death in the sixteenth and seventeenth centuries to a site where punishment was inflicted on an increasingly wide range of offenders during the course of the eighteenth and nineteenth centuries.

In the pre-industrial era, 'policing' was a community-based, less formal set of activities. In the UK, the establishment of formal policing was preceded by community-based systems, such as the 'hue and cry' in which local citizens took responsibility for raising the alarm and for chasing down the offender. Eighteenth-century England was characterised by increasing concerns about crime. By the mid- to late eighteenth century, crime and disorder were perceived to pose a threat to social stability, and it was around this time (in 1829 in London) that what we now understand as 'the police' emerged.

The nineteenth and early twentieth centuries saw the creation of the fundamental institutions of the modern criminal justice system: the prison, the police, the courts and related systems of criminal prosecution, probation and, in due course, an increasingly complex array of non-custodial penalties (fines, probation, community service, etc.). Towards the end of the nineteenth century separate systems for dealing with juvenile offenders also emerged. The first half of the twentieth century saw the consolidation and reform of the modern criminal justice system. This period drew to an end around the middle of the twentieth century, and was the era in which the 'solidarity project' – in which the state was the guarantor of full citizenship and security for all – was increasingly eclipsed by market forces. Recent decades have seen the emergence of a rapidly expanding mixed economy in many areas of criminal justice and, crucially, what also to many appears to be a decisive shift in what are believed to be the purposes and ambitions of our criminal justice and penal policies.

The Aims of Punishment

In pre-industrial/colonial times much punishment was public in character and, as such, was designed to shame, to bring forth expressions of guilt, remorse and repentance. Loss of freedom – through imprisonment – was far from a common response to criminal infractions and was not assumed, as yet, to be an effective method for stimulating reform. By the middle of the nineteenth century, this had all changed and in the UK a major public debate about the prison system was underway. The system, it was suggested, was failing in its objective of deterring criminals while simultaneously being too harsh. What emerged was a new system of punishment in which, while *deterrence* remained, an important goal of criminal justice policy, reform, and *rehabilitation* lay at its heart. The range of sanctions available to criminal courts expanded markedly, probation and other forms of training became established, and a range of new institutions were established or consolidated, many of which were conceived as direct alternatives to imprisonment.

The penal-welfare strategies that developed in the late nineteenth century reached their high point a little after the mid-twentieth century. However, there has been a radical restructuring and reorientation since that period. At the heart of this shift has been declining trust in the welfare and rehabilitative functions of criminal justice and the gradual rise to dominance of a set of discourses and practices that are more punitive, more politicised and more populist. By the late 1970s, there was a clear loss of faith in the power of the state to reform and, through reform, to reduce crime.

Criminal justice policy in this period was caught up in the battle between two competing versions of the role of the state. The first emphasised welfare and civil rights, and the reduction of social inequalities. The other railed against 'big government' and sought to limit state intervention in citizens' lives in most areas – with the exception of criminal justice. In this second model, the state has a much diminished role in managing and protecting social welfare, something increasingly left to the market, but has an increasingly enhanced role in the management of social order. Indeed, for commentators such as Charles Murray, rising crime and disorder were precisely a product of welfare dependency.

As a consequence, effective criminal justice and penal policy 'came to be viewed as a matter of imposing more controls, increasing disincentives, and, if necessary, segregating the dangerous sector of the population' (Garland, 2001: 102). Over the course of the past twenty years such punitiveness has become the standard political position on crime and order for politicians of all hues. Thus, the other great change in this field concerns the politicisation of criminal justice.

Criminal Justice and Penal Politics

Crime is now a staple of political discourse and of electoral politics. While this may not feel surprising, it is, in fact, a relatively new political phenomenon. Until the early 1970s, in the UK, for example, criminal justice policy barely featured in major elections and certainly was far from the 'wedge issue' it has often been since.

In the criminal justice arena, politicians' concern with how they are likely to be perceived has had a profound effect on policymaking in recent times. Crucially, as numerous commentators have noted, by the 1990s the old divisions between 'conservative' and 'liberal' political positions on crime had disappeared, and had been replaced by what appeared to be a straightforward 'tough on crime' message. The past two decades have seen a progressively intensifying battle by the major political parties to be seen as the party of law and order. A 'tough on crime' stance has come to be associated with electoral success and its opposite, being 'soft on crime', with electoral failure.

The lengthy political dominance of Conservatism during the 1980s in the UK led to vociferous debates within the British Labour Party over the possible sources of electoral success in what were clearly changed times. The Labour Party sought to dump its various hostages to fortune, not least of which was its previously more liberal policies on crime control. 'New Labour' in the UK embraced so-called third-way politics. In the criminal justice arena, this meant attempting to modify the old-fashioned liberal penal-welfarism that the party had largely clung to throughout the 1980s and into the 1990s by adding into the mix what was by now considered the *sine qua non* of successful electoral politics: a healthy dose of punitive rhetoric and the promise of similarly punitive policies. This mixture has never been more successfully captured than in Tony Blair's 1993 soundbite, 'tough on crime and tough on the causes of crime'.

Contemporary Penal Policy

The clearest change in penal policy can be seen in relation to the use of imprisonment. Figure 55.3 shows the prison population in England and Wales for the past half-century or so. The prison population stood at approximately 20,000 at the turn of the twentieth century; the prison population declined from the First World War through the Second World War and then began to rise. It reached its turn of the century levels again by the late 1950s and by the early 1980s reached a historic high in the low 40,000 s. The population was reaching 50,000 by the end of the decade, at which point various strategies were employed, successfully, to begin to reduce the numbers incarcerated. At roughly the point that crime reached its peak in England and Wales the prison population once again began to rise, and to do so markedly more quickly than at any point since the Second World War.

The reasons for the expanding prison population are complex. There are three main possibilities: an increase in the numbers being caught and sentenced; an increase in the seriousness of the crimes being prosecuted; and an increase in

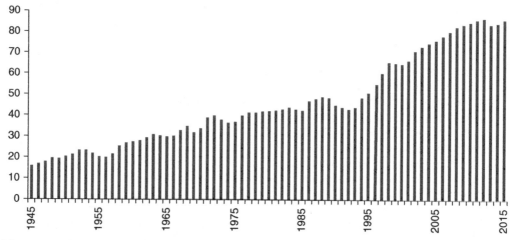

Figure 55.3 Prison population (000s), England and Wales, 1945–2015.
Source: HM Prison Services Statistics.

sentence severity. There is little or no evidence that the changes reflect an increase in the numbers of offenders being caught or convicted – these have remained relatively stable. Indeed, there does not appear to have been any substantial increase in the seriousness overall of the offences before the courts. Rather, the greatest change seems to have been in the severity of the sentences being passed by the courts: with prison sentences becoming more likely for certain offences, and also being imposed for longer periods of time than previously.

From 1997 to 2010, successive Labour governments introduced a considerable body of criminal justice legislation, much of which served to increase both the severity of the penalties attached to criminal offending and the reach of the penal system. Side by side with the increased use of formal criminal sanctions such as community and custodial penalties, there was a considerable spread of new forms of contractualised social control (most famously the Anti-Social Behaviour Order (ASBO)), all of which had the effect of drawing more people into the criminal justice system and, in many cases, keeping them there for longer.

In 2010, a government formed of the Conservative and the Liberal Democrat parties, came to preside over criminal justice and penal policy for the first time for over half a century. Quickly some mixed messages emerged. Initially, the most newsworthy was the policy shift in the Ministry of Justice, which questioned the wisdom of short

prison sentences, set targets for the reduction the overall number of people in prison, and argued for a return to a greater emphasis on rehabilitation. For students of penal politics this appeared to signal another sea-change. Here was a Conservative Justice Secretary eschewing the tough political rhetoric that had become the staple form of discourse in the previous twenty years. Furthermore, the main critics of the proposals turned out to be a combination of those on the right of the Conservative Party, together with ex-Labour Home Secretaries. It did not appear to be politics as usual. And so, in many ways, it proved. The so-called 'rehabilitation revolution' proved to be something of a damp squib, and although some modest reductions in prison numbers were achieved, prisons remained resolutely overcrowded.

But elsewhere some radical changes were set in train. Policing was subject to a radical overhaul of its governance procedures – with the introduction of directly elected Police and Crime Commissioners in England and Wales, and the merger of all forces into a single national force north of the border in Scotland. A radically reforming Home Secretary, Theresa May, also set about the police service, slashing its budget, criticising it for inefficiency and complacency, and appointing the first ever civilian Chief Inspector of Constabulary. Perhaps most unexpectedly, in the aftermath of the 2011 riots she announced a review of police powers to stop and search – arguably British policing's most sacred of cows. From 2012 onward, the marketisation of criminal justice grew in speed and penetration. It was the probation service that was most dramatically affected, and by June 2014 it was effectively split in two, with a National Probation Service managing 'higher risk' clients and advising the courts, on the one hand, and approximately twenty community rehabilitation companies doing the day-to-day supervision of the bulk of the probation service's extant clients.

In all this there are perhaps two main points to make about the politics of criminal justice and penal policy in the period since 2010. First, though the UK Coalition government policy was by no means uncontroversial, this became an area with distinctly less political 'heat' than had characterised some earlier periods. Indeed, in both the 2010 and the 2015 general elections, crime and punishment played relatively little part. To an extent, both terrorism and migration – both of which were quite significant electoral issues – served as proxies for some crime matters, but, by and large, the main parties were largely silent on law and order. Second, there are now at least three, if not four, quite distinct political jurisdictions as far as crime and punishment in the UK are concerned. Both Scotland and Northern Ireland now have criminal justice and penal systems that in many respects operate quite differently from that in England and Wales – and are moving in different directions. Moreover, although England and Wales are covered by a single legal system, and the police and prison services cover both countries, increasingly devolved power to the Welsh Assembly is opening up gaps between the two – perhaps most visibly in youth justice. Finally, it is clear that the politics of crime and punishment are quite dissimilar in a number of ways in England, Wales, Scotland and Northern Ireland, and this would appear to be a trend that can only increase.

Guide to Further Sources

There are numerous very helpful information sources on the web. Both the Home Office and Ministry of Justice websites contain a large amount of material. Criminal statistics are now produced by the Office for National Statistics, and the latest updates can be found at: www.ons.gov.uk/ons/taxonomy/index.html?nscl=Crime+in +England+and+Wales.

The International Centre for Prison Studies runs a website that contains a large amount of useful data on trends in the use of imprisonment around the world at: www.prisonstudies.org, and, domestically, a large amount of useful, sometimes provocative, material can be found at the website of the Centre for Crime and Justice Studies at: www.crimeandjustice.org.uk.

The most influential book in recent years in this area is D. Garland (2001), *The Culture of Control*, Oxford: Oxford University Press, which explores the changing nature of crime and penal policy and culture in America and Britain. A weighty, but definitive, volume is M. Maguire, R. Morgan and R. Reiner (eds) (2012), *Oxford Handbook of Criminology*, 5th edn, Oxford: Oxford University Press. This is an edited textbook with contributions from many leading criminologists covering their particular areas of expertise. In particular, those wishing to read more about penal politics should read the following chapter by D. Downes and R. Morgan, 'No turning back: the politics of law and order into the millennium'. An introductory textbook which covers the bulk of criminological topics, aimed at the new undergraduate student is T. Newburn (2016), *Criminology*, 3rd edn, London: Routledge. Finally, a provocative, thoughtful and persuasive book in which the reasons for the changing nature of crime control in contemporary Britain are explored is R. Reiner (2007), *Law and Order: An Honest Citizen's Guide to Crime Control*, Cambridge: Polity Press.

Review and Assignment Questions

1 What are the two main sources of data about crime?

2 What has been the general trend in crime over the past forty years?

3 How might the dominant characteristics of criminal justice policy over the same period be described?

4 What explains the rise in the prison population between 1990 and 2015?

5 In what ways have penal politics changed in recent times?

Visit the book companion site at www.wiley.com/go/alcocksocialpolicy to make use of the resources designed to accompany the textbook. There you will find chapter-specific guides to further resources, including governmental, international, thinktank, pressure groups and relevant journal sources. You will also find a glossary based on *The Blackwell Dictionary of Social Policy*, help sheets, guidance on managing assignments in social policy and career advice.

PART IX
Experiencing Welfare

56

Experiences of Out-of-Work Benefit Receipt

Ruth Patrick

■■

Overview

- Unemployment policy relies on welfare conditionality (attaching behavioural conditions to benefits receipt) in efforts to 'activate' individuals from 'welfare' into 'work'.
- The UK Conservative government (elected in 2015) has continued to extend and intensify conditionality, with inevitable consequences for those directly affected.
- More research is needed into how conditionality is experienced, but there is evidence that it can cause serious hardship.
- A rhetoric that divides the population around a work/non-work axis can add to the stigma and shame associated with benefits reliance.
- The focus on conditionality can be criticised for its neglect of broader societal barriers to engagement in the paid labour market.

■■

Unemployment and State Intervention

Social policy is centrally concerned with questions of employment and unemployment, with who is and who is not engaged in the paid labour market and on what basis. Unemployment matters because of the harm it can do to individuals, as well as its wider economic and societal costs. Being unemployed can have detrimental consequences for an individual's self-esteem, self-confidence, physical and mental health, and future employability. High rates of

The Student's Companion to Social Policy, Fifth Edition. Edited by Pete Alcock, Tina Haux, Margaret May and Sharon Wright.
© 2016 John Wiley & Sons, Ltd. Published 2016 by John Wiley & Sons, Ltd.

unemployment are problematic for the economy, and also adversely affect a government's tax revenues and levels of benefit expenditure. As a result, much policy energy is focused upon welfare to work, measures to support, encourage and even compel those on out-of-work benefits to make the transition into paid employment.

Unemployment is best understood as a descriptor of those working-age adults who want to be in paid employment, but do not currently have a job. The main social security benefit for those experiencing unemployment is Jobseeker's Allowance (JSA), the eligibility conditions of which demand that individuals are available for and actively seeking work. It should be noted that the JSA population is not a homogeneous group, and includes a growing number of lone parents and disabled people. In the UK, there are two main measures of unemployment. The claimant count measures the total number of people claiming JSA at any one time, and in the future will also include unemployed people claiming Universal Credit, a new benefit that will eventually replace JSA. In recent years, this figure has been much lower than the Independent Labour Organisation's (ILO) unemployment rate, which is based on survey evidence to estimate total numbers of people looking for and available for work. The disparity between the two figures is because not everyone who is unemployed is eligible for or chooses to claim out-of-work benefits. In the three months to December 2014, the claimant count stood at 823,900, while the ILO rate of unemployment was 1.9 million in November 2014 (DWP, 2015). Importantly, while media attention and political rhetoric might lead one to expect that a high proportion of benefit expenditure goes to unemployment benefits, it is in fact a very small proportion of the total. In 2011–12, £4.91 billion was spent on JSA, which represents just 3 per cent of total benefits expenditure.

This chapter focuses on the key social policy measures targeted at unemployed people in the UK, and – critically – considers how these measures are experienced by those directly affected. It seeks to provide a better understanding of the policy approach taken, and the impacts this can have on individual lives. In this analysis, discussion is focused on the experiences of JSA claimants, although it is recognised that many of the policy reforms discussed, such as the extension of welfare conditionality, also impact on the wider 'economically inactive' population. Welfare conditionality refers to attaching work-related behavioural conditions to benefit receipt, for example, requiring people to spend thirty-five hours per week looking for work in order to be eligible to claim Universal Credit (see Chapters 8, 47 and 48).

The Policy Approach

In recent years, policy attention has shifted away from concentrating efforts to encourage benefit recipients to find work on unemployed people alone to a much broader focus on the wider economically inactive population, on all those on out-of-work benefits. Today, many disabled people and lone parents are expected to take steps to seek work as a condition of continued benefit receipt, even where they are awarded disability benefits or Income Support. At the same time, eligibility for benefits has changed, meaning more and more lone parents and disabled people have been moved onto JSA, where they must comply with work-related conditions that encompass work search and various forms of work-related activity, such as skills and employability training and mandatory work experience. This shift in policy is best understood as a shift from a relatively narrow concern with 'unemployment' to a broader focus on 'worklessness'.

Throughout, political and media emphasis is placed on the supposed 'problem' of 'welfare dependency', with 'work' being the posited solution. In this analysis, paid employment is seen as transformative, with the scope to deliver rewards that extend beyond financial remuneration to improvements in health, well-being and family life. Further, paid employment is conceptualised as the primary duty of the responsible citizen, and governments characterise their welfare-to-work efforts as ensuring that this duty is being fulfilled. In the UK, a 'work-first' approach is taken, with movements into any employment prioritised (including, for example, zero hours contacts), rather than a focus on 'human capital' (used in many other countries) to improve people's longer-term prospects via training, for example.

Both the Conservative government and their predecessors across the political spectrum (the UK Conservative–Liberal Coalition 2010–15 and

Labour 1997–2010) argue that the role of intervention is to help people to help themselves, giving those out of work a 'hand up, not a hand out'. The 'work is the best form of welfare' mantra dominates, and is used to justify a reliance on both incentives and sanctions (such as removing essential benefit income for a month if an appointment is missed) to promote 'working behaviours'. At the same time, there is also a sustained emphasis on 'making work pay' to ensure that those in paid employment are financially better off than those on out-of-work benefits. Importantly, though, there are two ways to make work pay. First, it is possible to increase the rewards attached to paid employment, an approach that was favoured by Labour. In this respect, Labour introduced some of the most socially progressive measures of their time in office, such as the National Minimum Wage in 1999 and relatively generous forms of in-work support via tax credits (key reforms in 1999 and 2003). Second, though, it is also possible to make work pay by reducing out-of-work benefits, therefore widening the gap between the income received by those in and out of work. This has been the approach favoured by the UK Coalition government, which has legislated for a significant range of cuts and reductions in eligibility to out-of-work benefits. This welfare state retrenchment has occurred at the same time as a recourse to ideas of 'benefits as a lifestyle choice', a rhetoric that arguably stigmatises and undermines the inclusion of those who rely on benefits for all or most of their income.

In seeking to remedy the 'problem' of 'welfare dependency', the favoured policy tool remains welfare conditionality both in the UK and across the OECD. While welfare conditionality has long been a feature of the policy landscape, the past thirty-five years have seen it increasingly employed, with sustained efforts to both extend and intensify its application (Welfare Conditionality, 2015). First, it has been extended to include many disabled people and single parents. Second, there has been a notable intensification of conditionality, both in terms of possible sanctions for non-compliance with the regime, and the range and nature of job search and related demands being made of claimants. Today, jobseekers are expected to sign a personalised 'claimant commitment' on starting their claim, setting out these demands in a quasi-contract. The conditions

attached to out-of-work benefits include demands to engage in

- job search activities;
- welfare-to-work schemes, for example, the Work Programme; and
- mandatory unpaid work placements, sometimes described as 'Workfare'.

Following reforms since 2010, unemployed claimants must now seek work within ninety minutes travelling time of their home, and are expected to treat looking for work as a full-time job. Failure to comply with these demands include a range of possible sanctions, escalating for repeat 'offences' and of different lengths according to their judged severity. This includes the 'ultimate sanction' of three years without benefits for those who three times fail to accept a job offer, apply for a particular job or take part in a form of compulsory work experience, that is, Mandatory Work Activity. Figures show a considerable rise in the imposition of benefit sanctions under the UK Coalition government (2010–15) when compared with levels of sanctions during the UK Labour governments of 1997–2010.

Experiencing Welfare to Work

For those directly affected, conditionality is an approach that compels individuals to behave as the government would like or risk benefit sanctions. It is often presented as a welfare contract – responsibilities in return for support – but out-of-work claimants arguably have little choice but to sign up to this contract, giving it a particularly paternalistic and authoritarian flavour (see Chapter 10). Research suggests that welfare conditionality can have negative effects on physical and mental health, causing increased stress and reducing emotional well-being (Watts et al., 2014). Where there is a clash between an individual's own assessment of their work readiness and motivations and the state's expectations that they seek work, there are particular risks that conditionality will operate in negative ways.

International evidence on sanctions suggests that they increase exits from benefits and may increase short-term job entry, but there are signs that their longer-term outcomes around earnings, job quality and employment retention are more unfavourable (Watts et al., 2014). Inevitably, the imposition of sanctions can cause hardship (for the claimant and household members, including children), and there is growing research evidence of people being unable to afford to feed themselves, sometimes leading individuals to shoplift food as part of their struggle to get by.

In justifying the imposition of conditions and sanctions, governments frequently emphasise the help and support available to assist people in making the welfare-to-work transition. In 2010, the UK Coalition government introduced the Work Programme (WP), a single programme of back-to-work support, provided by third and private sector agencies, on a basis of payment for results in moving people into paid employment (see Chapter 48). However, there are concerns that the WP is failing to properly support those with the most significant barriers to employment, such as disabled people and those with the most entrenched barriers to employment. Work Programme participants sometimes do not find the support meaningful or helpful (Dole Animators, 2013; Patrick, 2014). In research into experiences of welfare reform, including the Work Programme, there were examples of people's longer-term employment aspirations going unsupported, perhaps as a consequence of the work-first approach (Patrick, 2014). Participants described being encouraged to look for *any* job, rather than focusing on those areas in which they were most interested, qualified or experienced.

'Strivers and Shirkers': The Consequences of a Divisive Rhetoric

The policy approach on welfare to work is justified with frequent recourse to characterisations of static groups of 'hard-working families' and 'welfare dependents', 'strivers' and 'shirkers'. These dualistic divisions re-imagine and re-create older distinctions between 'deserving' and 'undeserving' populations, and link in/exclusion and (ir)responsibility to whether or not individuals are engaged in paid employment. While politicians are active participants in the stigmatisation of 'welfare', there is also an increasingly dominant role for the media. In recent years, we have seen the

emergence of a growing number of 'documentaries' that promise to show the 'reality' of life on benefits. Shows such as *Benefits Britain* are dubbed 'poverty porn' given their edited and highly sensationalised depiction of what life is like for those reliant on out-of-work benefits. Such programmes contribute to the stigmatisation of benefit claimants, with stigma and shame a consistent feature of the experience of claiming benefits in twenty-first-century Britain.

Today, individuals who are often already coping with the shame of struggling to manage in poverty also have to contend with the consequences of a stigmatising rhetoric that increasingly associates non-work with irresponsibility and failure. Research has found signs that individuals are internalising negative narratives around benefit claiming, with some employing negative labels such as 'scrounger' to describe their own situation (Dole Animators, 2013; Patrick, 2014). Importantly, then, this rhetoric is affecting how people see themselves in ways that could be damaging to self-confidence, self-esteem and, thus, ironically, chances of securing paid employment. While these divisions remain powerful, there are questions about whether they actually reflect lived realities, with static characterisations failing to capture the fluid movements between low-paid employment and unemployment that are the norm for so many.

Navigating the Benefits System

In seeking to understand the stigma that is attached to benefits reliance, it is particularly important to highlight what some have described as the 'institutional stigma' around engaging with Jobcentre Plus (JCP), the Department for Work and Pensions (DWP) and associated officials, such as welfare-to-work providers. This institutional stigma can be defined as stigma that emerges from the processes of claiming benefits. Given the emphasis on welfare conditionality, relations between claimants and JCP advisers often place the adviser in a policing and surveillance role, as they ascertain continued eligibility for support and compliance with any work-related conditions. This can have a negative impact on these relationships, with the possibility of conditionality having a 'scarring effect' on the ways in which claimants experience their interactions with the welfare state. Under conditionality, claimants describe how they feel as if they are placed under suspicion, having to prove and demonstrate their 'deservingness'. This can prevent the development of a trusting and effective relationship, with claimants often reporting feeling judged and looked down on in these interactions and treated with an absence of respect. JCP appointments are often characterised by long waits, a lack of privacy and a dominant security presence, all further extending the ways in which these encounters can be generative of stigma and shame.

In navigating the benefits system, claimants have to deal with a bureaucratic system that has often been criticised for providing a poor service with particular issues around the provision of clear, timely and accessible information. Problems have been reported regarding misleading, contradictory and difficult to understand official communication, with inevitable consequences for individuals' understanding of their own rights. Individuals have reported finding out that they have been sanctioned when they go to try and withdraw their benefits money, only to find a zero balance. Poor levels of communication about forthcoming welfare reforms cause particular anxiety and worry, and contribute to feelings of fear and uncertainty about changes to the benefit system.

For out-of-work claimants, the work of engaging with officials can be time-intensive, emotionally draining and undermining of self-worth. There is the risk that these relationships, with their punitive and paternalistic edge, interfere with the potential for claimants to see such officials as people that might provide them with meaningful support to enter paid employment. The role of JCP can be seen as that of policing eligibility for benefits, rather than helping people to find work. This extends to relationships with WP advisers, with some claimants describing a service that is impersonal and alienating. This is sometimes explicitly linked to the payment-by-results model, with a suspicion that providers are only interested in securing outcomes in order to generate income and to meet individual targets for performance.

Overall, then, relationships between out-of-work claimants and the officials of the welfare state are frequently troubled and imbued in the institutional stigma of claiming benefits. Many would argue that these relationships are affected by the overall policy approach and narrative and

its emphasis on welfare conditionality and sanctions, and it is to an exploration of some emerging issues with this approach that this chapter now turns.

Emerging Issues

The policy approach to dealing with unemployment suggests that individuals require conditions and the threat of sanctions to activate them into employment, with the corrective lens firmly focused on individual claimants themselves. In this way, the policy problem is located at the individual level; on the supply-side of the labour market and the behavioural changes needed for individuals to make the welfare-to-work transition. This approach can be characterised as an 'individualisation of responsibility', with the 'problem' of unemployment conceptualised as an *individual* problem, requiring *individual* change. However, research evidence shows that individuals are often frustrated in their job searches, not by an absence of motivation or commitment to securing employment, but by demand-side barriers such as an absence of jobs or the lack of suitable childcare. The logic for a focus on the supply-side of the labour market is arguably contradicted by such research, which repeatedly finds strong aspirations to work amongst the unemployed, who are often hard at work trying to find jobs, albeit without success.

In May 2015, the Conservative Party won a majority in the Westminster general election, and pledged that their government would continue the welfare reform effort to make sure that work always pays, and that no one is able to 'choose' benefits as a lifestyle choice. They promised particular reforms to ensure that young people are encouraged to make the transition from education into employment, by extending mandatory forms of work experience and reducing their eligibility for benefits. These reforms further extend the policy emphasis on conditionality and reductions in social welfare provision, and will need to be closely monitored.

Critics of the approach taken by recent UK Governments argue that focusing on paid employment as the primary duty of the individual citizen is inherently exclusive, and serves to neglect the various forms of contribution in which so many of the economically 'inactive' are engaged. These include volunteering, caring, parenting work, and the informal care and support that is so often provided in low-income communities. Critics argue that a narrative that segments the population into two static groups according to their engagement in paid employment is incredibly divisive, and further devalues and undermines the contributions of those who are not currently in paid employment. The use of such categorisations has been described as operating to pit citizen against citizen, breeding ill feeling and threatening social solidarity.

Defending the approach taken, the incoming 2015 Conservative government, like its Coalition and Labour predecessors, focus on the transformative rewards offered by paid employment and their objective to share these rewards with more of the working-age population. However, this policy justification does not always recognise the continued existence of in-work poverty, a stubborn and persistent issue in the UK. More than half of the children living in poverty can be found in a household with at least one working adult. In addition, the non-pecuniary rewards of paid employment are not intrinsic to all employment. There are particular concerns here about the recent growth in insecure, temporary, low-paid and inflexible employment, given evidence that engagement in these forms of work can have very negative consequences, particularly for mental health and well-being.

Those who are critical of the government's approach argue that its emphasis on the 'problem' of 'welfare dependency' and proposed solution of 'work' is based on a simplistic and superficial analysis of the policy issues. This approach implies that 'welfare dependency' is always and inevitably negative, and neglects consideration of the ways in which we are all dependent on the state and each other. The giving and receiving of care is an intrinsic part of what it is to be human, and dependency is not necessarily and inevitably a negative characteristic. If we understand 'welfare' more broadly to include not just social welfare provided to out-of-work claimants, but the various forms of state support on which we all depend, such as education, healthcare and tax relief, then our understanding of who is welfare-dependent changes. A more inclusive picture emerges, and one that some would argue better captures the complex chains of interdependency between citizens and the state. However, the current policy approach shows little sign of changing, with all the main political parties committed to a continued prioritising of welfare conditions and measures to activate the 'inactive'. Against this context, it is critical to continue to monitor and explore the ways in which this policy approach is experienced by individual out-of-work claimants themselves.

Guide to Further Sources

The Department for Work and Pensions (DWP) website is a really useful resource for accessing government speeches, policy documents and statistics; see DWP (2015), *Department for Work and Pensions*, available at: www.gov.uk/government/organisations/department-for-work-pensions.

More details on the lived experiences of out-of-work benefit receipt can be found in R. Patrick (2014), 'Working on welfare: findings from a qualitative longitudinal study into the lived experiences of welfare reform in the UK', *Journal of Social Policy*, 43:4, 705–25. There is also a short film made by some of the participants in the study. Dole Animators (2013), *Dole Animators*, available at: www.doleanimators.org.

The stigma and shame associated with poverty and benefits is discussed in R. Walker (2014), *The Shame of Poverty*, Oxford: Oxford University Press.

A large research project is exploring how conditionality is experienced by those directly affected. More details can be found on their website, which also includes links to briefing papers and presentation slides; see Welfare Conditionality (2015), *Welfare Conditionality: Sanctions, Support and Behaviour Change*, available at: www.welfareconditionality.ac.uk.

A summary of the operation of welfare conditionality in the UK and research evidence into its impact is provided by B. Watts, S. Fitzpatrick, G. Bramley and D. Watkins (2014), *Welfare Sanctions and Conditionality in the UK*, York: Joseph Rowntree Foundation.

Review and Assignment Questions

1 What are the key features of the current unemployment policy approach?

2 What evidence exists around the impact of conditionality and sanctions?
3 How might divisions between workers and non-workers affect out-of-work benefit claimants?
4 What criticisms might be made of the current approach to unemployment policy?
5 What do we learn from looking at how unemployment policy is experienced by those directly affected?

Visit the book companion site at www.wiley.com/go/alcocksocialpolicy to make use of the resources designed to accompany the textbook. There you will find chapter-specific guides to further resources, including governmental, international, thinktank, pressure groups and relevant journal sources. You will also find a glossary based on *The Blackwell Dictionary of Social Policy*, help sheets, guidance on managing assignments in social policy and career advice.

57

Family Policy

Tina Haux

Overview

- There have been significant changes in patterns of family formation and dissolution in the UK in the past half-century. There have also been changes in employment patterns, with most mothers, especially those with older children, now in paid employment.
- Family values and norms about the 'right thing to do' have become more complex and dependent on context. But this does not imply a lack of commitment to family, although these commitments are subject to reflection and negotiation.
- Family policy can be defined in relation to policy goals, to areas of activity and to institutional structures. The key areas of activity include the regulation of family behaviour, cash benefits and tax credits or transfers for families, and the provision of services.
- In the UK, family policy has become more explicit in the last two decades, with a range of new policies introduced and existing provisions developed.
- Family policy is at the heart of important debates about the future direction for the welfare state, in particular in relation to the reconciliation of paid work and unpaid care.

The Student's Companion to Social Policy, Fifth Edition. Edited by Pete Alcock, Tina Haux, Margaret May and Sharon Wright.
© 2016 John Wiley & Sons, Ltd. Published 2016 by John Wiley & Sons, Ltd.

Family Change and Social Policy

Family policy has now become a significant and accepted part of the political and policy landscape in many industrialised countries. Family policy is usually defined to include the regulation of family behaviour, cash transfers to families and the provision of services to families (see Box 57.1). Family policy in the UK has become much more explicit, coherent and extensive in recent years. The political discourse behind these developments stresses the role of families as the 'bedrock' of society – the basic social unit, which carries values, brings up the next generation and sustains local communities.

Thus, families are very much at the centre of contemporary political and policy debate in the UK. All political parties claim to have policies that support families and sustain family life. Family life and personal relationships are the focus of media attention not only in the press and on television, but also in internet sites such as 'mumsnet', which attract millions of people. Academic interest in the relationship between family and state has made this a growing area of research and publication.

Much social policy is concerned with families and family life, and in the making of policy certain assumptions must be made about families and family roles. It has often been argued, for example,

that the provisions of the post-war British welfare state rested on a very clear model of family life, in which men were full-time workers and women were full-time carers. Families were assumed to be stable and long lasting, and the family roles of men and women were seen as being quite distinct.

The extent to which real families ever conformed to this idealised model is debatable, even in the 1950s, a decade in which family structures were unusually stable and homogeneous. Families today, however, are much more volatile and diverse. Although the 1960s are often characterised as the 'permissive decade', it was really in the 1970s that patterns of family life in the UK began to change very rapidly. The 1969 Divorce Reform Act, implemented in 1971, made divorce possible for a much wider range of people. Cohabitation also began to rise at that time, as did rates of extra-marital births. Table 57.1 summarises some key trends in family formation and structure since the 1970s. As can be seen, there have been some very significant changes over this period. Many more children are born outside marriage, more couples are cohabiting, first marriage is later, abortion is more common, women have fewer children and there is a higher risk of divorce. As a consequence, there are more lone-parent families (one in four families with dependent children are headed by a

Table 57.1   Family formation and family structure in England and Wales over 30 years.

	Early/mid-1970s	Early 2010s
Percentage of children born outside marriage	8	47
Percentage of single women cohabiting	8 (1979)	31
Median age at first marriage for women/men	21/24	30/32
Number of abortions, women aged 15–44	161,000	190,800
Fertility rate (live births per 1,000 women)	84	93
Number of divorces	79,000	118,140
Divorce rate per 1,000 married population	5.9	10.8
Percentage of families headed by lone parents	8	25*
Percentage of one-person households	18	28*
Average household size	3.1	2.4*
Percentage of population aged under 16	25	19*
Percentage of population aged over 65	13	17*

* Refers to UK figures; otherwise England and Wales only.

Sources: Families and Households, 2014 (2015); Live Births in England and Wales by Characteristics of Mother, 2013 (2014); Childbearing by UK and non-UK born women living in the UK, 2011 Census data (2014); Divorces in England and Wales, 2012 (2014); Marriage and Cohabitation (2013); Abortion Statistics England and Wales, 2013 (2014); Conceptions in England and Wales, 2013 (2015); Annual Mid-Year Population Estimates, 2013 (2014); National Population Projections, 2012 based (2013).

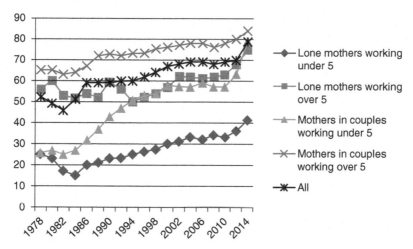

Figure 57.1   Employment rate of mothers by marital status and age of youngest child, 1977–2014. Sources: Living in Great Britain (1997); A. Walling (2005), *Families and Employment*, Labour Market Trends, July; ONS (2014), Families in the Labour Market, 2014; see www.statistics.gov.uk; ONS (2011), Mothers in the Labour Market.

lone parent), more stepfamilies (around one in ten of all couples with dependent children) and more people living alone, and the average household size is smaller. The population is also growing older. This also includes more of the very elderly, with more people now aged 85 and above than ever before.

Employment patterns for families with dependent children have also changed over this time period. In the early 1970s just about half of married mothers were employed, usually women with older children, since mothers at that period typically spent several years out of the labour market to provide full-time care for their husbands and children. In 2010, around three-quarters of married mothers were employed, including over half of mothers with pre-school children. As Figure 57.1 shows, employment rates remain lower for lone mothers than for married mothers, but have been rising rapidly in recent years, as has the employment rate of mothers in couples with very young children, that is, those under 5. Many employed mothers, both married and lone, are in part-time jobs. Most women who work part-time say that they prefer to do so, as it makes combining work and care easier, but part-time work does tend to be restricted to certain parts of the labour market and to be lower paid. Nevertheless, the

earnings that women contribute to family income are increasingly important in maintaining living standards and preventing family poverty. The income gap between no-earner, one earner and two-earner families is a key factor in widening economic inequality. In recent years, the proportion of the 'working poor' has increased substantially and has become a key issue to address for policymakers at all levels (see Chapter 48).

These family and employment trends have been characterised as the decline of the 'male breadwinner' family that was, as noted above, at the centre of the twentieth-century welfare state. It is important, however, to recognise that family situations change over time. Families form, break up and reform, and people move in and out of work. Thus, although the single- (traditionally male) breadwinner family is a minority at any one time, it is still an important stage in the family 'life course' for many people. This is also true of lone parenthood. The women (and, less commonly, men) who become lone parents do not usually stay lone parents for ever – many remarry or set up home with new partners, and even if they do not, their children grow up and leave home. Lone parenthood can therefore be characterised as a stage in the family life course, rather than as a fixed and separate family type.

The extent to which family relationships and values and norms about family life have also changed alongside changes in family structure has been the subject of much debate in the sociological literature. It is sometimes argued that family commitments have become weakened because people are now more 'individualised' and motivated by their own personal goals and aspirations. As people focus more on their individual needs and self-actualisation, they become less committed to sustaining family ties. This individualisation thesis has been challenged on both theoretical and empirical grounds. For example, Smart (2007: 189) argues that the concept of individualisation focuses attention on 'fragmentation, differentiation, separation and autonomy', rather than on the ways in which people 'connect' across family and other relationships, over time and place. Based on a major research programme, which explored issues of personal relationships, intimacy, family values and obligations, and love and care in family and friendship networks, Williams (2005: 83) argues that, while the 'new conditions' of more fluid and complex family structures and work/care patterns 'have changed the shape of commitments they have not undermined commitments itself'. Recent biological development, such as the increased availability and use of donor conceptions, presents a number of challenges. Nordquist and Smart (2013) have explored how the narratives of what constitutes family are constructed by couples who have used donor conception. On a different level, as with inter-country adoptions, the use of donors from other countries has proven challenging for policymakers and the families concerned as different cultures and regulatory frameworks collide.

At the same time, 'families of choice', that is, like-minded friends rather than (biological) relatives or 'family of origin' can play a big role in people's lives. Families, of origin and of choice, remain important, but family obligations are negotiated rather than fixed, family values are complex and there is no simple consensus about what is the 'right thing to do' with regard to parenting, caring and paid employment. In summary, it can no longer be assumed that all families are broadly the same, with the same sort of needs and resources. Nor can it be assumed that everyone shares the same values about family life. The issue of whether and how governments should respond to family change is thus an issue of ongoing debate. Some people see the welfare state as having weakened and undermined the family and call upon government to turn the clock back and restore 'traditional' family structures and roles. Others are more pragmatic and argue that policy should reflect these changes and seek to ensure that people are not disadvantaged as a consequence.

Family Policy in the UK

There is no simple way to define family policy. Some definitions include everything that affects families, whether intended or not. Others include only those policies directly targeted at families, with particular goals in mind. However, there are very different political and ideological views as to the role of government in relation to the family. Many governments do not explicitly identify the family as a target for policy, nor seek to influence family structure. It may be more useful, therefore, to define family policy in relation to areas of activity, as in Box 57.1

As noted above, family policy in the UK has become more extensive and explicit in recent years. In particular, the Labour governments of 1997–2010 introduced, or extended, family policy

---

Box 57.1 Defining Family Policy

Family policy can be defined by three main areas of activity:

1 *The legal regulation of family behaviour*: laws relating to marriage and divorce, sexual behaviour, contraception and abortion, parental rights and duties and child protection.
2 *Policies to support family income*: tax allowances, family and child benefits, parental leaves and benefits, enforcement of child support.
3 *The provision of services for families*: childcare provisions, subsidised housing, social services, community care.

in several directions. Daly (2010) summarises these under six main areas:

1 early education and childcare (the expansion of childcare and early years services as part of the National Childcare Strategy);
2 financial support for families with children (the introduction of tax credits and increased financial support for families with children);
3 services for young children and their families (the introduction of Sure Start);
4 employment activation (Lone Parent Obligation and welfare-to-work reform);
5 work–family reconciliation (the extension of maternity leave, introduction of paternity leave and right to request flexible working); and
6 parental responsibility and behaviour (greater intervention in family life, for example, parenting classes).

The extent to which this represents a fundamental shift in policy is the subject of ongoing debate. Daly (2010: 433) concludes that there were changes in policy instruments, but that 'the appearance of substantial change and innovation masks deep-seated continuities'. The underlying paradigm remains that of 'a market-oriented, family policy model'. However, focusing on specific policy areas

highlights more strongly the extent of change. For example, Lewis (2009) focuses on work–family reconciliation and argues that the level of expansion and innovation in this policy area has taken the UK in a new policy direction and closer to Europe (see Box 57.2). Haux (2012) examines the most substantial policy change affecting lone parents themselves, namely, the introduction of the Lone Parent Obligation requiring lone parents to be available for work once the youngest child reaches school age. Lister (2006) argues that the 'social investment approach' in respect of children (where all adults are or should be workers and children are workers of the future) of the previous Labour governments is indeed new as was setting a target to reduce child poverty (see Chapter 58).

From May 2010 to May 2015, the Conservative Party and the Liberal Democrats formed a Coalition government. Of the six themes identified as characterising the family policy changes of the preceding government, the Coalition government focused and reduced the scope of the first three (early years education and childcare, financial support for families and children, and services for young children and families) and expanded the latter three (employment activation of lone parents, work–life balance policies, and parental responsibility and behaviour). Overall, the focus shifted from ensuring that all families are better off to

---

Box 57.2   The Adult Worker Model and Work–Family Balance

Assumptions about families, and what families do, are an essential underpinning of the welfare state. Jane Lewis has analysed how the UK has moved from assuming a 'male breadwinner' to an individualised 'adult worker' model. Under the new mode, it is assumed that all adults have the duty and responsibility to engage in paid employment, and that such paid work can and should be carried out alongside caring responsibilities. This raises clear challenges for how care work can be combined with paid employment, and what policy measures are needed to enable this to happen.

Prior to Labour coming to power in 1997, the UK lagged behind other countries in Europe with regard to policies enabling families to combine paid work and family care

responsibilities. Lewis argues that there have been three dimensions to work–family policies under the 1997–2010 Labour governments – childcare provision, flexible working arrangements and parental leave – and that this has been a change in direction of family policy in the UK (see above). Yet, while claiming to be gender neutral and aiming to give parents more choice, many of these policies have, in effect, been targeted at mothers.

The Coalition government (2010–15) further expanded policy provisions in these three areas, most recently by introducing shared parental leave, that is, the possibility of extended leave to be taken by either parent and not only the mother as before.

identifying and supporting families in (potential) difficulty (often referred to as 'troubled families'). Policy initiatives (such as the Troubled Families Programme) are targeted at particular families with the intention of changing particular behaviours, such as smoking during pregnancy, truanting or not being in employment. However, the austerity-badged policies of the Coalition government hit families with children particularly hard. While there is some debate as to how balanced the austerity measures have been across the income scale, it is clear that policies such as the changes and freezes to the uprating of benefits, harsher means-testing and new policies such as the household benefit cap (a limit on the overall amount of benefits received in a year; see Chapter 47) have meant that families with children at the bottom of the income distribution were worse off in 2015 than they were in 2010. In addition, the UK Coalition government introduced a number of substantial changes by means-testing the previously universal child benefit, withdrawing from the enforcement of child maintenance collection for lone parents on social assistance, requiring a 'Family Test' for all new policies (to be assessed in light of their implications for family formation, transitions, separations and individual member's ability to be involved in family life) and pushing ahead with the introduction of Universal Credit (see Chapter 47).

The design of Universal Credit (UC) has implications for the reporting of (new) relationships, will increase the reach of conditionality and sanctions, which will affect women's access to social security, and will exacerbate the fact that women are likely to be the major losers as a consequence of the current social security and tax credit cuts (see Chapters 47 and 56). First, UC will be assessed on the basis of households rather than individuals. Payment to the household assumes fair distribution and equal power relationships within the household, neither of which can necessarily be assumed. Second, it will not necessarily be financially worthwhile for the potential second earner to move into work under UC. Second earners in families tend to be women, and thus UC is likely to reinforce a traditional male breadwinner model. Finally, UC extends conditionality, that is, the involvement of the state in people's life to those working part-time, as the goal is to move groups such as lone parents with older children into full-time employment.

Emerging Issues

The recent recession in the UK, triggered by the global financial crisis (2007–8), has put additional pressure on family budgets, and in-work poverty has become a key concern and challenge for families and policymakers. This has placed the spotlight more firmly on the high costs of childcare in the UK and its effect on the participation of women in the labour market. Yet public finances will remain constrained, thereby limiting the room for manoeuvre of the Conservative government. The interest in early years, parenting and long-term poverty, and in the promotion of marriage is likely to stay on the policy agenda. Family breakdown and poor parenting are being blamed for a number of social ills, despite the evidence showing the complexity of the causal factors involved. The 2015 Conservative government seem intent on continuing much of the family-related agenda of the previous Coalition government. If anything, the financial and moral support for particular family forms and economic behaviour (being married and in work) is set to increase. More broadly, key issues in family policy remain at the heart of important debates about the future direction of the welfare state. The long-standing feminist arguments for the importance of state policy in enabling the reconciliation of paid work and unpaid care are increasingly coming to centre stage in debates about future policy.

Guide to Further Sources

M. Daly (2010), 'Shifts in family policy in the UK under New Labour', *Journal of European Social Policy*, 20:5, 433–43, discusses the main developments in family policy under the 1997–2010 Labour governments and argues that they do not add up to a paradigmatic change.

G. Esping-Andersen (2009), *The Incomplete Revolution: Adapting to Women's New Roles*, Cambridge: Polity Press, analyses economic, social and demographic change, and argues that welfare states have not yet adapted to the revolutionary changes in the roles of women. Family policy, it is argued, should be seeking to 'accelerate the maturation of the female revolution'.

J. Lewis (2009), *Work–Family Balance, Gender and Policy*, Cheltenham: Edward Elgar, provides a detailed account of the emergence and success of work–family balance policies in the UK, as well as a comparison with policies in France, Germany and the Netherlands.

C. Henricson (2012), *A Revolution in Family Policy: Where We Should Go from Here*, Bristol: Policy Press, provides suggestions for the future of family policy based on the analysis of the past twenty years.

R. Lister (2006), 'Children (but not women) first: New Labour, child welfare and gender', *Critical Social Policy*, 26:2, 315–35, discusses the nature and implications of the children as 'social investments' approach to family policy under the 1997–2010 Labour governments.

T. Haux (2012), 'Activating lone parents: an evidence-based appraisal of the welfare-to-work reform in Britain', *Social Policy and Society*, 11:1, 1–14, examines the context and assumptions behind the introduction of the Lone Parent Obligation policy.

P. Nordquist and C. Smart (2014), *Relative Strangers. Family Life, Genes and Donor Conception*, Basingstoke: Palgrave Macmillan, explores the experiences and narratives of couples who have had children as a result of donor conception.

The Office for National Statistics gives access to social trends, population trends, etc. and to the various data sets that can be used to create tables and charts, see at: www.statistics.gov.uk.

Review and Assignment Questions

1 What have been the key changes in family patterns in the UK over the past thirty years?
2 What are the challenges for social policy arising from increased employment among mothers?
3 Define family policy.
4 Did the Labour governments from 1997 onwards transform family policy? If so, how?
5 What are the main challenges for family policy in the UK today?

Visit the book companion site at www.wiley.com/go/alcocksocialpolicy to make use of the resources designed to accompany the textbook. There you will find chapter-specific guides to further resources, including governmental, international, thinktank, pressure groups and relevant journal sources. You will also find a glossary based on *The Blackwell Dictionary of Social Policy*, help sheets, guidance on managing assignments in social policy and career advice.

58

Children

Tess Ridge

Overview

- Children are key recipients of welfare services across a wide range of policy areas, and their lives are considerably shaped by the type and quality of welfare systems available.
- Modern childhood is undergoing considerable social and economic change, and children of the twenty-first century live increasingly complex lives in a range of diverse family settings.
- Child welfare policies change over time, and depend on fluid and changing assumptions about the needs and rights of children, the needs and rights of parents, and the role of the state in children's lives.
- There is increasing recognition in policy that children are social actors and bearers of rights. There is also a trend towards 'social investment policies' which focus on children as 'citizen workers' of the future.
- The chapter examines a key policy area for children, the issue of child poverty. It explores the rise and fall of the Child Poverty Act and looks at the impact on children of a range of policy initiatives, and the implications for children of changes and continuities in policy when there is a change of government.

The Student's Companion to Social Policy, Fifth Edition. Edited by Pete Alcock, Tina Haux, Margaret May and Sharon Wright.
© 2016 John Wiley & Sons, Ltd. Published 2016 by John Wiley & Sons, Ltd.

Introduction

In the UK in 2015 there were around 12 million children under the age of 16 and they represented about 19 per cent of the population. The majority of these children were living in a family setting with their welfare needs being met by a range of informal and formal provision. Social policies for children need to be understood within the context of this informal/formal welfare mix. Children are often the target of policies and they are also important consumers of welfare. They are key recipients of welfare services across a range of policy areas, including education, health, housing and the environment, childcare, social services and financial support through the social security and tax system.

Children rely very heavily on welfare services for their present and future well-being, and their lives are affected by policies at local, national (including devolved administrations) and trans-national levels. Undoubtedly, in areas such as education, childcare, child protection and health policies the type and quality of services can have clear implications for children's well-being, but in other areas too, for example, the environment and transport, there can be intended or unintended impacts on children's lives. The ways in which children are treated by policymakers is also dependent on how childhood is perceived at any one time. This chapter will examine how changing conditions of childhood may affect policies and highlight some of the key debates and developments in this area.

Twenty-first-Century Childhood

In the twenty-first century, childhood in the UK is undergoing a further period of considerable social and economic change. These changes impact on the way that policies are developed for children and their families.

Demographic and social changes in the last half of the twentieth century have also wrought considerable transformation in family formation and structure. Trends towards reduced fertility and later child-bearing have led to an overall reduction in the number of children being born in economically developed Western societies. Increasing instability in family life has led to a growth in cohabitation and rising rates of family dissolution, and this in turn has resulted in greater diversity and complexity in family forms (see Chapter 57). As a consequence, children's lives are increasingly multifaceted and they can live in a variety of family settings. Clearly, it is difficult for the state to provide effective universal or targeted policies for children who are living increasingly diverse and complex lives.

Box 58.1 Childhood and Social Change in the Late Twentieth Century

Significant social changes affecting childhood since the last quarter of the twentieth century.

- Declining birth rates and increasingly ageing populations: here the implications for policy are still unclear, but may mean a shift of resources away from children towards older people.
- Increasing diversity in life circumstances and economic circumstances between children following social and demographic changes: this has resulted in growing income inequalities between children (see below for a discussion of child poverty).

- The impact of globalisation as children are exposed to global flows of people, products, information and images; this is also linked to 'transnational childhoods' as children move between households across national boundaries.
- The trend towards increasing institutional control over children's lives, resulting in longer periods spent in institutional settings such as schools and childcare.
- The emergence of children's voices in decision-making. This is explored further below in relation to children's rights.

Source: Prout (in Hallett and Prout, 2003).

Children's Rights

The issue of children's rights is an important one for social policy, as Box 58.1 shows there is increasing recognition in social policy that children are social actors and bearers of rights. This is part of a new trend towards including the voices of service users in policy and the increasing participation of children in research, practice and policy formulation. The UK has a series of rights-based legislative acts – such as the Children's Acts 1989 and 2006 – and wider international conventions – such as the United Nations Convention on the Rights of the Child (UNCRC). In line with changing expectations regarding children's interests Children's Commissioners have been appointed across the devolved administrations, with Wales leading the way in 2001 and finally England in 2005. Children's Commissioners have responsibility for promoting the views and interests of all children and young people at a national and devolved level within a rights-based framework informed by the UNCRC.

However, despite these advances there are still considerable areas of tension within policy regarding the rights of children. For example, although there is a positive policy to eradicate child poverty in line with Articles 26 and 27 of the UNCRC, marginalised children, such as the children of asylum seekers, tend to have far less attention paid to their welfare rights.

Devolution has resulted in a diverse range of policy developments across the different nations of the UK, with policies for children and young people particularly likely to show divergence. Increasingly, where you are born in the UK will affect the policies and laws that will have an impact on your childhood and, by extension, your future adulthood. These changes are also informed by different notions of children as rights bearers and citizens (see Box 58.2).

There are also different laws across the devolved administrations with regard to the age of criminal responsibility. In England, Northern Ireland and Wales, children are deemed to be criminally responsible from the age of 10 and can be tried in an adult court. In Scotland, the age of responsibility is 8 years, but children are not criminalised through adult systems as children up to 12 years are dealt with through the children's hearings system. There was also a radical change

> **Box 58.2** Children's Citizenship, Rights and Entitlements across the Devolved Authorities
>
> Children's rights and entitlements are linked to citizenship.
>
> - In England, children's rights are linked with duties rather than citizenship entitlements, and children are seen as in need of protection. Until they reach independence, any citizenship is 'by proxy' through their families.
> - In Scotland, welfare rights are important, but children are in effect 'citizens in the making'.
> - Northern Ireland has a rights-based approach, but an outcomes model that sees citizenship not as entitlement but as 'the by-product of good provision'.
> - In Wales, children's entitlements are strong, the Welsh Assembly has accepted the UNCRC as the fundamental underpinning for all its work with children and young people, and children are conceived as citizens in their own right.
>
> Source: Clutton (in Invernizzi and Williams, 2008: 179).

during the 2014 Scottish Independence Referendum when, for the first time, young people aged 16 and 17 were allowed to vote, although this right was not extended to UK young people in the general election of 2015, where the age of voting remained at 18.

Children, Family and Social Policy

To understand how policy can affect children's lives, it is first important to recognise that childhood, as we know it, is a relatively modern social construction, which changes over time. Like childhood, child welfare policies have also changed over time, and depend on fluid and changing assumptions about the needs and rights of children, the needs and rights of parents, and the role of the state in children's lives. They are also affected by the political economy of welfare and different perceptions and ideologies of childhood that prevail at the time. The state's value position in relation to childhood and family life has been an important factor when it comes to shaping policies. Historically, children's needs and interests have remained hidden within the private sphere of the family, and as a result they have tended to be invisible in the policy process. Their interests have been served mainly by social policies that are directed at the interests of the family. This 'familialisation' of children has meant that policies that respond directly to children's needs were unlikely to be developed. This is apparent, for example, in the provision of childcare, which has rarely been provided from the starting point of what is best for children, but rather as an important service for families, and in particular as a means to encourage mothers back into the labour market.

The assumption that children's best interests are consonant with their family's best interests is problematic, and, as a result, their needs and concerns are always in danger of being subsumed by the needs and interests of the family and of the state. There are also considerable 'tensions and contradictions' in the relationship between the state and the family, and this reflects an ongoing debate between the rights and responsibilities of parents for their children and the obligations of the state to provide services for children and intervene in their lives when they are deemed to be at risk (see below with regard to child safeguarding). Underpinning these tensions lies the fundamental issue of whether children are seen as a private good or whether society has a legitimate collective interest in investing in them and ensuring their well-being.

Children as a 'Social Investment'

Although children's needs have historically been hidden within the family, the position of children and families in welfare policy is changing. Ruth Lister (2006) argues that under the Labour administration there was a genuine attempt to focus on investment in children. This signals a profound change in the position of children and families in the welfare mix as the state moves towards the development of a 'social investment state'. The 'social investment state' entails a movement away from traditional welfare policies towards policies built on investment in social and human capital. In this welfare strategy children are central to future economic success; they are the 'citizen-workers of the future' (ibid.). In the 'social investment state' children are valued for the adults they will become, and policies are explicitly targeted towards ensuring that their potential is developed to ensure the economic prosperity of the country in the future in order to maintain national economic prosperity in a competitive global market. Therefore, childhood and the development of healthy and educated/skilled children are too important for the economic future of the country to be left solely in the hands of parents. The development of social investment policies has, in many ways, been beneficial to children's interests in the UK. For example, during the UK Labour governments of 1997–2010 there was a significant increase in investment in children through policies to eradicate child poverty (see below). However, despite such improvements, there is a tension between policies that focus on children as future adults and the quality of life that they experience in childhood. This highlights a key debate about whether children are treated in policy as 'beings' (children in childhood) or as 'becomings' (future adults and citizen workers). Too strong a focus on children as future adults is unbalanced without an equal concern for the well-being of children in childhood, and the quality of their social lives and opportunities for self-realisation (Prout, cited in Lister, 2006).

Child Safeguarding

Concerns about child protection and the safeguarding of children are key aspects of policy-making for children. This is a complex and sensitive area of policy where concerns raised about children's care and safety are the responsibility of a range of agencies and professionals (see Chapter 54). Children and families encounter safeguarding and interventions in a range of statutory settings, including social services, health services and schools. Social work with children and families can be particularly challenging. Box 58.3 sets out of some of the fundamental principles of good childcare social work practice.

Box 58.3 Principles of Relationship-based Practice in Working with Children and Families

- Recognising the 'child within'.
- Listening to the voice of the child: respecting their views and promoting their best interests.
- Working with children *and* families: understanding and acknowledging the tensions inherent in focusing on the needs of child while not overlooking the circumstances of the family.
- Acknowledging power and purpose: including the statutory power of social workers to remove children from their families.

Source: drawn from Wilson, Ruch and Lymbery (2011: 461).

In addition to child neglect and child protection issues arising within families, the first decades of the twenty-first century have been dominated by a series of public scandals resulting in an unprecedented period of investigations into historic and contemporary child abuse and child sexual exploitation. In 2015, there were over thirteen public inquiries and reviews of procedure in process across the UK involving core service providers such as the NHS, the Department of Education, the BBC, Social Services and the Home Office. The investigations are wide ranging and include historic cases involving sexual abuse of children by well-known celebrity figures and politicians, as well as statutory inquiries into historical and contemporary child abuse carried out within the public care system, children's homes, schools and other public institutional domains. In addition, a series of court cases revealed that a significant degree of grooming and sexual exploitation of children and young people was taking place in towns and cities across the UK. Such was the scale of the revelations that David Cameron, Prime Minister at the height of the scandals, described the sexual exploitation – especially in relation to that of young girls by gangs of men – as occurring

on an 'industrial scale'. The scandals have raised significant concerns about the ways in which public bodies handled child sex abuse claims. Allegations of cover-ups at the highest levels of governance fuelled a loss of confidence in statutory bodies, the police and prosecutors. Although new laws and policies will undoubtedly be developed following this period of scandal and moral panic, there are also likely to be considerable tensions between policies designed to respond to an increased demand for children's safeguarding services and the protection of children in a world where resources for social services at a local authority level are heavily constrained by budget cuts and austerity measures introduced at a national government level. The 2015 Ofsted annual review of children's social care found that over three-quarters of the forty-three local authority child protection departments inspected during 2013–14 were inadequate or requiring improvement, and that while the demand for child protection services had significantly increased, budget cuts from central government had resulted in intense pressure and a weakening of safeguarding services.

Policy in Action: Ending Child Poverty

Children are particularly vulnerable to poverty, and state support for them and their families through health, education, social services and the tax and social security system plays a vital role in their protection, especially for children who live in lone-parent households and/or where there is unemployment, low pay or long-term sickness and disability. The level of financial support provided by the state can be crucial in securing the economic well-being of children.

In 1999, faced with a child poverty rate of over 4 million, the Labour government pledged to eradicate child poverty within a twenty-year period. To do so, it developed a major programme of welfare reform, which had three key interrelated components, making work possible and making work pay, improved financial support for families with children, and investment in children.

The tensions between children as 'beings' and as 'becomings' were evident in Labour's Early Years programme, which included Sure Start in areas of deprivation and Children's Centres to deliver childcare and a range of parental support. These policies were formulated in recognition that early interventions in children's lives could be highly effective in preparing them for school and, as such, had a strong 'social investment' agenda. However, there can be real tensions between Early Years initiatives and the government's welfare-to-work policies, and it is not always clear whether the focus is support for parents and children or the pursuit of wider economic issues and concerns.

The Labour government struggled and ultimately failed to meet its poverty reduction targets, and in what turned out to be one of its final acts in power brought in unique legislation that bound all future governments of whatever hue to keep the child poverty pledge and eradicate child poverty by 2020. The Child Poverty Act 2010 set out a range of duties that required future governments to develop a child poverty strategy, present it to parliament every three years, and report every year on their progress (see Box 58.4).

Box 58.4 The Child Poverty Act 2010

Purpose of the Act:

- To enshrine in law the UK government's commitment to end child poverty by 2020.

Key elements:

- Every future government required to produce a child poverty strategy directed towards 2020 and due every three years. The strategy to be placed before Parliament.
- Annual report of progress towards target set before parliament, with the intention of holding governments to account.
- Independent Child Poverty Commission set up to advise policy and monitor government progress.
- Duty placed on local authorities, devolved authorities and their partners to tackle child poverty.

Critics of Labour's anti-poverty programme pointed to the dominance of the welfare-to-work agenda that underpinned much of the policy. For example, policies that encourage mothers, especially lone mothers, into employment will have an impact on children's lives (see Chapter 57). The intention is that children will experience increased financial security through their mother's income from work; however, the balance of work and care within families is affected, and as a result so too are children's experiences of childcare and after-school care, as well as the length and quality of time that they are able to spend with their mothers. Others have argued that greater redistribution of income from rich to poor would have been necessary to lift poorer families out of poverty.

Following Labour in 2010, the Coalition government, although bound by the Child Poverty Act, adopted a very different approach to child poverty, arguing that a transfer of income is not necessarily the route they wished to take to reduce child poverty. The first and second Child Poverty Strategies were developed in the midst of severe 'austerity' measures and resulted in significant cuts in social security, child services and housing support for low-income families. Each devolved administration (see Chapters 22–25) has its own child poverty strategy, but overarching policies such as 'austerity' measures and benefit and service cuts have undermined the capacity to protect children. Research has shown that these cuts have impacted disproportionately on low-income children and their families, and a report by the Social Mobility and Child Poverty Commission in 2015 indicated that the 2020 child poverty target was unlikely to be met. In 2015, following the election of a Conservative government, the Child Poverty Act – the law requiring government to abolish child poverty – was singled out to be repealed and the targets for raising children out of relative poverty scrapped. This will leave the UK as the only country in the OECD not to use a relative poverty indicator for measuring childhood poverty. New legislation will be developed to replace the 2010 Child Poverty Act, and will use measures of the proportion of children living in workless households and the educational attainment of disadvantaged 16-year-olds to assess progress on child poverty. This is a highly contentious move which was criticised by, among others, the Children's Commissioner for England. It is clear that in the context of changing economic, social and political values the future well-being of low-income children will depend very heavily on what economic and social welfare provision is made for them in the years ahead.

Emerging Issues

Childhood is undergoing considerable transformation, as social, demographic and economic changes impact upon the everyday lives of children and their families. Formulating adequate and effective social policies that respond to children's needs and concerns have presented considerable challenges for governments as they seek to reconcile the often divergent needs of the state, families and children. Despite the Child Poverty Act and the legal binding on future governments of every political stance to eradicate child poverty by 2020, it was apparent that a change of government could bring a change of policy direction, and this was the case in 2015 with the change from Coalition to Conservative government. Therefore, with significant welfare cuts in the pipeline and the proposed repeal of the Child Poverty Act, it is likely that the experience of poverty and disadvantage will continue to remain a severe problem for many children over the foreseeable future. The adequate provision of benefits and state support for families in employment and – most critically – out of employment will be a key concern. These are very sensitive policy issues that cut right to the heart of the child/parent/state welfare triangle. Income support policies for children reflect the tensions between the duties and responsibilities of parents and the duties and responsibilities of the state for ensuring children's well-being.

At the start of the twenty-first century, the interests of children slowly came in from the margins to the very heart of policy. However, there is no guarantee that their needs and concerns will stay at the centre of policy. Children are highly vulnerable to changes in government and the attendant potential for new policy directions driven by new political priorities. Child poverty concerns are already being redefined as the welfare landscape is redrawn in the context of changing government imperatives and the prospect of a lengthy period of 'austerity' policies. New concerns have also surfaced in response to revelations of widespread child sex abuse and child sexual exploitation. The policy responses to these events are unknown at this time, but may well be more likely to be informed by moral panics than by the needs and concerns of children themselves.

Guide to Further Sources

A key text that introduces child policy issues is H. Hendrick (2005), *Child Welfare and Social Policy, An Essential Reader*, Bristol: Policy Press. C. Hallett and A. Prout (2003), *Hearing the Voices of Children*, London: Routledge/Falmer, draws on the new social studies of childhood; it is a sociological approach but is focused on social policy and, in particular, on the emergence of children's voices in policy domains. Valuable texts about children's rights and citizenship can be found in H. Montgomery and M. Kellett (eds) (2009), *Children and Young People's Worlds: Developing Frameworks for Integrated Practice*, Bristol: Policy Press; and A. Invernizzi and J. Williams (2008), *Children and Citizenship*, Sage: London. A good overview of social investment policy can be found in R. Lister (2006), 'Children (but not women) first: New Labour, child welfare and gender', *Critical Social Policy*, 26:2, 315–35.

A valuable introduction to social work is K. Wilson, G. Ruch and M. Lymbery (2011), *Social Work: An Introduction to Contemporary Practice*, New York: Pearson Longman; ch. 16 covers working with children and families.

R. Eke, H. Butcher and M. Lee (2009), *Whose Childhood Is It? The Roles of Children, Adults and Policy Makers*, London: Continuum, provides a valuable insight into early years policies, the debates about 'being' and 'becoming', and their implications for children.

The devolved Children's Commissioners websites are good sources for rights-based research and analysis of policy. The English Children's Commissioner has carried out research into child protection and children at risk of sexual exploitation and gangs.

Government websites, including the Child Poverty Unit, the Department for Work and Pensions and the Department for Education, are valuable sources of policy documents and research. For further information about child poverty, see J. Waldfogel (2010), *Britain's War on Poverty*, New York: Russell Sage.

Look at the Joseph Rowntree Foundation website at: www.jrf.org.uk, and the Child Poverty Action Group (CPAG) website, which has a regular update on child poverty statistics, cpag.org.uk

The Child Poverty Act can be found at legislation.gov.uk/ukpga/2010/9/contents.

On a wider stage, the UNICEF website carries information about the UNCRC and many other issues that affect children: unicef.org.

Review and Assignment Questions

1 How has childhood changed in Britain over the last thirty years?
2 What role do children's rights play in policy?
3 What is the Child Poverty Act 2010, and what are the implications for children of this legislation?
4 How has devolution in the UK affected policies for children?
5 What are 'social investment' policies and how do they affect children?

Visit the book companion site at www.wiley.com/go/alcocksocialpolicy to make use of the resources designed to accompany the textbook. There you will find chapter-specific guides to further resources, including governmental, international, thinktank, pressure groups and relevant journal sources. You will also find a glossary based on *The Blackwell Dictionary of Social Policy*, help sheets, guidance on managing assignments in social policy and career advice.

59

Young People

Bob Coles and Aniela Wenham

Overview

The chapter describes a number of different positions taken by successive governments in five main phases:

- The first covers the arrival of youth policy in the period 1997–2000, mainly under the influence of the Social Exclusion Unit.
- The second period (2000–5) saw the birth, life and 'demise' of the 'Connexions Strategy' described by the Prime Minister at the time as 'our frontline policy for young people'.
- During the third period, youth policy became submerged in policy for 'children-and-young people' under the predominant discourses of the 2003 Green Paper, *Every Child Matters*.
- Fourth, we describe youth policy under the Coalition government 2010–15, which saw many of the pre-2010 structures for youth policy dismantled.
- Finally, we draw attention to developments in the European Union, suggesting that this might be a means through which some of the old Labour principles of youth policy can still be defended and promoted.

The Student's Companion to Social Policy, Fifth Edition. Edited by Pete Alcock, Tina Haux, Margaret May and Sharon Wright.
© 2016 John Wiley & Sons, Ltd. Published 2016 by John Wiley & Sons, Ltd.

Perspectives on Youth and Youth Transitions

It is often misleading and contentious to refer to youth as being defined by specific chronological ages. 'Youth' is, perhaps, better described as a phase in the life course between childhood and adulthood, and 'young people' are those at this phase in the life course. Different social sciences emphasise different aspects of this. The term 'adolescence' is often used in psychology to describe biological and psychological aspects of physical, emotional and sexual maturation associated with the teenage years. Sociologists have more often defined youth as associated with institutional transitions, three of which predominate. The first involves completing education and entering the labour market – the school-to-work transition. The second involves attaining (relative) independence of families of origin (including partnering and family formations) – the domestic transition. The third involves moving from the parental home, sometimes initially involving temporary transitional accommodation, but eventually achieving a 'home' independent of parents – the housing transition. Political scientists and others have focused on the ways in which different rights and responsibilities accrue to young people during their teenage years or early twenties. Indeed, some analysts have talked about youth citizenship as being distinctive from the full citizenship of adults. As an applied social science, social policy draws on all these perspectives in order to provide a critical appreciation of how, to what degree and in what ways the needs of young people are (or are not) met.

The Polarisation of Youth Transitions

The 'youth transition model' has proved especially useful in helping to understand the 're-structuration' of youth that occurred in the last quarter of the twentieth century and continued into the twenty-first. It helps highlight the ways in which 'traditional transitions' have been replaced by 'extended' and 'fractured' transitions. 'Traditional transitions', commonplace until the mid-1970s, involved most young people leaving school at minimum school-leaving age and almost immediately and unproblematically obtaining employment. As young people worked in their late teenage years, the majority continued to live in the parental home. They saved, formed partnerships, got engaged, then married, and on marriage moved to their own home and started a family, and usually in that order. In the twenty-first century, although significant numbers of young people still attempt some of the major transitions in their teenage years, traditional ones have been largely replaced by 'extended transitions'. These involve longer periods spent in post-16 and higher education, longer periods of family dependency, later parenting (the average age of a woman having her first child is now thirty), more complex partnering (often including cohabitation), and more complex and extended periods of living in 'transitional housing'.

'Fractured' transitions involve leaving school without finding work and/or leaving home without finding a secure alternative. They can be associated with unemployment, homelessness and social exclusion. They are also associated both with previous experiences of disadvantage (either in education, family life or both) and with other transition experiences, such as becoming a teenage parent, leaving home (often for negative reasons such as family disputes), or being involved in crime, drug misuse and/or the criminal justice system. This involved what governments since 1997 have referred to as 'social exclusion'. It is these 'problematic' transitions that are the focus of much youth policy.

The Emergence of Youth Policy in the UK, 1997–2001

Before the Labour government in 1997, it could easily be argued that Britain did not have a youth policy. Social policies did impact on the lives of young people. For instance, in the mid-1980s, half a million 16 year olds (a quarter of the age cohort) were denied unemployment benefits and recruited onto the Youth Training Scheme. Yet such policy was set by separate government departments responsible for the big institutions of the welfare state (employment, social security, health, education and the criminal justice system) with little if anything (no policy structures or mechanisms) to produce a coherent approach to particular client groups, such as young people. Some academics argued for the development of coherence, illustrating how failure to coordinate policy left different departments pulling in contradictory directions, despite often involving the same young people.

The chief instigating body of youth policy in the early years of the first Blair government was the Social Exclusion Unit (SEU) set up shortly after the 1997 general election. The Unit, which was part of the Cabinet Office, fulfilled tasks set for it by the Prime Minister and reported directly to him. One early report from the SEU in 2000 pointed out that Britain was alone in Europe in not having a minister, a ministry, a parliamentary committee or, indeed, any vehicle for cross-ministerial discussion of youth matters. It produced a radical new vision for the better coordination of youth policy across government.

The Connexions Strategy, 1999–2005

The fifth report from the SEU, *Bridging the Gap*, published in 1999, concerned young people aged 16–18 who were not in any form of education, employment or training (NEET). It was part of a concerted attempt by Labour to address 'social exclusion' amongst young people. The report confirmed that being disengaged at the ages of 16 and 17 was a good predictor of later unemployment, and was also closely linked to educational disaffection and disadvantage prior to the age of 16. It also correlated with an involvement in crime, misuse of drugs and teenage pregnancy. Other categories of young people that predominated amongst those who were NEET included care leavers, young carers, young people with mental health problems, young people with disabilities and special educational needs. The SEU report suggested the development of a new multi-professional service to help give guidance, advice and support for young people between the ages of 13 and 19 – a Connexions Strategy with, at the heart of that, a new Connexions Service. Whilst Scotland, Wales and Northern Ireland did not have a Social Exclusion Unit, and did not develop a service badged as 'Connexions', similar issues were addressed there, and similar patterns of multi-agency working were developed in those countries too (see Chapters 22–25).

Box 59.1   Connexions

The Connexions Service aimed to offer a *universal* service to all young people, and a *targeted* service offering intensive support to a minority of young people facing complex problems. The Connexions Strategy remit was much broader than that of the old careers services, which it absorbed or replaced. It aimed to provide (through forty-seven sub-regional Connexions Partnership Boards) the coordination of support and services across a range of different agencies. This included health agencies (including the drug prevention and advisory service, and teenage pregnancy and motherhood), education (including educational welfare and the youth service, as well as schools and colleges), social services (including leaving care teams), youth justice (including the police and youth offending teams), housing departments and the voluntary sector (including youth homelessness projects). The Connexions Strategy anticipated that it would deal with three tiers of need. Most young people would only require information, advice or guidance, on their education and learning, careers or personal development. Others, at risk of disengaging, needed in-depth support and guidance, and help to assess their needs, to develop and support action plans and to monitor progress. A smaller group needed specialist assessment and support, which may require services being 'brokered' from other specialist services. The service was to be delivered by a new profession of Personal Advisers (PAs). Connexions PAs were also expected to act as 'advocates' for young people, ensuring that appropriate services and benefits were obtained, playing the role of a 'powerful friend' where agencies were failing to comply with their duties and responsibilities.

Everybody Matters (But Some More than Others)

In September 2003, the UK Labour government published the Green Paper, *Every Child Matters*, which was to have immense significance for policy development on children and young people. It signalled a reconfiguration of the structures of policy at both national, local authority and community levels. It also heralded the appointment of a Children's Commissioner for England to act as an independent champion for children. The Green Paper further widened the responsibilities of the Minister for Children and Young People to deal with teenage pregnancy, the looked-after children system and family law. From 2007 to 2010 all these responsibilities were located within a new Department for Children, Schools and Families (although in Scotland this was devolved). At a local authority level, too, the Child Poverty Act 2010 required the coordination of services and responsibilities with local authorities to have a single Director of Children's Services. This new post was accountable for education *and* social services and the integration of all associated activities. This was accomplished through another new body, Children's Trusts, combining the local authority and health services and which had charge of the commissioning of Connexions and Youth Offending Teams. At a community level, a range of services for children and young people were to be co-located in Sure Start Children's Centres and Full Service Extended Schools. Given this new constellation of structures for children and young people, it was clear that some re-configuration of the Connexions Strategy would have to occur.

Under proposals made in *Youth Matters*, local authorities were left to decide whether or not to keep Connexions or to develop their own new version of a youth support system (HM Government, 2005). Whatever their choice, local authorities were once again put in control, this time through Children's Trusts, which received all government funding for services for children and young people. The old sub-regional Connexions Partnership Boards were abandoned. Careers education and guidance (CEG) was broadened to 'Information, Advice and Guidance' (IAG), with promises of a mixed media service (including new technologies such as the Internet and helplines), quality standards and opt-out permissive powers for schools. On targeted support for vulnerable young people, the government promised multi-agency working, a Lead Professional, a Common Assessment Framework and new patterns of information-sharing – all of which seemed strangely like the abandoned Connexions Strategy. In the event, many local authorities retained some form of a youth support service and addressing NEET was a key performance indicator for them.

Further Dismantling the Edifice: UK Coalition Government, Recession, Austerity and Cuts

Ominous signs of a radical change started on the first day of the incoming UK Coalition government in May 2010 when the old Department for Children, Schools and Families was replaced by the Department of Education, indicating a narrow focus which had not existed since the 1970s. A government committed to austerity, it seemed, had money to spare for the changes in signage this entailed. It was obviously important and symbolic. By 2013, young people's issues became even more marginalised when responsibility was handed from the Secretary of State for Education to a small, little known and poorly resourced unit inside the Cabinet Office.

Initially, the significance of such changes was masked by a seemingly new approach to young people signalled by the policy paper, *Positive for Youth* (PfY), which promoted a 'mixed economy of welfare' (see Part VI) to address young people's issues. Yet the champion of the proposals, Tim Loughton, who had spent years in opposition preparing his brief, was promptly sacked in 2012.

Even in the early days of the Coalition government (2010–15), austerity seemed to be the primary objective. The Educational Maintenance Allowance (EMA), a proven means of increasing participation in education of poorer young people aged 16–18 years, was cancelled abruptly in 2010. Despite increasing levels of youth unemployment, so too was the Future Jobs Fund (for 18–24 year olds). It was replaced only with a watered down Youth Contract. A variety of jobs working and supporting young people were also increasingly under threat as local authorities faced unprecedented cuts in their budgets. Young people were also subject to drastic reform to their

Box 59.2   Positive for Youth

Positive for Youth (PfY) encompassed a wide range of issues, including education, youth services, parenting, health and crime. Despite the multiplicity of issues receiving attention, the publication failed to demonstrate awareness of how these issues related to one another, but also how they would then be tackled as part of any overarching strategy. In line with the principles of social conservatism, emphasis was placed on individual responsibility (young people are encouraged to be entrepreneurial) rather than on state support for collective provisions, and, in particular, the role of the family (namely, parents) having primary responsibility for addressing or regulating young people's behaviour. Shrinking state responsibility for youth provision was most notable through an emphasis placed on 'a mixed economy of welfare', with business and the voluntary sector playing a crucial role in the delivery of services. This collaboration and partnership required professionals to adopt a more enterprising culture whereby the impact of their work must be demonstrated through the use of 'social impact bonds' and payment-by-results mechanisms to secure funding. The scale to which services and provision for young people have effectively been outsourced since 2010 is unprecedented. Where 'positive activities' for young people were included, it was in relation to the expansion of the National Citizen Service (a programme encouraging 16 and 17 year olds to be engaged in volunteering).

However, when compared with the youth-related SEU reports that framed the 'New Labour' era, it was striking how PfY paid little attention to the 'difference' of gender, class, ethnicity, disabilities or types of disadvantage. Instead, young people were represented as a homogeneous group. PfY chose to focus on the need to increase young people's aspirations (resulting in 'strong ambitions') without careful reflection on the resources needed to achieve these. There was also no mention of what we might have learnt through previous youth policy initiatives, such as Connexions, or the challenges surrounding multi-agency working and effective communication between professionals. You would be forgiven for assuming that policy-makers from 2010 onwards had experienced policy amnesia of any of the lessons learned prior to 2010.

welfare entitlement, something which is set to continue following the 2015 general election.

In 2010, an Audit Commission report indicated that the lifetime, public finance cost of NEET had already risen (2002–9) from £8 billion to £12 billion. The report demonstrated that much of this could be avoided by investing in well-targeted youth projects funded by local authorities at a cost of only a few thousand pounds each. Yet, even as early as 2010, in anticipation of the spending review, local authorities immediately started to cancel youth project contracts and to issue redundancy notices to youth workers. Throughout the five years of Coalition government, the youth service become a pale reflection of its previous ambitions, and Connexions was stripped of its wide manifesto and replaced by an all-age careers service. Some schools were reported to be training up classroom assistants and secretarial staff to fulfil the role.

Despite a clear historical narrative outlining the complexities of NEET, the UK Coalition government showed little sign of taking the issue seriously. The most recent comment from the Conservative Party for dealing with NEET, announced the introduction of a 'Youth Allowance' (replacing Jobseeker's Allowance), which would require young people to do unpaid community work whilst also job searching. As the election approached, although offering some modest investment in a Youth Guarantee Scheme, the Labour Party showed no real commitment to restoring its old vision of an holistic and integrated approach to youth policy. The Conservative Party won the general election on 7 May 2015. The first Conservative budget (July 2015) hit young people particularly hard. This included the withdrawal of JSA to be replaced by a 'Youth Obligation' for 18–21 year olds; the removal of the automatic entitlement to housing benefit for 18–21 year olds (with exemptions for vulnerable young people); and the abolition of student maintenance grants to be replaced with maintenance loans. The budget also announced the introduction of what was termed a 'national living wage', but this would apply only to workers over the age of 25.

Emerging Issues

In the UK, the five years up to the general election in 2015 was not a good time for youth policy. But the same period saw considerable progress within the European Union in establishing a framework (the EU Youth Strategy) to be followed by all constituent member states. This had two main aims: to provide more and equal opportunities for young people in education and the job market; and to encourage young people to actively 'participate' in society in a variety of ways. This was to be achieved across eight different fields of action, including education and training (including actions to discourage early school leaving and NEET up to the age of 25), employment and entrepreneurship, health and well-being, voluntary activities, and creativity and culture.

The European Union seems serious about confronting youth unemployment in recognition that young people have been hardest hit by the global recession. With a European average unemployment rate amongst under-25 year olds of over 20 per cent, there was particular concern in countries such as Greece and Spain where more than half the age group were unemployed. Europe too has embraced concern with the NEET issue, which provided the spur to action on youth policy in the UK at the turn of the century. But the focus in the EU is on a much wider age cohort (up to the age of 25) and is having a more profound impact in defining 'youth' and 'youth policy' away from the old narrow focus on 'teenagers' as occurred in England in 1998–2010.

To indicate compliance with EU policy, each member state is required to submit a periodic national report as to how it is complying with the EU Youth Strategy. It is notable that, in doing so, the UK government has been obliged to summarise the different developments in each of the home countries as there have been significant differences between them before, and especially since, 2010. The Conservative government, elected in 2015, has set a date of 23 June 2016 for a referendum on whether the UK should leave the European Union. But with further devolutionary pressures across the home countries, the non-English may simultaneously wish to be more positive about the youth initiatives emanating from Europe.

Guide to Further Reading

J. Coleman and A. Hagell (2013), *Key Data on Adolescence 2013*, 9th edn, Brighton: Trust for the Centre for Adolescence, provides a biannual compilation of useful statistics on young people.

Department of Education (2010), *Positive for Youth: A New Approach to Cross-Government Policy for Young People aged 13–19*, www.gov.uk/government/publications/positive-for-youth-a-new-approach-to-cross-government-policy-for-young-people-aged-13-to-19/positive-for-youth-the-statement; Audit Commission (2010), *Against the Odds*, archive.audit-commission.gov.uk/auditcommission/sitecollectiondocuments/Downloads/20100707-againsttheoddsfull.pdf; Eurofound (2012), *NEETs: Young People not in Employment, Education or Training: Characteristics, Costs and Policy Responses in Europe*, www.eurofound.europa.eu/pubdocs/2012/54/en/1/EF1254EN.pdf; European Union (2014), *The EU Youth Strategy*, ec.europa.eu/youth/policy/youth_strategy/index_en.htm.

HM Government (2005) Youth Matters. Green Paper (HM Government, Cm 6629) https://www.education.gov.uk/consultations/downloadableDocs/Youth%20matttters%20pdf.pdf.

A. Furlong and F. Cartmel (2006), *Young People and Social Change*, 2nd edn, Buckingham: Open University Press, is a re-written version of a very influential text.

R. MacDonald and J. Marsh (2005), *Disconnected Youth. Growing Up in Britain's Poor Neighbourhoods*, Basingstoke: Palgrave, reports on a specific study conducted in the North East, but contains excellent reviews of debates around young people, the 'underclass' and social exclusion.

Review and Assignment Questions

1 What are the key stages in youth policy development described in the chapter and what are the key features of each stage?

2 What were the main reasons for the development of a more holistic approach to youth policy between 1997 and 2010?

3 What is meant by 'social exclusion' and what were the main categories of young people thought to be at risk?

4 Why do you think 'NEET' became such a predominant policy concern after 1997 in the UK and in the European Union in the twenty-first century?

5 In the UK, do party politics matter when it comes to youth policy? How did youth policy change following the 1997, 2010 and 2015 general elections?

Visit the book companion site at www.wiley.com/go/alcocksocialpolicy to make use of the resources designed to accompany the textbook. There you will find chapter-specific guides to further resources, including governmental, international, thinktank, pressure groups and relevant journal sources. You will also find a glossary based on *The Blackwell Dictionary of Social Policy*, help sheets, guidance on managing assignments in social policy and career advice.

60

Older People

Kate Hamblin

■ ▪ ■ ▫ ■ ▪ ■ ▫ ▪ ■ ▫ ■ ▪ ▫ ■ ▫ ■ ▪ ■ ▫ ■ ▪ ▫ ■ ▪ ■ ▫ ▪ ■ ▫ ■ ▫ ■ ▪ ■ ▫ ▪ ■ ▫ ■ ▪ ■ ▫ ■ ▪ ■

Overview

- In the UK, people are living longer due to advances in healthcare and living standards (including nutrition and hygiene), and are projected in future to live longer still; at the same time, fertility rates are lower than in the mid-1900s.
- As a result, the old-age dependency ratio is increasing – there are fewer people of working age to provide for those beyond retirement.
- Changes to the old-age dependency ratio have raised concerns about the sustainability of pension and social care provision for increasing numbers of older people.
- 'Active ageing' policies and changes to social care funding have been policy responses to an ageing population.
- However, it should be highlighted that what it means to be 'old' is a social construct, in part influenced by social policy.

■ ▪ ■ ▫ ■ ▪ ■ ▫ ▪ ■ ▫ ■ ▪ ▫ ■ ▫ ■ ▪ ■ ▫ ■ ▪ ▫ ■ ▪ ■ ▫ ▪ ■ ▫ ■ ▫ ■ ▪ ■ ▫ ▪ ■ ▫ ■ ▪ ■ ▫ ■ ▪ ■

Introduction

This chapter focuses on the effect of social policies on older people, but also on the impact of an ageing population on welfare arrangements. First, then, it is important to define what is meant here by 'older people'. Those over the age of 50 are included in this definition, though in policy terms older people can be broadly split into those of working age and those over the state pension age.

However, even when divided along these lines, 'older people' as a cohort are not a homogenous group, nor do they experience ageing and social policy in the same way. Being old and the experience of ageing are not objective facts, but are constructed through interactions with others and social policy; what is it to be 'old' is therefore a social construct. Though people are living longer in general, there are important differences related to lifestyle, occupation, gender, income and

The Student's Companion to Social Policy, Fifth Edition. Edited by Pete Alcock, Tina Haux, Margaret May and Sharon Wright.
© 2016 John Wiley & Sons, Ltd. Published 2016 by John Wiley & Sons, Ltd.

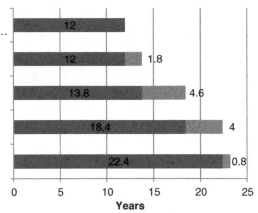

A manual worker, retiring in poor health with a low income and an unhealthy lifestyle would live for 12... **12**

...but if he retired in good health, he would live for another 1.8 years **12 1.8**

...and also had a healthy lifestyle, he would live for another 4.6 years **13.8 4.6**

...and a high income, he would live for another 4 years **18.4 4**

...and did a non-manual job, he would live for another 0.8 years **22.4 0.8**

Years

Figure 60.1 Post-65 life expectancy for males.
Source: S. Harper, K. Howse and S. Baxter (2011), *Living Longer and Prospering? Designing an Adequate, Sustainable and Equitable UK State Pension System*, Club Vita LLP and the Oxford Institute of Ageing, University of Oxford.

ethnicity. Figure 60.1 demonstrates how much life expectancies for men post-age 65 vary according to the work they did, their income, lifestyle and health. The *political economy of ageing* literature emphasises that a person's characteristics, such as their gender, occupation and ethnicity, all affect both how they experience getting older and their interactions with the welfare state. Titmuss (1955) identified 'two nations in retirement' as a person's work history determines the financial resources they have in later life. He argued those who are male and middle class would be best off as they were more likely to have occupational pensions, whilst those who are female, working class and single would be at a disadvantage in later years.

In spite of these nuances, the policy response to the ageing of the population both in the UK and further afield in EU nations is to encourage people to work longer and defer entering retirement for as long as possible. This, it is argued, is key to the sustainability of welfare arrangements at a time when there are fewer people being born, whilst people are living longer.

Welfare, Population Ageing and the Intergenerational Contract

Intergenerational solidarity – or the social contract between different generations – is implicit to the welfare state with transfers from working-age people to those beyond state pension age. However, as welfare state provision is reformed, this solidarity is altered and the contract between generations adjusted. Organisations, such as the World Bank, stress the potential for conflict between the generations, arguing that the growing numbers of young poor will create an intergenerational conflict as they fund the pensions of increasing numbers of (sometimes wealthy) retirees. Changes in life expectancy combined with reduced fertility and the 'baby boomer' generation entering older age have changed the 'old-age dependency ratio' (the number of people of working age versus the number who are over 65), which has been steadily rising in the UK, as Figure 60.2 shows. An ageing society leads to a decline in the working population, increasing pressure on pensions systems and social care, and the younger generations contributing through taxation. In particular, in countries like the UK which operates a 'pay-as-you-earn' (PAYE) pension system (those of working age provide the pension pot for those over the state pension age), the decreasing numbers of working age people increase their level of contributions in order to provide pensions for a disproportionate number of older people.

However, it also argued that concerns regarding the 'demographic time bomb' and integrational conflict over welfare resources have been inflated to justify welfare state reform. Studies

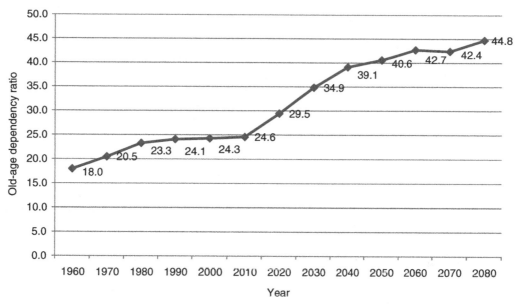

Figure 60.2 UK old-age dependency ratio, 1960–2080.
Source: Eurostat, Population Projections, 2010-based (EUROPOP 2010). The old-age dependency ratio here is the actual and projected number of persons aged 65 and over expressed as a percentage of the projected number of persons aged between 15 and 64 (argued to be of working age). So, in 2010, the dependency ratio was 24.3% (i.e., the number of people over 65 was 24.3% of those aged 15–64), and is projected to rise to 44.8%.

have found, at best, mixed results demonstrating that different age groups are self-interested when it comes to welfare arrangements and begrudge provision for other cohorts. Generally, it has been found that younger people are in favour of support for older generations and vice versa. In addition, the portrayal of older people as passive consumers of welfare ignores both the contributions made earlier in their lives and also as providers of care and voluntary support (see below). Nonetheless, provision and policies for older people approaching the state pension age (SPA) are changing and will be explored in the following section.

Pension Policy

The Old Age Pension Act 1908 (see Chapter 17) introduced a means-tested benefit for those over the age of 70, and seventeen years later, the first contributory pension scheme was created. Since then, as Table 60.1 indicates, the SPA has been amended several times, with a general trend since the 1990s towards increasing the age at which both men and women can receive their state pension.

The UK state pension system comprises a first tier, flat-rate Basic State Pension (BSP) and second tier with a benefit linked to earnings. Alongside these two tiers is the private pension market, with schemes funded by individuals and/or their employers. Traditionally, these were 'defined benefit' schemes or reflected an individual's final salary, but employers are moving towards the less generous and 'riskier' (in that they are dependent on stock market performance) 'defined contribution' schemes. The first tier is operated on a pay-as-you-go (PAYG) principle and the amount received depends on whether the person has met the minimum threshold for National Insurance contributions over their working life (which it is argued is unfair to those providing care and therefore unable to make these contributions). In 2003, the means-tested Pension Credit was introduced to supplement the pension incomes of those with very limited assets and incomes, yet take up of this benefit by those who are eligible is

Table 60.1   Changes to the state pension age in the UK.

Year	Changes
1908	Old Age Pension Act created a means-tested pension for those over 70.
1925	Widows', Orphans' and Old Age Contributory Pensions Act created the first contributory state pension scheme, funded by contributions from both the employee and employer and with an age threshold of 65.
1940	Old Age and Widows' Pension Act lowered the SPA for the contributory state pension scheme to 60 for women.
1995	Pensions Act introduced a timetable for the equalisation of male and female pension ages to 65. The SPA for women would slowly rise to 65 from April 2010 to April 2020.
2007	Pensions Act further increased the SPA to 66 between April 2024 and April 2026, then to 67 between April 2034 and April 2036, and to 68 between April 2044 and April 2046.
2014	Pensions Act altered the timing of the increase to SPA, with the rise to 67 now scheduled for between 2026 and 2028.

only around two-thirds. People are able to defer receipt of their BSP and in doing so increase the final amount by 10.4 per cent per year. In 2014, the Pension Act introduced a new single-tier pension, which will replace the BSP and Pension Credit and will be available to those retiring as of 2017 at the earliest.

There have been several incarnations of the second tier since it was introduced in 1961, and there are still some pensioners receiving the Graduated Retirement Benefit which closed to new entrants in 1975. It was followed by the State Earnings Related Pension Scheme in 1978, which was then replaced in 2002 with the State Second Pension. The second-tier pension is also PAYG, but the final amount received is dependent on the contributions made over the person's working life.

The second pillar was supplemented by a new pension scheme funded by employees and employers into which employees were 'auto-enrolled' as of 2012, with the option to opt out. These new Personal Accounts are defined contribution schemes, and it is argued that this policy reflects a move away from state provision towards individual responsibility for income and security in later life.

Work and 'Active Ageing'

In the light of demographic ageing and what is argued to be the corresponding pressure on current welfare arrangements, 'active ageing' policies have been presented as a solution. As the population ages, how 'older people' are defined and what is expected of them are being altered. When the state pension was initially created, retirement came at the end of a career, followed by at most a decade before death. The creation of a state pension at a set age provided a normative framework for retirement and a lower limit for the category of 'older'. Townsend argued in his seminal work (see Guide to Further Sources, below) that the creation of a state pension effectively 'fostered the material and psychological dependence' of older people due to the low levels of financial benefits in retirement.

With increased longevity, retirement does not generally accompany a period of decline as it once did. Retirement for some therefore has become the third stage in the life course, after education and employment and before dependent old age. The term 'troisième age' or 'third age' was coined in France to apply to this period of relatively good health and social participation and a time for 'active ageing'.

Active ageing is a relatively new term, increasing in popularity in the last fifteen years. It first originated in the US in the 1960s as 'successful ageing' in response to disengagement theory, which argued that as people age, they gradually withdraw from society. Activity theorists argued this presented an overly depressing picture and demonstrated ageing was not a barrier to leading a fulfilling and active life. Active ageing returned again in the 1980s under the guise of 'productive ageing', with a focus on labour-market participation. It has been adopted as a term by the EU, with their approach focusing on reinforcing the employability of older workers and adapting employment rules to the ageing population.

However, the portrayal of retirement as purely a period of passivity because it does not involve labour-market participation underestimates other social roles occupied by older individuals. Retirement does not necessarily indicate inactivity; often it is a period characterised by voluntary work or care for others, including grandchildren. The World Health Organization takes a more holistic approach to active ageing, with three pillars: health, participation (in more than just the labour market) and security.

In terms of the policies available to older people prior to retirement to encourage them to 'age actively' and to re-enter employment in the UK, April 2000 saw the national launch of the voluntary New Deal for the Fifty-Plus (ND50+) as part of Labour's drive for 80 per cent employment and a broader package of unemployment policies designed to encourage people to enter the labour market. In terms of eligibility, an individual had to be over 50 and receiving Income Support, Jobseeker's Allowance, Incapacity Benefit, Severe Disablement Allowance or Pension Credit for six months or more.

The ND50+ when initially introduced included:

- access to a Personal Adviser;
- a Training Grant up to £1,500 within two years of finding employment;
- a weekly Employment Credit of £60 for those whose wages were below £15,000 annually (however, this financial incentive was argued to have a 'deadweight' effect, that is, that any positive effect would have happened without the credit, and was replaced by the 50+ element of the Working Tax Credit in 2003).

However, in 2009 the various New Deal programmes (see Chapters 47 and 48), including the ND50+, were replaced by the Flexible New Deal, which in turn was disbanded in favour of the single Work programme.

Aside from encouraging older people themselves to enter and remain in paid employment, it is also acknowledged that if older people are to work longer, attention needs to be paid to employers: older workers cannot find and stay in employment in a climate of age discrimination. Factors influencing older workers' decisions around employment and retirement include both 'pull' factors (incentives such as occupational early retirement schemes) and 'push' factors, including employers' attitudes and policies. In October 2006, legislation to curb age discrimination in the workplace was introduced in the UK (Equality and Diversity: Coming of Age – Consultation on the draft Employment Equality (Age) Regulations 2006). Mandatory retirement ages and age-specific recruitment were prohibited unless justified. However, 65 remained the 'default' retirement age, but employees could submit a request to their employer to work beyond this. Employers had to write to their employees between six and twelve months before they intended to retire them, and their employees in turn had the right to request to remain in employment post-65, which their employer had a 'duty to consider'.

Further to these changes, in July 2010, the UK Coalition government announced that the default retirement age would be repealed gradually from April 2011 to be closed entirely by the end of 2011. The Employment Equality (Repeal of Retirement Age Provisions) Regulations 2011 Act stated that from 6 April 2011, employers would not be able to issue any notifications for compulsory retirement using the default retirement age procedure. Older workers could be compulsorily retired only if their employer had notified them by 6 April 2011 and if their retirement fell before October 2011.

Social Care Policy

While 'younger' older people may in general not need a great deal of support, advanced old age for some is correlated with chronic diseases such as diabetes, arthritis, congestive heart failure, dementia and disability, therefore, the increasing need for health and social care. While life expectancy is increasing, healthy life expectancy is not keeping pace, and gaps are widening between certain groups along lines of gender, employment, deprivation and ethnicity.

The care system in the UK is more complex than the National Health Service insofar as it involves assessments of need before services are provided, and charges may apply. Social care in the UK comes in many forms, including assistance with daily living activities (washing, bowel and bladder management, dressing, eating, functional mobility, personal device care, personal hygiene and grooming, and toilet hygiene) and instrumental activities of daily living (housework, taking medications, managing money, shopping, using the telephone, or other forms of communication, using (appropriate) technology, and transportation within communities), adaptions and adjustment to home environments as well as provision in day-care centres and residential care homes.

The nations of the UK operate slightly different systems for assessing need for social care. In Scotland, local authorities use the Single Shared Assessment Indicator of Relative Need (SSA-IoRN), which is a questionnaire comprising twelve questions to assess whether a person has low, medium or high needs. The person may then be entitled to 'Self-Directed Support', which can come in the form of a direct payment that can be used to meet their care needs. The Community Care and Health (Scotland) Act 2002 legislated that personal care for those over the age of 65 and living in their own homes should be free in Scotland, regardless of their income or assets.

In 2009, Northern Ireland launched its Northern Ireland Single Assessment Tool (NISAT), categorising needs as 'critical', 'substantial', 'moderate' or 'low', to be used across both health and social care with the aim of providing a more streamlined process of assessment. Local authorities in England and parts of Wales use the Fair Access to Care Services (FACS) banding system to determine whether an individual is entitled to social care, and the majority provide care only to those with 'critical' or 'substantial' levels of need. Those deemed in sufficient need are then offered a Personal Budget, which they can then use to fund their own care and can be paid to the individual as a direct payment. In policy terms, the 'personalisation' and 'self-directed support' agenda reflect a shift towards placing the individual at the centre of care decisions and promoting choice. However, individuals need local authority approval of what they intend to spend their payments on and some academics and health and social care professionals suggest personalisation creates new risks of exploitation and abuse.

In 2015, care provided by local authorities to individuals in care homes was not, however, free; individuals with assets in excess of £23,250 in England and Northern Ireland, £24,000 in Wales and £26,000 in Scotland must pay for their own residential care costs, while those with more than £14,250 in England and Northern Ireland and £16,000 in Scotland (in Wales there is no lower limit) pay a proportion of their care costs. If the person requires attention from a nurse or lives in a residential facility providing nursing, however, there is a contribution towards these costs as part of the NHS funded-nursing care (in England £110.89 per week, in Wales the rate is £120.55 per week, and in Northern Ireland the rate is £100 per week) or they will be paid for in their entirety if the person satisfies the NHS continuing healthcare assessment (including having complex medical condition and substantial and ongoing care needs; having a 'primary health need' where the primary need for care relates to health). If there is no one else living in the person's home at the time when they enter a care home, the local authority can also take the value of the property in account twelve weeks after entry.

In response to concerns about rising care costs and fairness, the 2014 Care Act included a number of changes which would come into effect in April 2016, including a 'lifetime cap' on what people contribute towards their care of £72,000 across their life course. This cap, however, does not cover 'hotel costs' (that is, bed and board) related to residential care; a separate cap would be introduced for the hotel costs of £12,000 per year. In addition, the upper threshold for the means-testing would be raised from £23,250 in England to £118,500, meaning that anyone with assets worth between £14,500 and the new upper limit would receive a deduction to their care costs on a sliding scale.

Emerging Issues

This chapter has explored the way in which social policy plays a role in the construction of what it is to be 'older'. Reflecting changes in the composition of the population and increased longevity, older people are being encouraged to work longer and remain 'active'. At the same time, provision for those in need of care and support is becoming 'personalised', while the amount an individual can be expected to contribute to their care costs will be capped.

In terms of emerging issues, while longevity in general is increasing, healthy life expectancy is lagging behind. We are in general living longer, but for some people these extra years are characterised by poor health. Policies with a focus on active ageing therefore risk creating a further 'two nations' in older age (aside from those identified by Titmuss with large pensions and those without): one nation for those who are actively ageing in good health and another for those are not. The whole life course influences the experience of old age, and therefore policy intervention early in life could result in better health and well-being in later years.

This chapter has focused on social policy provision for older people, but the provision of support and care *outside* of social policy also needs to be highlighted. An estimated 6.5 million unpaid carers in the UK provide support valued at £119 billion annually. As the population structure shifts and people live longer, there will be fewer people available to provide unpaid care to those who are frail. Greater support is needed for those providing unpaid care, especially in the face of competing demands from employment.

Guide to Further Sources

Essential reading includes P. Townsend (1981), 'The structured dependency of the elderly: a creation of social policy in the twentieth century', *Ageing and Society*, 1, 5–28, which examines how pension and social care policy have manufactured the dependency and 'passivity' of older people, and challenges policymakers to create supportive policies which are empowering.

A. Walker (1981), 'Towards a political economy of old age', *Ageing and Society*, 1:1, 73–94,

highlights the importance of the life course in shaping the experience of old age, and warns against treating older people as a homogeneous, amorphous whole.

P. Higgs and C. Gilleard (2010), 'Generational conflict, consumption and the ageing welfare state in the United Kingdom', *Ageing and Society*, 30:8, 1439–51, challenge the notion of intergenerational conflict over resources, and therefore counter some of the pessimism associated with population ageing.

Review and Assignment Questions

1 How is old age socially constructed?
2 What factors affect a person's life expectancy and healthy life expectancy?
3 If people are living longer, should everyone work longer? What might make this difficult?
4 Should older people fund their own care, even if it means they have to sell their home?
5 What are the biggest challenges related to a diverse ageing population facing policy makers?

Visit the book companion site at www.wiley.com/go/alcocksocialpolicy to make use of the resources designed to accompany the textbook. There you will find chapter-specific guides to further resources, including governmental, international, thinktank, pressure groups and relevant journal sources. You will also find a glossary based on *The Blackwell Dictionary of Social Policy*, help sheets, guidance on managing assignments in social policy and career advice.

61

Disability

Mark Priestley

Overview

- Policy interest in disability has grown and changed since the 1970s. Disability should now be viewed as an issue of human rights, citizenship and equality rather than one of care, compensation or rehabilitation.
- The claims of the disabled people's movement have been important in bringing about this change of view.
- Disabled people have become more active welfare citizens, taking control of resources to manage the support they need in place of traditional services.
- More countries have introduced policies to counter disability discrimination, based on civil and human rights, but legislation is not enough to guarantee full citizenship.
- Transnational governance has become more important through institutions like the European Union (EU) and the United Nations (UN).

Context

Disability became prominent in policy debates during the second half of the twentieth century, in the UK and globally, culminating in 2006 with a UN Convention to protect and promote the rights of disabled people throughout the world. Attention to disability as a policy issue has been characterised by three significant themes. First, there

has been a change of policy thinking. Where 'disability' was once seen as a deficiency within the person, it is now viewed as a form of discrimination arising from deficiencies in society. Second, there has been a shift from policies for care and compensation towards policies for equal rights and the removal of barriers to social inclusion. Third, there has been a groundswell of self-organisation amongst disabled people themselves,

The Student's Companion to Social Policy, Fifth Edition. Edited by Pete Alcock, Tina Haux, Margaret May and Sharon Wright.
© 2016 John Wiley & Sons, Ltd. Published 2016 by John Wiley & Sons, Ltd.

leading to greater representation in policy claims and greater involvement in the production of welfare.

Most contemporary debates begin from a distinction between different models of disability, or different ways of thinking about the needs of disabled people. Traditional approaches often treated disability as an individual problem caused by physical, sensory or cognitive impairment. The solution was to treat the person (through improved medical and rehabilitation services) or to compensate them for their 'limitations' (by arranging less valued social roles, such as sheltered employment, residential care, social security payments and so on). Both assume that the problem and the policy response should be focused on the individual. The alternative approach, usually termed the 'social model of disability', sees the disadvantage experienced by disabled people as caused by limitations in society rather than something within the person. As Oliver (1996: 33) puts it:

> disability, according to the social model, is all the things that impose restrictions on disabled people; ranging from individual prejudice to institutional discrimination, from inaccessible buildings to unusable transport systems, from segregated education to excluding work arrangements, and so on. Further, the consequences of this failure do not simply and randomly fall on individuals but systematically upon disabled people as a group who experience this failure as discrimination institutionalised throughout society.

Until the 1990s, this kind of thinking was a fringe concern in policymaking – strongly argued by disability activists, but at the margins of the policy community. Nowadays, the 'social model' and disability rights are often acknowledged as themes in the mainstream policy agenda, but inequalities persist and disability continues to raise a number of very challenging and controversial policy debates.

The Historical Context: Disability as an Administrative Category

Some understanding of history is essential in grasping the relationship between disabled people,

social policy and the welfare state. Today, in modern welfare states, almost all aspects of disabled people's lives are subject to some kind of distinctive public policy (for example, there are policies concerning disabled people's access to education, health, housing, transport, employment, welfare benefits, family life and civil rights). Yet, prior to the emergence of the welfare state, people with significant impairments were largely undifferentiated from the greater mass of 'the poor'. A key point then is to understand why disabled people exist as a separate category for policymakers at all.

Within disability studies, proponents of the social model provided a broadly materialist account of British history to show how urban industrial capitalism created disability as a welfare 'problem' for the state. These arguments suggest that early competitive wage labour markets and factory production methods excluded many people with impairments from paid work and consigned increasing numbers to lives of poverty and economic dependency. As policy historians have shown, the state's role in facilitating early industrial capitalism involved vigorous social measures to control the labour force and to remove incentives for idleness amongst the mass of the population. In this context, a key development for disabled people was the distinction made between the 'impotent' and the 'able-bodied' poor (or the 'deserving' and 'undeserving'). Whilst the idle poor were rigorously disciplined, those deemed 'unable to work' were provided with limited welfare. The earliest English definitions of those 'not able to work' made no mention of disability, but by the time of the 1601 Poor Law a new category of disabled people was emerging – and inability to work would become the key to deciding who was, and who was not, 'disabled'.

Governing this category, and entitlement to public assistance required a whole new system of surveillance, regulation and control, which brought responsibility for disabled people's welfare into the public policy domain. It is not necessary to chart this history in detail here and some of the key reading at the end of the chapter provides excellent overviews. One of the most important arguments is that disability has functioned historically as a flexible administrative category in the control of labour supply as well as in accessing public welfare. In particular, it is difficult to arrive at any fixed policy definition of who disabled people really are as disability policy definitions in countries such as the UK, Germany or the United States have changed or been interpreted differently over time.

A useful example is to consider why large numbers of disabled people who were considered 'unable to work' during times of high unemployment (for example, the 1930s) were quickly drafted as 'able to work' in times of labour shortage (for example, in munitions factories during the Second World War). Similar patterns are evident if we look at those encouraged to claim long-term out-of-work disability benefits during the lean times of the late 1970s and early 1980s, who were then targeted by vigorous back-to-work policies under Labour after 1997 and by the UK Coalition government after 2010 (see Chapters 47, 48 and 56). Thus, it is essential to see disability as a rather flexible policy category, determined more by economic and political circumstances than by personal capabilities.

Policy Claims: The Disabled People's Movement

Although state responses to the needs of disabled people have been driven by economic and political forces, they have also been shaped by the policy claims of disabled people themselves. Such claims and protests have a long history, but the modern disabled people's movement emerged from the growing political consciousness of the late 1960s and 1970s. The development of disabled people's organisations in the US, the UK and parts of mainland Europe has been well documented in the disability studies literature. Since the early 1980s, disability activists have organised globally under the umbrella of Disabled Peoples' International (covering more than 140 countries) and, since the 1990s, in Europe via the European Disability Forum.

The claims of disabled people's organisations have influenced both the form and content of policymaking. Four underlying principles are worthy of note. First, there has been strong advocacy for the principle of 'nothing about us without us' to ensure that disabled people have a voice in policy discussions that affect them. Where such debates were once dominated by medical and

rehabilitation professionals, or by welfare charities, it is now rare to find disability policy forums that do not include disabled people as significant actors. Second, there has been strong advocacy for non-discrimination laws based on equality and human rights. Most countries now have such laws in place (such as the disability provisions of the Equality Act in Britain), supported by similar provisions in the Treaty on the functioning of the EU and by the UN Convention on the Rights of Persons with Disabilities. Third, there have been demands to focus policy investments on creating greater accessibility for disabled people in the built environment, transport or information technologies. Finally, there has been greater involvement of disabled people in producing their own welfare solutions, resulting in policy changes towards increased choice and control in everyday life. Two of these themes merit further discussion.

Independent Living: New Modes of Welfare Production

The concept of independent living has been a prominent theme in disabled people's policy claims. The key struggles were aimed at freeing disabled people from oppressive long-term residential institutions and developing new mechanisms to support community living. In Britain, as in many other countries, there have been significant closures of traditional institutions and the widespread implementation of 'community care' since the 1990s. The movement for independent living was an important voice, challenging traditional models of 'care' and offering alternatives to support disabled people in practical ways. The aim was to place more resources in the hands of disabled people themselves to enable them to organise and purchase their own support for daily living, rather than relying on pre-arranged 'services' (for example, by employing personal assistants to help with everyday activities rather than attending a day centre or receiving home help from social services). Early independent living projects in Britain, Scandinavia and the US were often run by disabled people themselves, and provided new ways of thinking about welfare – blurring the traditional boundaries between purchasers, providers and consumers.

The success of such schemes, in offering disabled people more choice and control, gave rise to the emergence of 'direct payments' in the late 1990s and 'personal budgets', allowing people to arrange and purchase their own support in place of the services they might be otherwise entitled to. Direct payments and personalisation brought new opportunities for self-determination, but take-up still varies greatly in different parts of the country and with limited resources to achieve ambitious aims. This, in combination with an ageing population and public sector spending cuts since 2010, raises considerable questions about the viability of traditional 'services' and the sustainability of future funding for social care support envisaged in the Care Act 2014.

Non-discrimination: Policies for Civil Rights

As highlighted earlier, the rapid development of civil rights and anti-discrimination legislation has been a key feature of policy development, although different countries have taken different approaches. While non-discrimination legislation was secured in the US in 1990 (with the Americans with Disabilities Act) there was resistance to legislative change in Britain, especially from those concerned that equal rights for disabled people might impose unbearable costs on employers and service providers and thereby undermine national economic competitiveness. However, there was also mounting evidence that disabled people experienced discrimination institutionalised throughout society and, in 1995, a Disability Discrimination Act was passed.

With this law it became illegal for employers to discriminate against disabled employees or for service providers to treat disabled customers less favourably, but only insofar as this might be seen as 'reasonable' or 'justified'. Over time, the legislation was strengthened and extended to cover discrimination in education, business premises and transport. In 2006, a more general equality duty was placed on public authorities, mirroring policies to tackle institutional racism and gender inequalities. All public bodies (such as government departments, local authorities, hospitals, schools and colleges, etc.) have a duty to promote positive attitudes and equality and to eliminate disability discrimination.

The mere presence of anti-discrimination legislation has little impact without enforcement. In Britain, this began with a Disability Rights Commission (DRC), established in 2000 as an independent body to promote disability equality in England, Scotland and Wales (in Northern Ireland a single body covered disability equality and other dimensions of discrimination, such as racism and gender equality). The 2006 Equality Act paved the way for the abolition of the DRC and its incorporation within the Commission for Equality and Human Rights (which maintains a disability committee). The 2010 Equality Act then consolidated non-discrimination legislation across all areas. In 2009, the UK Government ratified the UN Convention on the Rights of Persons with Disabilities and its Optional Protocol, requiring the maintenance of independent mechanisms for policy monitoring and appeal.

The legal rights-based approach to policy shares much in common with the social model of disability discussed earlier, but, on its own, it offers a less radical strategy. The social model (as defined by its early authors) focused on the structural basis for disabled people's oppression, arising from the social relations of production and reproduction in modern capitalist societies. The implication was that real change could not be achieved without political struggle to challenge the infrastructure of disabling societies and institutions. By contrast, the campaign for legal rights drew more on a 'minority group approach' that emphasised claims within existing legal frameworks and constitutional law. Both approaches recognise disability as a human rights issue, but a social model interpretation suggests that disability requires structural changes beyond the law to solve the problems that disabled people face.

Globalisation and Governance: UN and EU Influences

There are at least half a billion disabled people in the world – one in ten of the population – and this number is set to rise dramatically. The issues in rich technological countries, with developed welfare provision, are often different from those in poorer countries, but disabled people remain amongst the poorest of the poor throughout the world. Access to resources is highly gendered, and the needs of disabled women and girls merit specific attention. Generational issues are also important, with reduced life chances for disabled children and disabled elders. Global problems demand global responses and the increasing significance of transnational policymaking is particularly evident in the EU and the UN.

The UN made its first Declaration on the Rights of Disabled Persons in 1975 and proclaimed an International Year of Disabled Persons in 1981. In 1985, the Universal Declaration of Human Rights was extended to include disabled people and work began on a longer-term strategy under the slogan 'towards a society for all'. The adoption in 1993 of international Rules on the Equalization of Opportunities for Disabled Persons led more and more states to introduce anti-discriminatory legislation and, eventually, to agree on a comprehensive human rights Convention on the Rights of Persons with Disabilities in 1996.

At the EU level, there was little early evidence of critical debates, although the mid-1970s saw some limited action programmes on vocational and social integration and a review of national policies. By the early 1980s, there were signs of a broader socio-economic understanding (including acknowledgement that disabled people are amongst those most adversely affected by the economic cycle in capitalist markets). The development of EU policy in the 1990s was then marked by the emergence of a legal rights-based approach, focused initially on employment rights. After pressure from disability organisations, disabled people were made 'visible' as European citizens in the Amsterdam Treaty of 1997 (now recognised in Article 19 of the Treaty on the Functioning of the EU). EU disability policy is focused more on market regulation than on redistribution, and attention has shifted towards the social model agenda and to social investment in the creation of barrier-free environments and products. The European Disability Strategy 2010–2020 takes a broad approach and articulates its key principles in terms of accessibility, participation and equality (with policy action across a range of fields such as employment, education and training, social protection and access to health). The EU is also party to the UN Convention.

Emerging Issues

Enactment of the UN Convention, from 2008, raised expectations and placed new responsibilities on states to ensure greater participation and equality of disabled people in society. There has been goodwill from governments, but major policy challenges remain. The claims of the disabled people's movement were fundamental to changing the way we think about disability policy, but, despite successes, there are uncertainties about the future. As disability is mainstreamed within the single equality agenda there may be fewer 'places at the table' for disabled people in the policymaking process. Whilst there are genuine public commitments to the human and social rights of disabled people, their realisation has been threatened by policy responses to the 2007–8 economic crisis. In resource-poor countries, the enormity of needs for poverty reduction and human development means that disabled people are often overlooked in policy investments. In richer welfare states, there have been intense fiscal pressures to shrink the flexible category of disability and thus to reduce the numbers eligible for financial support from the state.

Governments in European welfare states have become increasingly concerned by the number of people out of work and claiming disability benefits (for example, an estimated 2.52 million people in Britain in 2015) and sought to 'help' them into work through policy change. Following the election of a centre-right coalition UK Government in 2010, and implementation of its Comprehensive Spending Review, there have been significant changes. The personalisation agenda in health and social care, including personal budgets, continues, but austerity cuts have targeted disability benefits in particular, and reduced some benefit payments. Public sector cuts, particularly in local government, have impacted on the availability of many services used by disabled people. There has been a limiting of eligibility to out-of-work disability benefits with the introduction of tighter medical and 'work capability' testing (see Chapter 56). The aim is clearly to reduce the number of people receiving disability benefits, whilst being seen to offer some support for those judged more 'severely' disabled (reinforcing the arguments made at the outset about the 'flexible' nature of disability as a policy category in changing economic conditions).

Guide to Further Sources

For historical discussion of disability policy in modern welfare states, it would be useful to look at both D. Stone (1984), *The Disabled State*, Philadelphia: Temple University Press; and A. Borsay (2005), *Disability and Social Policy in Britain since 1750: A History of Exclusion*, Basingstoke: Palgrave Macmillan. The former is helpful in understanding the relationship between disabled people, welfare and the state, while the latter provides an itemised history of policy development in Britain. M. Oliver (1996), *Understanding Disability: From Theory to Practice*, Basingstoke: Macmillan, is useful as an introduction to different models of disability and their connection to theory and policy. The book also provides useful pointers to some of the most influential ideas and writings that influenced policy change.

A. Roulstone and S. Prideaux (2012), *Understanding Disability Policy*, Bristol: Policy Press, provide a helpful overview of British policy development. A. Lawson (2008), *Disability and Equality Law in Britain: The Role of Reasonable Adjustment*, Oxford: Hart, analyses the principles behind non-discrimination policies. S. Shah and M. Priestley (2011), *Disability and Social Change: Private Lives and Public Policies*, Bristol: Policy Press, reveal policy changes in Britain since the establishment of the modern welfare through the life stories of disabled people.

D. Mabbett (2005), 'The development of rights-based social policy in the European Union: the example of disability rights', *Journal of Common Market Studies*, 43:1, 97–120, shows how disability emerged in European policymaking. The following four books all provide important insights into the emergence of disabled people's self-organisation and the development of user-led policy alternatives to support independent living: J. Charlton (1998), *Nothing About Us Without Us: Disability Oppression and Empowerment*, Berkley, CA: University of California Press; J. Campbell and M. Oliver (1996), *Disability Politics: Understanding Our Past, Changing Our Future*, London: Routledge; C. Barnes and G. Mercer (2012), *Independent Futures: Creating User-led Disability Services in a Disabling Society*, Bristol: Policy Press; and M. Oliver and C. Barnes (2012), *The New Politics of Disablement*, Basingstoke: Palgrave Macmillan.

The academic journal *Disability & Society* and the *Yearbook of European Disability Law* are excellent sources. Online, the Disability Archive UK provides free access to several hundred papers by disability activists and researchers at: leeds.ac.uk/disability-studies, and the ANED website provides reports on disability policies throughout Europe, at: disability-europe.net. In the UK, current policy details are available at: gov.uk/browse/disabilities and the Government Office for Disability Issues publishes information about government strategy and equality indicators at: officefordisability.gov.uk.

Review and Assignment Questions

1 What is the difference between 'individual' and 'social' models of disability, and what are the implications for social policies?
2 How convincing is the argument that 'disability' is a flexible or fluid policy category and that who counts as 'disabled' changes in response to socio-economic conditions?
3 What combination of regulatory and redistributive policies is most likely to deliver equality and full participation for disabled people?
4 To what extent are national disability policies now influenced by compliance with European and global governance?
5 How are disabled people and their organisations represented in the policy process and how influential have their voices been?

Visit the book companion site at www.wiley.com/go/alcocksocialpolicy to make use of the resources designed to accompany the textbook. There you will find chapter-specific guides to further resources, including governmental, international, thinktank, pressure groups and relevant journals sources. You will also find a glossary based on *The Blackwell Dictionary of Social Policy*, help sheets, guidance on managing assignments in social policy and career advice.

62

Migrants and Asylum Seekers

Majella Kilkey

▪▫▪▪▫▪▪▫▪▪▫▪▪▪▫▪▪▫▪▪▫▪▪▫▪▪▫▪▪▫▪▪▫▪▪▫▪▪▫▪▪

Overview

- ■ The UK has a long history of migration and ethnic diversity.
- ■ Contemporary migration is linked to globalisation processes and is characterised by super-diversity.
- ■ People migrate for different reasons, including for employment, study, family reasons and to flee persecution, human rights abuses, war and conflict.
- ■ Migration and asylum policy has been concerned with curbing immigration, and is racialised and gendered.
- ■ Migration and asylum policy has produced a complex classification of migrants that is closely linked to a highly differential system of rights around entry, residency, settlement, family reunion, labour-market access and social welfare entitlements.

▪▫▪▪▫▪▪▫▪▪▫▪▪▪▫▪▪▫▪▪▫▪▪▫▪▪▫▪▪▫▪▪▫▪▪▫▪▪▫▪▪

Context

There are two types of migration: internal migration within the borders of a state, and international migration across state borders. This chapter focuses on international migration and social policy responses to migration and migrants. The chapter examines the UK solely as a migrant-receiving country. It should be noted, however, that significant numbers of UK citizens are themselves migrants living in other countries. In Europe, Spain and France are among the most popular destinations for people leaving the UK, while beyond Europe, Australia, Canada and New Zealand were historically significant destinations for UK migrants and continue to be so in contemporary times.

In terms of immigration, the UK has a long history, and this is evidenced in the large degree of ethnic diversity that is apparent in the UK today.

The Student's Companion to Social Policy, Fifth Edition. Edited by Pete Alcock, Tina Haux, Margaret May and Sharon Wright.
© 2016 John Wiley & Sons, Ltd. Published 2016 by John Wiley & Sons, Ltd.

Until the twentieth century, most migrants to the UK came from other European countries, especially Ireland, although as early as the sixteenth century, migrants were brought to the UK as slaves from Africa. The period following the Second World War saw the arrival of migrants from colonial and Commonwealth countries. Fuelled by processes related to globalisation, such as uneven economic development and cheaper and faster travel, contemporary migration to the UK is characterised by super-diversity in terms of countries of origin. While migrants come from all over the globe, linked to the enlargement of the European Union (EU) in 2004 and 2007, migration from European countries, particularly Poland, has become significant once again. Migrants come to the UK for a wide range of reasons – for employment, study, family reasons and to flee persecution, human rights abuses, war and conflict – and for any one person, migration is likely to entail a combination of those reasons. Many migrants leave family and friends behind in their country of origin, and the maintenance of ties back to their homeland can be an important part of migrants' lives while in the UK. These transnational relationships can be sustained long after settlement in the UK and by subsequent generations of the original migrant's family.

Migration and migrants have become increasingly problematised in public and official discourse. There is a widespread view that there are too many migrants and that migrants are a drain on welfare resources. While the policy environment around migration is complex, the direction of policy travel is one of deterrence and restriction.

This chapter moves on to examine the different definitions and categorisations of migrants. It then identifies some of the key themes in migration and asylum policy over time in the UK, before concluding with a discussion of some emerging issues in the social policy of migration and asylum.

Definitions and Categorisations of Migrants

The United Nations (UN) defines a migrant as:

a person who moves to a country other than that of his or her usual residence for a period of at least a year, so that the country of destination effectively becomes his or her new country of usual residence. From the perspective of the country of departure the person will be a long-term emigrant and from that of the country of arrival the person will be a long-term immigrant.

The above definition is a very generic one. It masks the huge diversity that exists in who migrants are, where they come from and why they move. Appreciating these differences is important from the perspective of social policy analysis because they inform the allocation of migrants into different categories, which in turn are linked to different sets of rights for both the migrant and his or her family members around entry, residency, settlement, labour-market access and social welfare entitlements. As we examine later in the chapter, as the UK tries to 'manage' migration more tightly in order to reduce the number of migrants entering and settling here, and to ensure that migration serves UK interests, the categorisation of migrants has become ever more complex. Box 62.1 maps some of the most important parameters and definitions in the UK Home Office's – the government department responsible for migration and asylum matters – contemporary classificatory system.

A long-standing fault-line in the categorisation of migrants in the UK, as in most other countries, is whether their movement is forced or voluntary. Forced or involuntary migration refers to the migration of refugees – a category with a legal definition in international law. The internationally accepted definition is that laid down by the 1951 UN Convention on the Status of the Refugee (the Geneva Convention), to which the UK, along with almost 150 other countries, is a signatory. Under the Geneva Convention, a refugee is defined as:

Any person who is outside the country of his nationality . . . because he has or had well-founded fear of persecution by reason of his race, religion, nationality, political opinion or membership of a particular social group and is unable or, because of such fear, is unwilling to avail himself of the protection of the country of his nationality . . . (Geneva Convention, UNHCR, 1951)

Box 62.1 Key Parameters and Definitions in the UK's Classificatory System of Migrants

Forced or voluntary

Forced migrants refers to *refugees*. Refugees have a legal status governed by international law. People can arrive in the UK with refugee status if they come through a refugee programme, or they can come to the UK and seek asylum. *Asylum seekers* are persons who have applied for refugee status and whose applications have not yet been concluded. For some the outcome of an asylum claim will be refugee status; others may be awarded intermediate-type protection status – *Humanitarian Protection* or *Discretionary Leave*; while still others will be unsuccessful in their claim and must return to their country of origin. All other migrants fit into the category 'voluntary' and are differentiated in a number of ways.

EU nationals

Within the architecture of European Citizenship – free movement, residency and equal treatment in all fields – *EU citizens* (nationals of EU member states) and their family members have the right to enter and reside in the UK and to access its labour market and social welfare provisions.

Third country nationals

Most of the rest of the world's population falls into the category of *Third country nationals*, whose rights are highly restricted and linked in the first order to the purpose of entry – *work*, *study* and *family* – and in the second order to a range of social and economic conditions, including the individual's level of capital and income, talent and skill level, having a UK sponsor, alignment to a shortage occupation and English language competence.

Irregular migrants

Some migrants do not have a recognised status in the UK. The catch-all term 'irregular' captures a diversity of routes to a wide range of situations positioned along a continuum from semi-compliant to non-compliant.

The definition emerged out of a very specific period in European history following the Second World War to address the problem of the millions of persons displaced as a result of war, and many commentators argue that it is too narrow in the context of the types of political and social conflict occurring across the globe in the twenty-first century.

Those recognised as refugees under the Geneva Convention are entitled to protection from return, to family reunion, and to the same social welfare and employment rights as the citizens of the country in which they now live. In the UK, until 2005, refugees were given indefinite leave to remain, but since then they are given a short-term stay of five years. A range of additional categories have also been introduced to offer temporary leave to remain to persons whom the Home Office judges to be in need of protection, but who do not qualify for refugee status. These include the categories of Humanitarian Protection and Discretionary Leave.

An asylum seeker is a person who has left their country of origin and formally applied for refugee status in the UK, but whose application has not yet been concluded. While a person is awaiting a decision on their asylum claim, they have very limited entitlement to social welfare, no right to do paid work and no right to family reunion. A person whose asylum application has been unsuccessful and who has no other claim for protection (Humanitarian or Discretionary Leave) awaiting a decision is required to return home. Some do so voluntarily, others are forcibly returned, while others remain in the UK as irregular persons with no rights (see below).

All other forms of migration are considered as voluntary migration. It should be noted, however, that the distinction between forced and voluntary is problematic, especially when we consider that structural problems that are beyond the control of individuals and households, such as poverty, inequality, unemployment and environmental destruction, are often heavily implicated in people's decisions to seek their livelihoods in another country.

A further dividing line in UK migration policy is between migrants from EU member states and countries outside the EU, so-called third countries. The Maastricht Treaty (1992) established the concept of the EU citizen in EU law. This treats nationals of EU member states as the bearers of a set of rights, encompassing, among other things, the right to move and reside freely in the territory of any other EU member state. This right, commonly referred to as the right to 'freedom of movement', can be traced back to the origins of the EU in 1957, but then it applied only to workers. Over time its scope has expanded, and now includes workers, students, pensioners and the unemployed, as well as their family members. Once resident in another EU member state, EU citizens are protected by a prohibition on discrimination on the grounds of nationality that applies to a wide range of areas, including the labour market and social welfare entitlements.

In contrast to nationals of other EU countries who can enter the UK virtually without restriction, nationals of third countries face a very tight entry regime, and, once in the UK, highly conditional and differentiated rights around residency, settlement, labour-market access, social welfare entitlements and family reunion. The rights of any particular third-country national depend on their purpose of entry, with policy distinguishing between those coming for work (including business), study and family reasons. Within each of those three categories, rights are further differentiated according to such factors as levels of capital and income, talent and skill level, alignment to a shortage occupation and English language competence.

A final fault-line is between 'regular' and 'irregular' migrants. The latter is a catch-all term for migrants who are non-compliant or semi-compliant with migration rules. The highly restrictive entry rules for third-country nationals results in some migrants crossing borders without the legal right to do so, while one-time regular migrants can become irregular because, for example, they do not leave the UK when their asylum claim fails or when their visa expires. The complex and ever-changing migration rules mean that regular migrants can become irregular unintentionally.

UK Policy: Key Themes over Time

Immigration policy has a long history in the UK, and has had different priorities at different times according to the shifting context in relation to migration flows, economic circumstances, and official and public discourse. Policy can be divided into four main phases:

- 1905–45: Control of mostly Jewish aliens from Europe.
- 1960s–1980s: Racialised control of immigration from Commonwealth and New Commonwealth countries.
- 1980s–2000: Control of asylum.
- 2000s onwards: Managed migration and migrant integration.

Taking together the numerous pieces of legislation passed over those phases, a number of key themes emerge.

One dominant theme is the intersection between migration and welfare policies. The welfare state is the product of the nation-state and is considered by many to be nationally bounded. As a result, what the rights and entitlements of non-nationals to social welfare should be is a question that has long troubled policymakers. This issue was apparent as far back as the beginning of the twentieth century in the 1905 Aliens Act, the first systematic immigration control. Under the Act, entry could be refused if a migrant lacked the means of subsistence, and if they were found to be in receipt of Poor Relief (the main social welfare provision at that time; see Chapter 16) within one year of entry, they could be expelled. Early twentieth-century social reforms such as the 1908 Old Age Pensions Act and the 1911 National Insurance Act also excluded 'aliens' by placing residency and citizenship conditions on entitlement; such conditionality remains a feature of many social welfare provisions in the UK today (see Chapters 47 and 56). The tightening of migrants' social rights (see Chapter 7) became sharply focused on asylum seekers during the 1990s, and through a series of legislative measures beginning with the 1993 Asylum and Immigration Appeals Acts successive governments curtailed asylum seekers' rights in relation to a host of areas, including access to the labour market; entitlements to Income Support; and through the dispersal system, choice of where in the country they could live. Those developments occurred alongside the emergence of an official and public discourse that most asylum seekers are 'bogus' and are trying to abuse the welfare state. Since the mid-2000s, the accusation of 'welfare tourism/ abuse' has been applied most vociferously to EU citizens arriving in the UK from those countries that joined the EU in the 2004 and 2007 enlargements. While freedom of movement provisions place limits on the UK's autonomy to restrict EU citizens' social welfare entitlements, the provisions do allow for some discretion, and beginning around 2013 a tightening of the entitlements of EU citizens to social security and social housing began to occur.

Another way of thinking about the intersection between migration and social welfare emphasises migrants' role as a source of labour in welfare services. This is a role that they have played since the inception of the welfare state in the post-Second World War period. The National Health Service in particular has relied on recruiting doctors and nurses from overseas in order to fill gaps in the context of poor workforce planning. As a result, it has faced criticism for creating a 'brain drain' and 'care drain' in some of the poorest countries of the world, and has responded by developing a more ethical approach to overseas recruitment. The evidence is, however, that it has simply shifted its recruitment strategy to 'less poor' regions, such as southern, central and eastern Europe.

A second theme is the economic instrumentalism of migration policies, which entails governments seeking to ensure that migration is in the interest of the UK economy. A key approach has been to link migration policy to labour-market needs, strengthening and loosening migration controls depending on labour demand. The first explicit effort to do this occurred with the Aliens Order in 1920, which, in the context of rising unemployment, introduced the requirement that an employer must be issued with a work permit for an alien and that this would only occur where no British labour was available. In the aftermath of the Second World War, when there was a shortage of labour, the UK, like many countries in northern Europe, actively recruited migrant workers. Initially, the UK looked to Ireland, and then to eastern Europeans residing in displaced person camps in the British zones in Germany and Austria. When that supply dried up, it began to recruit from the Caribbean and the Indian subcontinent. The economically instrumentalist approach to migration became increasingly sophisticated in the era of the UK's 'managed migration strategy' (see Box 62.2). This introduced a points-based immigration system (PBIS) in 2008, which streamlined eighty different sets of regulations and schemes relating to work

---

Box 62.2 Key Elements of the UK's Managed Migration Strategy

Managed migration in the UK

1 Labour migration is linked more explicitly to UK economic interests. Achieved through:
   - introduction of points-based immigration system;
   - establishment of the Migration Advisory Committee.
2 More control of all forms of migration. Achieved through:
   - tighter controls on entry;
   - reducing possibilities for long-term settlement;
   - enforcing removal through deportation and detention;
   - tighter internal controls, including by health and social welfare professionals.
3 Responsibility of migrants to integrate into UK society. Achieved through:
   - extending length of time someone must reside in the UK before settlement can be applied for;
   - passing 'Life in the UK' test as a condition of gaining citizenship;
   - passing an English language test as a condition of gaining citizenship.

and study migration into a system of tiers differentiated by labour-market and economic imperatives. The PBIS gives increased privileges to workers considered to be highly skilled and to business people and entrepreneurs with capital to invest in the UK. It also introduced time limits on skilled worker's rights to stay in the UK, in an effort to break the link between entry and long-term settlement. As part of the managed migration strategy, the Migration Advisory Committee (MAC) was established in 2007 and charged with advising government on labour-market needs. One of the many criticisms of the PBIS and MAC is that they approach the labour market from a UK-wide perspective, and do not take account of regional differences. This has been a particular issue for Scotland, where population decline has been experienced in recent years, especially in areas outside the large cities.

With the managed migration strategy a new theme of migrant integration emerged in UK migration policy. The emphasis on integration needs to be seen in a broader context of concern around a lack of community cohesion in the face of increasing ethnic, religious and cultural diversity. This concern arose in part from the 'race riots' in some cities in the north of England during the summer of 2001, and a perception on the part of some that migrants were living 'parallel lives'. It also relates to a broader debate in 'race relations' in the UK and a number of other European countries around the supposed failure of a multicultural approach to ethnic diversity, and the need for a more integrationist/assimilationist approach (see Chapter 32). In this vein, migrants, before they can gain permanent settlement rights in the UK, have been given new responsibilities to demonstrate their acceptance of 'British values' through, for example, attending a Citizenship Ceremony and passing tests related to English language competency and knowledge of UK society. The probationary period between arrival and claiming citizenship has also been increased in the case of some from two to five years, in part to give migrants a longer period of time to integrate before applying for citizenship.

A final theme is the relationship between migration policy and other social divisions, notably 'race' and gender (see Chapter 31). From the 1960s to the late 1980s, migration legislation in the UK was aimed at curbing migration from the

Commonwealth and New Commonwealth, and the controls that were introduced were racialised. The 1948 British Nationality Act had established two main categories of citizenship: citizens of the United Kingdom and Colonies (UKC) and citizens of Commonwealth countries. Both categories had the right to enter the UK and enjoy all social, political and economic rights, and increasing numbers arrived subsequently either as workers or as refugees from independence struggles and post-colonial conflicts. Public and official discourse, however, problematised the settlement of Black Commonwealth citizens, and legislation, beginning with the 1962 Commonwealth Immigrants Act and concluding with the 1988 Immigration Act, brought primary migration of Black Commonwealth citizens virtually to an end and made it more difficult for those already settled in the UK to bring family members for reunification purposes. The legislation, however, did not have the same impact on White Commonwealth citizens, demonstrating its racialised nature. UK migration policy has continued to have exclusionary effects, and the gender dimension of those is also important to highlight. The emphasis within the PBIS on the highly skilled and those with English language competence, for example, may be especially exclusive of women from countries where girls and women experience unequal access to formal education compared with boys and men. In addition, the extension of the probationary period between arrival and claiming citizenship, during which migrants' welfare entitlements are minimal, will put women sponsored to come to the UK under the marriage route in a situation of dependency on their male spouse, and make them vulnerable to exploitation; it will also create barriers to women in that situation who experience domestic violence to leave their spouses.

Emerging Issues

In the context of a restrictive stance towards immigration and a larger and more economically divergent European Union, EU migration has begun to be perceived as undermining migration control and to be in contradiction with selective migration policies. The issue of whether European freedom of movement rights can be renegotiated to allow the UK to restrict entry to all but the most desirable EU migrants – that is, the highly skilled – and to limit their entitlement to social welfare was a key part of Prime Minister David Cameron's efforts to re-draw the UK's relationship with the EU in advance of the referendum on the UK's membership of the EU in June 2016. It is important to acknowledge in this debate, however, that any rolling-back of freedom of movement rights will have implications for the estimated 2.2 million UK citizens living in other EU countries. The approach to third-country migration is likely to become ever more economically instrumentalist and, as a result, more exclusionary as to who can enter and tighter on their conditions of stay. In this context, the number of irregular migrants is bound to increase. In order to address this, the future will see detention and deportation measures having a greater role in the overall architecture of migration policy.

Guide to Further Sources

Overview texts on migration and policy responses in the UK can be found in R. Sales (2007), *Understanding Immigration and Refugee Policy*, Bristol: Policy Press; and A. Bloch, S. Neal and J. Solomos (2013), *Race, Multiculture and Social Policy*, Basingstoke: Palgrave Macmillan. B. Anderson (2013), *Us and Them. The Dangerous Politics of Immigration Control*, Oxford: Oxford University Press, focuses on the links through history between migration and welfare. The subject of irregular migrants, including accounts of the experiences of migrants themselves, is addressed in A. Bloch and M. Chimienti (2012), *Irregular Migrants: Policy, Politics, Motives and Everyday Lives*, London: Routledge. A good introduction to the European dimension is C. Boswell and A. Geddes (2011), *Migration and Mobility in the EU*, Basingstoke: Palgrave Macmillan. S. Castles,

H. de Haas and M. Miller (2014), *The Age of Migration*, 5th edn, New York: Palgrave Macmillan, gives a comprehensive overview of global migration patterns and policy responses in a vast range of countries. Government policies and research reports related to migration can be found on the Home Office web pages (gov.uk/government/organisations/home-office), and statistics can be found at the Office for National Statistics (ons.gov.uk). Organisations such as the Refugee Council and Migrants' Rights Network also produce regular summaries, commentaries and analyses of migration, refugee and asylum policies.

Review and Assignment Questions

1 What are the main processes underpinning contemporary migratory movements?
2 Why is it important to go beyond the generic category of 'migrant'?
3 Why does UK migration policy distinguish between EU nationals and third-country nationals?
4 Identify the key elements of the UK's managed migration strategy.
5 Giving examples, examine the ways in which immigration, asylum and welfare policies have intersected through history in the UK.

Visit the book companion site at www.wiley.com/go/alcocksocialpolicy to make use of the resources designed to accompany the textbook. There you will find chapter-specific guides to further resources, including governmental, international, thinktank, pressure groups and relevant journal sources. You will also find a glossary based on *The Blackwell Dictionary of Social Policy*, help sheets, guidance on managing assignments in social policy and career advice.

PART X

International and Comparative Context

63

Comparative Analysis

Margaret May

Overview

- Comparative analysis is a crucial constituent of social policy.
- Its development reflects shifts in the discipline and national welfare strategies.
- Comparative inquiry raises distinct conceptual and methodological issues.
- Cross-national comparisons can be framed in various ways.
- There are a range of explanations for variations in country welfare mixes.

Context

The study of welfare provision necessarily involves some form of comparison between current, past or alternative ways of meeting need or improving existing policies. This may not always be explicit and value bases may differ. But it is central to a discipline geared to evaluating welfare arrangements and ascertaining the factors that drive their design and varying, often conflicting, purposes and outcomes. Increasingly for analysts across the globe, addressing these issues effectively requires cross- as well as intra-national research.

Wherever they are, this enables not only appraisal through other lenses, but the identification of commonalities, differences and their implications. It also opens up questions about the genesis of welfare systems, the nature and direction of change in national social policies, the influence of different drivers and constraints, and what these might tell us about likely developments. Considering these facilitates what for many is the overarching value of comparative analysis, its potential for enhancing provisions in one country by drawing on the experience (and 'failures') of others. Such 'borrowing' may though be a way of legitimising desired change. It thus raises further questions regarding the selectivity and diffusion as well as the feasibility and effectiveness of policy transfers (see Chapter 64).

The Student's Companion to Social Policy, Fifth Edition. Edited by Pete Alcock, Tina Haux, Margaret May and Sharon Wright.
© 2016 John Wiley & Sons, Ltd. Published 2016 by John Wiley & Sons, Ltd.

Research on these issues is far from new and now extends internationally. Until recently, however, it focused primarily on 'western societies', where systematic study initially stemmed from awareness of the widespread expansion of state welfare in the immediate post-war era. Concern over signs of retrenchment in the 1980s added traction to this research, which was furthered from the 1990s by that over another wave of reconfigurations in response to seemingly similar problems.

Pre-eminent were the many processes associated with globalisation and the related threats to national autonomy and social expenditure (see Chapter 27). Linked with these were other new challenges, especially those posed by rising consumer expectations, growing diversity, demographic ageing, and new social risks emanating from post-industrialisation and shifting employment and family patterns. Policy design, moreover, appeared to be increasingly moulded not only by the operation of global markets, but by the widening remit of regional and international governmental organisations (IGOs) (see Chapters 1, 46, 64 and 71). Governments, too, extended their investment in comparative policymaking, a development driven in the UK by Labour's commitment to evidence-based welfare (see Chapter 2), as well as the broader spread of benchmarking as a lever for change.

The resultant welter of data and league tables demanded careful appraisal, as did other international developments. The deregulation of national financial markets, for instance, meant mortgages, pensions and other services in many countries were increasingly provided by local subsidiaries of multinational conglomerates. Care and higher education providers, too, moved into a global business that also involved an expanding international market for welfare personnel (see Chapter 35). Together these developments contributed to a growing interest in welfare arrangements beyond those hitherto framing comparative inquiry, which widened further in the aftermath of the 2007–8 banking crisis.

In highlighting the scale and instabilities of economic internationalisation, this raised awareness of the growth of a multi-polar global economy powered by China and other emerging economies, spurring research into social provisions in middle- and low-income countries (see Chapters 67–70). Together with welfare rescaling in many wealthier societies, this, as subsequent chapters indicate, added further dimensions to debates about the nature and outcomes of social policy cross-nationally.

Approaches to Comparative Analysis

In addressing these, comparative analysts use a range of approaches. Some concentrate on country-specific studies, providing a basis for cross-national evaluation. Those adopting an overt comparative approach may investigate particular sectors, programmes, 'problems', user needs, policy processes or attitudes, usually in countries with broadly similar socio-economic and political structures. Whatever the focus, these 'domain-specific' studies potentially involve comparing a number of inter-related elements (see Box 63.1).

Others take a macro approach, engaging in 'whole system' comparisons across a range of societies, often over time, entailing a consideration of key signature issues (see Box 63.2).

Box 63.1   Key Issues in 'Domain-specific' Comparative Analysis

- scale and nature of the 'need'/'problem';
- overall welfare context;
- policymaking processes;
- programme(s)/service(s)/benefit(s) aims;
- programme origins and development over time;
- entitlement criteria;
- provider/administrative structure;
- resource base;
- regulatory system;
- delivery/allocation processes;
- 'efficacy'/'outcomes' of current provision;
- pressures for change;
- policy proposals.

Box 63.2 Key Issues in 'Whole System' Comparative Analysis

- general welfare milieu;
- policymaking 'styles' and processes;
- key forms of welfare 'input' or 'effort';
- predominant patterns of welfare production;
- predominant processes of welfare allocation;
- main welfare outputs and outcomes.

Research Dilemmas

Researching these phenomena within one's home country is far from straightforward. Cross-national study, particularly of 'whole systems', is even more problematic, and ensuring like-for-like comparisons presents major conceptual and methodological challenges, not least those of selecting the countries, their number, policy indicators or domains for analysis. Social policy researchers are neither 'culture-free' in their interpretations nor in their research remits. Superficially similar terms can carry very different meanings and local practices are easily misread. The constructs 'welfare state' and 'social policy', for instance, are far from synonymous or similarly understood. Notions of 'social needs' and 'risks' too may differ. Indeed, one salutary feature of comparative study is the extent to which burning issues in one society may be differently perceived or discounted elsewhere.

In addition to the above conundrums, welfare programmes may have several, often conflicting, aims and inputs. Providers may be governmental, non-statutory or 'mixed'. Resource structures may vary in terms of staffing and funding (national or local taxation, direct and indirect; compulsory or private insurance; charges; or combinations of these) as may organisational arrangements, management cultures and informal 'street-level' practices. 'Domain'-level appraisal, whether of take-up relative to 'need', enhanced individual well-being, decreased inequality, cost-effectiveness or other possible criteria, is also highly value-laden and far from clear-cut, and assessing outcomes at a macro level particularly challenging.

In many ways, the methods utilised are those deployed in 'within-country' research and demand similar caution (see Chapter 2). But comparativists confront additional dilemmas. The well-documented limitations of official statistics, for example, are compounded by differing national conventions that may pre-empt direct comparison. Sources, categories and formats may vary. There may be gaps in coverage, changes in definitions or methods of gathering and classifying data possibly designed for other purposes. In many parts of the world, information may not be available or only in aggregate form. Moreover, the challenges are a matter of accessing, standardising or collecting empirically comparable data, but also those posed by differing investigative rules and epistemological traditions and moving beyond both 'methodological nationalism' and Euro-American frameworks.

Considerable effort has been invested in surmounting these problems. 'Safari' surveys of one or more countries by teams from another have given way to collaborative multinational projects designed to enhance cross-cultural 'literacy' and combine differing research styles, as in the World Value and European Social Surveys. Greater use is being made of multi-method strategies, cross-disciplinary investigations and more sophisticated quantitative and qualitative techniques, including enhanced data reduction systems, multiple correspondence, cluster and fuzzy set analyses. Fuller, more robust data sets and parallel national panel studies have also been developed by IGOs, governmental and non-governmental bodies, along with measures to improve access to micro-data and online facilities. More detailed social spending data have also become available, while, as with the UK's 'What Works' centres, governments have expanded their own cross-national research (see Chapter 64).

Given the cost of alternative studies, comparative researchers remain highly reliant on such databases, particularly the OECD's. Even these, however, may not readily relate to some policy concerns or allow particular comparisons (see Chapter 65), while studying non-OECD countries still demands considerable ingenuity. Nonetheless, substantial advances have been made, extending the comparative radar and ways of addressing the core debates within it.

Typologies and Regimes

One key issue is the use of classificatory frameworks to characterise and explicate the social policy landscape cross-nationally. The most influential early taxonomies were those advanced in the wake of the post-war welfare settlements by Wilensky and Lebeaux in America and Titmuss in the UK. The former distinguished two 'models of welfare', to which Titmuss (1974) added a third, typified, respectively, by the US, Sweden and the then West Germany:

- *Residual Welfare Model*: marked by extensive market-based provision and selective, means-tested 'safety net' public benefits and services, widely perceived as stigmatising.
- *Institutional Redistributive Model*, marked by universal, rights-based, non-stigmatising, redistributive state benefits and services, viewed as a 'normal' function of industrial society.
- *Industrial Achievement-Performance Model*: marked by work-based benefits and services, with state welfare functioning as an adjunct to the economy.

Current theorisation, however, is dominated by debates over the categorisation developed by the Danish analyst Esping-Andersen (1990). Covering eighteen OECD countries and based on largely post-hoc analysis of three international data sets, this encompassed differences in public provision, but also political and class formations. Unlike earlier modelling, it also considered social rights and the distribution as well as levels of social spending. Surveying these allocative issues he suggested welfare states varied along three interwoven dimensions:

- *Decommodification*: the extent to which people can uphold a socially acceptable standard of living independently of market participation.
- *Stratification*: the extent of class and status differentiation, segmentation and inequality.
- *Public–private mix*: the relative roles of the state, market and family in welfare provision.

To plot these Esping-Andersen used various indicators, including a decommodification index measuring the scope and generosity of three benefits (pensions, sickness and unemployment). His analysis led him to distinguish three qualitatively different ideal type '*welfare regimes*', epitomised, respectively, by Scandinavian, continental European and English-speaking countries, each having systematically different social outcomes:

- *Social-Democratic Regimes*: where a coalition of labour organisations and farmers secured a state committed to full employment and generous, redistributive, universalist benefits, incorporating both middle- and working-class interests.
- *Conservative/Corporatist Regimes*: where occupationally segregated benefits were introduced by conservative-dominated governments to secure working- and middle-class support.
- *Liberal Welfare Regimes*: where, in the absence of stable cross-class alliances, state welfare operated mainly on selective, residual lines.

As with any ideal-type framework some nations fitted these constructs more easily than others. But he concluded that the welfare systems of advanced economies could be subsumed within this trichotomy, which also had predictive value, indicating how different regimes moved along distinct trajectories.

This analysis inspired a torrent of research, becoming a reference point for comparative inquiry, which, as the many publications marking its twenty-fifth anniversary testified, is still framed by the controversies it triggered. While covering numerous theoretical, methodological and substantive concerns, these criticisms centre on the representativeness of his typology, the value of welfare modelling and his explication of regime differentiation, with varying studies questioning, upholding and extending his approach.

More specifically, Esping-Andersen's approach was initially challenged on four main grounds. First, it was argued, his focus on class and benefits masked other crucial differences. Feminist writers in particular contested his neglect of gender and care issues and, while he later included the concept of '*familialism*' (though not gender per se), this aspect of his typology continues to be questioned, as does its pertinence for other social cleavages.

Second, his policy canvass was criticised as overly narrow and belying the often different dynamics and impacts of public services, other forms of state intervention and non-governmental provision. These, and other indicators, did not always map neatly onto his triad and could alter country placings within it, whilst some national patterns appeared to be programme-specific or led to more intricate classifications. Third, it was argued the typology's country base too was overly narrow. As fundamentally opinion also varied on ways of measuring the impact of different provisions, countries' relative 'welfare performance' and 'generosity'.

For some analysts these and related methodological complexities meant the most fruitful approach lay with domain-specific comparison rather than further modelling. Whilst recognising in-country variations, others saw typologising as a valuable heuristic tool, enabling them to capture and compare a country's welfare 'DNA'. Research from this 'helicopter' perspective, however, posited more complex scenarios encompassing further 'welfare worlds', including the Antipodes, the Mediterranean, eastern Europe, East Asia, and, more recently, Latin America and the Middle East (see Chapters 67, 68 and 69) as well as hybrids and outliers.

On a different front, it also led to debates over the links between Esping-Andersen's typology and modelling in economics, particularly the distinction between two 'varieties of capitalism' ('liberal' and 'coordinated' market economies). More recently, further issues, such as its saliency in the face of the post-2008 welfare shifts in advanced economies, its constraining effects on other avenues of research, and a tendency to confuse 'typology' and 'ideal types' have also been raised. Others, however, continue to uphold its overall validity and the usefulness of a complexity-reducing 'big picture' approach.

Interest in the big picture has also been reflected in attempts to recast regime analysis as a way of understanding arrangements in the developing world, notably Gough and colleagues' account of meta 'social policy regimes'. Looking at an 'extended welfare mix' (including external aid, remittances, governmental and non-governmental provisions) and key welfare outcomes in sixty-five non-OECD countries in 2000, this distinguished:

- *Proto-welfare state regimes;*
- *Informal security regimes;*
- *Insecurity regimes.*

The first, 'proto-welfare state regimes' (encompassing ex-Soviet and southern South American countries), exhibited some characteristics of OECD welfare states. The second, 'informal security regimes', less distinct, comprised 'successful' regimes with relatively good outcomes despite low state inputs and external flows (China, much of East Asia, the rest of South-Central America, Iran, Turkey, Tajikistan) and 'failing' ones. Outcomes in the latter (mainly in the Indian subcontinent, southern and eastern Africa) were far lower, and in 'insecurity regimes' (predominantly in sub-Saharan Africa) contingent on unsustainable informal support and the vagaries of external aid.

On an international scale, the issues raised by this analysis in many ways echo those over regime theorisation generally and are still being addressed. In adding a global conspectus, however, it has also furthered the linked debate over the roots and sustainability of welfare formations and the wider applicability of accounts of their development in advanced industrial societies.

Convergence and Divergence

Here policy analysts divide again, differing over the factors powering policymaking, cross-national variation, continuity and change, and the extent to which welfare arrangements in advanced economies are converging along similar lines or retaining their distinctive features, and the implications for social policy elsewhere. Schematically, however, these controversies revolve around six broad themes, each with many permutations.

First, a long-standing line of thinking emphasises the key role of exogenous and endogenous *economic influences* in structuring social policy. Many early comparativists saw welfare statism as the concomitant of urban-industrialisation, necessitated by the destabilisation of traditional forms of social protection, the new needs and problems it generated, and the social infrastructure required for growth. Together with the wealth it produced, these pressures and the need to compensate for market failures were held to make for continuing welfare expansion and country convergence as differences in the timing of industrialisation ironed out.

Subsequent research, critical of its functionalist base, questioned this notion of linear growth and it has given way to more nuanced accounts of the interplay between economic change and social policy (see Chapter 27). It was echoed, however, in early studies of globalisation, which saw it as forcing downward neo-Liberal style convergence as governments strove to maintain economic competitiveness. Later analyses stressed re-engineering rather than retrenchment, but differed over whether the widespread turn to 'activation' and 'social investment' translated into equivalent interventions. Most recently, whilst underscoring the ongoing impact of post-industrialisation, fiscalisation and the 'great recession' in reshaping state welfare in advanced economies, research has again highlighted its variability, not least because of their differential exposure to these.

A second perspective singles out *socio-structural influences* as driving both common trends and national variations. Similarities in population profiles, composition and family patterns, such as demographic ageing or increased single-parenting, for example, are held to prompt analogous, though not identical, provision. More contentiously, highlighting the significance of social composition, some contend that, as in America, public provision is more constrained in diverse societies.

Many analysts, however, uphold *political influences* as the prime determinants of country welfare mixes and variations. Historically, this approach emphasised the correlation between the spread of democracy, working-class mobilisation and collectivism. Marxist writers in particular saw state welfare as the product of class struggle in industrial-capitalist societies, although also stressing its role in enforcing labour discipline and social stability.

For others, including Esping-Andersen, conflict between different social groups and the power resources they bring to bear explain both the genesis of welfare states and elemental differences between them. Residual regimes, for instance, reflected weak, often disempowered working-class organisations; others very different power balances, bargaining and trade-offs. Studies in this vein also point to the impact of feminist and other social movements and, more recently, to the complexities posed by increasingly volatile, fractured electorates and the differing social risks faced by skilled and unskilled workers. In essence, however, it is argued that 'politics matter' and partisan configurations, coalition-building and political choices determine social policy, maintaining national variations despite other pressures.

A closely aligned fourth view emphasises *institutional influences*, ranging from prerequisites for public welfare, such as strong administrative systems, to fundamental differentiators, particularly constitutional and electoral structures, related 'veto points' and the 'long shadows' or 'path dependencies' cast by initial collectivist provision. These, it is argued, account for the resilience of welfare formations, with measures once in place, and provider and beneficiary support for them, constraining paradigm change.

While some studies suggest incremental innovation can, over time, be 'path-breaking', this position has been attacked for overlooking the ways in which far-reaching reform can be instituted, particularly the 'blame avoidance' and other strategies used to secure electorally risky change. For some critics it also deflects attention both from the effects of external shocks such as war (see Chapter 18) and the extent to which reform is a continuous feature of welfare states.

It does, however, tie in with analyses emphasising *ideational influence*, contending welfare states reflect historically rooted differences in public value systems, cultures and religious affinities that can override political divisions and maintain general tendencies towards, for instance, Scandinavian universalism or American selectivism. A related sixth standpoint, however, views these as pliable in the face of *transnational influences*, especially the purveyance of particular strategies by IGOs (see Chapters 46 and 71) and the often neo-Liberal promotions of business consultants and other lobbies.

Compared with the global South, traditional welfare states may be more resistant to such pressure, raising questions about other influences on social policy. For example, public provision in some countries is the product of non-democratic administrations, while in many emerging economies it is seen as a lever for development, with governments investing primarily in workforce training and support.

In practice, however, although differing over their relative significance, many commentators offer a synthesis of these viewpoints, with one influential account (van Kersbergen and Viz, 2013) coming almost full circle positing an 'open functional approach', acknowledging the role of political agency and ideas, but emphasising the primacy of socio-economic imperatives in capitalist economies.

Emerging Issues

Debate on the issues touched on above will continue to dominate comparative analysis. It is likely though to focus more on the links between social and economic policy, a wider range of policy instruments and the role of non-state provision. Greater attention is also likely to be paid to intra-country differences, paralleled in the UK by further comparative study of its constituent nations.

Crucially, there are signs of a renewed interest in assessing the generosity of welfare arrangements and their 'real-world' outcomes for different groups. For many high-income countries, this is likely to build on the availability of finer-grained social spending records and the use of 'big data' such as that on benefit recipients; elsewhere researchers will have to find more innovative ways of tackling comparative study. Undoubtedly, the greatest challenge for future comparative research, however, lies in addressing the implications of global climate change. With its ramifications for individual well-being, social justice and notions of citizenship, this re-opens fundamental questions about the role of social policy within and across countries and the ways it is analysed.

Guide to Further Sources

Many of the issues outlined here are taken up in subsequent chapters. Fuller discussions can be found in R. M. Titmuss (1974), *Social Policy*, London: Allen & Unwin; G. Esping-Andersen (1990), *The Three Worlds of Welfare Capitalism*, Cambridge: Polity Press; the many retrospectives it elicited in 2015, particularly those in the *Journal of European Social Policy*, 25:1 and *Social Policy*

and Society, 14:2; I. Gough (2013), 'Social policy regimes in the developing world', in P. Kennet (ed.), *A Handbook of Comparative Social Policy*, 2nd edn, Cheltenham: Edward Elgar; F. Castles, S. Leibfried, J. Lewis, H. Orbinger and C. Pierson (eds) (2010), *The Oxford Handbook of the Welfare State*, Oxford: Oxford University Press (both of which include a consideration of methodological issues); and K. van Kersbergen and B. Viz (2013), *Comparative Welfare State Politics*, Cambridge: Cambridge University Press.

Current developments can also be tracked through the links on the SPA, the European Social Policy Association (ESPANET), the East Asian Social Policy group (EASP), OECD and UN websites (www.spa.org.uk; www.oecd.org; www.unrisd .org).

Review and Assignment Questions

1 How would you account for the growing interest in comparative social policy?
2 What are the main methodological problems faced by comparative policy researchers?
3 Taking any two countries and one social policy issue, what factors would you include in a comparative study?
4 What are the main drawbacks of using typologies in comparative analysis?
5 How would you explain cross-national variations in social policy?

Visit the book companion site at www.wiley.com/ go/alcocksocialpolicy to make use of the resources designed to accompany the textbook. There you will find chapter-specific guides to further resources, including governmental, international, thinktank, pressure groups and relevant journal sources. You will also find a glossary based on *The Blackwell Dictionary of Social Policy*, help sheets, guidance on managing assignments in social policy and career advice.

64

Policy Learning and Transfer

John Hudson

■■■

Overview

■ Many social policy challenges faced in the UK are also faced by governments in other countries, providing opportunities to improve policy by learning from the experience of other countries.

■ Policy learning and transfer can take many different forms. It is often facilitated by international bodies and networks established to encourage the sharing of knowledge and ideas.

■ There are many barriers to policy transfer in practice. Complete transfers, where a country copies the whole of a policy used somewhere else, are rare.

■ Cross-national policy learning and transfer are often messy and complex processes in practice, with knowledge developed over many years and policy ideas taken from many places.

■ Policy learning and transfer are ultimately political processes. Power plays a central role in shaping the content of policies that move around the globe.

■■■

Context

Many countries face ostensibly similar social policy challenges such as how to adapt social provision in the light of demographic changes such as ageing (see Chapter 26), how to address issues around poverty and inequality (see Chapter 33) or how to respond to economic pressures (see Chapters 21 and 27). Given the number of common policy challenges, it is no surprise that countries are looking to improve policy outcomes by sharing knowledge of their experiences and learning from

The Student's Companion to Social Policy, Fifth Edition. Edited by Pete Alcock, Tina Haux, Margaret May and Sharon Wright.
© 2016 John Wiley & Sons, Ltd. Published 2016 by John Wiley & Sons, Ltd.

examples of best practice that have been implemented elsewhere.

Though a country can draw policy lessons from its past experience or across its localities/regions, the process of policy transfer is most commonly understood as referring to instances where policy lessons are drawn from one country and transplanted into another. It is such cross-national processes of learning and transfer that form the focus of this chapter.

Chapter 63 examines the growth in comparative analysis of social policy in recent years, but, as it makes clear, much of the debate in academic circles has focused on theoretical questions such as how and why countries develop different welfare regimes. Those engaged in policy learning and transfer research adopt a more applied approach to comparative analysis, focusing less on how, why and in what ways countries differ from each other, and more on how, why and in what ways countries can and do learn from each other. Indeed, for those undertaking comparative research in governmental and/or policy facing organisations, these applied questions tend to be uppermost in their mind. For them 'the purpose of learning what foreigners do is not to collect exotic information, but to draw practical lessons that can improve public policy at home' (Rose, 2005: 4).

However, learning from abroad is challenging in practice. First, there is the difficulty in establishing what kind of lessons might be drawn and where from. Then, there are major challenges in translating lessons into policy change. Indeed, while there is a strong intuitive appeal to the idea that policy will be improved if we draw lessons from exemplars of best practice around the world, in truth, examples of successful and straightforward policy transfer can be hard to find (Page and Mark-Lawson, 2007). Moreover, while the phrase 'policy learning and transfer' conjures images of a rational and reflective process freely entered into by enlightened policymakers, in practice policy transfer is a political process in which power often plays a more decisive role than evidence.

Types of Learning and Transfer

Cross-national policy learning and transfer can take many forms, and much of the literature has been dedicated to classifying different types of learning and transfer. A number of useful distinctions have been drawn.

First, we can differentiate types of policy transfer. The starkest distinction is that between voluntary and coercive policy transfer. While the former is entered into freely when decision-makers opt to draw lessons from another country, the latter occurs when external bodies force a country to adopt policy frameworks used elsewhere. While both involve policy ideas being transferred from one country to another, the dynamics in each are radically different. Coercive transfer most commonly occurs when a country requires financial aid from an external body such as a foreign government or international governmental organisation such as the IMF or World Bank (see Chapter 71); often aid comes with strings attached such as a requirement to pursue a particular set of policy reforms. While the voluntary/coercive distinction is helpful, it has been suggested that policy transfer often involves a mixture of the two in practice; for instance, a country may be obliged by international treaties to strengthen environmental protection, but voluntarily search abroad for policy frameworks it might draw on in order to meet these obligations.

As well as differentiating types of policy transfer, we can also distinguish different processes of learning that underpin them. We can, for instance, draw a distinction between ad hoc and institutionalised processes of learning. Ad hoc approaches are common, often the result of politicians or bureaucrats having close links with their counterparts in other countries. For example, when Bill Clinton was the US President and Tony Blair was the UK Prime Minister, the two leaders and their advisers often shared ideas about how their 'Third Way' approach might be taken forward (see Chapter 20). Institutionalised processes are usually more bureaucratic, tied to the mission of organisations that exist to foster cross-national cooperation or working on a more permanent basis. The European Union (EU), for example, has developed the Open Method of Coordination (OMC) as a processes for facilitating cross-national policy learning and transfer in areas where common EU-wide policy agendas exist (see Chapters 43 and 65). Indeed, some international bodies exist primarily to coordinate and foster the sharing of policy-relevant

Box 64.1 The OECD

The Organisation for Economic Cooperation and Development (OECD) describes its mission as promoting policies that will improve economic and social well-being by providing a forum for countries to 'work together to share experiences and seek solutions to common problems'. It does so in many ways, but chiefly through collecting and harmonising social and economic data from its members; conducting analyses of this data; organising high-level discussion and debate of such analyses amongst member states; and publishing regular reports based on these analyses and discussions. It also conducts regular reviews of key policy areas across its membership and facilitates peer review of the performance of individual member states in particular areas of policy. Established in 1961, it has thirty-four member countries today, including many of the advanced economies of the world.

knowledge. A key example here is the Organisation for Economic Cooperation and Development (OECD), whose mission is focused on the sharing of knowledge about policy problems and solutions (see Box 64.1).

In short, if cross-national policy learning and transfer is to take place, then it usually requires a cross-national policy transfer network to support the movement of knowledge and ideas between countries. However, the precise form and nature of these networks varies widely and this, in turn, impacts on the nature of any cross-national policy learning and transfer that takes place.

Barriers to Transfer

Looking at the experiences of other countries can offer a quick way to generate new policy ideas and/ or to provide evidence on what has been effective elsewhere. However, evidence and ideas alone rarely lead to policy change. Indeed, there are many barriers to cross-national policy learning and transfer taking place in practice. Consequently,

examples of policies being moved directly from one country to another are relatively rare. Moreover, there are numerous examples of attempted transfers that have failed following their transplantation from one country to another.

A wide range of barriers to cross-national policy transfer and learning have been identified. These include simple factors that may impede learning such as the fact that policymakers in different countries may not share a common language. While this may seem like a small issue that is easy to overcome, some research has suggested that it nonetheless often serves to restrict the search for policy solutions to countries where communication barriers are minimal. It has been argued, for example, that policymakers in the UK often look first at the experience of other Anglophone countries such as Australia, Canada and the US, leading to a bias in the source of policy lessons (see Box 64.2). A bigger issue still in terms of policy learning is that the complexity of policy itself makes it difficult to ascertain the precise nature of the lessons that might be drawn from another country's experiences. For example, while there are relatively objective data we can use to establish which countries lead the world in terms of educational attainment in mathematics at high school level, these data do not tell us what it is that makes a country particularly successful here. Indeed, a wide range of factors might be important, including the style of maths teaching in schools, the level of resources allocated to education by government, the amount of time students spend studying maths in and out of school, and perhaps even cultural factors such as the esteem of science in each country or social factors such as the level of inequality in each country. We might also add that even though we might be able to point to a group of countries that lead the way in maths, we cannot be sure that this means we should simply follow their example: it could be, for instance, that these countries have sacrificed an emphasis on other important areas such as language training, arts or physical education. In short, it is rarely the case that there is a country we can clearly flag as providing the definitive example of 'best practice' and, moreover, even when there is a clear exemplar we cannot always explain why that country has done so well.

The barriers to transfer do not stop at the level of cross-national policy learning: even when

Box 64.2   Learning from the US

Scholars have detailed many examples of UK governments transferring social policies from the US. When Margaret Thatcher was Prime Minister of the UK (1979–90), her closeness – personally and ideologically – to the US President Ronald Reagan (1981–9) was often noted, and it is little surprise that some almost complete policy transfers occurred during this time. Perhaps the most notable example was that of 'Job Clubs' that aimed to provide hands-on support to unemployed jobseekers; they were an almost direct copy of a US initiative.

A similarly close relationship existed between Tony Blair and Bill Clinton when the former was Prime Minister of the UK (1997–2007) and the latter President of the US (1993–2001). During the Blair years some major policies clearly drew on US experiences: Sure Start was similar to the US Head Start/Early Head Start programmes; zero tolerance policing initiatives in New York influenced similar practices in the UK; and the increased conditionality in US social assistance programmes matched elements of Blair's social security reform (see Chapters 47, 48, 55 and 56). However, many argue the transfers were less direct during this area, there being significant differences in policy detail in the US and UK despite the very similar slogans often being used by Clinton and Blair.

more subtle than the short-term issues, but are often seen as crucial in preventing transfer; the key point here is that it is rarely the case that two counties will have the same institutional, political, technological and cultural contexts, and that differences in any of these areas may lead to a policy that worked well in one country being rejected in another.

Degrees of Transfer, Types of Learning

So far this may feel like a gloomy perspective on policy transfer and learning: a good idea in principle but tricky to execute in practice. But this is in part because we have so far mainly considered the 'purest' form of the notion in which learning is a discrete, rational and voluntary process that results in the complete transfer of a policy from one place to another. The complexities outlined above make this rare, but this does not mean that learning and transfer are not taking place, rather that they are taking place in more subtle ways. To this end, Dolowitz (2000) argues that we can observe different degrees of policy transfer in practice, ranging from copying (transfer of the whole policy) and emulation (copying of the ideas behind a policy but not the details) through to combinations (copying parts of a number of policies to create a new one) and inspiration (a policy in another country providing ideas to work from but the finally transferred policy differing greatly from the original).

As the above hints, this also means that there can be different objects of transfer, too, with Dolowitz (2000) suggesting a continuum from the highly specific transfer of policy content, policy instruments, policy programmes and institutions, through to the much less specific transfer of ideologies, ideas and attitudes and policy goals. Significantly, much of the research on social policy transfer has highlighted instances of the latter rather than former; for example, while the UK borrowed the notion of 'zero tolerance' policing from the apparently successful New York model, in practice it was the language of zero tolerance rather than the substance of the policy that was transferred (Page and Mark-Lawson, 2007: 52). Finally, in terms of objects of transfer, Dolowtiz (2000) also suggests that negative lesson drawing

policymakers feel confident in drawing policy lessons from abroad, major barriers to policy transfer remain because of the often fraught nature of policy making (see Chapter 42), for transfer is ultimately a political process rather than a technical exercise. Short-term barriers here might be factors, such as political conflict between key figures within the government leading to policy reforms being blocked, while longer-term issues might include the way in which the long historical development of policies in each country leave institutional legacies that can restrict the range of options open to policy makers (see Chapters 16–21). The longer-term issues are can take place whereby policymakers looking to introduce reforms may identify flawed approaches when searching abroad and consciously eliminate them from their menu of options as a consequence.

More recently Dolowitz (2009) has argued that we can observe different types of learning, too, drawing a distinction between simple forms of learning (for example, *mimicry*) and more complex forms of learning (for example, *concept formation*). This hints at one of the challenges we face in understanding cross-national policy learning in practice: learning itself is often a lengthy process. Some of the most recent policy learning and transfer research has tried to unpack the ways that policymakers pick up information, develop it and apply knowledge. In truth, there are no hard and fast rules here, but we might usefully point to some important distinctions between information and knowledge and, similarly, between lessons and learning. While there has perhaps been a tendency to look at processes of policy learning and transfer as involving the 'discovery' of new information from abroad that can provide policy 'lessons' to implement at home, in practice policymakers (particularly specialist experts) will have a good knowledge of policy frameworks in key countries that they have built through a career long process of learning.

All this underlines that cross-national lesson drawing involves much reflexive thinking on the part of policymakers. Rose (2005) suggests that successful cross-national policy learning and transfer involves a good deal of fresh thinking extending beyond the simple identification of a lesson from abroad. This typically includes developing a model that explains what makes a programme work well in its host country and then adapting this foreign model to create one suitable for the context to which it is being transferred. As such, there is much complex theoretical knowledge underpinning most instances of transfer. Rose (2005) argues that good models should be based on tested knowledge and the evaluation of the outcomes of transfer too, with flexibility in the detail of the transfer during implementation – removing or adding elements based on feedback – boosting the chances of a transfer being successful.

In short, the reality of cross-national policy learning and transfer may be a rather messy one. Rather than whole policies being imported

---

Box 64.3 Interrogating Policy Transfer

Dolowitz and Marsh have suggested that we can understand instances of policy transfer by posing straightforward questions for interrogating the process such as:

1 Why did policymakers engage in policy transfer?
2 Who was involved?
3 Where did the transferred policy originate from?
4 What was being transferred and how complete was the transfer?
5 Were there barriers that prevented successful transfer?

---

following a deliberate attempt to learn from another country, we can point to a permanent and ongoing exchange of evidence and ideas. Policymakers tend to draw on examples from abroad in an often haphazard way, typically using them to develop new ideas and/or combining them with ideas from elsewhere to create new policies suitable for their own context and needs (see Box 64.3). As one policymaker put it when explaining some recent UK labour-market reforms: 'we nicked stuff from all over the place' (Dwyer and Ellison, 2009: 402). All this can make policy learning and transfer complex processes for us to grasp as students of social policy. Dolowitz and Marsh's key questions are a good place to start interrogating policy transfers (see Box 64.3). However, where policymakers engage in a long-term process of policy learning in which transfer is selective and appropriate to context, then it ought to lead to better policy outcomes than a quick-fix search for lessons and the wholesale import of an idea from abroad.

Emerging Issues

Policy learning and transfer are ultimately political, rather than technical, exercises, meaning issues of power are central in shaping outcomes. While examinations of policy learning and transfer have always acknowledged that these processes are political, more recent work has focused on unpacking the subtle ways networks and institutions may shape the content of policy learning and transfer. This involves not only looking beneath the bonnet of important international organisations such as the EU, IMF, OECD and World Bank, but also looking at what have been dubbed the 'mundane practices' of officials: the conferences they attend, the people they connect with overseas, the places they travel to in the course of their work. Greater attention is being paid to informal, private and even secret networks that policymakers use to share ideas and knowledge. In some ways, this new work serves to highlight the importance of technical elites in shaping the movement of policy ideas across borders, but it has also shown how reference to a limited number of key examples can lead to policy converging around certain norms or key ideas that reflect the dominant views of this elite. By exploring cross-national policy learning and transfer in this way, recent work has helped further our understanding of the spread of key ideas and ideologies, particularly overarching frameworks such as neo-Liberalism (see Chapter 9).

Guide to Further Reading

One of the most extensive reviews of policy transfer literature and social policy is found in D. Dolowitz (2000), *Policy Transfer and British Social Policy: Learning from the USA?* Open University Press, Buckingham. Dolowitz's book is an excellent place to start, offering useful case studies and primer on key concepts. Those wanting a more practical angle will find it useful to read it alongside R. Rose (2005), *Learning from Comparative Public Policy*, London: Routledge. Dolowitz reflects on different forms of policy learning, going beyond ideas in his earlier book in D. Dolowitz (2009), 'Learning by observing: surveying the international arena', *Policy & Politics*, 37, 317–34.

P. Dwyer and N. Ellison (2009). '"We nicked stuff from all over the place": policy transfer or muddling through?', *Policy & Politics*, 37, 389–407, outlines the messy nature of transfer and learning in practice, drawing on insightful interviews with policymakers. In a similar vein, E.

Page and J. Mark-Lawson (2007), 'Outward-looking policy making', in H. Bochel and S. Duncan (eds), *Policy Making in Theory and Practice*, Bristol: Policy Press, examines how far policy transfer takes takes place in practice, drawing on the experience of the Blair governments in particular.

Two more recent articles capture the latest debates well, the first, a wide-ranging review of key work, the second, a challenging read written in response: D. Benson and A. Jordan (2011), 'What have we learned from policy transfer research? Dolowitz and Marsh revisited', *Political Studies Review*, 9, 366–78, and E. McCann and K. Ward (2012), 'Policy assemblages, mobilities and mutations: toward a multidisciplinary conversation', *Political Studies Review*, 10, 325–32

The OECD website (www.oecd.org) details how they foster cross-national learning. Much of the data they collect can be accessed at data.oecd.org and their social and welfare issues page at/www .oecd.org/social list many useful publications.

Review and Assignment Questions

1 Why might policymakers engage in cross-national policy learning and transfer?
2 How do coercive and voluntary processes of transfer differ?
3 What are the common barriers to cross-national policy transfer?
4 Why might a policy that appears to work well in one country not work well in another?
5 Why are processes of cross-national policy learning and transfer more complex than they might appear at first sight?

Visit the book companion site at www.wiley.com/ go/alcocksocialpolicy to make use of the resources designed to accompany the textbook. There you will find chapter-specific guides to further resources, including governmental, international, thinktank, pressure groups and relevant journal sources. You will also find a glossary based on *The Blackwell Dictionary of Social Policy*, help sheets, guidance on managing assignments in social policy and career advice.

65

Social Policy in Europe

Jochen Clasen and Daniel Clegg

■■

Overview

- European countries have consistently been the highest spenders on social policy within the economically advanced groups of OECD countries.
- European countries provide the most generous benefit levels within the OECD.
- Typically European (but not British) is the use of employment protection as a mechanism for securing income for wage earners.
- Typically European (but not British) is the involvement of social partners in social policymaking.

■■

What is Europe?

Geographically, Europe is a vague entity. Its eastern border is especially ambiguous. Russia is a European country, but is all of Russia part of Europe? Is Turkey European, or Asian or both? Politically, things are not much simpler. The idea that 'Europe' can be regarded as synonymous with the European Union (EU) is unduly reductionist. Even if, in 2015, the EU covers twenty-eight countries and thus represents most people who live in Europe, it excludes not only very small states such as Liechtenstein, but politically important countries such as Norway and Switzerland.

From a British perspective, 'Europe' is often portrayed as both different from the UK and homogeneous in its non-British character, as popular references to things 'European' with regard to food or football indicate. In some respects, the former notion might have some substance given the linguistic and partly cultural affinity of the UK with the US, Australia, Canada and New Zealand as the economically advanced English-speaking 'family of nations'. As for the latter point, however, culturally, linguistically and socio-economically

The Student's Companion to Social Policy, Fifth Edition. Edited by Pete Alcock, Tina Haux, Margaret May and Sharon Wright.

Europe is rather heterogeneous. Since this applies to social policy too, it is rather difficult, if not impossible, to capture the variation of 'social policy in Europe' within the space constraints of this short chapter.

European Social Policy?

Is there such a thing as European social policy? This is a difficult question to answer. The large academic literature on welfare state models emphasises the fundamental differences in the goals, instruments and outcomes of social policies across the continent, identifying at least three distinct types of welfare state within western Europe alone (see Chapter 63). At the same time, though, the idea of a 'European social model' is regularly invoked by both scholars and policy-makers, pointing at shared values of solidarity and social justice that bind the countries of the old continent together and set it apart in the modern world. Furthermore, although most social policy remains a national competence, the progressive deepening of European integration since the 1950s has created direct and indirect pressures for social policy convergence between member states of the European Union (see Chapter 43).

Within the set of economically advanced countries in the world, is it therefore possible to identify characteristics that are typical of social policy in Europe? Asking a similar question, and applying financial, institutional and ideological criteria, Baldwin (1996) firmly arrived at a negative conclusion. Indeed, taking public social spending as a point of departure, the range of social policy effort across European (and even EU) countries was very wide indeed in the 1980s and early 1990s. Equally, there was hardly any distinctively European pattern in which resources were distributed, that is, as universal, insurance-based or means-tested support. The level of benefits, such as public pensions or unemployment compensation, was neither consistently higher nor lower in European countries than in other OECD countries. On average, Baldwin conceded, welfare spending might be more generous in European than in non-European countries, but with so broad a range within the European social systems, he questioned what 'the average' actually indicated. Similarly, Alber (2010) queried the notion of 'residual' American

social policy which often tends to be contrasted with a more generous or comprehensive European idea of social protection. Alber demonstrated that in some areas, such as public pensions, US social policy is more generous and redistributive than many European countries. If anything, he argued, due to a dominant discourse on 'activation' at the expense of social protection European countries have become more 'American' in recent years, while US social policy has become somewhat more European with respect to the debate on public healthcare.

How could we broadly assess these arguments? If we take the EU as a point of departure, the processes of enlargement since 2004 (adding ten countries), 2007 (when Romania and Bulgaria joined) and 2013 (Croatia) have certainly created more rather than less diversity in the scope, depth and institutional range of social policy provision. However, if we consider the level of public social expenditure (as a proportion of national income) as a measurement of the relative emphasis countries put on social policy and assess the economically most advanced countries in the world, European nations have consistently been the highest spenders on social policy since 1980. Similarly, throughout the past two decades there has always been a gap between the economically advanced European countries and the richer non-European countries such as the US, Canada, Australia, New Zealand and Japan. Aggregate public social expenditure across the EU-15, that is, member states prior to the EU expansion towards central and southern Europe in 2004, has been consistently higher than aggregate spending in these five non-European countries. In 2013, the ten countries that spent at least 25 per cent of their GDP on social protection were all EU members (OECD, 2015).

Of course, there are questions of comparability. Some social policy domains (such as education, for example) are often excluded from aggregate social spending and, while taking account of different sizes of national economies, measuring social expenditure as a share of GDP is always vulnerable to fluctuations in national business cycles. Ideally, differences between demographic patterns or unemployment levels should be considered in order to arrive at 'adjusted' levels of spending (Siegel, in Clasen and Siegel, 2007). Analyses of 'net' social spending have pointed out that cross-national differences are less marked once the effects of taxation on benefit income, indirect taxation on consumption financed by benefits as well as tax breaks are considered (Adema et al., 2011, 2014). If voluntary social spending is also considered, the variation in levels of 'net total social expenditure' between European and non-European OECD countries narrows considerably (see OECD, 2015).

However, such a broad measure might be less useful since it conceals redistributive efforts, which is a major objective of social policy (on this see Castles and Obinger, 2007). Thus, taking account of the effect of taxation, but leaving aside voluntary spending, differences between the higher European spenders and lower spending non-European countries remain distinctive. However, using 'net publicly mandated social spending' as an indicator suggests some repositioning of European countries, with France and Belgium reaching the top of the OECD table as a result of the fact that tax systems in other countries conventionally ranked highly, such as Denmark and Sweden, claw back more money handed out for social purposes (Adema et al., 2014; OECD, 2015).

How could we assess whether European countries are more generous than other countries? One indicator is the so-called 'net replacement rate', that is, the level of net benefit income in relation to previous net earnings. The OECD provides such calculations for different risks (such as unemployment, sickness, etc.), income levels and family constellations (OECD, 2015). A quick glance at, in this case, unemployment compensation during the first phase out of work indicates a significant degree of variation and, at first sight, little sense of a European pattern. However, it is noticeable that across eighteen different combinations of family types and earnings levels, the five most generous countries are always European, albeit not always the same five countries. By contrast, while European countries, including the UK, can sometimes be found amongst the least generous five countries, this group is generally dominated by non-European countries.

Another often suggested trait of social policy in Europe is the emphasis on a broad rather than narrow notion of social citizenship. Some data appear to confirm this. For example, eighteen out of thirty-one OECD countries distributed more than 90 per cent of their total cash transfers without an income test in 2012, and they were all European. At the other extreme, a third or more of all cash transfer payments were subject to a means-test in five countries, all of which were non-European (OECD, 2015). However, this picture applies more to continental European countries, given that means-testing was also fairly common in Ireland (31 per cent) and the UK (26 per cent).

The strong role of publicly provided rather than privately purchased social policy is yet another characteristic associated with European social policy. In fact, the picture is much more blurred, which is partly due to the problem of delineating public (and thus assumed to be mandatory) and market-based private (and thus voluntary) social spending. The OECD makes a distinction between voluntary private and mandated private protection expenditure, but difficulties remain. Nominally private occupational pensions based on collective agreements, for example, can be fairly comprehensive and regulated in a way that makes them all but mandatory. Equally, sickness or disability benefits provided by employers are generally categorised by the OECD as private mandatory social spending, but not in all cases, thereby creating anomalies. For example, the OECD (2015) deems the Netherlands to have the second highest level of private voluntary social spending across thirty OECD countries, surpassed only by the US and Switzerland. However, some authors consider the OECD's categorisation of some 'private' Dutch spending as a 'misnomer' (De Deken and Kittel, in Clasen and Siegel, 2007). In short, in the absence of satisfactory conceptual clarity and good comparable data, it is difficult to substantiate the OECD's claim that market-based voluntary social protection is as relevant in some European countries (the UK, the Netherlands and also France) as it is outside Europe.

Turning to outcome measures of (not only) social policy, a consistent pattern emerges which indicates that some, but not all, European countries are maintaining relatively low levels of poverty and income inequality. Defining poverty as the proportion of individuals with below a certain percentage of median disposable income, say 50 per cent or 60 per cent of the median, OECD data (2015) indicate that across thirty-four economically developed countries, the ten best performing countries are European. The picture is similar for various measures of inequality (of disposable income; that is, after tax and benefits), with northern and some central European countries, such as Slovenia, Slovakia and the Czech Republic, having the lowest levels of all OECD countries. At the same time, however, there are some European countries, including Spain, Portugal, Greece and also the UK, which tend to have levels of inequality that are above the OECD average (OECD, 2015).

Baldwin (1996) pointed to institutional cross-national variation in, for example, the organisation of healthcare or the role of family allowances. Here, his assessment of the absence of a European identity remains valid because of continuing diversity across and within countries, as well as within individual social policy arrangements. This is perhaps most visible in pension systems, which tend to be multi-tiered, with or without a minimum public pension, at times means-tested but often not, and supplemented by mandatory or voluntary occupational systems (see also Alber, 2010). Categorising healthcare systems too, a range of regulatory and financial models can be found across the OECD, but no distinctively European identity.

In sum, from a macro-perspective, social policy in Europe is distinctive in the sense of relatively high levels of public social spending, a broad notion of social citizenship and benefit rates that are typically, but not in all cases, more generous than in other economically advanced countries. Several European countries come out on top in terms of reducing poverty and containing income inequality. However, there is no European social policy identity in the ways in which social protection is organised or in the mix between public and private provision.

Typically European and/or Typically British?

There is too much diversity of social policy arrangements even within the EU member states for it to be possible to postulate any sense of uniformity. However, while diverse in settings and outcomes, there are social policy characteristics that are either exclusively, or predominately, found in Europe. In the remainder of this chapter we address some of these and, in this context, we

reflect on the relative position of British social policy as typically (or atypically) European.

Social policy needs resources that are collected via direct and indirect taxation or social security contributions, sometimes referred to as 'payroll tax'. Typically, European countries devote a greater role to contributory (social insurance) as opposed to tax funding of the welfare state, as indicated by the combined (employee and employer) share of social security contributions. In 2012, social security contributions in European countries typically amounted to between 10 and 16 per cent of GDP, but were well below 10 per cent in all non-European OECD countries (except for Japan). However, there are European exceptions such as Denmark, Ireland, Switzerland and the UK (OECD, 2015).

Applying a broader understanding of social policy, typically European is the use of employment protection as a mechanism of providing income security to workers. Across twenty-three European countries for which data exist, the UK had the lowest level of general employment protection (applying to permanent workers and individual as well as collective dismissals) in 2013, followed by Ireland (OECD, 2015). Using particular measures, Denmark too provides relatively little employment security, but this is compensated by generous unemployment benefits and a strong profile of active labour-market policies such as training. By contrast, the UK is a very low spender on active labour-market policies compared with other EU-15 countries (OECD, 2015). Equally, the UK and Ireland focus benefit support on low-income groups and are significantly less generous to middle- and higher-income groups. This is also reflected in the relative scope of means-tested benefits, which in Ireland and the UK is significantly above the EU average as indicated earlier. A quick glance at the generosity of benefits (such as unemployment protection and public pensions) underlines the fact that average- and higher-income groups are invariably better protected in northern and particularly in western continental European countries compared with the UK (see OECD, 2015). In short, low levels of both job and income security, which are due to an only weakly regulated labour market, make the UK (and Ireland) somewhat atypically European and puts the countries firmly within the camp of economically advanced 'liberal market economies' otherwise found outside Europe – in the US, Canada, Australia and New Zealand.

In many European countries, trade unions and employers have long played pivotal roles in the administration of social policy, and in particular social insurance programmes, such as pensions, unemployment, injury or sickness insurance. The actual range and scope of involvement differs, of course, and the role of social partners in the governance of social protection has declined in some countries. Nevertheless, employers and trade unions in Germany, for example, collaborate within quasi-public but legally independent and financially separate organisations of social insurance, at times joined by state officials. Social partners in Austria, Belgium, the Netherlands and Switzerland play similar roles. In France, employees and employer are jointly in charge of social insurance schemes such as the unemployment benefit and pension funds. In Sweden, Denmark and Finland trade union-affiliated organisations are solely responsible for administering unemployment insurance. Related to this, the idea of social security acting as a form of 'social wage', that is, reflecting former earnings as a way of at least partially preserving accustomed living standards, is common in most European countries. In the UK, neither such arrangements nor the notion of social policy as part of industrial relations apply. Finally, collective bargaining is another important social policy instrument that central and north European countries, but much less so the UK, rely on as a means for securing not only income but regulating working conditions.

In sum, in the context of economically advanced countries in the EU, the UK (and Ireland to a lesser degree) is somewhat atypical in a European sense because of a narrower notion of social policy focused on the redistribution of market income via taxation and benefits and services (Bonoli, in Clasen and Siegel, 2007), as opposed to a broader understanding which pursues social policy goals also via channels such as employment protection or collective agreements.

Emerging Issues

Though Europeans traditionally engage more in social policy than countries in any other region of the world, there has never been either a European welfare state or a single distinctive European social policy identity. Furthermore, European diversity in social policy seems set to increase rather than decrease in the coming years. While economic growth rates declined across the developed world in the wake of the 2007–8 financial crisis (see Chapter 27), European economies were affected to very differing degrees. Europe contains some of those countries that recovered most quickly from the economic crisis (including Austria, Germany, Norway and Sweden), but also all of those that were the hardest hit (including Estonia, Greece, Ireland, Italy and Spain). In the latter countries, pressures to reduce budget deficits have led governments to commit to very substantial reductions in social spending in the coming years, even though the social impacts of the crisis are still highly visible. While the best performing countries in combating poverty or containing income inequality will continue to be European, many other European nations will increasingly fail to emulate them in both respects.

Not least due to improved efforts in some areas (such as education and health), the UK moved in recent times from the edge to the middle of the range of European social policy as far as social expenditure is concerned. Though the commitment of all the main UK political parties to reducing the deficit will likely mean large reductions in some areas of social spending in the years ahead, similar developments elsewhere in Europe may mean that the UK's position relative to the average will not change much. The UK could, however, be expected to fall further behind the best performing European countries with respect to goals such as poverty reduction. Moreover, in many other respects, and particularly with regard to the link between social policy and other policy fields such as industrial relations and employment protection, British social policy will continue to be somewhat atypically European.

A European outlook serves as a reminder that social policy can (and perhaps should) be regarded from a broad perspective, involving more policy areas than the conventional welfare state domains. Similarly, more nuanced data on social spending are now available that, despite methodological challenges, allow for more meaningful cross-national comparisons within and beyond social policy in European countries (see Chapter 63).

Guide to Further Sources

Both Eurostat (epp.eurostat.ec.europa.eu/portal/page/portal/statistics/themes) and OECD (2015) (stats.oecd.org/Index.aspx?DataSetCode=SOCX_AGG) are indispensable for data on social policy. For the debate on which indicators of social spending are most suitable for comparisons, see F. G. Castles and H. Obinger (2007), 'Social expenditure and redistribution', *Journal of European Social Policy* 17:3, 206–22; W. Adema, P. Fron and M. Ladaique (2014), 'How much do OECD countries spend on social protection and how redistributive are their tax/benefit systems?' *International Social Security Review*, 76:1, 1–25; and W. Adema, P. Fron and M. Ladaique (2011), 'Is the European welfare state really more expensive?: indicators on social spending, 1980–2012; and a Manual to the OECD Social Expenditure Database (SOCX)', OECD Social, Employment and Migration Working Papers, No. 124, OECD, at: dx.doi.org/10.1787/5kg2d2d4pbf0-en.

The volume by J. Clasen and N. A. Siegel (eds) (2007), *Investigating Welfare State Change. The 'Dependent Variable Problem' in Comparative Analysis*, Cheltenham: Edward Elgar, includes several contributions that reflect on the problems of conceptualising and empirically comparing national social policy arrangements (including the chapters by G. Bonoli, J. De Deken and B. Kittel, L. Scruggs and N. A. Siegel referred to in this text).

The two texts mentioned that deal with the discussion of the distinctiveness of European versus US social policy are J. Alber (2010), 'What the European and American welfare states have in common and where they differ: facts and fiction in comparisons of the European social model and the United States', *Journal of European Social Policy*, 20:2, 102–25; and P. Baldwin (1996), 'Can we define a European welfare state model?', in B. Greve (ed.), *Comparative Welfare Systems: The Scandinavian Model in a Period of Change*, Basingstoke: Macmillan, 29–44.

For more information on social policy in European countries, the European Social Policy Analysis network (ESPAnet) provides links to relevant national social policy associations and organisations and national research centres within Europe at: www.espanet.org. The European Data Centre for Work and Welfare (EDAC) is a web portal with direct links to information on quantitative and qualitative comparative and national data at: www.edac.eu. For EU social policy involvement and documentation the Directorate General for Employment, Social Affairs and Inclusion is a good starting point, at the EU webportal: ec.europa.eu/social/main.jsp?langId=en&catId=656.

Review and Assignment Questions

1 Does it make sense to contrast US American with European social policy?
2 What is typical for European welfare states?
3 In what sense is the UK a typical European welfare state?
4 In what sense is the UK different from most other European welfare states?
5 Critically discuss the claim that there is no such thing as European social policy.

Visit the book companion site at www.wiley.com/go/alcocksocialpolicy to make use of the resources designed to accompany the textbook. There you will find chapter-specific guides to further resources, including governmental, international, thinktank, pressure groups and relevant journal sources. You will also find a glossary based on *The Blackwell Dictionary of Social Policy*, help sheets, guidance on managing assignments in social policy and career advice.

66

Social Policy in the United States

Phillip M. Singer and Scott L. Greer

Overview

- Social policy in the United States is marked by distrust of government, tension between private and public markets, and a lack of comprehensive coverage for citizens.
- Most individuals in the US receive insurance coverage through the private sector. Continued high costs, lack of universal coverage and poor quality of healthcare led to health reform in the US.
- Education can be divided between primary and higher education. In both instances, there are concerns about future funding, student outcomes, and the role of private and public institutions of learning.
- Income security is highly fragmented; eligibility for programmes is predicated on age, income and gender, leading to a patchwork of programmes and a lack of a universal safety net.

Social policy in the United States is unique in comparison with other Organisation for Economic Co-operation and Development (OECD) countries. The uniqueness of the US is a result of several themes present throughout this chapter. First, the American public is distrustful of centralised government power. This distrust has led to a tension in the role of the private and public sector in the implementation and administration of social policy. Second, the combination of fragmented power and a lack of centralised government have led to significant variation in

The Student's Companion to Social Policy, Fifth Edition. Edited by Pete Alcock, Tina Haux, Margaret May and Sharon Wright.
© 2016 John Wiley & Sons, Ltd. Published 2016 by John Wiley & Sons, Ltd.

programmatic eligibility, benefits and governance. Third, social policy in the US is incomplete. The US lacks a comprehensive social policy, instead focusing on segments of society.

The distinctiveness of American social policy is further shaped by several institutional factors. First, the American federal and state systems are formally divided into three branches of government: executive, legislative, and judicial. Each branch has its own delineated powers and a check to keep other branches from overextending their power. Second, the passage of social policy in the US requires each of the branches of government to work together; the preferences of the executive branch (president) are not enough to make policy. Political parties bridge the branches of government, but not as reliably as in most of Europe. Lastly, responsibilities for specific policy domains are divided between the federal and state governments, with increasing overlap between the two levels of government.

The passage of legislation in the US involves so many players and such complexity that it rarely produces coherent legislation or encompassing programmes – as can be seen in a comparison of the complexity of health insurance, personal tax returns or pensions in the UK and the US. A US society fragmented in many ways, from race and religion to geography and economics, combines with a fragmented political system to produce sectional policies for groups such as veterans or the elderly rather than overarching, coherent programmes such as the NHS. These programmes then further fragment society by dividing their interests with special health programmes for veterans and the elderly, or highly localised school districts that effectively ration education by house price.

Health Policy

Healthcare coverage and programmes

Healthcare coverage is not guaranteed in the US. Eligibility for social policy programmes is segmented based on the attributes of an individual, including age, income and employment status. Over 40 million individuals in the US lack insurance coverage of any kind. For the rest of the US population, insurance coverage comes through several different types of private and government backed programmes.

The largest segment of insurance coverage comes from the private market. Nearly 60 per cent of people with insurance receive coverage through their job. Although this type of insurance has traditionally been financed mainly through the employer, recent trends show the growing share of employee cost-sharing. Further, over the past decade the number of employees receiving employer-sponsored insurance has declined significantly, with projections of further erosion in the future.

Government is also an active provider of healthcare in the US. Responsibility for health policy is divided between programmes operated by the federal government and programmes operated through a federal–state government partnership.

Medicare is the largest federally operated provider of health insurance, with nearly 50 million beneficiaries enrolled in it. Medicare is a social insurance programme which provides healthcare services for the elderly population and individuals with specific chronic health conditions. It is funded through a combination of payroll taxes on business and employees and monthly premiums. Medicare provides coverage for three types of services: hospital, physician and prescription drug insurance. A second federally administered health programme is for military veterans and current military members. Collectively, the Veterans Health Administration and TRICARE are the largest health systems in the US, providing care for nearly 20 million individuals.

States in the US, in partnership with the federal government, operate Medicaid and the Children's Health Insurance Program (CHIP). Both programmes are jointly funded between the two levels of government, with the federal government providing more funding for poorer states. The federal government provides the majority of the funding and sets minimum eligibility requirements, whereas the state is responsible for its administration. Medicaid is a means-tested welfare programme, with eligibility tied to disabilities or income below a certain poverty threshold. CHIP provides insurance coverage for children whose families are not eligible for Medicaid, yet lack affordable employer-sponsored insurance.

Healthcare costs

The growing cost of healthcare is a major concern for policymakers in the US (see Chapters 49 and 50). The US spends 18 per cent of its Gross Domestic Product (GDP) on health expenditures, which is two and a half times what other OECD countries spend on healthcare. There are several reasons why the US spends more money on healthcare. Most notably is that the price of medical services and prescription drugs in the US is much more expensive than the same services and products in other countries. Further, there is no mechanism for financial control. No government entity is charged with negotiating lower prices for beneficiaries, leaving negotiations with private insurers and physician practices, which lack the ability to lower prices.

Healthcare quality

Comparing patient outcome measures from the US healthcare system with other OECD countries, the US is wanting. Of eleven OECD countries, the US was ranked as the fifth in terms of the quality of care received. However, these rankings mask the great variability in quality outcomes within the US. Patients have the freedom to seek care from hospitals and physicians which provide high-quality medical care, if they are able to pay for that quality. Within the healthcare system in the US there are islands of high-quality care and patient outcomes surrounded by an ocean of poor and mediocre care.

Health reform

In 2010, with costs increasing quickly, the numbers of uninsured mounting and poor health outcomes rising, the US passed legislation to reform its healthcare system. The Patient Protection and Affordable Care Act (ACA) is the most significant reform to social policy in the US in the past fifty years.

The ACA confronts the challenges facing the US healthcare system in several ways. The law increased the number of individuals with insurance through three primary mechanisms. First, states have the option to expand their Medicaid programmes to cover additional segments of low-income individuals. Second, the federal government provides a subsidy for people to purchase affordable insurance on the online marketplaces. Lastly, individuals who are not eligible for Medicaid or a subsidy are required to purchase insurance or pay a tax. The ACA seeks to control costs through increasing competition among health plans and changing how clinicians are reimbursed for care. Quality is addressed through payment reforms which incentivise coordination of care for patients and tie payment to patient outcomes.

Education Policy

Education policy in the US can be divided between two types of institution. Primary and secondary education is concerned with mandatory schooling completed before adulthood. Higher education is related to optional schooling received after the completion of secondary education (see Chapters 51 and 52).

Primary and secondary school enrolment

This section focuses on three types of primary and secondary schools: public, private and charter schools. The majority of primary and secondary students are enrolled in public schools. Enrolment in public schools is geographical. Students are assigned to schools located nearest to their home and public schools cannot refuse enrolment of any student. Private schools enrol a much smaller percentage of primary and secondary school students. Enrolment in private schools occurs through an application process and the selection of students for admittance. Lastly, charter school enrolment has grown substantially in the past decade in the US, but is still the smallest of the three types. Similar to public schools, charter schools cannot refuse enrolment for any student, but these schools are not restricted by geography in their selection of students.

Primary and secondary school governance

Traditionally, primary and secondary education policy has been under the control of state and local government. Public schools are governed by elected public officials in school districts. School districts are special arms of the local government tasked with the operation and curriculum for all schools within the municipal government. Private schools are operated by private institutions, rather than through the government. These schools have more freedom of choice related to curriculum, hiring and learning models than public schools. However, state government is involved in regulating aspects of private schools, including accreditation and teacher certification. Charter schools are a hybrid between traditional public and private schools. Similar to public schools, charter schools must accept all students who apply for places, but they are governed by private organisations. Charter schools also have more freedom than public schools in their curriculum development, staffing requirements and learning models. They pose much more complex regulatory problems than traditional public schools because of the diversity of their governance, which can include for-profit companies and politically polarising ethnic or religious groups. Their overall contribution to improved educational outcomes, controlling for student characteristics, is small.

Primary and secondary school financing

The financing of primary and secondary education highlights the diverse role of government in education policy in the US. Publicly funded and operated schools are universal and free for students. The majority of primary and secondary education funding comes from state and local governments, and the cost of operating these schools is high, with government expenditure reaching half a trillion dollars annually. In recent years, the federal government has used the promise of increased funding for public schools to influence the governance of education (as in the EU, a surprisingly small amount of money buys a great deal of influence). The No Child Left Behind Act 2001 increased the presence of the federal government in the learning standards, curriculum and testing of students. Schools that met performance metrics and student-learning goals receive increased funding from the federal government.

Public schools are funded through local property taxes and general state revenues. Schools that are located in areas with more expensive real estate markets have higher property taxes, while poorer schools have lower property taxes and fewer

available funds. To augment the local tax base, state governments primarily procure funding for education through income and sales tax, and redistribute those funds to schools. Charter schools are similar to public schools, with their funding coming through state and local tax revenues. The amount of funding for charter schools is determined by the number of enrolled students. Private schools do not receive any public funding assistance. Rather, they must rely on student tuition fees and private donations for the continued operation of their schools.

Primary and secondary school quality

Compared with other OECD countries, the US spends more on primary and secondary education than most other developed countries. Yet comparison of the outcomes of students in the US with their global counterparts indicates that the quality of education is wanting. An international assessment measuring student performance from sixty-five countries across the globe found that the US ranked thirtieth nationally in mathematics, twenty-third in science, and twentieth in reading.

Higher education governance

The first universities in the US were private and religiously founded. The trend of private universities dominating the higher education landscape continued until the end of the nineteenth century. Passage of new legislation provided real estate and federal funding for states to establish their own public universities. The total number of public institutes of higher education has continued to grow. While there are more than double the number of private universities and colleges in the US, public schools of higher education enrol three times as many students.

Higher education financing

Similar to their primary and secondary counterparts, traditionally much of the funding for higher education in the US has come from governmental sources. However, in the past decade public colleges have faced steep budget cuts from state governments. Due to diminished governmental support for higher education, public colleges have become increasingly reliant on student tuition fees and federally provided research grants for continued operation. In response to state cuts to higher education, the cost of tuition, room and board has grown exponentially.

Higher education quality

The quality of higher education in the US is varied. The upper echelon of private and public schools rank highly in international comparisons. Yet there has been growing concern about learning outcomes and the ability of higher education to produce students with a skillset to compete in a global economy. The positive effect of education is shown in increased educational achievement for students, leading to increased levels of employment and annual earnings. However, the increasing cost of higher education to students, driven especially by reductions in state appropriations, has led to increasing pressure on universities to demonstrate effective learning.

Income Security Policy

The most significant social policy related to income security in the US was the Social Security Act 1935. Signed during the height of the Great Depression, for the first time in the history of the US income security benefits became available. However, only certain segments of the US population were eligible for benefits. Broadly, the Social Security Act and its subsequent amendments provide three forms of income security: old-age assistance, unemployment benefits, and assistance for low-income families and children (see Chapter 47).

Old-age and disability insurance

There are two federally administered social insurance programmes which are geared primarily towards the elderly. The first, as discussed earlier, is the Medicare health programme. The second is old-age insurance through the Social Security programme. Funding is the same for Medicare and old-age assistance, payroll taxes are collected from all current employers and employees, and those funds provide benefits for currently eligible recipients.

Eligibility for old-age assistance results from meeting two requirements. First, an individual must have met the minimum financial contributions to the programme by completing ten years' worth of payroll tax payment to the federal government. Second, an individual must meet the age requirements. Due to financial pressures on the financing system, the minimum age for eligibility for old-age insurance has gradually been extended.

Social Security offers two types of disability insurance. First, individuals who have met the minimum financial contribution to the Social Security programme and have a disability that has kept them out of work for over a year are eligible for disability benefits. The second programme is Supplemental Security Income (SSI), which is funded through general tax revenue, not payroll taxes. Individuals eligible for SSI are those that have not met the minimum financial contribution to Social Security, are aged, blind or disabled, and are low-income or lack other resources.

Old-age and disability benefits are not designed to cover the full cost of living for the elderly and disabled. On average, Social Security provides about 40 per cent of the wage earners income. The amount of benefits is predicated on how much money was earned during the working career of an individual; individuals who receive higher lifetime earnings receive higher benefits. On average, SSI benefits are even lower for beneficiaries than disability benefits through Social Security.

To cover deficiencies in Social Security benefits for the elderly and disabled, private income replacement programmes have grown. Private income replacement offers several different types of plan for income security. Employer retirement plans come in two categories. First is a defined contribution plan, where an employee makes contributions and the employer matches with a contribution and the money is invested in eligible securities. Second is a defined benefit plan, which provides a predetermined pension to all employees, paid for by the employer. The number of employees who participate in defined benefits plans has dropped dramatically in the previous quarter of a century. Instead, the trend in private market income replacement in the US is towards more defined contribution plans. However, this trend increases the financial risk associated with market fluctuations on retirement savings.

While Social Security is a popular programme in the US, there have been attempts to privatise it. Due to the financing structure of the programme and a demographic shift, there are concerns about its future viability. The proposed privatisation reforms would have allowed workers to invest their payroll taxes in the stock market instead of in the Social Security trust fund. However, objections concerning the effect of economic downturns on the retirement savings for Social Security ended attempts at reform.

Unemployment benefits

To assist eligible workers who are involuntarily out of work, Social Security provides a programme for temporary unemployment benefits. This is operated through a federal–state partnership programme. The federal government establishes broad guidelines for the operation of the programme and the state administers it, with each state having varying types of eligibility, standards and benefit amounts. The programmes are funded via contributions from employers located in the state and most allow six months of eligibility.

For individuals who are out of work for longer than six months, the 'long-term unemployed', the federal government operates a separate programme. The 'Great Recession' has driven the numbers of the long-term unemployed to historically high levels; there are nearly 3 million long-term unemployed in the US, with 1 million of those individuals lacking employment for more than two years. However, political gridlock in the federal government has allowed unemployment benefits to lapse, leaving a growing segment of the population without further assistance.

Low-income families and children

There are two federal programmes which are geared towards providing income security for low-income families with children in the US. The first, is Temporary Assistance for Needy Families (TANF). TANF was formed in the ashes of the programme Aid to Families with Dependent Children (AFDC). AFDC was initially constructed as a programme to provide money for needy dependent children and was funded through the provision of federal block grants to the states. These grants give broad discretion to each state

in the operation of their programme and ensure that there is great variability amongst the states in the eligibility and benefits of TANF. However, critics of AFDC argued that it incentivised mothers to have children and to stay out of the labour market, and instead to rely on government largesse. In response to these concerns, TANF was created. TANF requires beneficiaries to engage in work activities to remain eligible for the programme and added strict lifetime caps on the length of eligibility for the programme.

The second programme is the Supplemental Nutrition Assistance Program (SNAP), which provides food assistance for indigent families and children. The federal government funds SNAP and state and federal government share the cost of administration. In 2014, the programme cost the federal government nearly $77 billion and helped to provide assistance to nearly 46 million low-income Americans. Eligibility is determined by each state, but in general eligible recipients must have a monthly income and assets below a certain threshold.

Emerging Issues

Social policy in the US can be difficult to characterise – whether it is primary and secondary education, with tens of thousands of administrative units overseen by fifty divergent states, or health, with its variety of federal, federal–state, state, private and charity systems for providing care. This programmatic fragmentation is a result of a political system designed to fragment and restrain majorities in a country that is socially fragmented in many ways. Programmatic fragmentation feeds on itself, creating new constituencies for different small programmes. The result is a creative social policy environment, but one whose coherence, efficiency and equity is often poor.

There are several reasons why extensive change to social policy in the US is unlikely to occur. First, the American political system is fragmented, and administration and financing responsibility for social policy is diffused to federal, state and local governments. Modification of American social policy requires agreement between these different levels of government, which is not common. Second, political polarisation, amongst the American electorate and its elected officials, increases the difficulty of agreement on any desired policy outcome. Lastly, social policy inertia: the longer a policy is enacted the more politically challenging it is to repeal or alter, and this makes change more unlikely to occur. Yet, as outlined in this chapter, tensions between public and private markets, distrust of centralised government, and lack of comprehensive policy coverage could propel extensive reform to education, income security and healthcare in the US.

Guide to Further Sources

There are many strong textbooks on American government and public policy in genera, for example, M. E. Kraft and S. R. Furlong (2014), *Public Policy: Politics, Issues and Alternatives*, Washington, DC: CQ Press. Walter Trattner (2007), *From Poor Law to Welfare State*, New York: Free Press, is a classic history. For the way race, politics and fragmentation shaped US public policy, see Ira Katznelson (2005), *When Affirmative Action was White*, New York: W. W. Norton; and Michael B. Katz (2008), *The Price of Citizenship: Redefining the Welfare State*, Philadelphia: University of Pennsylvania Press. The relationship between public and private welfare in the US is the subject of important literature, including Jennifer Klein (2003), *For All These Rights*, Princeton: Princeton University Press; Marie Gottschalk (2000), *The Shadow Welfare State*, Ithaca, NY: Cornell University Press; and Suzanne Mettler (2011), *The Submerged Welfare State*, Chicago: Chicago University Press.

For detailed discussions of US programmes, the best official source is the Government Accountability Office at: www.gao.gov. The Kaiser Family Foundation (www.kff.org) and the Commonwealth Fund (www.cmwf.org) are excellent sources for health policy information. The US is enjoying an efflorescence of online public policy journalism, www.vox.com, with the *New York Times* 'Upshot' section and the *Washington Post's* 'Monkey Cage' and 'Wonkbook' sections being especially useful.

Review and Assignment Questions

1 In what sense does social policy in the US differ from other OECD countries?
2 In what sense is social policy in the US similar to other OECD countries?
3 What are the institutional features which influence social policy in the US?
4 How does social policy in the US exhibit the tension between market and state interventions?
5 What do you consider the distinguishing characteristics of social policy in the US?

Visit the book companion site at www.wiley.com/go/alcocksocialpolicy to make use of the resources designed to accompany the textbook. There you will find chapter-specific guides to further resources, including governmental, international, thinktank, pressure groups and relevant journal sources. You will also find a glossary based on *The Blackwell Dictionary of Social Policy*, help sheets, guidance on managing assignments in social policy and career advice.

67

Social Policy in East Asia

Misa Izuhara

Overview

- East Asia is a dynamic and diverse region which contains societies of different sizes, with different political structures and levels of socio-economic, as well as social policy developments.
- The strong regulatory role of the state, which was once characterised as the distinctiveness of East Asian welfare approaches, is now shifting towards more market-oriented approaches.
- In response to recent financial crises, more differentiated trajectories of social policy developments and reforms have been observed across East Asian societies.
- Rapid demographic transitions, such as ageing society and changing families, require East Asian societies to re-examination their existing welfare systems.
- There are growing social divisions and inequalities in different sections of society as a result of contemporary social and economic change.

Introduction

In East Asian societies, there have been substantial developments and reforms in various areas of social policy in response to both domestic and external pressure in recent years. The 'remarkable rates of economic growth with the limited public expenditures on welfare' – albeit staggered from Japan's early post-war economic miracle of the 1960s, to the rise of the newly industrialised 'Tiger Economies' of Hong Kong, Singapore, South Korea and Taiwan in the 1970s and 1980s, to the more recent re-emergence of the People's Republic of China to global prominence in the

The Student's Companion to Social Policy, Fifth Edition. Edited by Pete Alcock, Tina Haux, Margaret May and Sharon Wright.
© 2016 John Wiley & Sons, Ltd. Published 2016 by John Wiley & Sons, Ltd.

1990s onwards – all have continuously attracted academic and popular discourse in the analysis of economy and social policy in the region over the last few decades.

Since the early 1990s, however, Japan has been experiencing a prolonged period of 'post-bubble' recession. The economic downturn has helped to transform their conventional systems of the male breadwinner family model, life-long employment and occupational-based welfare, which used to provide the foundation of welfare for the majority of households. Preceding the global financial crisis of 2007–8, the Asian financial crises in 1997 and 1998 taught the Tiger Economies a lesson about the volatility and vulnerability of economy and property asset values, and have forced governments to reconsider their welfare approach. Moreover, the major system transitions taking place in contemporary East Asia include China's adaptation from a planned economy to a more market-orientated system since the 1980s. The introduction of a market approach for employment, housing and social security has shifted the state responsibility to individuals and families in securing their own welfare in the private market, producing new social risks. The uneven impact of and response to economic change have thus provided a distinctive context for the comparative analysis of social policy developments and reforms across East Asian societies. Their experiences are indeed shaping contemporary social policy debates on the importance of safety nets, and social protection more generally.

What is East Asia? What is Social Policy in East Asia?

Like Europe, defining East Asia as a region is a debate in itself. East Asia is a diverse and dynamic region, including a number of different countries in terms of the size, political structure, the level of social and economic development, type of institutions, colonial histories, ethnic composition, religions and cultures. The region includes both the small city-states such as Singapore, Macau and Hong Kong Special Administrative Regions (SAR) and the large and world's most populated country of China (see Figure 67.1). There are complex relationships among 'Chinese societies', including China's 'One Country, Two Systems' since the

transfer of sovereignty of Hong Kong from the UK to China in 1997. The political economy of the nations in the region differs from the capitalist democracy found in Japan, to 'soft-authoritarian' Singapore, to the transitional economy of China now ambiguously known as 'market socialism' or 'state capitalism', which shares some elements with other transitional societies such as Vietnam in wider East Asia (see Chapter 68). The different stages of socio-economic development are also evident in the region. According to the Human Development Index by the United Nations Development Programme based on indicators including life expectancy, literacy and the standards of life, for example, Singapore was ranked the highest in the region at 9th, followed by South Korea and Hong Kong at 15th, and Japan at 17th, while China was ranked at 91st and Vietnam 121st in 2014 (see Chapter 70).

Social policy approaches tend to vary widely across the societies. For example, a variety of social protection approaches are found in East Asia in terms of funding mechanisms, eligibility and the level of resources to respond to contemporary social issues: that is, from the contributory social insurance-based approach of Japan, South Korea and Taiwan, to tax-based means-tested social assistance in Hong Kong, to individual saving schemes (provident funds) in Singapore. Nevertheless, certain shared characteristics in welfare systems among many East Asian societies stimulated the development of comparative social policy analysis in the region. 'Small state' derived from a residual element of direct state welfare provision such as low public expenditure and low state benefits despite the dominant role of the state as a facilitator and regulator of welfare provision. In a similar vein, limited commitment of the state to social citizenship has also been highlighted. Across policy fields, the strategic role of social investment in education and health is another characteristic of the East Asian welfare approach. Overall, employment-based welfare is a popular approach as opposed to programmes that tend to 'undermine work ethics' such as cash-based public assistance. The distinctive roles played by non-state sectors in the welfare mix are equally crucial in East Asia, especially the role of families as a key welfare provider, and the role of large corporations in providing generous welfare to their core employees in countries like Japan and South Korea.

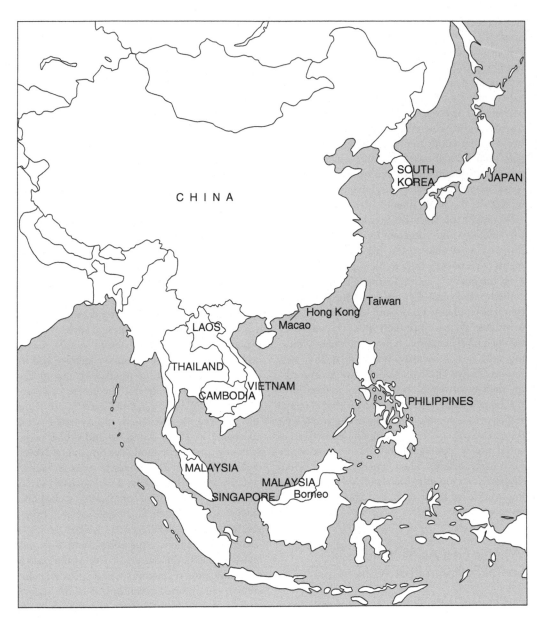

Figure 67.1 South East Asia.

There are, however, limitations confronting comparative and international social policy analysis involving East Asian societies due partly to the availability of comparative data, produced by, for example, international organisations such as the Organisation for Economic Cooperation and Development (OECD) and the World Bank, as well as commonly used measurements and concepts. Comparison is often based on available quantitative data and on more measurable state

expenditure, such as on healthcare and education. Until recently, comparative analysis of East Asian social policy tended to focus on the established welfare state of Japan (with mature key welfare programmes such as pensions, education and healthcare) and the emerging welfare systems of the four Tiger Economies. Some commentators argue that the birth and subsequent development of the Japanese welfare systems since the 1960s are located somewhere between the West and the rest of East Asia. Only two countries – Japan (which joined in 1964) and South Korea – are currently members of the OECD, and the more recent entry of South Korea in 1996 limits the comparative analysis of certain trends. Although geographically dispersed, the Tiger Economies of Hong Kong, Singapore, South Korea and Taiwan provide a comparative cluster for the analysis of social policy within the region. The similarities and variations found in their welfare approaches have stimulated the debate around the validity of an East Asian model of welfare. Malaysia is sometimes included in the discussion due partly to its British colonial legacy, while Vietnam and other transitional societies of South East Asia have started attracting comparative analysis in a developmental context. In recent years, China has been brought more fully into social policy debate in East Asia with a growing body of academic literature (see Chan et al., 2008). China's remarkable transition from a planned economy with a low-level but universal welfare provision through *danwei* (work units) to a more privatised and marketised approach adds further dynamism to existing comparative analysis in the region.

Moreover, complexity has been also observed in other aspects such as governance, citizenship or social security in association with a series of policy reforms in East Asian societies. Although western conceptions and theories tend to dominate comparative analysis of welfare systems through preconceived frameworks, such as welfare typologies and the analysis of state activities, such frameworks and terms are not necessarily universally applicable to the analysis of East Asia. There are many issues associated with definitions and use of the terms; for example, 'social security' has a different meaning in different societies; and the notion of 'citizenship' may not be well developed in those societies (see also Chapter 70).

Welfare Systems in East Asia

There has been debate around distinctive natures of welfare systems in East Asia, and whether or not there is a regional model that can capture the common features of East Asian welfare systems. Much of the debate stems from a strand of comparative social policy research, namely, welfare regime theories. Theorising welfare systems

originated in the 1980s or earlier, but was provoked by Esping-Andersen's (1990) seminal work, *Three Worlds of Welfare Capitalism* (see Chapter 63). Japan was the only East Asian society included in his analysis and was originally classified in the 'Conservative-Corporatist' regime cluster with Germany and other continental European societies due to its characteristics, including social rights based on employment and contributions. Subsequent critiques, however, highlighted Japan's misfit in the given regime cluster by suggesting a possible 'fourth' regime together with family-centred Mediterranean societies; or clustering Japan with other East Asian societies to create the 'East Asian welfare regime'. Esping-Andersen himself also revisited the original analysis and suggested that potentially Japan was a hybrid case between the 'Conservative-Corporatist' and 'Liberal' regimes. Since then, the debates have moved on significantly and have expanded to include more societies in the region when theorising the shifts in the welfare systems and differentiated developmental trajectories within the changing socio-economic context. Two key theses – *developmentalism* and *productivist welfare capitalism* – are briefly introduced below.

Examining Japan's economic miracle in the first half of the post-war period, the 'developmental state' thesis was predominantly concerned with the role of the state, in particular, in relation to its financial capacity and regulatory power in achieving great economic growth. The developmental state was to embrace the bureaucratic autonomy of the state in key areas such as financial control over the economy. In this scenario, economic progress was not the product of classical liberalism, but the state in conjunction with the dominant political party, business and bureaucrats generated governed markets. Subsequent analysis highlighted more complex and mixed influences of other sectors including corporations. In principle, such states encouraged that welfare should be provided through employment, and would oppose programmes to undermine work ethics such as unemployment benefits and means-tested public assistance. As some commentators argue (see Choi, 2013), however, *developmentalism* was a product of particular socio-economic conditions, including the relatively younger population (focusing on job creation over old-age income and care), family solidarity (which produced a high volume of welfare) and the strong manufacturing industry (guaranteeing full (male) employment). Recent social-economic shifts towards an ageing society, changing families and the restructuring of the labour market have thus been diminishing these conditions and, in turn, have transformed the once dominant system.

In contrast, the dynamics of capitalist market economies rather than an 'autonomous state' lie at the core of the 'productivist welfare capitalism' thesis. The thesis defines a welfare state as a by-product of economic growth and explores the close relationship between the economy and social policy (see Holliday, 2000). The key features include that social policy is subordinate to the overriding policy objective of economic growth. The *productivist* principles are based on minimal social rights with extensions linked to productive activity, reinforcing the position of productive elements such as education and skill training, and state–market–family relationships being directed towards growth. The introduction of the 1973 Pension Act in South Korea is a case in point as being partly in order to raise funds for industrial investment. The post-Asian financial crisis (AFC) debate around productivism has been, however, in stark contrast in different recovery paths across the four Tiger Economies, which further delineated their 'productivist' positions within the region. Many authors have challenged whether the welfare approaches discussed above are necessarily all uniquely East Asian. Economic activation policy through human capital investment has been, for example, found in Anglo-Saxon liberal regimes, albeit in different rationales and approaches. The US can be defined as 'productivist' in the sense that it is a residual state that emphasises investment in education and skills training over traditional forms of social protection. The stronger presence of the informal sector on the delivery of welfare is highly common in southern European states, and those 'familial' states are similarly suffering from the recent demographic transition of extremely low fertility.

Contemporary Shifts

The productivist notion of welfare arrangements has experienced both continuity and change, with interesting divergence among the societies. This therefore poses a question of whether 'productivism' is still an appropriate label to define welfare systems in East Asia. The post-AFC developments and reforms in social policy, for example, began to witness further divergence within the Tiger Economies. On the one hand, societies that foster the self-help principle for social protection through individual saving schemes such as provident funds in Singapore and Hong Kong tend to remain a residual state, thus 'productivist', with evident welfare retrenchment of cutting back the state or employers' contributions to the schemes in response to the financial crisis. On the other hand, South Korea and Taiwan demonstrate different trajectories. with paradoxical welfare expansion in the era of globalisation. These societies have developed redistributive social insurance schemes, similar to those in Japan, on pensions and, more recently, long-term care for older people, and expanded their programmes, shifting away from a residual 'productivist' approach. With contemporary shifts in new global environment, financial deregulation and changing demographic profiles, however, welfare provision is in general shifting towards more market-orientated liberalism, expanding means-tested programmes, and even increasing the expectations on individuals and families to secure their own welfare. Overall, as Choi (2013) argues, state-driven developmentalism has been weakening in the current economic climate, giving way to a more market-orientated productivism in East Asia.

Another contemporary shift that is salient and highly relevant to social policy is demographic transitions and its phenomenal pace of change in East Asia. A combination of increased longevity and a decline in fertility has accelerated societal ageing in many parts of East Asia. Compared with developed European societies, the process of societal ageing started much more recently and much more quickly; and fertility rates are below the average even for low-fertility societies in Europe. A quarter of Japan's population had already reached 65 and over in 2013, making Japan the world's oldest society. Ageing issues thus tend to dominate the policy debates, which is evident in the introduction of social insurance on long-term care in Japan, South Korea and Taiwan. A continuous decline in fertility rates is, however, another side of the same coin, as the average number of children born to women at reproductive age is as low as 1.1 to 1.4 across East Asian societies. Developing pro-natalist policies is also one of the urgent policy priorities. Furthermore, increasing numbers of divorces, late/never-married, female labour market participations and elderly-only households all mean that the 'conventional' model of families, which once contributed as welfare providers to the low level of public expenditure, substituting, for example, social services, has been disappearing. Welfare organised around 'standard families' is indeed no longer sustainable.

Emerging Issues

Differentiated impacts of the economic crisis and rapid social transitions on these societies have meant that there are growing social divisions and inequalities in different sections of society. Inequalities exist in many areas, such as access to education, access to the labour market and differentiated employment status, access to welfare, leading to wealth inequalities. How such social inequality has become increasingly fixed over generations, with the system restricting social mobility, has become one of the major concerns in some societies. This debate strongly reflects shifting employment patterns and privatisation and marketisation processes during the recent economic reforms and recessions in many parts of East Asia, including China and Japan. In Japan, for example, economic growth and labour market stability enjoyed by the current older generation are simply not available for younger people today, and their struggle to access stable employment and income has been well documented. Mass graduate unemployment is a major issue in urban China, indicating a mismatch between labour demand and supply. Patterns of migratory movements, including rural-to-urban migration in China, are increasingly becoming complex in the region, which challenges the notion of social rights especially for temporary workers. The post-bubble or post-AFC recession, which led to a more flexible labour market, has brought increasing instability among the younger generation. Younger people now struggle in the transition from education to employment, from parental home to an independent household, and to home ownership. The competitive and hierarchical education system could be another incubator for reproducing social

inequality over the generations. This is also an inevitable outcome of the systems in which the redistributive effect of taxes and social security has been minimal in those societies. In this context, 're-familisation' (taking family resources into account) is an emerging discourse to absorb new social risks facing younger people, especially policy measures which tend to be absent for young adults – those in the middle of their life course. Debate around intergenerational justice over resource allocation has not been well developed in East Asia. When family resources become more important in the neo-Liberal policy context, the emphasis on the micro-level family redistribution will further accelerate the wealth gap between families within and across the generations. Overall, greater safety nets and better social protection to address new social risks for those who fall out of the available measures developed around 'standard families' and 'stable employment' need to be considered.

Guide to Further Sources

The many issues and debates introduced in this chapter are explored more fully in M. Izuhara (ed.) (2013), *Handbook on East Asian Social Policy*, Cheltenham: Edward Elgar. This handbook provides contemporary analysis and perspectives to the study of social policy in East Asia from welfare state developments to theories, to current social policy issues. A chapter in the handbook by Y. J. Choi (2013), *Developmentalism and Productivism in East Asian Welfare Regimes*, Cheltenham: Edward Elgar, offers a succinct summary and analysis of the trajectories of the two theories. The key original authors for the debates of *developmentalism* and *productivism* are C. Johnson (1987), *MITI and the Japanese Miracle*, Stanford: Stanford University Press, and I. Holliday (2000), 'Productivist welfare capitalism: social policy in East Asia', *Political Studies*, 48:4, 706–23, respectively.

There has been a growing body of academic literature (in English) on various fields of social policy developments in the People's Republic of China for the last decade or two. C. K. Chan, K. Ngok and D. Phillips (2008), *Social Policy in China: Development and Well-being*, Bristol: Policy Press, provides a good overview of China's policy development in the reform period.

More recently, the theme of social policy developments in the region centres on the impact of globalisation, (uneven) recovery from various economic crises; see, for example, K. H. Mok and R. S. Forrest (eds) (2009), *Changing Governance and Public Policy in East Asia*, London: Routledge; and G-J. Hwang (ed.) (2011), *New Welfare States in East Asia: Global Challenges and Restructuring*, Cheltenham: Edward Elgar.

Some OECD data include Japan and South Korea in international comparison of member countries in social expenditures, healthcare, education and so on (www.oecd.org); and other data involving East and South East Asian societies are found in the Asian Development Bank/World Bank – each tends to draw different groups of societies in the region.

Some social policy journals have published special issues around the themes involving social policy and East Asia; for example, *Social Policy & Administration*, Regional issue: Japan and South Korea – Asian Welfare States (2014, 48:6); *International Journal of Japanese Society*, Social change and social policy in East Asia (2009, 18:1); *Social Policy and Society*, Themed Section: Moving towards human rights based social policies in China (2011, 10:1).

Review and Assignment Questions

1 Explore the distinctiveness of East Asian welfare regimes in relation to the role of each sector
2 Are 'developmentalism' and 'productivism' still useful labels to examine welfare systems in East Asia?
3 What are the major implications of demographic change (such as ageing of the population, changing families) for future social policy in East Asia?
4 How do you explain causes and consequences of widening social inequalities in East Asian societies?

Visit the book companion site at www.wiley.com/go/alcocksocialpolicy to make use of the resources designed to accompany the textbook. There you will find chapter-specific guides to further resources, including governmental, international, thinktank, pressure groups and relevant journal sources. You will also find a glossary based on *The Blackwell Dictionary of Social Policy*, help sheets, guidance on managing assignments in social policy and career advice.

68

Social Policy in the BRICS Countries

Rebecca Surender

Overview

- The BRICS (Brazil, Russian Federation, India, China and South Africa) are a group of rising and influential countries.
- They are distinguished by their fast growing economies and escalating visibility in global social policy affairs.
- They have achieved rapid and unprecedented development and poverty alleviation within their own borders.
- As 'aid donors', the BRICS are having a significant impact on the institutions and ideas of western development agencies, as well as on the quantity and types of aid to other developing countries.
- Academics and policymakers disagree about the impact that the BRICS are having on welfare outcomes and debates, and whether the BRICS group is sustainable in the longer term.

Background and Definitions

The acronym BRICS stands for Brazil, the Russian Federation (Russia), India, the People's Republic of China (PRC) and South Africa. It was first used in 2001 by investment bankers to refer to what was predicted would be the fastest growing emerging economies at that time. With over 40 per cent of the world's population and 20 per cent of global GDP, it was forecasted that the four largest BRIC nations would join the US as the five largest economies in the world by 2050. The initial interest in this group was for financial investment purposes. However, their rising visibility and

The Student's Companion to Social Policy, Fifth Edition. Edited by Pete Alcock, Tina Haux, Margaret May and Sharon Wright.

power in global governance and international affairs, together with their success in reducing poverty, have meant that there is now wider interest in the group's influence on global social policy debates and processes.

The formal political association of the group can be traced to high-level meetings between the initial four states in 2006. South Africa (SA) was invited to become a member in 2010 and the BRICS Summit was formed. Many queried the inclusion of SA since, compared with the other BRIC countries, it has considerably less economic power and lower overall living standards. However, its per capita income is higher than China's and India's. SA is also the wealthiest and most politically influential country in Africa. Some argue it therefore generates representation and voice for the entire continent with a population of over 1 billion. Others question whether Russia legitimately belongs to the group not only because of its lack of shared identity as a developing country, but also because it can no longer claim to be among the largest and fastest growing economies. Though Russia's role was less questioned when the main BRICS's purpose was for financial investment, its recent experience of economic retrenchment and decline has again called into question its participation within the group. Despite these tensions, in 2014 the sixth BRICS Summit took place in Brazil, where all five countries signed agreements to establish a development bank and discussed issues directly relevant for social policy and welfare in the global South.

Varying Challenges and Differing Responses

In contrast to most of the other regional groupings in this volume, BRICS countries are a highly heterogeneous and diverse 'cluster': two are authoritarian, three are 'noisy' democracies, three are nuclear powers, two have permanent seats on the UN Security Council and so on. More importantly, they do not share the legal, historical or geographical similarities as that of the European Union (see Chapter 65), East Asia (see Chapter 67) or the Middle East (see Chapter 69). Each of the BRICS will also face different demographic, economic and societal changes and external pressures in the future. It is unsurprising, then that in terms

of social policy approaches, it is hard to identify a single 'BRICS brand' or model. Rather, we see significant variation in terms of the quantity and type of internal (domestic) welfare arrangements across the five countries, and the instruments and mechanism used to deliver services. For example, SA's domestic social policy has been characterised as an 'activist' approach; driven less in terms of social investment and economic development functions and more in terms of citizenship, social rights and social justice. To this extent, it stands in contrast to the 'productivist model' of China, the social insurance approach in India and the 'social investment model' typical of Brazil (see Chapter 63 for a discussion of different welfare state typologies).

Why then do BRICS Matter for Social Policy?

Despite this heterogeneity, the BRICS have caught the attention of the social policy community and are influencing global social policy debates for several reasons. Chief among these is that they have achieved unprecedented success in lowering poverty and raising living standards for their respective populations. In addition to economic growth and employment, impressive social protection and welfare systems have contributed to this development. China has extended its pension coverage, health insurance, social insurance, social assistance and welfare services, while India has expanded its works programmes, minimum wage guarantees and health insurance for those below the poverty line. SA has one of the largest redistributive social transfer systems in any developing country with social grants available to all those who, due to age or disability, fall outside the labour market (28 per cent of the population). Brazil has championed conditional cash transfers as a primary instrument of hunger and poverty alleviation, and by 2012 the *Bolsa Família* programme was being delivered to over 13 million families, in poverty (nearly 30 per cent of the population). The rapid development and poverty alleviation within their own borders meant that between 1981 and 2005, three of the BRICS (Brazil, China and India) had experienced a massive drop in the percentage of their populations living below the poverty line; China dropped from

84 to 16 per cent; India from 60 to 42 per cent; and Brazil from 17 to 8 per cent.

In addition to successfully reducing their own domestic poverty rates, the BRICS have also become significant actors in international development assistance and major contributors of aid to other developing nations.

Key Trends in Social Protection within Each of the BRICS

Despite common challenges for social security administration, there exist clear differences in the issues and environment in each country, which in turn determine the different social policy approaches adopted by each country (ISSA, 2013).

Brazil

Brazil is a country with a young population, but which is ageing relatively rapidly. Although social security is generally well developed, due to the large informal sector and the fragmentation and inconsistency in benefit provision across different levels of government, coverage varies significantly between rural and urban areas and between the formal and informal sector. The 1988 Brazilian Constitution, however, requires universal coverage and services and equivalence for the entire population, and this has driven 'extension coverage' initiatives in the last twenty-five years. Most famous are the conditional cash transfer schemes (for example, the well-known *Bolsa Família* programme) and in-kind transfers (see Box 68.1). Considerable efforts since the turn of the century have focused on increasing the scope of the *Bolsa Família* and other such social assistance. Between 2005 and 2009, the number of recipients of contributory social insurance benefit increased by 11 per cent, whilst non-contributory social assistance recipients increased by 25 per cent.

The Russian Federation

Russia differs from other BRICS countries in being able to build on its universal social security system from Soviet times. Consequently, Russian social security encompasses a wide range of statutory programmes, including mandatory and voluntary

Box 68.1 Brazil's Bolsa Família Programme (BFP): Goals, Structure and Outcomes

- The BFP is a welfare programme implemented in 2003 by the Brazilian government to provide financial aid to poor families.
- It is a conditional cash transfer – in order to receive cash benefits families must ensure that the children are vaccinated and attend prenatal clinics and school.
- It attempts to reduce short-term poverty through cash transfers and long-term poverty by increasing human capital and health and education resources.
- It has become the largest cash transfer programme in the world, reaching over 13 million families in 2012.
- Research shows that the programme is positively associated with increased school attendance and reduction in chronic child malnutrition in the poorest regions.
- It has been credited with reducing income inequality in Brazil, accounting by 20–25 per cent, with 73 per cent of the transfer going to the poorest quintile.
- The money is given to a female head of household through *Citizen Cards* which operate like a debit card.

pension schemes, health, family and maternity programmes, unemployment and work injury provision. These schemes have been augmented with various social assistance measures which target certain vulnerable groups. However, the country arguably faces more deep-seated and disruptive social, economic and demographic changes than the other BRICS. These changes have put a number of strains on existing schemes, leading to a reduction in the level and quality of benefits, particularly for those working in the informal sector and new migrant workers.

A particular social policy priority is the rapidly shrinking population, which has decreased by over 5 million over the last twenty years. Emphasis has therefore been placed on policies to improve the birth rate in the country, including improvements in maternity and family benefits and a number of innovative approaches such as the one-off 'Family Capital' payment worth around €10,000, which can be used for educational or housing needs or to supplement retirement savings.

India

India is a 'young country' with a high birth rate and will age much less quickly than most other BRICS countries. Nevertheless, due to the extent of its poverty and weak state capacity for delivering basic public services, the potential for using social policy redistributive measures is far more limited than for other BRICS. The country's large informal or 'unorganised' sector makes up over 90 per cent of the workforce and it continues to be a largely rural economy. Although a number of social security laws and compensation schemes (for work injury, disability, death, maternity coverage and old-age) formally exist, they are unevenly implemented.

There are also a number of non-contributory and means-tested schemes such as the National Old Age Pension providing benefits to those earning less than US$7.00 per month and reaching 17 million poor people. Two notable initiatives are the *Rashtriya Swasthya Bima Yojana* Universal Health Insurance Scheme, established in 2007 to provide health coverage for those below the poverty line using a SmartCard system for beneficiaries (now with more than 10 million members) and the *National Rural Employment Guarantee Scheme*, which provides up to 100 days of unskilled manual labour per family per year at the statutory minimum wage to anyone who wants it.

Traditionally, in the absence of formal social security, extended family support and ad hoc systems of provision address the welfare needs of the population. However, given increasing rural-to-urban migration – a trend also seen in other BRICS countries – and changes in family structures, this informal system of protection is starting to break down.

China

Until recently, direct redistributive interventions have not been prominent in China's efforts to reduce poverty and instead enterprise-based social security remained the norm. Over the last decade, however, China has taken advantage of its current favourable demographic situation and healthy government finances to improve coverage of its population through the introduction and extension of different social security programmes. Coverage levels of old-age benefits and a basic pension, medical care, unemployment insurance, employment injury coverage and maternity benefit have all extended. It has managed to address the challenges of large regional differences and significant rural-to-urban migration, providing almost 100 per cent of its population with medical coverage and about half the population with old-age benefits.

One particular policy that has caught widespread attention is the Minimum Livelihood Guarantee Scheme (*Dibao*). A non-conditional cash transfer programme, it provides a social security net for residents whose income falls below a certain level. It covers both rural and urban residents, which is often not the case for most government policies and is implemented across China, unlike employment, housing, environmental and other issues where no national policy exists.

South Africa

In response to its specific history of colonialism and Apartheid, the SA Government began a programme of unprecedented social policy initiatives and legislation designed to achieve better living standards and opportunities for its poorest citizens. There was a significant increase in expenditure on both social services and social transfers – from 44 per cent of government expenditure in 1993 to 57 per cent in 2002/3. Most radical was the introduction of wholesale social assistance providing social grants to millions of citizens. Covering 13.5 million beneficiaries in 2009, the net includes non-contributory and means-tested social security transfers, mostly to those who for reasons of age or disability are not in work. Four main cash transfers (the Child Support Grant (CSG), Disability Grant, Old Age Pension and

Foster Care Grant) account for over 12 per cent of government expenditure or approximately 4 per cent of GDP.

Amongst developing nations, this makes SA one of the world's biggest spenders on social grants. Also, in contrast to other BRICS countries, underpinning SA's social policy framework is its Constitution, which formally guarantees social protection and rights of citizenship in a manner not inconsistent with a West European-style social democratic tradition.

The Role of BRICS in Shaping Global Social Policy

The BRICS have become significant actors in international development assistance and major aid donors to other developing nations. Though none of the five countries reaches the 0.7 per cent of the Gross National Income target set by the Development Assistance Committee (DAC) donors and the absolute amount of assistance remains relatively small compared with DAC totals, the rate and pace of the rise in BRICS aid expenditure remain impressive. This aid has important implications for the policy landscape of developing countries, especially in Africa. While welfare and social policy sectors such as health, housing and poverty relief are largely funded by taxes in rich nations, in poorer countries, social programmes and interventions are funded primarily by donor aid.

However, more important than the volume of aid that BRICS contribute, is the impact the BRICS 'model' is having on the instruments and mechanisms of aid and the normative objectives underpinning it both within developing countries and Western donor organisations. While there is no single social policy model within each country, we see that as a consortium, there is a 'BRICS brand'. It is guided by a social development approach, which establishes stronger links between the economic and social dimensions of development than traditional donor organisations. Thus, although in the last few years all BRICS members have expanded their own internal social welfare programmes, in their capacity as overseas donors the BRICS have pursued a different approach. The approach also diverges from current 'North–South' models. Western multilateral institutions

now appear to be embracing a post-'Washington consensus' social policy agenda for developing nations, promoting 'pro-poor' and redistributive frameworks. The ideas and activities of the new donor group, however, appear to have moved in a different direction. Instead, the BRICS have chosen to combine trade, investment and technical support in an integrated package that cannot be untangled easily, reflecting the view that economic development should be prioritised in the development process. This shift in emphasis from income poverty and social exclusion to 'productive enhancement and enterprise' reflects the view that social development is ultimately achieved by productive activities which add to economic development. BRICS countries therefore tend to prioritise training, scholarships and technical cooperation (productive sector investments) rather than social assistance cash transfers characteristic of DAC donors. There is some evidence that BRICS activities are generating new ideas and gaining influence in Western multilateral institutions such as the OECD, the World Bank, the International Monetary Fund and the World Health Organization. This raises interesting questions about the traditional analytical frameworks used by Western social policy for understanding global welfare dynamics and the processes and politics of social policy formation in developing countries (see Chapter 71).

Emerging Issues

In less than a decade the BRICS have begun to significantly impact the welfare arrangements and outcomes within their own countries as well as the volume and kind of aid and polices in other developing countries. A new approach or model, embedded in a framework of 'South–South cooperation' (described by the United Nations as a process designed to promote cooperation among developing countries in pursuit of common development goals), appears to be emerging (see Box 68.2). There are doubts, however, about the extent to which these developments are positive. Some policy analysts have welcomed the injection of new ideas and norms, arguing that they hold traditional actors and ideas to greater account. Others predict that the motivations of the BRICS are the same as

> **Box 68.2** Principles and Objectives of South–South Cooperation
>
> ■ 'South–South cooperation' is a broad term used to describe diverse types of political, economic and social cooperation among developing countries.
> ■ Emphasises strong political and economic solidarity between developing countries.
> ■ Stems from the belief that developing states share common historical legacies and experiences of colonisation, limited power in the prevailing global order hierarchy, and challenges of underdevelopment.
> ■ Key guiding principles are equality, self-determination and non-interference in the internal affairs between states.
> ■ Mutual benefit, mutual respect and partnership among equals are paramount.
> ■ Cooperation takes different forms: development aid and in-kind contributions, preferential trade arrangements, sharing of knowledge and expertise, training, technology transfer, financial and monetary cooperation.

existing donors and will simply reproduce traditional donor–recipient hierarchies.

Critics argue that South–South cooperation is no less self-interested than the West's and BRICS development activities are mostly to gain political influence in regional affairs or driven by economic motives; primarily raw material extraction, low labour costs and economic prospects (Lo, 2014). Some forecast that as the BRICS grow in power they may shut out, rather than strengthen, the voices of weaker nations and over time a 'South within the South' trend will occur.

Another set of debates focuses on inequality as opposed to poverty alone. Here critics contend that despite widespread poverty reduction, income inequalities in all BRICS countries have increased steeply and have remained well above the OECD average. Although there are many

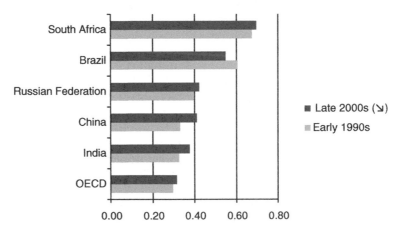

Figure 68.1 Change in inequality levels, early 1990s versus late 2000s.
Notes: (1) Figures for the early 1990s generally refer to 1993, whereas figures for the late 2000s generally refer to 2008.
(2) Gini coefficients are based on equivalised incomes for OECD countries and per capita incomes for all emerging economies, except India and Indonesia for which per capita consumption was used. A score of 0 signifies complete equality and a score of 1 complete inequality.
Source: OECD–EU database on Emerging Economies and World Bank Development Indicators database.

reasons for this, a recent OXFAM report (2014) emphasises the fact that as a proportion of GDP, spending on social protection is generally lower in BRICS countries than OECD averages, and that targeted public expenditure and policy frameworks are needed if the benefits of growth and economic development are to be realised both within and beyond the BRICS.

Finally, many question how sustainable the BRICS collective is in the long term (UNDP, 2010). Some predict that internal divisions and tensions will ultimately stall the group's evolution as a cohesive actor. In addition to the long-standing rivalries between China and India, wider strategic rivalries between members around securing permanent seats on the UN Security Council or nuclear capabilities are also evident. China's position as the most powerful member of the BRICS also leads some to predict that Chinese dominance of global development will ultimately threaten the long-term coherence and robustness of the alliance. In addition to power rivalries, there are also strong ideological differences between the five nations, in their development approaches and their respective relationships to the West.

It is not obvious that the BRICS alliance has inevitably minimised the inherent conflicts between recipient needs and donor interests or whether its new 'productivist' approach will translate into a positive impact for the poorest within its or other nations. It is too early to make definitive prescriptions about these debates or what it means for the conditions, processes and politics of global social policy. It is clear, however, that the entrance of the BRICS as South–South development actors has meant that international development is in a period of major transition and undergoing an upheaval in its social policy ideas and practices.

Guide to Further Sources

There are currently few general books concerning BRICS social policy, and most literature is in the form of journal articles and government and international organisation reports. A good source of material can be found at www.bricspolicycenter .org, including the Oxfam Report (2014), 'Inequality matters: BRICS inequalities fact sheet' (www.oxfam.org/sites/www.oxfam.org/files/brics-inequality-fact-sheet-oxfam-03-14-2013_0.pdf).

The Report outlines key dimensions of socio-economic inequality in the BRICS, highlighting trends and debates relevant for public policies. The International Social Security Association report, 'BRICS: social security coverage extension in the BRICS' (www.issa.int/topics/brics/report), is a comprehensive study of social security in member states in both qualitative and quantitative terms. UNDP (2010), South–South cooperation, *The Same Old Game or a New Paradigm?*, Poverty in Focus No. 20, Brasilia: Bureau for Development Policy, has a number of useful chapters, including Ladd's chapter on the politics of the G20 and Malhotra's chapter on the benefits of South–South cooperation for the Least Developed Countries. Some general texts on social policy in developing countries will have chapters relevant for BRICS analysis, including R. Surender and R. Walker (2013), *Social Policy in a Developing World*, Cheltenham: Edward Elgar; and I. Gough and G. Wood (04), *Insecurity and Welfare Regimes in Asia, Africa and Latin America*, Cambridge: Cambridge University Press. For an interdisciplinary introductory text on BRICS, see V. Lo (2014), *The Rise of the BRICS in the Global Political Economy*, Cheltenham: Edward Elgar.

Review and Assignment Questions

1 Is there a BRICS model of social policy?
2 What are the key trends in social protection policies and instruments in BRICS countries?
3 Does the BRICS group have legitimacy when it comes to global social policy matters?
4 What are the main principles guiding South–South cooperation?
5 What are the challenges to the sustainability of the BRICS alliance in the long term?

Visit the book companion site at www.wiley.com/ go/alcocksocialpolicy to make use of the resources designed to accompany the textbook. There you will find chapter-specific guides to further resources, including governmental, international, thinktank, pressure groups and relevant journal sources. You will also find a glossary based on *The Blackwell Dictionary of Social Policy*, help sheets, guidance on managing assignments in social policy and career advice.

69

Social Policy in the Middle East and North Africa Region

Rana Jawad

▪▪

Overview

- The study of social policy in the Middle East and North Africa Region (MENA) is in its infancy, but the welfare systems of the region may be broadly categorised as corporatist/residual. The Rentier state concept continues to be a salient paradigm.
- A major challenge facing the formulation of social policy in the region is the lack of government commitment to universal social justice and social welfare issues.
- International organisations exercise a major influence on social policy agendas in MENA. They have begun to advocate a new policy discourse around social protection in the region with cash transfer programmes and the extension of social security coverage as key programmes.
- The events of the 'Arab Spring' in 2011 brought a glimmer of positive social change to the region. Four years on, only Tunisia has managed a stable transition, while the rest of the region has fallen prey to new waves of religious extremism and political disintegration.

▪▪

Introduction

This chapter provides a historical and analytical perspective on social policy in MENA societies.

Does it exist? What does it mean? How does it operate? Who provides it and who uses it? These questions underpin this chapter, since it will be clear from very early on that the study of social

The Student's Companion to Social Policy, Fifth Edition. Edited by Pete Alcock, Tina Haux, Margaret May and Sharon Wright.
© 2016 John Wiley & Sons, Ltd. Published 2016 by John Wiley & Sons, Ltd.

Figure 69.1　The geographical area known as the Middle East.
Source: R. Jawad (2010), *Social Welfare and Religion in the Middle East*, Bristol: Policy Press.

policy in MENA is somewhat new, even though in practice governments and civil society organisations have been engaged in social welfare activities since the 1940s (the time of state independence in the region). As the map (Figure 69.1) indicates, the MENA extends from Morocco to Turkey along the southern and eastern shores of the Mediterranean, as far east as Iran and south to Sudan, Saudi Arabia and Yemen. The region has a population of half a billion, which is Muslim in the majority. However, it is home to the world's three largest monotheistic religions, and it continues to have substantial Christian and Jewish populations.

It is worth noting that this is a region still very much in the making: disputes over territorial borders, recognition of ethnic minority status and concerns with nation-building remain alive, with very real implications for whose interests social policy represents. From a Western perspective, the overriding public perception of the MENA as a place of backward social and economic practices and extremist religious ideologies makes it harder to discuss the existence and role of social policy there. The cycle of spiralling violence epitomised by terrorist groups like Islamic State and the political disintegration which is engulfing large numbers of countries, including Syria, Iraq, Yemen and Libya, intensifies the long-held claim of 'Arab/Islamic exceptionalism'. But the academic and policy tides are changing, and somewhat like the turning of a large freight ship, this chapter seeks to dispel some of the myths that surround the study of social policy in MENA, and to provide some useful first understandings of what it means and how it works. Moreover, it argues that social policy as a subject area can greatly contribute to academic knowledge and public understandings of the socio-political dynamics in the MENA. This is because the key units of analysis in social policy, such as social welfare, citizenship, equality, poverty, rights, mixed economy of welfare and human well-being, can allow us to focus on the key dimensions of MENA societies whereby our view of the region becomes more open to beneficial forms of social action.

A Historical Overview: Oil, Independence and Lost Opportunities

With the aims of nation-building and state legit-imisation as their primary objectives, MENA states pursued various policies in the era of inde-pendence (1940s). These had a redistributive char-acter as follows:

■ nationalisation of foreign assets and large domestic enterprises, such as the Suez Canal in Egypt;
■ land reform;
■ mass education and, in some cases, secular-isation of the education system;
■ support of low-income groups through direct financial transfers by the state, with Turkey leading the way

The 1940s and 1950s in the MENA region were therefore deeply imbued with secular and socialist sentiment, the vestiges of which can still be found in countries such as Egypt, Syria and Iraq. Until the 1980s, the region experienced immense social transformations, due almost entirely to the sudden oil windfall. This was used to establish and fund state social services, such as guaranteed govern-ment employment for graduates; new labour legislation (favouring workers in large public enterprises) such as health insurance, retirement pay, maternity pay; free education; free hospital care; and basic consumer subsidies, the most important of which were food and housing. Urbanisation and economic development were accompanied by significant attainments in educa-tion and enhanced female labour participation. But this was a short honeymoon. The easy access to capital that resulted from oil revenues concen-trated wealth amongst the urban elite, and left the majority of the populations poorly skilled and ruled primarily via patrimonial and tribal struc-tures. This reliance on natural resource rents for social spending has earned the welfare regimes of the MENA the label of 'Rentier', which is discussed in the section below.

Theoretical Overview: A New Ethic of Welfare Beyond Rentierism

'Rent' is not 'an earned income' like wages and profit because it does not depend on reward for participation in the process of economic produc-tion. It is a gift resulting from ownership of natural resources. Four key characteristics define the Ren-tier state:

■ rent income dominates the economy;
■ the rent comes from outside of the country;
■ rent wealth is generated by a minority group in the population, but distributed and utilised among the majority;
■ the government is the main receiver of exter-nal rent.

Thus, oil-producing economies such as Saudi Arabia and Kuwait are characteristic examples of Rentier economies. But there is also a Rentier mentality in the region whereby the state becomes a provider of favours and benefits as opposed to the upholder of citizenship rights and obligations. Rentier behaviour can be found in the form of dependence on military or political aid, workers' remittances and tourist expenditure, all of which are forms of external rent.

However, both empirically and analytically, the Rentier concept is inadequate. It misses the way in which the social order is itself negotiated and how the state also exercises influence on the formation of national identity and its symbols. Indeed, a more culturally sensitive analysis of social policy would suggest that non-state actors, especially in

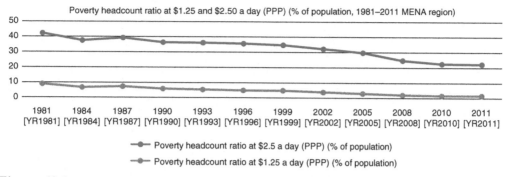

Figure 69.2   Poverty headcount ratio in MENA region, 1981–2011.
Source: World Bank Poverty Database, last accessed 24 August 2015 (povertydata.worldbank.org/poverty/region/MN).

the form of religious movements, have a large stake in the social welfare settlement in the MENA (see Chapter 23).

Beyond the concept of the Rentier state, the welfare regime approach propagated by Esping-Andersen (see Chapter 63) may help to provide some tools for classifying social policy in the MENA. These include the notion of a 'regime' of welfare; the departure from social welfare expenditure as the key denominator of social policy classification; the emphasis on a 'welfare mix' which highlights the role of non-state actors, especially the market; and the political economy approach which allows analysis of power structures and social norms. With regard to the three welfare regime types proposed by Gough et al. (see Chapter 63), it is noteworthy that their study excluded the MENA and they over-emphasise the role of the state in their approach. We should also not forget the issue of terminology; MENA countries tend to speak of an ill-defined 'social sphere' or 'social strategies' as opposed to a fully-fledged welfare state and social policy. Jawad (2009) has begun to develop new conceptual frameworks emphasising the agency of social and political actors and limited legitimacy of governments.

A Brief Socio-Economic Profile of the MENA Region

Economically, the region has the lowest labour force participation rates in the world at 54 per cent in 2010 due to the low level of female participation. It is also experiencing the lowest rate of economic growth, which averaged at 2 per cent in the 1990–2011 period. The growth that has taken place has not led to higher incomes or higher household consumption, which confirms the persistence of social inequalities. Unemployment is estimated at 14.8 per cent for the region, the highest in the world. Vulnerable unemployment as a share of total employment is, however, below the world averages. Estimates of poverty rates vary according to what baselines are used. Generally, the Arab region has among the lowest levels when regression poverty-based lines are used. At 22.1 per cent, poverty levels have remained unchanged since 1990 and are equivalent to those of Europe and Central Asia, though the dynamics impoverishment processes in MENA need to be studied further (UN/LAS, 2013).

Only 30–40 per cent of Arab populations are covered by formal social protection systems. Large swathes of the population are excluded, such as agricultural workers, the self-employed and informal sector workers.

Figure 69.2 gives an overview of poverty trends for populations living below US$1.25 and US$2.50 between 1981 and 2011. These trends show that while the poverty rates are lower on average than other regions of the world, most notably sub-Saharan Africa, the rate of decline has begun to stagnate since 2008, with on average a third of the populations in this region living on less than US$2.50 per day. This signals the ineffectiveness of social policies in the MENA region in addressing the root causes of poverty and social inequalities.

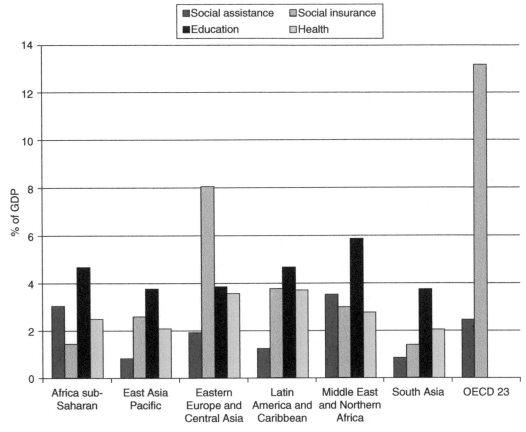

Figure 69.3 Social spending as a percentage of GDP – all regions.
Source: World Bank, 2008.

Revitalising Social Policy in the MENA: The Contemporary Context

The MENA region is providing very similar types of social protection programmes to other world regions and faces many similar challenges to those found in India, China, Brazil and South Africa. These range from cash transfers and targeted social assistance to vulnerable groups to earnings-related social insurance schemes (see Chapters 68 and 70). The appetite for universal social protection schemes in the Arab region is small, with the exception of an over-reliance on inefficient and ineffective food and fuel subsidies. Gulf Cooperation Council (GCC) states have made the biggest strides in extending health insurance, while various other countries such as

Yemen, Jordan and Gaza and West Bank have focused more on improving social assistance programme targeting.

Figure 69.3 shows social expenditure as a percentage of GDP for the MENA region in comparison with other world regions. It shows that education expenditure occupies the largest share of the Arab region countries' GDP and that social insurance remains among the lowest. Figure 69.3 also shows, that after education, spending on social assistance occupies the second largest share of GDP. In fact, the MENA region is considered to be the world's highest spender as a region on social assistance. This situation reinforces the interpretation of social protection in terms of social assistance.

Figure 69.4 shows the distribution of expenditure as part of the Gross Domestic Product (GDP)

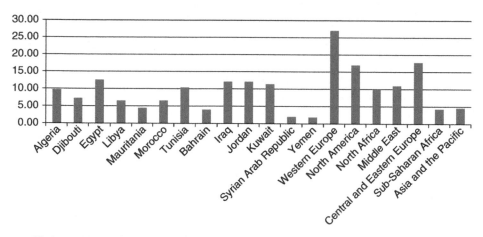

Figure 69.4 Public total expenditure as a percentage of GDP on social protection in Arab countries compared with other world regions.
Source: ILO World Social Security report, 2014–2015 (cited in Jawad, Coutts and Anouar, 2016 forthcoming).

on social protection of the individual MENA societies, ranging from very small proportions in Yemen to more substantial proportions in Iraq, Kuwait, Jordan and Egypt. Yet western Europe, North America and central and eastern Europe spend a substantially higher proportion of their GDP on social protection than any of the MENA societies.

More recently, international development agencies have begun to promote an agenda around social protection in the MENA, which has met with greater interest by MENA governments in part due to the concerns posed by the Arab uprisings, but also as a result of the need to propose new policy objectives in the post-2015 Millennium Development Goals era. New policies are appearing which include the extension of employment-based health insurance, unemployment benefits for university graduates, reform of food and fuel subsidy programmes and unconditional cash transfer programmes. These do not constitute a revolution in social policy but are a step in the right direction, though they are policies that complement a neo-Liberal perspective on social welfare duties and responsibilities.

The emphasis on private sector investment and employment-based social insurance in the MENA is also made clearer when we look at what kinds of social security legislation are available in the region (Table 69.1). These are all employment-based schemes and are primarily restricted to old age, disability and work injury.

Based on the above analysis, the institutional mix of social policy in MENA countries relies heavily on the market, the family, the charitable and religious welfare sector and, finally, a state role that is primarily in the form of financing and less in terms of direct provision.

A Residual/Productivist and Corporatist Approach to Social Policy

In terms of welfare regime analysis, we may pitch MENA countries somewhere between residual and corporatist models. With some minor exceptions of countries with long socialist traditions such as Syria and Egypt, most are now adopting a strong neo-Liberal stance whereby the private sector is the main engine of social and economic prosperity, the state provides social safety nets for poor and vulnerable groups, and the family (mainly the nuclear family) and charitable/religious organisations are expected to play a role in offering social support services. This exemplifies the classic definitions of residual or 'productivist' social policy where economic growth is given priority over more equitable mechanisms of redistribution and universal non-contributory coverage.

Table 69.1   Available data on formal contribution-based social security schemes for selected countries (public and private sector employees only).

Country \ Scheme	Old age	Disability and survivors	Work injury	Unemployment	Sickness	Maternity	Family
Bahrain	X	X	X	X	–	–	–
Iraq*	X	X	X	X	X	X	X
Jordan	X	X	X	–	–	–	–
Kuwait	X	X	X	–	–	–	–
Lebanon	X	X	X	–	–	X	X
Oman	X	X	X	–	–	–	–
Saudi Arabia	X	X	X	–	X	X	–
Syria	X	X	X	–	–	–	–
Yemen	X	X	X	–	X[†]	X[†]	–
Egypt	X	X	X	X[‡]	X	X	–
Morocco	X	X	X	–	X	X	X
Libya	X	X	X	X[‡]	X	X	–
Tunisia	X	X	X	X[‡]	X	X	X
Algeria	X	X	X	X[‡]	X	X	X

Source: International Social Security Association (www.issa.int).

* Information on Iraq is more than ten years old.

[†] Public sector employees only.

[‡] Very strict rules apply.

The Gulf States have traditionally occupied the category of Rentier economies, whereby social welfare provision is primarily funded by oil revenues and is divorced from notions of citizenship rights and obligations. There is evidence of positive intentions in some of the Gulf States to diversify their economies in view of the eventual disappearance of oil and hydrocarbon resources. Indeed, positive moves in societal security in these countries may be found in Bahrain, which has now implemented an unemployment scheme.

But there is also a difficulty in the region in relation to the basic intellectual ground work and policy evaluation process. With the exceptions of Turkey and Israel perhaps, most governments of the MENA do not have clear definitions of poverty or social protection, nor have they developed adequate statistical data to analyse the problem of poverty in their countries. There is a general lack of harmonised social welfare expenditure data. Moreover, the definition of social welfare is based primarily on the fulfilment of human needs as demonstrated by the precedence given to social safety nets in social policy. MENA countries

are far away from the discourse of social rights and citizenship that is more familiar in the West. Yet the focus on needs and social safety nets contradicts government policy rhetoric in some MENA countries that seek to 'help citizens achieve their full potential'. Thus, MENA countries remain socially conservative societies where it is envisaged that the family will play the central role in issues of moral and social identity.

In conclusion, MENA governments have two overarching tendencies in social policy: on the one hand, they are focused on employment-based social security, which means that formally employed private sector workers and the public sector are the most likely to receive protection, primarily in terms of end-of-service indemnity pay, health and education. Indeed, some countries such as Lebanon do not even have old age pension schemes, and when we consider that almost two-thirds of labour is in the informal sector in the MENA region, then the challenge to extend social security becomes even more urgent. On the other hand, there is an over-reliance on social safety nets such as food and fuel subsidies and social care services to vulnerable groups. This exemplifies the other dominant tendency in MENA states, which is the residual/approach that emphasises the role of the family and community groups in social welfare as well as a male-breadwinner model of social protection. Though the inverse of this is that populations in this region enjoy strong social support networks and have the support of their communities in times of need, there are increasing social, demographic and economic pressures that make family and community-based support increasingly problematic.

Emerging Issues

It is an important time for social policy in the MENA both as a field of study and also as a legitimate arm of state action. Some key emerging issues are:

- The more politically stable countries in the region are now engaging with the social protection policy agenda and attempting to set out the kind of societies that they aim to construct. Though modest, and in most cases still favouring a private sector-led economic development path, MENA governments are facing up to the significant socio-economic challenges and problems that their societies now face, which the 'Arab Spring' made even more pronounced. Political will and an articulate plan for social policy have yet to be formulated by most Arab countries in the region.
- How countries move beyond oil revenue to finance social services is a key issue for the future. Iran and the other Gulf countries are keen to find alternative ways of diversifying their economic bases further.
- Political instability in the region stands in the way of social policy: countries such as Iraq, Syria, Yemen and Libya and to some extent Lebanon are partially if not fully consumed by civil conflict, and emergency relief often impedes social policy development. The Syrian refugee crisis is now one of the worst humanitarian crises, and the influx of Syrian refugees to neighbouring countries has posed added pressure on social and public services.

- It is important to conduct further quantitative and qualitative research to produce a classification of the welfare systems in the MENA.

Guide to Further Sources

IPR-MENA social policy network at: www.bath.ac.uk/ipr/our-networks/middle-east-social-policy.

R. El-Ghonemy (1998), *Affluence and Poverty in the MENA*, London: Routledge, provides a comprehensive account of the political, economic and social factors that have produced the contemporary social inequalities in the region. M. Loewe (2004), 'New avenues to be opened for social protection in the Arab world: the case of Egypt', *International Journal of Social Welfare*, 13, 3–14, critically explores the social security system in Egypt.

G. Luciani (ed.) (1990), *The Arab State*, London: Routledge, though out of date, provides an authoritative original analysis of the nature of the Arab state, including Rentierism.

S. P. Heyneman (ed.) (2003), *Islam and Social Policy*, Nashville, TN: Vanderbilt University Press, offers an overview discussion of how Islamic values shape social policies in a variety of Muslim countries, including Iran and Pakistan.

R. Jawad (2009), *Social Welfare and Religion in the MENA: A Lebanese Perspective*, Bristol, Policy Press, gives a detailed empirical analysis of social policy in the MENA region based on a case study of Lebanon (and supplementary research on Egypt, Iran and Turkey) with special focus of the role of religion.

Contributors to M. Karshenas and V. M. Moghadam (eds) (2006), *Social Policy in the MENA: Economic, Political and Gender Dynamics*, United Nations Research Institute for Social Development, Basingstoke: Palgrave Macmillan, discuss social policy from a development perspective in various countries in the MENA.

United Nations Economic and Social Council for Western Asia (2009), *Integrated Social Policy Report III: Visions and Strategies in the ESCWA Region*, UN: New York, gives UNESCWA's perspective on social policy in the region of the MENA.

UN/League of Arab States (2013), *The Arab Millennium Development Goals Report – Facing*

Challenges and Looking Beyond 2015, ESCWA: Beirut.

Review and Assignment Questions

1   What is a Rentier state? Does the concept help or hinder the classification of social policy in the MENA?
2   Why is it important to consider the role of international development institutions such as the World Bank or the United National Development Project (UNDP) when studying social policy in the MENA?
3   How well does Esping-Andersen's typology of welfare regimes help us to understand the nature and scope of social policy in the MENA?
4   What are the shortcomings of a state-centred approach to social policy in the MENA?
5   In what ways do the MENA countries demonstrate corporatist and residual social policies?

Visit the book companion site at www.wiley.com/go/alcocksocialpolicy to make use of the resources designed to accompany the textbook. There you will find chapter-specific guides to further resources, including governmental, international, thinktank, pressure groups and relevant journal sources. You will also find a glossary based on *The Blackwell Dictionary of Social Policy*, help sheets, guidance on managing assignments in social policy and career advice.

70

Social Policy in Less Developed Societies

Patricia Kennett

■▪■▫■▪▫■▫■▪■▫▪■▫■▪▫■▪■▫▪■▫■▪■▫▪■▫■▪■▫▪■▫■▪■▫▪■▫■▪■

Overview

- ■ The study of welfare arrangements in less developed societies is a relatively new and expanding domain within mainstream social policy.
- ■ A range of classification systems have been devised to explore and account for these arrangements.
- ■ International institutions and overseas development assistance play a key role in shaping social policy in less developed societies.
- ■ The scope and role of cash transfer programmes in developing countries have expanded in recent years.
- ■ Growing recognition of the need for more predictable and sustainable forms of social protection and expansion of social assistance programmes.

■▪■▫■▪▫■▫■▪■▫▪■▫■▪▫■▪■▫▪■▫■▪■▫▪■▫■▪■▫▪■▫■▪■▫▪■▫■▪■

Introduction

An understanding of social policy in any part of the world can be achieved most successfully through analyses that incorporate historical, political and economic, as well as social dimensions. This is particularly the case when attempting to understand social policy in less developed societies, where the experiences of colonialism, independence and nation-building, the degree of influence exerted by international financial institutions, and the extent and nature of poverty and inequality have had a major impact on shaping social policy debates and systems of welfare.

There has often been a lack of a clear identity for social policy in less industrialised countries and a much greater emphasis on the broader notion of social development. Since the 1950s,

The Student's Companion to Social Policy, Fifth Edition. Edited by Pete Alcock, Tina Haux, Margaret May and Sharon Wright.

Table 70.1   Country classification by GNI per capita, 2014.

Name	Amount of GNI per capita	Number of countries	'Developing societies'
Low income	Less than $1,045	34	Yes
Lower middle income	$1,045–$4,125	50	Yes
Upper middle income	$4,126–$12,735	55	No
High income	More than $12,736	75	No

Source: World Bank, 2015 (data.worldbank.org/about/country-and-lending-groups).

the main tenet of development thinking has been premised, either explicitly or implicitly, on the role of modernisation as a vehicle for facilitating economic growth through urbanisation, industrialisation and capital investment. The phrase itself and the perceived strategies for achieving it have implied the desirability of adopting a unilinear and universal development trajectory replicating and perpetuating the structures and systems dominant in Western industrial countries to the developing world. The development discourse has, until recently, tended to subordinate or subsume social policy within economic policy and to focus on homogeneity across developing societies, rather than diversity. The first section of this chapter will examine the conceptual distinctions that have been used to define, categorise and separate different parts of the world (see Chapter 63). It will then go on to distinguish patterns of welfare, focusing specifically on Latin America and Africa. The role of international institutions and overseas development aid (ODA) in relation to the shaping of social policy instruments, and the growing interest in and expansion of social protection programmes, will then be considered. The discussion concludes with a consideration of future challenges for less developed societies and the role of social policy in sustainable development.

Concepts and Categories

A variety of imprecise and inconsistent conceptual distinctions have been used to categorise and differentiate areas of the globe, such as First–Third World, Developed–Developing, North–South, industrialised–less industrialised, which have usually involved poorer countries being contrasted, negatively, with the more developed, advanced, industrialised, richer countries of the North.

The World Bank's main criterion for classifying countries is the size of their economy measured by gross national income (GNI) per capita, with every country classified as low income, middle income (subdivided into lower middle and upper middle) or high income (see Table 70.1). In 1971, the United Nations (UN) established the Least Developed Countries group. At the time, twenty-four countries were identified as having a low per capita income, a low level of human resource development based on indicators of nutrition, health, and education and adult literacy, and a high degree of economic vulnerability. In 2013, fifty countries were designated by the UN as the Least Developed Countries, of which thirty-four were in Africa, ten in Asia, five in Australasia and the Pacific, and one in the Caribbean, representing a projected total population of 950 million people in 2015.

Social Policy in Context

The developing world incorporates a range of diversity in terms of colonial history, political profile, social structure, levels of development, and state and institutional capacity. As one might expect, social policy instruments are wide ranging and, as well as more traditional welfare measures, have come to include land reform, subsidy for food and water, and the regulation of the private sector. The choice and combination of instruments are likely to be unique to each country, as they involve the interplay of a range of forces, including ideological predisposition, institutional structures, and the political and economic context.

A major factor impacting on the structures of provision and choice of social policy instruments has been the history and current context of geopolitical relationships between the North and the

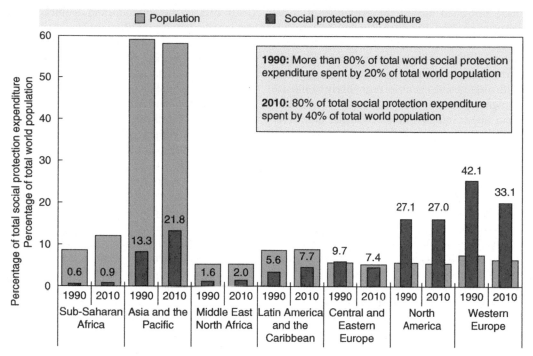

Figure 70.1 Percentage of total world social protection expenditure and of total world population across country groups in 1990 and 2010.
Source: OECD (2014), *Society at a Glance: Asia/Pacific*, available at: dx.doi.org/10.1787/9789264220553-en, last accessed 13 March 2015.

South, which have manifested through imperialism, colonialism, the institutionalisation of relations of political and economic dependency, and development strategies and programmes which have in combination aggravated and perpetuated ethnic and religious tensions and conflict, and contributed to many of the negative aspects of social life in Africa, Asia and Latin America.

Figure 70.1 gives an indication of the distribution of total world population and social protection expenditure across country groups in 1990 and 2010. It demonstrates that social protection expenditure distribution has become slightly more equal, a shift that can be accounted for by the gradual development of more comprehensive social protection systems in developing counties, mainly middle-income countries of Asia and Latin America. The figure also highlights the wide disparities in social sector spending between different regions. In general, western European countries spend an average of 25 per cent of Gross Domestic Product (GDP) on the social sector, compared

with 12.5 per cent in Latin America and the Caribbean, and 8.7 per cent in sub-Saharan Africa (OECD, 2015). The widest disparities in expenditure between regions are found in the area of social protection, which include, for example, pensions, unemployment and disability benefits. In western European countries, approximately 18 per cent of GDP is spent on social security, compared with approximately 8 per cent in Latin American countries (LACs) and approximately 4 per cent in sub-Saharan Africa. The development and maintenance of social security systems require, in the first instance, an appropriate and complex infrastructure, state capacity and a formal labour market through which to raise and collect taxes to finance social sector programmes and to implement them. Poorer countries are usually characterised by limited state capacity and infrastructure, and budget and policy restrictions, particularly from international financial institutions (IFIs). In addition, traditional labour structures, and massive and chronic levels of poverty and inequality, have mitigated against the evolution of social security systems. The disparities in health spending are not so great, but there is still variation between different regions of the world. The pattern is a little different in the case of education, with low-income countries more likely to allocate a higher proportion of their GDP to education than upper middle-income countries and lower middle-income countries. This highlights the trend towards growing investment in education in poorer countries.

Policy Issues and Regimes

Whilst the aggregate data introduced above provides a useful starting point for analysing social policy in less developed countries, more important is an appreciation of the structures of welfare, its composition, and the complex and changing patterns of relationships between different producers. Although patterns of social policy across the South vary depending on each country's distinctive historical pathway, focusing on Latin America and Africa, it is possible to identify two broad categories of social policy and welfare system, which can be characterised as clientelistic and residual (see Chapters 63 and 71). These different models can be linked to the levels of regulatory and institutional capacity achieved by particular states and the ways in which society has been organised.

The *clientelistic model*, predominant in Latin America, emerged as a consequence of the power of elites and interest groups and their ability to 'colonise' the state apparatus. Welfare systems developed relatively early in Latin America compared with other developing regions, and by the 1980s many countries in the region had long-standing, and in some cases well-developed, formal welfare. Whilst social assistance has remained underdeveloped, formal social insurance programmes were introduced during the first half of the twentieth century and focused on providing insurance for specific groups of workers through earnings-related contributions. Barrientos (2004) highlights the importance of the extensive array of employment protection regulation, and its key role as a central component of the Latin American 'welfare mix'. Whilst there have been aspirations towards the universal provision of education and healthcare, the adverse economic conditions in the 1980s curtailed this ambition, and significant gaps and inequalities in provision remain.

The *clientelistic model of welfare*, which Barrientos categorises as 'a liberal-informal welfare regime', can be characterised as occupationally stratified in terms of social insurance and employment protection, and highly segmented in health insurance and healthcare provision. For the most part, this model benefits only a small proportion of the population who are in privileged positions in the formal sector. The majority of those in rural areas, and those who attempt to earn a living in the urban informal sector and their households (approximately 52 per cent of the population in Latin America), are excluded. Thus, the majority of the population relies on informal support networks to protect them against social risk, and the sparse networks linked to national and international non-governmental organisations (for a discussion of the role of international organisations in developing countries, please refer to Chapter 71).

Residual social policy and welfare systems are most evident across much of Africa, particularly sub-Saharan Africa, the origins of which can be located in the history and experience of colonial rule through which the first limited social services were introduced. Akin Aina (1999) has argued that the expansion of formal social policy under the colonial administration was largely determined by economic factors and the exploitation of the resources of the colonies, as well as the maintenance of social order. Social policy provision was minimal, residual and discriminatory, and more concerned with providing for the needs of, and thus supporting, the colonial administration. Following independence in the 1960s and 1970s, social policy was to play an important role in legitimising many post-colonial governments, with the development of social programmes in education, housing, health, and price subsidies and controls. This was supported by the Keynesian model of development, dominant up until the 1970s, which incorporated a combination of international economic laissez faire and state intervention to promote economic development, the social rights of the population and social order. Social policy measures were seen as appropriate and desirable and, in tandem with economic growth, were key instruments for social development and the elimination of poverty.

Development, International Institutions and Social Policy

By the early 1980s, the perception that the relationship between macro-economic policy and social policy could be a positive one had been completely rejected and devalued. Most countries in Latin America and Africa were experiencing a decline in economic growth rates, high inflation levels, a growing debt burden and an increasingly competitive international environment compared with the 1970s. The Debt Crisis and economic decline became the key issues across the globe, and rolling back the state, reducing public expenditure, privatisation, the elimination of subsidies and opening up economies became fundamental components of the development paradigm.

The dominant discourse emerging at the global level was that the problems of development were primarily ones of economic (mis-)management, inefficiency and state corruption. From this perspective, improvements in social policy could only flow from improved economic performance. This was a reflection of the new economic orthodoxy emerging in the North, which was subsequently transmitted to developing societies through the influential IFIs and promoted monetarist economic policy, deregulation and privatisation. These themes were reflected at the global level and a consensus emerged on the most appropriate model of economic and political management for developing countries, including deregulation, privatisation of state-run organisations, liberalisation of the economy, the free market and retrenching of the public sector. There was also the commitment to channel aid through non-governmental organisations, rather than through country governments (see Chapter 37). This package of measures has often been termed the 'Washington Consensus', a phrase coined by economist John Williamson in 1990 when referring to appropriate development strategies for South America. Its strategies were promoted by global institutions and the most powerful state players, and took the form of structural adjustment programmes through which loans to poor countries were conditional on policy changes proposed by the World Bank.

By the end of the 1990s, there was recognition that structural adjustment had done little to improve the economic circumstances and social well-being of people in less developed countries. A radical rethinking of the national and international policies needed to tackle the problems of poor countries that were failing to prosper was called for by civil society organisations and national governments in both the North and the South. There was a shift in the terrain of intervention from the economic to the political sphere as the term 'governance' became a dominant theme in international institutions. There was also a growing recognition and the emergence of a global discourse that social rights should be respected in the development process, and that poverty reduction should be adopted as a central objective of international development cooperation. IFIs, such as the World Bank, began to incorporate much more explicit references to poverty reduction and social development in their approach to concessional assistance to low-income countries, and, in 2000, 189 UN member states agreed a set of specific targets for reducing poverty, hunger, disease, gender inequality, illiteracy and environmental degradation, which were incorporated in the Millennium Development Goals. Yet the BRICS countries (Brazil, Russia, India, China and South Africa) are playing an increasingly important role in this region and their economic links and aid efforts are firmly based on the old maxim of focusing on economic development first and foremost (see Chapter 68).

Many developing countries, particularly the less developed countries, are highly dependent on external resources. However, there has been increasing concern that the amount of aid from richer countries is failing to reach specified targets or to match pledges made by national governments. In addition to concerns about the quantity of aid, the quality of overseas development aid has also been called into question. Aid is often unpredictable, has numerous strings attached and usually involves the recipient incurring transaction costs. According to the UN, international aid continues to be underused, inefficiently targeted and in need of repair. The practice of tied aid, linking development assistance to the provision of supplies and services provided by the donor country, remains widely prevalent, as does the economic conditionality imposed by IFIs.

Table 70.2   Examples of large-scale cash transfer programmes in operation, 2014.

China	Minimum Living Standards Scheme	22 million (2006)
Mexico	Oportunidades (began in 1997)	5 million households
Brazil	Bolsa Familia	12 million households
	Old Age Pension	2.4 million households (2008)
South Africa	Child Support Grant	Expected to reach 10 million children by end 2009
	Old Age Pension	2.4 million households (2009)
Indonesia	Safety Net Scheme	Expected to reach 15 million households
India	National Rural Employment Guarantee Scheme	48 million households (2008)
Ethiopia	Productive Safety Nets Programme (PSNP)	1.5 million households (est. 8 million people)

Source: DFID (2011), 'Cash Transfers', Evidence Paper Policy Division, London: Department for International Development.

Extending Social Protection

More recently there has been a growing interest in the provision of social protection in developing countries, accompanied by an interest in the potential of cash transfer programmes to alleviate poverty and as an instrument through which to address the Millennium Development Goals and post-2015 Development Agenda that is cost-effective and fiscally sustainable. The system of delivering social assistance originated in Brazil in 1995, but has expanded through Latin America and the Caribbean, and to Africa where the National Social Protection strategy incorporates the commitment to the provision of basic social assistance through cash transfer programmes (see Table 70.2; see also Chapter 68 on the BRICS countries).

Over fifty national cash transfer programmes have been established globally and cover between 750 million and 1 billion people in the developing world. The expansion of these programmes has, in part, been a result of the recognition of the need for regular and predictable social protection programmes, rather than dependency on repeated humanitarian intervention and intermittent and unpredictable aid. Cash transfer programmes vary in their scope, aim to protect the very poorest in a society and promote human capital development. Conditional cash transfer programmes impose certain requirements on potential beneficiaries, such as school attendance, immunisation and visits to health clinics, and are more fully developed in Latin America than in sub-Saharan Africa. Whilst initial evaluations have shown positive results in terms of school enrolment, levels of immunisation and attendance at health centres, there is some concern regarding the quality and quantity of education and health services received by recipients and their long-term impact. Whilst the impact and extent of these programmes should not be over-stated, nor problems with implementation and conditionality overlooked, cash transfers could be viewed as the foundation of a broader commitment to strengthening and integrating systems of social protection in less developed countries.

Emerging Issues: Crisis, Human Security and Sustainable Development

The focus of this chapter has been on developing societies, a contested concept and a category that incorporates enormous diversity and heterogeneity. Nevertheless, the recent global financial crisis, combined with rising food prices and concerns regarding the impact of global warming, has highlighted the inadequacies of the existing development paradigm and its inability to enhance and sustain well-being for a substantial proportion of men, women and children living in the South. Historically, the highest levels of income inequality have been found in Africa and Latin America, a situation that worsened during the

Table 70.3   Number of countries with rising and falling income inequality by region, early 1990s to late 2000s.

Region	Falling	No change	Rising	All
Africa	16	3	7	26
Arab States	3	1	2	6
A&P	5	2	6	13
ECIS	2	1	16	19
LAC	8	5	7	20
Low- and middle-income countries	**34**	**12**	**38**	**84**

Source: UNDP calculations using data from Solt (2009).

1980s and 1990s. However, as Table 70.3 shows, trajectories of inequality are not linear, with a decline in income inequality in a number of countries in sub-Saharan Africa since the late 1990s, and in Latin America since the early 2000s. Nevertheless, 'the majority of the world's population is still living in countries with stable or rising inequality' (UNDP, 2014). Drivers of income inequality and vulnerability include the impacts and dynamics of global economic integration into world trade and financial markets, as well as an over-emphasis on macro-economic policies and price stability, rather than on labour market and social policy reforms, progressive taxation and public investment (see Chapter 68).

Whilst recognising the specificity of individual developing counties, the chapter has also considered more general trends in social policy development, particularly in terms of the relationship between North and South and the role of international institutions. The challenge for the international community, national governments and civil society is overcoming the democratic deficit evident in international institutions, strengthening the voice of developing country representatives, reforming the aid infrastructure and exhibiting a genuine commitment to social policy and sustainable development. A deepening and widening of appropriate country-owned social protection programmes, combined with an improvement in access to and the quality of health and educational services, as well as labour market opportunities would provide the multidimensional framework through which to support human security and sustainable development and address the multidimensional nature of vulnerability and disadvantage in developing countries. Social policy not only has the capacity to contribute to social capital and social cohesion, but also can play a significant role in reinforcing the legitimacy of the political order and contributing to political stability.

Guide to Further Sources

The many issues and debates touched on in this chapter are explored in United Nations Development Programme (2013), *Humanity Divided: Confronting Inequality in Developing Countries*, New York: UN Bureau for Development Policy; T. Akin Aina (1999), 'West and central Africa: social policy for reconstruction and development', in D. Morales-Gomez (ed.), *Transnational Social Policies. The New Development Challenges of Globalisation*, Earthscan: London; I. Gough and G. Wood, with A. Barrientos, P. Bevan, P. Davis and G. Room (2004), *Insecurity and Welfare Regimes in Asia, Africa and Latin America*, Cambridge: Cambridge University Press (which includes A. Barrientos' chapter 'Latin America: a liberal-informal welfare regime?').

Some useful general sources include R. Surender and R. Walker (eds) (2013), *Social Policy in a Developing World*, Cheltenham: Edward Elgar; R. Holmes and N. Jones (2013), *Gender and Social Protection in the Developing World. Beyond Mothers and Safety Nets*, London: Zed Books; and A. Hall and J. Midgley (2004), *Social Policy for Development*, London: Sage.

International governmental and non-governmental organisations, such as the UN Development Programme (UNDP), the UN Research Institute for Social Development (www.unrisd.org), the

World Bank (www.worldbank.org), the International Labour Organization (www.ilo.org), and the World Health Organization (www.who.int), as well as Oxfam International (www.oxfam.org) and Save the Children (www.savethechildren.org), produce substantial amounts of material on developing societies, much of which is relevant to the study of social policy.

Review and Assignment Questions

1 What have been the role and impact of international institutions in shaping social policy in developing countries?
2 How effective has social policy been in promoting well-being in developing countries?
3 Are cash transfers the answer to vulnerability and inequality?
4 Are categorisations of different parts of the globe or types of welfare systems helpful in developing social policies to address vulnerability and inequality?
5 What are the drivers of inequality and vulnerability in developing countries and how can they be overcome?

Visit the book companion site at www.wiley.com/go/alcocksocialpolicy to make use of the resources designed to accompany the textbook. There you will find chapter-specific guides to further resources, including governmental, international, thinktank, pressure groups and relevant journal sources. You will also find a glossary based on *The Blackwell Dictionary of Social Policy*, help sheets, guidance on managing assignments in social policy and career advice.

71

Globalisation, International Organisations and Social Policy

Nicola Yeates

Overview

■ Globalisation has brought International Organisations (IOs) to the foreground of social policy.

■ There are many different kinds of IO. Some are primarily oriented towards economic objectives and concerns, others towards social objectives.

■ IO are key social policy actors; they:
- ■ shape the (re)distribution of resources within and between countries,
- ■ finance, regulate and provide welfare goods and services,
- ■ promulgate ideas about what kinds of social policies are needed, and
- ■ influence the content of national social policies.

■ IOs have a key role to play in bringing about a democratically governed global economy based on social justice for as long as social inequality and poverty exist.

■ Thinking globally challenges traditional ways of thinking about social policy concepts such as fairness, choice, reciprocity and obligations.

The Student's Companion to Social Policy, Fifth Edition. Edited by Pete Alcock, Tina Haux, Margaret May and Sharon Wright.
© 2016 John Wiley & Sons, Ltd. Published 2016 by John Wiley & Sons, Ltd.

Globalisation and the Study of Social Policy

'Globalisation' is the term given to economic, technological, cultural, social, and political forces and processes that are said to have collectively produced the characteristic conditions of contemporary life. Foremost among these characteristics are dense and extensive economic, political, and social interconnections and interdependencies routinely transcending international state borders. The economic and social dynamics these unleash impact on human welfare, welfare states, the content of social and economic policy and policymaking processes.

The kinds of trans-border connectedness we are witnessing presently is different than in previous periods. The interconnections are expressed in ways that appear to 'bring together' geographically distant localities worldwide, with events happening in one part of the world able to quickly reach and affect other parts. The global financial crisis of 2007–8 illustrated how fluctuations in one economy quickly reverberate around the world, jeopardising economic security on a mass scale.

This 'enmeshment' is said to give rise to consciousness of the world as a shared place. Social issues are increasingly perceived as global in scope and require global solutions. Key social, economic and environmental issues are beyond the scope of any one individual country to address by itself, and this is generating forms of concerted coordination and cooperation in the form of global institutions. International Organisations (IOs) function as shared platforms and fora in which countries debate how to address common social and economic issues and collectively govern themselves. Much of what is discussed in these fora pertains to social policy, while IOs develop their own proposed responses to these questions (Box 71.1).

International Organisations and Global Governance

IOs have been active in social security and health policy since the early twentieth century, but the number of IOs and scope of their social policy competences have grown since the end of the Second World War when the Bretton Woods

Box 71.1 Globalisation and Social Policy

- The causes of many current social policy issues reside outside the control of any one country, but their effects can have worldwide effects.
- Cross-border flows of goods, services, capital, ideas and people link economies and welfare systems in a multitude of ways.
- New forms of cross-border collective action are needed to address the causes of key social policy issues and responses to them.
- International organisations instantiate how cross-border forms of collective action are being developed to address social problems.
- Governments, civil society organisations, business groups, professional organisations, trade unions and social movements act upon and through IOs to influence how social issues are framed, and which social policy issues should be addressed and how.
- As global actors are brought into social policymaking so new alliances and coalitions emerge within and between countries (regionally and globally) around key social policy issues. In seeking to bringing about social change through social policy reform they reframe national issues as global ones, propose solutions to identified issues and change the balance of power between and within countries.

institutions and an international trade regime, the General Agreement on Tariffs and Trade (GATT), were established. IOs grew from about seventy in 1940 and now number more than a thousand. They are central in the system of global governance – the complex legal, institutional and political framework of public and private international agreements, treaties, regulations and accords that regulate social, political and economic life worldwide.

Table 71.1   Examples of global and regional IGOs and INGOs.

IGOs	INGOs
Global	
World Bank (WB); International Monetary Fund (IMF); United Nations (UN) and its agencies, e.g. International Labour Organization (ILO), World Health Organization (WHO).	World Economic Forum; World Water Forum; International Confederation of Free Trade Unions; International Planned Parenthood Federation; Oxfam; International Pharmaceutical Industries Association.
Regional	
European Union (EU); North American Free Trade Agreement (NAFTA); ASEAN (Association of South East Asian Nations).	European Services Forum; European Trade Union Confederation; Asian Social Forum, African Social Forum.

International *governmental* organisations (IGOs) are international fora through which sovereign governments enter into collaborative political and legal relationships. International *non-governmental* organisations (INGOs) are entities through which voluntary, charitable, trade union, professional associations, industry organisations and business groups operate internationally. Some IOs operate on a worldwide scale; others do so on a regional scale (Table 71.1).

IOs vary considerably in terms of power and resources, and this affects how effective they are in realising their policy objectives (Table 71.2). INGOs can command significant budgets and may be better staffed than some IGOs (compare, for example, the WTO's 630 staff with Oxfam's

Table 71.2   Examples of social governance at national, world-regional and global levels.

	National	EU	Global
Economic stability	Central banks	European Central Bank in Eurozone	IMF/Bank of International Settlements
Revenue	Taxation	Customs revenues, plus member state donations (note discussion of tax harmonisation)	Mix of UN appeals, ad hoc global funds, multilateral overseas development assistance
Redistribution	Tax and income transfers policy	Structural funds, Common Agricultural Policy	Ad hoc humanitarian relief, special global funds, debt relief, differential pricing of drugs
Regulation	State laws and directives	EU laws, regulations and directives, including Social Charter	UN conventions, WTO trade law, Corporate codes of conduct
Citizenship rights	Court redress, Consumer charters, Tripartite governance	Court redress, Tripartite governance	UN Commission for Human Rights but no legal redress

Source: Yeates (2010), adapted from Deacon (2003).

2,800 staff). Some IGOs have no independent legal force or permanent secretariat; others have the force of international law behind them (WTO, EU, UN) and/or substantial bureaucracies (ILO, WB, EU, UN).

International Governmental Organisations (IGOs)

IGOs have a substantial role in regulating, financing and providing health, education and welfare services. The UN and its agencies (for example, ILO, WHO) have a regulatory role through international social standard-setting. Forms of international welfare financing are instantiated through regional social funds, international development loans and international development aid. International trade treaties, such as the WTO's General Agreement on Trade in Services (GATS), stipulate what kinds of public regulation, finance and provision are lawful and what are not. The EU is the most 'advanced' regional organisation in terms of social policy, though many others around the world have also developed an active role in social policy (see Chapter 46). All IGOs struggle with the question of how to achieve a balance between economic growth, social equity, social solidarity, democratic rule and environmental sustainability.

International Non-Governmental Organisations (INGOs)

INGOs are involved in all parts of the global policymaking process, from agenda-setting through to policy implementation. Some enjoy official consultative status, working, for instance, through various UN and World Bank NGO committees. They play a key role in delivering global social programmes, notably humanitarian aid, as they can provide access to areas and populations that IGOs cannot always reach. They also fill gaps in provision for poor, rural and conflict-ridden communities where political and economic conditions do not attract for-profit providers. Some INGOs play prominent advocacy roles, whereas others are involved more at the level of service provision. Philanthropic organisations are amongst the largest and most influential INGOs. The Melinda & Bill Gates Foundation is a major contributor to global health funding.

The growing influence of INGOs in global policymaking is sometimes seen as heralding a 'global civil society' and the democratisation and socialisation of global politics. Certainly, INGOs and the social movements from which they emerge have been at the forefront of campaigns against neo-Liberal globalisation and the protection of social rights. At the same time, their involvement in global policymaking can promote the values of self-interest, hard work, freedom of choice, private property and a distrust of state bureaucracy. As many INGOs are associations of industrial and for-profit organisations, an enhanced role in global policy formation may amplify commercial interests and facilitate welfare residualisation, privatisation and corporatisation.

Impacts of International Organisations on Social Policy

There are four principal ways in which IOs shape the content of social policy. They can:

1 provide a forum for mutual education, analysis and debate, which promotes shared analyses and beliefs that inform policy debate and provide a platform for future collaboration;
2 define international social standards and common frameworks for national social policy (for example, UN human rights charters, the ILO's labour conventions and the WHO's health conventions);
3 provide resources to support policy development and implementation (for example, stimulus finance, technical assistance, policy advice and expertise); and
4 promote regulatory reform; for example, promoting labour mobility removes some restrictions on cross-border migration and stimulates the development of entitlements to migrants' social security and healthcare abroad.

The social policy impacts of IOs' economic policies may be far-reaching. Policies that enable the 'free' movement of capital may trigger a competitive welfare 'race to the bottom' as countries compete to attract overseas investment by lowering their social (labour) standards. Creating international markets in welfare goods and services that enable more affluent groups to opt out of public provision and into private (commercial) provision to meet their welfare needs may undermine the kinds of cross-class social solidarity that were historically important to the development of welfare states.

IOs are often seen as all-powerful, but they are not universally successful in achieving their objectives. Their successes vary considerably between different policy areas and countries. Governments often seem able to selectively choose from a range of proposals and courses of action offered to them by IOs. However, sometimes IOs place strong pressure on governments to steer them along certain social policy paths, inducing them by providing financial aid or threatening penalties and sanctions. The World Bank and its allies have been highly influential in persuading a range of countries to privatise their pensions systems. However, they were not universally successful in all cases, while some of the early adopters of pension privatisation have since reversed those reforms. Leftist electoral successes and the sustained efforts of social movements have been an important factor in countries where this has happened.

In sum, IOs actively participate in the political and policy processes shaping:

- the terms of international trade, aid and development policies;
- the allocation and use of aid, development and social funds;
- international social standards and norms; and
- the definition of which social policy reform initiatives are effective, affordable and desirable.

IOs also oversee and are sometimes directly involved in the implementation of social policies and programmes. Through these activities they:

- shape the distribution and redistribution of resources worldwide;
- frame social policy debate in national and global spheres of governance;
- influence the nature of social provision in individual countries; and
- contribute to social policy outcomes: who gets what resources, how people are treated, under what conditions and with what effects.

Social Policy Concepts in a Global Context

Equality, Rights and Justice

Thinking globally about equality, rights and justice necessitates asking to what extent the world is a 'fair' place. Is it socially just that access to resources, life chances, opportunity and quality of life are determined by which country you happen to be born in or live in, rather than by hard work, skill, talent or merit (see Chapters 4 and 5)? What would be a just basis for participation and representation in the institutions of global governance? Northern states have more voting rights in Bretton Woods institutions than those in the South, while the UN is often also criticised for being dominated by the North (in particular the US). The WTO at least enshrines formal political equality between member countries, though in practice this is not realised.

We might also consider differences in the extent to which citizenship rights are differentially embodied and guaranteed by global institutions. The Council of Europe provides European citizens with the right to equal treatment before the European Court of Human Rights in Strasbourg; the UN identifies similar rights through the International Covenant on Economic, Social and Cultural Rights and the Declaration of Human Rights, but it has no mechanism for their legal enforcement nor does it allow individual rights of petition. Some international treaties (for example, WTO GATS, NAFTA) have established enforceable corporate trade and investment rights, but eschewed citizen social and labour rights.

To what extent are social rights inherent rights that attach to all human beings, irrespective of cultural and economic context? 'Cosmopolitans' argue that some or all of the presently defined labour standards defined by the ILO Philadelphia Declaration (1944) are universal rights. 'Nationalists' advocate a kind of global relativism, arguing that it is for individual countries and communities to decide what constitutes an appropriate set of rights and what mix of rights carry corresponding social obligations.

Efficiency, Equity and Choice

In a global context, debates about efficiency, equity and choice become a discussion about whether global production and trade should be subject to 'social rules' (see Chapter 6). 'Free' trade advocates argue that international trade is the best way of improving individual and collective welfare, as globally competitive countries and businesses will attract more investment, and more jobs will be created. Critics point to how global competition often involves the super-exploitation of vulnerable labour forces, especially in poorer countries, and how rich Northern countries maintain protectionist trade regimes while demanding that developing countries dismantle theirs. 'Free trade' policies may encourage countries to engage in competitive social deregulation to attract foreign investment or prevent capital flight overseas, and in other measures which produce inefficient, sub-optimal social and economic outcomes.

Some advocates of 'free trade' policies are beginning to appreciate the benefits of certain kinds of social regulation, if only to avoid the damaging effects of political activism against consumer goods produced by exploited labour. But attempts to establish coherent global social regulation have seen limited success, and recent regulatory measures have inscribed principles of voluntarism. The OECD Guidelines for Multinational Enterprises set out principles for socially oriented business practices, but corporations can choose whether to observe them or not. Voluntary codes of corporate conduct have proliferated, but monitoring their implementation relies on the efforts of resource-limited NGOs.

Altruism, Reciprocity and Obligation

Altruism, reciprocity and obligation are enshrined in many of the policies and programmes of IOs and international agreements. The World Bank embodies these insofar as it finances development projects in poorer countries, while the UNHCR has overall responsibility for the care of refugees worldwide. Other examples of global social solidarity are a target of 0.7 per cent of Gross National Income that countries should allocate for Overseas Development Assistance (ODA), debt relief packages for low-income highly indebted countries, and the Millennium Development Goals (MDGs) and their successor, the Sustainable Development Goals (SDGs). International financing of social goods includes international

agreements on the differential pricing of drugs. The WHO has a global ethical code of conduct to regulate the international recruitment of medical personnel.

Philanthropic and charitable (including faith-based) groups play an important role. Northern foundations (Ford, Volkswagen, Soros, Gates) fund global programmes of social research and social provision. Many of the recently created global funds and programmes, such as GAVI (the global vaccinations programme) and the Global fund to Fight AIDS, Tuberculosis and Malaria (GFATM), are financed by the private sector. UNICEF's activities and campaigns (for example, Save the Children appeals) receive charitable, citizen and commercial finance.

Do these expressions of altruism, obligation and humanitarianism amount to little more than donor self-interest? Grant aid often contains conditions requiring the purchase of goods and services of businesses based in the donor country, so many of the benefits flow back to the donor country. Donor influence on the policies of recipient countries has also been raised as a concern. Whether mandatory forms of social regulation and redistribution underpinned by clear financial commitments and targets should replace the reliance on voluntarism and philanthropy, and whether the aim should actually be to strengthen the trading position of poorer countries rather than encourage them to rely on donor aid are regularly debated.

Global Social Reform

Addressing the weaknesses of IOs is an indispensable part of global social policy reform campaigns. One problem with IGOs is that while they may have commendable social policy objectives, they do not possess the state-like powers needed to realise them. There is no centralised international mechanism to negotiate and enforce treaty obligations worldwide and there is no coherent means for legal redress by aggrieved citizens. There is no central bank. IGOs do not have independent revenue-raising powers and are dependent on donor funding. The IMF comes closest to a nascent international state insofar as it carries out a number of state functions, such as the allocation of funds and the regulation of some aspects of international finance, but it lacks the political resources and coercive capacities of states.

A reformed, democratised UN system is regarded by some as the best means for developing a more coherent and effective global social policy. An independent source of funding (perhaps out of global taxes) and stronger legal powers could strengthen its hand as a global social policy actor, capable of instituting a coherent and progressive approach to social development founded on human rights. Others argue that reforming existing organisations does not go far enough and that entirely new kinds of international organisation need to be constructed. Either way, there is a good deal of agreement that the representation of poorer and developing countries in them needs to be addressed as a priority. While some campaigners look forward to the reinvention of global organisations, others seek an enhanced role for regional associations of nations in developing social policies more attuned to the needs of the populations of the region concerned.

Others are sceptical about the extent to which IOs (whether on a global or world-regional scale, new or reformed) can ever work in the long-term interests of social development and instead seek to dismantle them. 'De-globalisers' would prefer to promote smaller-scale, localised and diversified economies governed by institutions closest to the populations concerned. This would involve inventing (or returning to) forms of economic and social organisation that are hooked into, but not dominated by, outside forces. The impending ecological crisis and the search for alternative models of social and economic development mean these ideas are gaining ground.

Emerging Issues

The failure of the global regulatory system to prevent the global financial crisis of 2007–8 and the troika's ('troika', the tripartite committee led by the European Commission with the European Central Bank and the International Monetary Fund) role in supporting (and prolonging) post-crash austerity in Europe and beyond intensify the need for IOs to define pathways for social sustainability. The environmental and ecological limits to economic growth models require IOs (and others) to revisit their expectations and assumptions

about the nature of development and its relationship to human welfare. The successes and failures of global policy in relation to the Millennium Development Goals will need to be applied as the Sustainable Development Goals are implemented post-2015. Probing questions will need to continue to be asked about the efficacy and desirability of commercial and philanthropic responses to global inequality and poverty. In a world marked by severe social and economic inequality, universal access to adequate shelter, income, medicines, healthcare, education, clean water, food and sanitation will continue to be at the forefront of campaign agendas, together with questions about how to finance this sustainably and on the scale needed.

Guide to Further Sources

Two student texts discuss the themes and issues covered in this chapter: N. Yeates (2014), *Understanding Global Social Policy*, Bristol: The Policy Press, provides an accessible introduction to key issues and debates in a wide range of global policy areas, while N. Yeates and C. Holden (2009), *The Global Social Policy Reader*, Bristol: Policy Press, collates key readings. You can also consult N. Yeates (2012), 'Global social policy', in John Baldock et al. (eds), *Social Policy*, 4th edn, Oxford: Oxford University Press; R. Deacon (2007), *Global Social Policy and Governance*, London: Sage; and V. George and P. Wilding (2002), *Globalisation and Human Welfare*, Basingstoke: Palgrave. *Global Social Policy: Journal of Public Policy and Social Development* (Sage) covers a wide range of issues discussed in this chapter. For further information about the Millennium Development Goals (MDGs), see: www.unmillenniumproject .org/goals. Information about the Sustainable Development Goals, adopted September 2015, can be found at: sustainabledevelopment.un.org/ focussdgs.html.

Review and Assignment Questions

1   Why are IOs important in the study of social policy?
2   How are IOs important in shaping social policy as a political practice?

3 How influential are IOs in matters of social policy?

4 Social policy concepts are often developed and discussed in relation to national welfare states. How can these be adapted to the global dimensions of social policy?

5 What are the key challenges for social policy in a globalising world? Are international organisations and the international community addressing them? How are they doing this? What more should they be doing? What should they be doing differently?

Visit the book companion site at www.wiley.com/go/alcocksocialpolicy to make use of the resources designed to accompany the textbook. There you will find chapter-specific guides to further resources, including governmental, international, thinktank, pressure groups and relevant journal sources. You will also find a glossary based on *The Blackwell Dictionary of Social Policy*, help sheets, guidance on managing assignments in social policy and career advice.

Appendix: The Social Policy Association

The Social Policy Association (SPA) is the professional association for academics, researchers and students in social policy and administration. It was founded in 1972 and has a large membership in the UK and, increasingly, internationally. Its aims are to promote the discipline of Social Policy as an academic discipline, to represent its members' interests, as well as to enhance the communication and learning between its members, policymakers and the public. Key activities of the SPA include an annual conference with 250–300 delegates, support for two leading international academic journals, the *Journal of Social Policy* and *Social Policy & Society* and policy analysis in form of *In Defence of Welfare* publications, joint projects such as the online publication *Discovering Society* (discoversociety.org) with the British Sociological Association, an active network of seminars and conferences for postgraduate students as well as regular *Policy Round Tables* on current topics bringing together policymakers, thinktanks and academics.

The SPA is a membership organisation, and membership is open to all students, teachers and others with work in the social policy field. All members pay an annual fee, with the cost of the membership varying according to income bands and location. Benefits of membership are:

- free subscription to leading policy journals, the *Journal of Social Policy* and *Social Policy & Society*;
- free copy of *Social Policy Review*, published annually by Policy Press – an edited collection of articles reviewing developments and debates in social policy in Britain and internationally;
- a number of grant schemes to support the setting up and attendance of seminars and conferences for members;
- discount at the annual conference held in July each year in the UK;
- discounts to subscriptions to other leading journals and learned societies; and
- benefit from international links of the SPA.

The majority of the SPA members live and work in the UK. However, the Association has active members and liaises with social policy associations all over the world, in particular in Europe, North America and Australia. More recently, it has expanded its formal links with social policy associations, networks and scholars from East Asia, India and Latin America.

The Student's Companion to Social Policy, Fifth Edition. Edited by Pete Alcock, Tina Haux, Margaret May and Sharon Wright.
© 2016 John Wiley & Sons, Ltd. Published 2016 by John Wiley & Sons, Ltd.

The Association is managed by an Executive Committee made of up members elected at the Annual Conference, with members serving on the committee for a period of three years at a time. In addition, there are officers – Chair, Secretary and Treasurer – also elected and serving on a three-year basis. Students of social policy at both under-graduate and postgraduate level are very welcome to join the Association. The SPA can be contacted through its web pages at: www.social-policy.org.uk.

Index

The Student's Companion to Social Policy, Fifth Edition. Edited by Pete Alcock, Tina Haux, Margaret May
and Sharon Wright.
© 2016 John Wiley & Sons, Ltd. Published 2016 by John Wiley & Sons, Ltd.

Index compiled by Terry Halliday